Edinburgh

Glasgow, Lothian & Fife

Penguin Books

PENGUIN BOOKS

Published by the Penguin Group
Penguin Books Ltd, 27 Wright's Lane, London W8 5TZ, England
Penguin Putnam Inc., 375 Hudson Street, New York, New York 10014, USA
Penguin Books Australia Ltd, Ringwood, Victoria, Australia
Penguin Books Canada Ltd, 10 Alcorn Avenue, Toronto, Ontario, Canada M4V 3B2
Penguin Books (NZ) Ltd, Private Bag 102902, NSMC, Auckland , New Zealand

Penguin Books Ltd, Registered offices: Harmondsworth, Middlesex, England

First published 1998
10 9 8 7 6 5 4 3 2 1

Colour reprographics by Precise Litho, 34–35 Great Sutton Street, London EC1
Printed and bound by William Clowes Ltd, Beccles, Suffolk NR34 9QE

Edited and designed by

Time Out Guides Limited
Universal House
251 Tottenham Court Road
London W1P OAB
Tel +44 (0)171 813 3000
Fax +44 (0)171 813 6001
Email guides@timeout.co.uk
http://www.timeout.co.uk

Editorial

Managing Editor Peter Fiennes
Editor Thom Dibdin
Deputy Editor Kevin Ebbutt
Researcher Sarah Sharma
Proofreader Tamsin Shelton
Indexer Margaret Cronan

Design

Art Director John Oakey
Art Editor Mandy Martin
Designers Benjamin de Lotz, Scott Moore, Lucy Grant
Scanner Operator Chris Quinn
Advertisement Make-up Paul Mansfield
Picture Editor Kerri Miles
Picture Researcher Emma Tremlett

Advertising

Group Advertisement Director Lesley Gill
Sales Director Mark Phillips
Advertisement Sales (Edinburgh & Glasgow) AIDA Advertising
Advertising Assistant Ingrid Sigerson

Administration

Publisher Tony Elliott
Managing Director Mike Hardwick
Financial Director Kevin Ellis
Marketing Director Gillian Auld
General Manager Nichola Coulthard
Production Manager Mark Lamond

Features in this guide were written and researched by:

Introduction Thom Dibdin; **Edinburgh: Edinburgh by Season** Thom Dibdin; **Key Events** Barry Didcock; **History** Barry Didcock; **Architecture** Susanna Beaumont; **Politics** Barry Didcock; **Tartan & Shortbread** Keith Davidson; **Sightseeing** *Royal Mile, Arthur's Seat, Leith* Alistair Mabbot; *The Castle* Stephanie Noblett; *New Town, Stockbridge* Susanna Beaumont; *Southside, Western Rim* Keith Davidson; *Murder & mayhem on the mile* Matthew Reason; **Museums** Thom Dibdin, Olaf Furness; **Art Galleries** Susanna Beaumont, Olaf Furness; **Accommodation** Emma Protopapadakis; **Pubs & Bars** Thom Dibdin, Brian Donaldson, *The List;* **Shopping & Services** Katrina Dixon; **Restaurants** Sue Wilson, *The List;* **Cafés & Bistros** Sue Wilson, *The List;* **Children** Jane Ellis, Keith Davidson; **Comedy** Sue Wilson; **Film** Thom Dibdin; **Gay & Lesbian** Bob Orr; **Music: Classical & Opera** Carol Main; **Music:** *Rock* Alistair Mabbot, *Folk* **Kenny Mathieson,** *Jazz* Sue Wilson; **Nightlife** Thom Dibdin; **Sport & Fitness** Mike Wilson, Kevin Ebbutt; **Theatre** Sue Wilson; **Glasgow: Glasgow Today** Fiona Shepherd; **History** Andy Denholm; **Architecture** Caroline Ednie; **Sightseeing** Alistair Mabbot, Andrea Mullaney, Fiona Shepherd; **Accommodation** Deirdre Molloy; **Restaurants & Cafés** Caroline Ednie, *The List;* **Pubs & Bars** Fiona Shepherd; **Shopping & Services** Deirdre Molloy, Rory Weller; **Arts & Entertainment** Dominic D'Angelo, Andrea Mullaney, Fiona Shepherd, Rory Weller; **Trips Out of Town** Kirsty Walker; **Directory** Sarah Sharma, Thom Dibdin, Alistair Mabbot, Claire Prentice, Sue Wilson.

The Editor would like to thank the following:

Alison Burden, Jamie Byng, Daniel Dibdin & Susanne Frost, Katrina Dixon, Kevin Ebbutt, Louise Gray, Harriet Johnson, Robin Hodge, Ruth Jarvis, Alan Nicholls & Maggie McKeown, Stephanie Noblett, Wendy Schofield, Jonathan Trew, Sue Wilson.

Maps by JS Graphics, 17 Beadles Lane, Old Oxted, Surrey RH8 9JG. Edinburgh Map based on material supplied by Alan Collinson through Copyright Exchange.

Photography by Marius Alexander, except: pages 15, 20, 81 **Scottish National Portrait Gallery**; pages 16, 18, 22 **AKG**; page 21 **National Gallery of Scotland**; page 175 **Annan Photographic Library**; page 33 **Still Moving**; page 173 **Susan Collin**; page 173 **Andy Wiltshire**; page 169 **Douglas Robertson**; page 153 **Bill Cooper**; page 158 **B.J.Stewart**; page 160 **Redferns**; page 147 **Liam Longman**; page 229 **Edinburgh & Lothians Tourist Board**; pages 230, 245 **Emma Tremlett**; pages 232, 235 **Thirlestane Castle Trust**; page 239 **Scottish Borders Tourist Board**; page 241 **Robert Lees/Still Moving Picture Co.**

Contents

About the Guide

The *Time Out Edinburgh Guide* is one of an expanding series of city guides produced by the people behind London's successful listings magazine. Our hard-working team of local writers has striven to provide you with all the information you'll need to explore Edinburgh – with a bit more besides in case you fancy popping over to Glasgow or taking a trip out of town.

CHECKED AND CORRECT

Above all, we've tried to make this book as useful as possible. Addresses, telephone numbers, transport information, opening times, admission prices and credit card details are all included in our listings. And, as far as possible, we've given details of facilities, services and events, all checked and correct at the time we went to press. However, owners and managers can change their arrangements at any time. Before going out of your way, it is always best to telephone and check opening times, dates of exhibitions and other particulars.

PRICES

The prices we've supplied should be treated as guidelines, not gospel. Fluctuating exchange rates and inflation can cause charges, in shops and restaurants particularly, to change rapidly. If prices vary wildly from those we've quoted, ask whether there's a good reason. If not, go elsewhere. Then please write and let us know. We aim to give the best and most up-to-date advice, so we always want to know if you've been badly treated or overcharged.

CREDIT CARDS

The following abbreviations have been used for credit cards: **AmEx**: American Express; **DC**: Diners' Club; **Disc** (Discovery); **JCB**: Japanese Credit Bank; **MC**: MasterCard (Access); **TC**: travellers cheques in any currency ($TC, £TC denotes currencies accepted). **V**: Visa (Barclaycard).

TELEPHONE NUMBERS

All phone numbers in Edinburgh are prefixed by the code 0131. All telephone numbers printed in this guide take this code, unless otherwise stated. Numbers preceded by 0800 can be called free of charge from within the UK. Numbers preceded by 0345 are charged at a local UK rate.

RIGHT TO REPLY

It should be stressed that the information we give is impartial. No organisation has been included in this guide because its owner or manager has advertised in our publications. We hope you enjoy the *Time Out Edinburgh Guide*, but we'd also like to know if you don't. We welcome tips for places that you think we should include in future editions and take notice of your criticism of our choices. There's a reader's reply card at the back of this book.

TRANSPORT DETAILS

In both Edinburgh and Glasgow we have specified the buses that pass closest o the place being listed, but there are several central points which are served by such a large number of buses that we have decided to group them together in the interests of space.

Edinburgh

All buses listed are operated by Lothian Region Transport.
Bridges: 3, 7, 8, 9, 14, 21, 30, 31, 33, 36, 62, 64, 69, 80, 87, 88.
Bruntsfield: 11, 15, 16, 17, 23, 37, 45.
Dalry Road: 2, 3, 4, 12, 21, 22, 25, 28, 30, 33, 43, 44, 61, 65, 66.
George IV Bridge: 23, 27, 28, 37, 40, 41, 42, 45, 46, 47.
George Street: 13, 19, 34, 35, 39, 40, 41, 43, 47, 55, 82.
Great Junction Street: 1, 6, 7, 10, 14, 17, 22, 25, 87, 88.
Haymarket: 2, 3, 4, 12, 18, 21, 22, 25, 26, 30, 31, 33, 36, 37, 38, 43, 44, 61, 63, 66, 69, 85, 86.
Leith Walk: 2, 7, 10, 11, 12, 14, 16, 17, 22, 25, 87, 88.
London Road: 4, 5, 15, 26, 43, 44, 45, 51, 63, 66, 75, 85, 86.
Princes Street: 2, 3, 4, 11, 12, 15, 16, 17, 21, 25, 26, 30, 33, 36, 37, 38, 43, 44, 63, 69, 85, 86.

Glasgow

All buses listed are operated by Greater Glasgow.
Bath Street: 11, 16, 18, 23, 42, 44, 57, 59, 66, 74.
Hope Street: 4, 18, 21, 23, 38, 39, 41, 44, 45, 48, 53, 54, 55, 57, 59, 61.
St Vincent Street: 6, 8, 14, 16, 20, 31, 66.
Sauchiehall Street: 11, 18, 20, 21, 23, 42, 44, 48, 51, 53, 54, 55, 57, 59, 61, 66.

There is an online version of this guide, as well as weekly events listings for several international cities, at:
http://www.timeout.co.uk

Introduction

You can see the sky in Edinburgh. And it is not the insipid, smog-laden sky that you might glimpse from the skyscraper-vaulted canyons of so many modern cities, either. It is a full-on, edge-to-edge expanse – whether it is seen from the Mound as the summer evening sun shines over the Caledonian Hotel on to the north face of Castle Rock or on a crisp winter morning, when the frost glistens on Arthur's Seat and the sharp stench of brewery yeast tangs the nostrils.

It is skies like these that set off the city's natural peaks and man-made monuments to their best advantage. But when the clouds dip down, low, grey and brooding, then the city's neo-classical architecture comes into its own. Here are buildings that can confound elemental forces. Buildings that were made to keep the weather out but that can also absorb a population bent on cultural improvement. Because, behind the façades and the grey imperiousness, inside the places of entertainment – whether the most genteel, high-brow palace or the most raucous, populist dive – there is an audience that is willing to be educated and, more importantly, one that has an opinion.

Edinburgh's residents have a reputation for tight-lipped indifference – just as Glasgow's have a reputation for vivacious chat and comment. Yet the truth about Edinburgh is that, just as the grey architecture houses a beating social heart, so the tight faces of its people hide a cosmopolitan outlook that has embraced and absorbed a multitude of opinions and ideas.

Edinburgh is, after all, a capital. For centuries it has been the sort of cultural melting pot that a fully functional capital should be. Of course this is sometimes in spite of, rather than because of, the city's institutions. But even they have generally begun to understand that diversity is a good thing. It was institutions that allowed the Edinburgh International Festival to start up, after all – although if the people who agreed to the original proposals could see what the Fringe has become today, they might not have been so forthcoming. The diversity of the city's festivals is a way for it to keep that pot bubbling away, brimful with international influences.

The city is not just any old capital, either. It is the capital of Scotland – a nation that yearns not so much for independence from England, as for the differences between it and its more populous southern neighbour to be universally and automatically acknowledged. With a Scottish Assembly in sight, Scotland, or rather being Scottish, seems to impart a maturity on all who claim it. Scotland is a nation that is ready to acknowledge and grasp the responsibilities of its semi-devolved state.

But for all the beauty in Edinburgh's heart, you should not forget that it is a city that is inside out. No area of inner-city deprivation surrounded by plush enclaves here, thanks to the work of the architect James Craig and the builders of the New Town in the nineteenth century. No, Edinburgh has a beautiful centre – surrounded by an outer ring of deprivation. Places like Pilton, Wester Hailes, Niddrie and Craigmillar are depressed housing schemes on the city's periphery – and don't start to think you've seen all of Edinburgh until you've been here. For an antidote to the barrage of confusing facts from the city centre bus tours, head for the city edge and then take a 32 or a 52 bus: their circular routes go in opposite directions round the outskirts of the city.

This is the side of the city that writers such as Irvine Welsh and the Rebel Inc crew have had the temerity to chronicle, although one particular international influence – the heroin trade – is not as pervasive as it was in the 1980s. What is most positive about this new writing is that it gives proper acknowledgement to the influence of Edinburgh's counter-culture as its culture. The house parties of East Craigs may be a world away from the tea parties of Morningside but, like it or not, they both have an effect on each other. And, no matter where you stay in this brilliant, beautiful, inside-out city, you can always see that sky.

Editing this book has been both an exhilarating and an invidious experience. Exhilarating, because it has been a pleasure to write about Edinburgh and commission writers who know and love the city. But it didn't seem right to have only one city guide for Scotland and not include anything at all about Glasgow. So the invidious choice was how much space to give to Glasgow and how much to include. In the end, it was decided to give the greatest weight in the Glasgow section to the aspects of the city that are of most interest to the visitor: architecture, style and, of course, drinking culture. But there is still far too much that has had to be overlooked. Thankfully *Time Out*'s decision-makers now have plans to produce a separate Glasgow Guide, which, when it comes out, will benefit both cities.

Thom Dibdin

The Ancient Peat Bed of Orkney.

On only one island are peats cut shallow on the heather moor called Hobbister to maintain the unique character of its malt.

Orkney's gold

In Context

Edinburgh by Season

First footing fun and festival frolics. Any excuse for a party.

Sometimes it feels as if you are experiencing a whole year of seasons in a day in Edinburgh – such are the vagaries of the weather. Snow, sun, wind and rain can all have their hour during a walk around the city. Likewise, there is always something going on, whether it is a talk at the Royal Museum of Scotland, an organ recital at St Giles' Cathedral or a behind-the-scenes tour at the Traverse Theatre. It is probably the influence of the Edinburgh Festival itself, but Edinburgh folk do have a penchant for putting events into festivals. And there is an ingrained beauty to Edinburgh, whatever the weather.

Winter

The nights are long, the days are dark and the wind can come howling in off the North Sea with a bitter Siberian after-taste. Visitors should pack accordingly – but be prepared for the odd day of deceptive sun. Exactly when the Edinburgh year begins depends on whether it is viewed from the aspect of a pessimist or an optimist. The former will choose 1 January – Ne'er Day – when most folk are reflecting on the hangover caused by the past night. The optimist will plump for Hogmanay itself: the last night of the year, the first of the new and cause for much public merrymaking. Hogmanay it is, then.

Edinburgh's Hogmanay

Various venues around central Edinburgh. Box Office & Information c/o 21 Market Street, EH1 (473 1999). Princes St buses, then 5-min walk. For millennium enquiries contact the Edinburgh & Scotland Information Centre (473 3800). **Dates** 29 Dec 1998-1 Jan 1999; 27 Dec 1999-2 Jan 2000.

Technically, Hogmanay is New Year's Eve. The night when the people throughout Scotland take to the streets, meet by the market cross, kiss everyone within sight when the bells ring out and thence go 'first footing' with a lump of coal, a

*Thousands take to the streets for **Edinburgh's Hogmanay**, Europe's biggest winter festival.*

*Fertility and seasonal rites are the order of the night at **Beltane** on Calton Hill. Page 9.*

bun and a drop of the hard stuff. But Edinburgh became so notorious for its good-natured celebrations that in 1993 the City Council took paid advice from local entrepreneur, Pete Irvine, and instigated a three-day festival. Borrowing wisely and widely from Scottish tradition, Edinburgh's Hogmanay now features the burning of a long boat, processions lit by firebrands, street theatre and several events for the more foolhardy and extrovert on Ne'er Day itself. This is Scottish hospitality at its best. Families with children are well catered for, while those without such ties are often in danger of meeting their life partners. Besides the official celebrations, every local place of revelry is ringing with clubs, ceilidhs, live acts, dancing and general merrymaking until the wee small hours. As the biggest winter festival in Europe, the main street party almost became a victim of its own success in 1996. A succession of mild winters, combined with the prospect of dancing drunkenly in the streets to top musical entertainers, provoked such a huge crowd that crushing almost caused a tragedy. In 1997, it was decided to limit the numbers in the town centre and make access from 8pm on New Year's Eve restricted to those with advance tickets. From 1999, unless there is a major change of heart, revellers will have to pay to be in the town centre after 8pm.

Turner Watercolours

National Gallery of Scotland, The Mound, EH2 (624 6200). Princes St buses. **Open** 10am-5pm Mon-Sat; 2-5pm Sun. **Admittance** free. **Dates** 1-31 Jan annually.
Over 40 Turner watercolours were bequeathed to the National Gallery of Scotland in 1900 by Henry Vaughan, who stipulated that they should only be exhibited in January when the light is at its weakest and least destructive to works of art on paper. These are exhibited every January at the National Gallery of Scotland (*see chapter* **Art Galleries**) at the bottom of the Mound, along with Turner's illustrations of Thomas Campbell's poems.

Burns Night

Date 25 January.
It is the custom of Scots the world over to foregather on 25 January, consume the sacred foods – haggis, neeps (turnips) and tatties (potatoes) – sup of the sacred whisky and recite the sacred texts. For this night is the birthday of Robert 'Rabbie' Burns, Scotland's Bard. In Edinburgh, such Burns Suppers happen in private homes, among members of Burns associations and, in public, at restaurants and hotels around the town. It is best to get invited to someone's home if possible, otherwise things can appear over-formal (at least at the outset) or unbearably laced with tartan kitsch. If a native invitation is not forthcoming, find a few fellow travellers, grab a haggis supper each from the chip shop, pass round the whisky (one bottle per person should be enough) and read from a book of Burns' poems until the drink has loosened the tongues. Some are extremely bawdy, although *Tam o' Shanter* is a great story and the *Address to a Haggis* a true celebration of the working man.

Spring

Coats come off, scarves go back in the drawer and vegetation across the city bursts into bloom. The daffodils on Castle Hill, seen from Princes Street, would send Wordsworth searching for a better collective noun than 'host'. The cherry trees in St Andrew's Square and across the walks of the Meadows bring a secret smile to all that see them. As for the Botanics, the rhododendra are a sight to behold. British Summer Time begins – and the clocks go forward an hour – on 28 March in 1999 and 26 March in 2000.

Easter Day is Sunday 4 April 1999 and Sunday 23 April 2000.

Shoots & Roots

Various venues (554 3092). **Dates** 1-4 Apr 1999; 20-23 Apr 2000.

Surviving the Festival

Surviving a full-blown encounter with the Edinburgh Festival can be compared to white-water rafting on particularly rocky rapids. You can do any amount of planning to make sure you'll come out of the experience alive, but once started, you don't have much control over what goes on – best just to cling in there and enjoy the ride.

The first directive of Festival-going is to make like a boy scout and be prepared. Get as many programmes as you can before coming to Edinburgh. If you are intent on seeing a specific performer or performance in the International Festival, particularly on the musical side, it is wise to buy those tickets early. The best seats for the big concerts sell out quickly.

If, however, you simply want a blast of top cultural entertainment to round off a few days of Fringe-going, then it is quite safe to wait until you arrive to choose your fancy.

The really hot tickets of every year's Festival are for the firework concert in Princes Street gardens, which takes place on the last Thursday of the Festival. These are for the best seats of all, in the gardens themselves and are mostly only available by postal application, although a few are held back until the Sunday before. The views are good, however, from all over town. Princes Street and the Mound offer the best close-up views, while North Bridge and Calton Hill allow for a bit more perspective.

Take a portable radio and tune into the local station, Radio Forth (97.3 FM), which carries the concert live. Some people rate the view from even further afield – the Botanics or the far shore of Fife. But they don't get the full-on experience of the ground quaking as the big mortars thrust their pyrotechnic loads into the night sky.

Having procured the various festival programmes, peruse them thoroughly. This is the time to work out how the programmes – particularly the Fringe's – actually work. Make a wish list of must-see performances and perform some serious time management yourself. Make lists. Make more lists. A top tip is to work out an itinerary based around the Book and Film Festival events, which are mostly one-offs. You might even consider booking ahead for both these festivals, as they are renowned for being places where authors and directors get to meet their public.

Having programmed every available second of your days in Edinburgh – performances start at breakfast time and finish well after most sane people are tucked snugly up in bed – work out how much it will all cost and how much time you will have to travel between each different venue. At this point, you'll probably start day-dreaming about a large bank error in your favour and the invention of a simultaneous matter transmitter.

It is wise not to book tickets for every show you want to see at this juncture. Your perceptions will change once you are in town. Also avoid shows that sell themselves on their nudity factor. It's a cheap form of publicity that masks more bad acting than it reveals naughty bits.

What will also change is the shape of your bottom. While Festival and Fringe have evolved out of all recognition over the last 50 years, many of the seats have not. Before leaving make sure you pack something that can add just a little bit of comfort and padding. Best not to bring something too soft or you will end up falling asleep, but that cross-stitch cushion Aunty Betty gave you for Christmas seven years ago will do fine. Also pack a few spare rolls of toilet paper, particularly if you are staying in a friend's flat.

Immediately on arrival make two purchases: *The Scotsman* and *The List*. The former carries more reviews than any other paper, the latter more previews and reviews than any other magazine and are good ways to start to understand the various time zones. Now you can find your accommodation, dump your kit and get going to your first show. You should also find yourself a good supply of very strong coffee. It is likely that you will need a large hit at regular intervals, as the pressure to overdo things will be intense. The California Coffee Company and the Elephant Tea House are both recommended (*see chapter* **Bistros & Cafés**).

There are two extremes of Festival-going: the itinerary-bound believer in firm plans and the laid-back follower of the coolest vibe. An itinerary allows you to remain focused and optimise your show-going potential. Waver towards this if time is limited or the number of shows you see is important. Hanging around in the bar after a show to find out what the best tips are can send you off to some unexpectedly groovy treats. Favour this option if you are in town for more than a weekend or the hipness factor of the shows you see is important to you.

The best time is obviously to be had by holding both these attitudes while making yourself aware of what the reviewers are saying. So be prepared to ignore all your lists. Although your first day in Edinburgh will leave you buzzing with cultural input and ready to drop after running from show to show, by the second day, you will be an old hand. Your opinion will be sought from new arrivals and you will be able to compare your opinions with those in the papers.

One of the saddest trends over the last few years of the Festivals has been for Fringegoers to concentrate on guaranteed laughs and hang around the big three comedy venues: the Gilded Balloon, the Pleasance and the Assembly Rooms. Which is all very well, but leaves the rest of the Fringe starved of an audience – and the potential audience itself bereft of some very fine performances.

It should be every Fringe-goer's duty, nay, desire, to see at least one idiosyncratic show in one wee hall on the edge of town. Not only might it be superb, but it will almost certainly be far cheaper than the central venues. Moreover, the kudos of having seen *Macbeth* performed in Scots at St Ninian's Hall is far greater than dozing through half an hour of duff stand-up at a London-programmed venue.

There are two problems with venues away from the centre of town. If you are the only member of the audience, do not panic: you owe the performers nothing. You have paid for your ticket and have every right to be entertained. And, if you are prepared to appear a bit strange and give a solo standing ovation at the end, the performers might buy you a drink. Besides, you had to overcome the second problem: getting there. A bicycle is useful if you are fit. Taxis are not too expensive if you are not. A good idea is to try a non-central venue after you've been around a few days. The walk will actually help you clear your brain of the Festival-induced psychosis that will have built up. You can often spend a whole day seeing a variety of genres, from comedy to straight theatre, by the same company – an experience that carries its own special satisfactions.

Nor should Edinburgh's non-festival events be ignored. Club runners always try to attract the Festival crowd but, in the fast changing world of dance music, only the most mainstream can get their DJs booked far enough ahead to get in the Fringe brochure. Check out the flyers in central bars and pubs for some idea of what is really going on. As with the whole of the Festival, keeping your ear to the ground and your feet ready to go where the vibe is most appropriate is the best way to enjoy the rocky rapids of Edinburgh in August – with your sanity intact.

Edinburgh's folk festival has undergone a change of emphasis in recent years, splitting into a spring and an autumn weekend. The spring weekend encompasses music that uses modern variations on traditional forms. An autumn festival (*see below*) is also held.

Edinburgh Science Festival

Various venues (information line 220 6220). **Open** 9am-5pm Mon-Fri. **Dates** 3-18 April 1999.

Edinburgh has long been a city of scientific excellence: its scientifically minded children reach back to 1550 and the birth of Napier, inventor of logarithms; and since the Enlightenment the city has been associated with the cutting edge of science, thanks to the universities and the Scottish school system. The Science Festival, founded in 1987, is a bold and largely successful attempt to continue this trend by providing lectures and events that popularise all branches of science and technology. Without dumbing down, the Festival has become adept at putting a controversial and topical slant on the average of 250 events held in 40 venues around Edinburgh, thus ensuring maximum media exposure and continuing to attract scientific heavyweights from around the world. Much of its success must also be ascribed to the trick of presenting what could otherwise be dull and exceedingly dry material as part of a festival – which helps to put a positive slant on events. Two measures of the Festival's success are that, notwithstanding the strength of the schools and children's programmes, it reaches more adults than it does children and that slightly more than half its 175,000 visitors are women.

Beltane

Calton Hill. Princes St buses. **Times** 10pm-dawn. **Dates** 30 April 1999.

As the winter nights shorten and the spring sap starts rising, in Edinburgh as elsewhere, people's thoughts turn to lust and wooing. Beltane captures some of this innate sensuality in a modern ritual, reinvented in 1988 by Angus Farquar of the radical art activists NVA. It takes place on Calton Hill from about 10pm, lasts until dawn and incorporates all sorts of fertility and seasonal rites including the passage of winter into spring. The centre piece of the night is the ritual procession of the May Queen to four elemental points around the hill, followed by the death and rebirth of the Green Man and the lighting of a huge bonfire. The ritual changes every year, as the loose group of people who organise it changes. It can get crowded on the hill top. But the event, which makes liberal use of fire, dressing up, drumming and acting, is best enjoyed by those who stray from the role of spectator to participant – in however minor a way. This is the sort of anarchic event at which everyone makes their own impression: it won't do any harm to take a flask of whisky to toast the May Queen, something flammable to add to the bonfire and the inclination to stay up all night.

Radical Book Fair

Based at Word Power Bookshop (662 9112). Bridges buses. **Dates** mid-May 1999.

A long weekend based at Word Power bookshop (*see chapter* **Shopping & Services***)* consisting of readings, book launches, panel discussions and general promotion of books from small, independent and radical publishers.

Scottish International Children's Festival

City centre theatres (554 6297). **Open** 9am-5pm Mon-Fri. **Dates** mid-end May annually.

Taking children's theatre seriously does not mean serious theatre, but some of the best theatre for children in the world, all happening at the same time. After the tented village at Inverleith Park was all but washed out in 1987, the Festival moved into Edinburgh's purpose-built theatres and widened both scope and breadth in 1988. At its best, this is powerfully evocative stuff.

*Moove on up to the **Royal Highland Show** at Ingliston in June.*

Meadows Festival

George IV Bridge buses. **Dates** first weekend in June annually.

The walkways of the Meadows become lined with stalls for this mini-festival, which also encompasses live musical entertainment, kids' amusements and fairground rides.

Summer

None of your 'I went to the matinee of *Titanic* and missed the summer' for Edinburgh. While summer showers might wet you slightly, the long days more than adequately make up for it. Around the end of June the nights are truly dark for no more than an hour if, that is, the sky is clear.

Caledonian Beer Festival

Caledonian Brewery, 42 Slateford Road, EH14 (337 1286). Slateford rail. **Dates** first weekend June annually.
Edinburgh's only independent brewery has a great deal to shout about with its fine selection of real ales. But that doesn't deter it from welcoming some 50 of its competitors' brews to join its own over a long weekend that is becoming a bit of a tradition with excellent catering and bands every evening.

Pride Scotland

Edinburgh Meadows (556 8822). **Dates** June 1999, 2001.
Founded to 'celebrate the pride in the lifestyles of lesbian, gay, bisexual and transgender people, expressed in an annual march and festival', Pride Scotland is really an excuse for a big party on the last weekend in June. Not as outrageous as London Pride, it's still a great, affirming day out with the partying continuing into the small hours. In 2000, it'll be held at Glasgow Green.

Royal Highland Show

Royal Highland Showground, Ingliston (0930 100 444). 16, 18, 19, 31(A), 37, 38(A/B) buses. **Dates** 24-27 June 1999; 22-25 June 2000.

Held out at the Royal Highland Showground, Ingliston (10 miles west of the city centre, by Edinburgh Airport), the Royal Highland Show is the biggest and probably the best place to see everything Scottish that is vaguely agricultural. This is the place to be for those who want to smell the animals that end up on their plates, see the machines that help grow the crops and ogle the food that results from all the farmers' efforts. The judged farm animal sections – all 400 of them – attract thousands of entries; there is some serious consumerism to be had – from combine harvesters to high-street goods; and the ring events are of top quality. It's a solid family day out for you and 150,000 other visitors.

T in the Park

Balado, by Kinross, Perthshire. **Dates** July 1999; July 2000 tbc.
Scotland's big outdoor music festival is pulling in both the punters and the bands as never before since starting in Strathclyde Park in 1994 and moving to a rural venue in Perthshire in 1997. As is the way with these things, nothing is confirmed until a month or so before the event, but expect the full range of festival names. Oasis, Underworld, Prodigy, Ritchie Hawtin, and Nick Cave and Kylie Minogue have all trod the stages in years past.
http: *www.tinthepark.com*

The Festival

What is known, colloquially, as 'The Festival' is, in fact, a collection of six different festivals and events, each with its own distinct feel and organisation, but all held in Edinburgh during August.

Edinburgh International Festival

Various venues around Edinburgh (473 2001). **Dates** 16 Aug-5 Sept 1998; 15 Aug-4 Sept 1999; 13 Aug-2 Sept 2000; 12 Aug-1 Sept 2001.
The first, although not, now, the biggest, was the Edinburgh International Festival. It was founded in 1947

following the concerted efforts of the Lord Provost John
Falconer, Harry Wood of the British Council and Rudolph
Bing, who became its first director. The major arts festi-
vals of continental Europe were still in turmoil after World
War II. The aim was, and still is, to 'provide the world with
a centre where, year after year, all that is best in music,
drama and the visual arts can be seen and heard in ideal
surroundings'. Festival performances take place in most of
Edinburgh's large venues. The programme is published in
April. In March 1998 the Festival bought the former
Highland Tolbooth at the top of the High Street at Castle
Hill and started work to turn it into a permanent ticket
office and year-round focus for Edinburgh as a festival city
in time for the 1999 Festival.

Edinburgh International Film Festival

*Most Edinburgh cinemas, but centred at Filmhouse, 88
Lothian Road (229 2550/228 4051). Bruntsfield buses.*
Dates 16-30 Aug 1998; 15-29 Aug 1999; 13-27 Aug 2000.
Immediately the folk at the Edinburgh Film Guild got wind
of the plans for the International Festival they were
incensed. A modern festival that did not celebrate film, the
quintessential artistic medium of the twentieth century?
The Guild, with its founder Norman Wilson and The
Scotsman's film critic Forsyth Hardy at the controls, funded and staged the first Edinburgh International Festival
of Documentary Films. Since 1947, it has broadened out
from its tight documentary remit. Although it is no longer
'the only film festival worth a damn' as John Huston said
in 1972, the two weeks of screenings are invariably a
hotbed of young British filmmaking talent, an important
showplace for new British and continental films and a
forum for a Hollywood blockbuster or three to hold their
European openings.

The Fringe

*The Fringe Office, 180 High Street, EH1 (226 5257). 1,
6, 34, 35, Bridges buses.* **Open** box office 27 July-31 Aug
10am-7pm daily. **Dates** 9-31 Aug 1998; 8-30 Aug 1999
(tbc); 6-28 Aug 2000 (tbc).
At the very first International Festival there were eight officially uninvited companies. But the term 'Fringe' was not
used until 1948 when Robert Kemp wrote in the *Evening
News* of 14 August that 'Round the fringe of official Festival
drama there seems to be more private enterprise than ever
before'. By the end of the 1950s, performers were describing themselves as being on the Fringe. From day one, the
Fringe has been self-selecting. All a performer needs is a
venue and enough money to buy a listing in the Fringe programme. Which means that the truly 'out-there' and avant-
garde rub shoulders with the most steadfastly traditional,
the truly appalling with the most professional, the never-
will-be hopefuls with the Gielguds of the next generation.
Indeed, members of the Monty Python team performed in
1964 and Rowan Atkinson's review of 1977 closed after the
first night as a flop. It certainly lives up to its reputation as
the greatest arts festival in the world. In 1998, it decoupled
itself from the EIF and now starts one week earlier.

Edinburgh Military Tattoo

Castle Esplanade (225 1188). 1, 6, 34, 35 buses. **Open**
10am-4.30pm Mon-Fri. *Festival* 10am-9pm Mon-Fri;
10am-10.30pm Sat. **Dates** 7-29 Aug 1998; 6-28 Aug 1999;
4-26 Aug 2000; 3-25 Aug 2001.
First performed in 1950 as the army's contribution to the
Festival, the Tattoo has become its single most popular
event with 200,000 tickets sold every year. By show-time,
there is rarely an empty seat on the temporary stands that
line the Castle Esplanade. Although an overtly militaristic
display, it is also a pageant of colour that uses its hundreds
of performers and the Castle backdrop to stunning effect.
Beware the tide of people entering and leaving the Tattoo
in the early evening who cause serious traffic problems in
the Royal Mile.

Book Festival

*Charlotte Square, EH2 (228 5444/24-hour hotline 0897
500 010; calls cost £1 per min/box office 624 5050).
Princes St or George St buses.* **Open** *Festival* 10am-6pm
Mon-Sat. **Dates** 15-31 Aug 1998; 14-30 Aug 1999.
A bit of a newcomer to the Festival scene, the Book
Festival occupies a tented village in the centre of Charlotte
Square and is usually at the same time as the Film Festival.
Notable for the number of authors it attracts and its lack
of publishing trade professionals. It became an annual
event in 1998.

Jazz & Blues Festival

*Various venues around Edinburgh (admin 225 2202/box
office 667 7776).* **Open** *admin* 9am-5.30pm Mon-Fri; *box
office* 10am-6pm Mon-Sun. **Dates** 31 July-9 Aug 1998; 30
July-8 Aug 1999; 28 July-6 Aug 2000 (tbc).
Presenting 'the best of jazz to the biggest audience', the Festival
covers most of its remit with the free Jazz on a Summer's Day
in Princes Street Gardens and Mardi Gras in the Grassmarket.
It also manages to cover the full range of jazz forms, in venues
from the Playhouse to pubs and cabaret bars.

Autumn

As the haar – or sea mist – starts creeping up from
the Forth and drizzles set in, Edinburgh folk's
thoughts turn to indoor entertainment. Ceilidhs
abound across the town. Much whisky is tasted
and savoured. But that steel-grey sky still brings
a remarkable beauty to the city. British Summer
Time ends – and the clocks go back an hour – on
25 October in 1998, 31 October in 1999 and 29
October in 2000.

Open Doors Day

*Various sites around Edinburgh. Details from Cockburn
Association, Trunk's Close, 55 High Street, EH1 (557
8686).* **Open** 9am-5pm Mon-Fri. **Dates** 26 Sept 1998;
Sept 1999, 2000 (dates tbc).
One day a year, the Cockburn Association persuades the
owners of many of Edinburgh's finest private buildings to
open their doors to the public. These change, so contact the
association for details.

Hallowe'en: Samhain

High Street. 1, 6, 34, 35, Bridges buses. **Date** 31 Oct.
In recent years, the Beltane organisation (*see above*) has
attempted to revive the other three quarter days of the
ancient calendar. Samhain, which coincides with Hallowe'en,
is the most obvious and they take to the streets with much
frenzied dancing and beating of drums.

Bonfire Night

Date 5 November.
Modern Scots have a certain ambivalence towards Guy
Fawkes. The fact that his gunpowder plot of 1605 was
against Scotland's own James IV is somehow masked by
the fact that it was also against the English Parliament, a
sentiment secretly supported in many a Scottish heart –
at least up to the granting of the Scottish Parliament. But
there again, any excuse for a party. The biggest firework
displays are generously organised by the Council in
Meadowbank Stadium.

Shoots & Roots

Various venues (554 3092 for details). **Dates** 20-22 Nov
1998; 21-23 Nov 1999; 23-25 Nov 2000.
The autumn folk weekend encompasses music which is traditional in format and presentation (*see above*).

Key Events

c638 Southern Scotland under the control of Northumbria.
c950 The MacAlpin kings repel the Northumbrians.
1018 Malcolm II defeats the Northumbrians at Carham and Edinburgh Castle becomes Scottish.
1093 Malcolm III killed in ambush. Civil war follows.
c1150 Brewing practised in the area around Holyrood.
1128 Augustinian Abbey of Holyrood founded by David I.
1314 Robert the Bruce's nephew, Thomas Randolph, re takes the castle from the English.
1329 Edinburgh receives royal charter from Robert the Bruce.
1333 Berwick lost to the English.
1349 The Black Death arrives, returning in 1362 and 1379: a third of the Scottish population is estimated to have died.
c1430 St Anthony's Chapel built on Arthur's Seat.
1456 James II gifts Greenside to the town's citizens.
1457 James II decrees against the playing of 'Fute-ball and Golfe' because they interfere with the practice of archery.
1477 James III charters markets to be held in the Grassmarket.
1482 James III grants the Blue Blanket to the town.
1489 Mons Meg used at the siege of Dumbarton.
1498 Holyroodhouse built by James IV.
1503 The basin at the foot of the Mercat Cross filled with wine to celebrate James IV's entrance into the town.
1513 Citizens muster under the Blue Blanket at the Mercat Cross to march to Flodden. James IV is killed in the battle. Following the defeat, the Flodden Wall is built to defend the city. It is completed in 1560.
1519 Earliest reference to a Grammar School, later the Royal High School. Leper colony set up at Greenside.
1544 English army attacks from the sea, sacks Holyroodhouse and its Abbey, but fails to gain entrance to the city.
1566 David Rizzio murdered in Holyroodhouse.
1582 James VI issues charter for the Townis College, later Edinburgh University.
1590-1 Witches burned at Castlehill.
1603 James VI accedes to the English throne and removes the Court to London.
1633 Edinburgh formally becomes capital of Scotland.
1637 Building started on the Tron Kirk.
1639 Parliament House finished. Used by Scottish Parliament until 1707. Now used in connection with the Court of Session.
1658 Stagecoach between Edinburgh and London once every three weeks.
1673 First coffeehouse opens, in Parliament Close.
1675 Physic Garden founded by the Nor' Loch.
1677 Town council decrees all chimneys must be swept four times a year to prevent fire.
1681 Tea tasted in the city for the first time; James Dalrymple, the father of Scots law, publishes his *Institutions of the Law of Scotland*.
1685 Duckings cease in the Nor' Loch.
1695 The Bank of Scotland chartered. It moved to its present position at the top of the Mound in 1805.
1698 A run of seven disastrous harvests begins, increasing discontent and rioting in the city.
1702-7 Scottish Parliament sits in Edinburgh discussing the Act of Union. It is ratified in 1707.
1726 Last burning of a witch in Edinburgh.
1727 Royal Bank of Scotland founded.
1736 Porteous riots.
1749 William Younger founds his brewery at Holyrood.
1751 The collapse of a High Street 'land' leads the Town Council to survey others and demolish some.
1767 James Craig's plans for the New Town adopted. Theatre Royal opens, Edinburgh's first licensed theatre.
1769 First house on Princes Street built.

1770 Queen Street begun.
1771 *Encyclopedia Britannica* published by William Smellie in Anchor Close; Sir Walter Scott born in College Wynd.
1780 First umbrella seen in the city.
1784 Last execution in the Grassmarket.
1787 The Edinburgh edition of Robert Burns's poems published. The opening lines of his *Address to Edinburgh* are: "Edina, Scotia's darling seat". A firm of bathroom manufacturers named a certain porcelain appliance Edina.
1788 Deacon Brodie hanged at the Tolbooth.
1792 Riots in George Square.
1802 *Edinburgh Review* founded at 18 Buccleuch Place.
1817 *Blackwood's Magazine* founded; *The Scotsman* founded and published from 347 High Street.
1820 Radical Road built. 'Round and round the Radical Road the ragged ragster ran'.
1821 Edinburgh School of Arts formed.
1822 Work begun on the National Monument.
1824 The Great Fire destroys much of the High Street, lasts three days and results in the formation of the world's first municipal fire service; Botanic Garden moves to Inverleith.
1832 Dean Bridge built; New Town extended across it in 1850.
1833 Burgh Reform Act sees the city divided into wards.
1836 Waverley Station begun.
1843 The Disruption splits the Church.
1843-7 Five new large public cemeteries open.
1847 Alexander Graham Bell, the inventor of the telephone, born in South Charlotte Street.
1864 Last public hanging in Edinburgh.
1869 Last public cockfight (in Leith).
1876 Town takes over the Princes Street Gardens from the owners of the houses on Princes Street.
1886 Edinburgh International Exhibition held on the Meadows.
1890 Forth Rail Bridge opened.
1893 Monument to Scottish soldiers killed in American Civil War raised in the Old Burying Ground.
1895 Royal National Observatory built on Blackford Hill. Electric street lighting introduced.
1903 First private car registered in Edinburgh.
1904 *The Scotsman* moves to new site on North Bridge.
1908 Scottish National Exhibition held in Saughton Park.
1912-14 Suffragette attacks in the city.
1916 A German zeppelin bombs Edinburgh.
1925 Murrayfield Stadium opens for rugby matches.
1947 The first Edinburgh International Festival takes place.
1956 Last tram runs. National Library opened by Elizabeth II.
1960 Elizabeth II attends the General Assembly to celebrate the 400th anniversary of the Reformation.
1962 Traverse Theatre opens in the Grassmarket.
1964 Heriot-Watt University founded.
1969 Royal Commonwealth pool opens on Dalkeith Road.
1970 Commonwealth Games held in the city; Meadowbank Stadium opened.
1971 New St Andrews House and St James Centre opened.
1977 New terminal opened at Turnhouse; Old Royal High School earmarked for Scottish Parliament.
1980 *Blackwood's Magazine* folds. Sir Compton Mackenzie had stated in 1967 that 'as long as Blackwood's Magazine continued to appear I had no fears for Edinburgh's supremacy as a city'.
1986 Commonwealth Games held in the city. Again.
1993 Irvine Welsh's novel *Trainspotting* is published.
1997 Scotland votes Yes for the return of a Scottish parliament with tax-varying powers. Edinburgh International Festival celebrates 50 years in showbusiness.
1998 Holyrood announced as site of Scottish Parliament.

History

From mob rule to home rule, the past of the city of 'fur coat and nae knickers' has been fraught with strife and schism.

Early history

CASTLE IN THE AIR

With its sprawling fortress perched high on a volcanic outcrop, there can be few cities in the world that have as dominant or as historically important a focus as Edinburgh. That this castle in the air is joined to a palace on the ground by an ancient road, along whose route history has been made a hundred times over, only adds drama to the story.

But strip away the clutter of the Old Town in your mind's eye, ignore the grandeur of the Georgian New Town, the rigid Victorian tenements and the bleak 1960s architecture, put back the man-made loch that skirted the Castle Rock's northern edge for centuries and you have a sense of the breathtaking physical geography that has drawn people here for thousands of years.

There is no evidence that the Romans occupied the Castle Rock, although from their fort at Inveresk, five miles away, they would have had a fine view of its imposing bulk. But it is known to have been a stronghold for Celtic tribes such as the Gododdin. King Mynyddog ruled from the Castle Rock around the start of the seventh century, and it was the Gododdin who named it Dunedin, meaning 'hill fort'.

In AD638, southern Scotland was conquered by the Northumbrians, who built on the rock and Anglicised its name to Edinburgh. Later the Castle became known as Castrum Puellarum, or Maidens' Castle. In the mid-tenth century, the MacAlpin kings repelled the Northumbrians southwards again and, in 1018, Malcolm II (1005-34) defeated them at Carham. The Castle Rock and the surrounding area became Scottish.

Malcolm III (1058-93) built a hunting lodge on the rock. It is Malcolm, also known as Malcolm Canmore ('big head'), who is commemorated in Shakespeare's *Macbeth*. But in Edinburgh, Malcolm is best remembered as the husband of Margaret, the Saxon princess he married in about 1070. The union produced three daughters and six sons, three of whom ruled as King of Scotland.

Margaret built a chapel on the rock, St Margaret's Chapel, now the oldest building in Edinburgh. She died there after her husband was killed in an ambush near Alnwick in 1093. A power struggle ensued and Malcolm's brother Donald Bane (also featured in *Macbeth*) laid siege to the Castle. Margaret's sons took her body and escaped down the western side of the rock.

David I (1124-53) was the last of Margaret's sons to assume the throne of Scotland. He ruled for nearly 30 years and was the first Scottish king to strike his own coinage. In 1128, he founded the Augustinian abbey at Holyrood – Edinburgh folklore has it that he was hunting one day when he was knocked from his horse and attacked by a stag, only to be saved when a cross (or 'rood') appeared in his hand. To show his thanks to God he founded the abbey. In truth, Holyrood Abbey was only one of several founded by David I at established royal centres throughout his reign, part of the 'Davidian Revolution'. This also saw 15 or so Scottish towns granted the status of royal burgh.

Edinburgh was not the most important of these – Berwick, Scotland's largest town, and Roxburgh were described as burghs even before 1124, and Perth had a long-standing importance. But by 1153 Edinburgh had its own mint and could be said to be one of Scotland's major towns.

GETTING RELIGION

Holyrood Abbey was completed in 1141 and Augustinian monks brought from St Andrews to fill it. The presence of the canons led to the lower half of what is now the Royal Mile being named the Canongate. It was separated from Edinburgh by the defensive gate at the Netherbow and remained a separate burgh until 1856. The monks also brewed beer, and others in the area followed suit: the future site of the Scottish Parliament, opposite Holyrood, is a former brewery.

The **Palace of Holyroodhouse** wasn't built until 1498, but with the abbey in place, Edinburgh began to creep down the spine of the volcanic ridge that leads from the Castle Rock. The Cowgate, running parallel to the Canongate, began to develop as the entrance through which cattle were herded to market. In 1230, the Black Friars (Dominicans) arrived in Edinburgh and established a friary in the east end of the Cowgate. With the Abbey already in place and a succession of religious orders arriving in the town (the Dominicans were followed by the Franciscans, or Grey Friars, in 1429), Edinburgh became an ecclesiastical centre.

The other main religious building in the town was the Church of St Giles (today's **St Giles' Cathedral**). Historians have found mention of a church in Edinburgh as early as 845, but whatever was on the site of St Giles was replaced by Alexander I in 1120 and the church was formally dedicated by Bishop David de Bernham of St Andrews in 1243.

Royal associations

THE RULE OF LAWLESSNESS

Despite the Castle, Edinburgh and its environs had seen relatively few battles. It was only during the fifteenth and sixteenth centuries that the town came to be associated with royalty, and its strategic importance in this earlier period was limited as it was easy to bypass (unlike Stirling Castle, where many of the defining battles of the late thirteenth and early fourteenth centuries were fought). The English king, Edward I, did take up residence in the Abbey during his siege of Edinburgh in 1296 and by 1311 it was in English hands. But even its defensive capabilities were questioned: Robert the Bruce was so appalled at the ease with which his nephew, Sir Thomas Randolph, recaptured it in 1314 that he had it rebuilt.

In 1328, the Treaty of Edinburgh was signed, ending the wars of independence with England (in Scotland's favour). The following year Robert the Bruce granted Edinburgh the status of royal burgh, thus giving it an important degree of fiscal independence. Bruce died the same year.

His heir, David II, was only five in 1329, so Edward III once again tried to conquer Scotland. In 1337, the Countess of March – known as Black Agnes – led the defence of the Castle for five months before Edward took it. The English king rebuilt it in parts, but only four years later Sir William Douglas recaptured it for the Scots. The Canongate was less lucky in this period: it was burned by Richard II's troops in 1380.

David II died in 1371 with no heir and Robert the Steward, who had already been Guardian of Scotland twice, became Robert II. The Stewart succession had begun.

This was a period of lawlessness that saw successive kings murdered or killed in battle, to be succeeded by children who were too young to rule in their own right. It was also the period in which Edinburgh came to be recognised as a royal city. The need for strong regents was vital and the people of Edinburgh witnessed some bloody power plays as the various court factions slugged it out in a succession of reigns. James I (1406-37) tried to curb the power of the nobles, but was murdered in Perth in 1437 for his troubles. His son, James II (1437-60), was only six at the time and was crowned hastily in Holyrood Abbey by his mother. Three years later, in 1440, James himself witnessed a political assassination in Edinburgh Castle when the young Earl of Douglas was murdered by Sir William Crichton and Sir Alexander Livingstone, the acting regents.

ALL MAPPED OUT

The Old Town began to take shape during this period; the Grassmarket and the Cowgate started to form more fully, though development to the south and north was made difficult by physical features such as the Craig Burn, which was dammed in the mid-fifteenth century for defensive purposes and became the Nor' Loch. At the same time, the town's first defensive wall was built: called the King's Wall, it ran from half way down the south side of the Castle Rock, above the Grassmarket and the Cowgate, to the Netherbow, and then dipped down to the Nor' Loch. As the town crept along the spine of the ridge, the familiar herring bone pattern of closes and wynds began to emerge, still visible today in parts.

The principal landmarks in this medieval Edinburgh were the Castle, the Lawnmarket immediately east of it, the High Kirk of St Giles, the Mercat Cross and the Tolbooth, on the south side of the High Street. A prison was added to the Tolbooth and by the fifteenth century both Parliament and the Court of Session would meet there.

The reign of James III (1460-88), like that of his father, was turbulent. He was nine when he came to the throne and struggles over the regency soon broke out. His mother, Mary of Gueldres, demanded that Parliament (sitting in the Castle) name her regent. Meanwhile, the young king was at the bottom of the hill in Holyrood Abbey, with the Bishop of St Andrews. The precarious situation caused the Edinburgh mob to riot. It was the first recorded glimpse of the volatile and well-organised body that would regularly cause havoc over the next few hundred years.

Despite the turbulence, it was during James III's reign that the Cowgate began to be seen as the fashionable place to have a house. Dwellings were also built in the Canongate, beginning in 1485. Hemmed in by its defensive walls, Edinburgh was already becoming overcrowded; the Canongate houses were notable for their spacious rooms and back gardens. But the absence of a defensive wall left the Canongate open to attack: the Abbey it had grown up around was sacked and looted by a host of interlopers over the centuries.

The area round about the town was sprinkled with small villages. Restalrig, for instance, is now part of Edinburgh but its church dates back to the twelfth century. Merchiston was where the inventor of logarithms, John Napier, was born in 1550.

COMMERCIAL BREAKS

Commerce flourished under James III. Between 1320 and 1450, Edinburgh's share of wool exports rose from 21 per cent to 71 per cent – as the only

Commerce was king under James III.

major town with a port between the Tweed and the Forth, it was ideally placed to capitalise on foreign trade opportunities. In 1469, the town ceased to be ruled by the merchant burgesses and became a self-electing corporation. In 1477, James III chartered markets to be held in the Grassmarket, partly because of the congestion on the High Street, where the cloth sellers, beggars and fishwives plied their trade from stalls and booths around St Giles. When these became permanent and could be locked they were called luckenbooths.

In 1482, James granted the Blue Blanket to the citizens of Edinburgh. This was a symbol of the independence of the municipality, of its right to levy customs at the port of Leith and of the exclusive rights of the town's craftsmen. Such craftsmen included the candlemakers, who are known to have been organised by 1488 and who worked in the area around Candlemaker Row.

There was a reason for James's kindness to Edinburgh. Three years earlier, in 1479, he had imprisoned his two brothers at the behest of his Flemish astrologer. One, the Earl of Mar, had died in the Canongate Tolbooth; the other, the Duke of Albany, had escaped from the Castle by drugging his jailers and fleeing to France. The English then attempted to put Albany on the throne. James mustered an army to face them, but a group of disgruntled nobles took the opportunity to hang his

favourites and imprison him in the Castle. The English, under the command of the future Richard III, then entered the Tolbooth and demanded that James be released into Richard's hands. Once more the Edinburgh mob rioted, causing Albany to realise that his brother still had popular support. James kept the throne.

His son, James IV (1480-1513), repaid their support in bricks and mortar when he founded the Palace of Holyroodhouse in 1498, though the monks of the Abbey were less pleased at being displaced by the building work.

CAPITAL IN WAITING

With the Scottish kings increasingly treating the town as their royal residence, the idea that Edinburgh should become Scotland's capital began to gain currency.

James IV's reign coincided with the end of the medieval age and he was eager to seem modern and forward-looking. In keeping with this spirit of the new age, James allowed the barbers and surgeons of Edinburgh – both already allowed to practise medicine – to form a guild. He gave them the sole right to sell whisky (which was regarded as a medicine) and decreed that once a year they should be given the body of a hanged criminal from which to learn more about human anatomy. James also founded the Scottish navy.

The arts benefited as well. The first Scottish printing press opened in 1507, at the foot of Blackfriars Wynd, the narrow street that led from the High Street down to the Dominican Friary. It was founded by Andro Myllar and Walter Chapman and published books on law and government and works by two of Scotland's greatest poets, William Dunbar and Robert Henryson.

The first of Dunbar's work to be published was in 1508 and his words offer a snapshot of life in the town. In one vitriolic passage he attacks the city fathers for their tight-fisted attitudes and in another voices a concept that has currency to this day: Edinburgh is a city of two contrasting faces, one rich and one poor. Among Edinburghers the distillation of that idea can be found in the phrase 'fur coat and nae knickers', and writers from James Hogg to Robert Louis Stevenson have found mileage in the idea that behind the elegant façade lurks something demonic.

'PERPETUAL' PEACE, CONTINUAL WAR

Holyrood saw an event of some splendour on 8 August 1503, when James married Henry VII's 12-year-old daughter, Margaret Tudor. Less splendid were the events that followed. As part of the marriage settlement, James had signed the Treaty of Perpetual Peace with England. The grand title failed to live up to political reality, however, and only a decade later the countries went to war again when the French persuaded James to attack

England. In early autumn 1513, the citizens of Edinburgh mustered at the Mercat Cross on the High Street to join an army that, when it took its fateful position on Branxton Hill in Northumberland, was 20,000 strong. The Battle of Flodden was a disaster for the Scots. The army was routed and 10,000 Scots were killed, James among them.

In Edinburgh, the shock of the defeat was palpable. Disbelief turned to panic when the townspeople realised the English might press north and attack Edinburgh. Work on the Flodden Wall began, though the attack never materialised. Still visible in parts today, it had six entry points and, while not completed until 1560, formed the town's boundary for a further two centuries.

The death of James V, in 1542, continued the dynastic turmoil and added a religious element. It was thought that stability could be ensured by marrying off his infant daughter, the future Mary, Queen of Scots. But to whom? The Scots were split between those who wanted a French alliance (Cardinal Beaton and Mary's mother, Mary of Guise) and those who wanted an English one. Henry VIII of England sent the Earl of Hertford's army to Scotland to 'persuade' the Scots that a marriage to his son, Edward, was preferable. Hertford landed at Leith in the early summer of 1544 and looted both Abbey and Palace in an episode that has come to be known as the 'rough wooing'. Hertford's force of 10,000 men then stormed the Netherbow but were repulsed; instead they seized £50,000-worth of grain and two ships.

Three years later, the English returned with an army commanded by the Duke of Somerset. They set up a base at Haddington, 18 miles from Edinburgh, and, in September 1547, the Battle of Pinkie Cleuch was fought at Musselburgh, just outside the town. The Scots lost and were chased back to the gates, but the Castle was held. The harassment only stopped in 1548, when a force of French and Dutch troops landed at Leith. Mary was sent to live in France and, in 1549, the port was fortified against further attack. She eventually married her cousin, Lord Darnley, in 1565. By that time the religious turmoil had begun.

REFORMING ZEAL

In 1560, the famous Reformation Parliament declared Protestantism Scotland's official religion. The faction that had previously been pro-French and pro-Mary now also became pro-Catholic, while the Protestant forces rallied against them.

John Knox, a legendary figure in Edinburgh history and the architect of the Reformation in Scotland, became the leader of the Reformed Church. He hated Mary, and the period between her arrival at Leith from France in August 1561 and her abdication in 1567 saw much friction between the Catholic monarchy and the Protestant Church.

John Knox, architect of the Reformation.

Mary remains one of Scotland's most romantic figures. Much of the myth-making turns on the events of 1566, when her favourite, the Savoyard David Rizzio, was murdered by a group of noblemen in Holyroodhouse – a group led by her husband, Lord Darnley. Not long afterwards, Darnley was killed in an explosion at his house and Mary married Lord Bothwell. But the marriage was opposed and a rising of the nobles caused Mary to flee to England after relinquishing the throne to the son she had borne Darnley, the future James VI (1567-1625).

James was born in a tiny room in the Castle, which can still be seen today. He proved to be a man of great learning and wrote the first anti-tobacco tract, *Counterblast Against Tobacco*, in 1604. But if he was forward-looking in that respect, he was less so in others: Knox believed James ruled Scotland for God, whereas James believed in the divine right of kings.

James later forced through the Five Articles of Perth, which tempered the power of the Kirk as a Protestant vehicle, and hankered after the throne of England. On 26 March 1603, the King was woken by a banging on the outer gate of Holyroodhouse. It was Sir Robert Carey, who had ridden for 36 hours with news from London: Queen Elizabeth was dead. James VI was to be crowned James I, King of England.

Rule from England

Three years into the seventeenth century, Scotland lost its king to London when James VI (or 'Jamie Saxt' as he was known) succeeded to the throne of England. History remembers him as James VI (of Scotland) and I (of England). A century later Scotland was to lose its Parliament, too, when the Act of Union was signed and the Scottish Parliament was dissolved.

The years between 1603 and 1707 were ones of social unrest and religious turmoil as Scotland came to terms with absentee rule. James said he would return every three years, but it was 14 years before he set foot on Scottish soil again. The country suffered a loss of national identity and a feeling of uncertainty. One aspect of this 'crisis of the intellect' was the witch hunts. These were initiated in James VI's reign but took place regularly until 1670. They resulted in hundreds of (mainly) women being burned at the stake in Edinburgh, after first being half-drowned in the Nor' Loch.

But the first years of the seventeenth century were not unprofitable for Edinburgh. Merchants such as George Heriot were thriving, as was the University of Edinburgh, founded in 1582 as the Townis College. Other building work in the early seventeenth century bears testament to the town's prosperity: the east wing of the Castle was rebuilt by Sir James Mason, Parliament House was begun in 1632 (the Scottish Parliament was by then resident in the city) and a year later Holyroodhouse was extended. **Gladstone's Land**, one of many merchant houses erected in this period, was built in the early decades of the century.

Goldsmiths, watchmakers and bookbinders flourished in Parliament Square and with Edinburgh now the legal centre of Scotland the town's lawyers amassed great wealth. In 1609, James ordered that the magistrates should wear robes like those of the aldermen of London and gave the royal assent for a sword to be carried in front of the provost on official occasions.

THE NATIONAL COVENANT

But, in 1637, something happened to reignite a religious passion not seen in Scotland since the days of the Reformation, 90 years earlier. And Edinburgh and its mob played a significant role. James died in 1625 and was succeeded by his son, Charles I. He was crowned King of Scotland in 1633 at Holyroodhouse.

In an effort to impose religious uniformity on both countries of his domain, Charles introduced a new prayer book to Scotland. Called the Book of Common Prayer, it followed the pattern of the Episcopalian church service, unpopular with the Presbyterians.

So unpopular, in fact, did the new prayer book prove that on the occasion of its first use in St Giles, 23 July 1637, an old cabbage seller called Jenny Geddes threw her stool at Dean Hanna shouting: 'Dost thou say Mass at my lug?' The Bishop of Edinburgh mounted the pulpit to calm the crowd but was mobbed. The riot spread outside and into the streets. This 'spontaneous' uprising is another great Edinburgh folk story – but in truth, trouble had been brewing for some time and it is likely that the riot was carefully planned beforehand.

Either way, Charles was furious. But the Book of Common Prayer and the heavy taxes the King had levied on Edinburgh still irked the Scots. A document called the National Covenant was drawn up, signed in blood by some, asserting the Scots' rights to both spiritual and civil liberty. On the last day of February 1638, it was read from the pulpit of Greyfriars Church. Over the next two days a host of lairds and burgesses came to sign it.

The Castle was held by forces loyal to the King, but in the town the rule of the Covenant held sway. Meanwhile, Charles was distracted in England when civil war broke out. By 1649, Oliver Cromwell had assumed power in England and on 30 January, Charles I was executed in London. The Scots were outraged that their Parliament had not been consulted – after all, Charles had been King of Scotland as well as England – and six days later the Scots proclaimed Charles II king if he would accept the Covenanters' demands. Instead, Charles asked the Marquis of Montrose, who had been loyal to his father, to conquer Scotland for him. But Montrose was defeated and captured. Brought to Edinburgh, he was paraded up the High Street and, on 21 May 1650, executed in front of a crowd that was not entirely unsympathetic towards him. Nevertheless, Charles came to Scotland, landing at Leith later that year. No other monarch would visit Edinburgh until George IV in 1822.

Cromwell's response was to invade. He defeated the Scots under General Leslie at the Battle of Dunbar on 3 September 1650. While Charles escaped to be crowned King of Scotland, in January 1651, Cromwell's troops burned Holyroodhouse and he imposed crippling taxes for the maintenance of his army.

PESTILENCE & PLAGUE

Those 13 years of rebellion and religious turmoil hit Edinburgh hard: trade dropped off dramatically and plague ravaged the city in 1644, killing 20 per cent of the population. Nevertheless, it remained a lively place throughout the seventeenth century.

Golf was played in virtually any open space, archery was practised and the young men of the town were apt to use their pistols to shoot fowl from their windows. The Kirk, meanwhile, was forever berating the townspeople for spending Sundays in ale houses.

Sanitation got no better, though: plague visited the city again in 1645 and it wasn't until 1687 that Parliament decreed that the council provide 20 carts to remove refuse. Water was still being carted around in barrels by the water caddies, or drawn from private wells.

Meanwhile, tea was tasted for the first time in the city in 1681, the same year James Dalrymple published his *Institutions of the Law of Scotland*. He is remembered as the 'Father of Scottish Law', an important sobriquet as it was Scotland's independent legal system (along with its separate religious and educational set-ups) that came to be seen as proof of nationhood after 1707.

A map drawn in 1647 shows a bewildering number of closes running off the High Street and down through the Cowgate, with St Giles and the old burying ground behind. Edinburgh spread a little beyond the Flodden Wall in 1617 when High Riggs was bought by the town; further areas were added in 1639, notably the Pleasance and Calton Hill.

MURDER MOST FOUL

When Charles II was returned to the throne in 1660 after Cromwell's death – the period known as the Restoration – he reneged on acts made in favour of Covenanters and discontent simmered once again. Revolt broke out in Galloway in 1666 and, in 1679, the Covenanters won a victory at the Battle of Drumclog. Charles sent the Duke of Monmouth to crush the Covenanters, which he did at the Battle of Bothwell Brig later that year. In a period of history that has become known as 'the killing time', the survivors were marched to Greyfriars Kirkyard in Edinburgh and imprisoned there for five months. They had little food, shelter or water and many died or were executed.

James VII and II ascended to the throne in 1685 on the death of his brother Charles, but his Catholicism made him unpopular. The Dukes of Argyll and Monmouth tried to unseat him and failed; James's reign stuttered on. In 1688, when he fathered an heir, English noblemen sought to replace him with a Protestant, William of Orange, and his wife Mary, who was James's daughter. James fled to France and the protection of Louis XIV.

William and Mary came to the throne in 1688. Many in Edinburgh and in the Scottish Parliament favoured William – they burned effigies of the Pope on news of his landing – but Scotland as a whole was largely pro-James, especially in the Highlands. This lobby became known as the Jacobites, after 'Jacobus', the Latin word for James. The Duke of Gordon did hold Edinburgh Castle for James, but only until 1689.

Mary, Queen of Scots, the country's most romantic historical figure, who fought bitterly with the church in Scotland.

The 1690s were bad for Edinburgh. A series of terrible harvests affected food supplies, an English war with France affected trade, Catholic and Protestant factions were once more circling each other warily and, in 1698, the failure of the Darien Scheme virtually bankrupted the nation.

Funded partly by the Edinburgh financiers and merchants who had helped set up the Bank of Scotland in 1695, the Darien Scheme involved sending an expedition from Leith to the Caribbean to set up a trading link between east and west. Through a combination of misfortune and English hostility, it was a disaster.

When news of the failure reached Edinburgh there was rioting on a massive scale: the Tolbooth was stormed and all the prisoners released, while much of the Cowgate and the Royal Exchange were torched.

The collapse of the scheme strengthened the hand of those south of the border who sought to bully Scotland into a union with England.

END OF AN AULD SANG

On 3 October 1706, a crowd gathered on the High Street to watch, for the last time, the 'Riding', the ceremony that preceded the opening of Parliament. Eventually the Act of Union became law in January 1707, and the dissolution of Parliament followed in April. When the Lord High Chancellor of Scotland, Lord Seafield, was presented with the Act for royal assent, he is said to have touched it with his sceptre and said the words: 'There's an end of an auld sang'. It would be nearly 300 years before the Scottish Parliament sat again.

The Age of Improvement

The eighteenth century is known in Edinburgh as the 'Age of Improvement'. The phrase refers to the massive building programme started in the 1760s and to the spirit of intellectual inquiry that flourished among the town's lawyers, academics and churchmen (known as 'the Enlightenment'). Edinburgh was buzzing with the words of men like the philosopher David Hume and Adam Smith, author of *The Wealth of Nations*.

By 1720, the city had two newspapers, and the formation of a school of design, in 1760, pre-dated London's Royal Academy by eight years. The Honourable Company of Edinburgh Golfers was founded in 1744 and, in 1777, the Royal High School moved to grand new premises in High School Yards, at the foot of Infirmary Street. The number of students at the university doubled between 1763 and 1783 (the year the Royal Society of Edinburgh was founded); it had quadrupled by 1821. Lawyers were everywhere – there were 65 wig-makers in the city by 1700 – and the Faculty of Advocates became pivotal in the city's social and intellectual life.

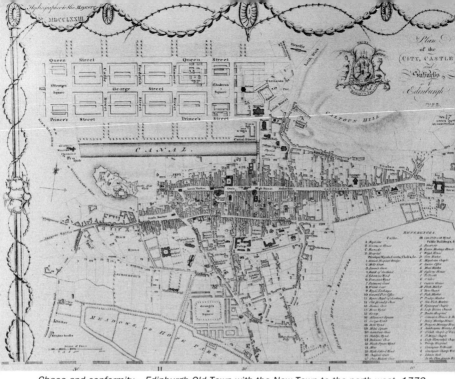

Chaos and conformity – Edinburgh Old Town with the New Town to the north west, 1772.

In 1725, the Lord Provost, George Drummond, drew up plans for a new medical school and, in 1729, the first infirmary opened at Robertson's Close. In 1731, the Medical Society was founded and, in 1736, the infirmary was granted a royal charter. A second hospital opened in College Wynd in the same year.

But at the start of the century, the city was still medieval in its geography. Edinburgh gave the appearance of being one cramped, towering, organic whole, clinging grimly on to the hillside with an enormous channel – the High Street – running down the middle.

The old city walls still formed the town boundaries, by and large, so as the population grew to well over 50,000 in the eighteenth century, the only way to build was up. This practice resulted in the 'lands'; six, seven, eight storeys tall and prone to collapse with great loss of life.

Nobles and lairds lived almost side-by-side with the common people, and visitors regularly commented on the well-established Edinburgh tradition of emptying chamber pots out of the top windows. 'Gardey loo', was the famous warning shout, often matched by a hasty 'Haud yer haun!' (Hold your hand!) from the pedestrians getting showered beneath.

BIRTH OF THE NEW TOWN

So it was with a lungful of fresh air that Edinburgh finally burst out across the valley to the north, creating one of the finest architectural enclaves in the world – the New Town. Progress, harmony, rationalisation – and claret – were the order of the day as far as the Enlightenment was concerned. And three of those four principles were brought to bear on the competition, announced in 1766, for the best plan to extend Edinburgh to the north and from which the New Town grew.

The competition was won by a 21-year-old architect called James Craig. The prize-winning plan has not been saved, but a later plan, from 1767, shows three main streets – South, North and Principal – crossed by smaller streets and positioned between two Grand Squares. These streets eventually became Princes Street, George Street and Queen Street. Princes Street was originally meant to be called St Giles' Street after the city's saint, but George III objected.

As part of the overall scheme, the Nor' Loch was drained and the North Bridge, which spanned the valley, was started in 1763. In 1781, the Mound was begun, using the earth from the work going on to the north. By the time the Mound was completed, in 1830, an estimated two million cartloads of earth had been dumped on it. The city also pushed south up to the old Kirk O'Fields, where a new college for the university was built in 1789 and, in 1768, the Theatre Royal went up in what was known as Shakespeare Square. It was the first licensed stage in Scotland and stood on the site of the old post office at the east end of Princes Street.

Overspill from the Old Town to the New Town was considerable and, by 1791, there were 7,206 people living there. The city had also pushed southwards and George Square was laid out in 1766, but, with its panoramic views over the Forth, it was the New Town that became a haven for lawyers and merchants. David Hume was one of the first people to move to the New Town: he built a house at the corner of St Andrew's Square. The result of this movement of the wealthier classes northwards was that a type of social apartheid formed. Once more, the notion of the city with two faces surfaced.

The late eighteenth century also provided Edinburgh with one of its most fascinating characters: Deacon William Brodie, town councillor by day, burglar by night. Hanged in 1788, it is his double life that Stevenson is said to have used as the model for his novel *The Strange Case of Dr Jekyll and Mr Hyde*.

With the easing of congestion in the Old Town, tempers seemed to cool a little – the mob saw relatively little action in the eighteenth century. The Porteous Riots of 1736, however, were a notable and violent exception. Irritated by the decision to hang two smugglers and incensed by the shooting of several townspeople by soldiers at the hanging, the mob stormed the Tolbooth and 'arrested' the unpopular captain of the guard, Captain Porteous. He was marched down to the Grassmarket, lynched and left dangling from a dyer's pole.

Neither was Edinburgh much affected by the two significant Jacobite rebellions of 1715 and 1745, though Prince Charles Edward Stuart – aka Bonnie Prince Charlie – did spend six weeks in Edinburgh in 1745 after his victory over Sir John Cope at Prestonpans. Charlie's dream of reclaiming Scotland for the Stuarts died at Culloden a year later. After the defeat, 14 of the standards carried by the clan chiefs at Culloden were taken into the town by chimney sweeps and burned.

But violence came knocking again at the end of the century, when revolution broke out in France and many in Great Britain feared an invasion. The Edinburgh Volunteers were formed to defend the city. With the violence came political discourse and parliamentary reform was discussed. In 1802, the

Old Parliament House with St Giles' Cathedral during the age of Enlightenment.

Edinburgh Review was founded and it became a forum for anti-government opinions; other publications followed as Edinburgh became preeminent in the world of publishing and bookselling.

GREAT SCOTT

Edinburgh-born Sir Walter Scott was a titan of the later years of this era. He was internationally respected and, in early-nineteenth century-terms, a blockbusting novelist. It was pressure from him that led to the 'Honours of Scotland' – the crown, sceptre and sword of state – being searched for and uncovered in the Castle in 1818. They had been lost since 1603. Meanwhile, Scott was able to entice George IV to Edinburgh, in 1822, for what was the first official visit of a monarch to Scotland since Charles I in 1641. If he could have seen beyond the pomp of this curious occasion, George would have discovered a city on the slide. In 1818, work began on the Union Canal to join Edinburgh with the Forth and Clyde Canal, but the National Monument to the dead of the Napoleonic Wars, which was begun in 1822 on Calton Hill, was never finished. The Parthenon-like structure stands there still, long ago dubbed 'Scotland's Disgrace', but now also a reminder that Scotland was once more losing its way. Power was in London and the intellectual activity of the Enlightenment was declining – Edinburgh's glory days were behind it.

The Victorian era

Edinburgh underwent a third period of expansion during the Victorian era, when suburbs such as Marchmont, Morningside and Bruntsfield were built. The city that had become two when the New Town was built found itself with a third face. Each 'city' had its own characteristics and type of inhabitants: the solid Victorian suburbs were peopled by the growing middle class, the grand New Town remained the area of choice for lawyers and judges, while the teeming Old Town became a slum.

Edinburgh also witnessed one of the most significant moments in nineteenth-century Scottish history in 1843, when the Church was split in two and a breakaway group, the Free Kirk, was formed. But unlike the religious turbulence of previous centuries, this 'revolution' was peaceful.

Meanwhile, the city retained its reputation as a place of law and learning, while Glasgow to the west became the country's industrial powerhouse. It is a distinction that remains to this day.

URBAN BLIGHT

At the start of the nineteenth century, the population of Edinburgh and Leith was 102,987. By 1881, the population of Greater Edinburgh was 320,549. One of the reasons for the dramatic increase was the influx of people from other parts of Scotland and from Ireland. Indeed, Burke and Hare, two of Edinburgh's most infamous criminals, were both Irish immigrants.

With the population rise came unemployment. The riots of 1812 and 1818 both had economic causes at their root and by the 1830s outbreaks of cholera and typhoid had decimated the Old Town. That was compounded, in 1824, by a fire that destroyed much of the High Street with great loss of life and resulted in the formation of the world's first municipal fire service.

Meanwhile, a study conducted by Dr George Bell in the 1850s found 159 of the Old Town's closes lacked drainage and fresh water and concluded that Blackfriars Wynd was home to 1,000 people sharing just 142 houses. Cholera returned to the city in 1848.

Bell also bemoaned the alcoholism endemic in the Old Town's inhabitants. A separate study undertaken in 1842 by a young Edinburgh doctor, William Tait, found that of Edinburgh's 200 brothels, most were in the Old Town.

Attempts were made to restore the Old Town, particularly by William Chambers (Lord Provost from 1865-69), but the area was on a downward spiral that continued into the twentieth century.

In contrast to the decrepitude of the Old Town were the public buildings thrown up during the nineteenth century: schools, churches, galleries, railway stations, hospitals, banks and bridges – the Victorians had a zeal for them all.

It was matched, after the 'Disruption' of 1843, by the missionary zeal of the Free Kirk, which came into being in May 1843 when 474 ministers seceded from the Church to form a breakaway organisation. The occasion was the General Assembly, the grievance was the right of congregations to choose their own minister, and the scene of the split was the Church of St Andrew and St George on George Street. Led by Dr David Welsh, Dr Thomas Chalmers and Dr Thomas Guthrie, the dissenting churchmen marched down Hanover Street to Tanfield Hall in Canonmills. 'No spectacle since the Revolution,' noted Lord Cockburn in his journal, 'reminded one so forcibly of the Covenanters.' The split wasn't resolved until 1929.

MAKING PROGRESS

In 1847, Guthrie helped set up three charity schools after meeting some boys in Holyrood Park who said they had never been to school. Guthrie also became active in the temperance movement, which sought to curb the kind of drinking that Dr George Bell had identified as a social ill some years earlier. This movement had some success, in 1853, when a bill was passed that shut the inns on Sundays. Meanwhile, public hangings were stopped, in 1864, and moved to within the walls of Calton jail, which had been opened in 1817. George Bryce was the last criminal to suffer the indignity of a public execution and it is said that 20,000 people turned up to watch him die.

Fewer turned up to the early meetings of those engaged in the struggle for women's suffrage. Nevertheless, one of the first three women's suffrage societies was formed in Edinburgh, in 1867. The same year saw the Improvement Act, which stripped the old wooden fronts from the lands (a terrible fire hazard) and opened up some of the most crowded areas. The move was initiated by Lord Provost Chambers, who lent his name to Chambers Street, which was built in 1871.

This moral and ideological progress was matched by technological advances, particularly in the fields of transport and medicine.

In the early seventeenth century, London was 13 days away by coach; towards the end of the century the journey could be done in four. But, with the age of steam, transport became far easier – 1850 saw the first public train from London to Edinburgh and, in 1862, the famous *Flying Scotsman* did the run in just ten-and-a-half hours. In 1890, the Forth Railway Bridge was built, an imposing structure spanning the Forth at South Queensferry. Unusually for a nation that has made understatement an art form, it has long been hailed by Scots as the 'Eighth Wonder of the World'.

Between 1845 and 1846, rail tunnels were built between Haymarket and Waverley Stations, through the south flank of Calton Hill and under the Mound. These brought tourists and travellers straight into the heart of the city, where they would emerge to face the Castle, the Gothic bulk of the Scott Monument (begun in 1840), the galleries at the foot of the Mound and the splendour of Princes Street gardens. A century and a half later, this is still the best way to arrive in the city.

In the world of medicine, men such as James Young Simpson and Joseph Lister gained international renown for their work in the fields of anaesthetics and antiseptics.

Towards the end of the Victorian era, Glasgow had begun to assume increasing importance in Scotland, to the detriment of Edinburgh. The two international festivals Glasgow held – in 1888 and 1901 – outshone the one on the Meadows in Edinburgh in 1886, and men such as the designer Charles Rennie Mackintosh were creating an artistic and architectural legacy that is still revered today. The appearance of Gladstone in Edinburgh, in 1880 and 1881, to fight campaigns in Midlothian gave the city some political kudos, but as the historian and journalist Allan Massie has pointed out, Edinburgh at the end of the nineteenth century was just the biggest small town in Scotland.

The Modern Age

Look around Edinburgh today and the most significant twentieth-century buildings are the hideous, grey edifices thrown up in the 1960s. Very little has been added architecturally to the city this century. The suburbs have continued to creep outwards, but buildings were more likely to be pulled down than put up, as the city fathers (and private contractors) finally got to grips with the decaying Old Town and moved the population outwards to areas such as Niddrie and Craigmillar. In fact, the greatest construct of twentieth-century Edinburgh has been the arts festival.

Some major building work has been undertaken, however. The two great station hotels at either end of Princes Street were opened in the early years of the century, though Princes Street Station – served by the **Caledonian Hotel** – is long gone. Meanwhile, the **King's Theatre** opened in 1906, and the Usher Hall followed in 1913. And then, in 1939, St Andrew's House opened to house the Scottish Office and later became the headquarters of the Secretary of State for Scotland. It resembles a Stalinist blockhouse, though it compares favourably with many that came after. The worst of these are the **St James Centre** and New St Andrew's House, built at the east end of Princes Street in 1971. Leith Street was flattened to make way for these buildings and, in the process, Edinburgh lost the house in Picardy Place in which Sherlock Holmes creator Arthur Conan Doyle was born, in 1859.

The author was Catholic and his nineteenth-century childhood was plagued by sectarian taunts. However, the civil unrest that broke out in

Ireland in the second decade of the twentieth century caused even greater religious intolerance in the city. This exploded in the 1930s, when Edinburgh-born John Cormack, who had served in Ireland with the British Army, founded the Protestant Action League, though as an organisation it was short-lived and little-remembered.

Longer lasting were the effects of the women's suffrage movement. Between 1912 and 1914, supporters in Edinburgh regularly damaged letterboxes, though their more adventurous exploits included attempts to blow up the Royal Observatory and Rosslyn Chapel, and the setting of a fire at Fettes College. Letterboxes came under attack again in Edinburgh in the 1950s, when they were defaced by Scottish Nationalists after the coronation of Queen Elizabeth II.

Meanwhile, Edinburgh's infrastructure was being upgraded. New reservoirs were opened to bring more water into the city, the telephone service was expanded and, in 1924, a radio station opened. Fashions changed, fewer women were employed in domestic service, nursery schools opened and, in 1912, the World Council of Churches was formed as a result of a meeting in the Assembly Hall.

Edinburgh's lack of heavy industry saved the city twice during this century's middle years. It allowed it to avoid the ravages of the Depression and, a decade or so later, the bombs of the Luftwaffe. Leith was one of the few areas that was badly affected.

LEISURE CENTRE

Sport has become woven into the fabric of Edinburgh life this century. Most of the city's sporting teams were born in the nineteenth century. The city's two football teams were founded within a year of each other – **Heart of Midlothian** in 1874 and **Hibernian** in 1875 – and both have enjoyed (occasional) periods of success over the years. Support is divided partly according to religion – Hearts are Protestant, Hibs are Catholic – and partly according to geography, with Hearts to the west, Hibs to the east.

Rugby Union has been played in the city since the nineteenth century, with internationals held on the pitches at Raeburn Place. In 1922, the Scottish Football Union (as it was then called) bought a plot of land at Murrayfield and built a stadium. It was inaugurated on 21 March 1925, when Scotland played England for the Grand Slam.

Oldest of all these sports, however, is curling. Its origins are lost in time, but the Royal Caledonian Curling Club was formed in Edinburgh in 1838 and is now regarded as the sport's 'mother club'. The World Curling Federation is also based in Edinburgh.

But if sport didn't appeal there were other leisure pursuits to follow. In 1913, the **Zoological Gardens** were established and, in 1933, a huge Olympic-size open-air swimming pool opened on the coast at Portobello. City folk could now catch a tram to the seaside (the system was city-wide by 1922), spend their days in the sun and enjoy a view over the Forth.

But Edinburgh being Edinburgh, life wasn't always thoroughly modern: the privilege of sanctuary for debtors in Holyrood Abbey, established back in 1128, was still in existence as late as 1904.

EDINBURGH TODAY

Many traditional Edinburgh industries, such as publishing, have declined throughout the twentieth century. The addition of two universities (Heriot-Watt and Napier) has strengthened the city's academic reputation, however, and Edinburgh is one of Europe's top financial centres, with fund management and insurance specialities.

The International Festival has kept Edinburgh on the artistic map since 1947. In the inter-war years the 'Scottish Renaissance' saw a flowering of literary and artistic talent. It centred around writers and artists such as Hugh MacDiarmid, James Bridie, Edwin Muir, Naomi Mitchison, Lewis Grassic Gibbon and Neil Gunn. Milnes Bar on Hanover Street was a regular meeting place.

Something of that feel has returned in recent years thanks to the success of a few vibrant publishing houses and, of course, the international success of Irvine Welsh's novel *Trainspotting*. It has helped throw the spotlight on Edinburgh's ills, such as the heroin epidemic that swept through the city in the 1980s, and undermine the tartan-and-shortbread image fostered by the shops that today throng the Lawnmarket.

The Commonwealth Games have come twice to Edinburgh (1970 and 1986), though with a burgeoning number of conference facilities in the city, it is delegates rather than athletes who will congregate in Edinburgh in the future. It is all part of a tourist industry that now brings £2.4 billion to Scotland annually, and on which Edinburgh's economy largely depends.

The modern Edinburgh – now spread wide over seven hills – would be unrecognisable to the earliest settlers of the Castle Rock. The population of Edinburgh in the 1991 census was 418,914, and many of them will be unable to see either the castle in the air or the palace on the ground from where they live in their high-rise flats or low-lying tenements. But the ghosts of Scott, Stevenson, St Margaret, Queen Mary, Hume and the rest – as well as the buildings, books, ideas and memories they left – will remind both populace and visitors that the city's history is a living thing that continues with them. Edinburgh may be a place in love with its own past, but with a new millennium and a new Parliament about to open, it can do no harm to flirt with the future.

Architecture

Defined equally by its dramatic setting and a willingness to adopt and adapt, Edinburgh has developed a strong architectural identity.

Edinburgh is justifiably classed as one of Europe's finest cities, so it's not surprising that it has a knowingly handsome air. A 'dream of a great genius', wrote one 1820s visitor, while Mary Shelley had the narrator of her Gothic classic *Frankenstein* comment on 'the beauty and regularity of the New Town of Edinburgh, its romantic castle and its environs, the most delightful in the world…'.

Topographically, Edinburgh has been dealt a spectacular hand. The Pentland Hills lie to the south and a coastal plain stretches north to the Firth of Forth, while Arthur's Seat and the Castle Rock, impressive remnants of volcanic action, lend geographical drama to the inner city. This setting has shaped a city of two distinct characters. Crowned by **Edinburgh Castle**, hugging tightly to the Castle Rock, the Old Town looks across to the New Town, a triumph of classical formality played out in a gridiron of well-disciplined streets.

Remarkably well-preserved – in 1995 UNESCO designated the Old Town and New Town a World Heritage Site – Edinburgh has a knack for seducing the visitor. It is a city that demands to be walked. Calf-muscles can take a battering on its many slopes, but Edinburgh's architecture, a glorious embodiment of its history and character, more than compensates for the pain.

PREHISTORIC TO MEDIAEVAL

Bronze Age settlers first colonised the natural citadel of the Castle Rock in around 900BC. In the first century AD, after centuries of relative inactivity, the rocky outcrop became home to a succession of settlements.

Under the ambitious rule of the House of Canmore, the Castle Rock emerged as a fortified stronghold (today's Edinburgh Castle). The small but squatly Romanesque St Margaret's Chapel (c1110), with its characteristic rounded, chevron-decorated chancel arch, is the earliest architectural survivor.

In 1125, the expanding settlement was declared a royal burgh and, in 1128, the Abbey of Holyrood was founded. Linear development gradually linked Holyrood to the Castle Rock along the rocky spine of the Old Town, defining the route of today's **Royal Mile**.

Architecturally, little remains from Edinburgh's infant years. Instability and limited funds meant that few structures were built of stone. Most of the houses were crudely made from wattle and post,

covered in clay for insulation and thatched with straw, rushes or heather. Their lifespan was no more than a couple of decades, even assuming they escaped the fires that were a common occurrence during the frequent sacks by the English.

Of the handful of stone structures, St Giles (today's **St Giles' Cathedral** on the Royal Mile), the only parish church in the burgh, dates from 1120, but little remains of the original building. It was extensively remodelled in the late fourteenth century, when Gothic transepts and a series of chapels were added. Holyrood Abbey was also virtually rebuilt, between 1195 and 1230, the addition of arcades of pointed arches emphasising the vertical. The Castle fell twice to the English during this period, prompting a huge rebuilding programme in 1356.

SCOTTISH RENAISSANCE

As its national stature grew during the reign of James III (1460-88), Edinburgh witnessed a surge in confidence and building activity. Holyrood Abbey became a royal residence and was expanded, leading to the 1498 addition of the **Palace of Holyroodhouse**, and Edinburgh Castle was augmented by Crown Square and its baronial Great Hall, topped with a hammerbeam roof. Money was pumped into churches, most notably the now-demolished Trinity College Church, and in around 1500 a crown spire was added to the central tower of St Giles. An array of flying buttresses bedecked with gilded pinnacles, it became a template for crown spires across Scotland.

Further invasion attempts by the English in the 1540s prompted Scotland to improve relations with France and open up trade with Europe, heralding the Old Town's mercantile boom years. The city's growing internationalism was mirrored in a fusion of local and continental building patterns.

THE RISE OF THE TENEMENT

As the population increased, more housing was required. But the uneven terrain, combined with the ancient 'feu' system of land tenure, which granted leases in perpetuity, made horizontal development problematic. Thus expansion was forced upwards, leading to the birth of the tenement. Originally denoting a holding of land, the word came to mean separate dwellings stacked in storeys, linked by a common stairwell.

IN 1656 KING JAMES VII
ORDAINED THAT THE MORIFICATION OF
THIS MOORE GRANTED IN 1649 TO
BUILD A CHURCH SHOULD BE APPLIED
TO THE ERECTION OF THIS STRUCTURE

Wynds and closes developed rib-like from the Royal Mile. Houses already standing had additional storeys tacked on, often haphazardly, to become tenements with jutting windows and a confusion of roof levels. **John Knox's House** (c1490), with its protruding upper windows and storeys, is one of the few remaining examples, but it's a relatively restrained one – some timber-framed storeys protruded as far as seven feet (two metres) into the street.

Building regulations, however, reined in the quick-buck property speculators, stipulating, from the 1620s, tile or slate roofs and, in 1674, stone façades as fire precautions.

Daringly exploiting the ridge of the Old Town, tenements frequently bridged different levels, making them some of the tallest domestic buildings in Europe. The cheek-by-jowl tenements along the Royal Mile had more in common with the architecture of northern Europe than that south of the border.

By the late seventeenth century, tenements built in sandstone or harling (a mix of rubble and plaster) and characterised by flat frontages and a verticality accentuated by gables and dormer windows soared up along the Royal Mile. The Lawnmarket, below the Castle, was home to the grander examples. The five-storey **Gladstone's Land** (c1620-30) retains the once-commonplace street arcade and an oak-panelled interior.

With the upper Royal Mile awash with merchants, its lower reaches had become the choice location of the nobility, and mansions flanked the approach to the Palace of Holyroodhouse.

Moray House (c1628), with its pyramid-topped gate-piers, and the vast Queensberry House (c1634), now a redundant hospital, are the grandest survivors. The Palace itself was rebuilt in the 1670s. In a triumphant blend of Scottish and European influences, a thick-set façade with turreted towers fronted an inner courtyard with classical arcades.

With the city becoming increasingly wealthy, a new Parliament House (given a classical overhaul in the early nineteenth century) was built next to St Giles in 1637, giving weight to Edinburgh's role as Scotland's capital.

Elsewhere the city flaunted its internationalism, as with the easy handling of Renaissance style in the grandly ornamented George Heriot School (1628), south of the Royal Mile.

Along the Royal Mile, churches were built, namely John Mylne's **Tron Kirk** (1663, today the Old Town information centre) and the aristocratic-looking Canongate Kirk (1688), with its delicate, curving gables.

The Old Town's Canongate Kirk flaunts its Renaissance style. Burns' muse, Clarinda, is buried in the kirkyard.

Stained glass window in St Margaret's Chapel.

IDENTITY CRISIS

The 1707 Act of Union with England provoked an identity crisis for Edinburgh, and some dubbed the city 'a widowed metropolis'. But Edinburgh, not given to extended periods of mourning, eventually came to see architecture as pivotal to its reinvention.

The collapse, in 1751, of a Royal Mile tenement highlighted the antiquity of the Old Town and the need for 'modern' living quarters.

In 1752, the city's Lord Provost, George Drummond, drew up some proposals to expand Edinburgh, creating the grandiose Exchange (now the City Chambers) on the Royal Mile and, in 1765, the North Bridge.

The bridge, the first to cross Nor' Loch, gave easy access to Leith and, importantly, a swathe of redundant land to the north of the Old Town. This was to become the site of the 'new towns' that are collectively known as today's New Town.

Conceived as Edinburgh's 'civilised' face, the first new town, designed in 1766 by James Craig, was built to a regimented layout, with George Street flanked by Princes and Queen Streets. The name of the game was now classicism.

Influenced by the growing Europe-wide fascination with Greek and Roman civilisations, Edinburgh's new architecture adopted proportion, grandeur and classical trimmings as its hallmarks.

A leading practitioner, Robert Adam, designed Charlotte Square (from 1792). A residential enclave acting as a grand full stop to George Street, it boasted rooftop sphinxes, balustrades and fanlights (semicircular windows above the front door) and, importantly after the cramped conditions of the Old Town, the space of the square itself. **Register House** (c1788), on the axis of North Bridge, is another example of Adam's well-mannered classicism. Its cupolas and pedimented portico are a gracious retort to the haphazard gables of the Old Town.

CLASSICAL REINVENTION

By the early 1800s, architecture had an increasingly crucial role in expressing the city's newly cultivated identity. As early as 1762, Edinburgh was called the 'Athens of the North'.

As the Scottish Enlightenment held sway, the architect William Playfair gave stone and mortar representation to Calton Hill's status as Edinburgh's 'acropolis'. His **City Observatory** (1818), a mini-cruciform temple capped by a dome, stands next to his Parthenon-esque National Monument. Started in 1826 to commemorate the Napoleonic Wars, its 12 huge columns, set on a vast stepped plinth, were an attempt to provide the classical illusion to end all further classical illusions. But it remained unfinished due to a funding crisis – earning it the nickname 'Edinburgh's Disgrace'. Later it formed a visual link to Thomas Hamilton's Royal High School (1829), on the lower slopes of Calton Hill. Described as the 'noblest monument of the Scottish Greek revival', it was classicism at its most authoritarian, with a central 'temple' flanked by grand antechambers.

On the Mound, the prolific Playfair delivered further classical rhetoric with the **Royal Scottish Academy** (1823) and the **National Gallery of Scotland** (1850), a monumental, temple-inspired duo parading an army of columns and classical trimmings.

On the residential front, a succession of upmarket new towns clustered around Craig's original. The ostentatiously wide Great King Street and the columned residences of Moray Place contributed to what was, by the 1840s, one of the most extensive and well-ordered suburbs in Europe.

Punctuated by private 'pleasure gardens', the New Town gave urban living a picturesque rural charm and trumpeted Edinburgh as an ambitious and inspired city.

SCOTTISH BARONIAL & ECLECTICISM

In 1822, George IV visited Edinburgh dressed in tartan stockings and a kilt. His sartorial advisor was Sir Walter Scott, author and campaigner for the 'tartanisation' of Scotland.

With its internationalism established in the determinedly classical New Town, Edinburgh turned its attention to the home-grown heritage of

Fettes College – Tony Blair's former school.

the Old Town. The city's commercial, political and legal centre needed upgrading.

As recommended by the 1827 Improvement Act, new buildings and those in need of a facelift adopted the 'Old Scot' style. Turrets, crenellations and crows feet, à la Scots baronial, elbowed a return into the architectural language; Cockburn Street, the first vehicular link between the Royal Mile and Waverley Station, is a determined example.

Elsewhere, new public buildings masqueraded as rural piles airlifted from the Scottish Highlands. The Royal Infirmary (1870), to the south of the Royal Mile, sported a central clock tower and an array of turrets. Fettes College (1865-70), north of the New Town, was an exuberant intermarriage of local baronial and French chateau. The 'tartan touch' also hit the expanding tenement suburbs – Marchmont to the south of the city became sprinkled with turrets and gables.

Growing adventurousness gave way to architectural promiscuity. The city's well-off institutions showed confident but florid excess, with a 'pick and mix' approach to style. The headquarters of the Bank of Scotland, grandly posed on the precipice of the Mound, adopted full-on baroque; the British Linen Bank (now a Bank of Scotland branch) on St Andrew's Square opted for the Renaissance palazzo look, its Corinthian columns topped by six colossal statues.

Gothic revival made its mark courtesy of Augustus Pugin, master of the decorated pinnacle and soaring spire and designer of Tolbooth St John's Kirk (1844), below Castle Esplanade. But the finest line in romantic Gothic came in George Meikle Kemp's **Scott Monument** (1840), on Princes Street, an elaborate, filigreed, spire-like affair enshrining a statue of Sir Walter Scott.

MUSCULAR POST-MODERNISM

Little disturbed by industrialisation, turn-of-the-century Edinburgh saw no huge bursts of construction. The impetus to build was further anaesthetised by two world wars. The Euro-wide, clean-cut 1930s style made little impression, save the robustly authoritarian St Andrew's House (1937-39), on the lower reaches of Calton Hill. The former home of the Scottish Office is a true architectural heavyweight, with an imposing, symmetrical facade. In the suburbs a few avant-garde adventurers experimented. Architect William Kininmonth's house (1933), in Dick Place, with its cool play of curves and verticals, is one of the finest examples of the International style in Scotland.

The redevelopment of the Old Town was the major planning and social issue during the first half of the century. With the upwardly mobile residents siphoned off to the New Town, a large part of the Old Town had, by the Victorian era, developed into an overcrowded, disease-ridden slum. As early as 1892 the urban planner Sir Patrick Geddes (who inspired the saccharine revamp of Ramsey Gardens, just below Castle Esplanade) had proposed seeding the area with members of the university. But his plan was not adopted. Instead, by the inter-war years, residents were being encouraged to decamp to a series of council-built satellite townships on the periphery of the city, first among them the Craigmillar estate. This social engineering, achieved through town planning, was a crude mirror of the earlier, wealthier New Town model of urban displacement.

The fate of the increasingly depopulated Old Town was still in the balance. In 1949, the Abercrombie Plan saw slum tenements demolished, along with the grander George Square, to make way for a new university campus. The sacrifice of George Square, particularly, to the unpopular 1960s idiom that replaced it sent a rallying call to the preservation troops, with the effect that much of the Old Town was saved – but thereafter resolutely contemporary architecture has dared make only rare appearances in the Old Town. Even outside it there are few notable exceptions save the low-slung, glass-panelled **Royal Commonwealth Pool** (1967) and Basil Spence's University Library (1965) to the south. The city instead suffered explosions of 1960s brutalism, as seen in the ugly, blockish **St James Centre**, just off Princes Street. The subsequent backlash sent

the city planners into cautious mode, inviting accusations of architectural timidity. These reached their height in 1989 when a redundant site on the Royal Mile was filled by the Scandic Crown Hotel (now the **Crowne Plaza Edinburgh**), built in the Old Town-imitation style.

A flirtation with a late-twentieth-century idiom is shown in the Exchange, the city's new financial quarter on Lothian Road, outside the confines of the Old and New Towns. Terry Farrell's International Conference Centre forms the nucleus, with big-name companies (Edinburgh is the fourth largest financial services centre in Europe) inhabiting the surrounding office blocks. Built in the 1990s but in 1980s style, the Exchange's Festival Square and the Standard Life Building are one-liners in overly muscular commercial architecture and sad examples of modernism at its most mediocre.

DEVOLUTION & BEYOND

Debate over the location of the new Scottish Parliament highlighted Edinburgh's ongoing architectural sensitivity. Calton Hill, long seen as the symbolic heart of Scotland's nationhood (the Royal High School was converted in 1979 to house the proposed Scottish Assembly) had the historical upper hand.

The decision by the Scottish Office to site the Parliament in Canongate, near the Palace of Holyroodhouse – the British monarch's official residence in Scotland – was viewed in some quarters as a sign of political complaisance.

Canongate is, however, witnessing an extensive programme of new building. Its central location, to the east of the Old Town, with scenic views to Arthur's Seat has made it a prime target for redevelopment. Michael Hopkin's translucent, tent-like William Younger Centre, which will house an interactive exhibition of the earth's history, is to open in 1999. *The Scotsman* newspaper is relocating to a new home next door and a swathe of land sandwiched between Canongate and Holyrood Road is being redeveloped with a mix of housing and public buildings. Here it appears that commercial concerns are to be balanced with the need to maintain the Old Town's residential population.

At the time of writing, five international architectural practices (three working in collaboration with Scottish practices) had been shortlisted to design the new Parliament. The consensus is that Scotland should demonstrate its new status with a building that respects the city's past while embracing the contemporary.

Having been accused of suffering from the 'post-New Town siesta' syndrome by some critics, Edinburgh is now perhaps more conscious of the need to protect its architectural heritage, wake up to the future and turn that dream of genius into an architectural reality.

Politics

Who rules Scotland?

No matter the political hue of the government of the day or the currently burning political topic, one question has long been central to Scottish political debate: 'Who rules Scotland?'

It is a question that was asked when James VI acceded to the English throne and moved his Court from Edinburgh to London in 1603. It was asked over a century later, in 1707, when the parliament took the same journey after the Act of Union was ratified. It was asked when the Scottish National Party was formed in the 1920s. It was repeatedly asked during the Thatcher administration of the 1980s, particularly when the Poll Tax was imposed in the late 1980s. It is still being asked today.

Immediately after World War II, the Scottish Labour Party and the Scottish Conservative and Unionist Party dominated the political scene. In the 1960s and particularly the 1970s, the Scottish National Party (SNP) made gains and today those three parties are joined by the Scottish Liberal Democrats in the power-balance.

All the parties have approached the issue of home rule with a degree of fluidity; political pragmatism has seen successive generations of the same party edge towards or away from it. The Conservatives, for instance, were once in favour, but made an anti-devolution stance a central plank of the manifesto on which they fought the general election of 1997 – and lost every single Scottish seat in Westminster. Their traditional heartlands are the well-heeled farming areas of the Lowlands, Perthshire and the more affluent districts of the major cities.

The SNP are presently the second most powerful force in Scotland, despite opinion polls indicating that more than 50 per cent of Scots are in favour of independence. The north and the Highlands and Islands tend to vote SNP or Liberal Democrat, though rogue patches of this or that political hue crop up all over the country – the SNP took Galloway and Upper Nithsdale in the 1997 election and the Liberal Democrats have strong pockets of support in the Borders.

But it is Labour that has the firmest hold on both the Scottish psyche and Scotland's political institutions, particularly in the urban and industrial areas of the central belt. In the general election of 1945, Clement Attlee's Labour government swept to power with a huge majority and set about building the welfare state and nationalising heavy industry. It was a victory for a party whose roots lie firmly in Scotland, the Scottish Parliamentary Labour Party having been established by Lanarkshire-born trade unionist Keir Hardie in 1888. Accordingly, the Scottish branch of the Labour Party has always enjoyed a degree of independence within the Labour movement.

However, the Labour Party has yet to match the 50.1 per cent polled by the Scottish Conservative and Unionist Party in the 1955 general election (or indeed the massive 58 per cent who came out for the Liberal Party in 1908) and it has often been riven by internal argument. This was most obvious during the Poll Tax debacle in 1988 when many party hardliners wanted to follow a policy of non-payment but were opposed by the leadership. The Conservatives never got near that 50.1 per cent figure after 1955.

Unemployment in Scotland rose in the late 1950s and early 1960s and Labour came to be seen as the party of the Scots, while the Conservatives were viewed as English. This trend became most pronounced during the Thatcher years.

Another factor during this period was the rise of the other parties, most notably the SNP. The Scottish National Party was formed in 1928. Originally called the National Party of Scotland, it was a response to the failure of both the Liberal Party and the Labour Movement to fully support home rule bills in the early 1920s.

In its original form it drew support from literary figures such as Compton Mackenzie (author of *Whisky Galore*) and the poet Hugh McDiarmid. In 1934, it became the Scottish National Party, but in the late 1930s its popularity dipped as a result of the unpopularity of fascist nationalism in Europe. The party won its first parliamentary seat at Motherwell in 1945 but lost it in the general election a few months later.

In 1950, a group of young Nationalists 'stole' the Stone of Destiny from Westminster Abbey. The stone is a potent political symbol to the Scots. Stolen from Scotland by Edward I in 1296, it was finally returned in November 1996 by the Conservative Party in an act that the Conservative supporter and lawyer Ian Hamilton called 'cynical political jobbery'.

The SNP fared comparatively well in by-elections in the early 1960s and in the 1966 general election it fielded 23 candidates. Winnie Ewing won a notable by-election in Hamilton in 1967, set-

There's no doubt about it: the Scottish people want a Scottish Parliament.

ting a pattern of sporadic, spectacular wins alternating with reversals of fortune.

The discovery of oil in the North Sea in 1970 pushed the independence question high enough up the Scottish political agenda for the SNP to take 11 MPs to Westminster after the 1974 general election. A referendum on home rule was held in 1979 and narrowly defeated.

After the fall of the Callaghan government in 1979, Margaret Thatcher came to power. She would later be demonised by all on the Scottish left for a series of policies that were viewed as avowedly anti-Scottish. Ironically, the Poll Tax, which was the most hated of these policies, was dreamed up by a Scot, one of a group of economists who had flourished at St Andrews University.

The Thatcher government also waged war on high-spending Labour councils, of which Lothian Regional Council was the most notable.

Much administrative work was devolved to Scotland when the Scottish Office opened in 1939. A hundred civil servants came then; by the time New St Andrews House opened in 1971 there were 10,000. But during the Thatcher era the position of Secretary of State for Scotland changed: successive Scottish Secretaries came to be seen as viceroys of a colonial rule rather than as politicians representing Scottish interests at Westminster.

Today, there are 72 Scottish MPs and the Scottish Office has a permanent staff of over 13,000. Scotland also has eight MEPs (Members of the European Parliament).

Since the end of World War II, the balance of power in Scotland has swung to the right and the left, new parties have come to the fore and political infighting at both party and local level has been vicious. But that one central question still remained unanswered. The conflict that was set up when first a king and then a parliament left Edinburgh to sit in London has never been fully resolved.

On 11 September 1997, following Labour's win in the general election of May that year, another referendum was held to see if the Scottish people wanted a parliament and, if so, whether they wanted it to have tax-varying powers. Scots voted yes on both counts. The first elections for the Scottish Parliament are due to take place in 1999. The Parliament building, which is to be built at Holyrood in Edinburgh, will open in the early years of the twenty-first century. But doubtless, that ancient question as to who rules Scotland will still be being asked. And, given the limited powers given to the Parliament, it is unlikely that the answer will be the Scottish people.

Edinburgh by Numbers

20,000 The estimated number of people who attended the last public hanging in Edinburgh – of George Bruce of Ratho on 21 June 1864.
25,000 The number of people who marched in Edinburgh in 1992 to campaign for democracy for Scotland.
65 The number of wig-makers in Edinburgh in 1700.
180,000 The number of tickets sold for shows during the first Edinburgh International Festival in 1947.
420,00 The number of people who saw one or more performance during 51st Edinburgh International Festival in 1997.
169 The number of Fringe shows seen by Nigel Tantrum in 1994.
8 The number of groups taking part in the first Fringe.
194 The number of groups taking part in the Fringe in 1977.
494 The number of groups taking part in the Fringe in 1986.
605 The number of groups taking part in the Fringe in 1987.
18,500 The number of beds to hire in Edinburgh.
37,500 The number of seats in venues with a public entertainments licence in Edinburgh during August.
71 the number of mills powered by the Water of Leith along the ten mile stretch between Balerno and Leith in 1828.
257 The number of Covenanters shipped as slaves to Barbados in 1679.
2,000,000 The estimated number of cartloads of soil removed from the foundations of the New Town and deposited on the Mound between 1781 and its completion in 1830.
6,000,000 The number of oysters harvested a year from their beds in the Forth at the height of the trade. There are no longer any oysters to be had in the Forth.
35,000 Population of Edinburgh in 1678.
40,420 Population of Edinburgh in 1722.
64,479 Population of Edinburgh in 1755.
102,987 Population of Edinburgh and Leith in 1811.
175,407 Population of Edinburgh in 1831.
320,549 Population of Edinburgh in 1881.
439,101 Population of Edinburgh in 1931.
467,000 Population of Edinburgh in 1951.

418,914 Population of Edinburgh in 1991.
447,550 Population of Edinburgh in 1995.
1,000,000 The estimated population of Edinburgh during August in 1997.
13 days Edinburgh-London stagecoach journey time in 1712 (the fare was £4/10/- or £4.50).
4 days Edinburgh-London post-coach journey time in 1773 (the fare was £4/14/6 or £4.73).
14 hours Edinburgh-London service on North British Railways in 1847.
10 and a half hours Edinburgh-London run of the *Flying Scotsman* (the oldest named train in the world) in 1862.
5 hours, 22 minutes Edinburgh-London run by British Rail in 1977.
3 hours, 59 minutes Edinburgh-London run by GNER's Scottish Pullman service, summer 1988.
£21,000 The amount of public subscriptions given towards the National Monument on Calton Hill, started in 1822. £42,000 was needed and the half-completed monument was dubbed Scotland's Disgrace.
£20,000 The amount of money pledged in 1945 by Sir John Falconer, Edinburgh's Lord Provost, for the purpose of an International Arts festival.
£42,000 The cost of a one-bedroom, basement flat in the New Town in 1988.
2,700 The number of plants in the Edinburgh Physic Garden when at its one-acre site at Trinity Hospital (now Waverley Station) in 1689.
4,000 The approximate number of species in the Royal Botanic Garden at the Leith Walk site in 1812.
14,000 the number of species in the Royal Botanic Garden and its three outstations at Benmore, Dawyck and Logan 1994.
1,984 The number of yards in a Scots Mile.
914 miles The total length of the streets of Edinburgh.
22 miles The length of the Water of Leith.
12 The average number of days a year when snow was lying at 0900 hours at Edinburgh Airport (1961-90).
106mm The greatest rainfall recorded in a single day in Edinburgh (1787).
238mm The greatest rainfall recorded in a single month in Edinburgh – August 1948.
65mm The average rainfall at Edinburgh Airport during August (1961-90).
42mm The average rainfall at Edinburgh Airport during February (1961-90).
4.67 hours The average sunlight per day in August at Edinburgh Airport (1961-90).
39% The percentage rise in car ownership in Edinburgh, 1986-94 (UK average: 19%).
3% The percentage of vehicles that are buses on the streets of Edinburgh.
50% The percentage of journeys in Edinburgh taken by bus.
83% The percentage of vehicles that are cars on the streets of Edinburgh.
640 acres (259 hectares) The size of Queen's Park (Arthur's Seat).
3,5000 acres The total area of Edinburgh public parks owned by the City Council.
141 The number of police boxes built throughout the city in 1933.

Scotland the teatowel

Tartan – never mind the marketing scam, just feel that expression of Scottish identity.

Cliché and kitsch at the Edinburgh Commonwealth Games in 1986.

Over the the last decade or two there has been a growing self-consciousness in Scotland about the myths perpetuated in the name of national identity. The result has been a peculiar, post-modern embracing of cultural icons – despite revelations about their lack of authenticity. It's as if Scots have cottoned on to the fact that some of them are quite good after all, whatever their provenance. The country still has a frightening capacity for lapsing into a cartoon version of itself, but there are hints of a New Caledonia if you know where to look.

Take tartan. Any claims that Highlanders of old traipsed through the heather in distinctive kilts with everyone of the same clan sporting the same design is nonsense. Up until the late eighteenth century, Scotland was split in two. Lowlanders saw themselves as cultured, forward-looking and fond of trousers, while they regarded the Highlanders as

Gaelic-speaking hoodlums in barbaric attire. Highland costume included a great length of material wrapped round the upper body and thighs, fastened at the waist so the lower part formed a skirt – the belted plaid. Those who had money wore a plaid of ostentatious design; those who did not wore brown. Tartan-style designs, even for the rich, didn't reach Scotland until the sixteenth century and probably came from Flanders.

It wasn't until the 1720s that the kilt as we know it today was invented. An English businessman struck a deal with a clan chief near Inverness to smelt iron ore on his land. Local men were employed and their belted plaid proved such a hindrance when it came to felling trees or working a furnace that the inventive Englishman came up with a sawn-off plaid that dispensed with the upper portion and left just the skirt. The kilt was born, but still there was no relation between tartan and clan identity.

Use of the kilt spread and, by the time of the Battle of Culloden (the defeat of Bonnie Prince Charlie), it was seen as part of traditional Highland dress – so subsequently banned by a London-based government intent on wiping out all traces of a culture that could lend armed support to Catholic rebellion against the British crown. In a generation, the Highland way of life – let alone its fashion sense – was destroyed. But once the clan structure had been broken, the people 'pacified', and the men directed into Highland regiments of the British Army, public opinion in the Lowlands and England started to feel more comfortable with the now harmless 'noble savage' from the north. The Highlands became hip…

The crucial turning point, when Highland imagery became the basis of a national identity for all Scots, came in 1822 with George IV's visit to Edinburgh. A reigning British monarch hadn't set foot over the border in two centuries and novelist and arch-romantic Sir Walter Scott was entrusted with the organisation of the visit.

The result was a sick joke. The King, a preposterous, ailing blimp with a taste for cherry brandy and opium, arrived in Edinburgh to take part in a caricature of a Highland pageant entirely invented by the novelist. The Scottish aristocracy and bourgeoisie, clad in a comical pastiche of Highland costume (as directed by Scott, with an arbitrary choice of garish tartans), fell over themselves to fawn before the King, quite happy to forget that his great uncle (Butcher Cumberland) had bloodied the glens 76 years before.

From then on, manufacturers provided tartans for all. Any linkage to clan names was, in effect, one giant nineteenth-century marketing scam.

So have modern Scots dropped tartan? Not a bit of it. Despite its chequered history, it's fun. And, frankly, you're better off with a kilt at a wedding rather than looking like a geek in a top hat and tails. Tartan features on the international fashion scene and football clubs have been getting into the act.

It's just one example of how the Scots have realised that when intelligence and style are applied to icons of their constructed culture, they can actually become worthwhile.

Scottish icons

The kilt – national dress

There are several outfitters on the Royal Mile that cater to passing tourists, but if you want to get away from the hustle and bustle, head for Leith. A made-to-measure kilt from **Kinloch Anderson** in Commercial Street will cost around £300, but should last longer than you will. The shop also has a small area set aside on the history of tartan with a couple of exhibits dating from the time of George IV's visit.

Haggis – national dish

Haggis is minced lung, heart and liver from a sheep, mixed with oatmeal and pepper and çooked in a sheep's stomach. The world regards haggis as Scottish, but all kinds of peoples from ancient times have eaten animal bits in a wrap of skin, stomach or intestine. Haggis was on the menu from at least the thirteenth century in Scotland, but it took a Robert Burns poem, *Address to a Haggis*, to fix it as a national comestible. Eaten occasionally throughout the year, sales rocket for 25 January, when the country celebrates Burns' birthday. Try one from **Macsweens of Edinburgh** in Bruntsfield Place. A vegetarian version is also available.

The Ceilidh – national rave

It used to mean 'gathering', but now means lots of people hopping around to traditional dance tunes played by everyone from muscular rock 'n' reel bands to a dextrous auld mannie with an accordion. Ceilidhs are in vogue and several venues host regular nights. The Robert Fish Band play the **Assembly Rooms** on George Street every month and the venue also hosts charity ceilidhs. St Bride's Centre, 10 Orwell Terrace, EH11 (346 1405) has fundraising ceilidhs, too, while the Caledonian Brewery in Slateford Road has a bash every Saturday.

Shortbread – national biscuit

Many of the mass-produced brands taste like tinder-dry bits of Scots pine, so go for the best. Shortbread House of Edinburgh (14 New Broompark, EH5; bakery 552 0381) keeps winning awards. It's neither widely available nor cheap, but you can usually find some in the food hall at **Jenners** department store or **John Lewis**.

Whisky – national drug

Irish is good, American is more rock 'n' roll, but Scotch whisky, with its unequalled variety and character, blows the opposition away. Single malts have a complexity that rewards careful drinking but special cask whisky is something else again. For these, try Cadenheads shop at 172 Canongate, EH8 (556 5864) or join the **Scotch Malt Whisky Society**. Expect to pay at least £30-£35 for a bottle of cask-strength malt and sometimes much, much more.

Bagpipes – national squeeze

Bagpipes are indeed the traditional sound of the Highlands, although trace further back and the Irish harp was once the instrument of choice. The international reputation of Highland pipes was probably fixed by their association with British imperialism in the nineteenth century – when the army came to town it was often to a pipe accompaniment. Bagpipe-style instruments from India, North Africa and the rest of Europe never enjoyed such prominent advertising. Musically primitive, a massed band of pipers can be irritating or downright scary. But a lone piper playing a lament is one of the most haunting sounds in world music. A set of pipes from the likes of MacMurchie of Kirknewton (01506 872 333; 10am-6pm Mon-Fri) can cost from £475 to £2,775.

Highland Games – national sport

The first recorded instances of the games as we know them today date to the second decade of the nineteenth century and many gatherings overseas are as long-lived and authentic as anything in Scotland. The actual events do have a longer pedigree in that people have danced, played music and thrown things around in the Highlands for centuries, but modern games are no more authentic than the average tartan. Any gathering will have its own local flavour, but visitors should find caber tossing, weight putting, dancing and piping competitions at all of them. In the last few years, a games has been run at Stewart's-Melville playing fields on Ferry Road (319 2005). This is put on in July and August with an eye to tourists. Glasgow hosts the world pipe band championships (15 Aug 1998; 14 Aug 1999), which also incorporates a games on Glasgow Green (0141 287 5190).

Sightseeing

The Royal Mile

From Castle to Palace: Castlehill, Lawnmarket, High Street and Canongate make up the Royal Mile – the backbone of the Old Town and heart of Edinburgh's tourist trail.

The Royal Mile, the oldest part of Edinburgh, is built on the ridge that slopes from **Edinburgh Castle** down to the **Palace of Holyroodhouse**. Protected by the Castle Rock on the west and the now-drained Nor' Loch on the site of Princes Street Gardens, the Old Town was hemmed within city walls in the Middle Ages. As population growth forced housing to be built higher and higher, the long gardens that once ran either side of the ridges were also built over, making this a densely housed area. The dramatic descents on either side mean that buildings that look a few floors high from the High Street can tower many storeys on the other side.

All these tenements, known as 'lands', being packed so tightly together inside the city walls meant that different parts of society shared the same houses, usually with the prosperous and noble on the upper floors. After the North Bridge was opened in 1772, the gentry moved to the New Town and although the tenements started to fall into disrepair, their decay was checked and they still predominate on the Royal Mile, interspersed with the remaining 60 or so 'closes' (alleys) of the hundreds that once riddled the area.

The Royal Mile is still infused with the intrigue and drama that comes from a capital city that has been through turbulent times and has seen more than its fair share of historical figures and events. The lack of sanitation facilities, which gave rise to the famous Old Town cry of 'gardey loo' (a corruption of the French 'gardez l'eau') when flinging household waste out the window, led to a third of the population being wiped out by bubonic plague.

The chaotic, crowded, smelly, noisy Edinburgh of the seventeenth and eighteenth centuries still seems to lurk just under the surface. With such an atmosphere, the area lends itself to ghost tours (*see box* **Murder and mayhem on the Mile**). Inevitably, the vast majority of the shops are aimed at the tourist market: woollen mills, craft shops, tartan outfitters; they're all here.

A tenement in **Ramsay Gardens**.

Edinburgh Castle

Unlike so many ruins, the grey and imposing fortress that is **Edinburgh Castle** has been in constant use for a thousand years. It is extraordinarily well preserved, kept scrupulously tidy and

the military presence gives it an atmosphere that's brisk (although that could just be the wind) and devoid of the tackiness found at other historic sites. It was a royal residence until the Lang Siege of 1571-3 when Mary, Queen of Scots' supporters in the Castle were bombarded by the regent governing on the behalf of her son, the infant King James VI of Scotland and I of England. The following refurbishment was meant to turn the Castle into an impregnable military fortress and the royal residence moved down to Holyroodhouse.

The Castle is entered from the Esplanade, where the world-famous and nearly always sold-out **Edinburgh Military Tattoo** has been held every Festival since 1950. When the Esplanade is not covered by the seats set up for the Tattoo, the most impressive visible feature of the Castle is the curve of the massive artillery emplacement, the

Half Moon Battery, built to protect the Castle's vulnerable eastern side after the Lang Siege. The Gatehouse immediately below – with the bronze statues of Robert the Bruce and William Wallace on either side of the gate – was added in 1886-8 as a conscious attempt to make the Castle look more picturesque. Behind the Half Moon Battery, the Old Palace buildings drop sheer down to Johnston Terrace. The Mills Mount Battery, from where the one o'clock gun is fired, is not visible from here – it's behind the trees to the right, facing out over Princes Street. Cliché though it is, you can always tell Edinburgh natives because, instead of flinching when the gun goes off, they automatically check their watches.

The military memorials on the Esplanade are self-explanatory. But on the left of the gate on the way out on to the Royal Mile is a most poignant memorial, in the shape of a small bronze well, which marks the place where over 300 women were burned as witches between 1479 and 1722.

Castlehill

Also visible from the Esplanade – on the extreme left as you face away from the Castle – is Ramsay Gardens, an octagonal, irregular complex of baronial buildings bristling with spiral staircases and overhangs, built by the poet Allan Ramsay in the early eighteenth century. The low, flat building beside it was once the Castlehill reservoir, built in 1851, which supplied water to Princes Street. Nowadays, it houses **Edinburgh Old Town Weaving Company**. The **Camera Obscura** (*see below*) is in the black-and-white tower on the roof of the next building down. It contains a system of lenses and mirrors that projects images of the surrounding area on to a disc inside. Just over the narrow cobbled road is the **Scotch Whisky Heritage Centre**. There are guided tours through a three-floor exhibition culminating in the Tasting Bar. The Tolbooth St John's Kirk stands where Castlehill meets the top of Johnston Terrace, designed by Augustus Pugin in 1844 its Gothic spire is the tallest in Edinburgh at 240 feet (73 metres). The building was bought by the Edinburgh International Festival in 1998 and is being refurbished as an information and ticket centre for the Festival in 1999. The view from Johnston Terrace emphasises the grandeur of the Castle Rock and is particularly impressive at night when the Castle is illuminated.

Lawnmarket

The Lawnmarket, so named because cloth, known as 'lawn', was sold here, boasts a fine example of an Edinburgh townhouse. **Gladstone's Land**, a property dating from 1550, was extensively rebuilt by an ancestor of Prime Minister William Gladstone 70 years later. The sixteenth-century interior, with its oriel-shaped balcony and segmental arch are all well preserved, but the house is only open between April and October.

There are numerous closes to investigate on the Lawnmarket, such as James's Court, where James Boswell lived and was visited by Dr Johnson. While in the restored eighteenth-century courtyard at the bottom of the close, one might feel the tug of the **Jolly Judge**, a cosy pub with an open fire and a wooden ceiling painted with flowers and fruit. Robert Burns stayed in a house on Lady Stair's Close on his first visit to Edinburgh, so it's appropriate that Lady Stair's House, built in 1622, has been turned into the **Writer's Museum**, which displays relics of Burns, Sir Walter Scott and Robert Louis Stevenson. Brodie's Close was the home of the notorious Deacon Brodie, a respected member of Edinburgh society who led a double life as a burglar. He was put to death outside **St Giles' Cathedral** (*see below*), ironically on a gibbet he had designed himself. The ugly City of Edinburgh Council headquarters on the corner of George IV Bridge is the only modern architectural carbuncle on the Royal Mile.

It's at this point that the Royal Mile is intersected by George IV Bridge on the right and Bank Street, winding down to the Mound and Princes Street, on the left. Formed by the soil dumped when the New Town was built, the Mound is dominated by the Royal Bank, which looks more like a palace and gazes imperiously over the New Town. It, too, is striking when floodlit at night. Opposite it is a relaxed coffeehouse, **Common Grounds,** which has a daunting range of coffees, some delicious. Further along North Bank Street is the Church of Scotland's Assembly Hall and New College, which the Kirk shares with the university's Faculty of Divinity.

High Street above the Bridges

Daniel Defoe called the High Street 'the largest, longest and finest street for buildings and number of inhabitants, not in Britain only, but in the world'. The section above the Bridges is undeniably impressive and was used in the film version of Thomas Hardy's *Jude the Obscure* to stand in for Oxford. The High Court of Justiciary, the supreme criminal court in Scotland, stands at the crossroads, newly graced with a bronze statue of David Hume, absurdly (for a 1997 statue of an eighteenth-century philosopher) garbed in classical dress. Round the back of the Court, in Giles Street, **Patisserie Florentin** is a fashionable place to down coffee and cake. It's worth remembering its extended opening hours if you're partial to a coffee in the late evening.

The three brass bricks laid into the pavement opposite Hume mark the place where the last pub-

lic hanging in Edinburgh took place: of George Bruce on 21 June 1864 and watched by 20,000 people. Next to them is the City of Edinburgh Council Chambers, built in 1818 to a design based on the Acropolis in Athens. It is still used by the Council and forms one wall of Parliament Square. Parliament House, the home of the Scottish Parliament until the Union of the Crowns in 1707, runs along the back. The great hall inside is used by lawyers from the adjoining District Court, Court of Session and High Court.

The Heart of Midlothian, laid out in cobblestones by the roadside near the entrance of St Giles' Cathedral, marks the spot of the old Tolbooth Prison where executions took place, the victims' heads frequently being displayed afterwards. It is a local custom to spit on this spot. For the pedantic, the fabric of the building itself is refered to as St Giles', while the church is known as the High Kirk of Edinburgh. The **Lower Aisle Restaurant** downstairs is good for a reasonably priced lunchtime bite among lawyers over from the courts.

Although it's an open square now, Parliament Square used to be crowded by many shops and 'lucken booths' – which were the lockable shops or booths built in the fifteenth century to offset the cost of building St Giles'. In the shadow of the Mercat Cross, east of the cathedral, traders struck deals in a thriving commercial climate. Executions and royal proclamations were carried out here, too.

The City Chambers face St Giles' and the Mercat Cross from the other side of the road. Completed in 1761, and thus one of the first truly Georgian buildings in Edinburgh, it was originally the Royal Exchange but failed because traders still preferred to do their business in the open air at the Mercat Cross. The building was also an attempt to bury Mary King's Close, both literally and in people's memories. During the plague in 1645, Mary King's

Close was subjected to a brutal form of quarantine that involved the whole close being blocked up and all its inhabitants left to die. Butchers were sent in later to dismember the corpses. Large sections of the buildings are still intact amid the City Chambers' foundations. The close is reputed to be one of the most haunted places in Scotland and even sceptics can find it eerie. In one room the ghost of a little girl has been placated with gifts – small dolls, sweets, coins – left by visitors.

SNAKING QUEUES

Further down the High Street is the Fringe Office, the epicentre of Edinburgh Festival Fringe activity. For three weeks in the summer, the pavements are close to impassable due to snaking queues for tickets and performers in weird costumes pressing handbills on passers-by. The atmosphere of Cockburn Street, on the left, tends to fluctuate with the vitality of youth culture, but it's been looking tired in that regard for a few years now. A range of identikit clothing stores notwithstanding, it veers towards the biker end of hippie. The arrival of shops selling upmarket craft items and two modern art spaces, the **Collective Gallery** and **Stills Gallery**, hasn't completely shaken off the scent of patchouli.

The area around the **Tron Kirk** (*see below*), on the corner with South Bridge, was the traditional gathering place for revellers bringing in the New Year until Edinburgh's official Hogmanay celebrations began and the focus moved down to Princes Street. The Kirk is now used as the **Old Town Information Centre** (*see below*) from March to October. Hunter Square, beside it, was given an overhaul a few years ago to make it a pleasant place to sit and watch the world go by. The **City Café**, one of Edinburgh's hippest bar-and-café joints, is close by on Blair Street.

*Charles II rides forth in **Parliament Square** behind St Giles' Cathedral.*

At the traffic lights here, the High Street is cut in two by North Bridge and South Bridge, known together as the Bridges and built to open up the New Town in the late eighteenth century. Although South Bridge looks like a continuous street, it is in fact propped up by 19 massive arches, only one of which is visible. The last building on the left of North Bridge, looking towards the New Town, is the rugged, iconic building that has housed Scotsman Publications (publishers of *The Scotsman, Scotland on Sunday* and the *Evening News*) for the past century. Purpose-built for the company, it is being vacated in 1999 for new premises at Holyrood. At the front of the building, there's an enclosed spiral staircase that provides a shortcut down to Market Street and Waverley Station, but don't use it unless you have to or actually enjoy the stench of stale urine. It is the entirely believable setting for foul murders in several Edinburgh-set detective thrillers.

High Street – below the Bridges

Over the traffic lights, just behind the upmarket but welcoming **Bank Hotel**, Niddry Street dips steeply down towards the Cowgate. Its shabby walls have been done up to represent nineteenth-century Edinburgh in at least one BBC drama, and behind them is a rabbit warren of cellars built into the arches of South Bridge and forgotten. It's an atmospheric place, open to guided tours, but still in the early stages of commercial exploitation. In the last ten years the commercial potential of these subterranean expanses for clubs and art spaces has been noted. The **Vaults**, just up Niddry Street from the cellars, is a popular night spot.

The **Crowne Plaza Edinburgh** (still referred to as the Scandic Crown, the name it opened under in 1990) has been maligned for its individual interpretation of Scottish baronial style. Actually it's a valiant and largely successful attempt to blend in to its surroundings. Blackfriars Street runs off the High Street and is home to the **High Street Hostel**, a cycle-hire shop, two backpackers' centres and two good pubs, **Black Bo's** and El Bar.

A tasteful and well-designed glass façade fronts the **Museum of Childhood**, opened in 1955 as the first museum in the world to examine the history of childhood. Its founder used to make sure that visitors understood the difference between a museum of childhood and a museum for children, but the multitude of toys, games and displays are good enough to fascinate both kids and adults.

All that saved the awkwardly positioned house that is now the **John Knox House Museum**

Time has not taken too much toll on the **Canongate Tolbooth***, now home to the* **People's Story***.*

from demolition in 1830 was reverence for its illustrious former occupant. Now it's widely believed that the leader of the Reformation, who turned Scotland from a Catholic to a Protestant country, never lived there at all, but it's a good job that someone sought to preserve it. It sports many features of fine Old Town houses: timber galleries and gables, overhanging beams and religious quotations and carvings around the outside walls. The house was built by goldsmith James Mosman, and inside, as well as exhibits associated with Knox, is a reconstruction of Mosman's workbench. The house is connected to the adjacent **Netherbow Arts Centre**, which contains a 75-seat theatre, storytelling centre and café.

This end of the High Street is the point where the east gate of the city, the Netherbow, used to stand. Down Tweeddale Court, you can see a surviving length of the city wall, and sheds that were once used to store sedan chairs. Opposite them is the **Scottish Poetry Library** (*see below*). Back out on the High Street, there's a reference to the city boundary in the name of the pub on the corner: the **World's End**.

Canongate

The next section of the Royal Mile, the Canongate, takes its name from the route taken by the Augustinian canons to the gates of Edinburgh after their arrival at Holyrood in 1128. Outside the city wall, Canongate was an independent burgh from Edinburgh until as recently as 1856.

Recognisable from its clock, bell tower and outside stair, the Canongate Tolbooth was built in 1592 to collect tolls from people entering the city, but it also served as council chamber, police court and prison for the burgh of Canongate. It now houses the **People's Story**, an absorbing museum of Edinburgh's social history so dedicated to getting the feel right that you can actually smell woodsmoke as you enter. Beneath it lies the Tolbooth Tavern, a classic Edinburgh watering hole. **Huntly House**, opposite, is three timber-framed houses joined into one in 1570 and surmounted by three overhanging white-painted gables of a kind that were once common in the Old Town. It is also a museum, exhibiting artefacts from the earliest-known inhabitation of the area right through the ages.

Few know of Dunbar's Close Garden, a secret little park at the end of an unassuming close on the north side of the Canongate, laid out in the manner of a seventeenth-century garden with ornamental flowerbeds and manicured hedges. It's a beautiful refuge from the summer crowds, with a view of the old Royal High School, for many years intended as the site for the Scottish Parliament.

The bell-shaped, Dutch design of Canongate Church marks it out strongly from the rest of the

Royal Observatory Visitor Centre
Blackford Hill, Edinburgh EH9 3HJ
Tel: 0131-668 8405 Fax: 0131-668 8429

Discover the latest about space and astronomy

OPENING HOURS
Monday to Saturday 10am to 5pm
Sunday 12 noon to 5pm
Public Observing (October to March)
Fridays at 7.30pm (£1.00)
(Weather Permitting)

ADMISSION
Adults £3.00; Children £2.00;
Concessions £1.50;
Family Ticket £6.00
Disabled Ticket £1.00 (partial access)

buildings on the Royal Mile and makes it one of Edinburgh's most individual and attractive churches. It was built for the displaced congregation of Holyrood Abbey, destroyed in 1688. It's Edinburgh's military church, but also buried in the churchyard are David Rizzio, murdered secretary of Mary, Queen of Scots, economist Adam Smith and Robert Burns's beloved 'Clarinda' (Mrs Agnes McLehose), for whom he wrote *Ae Fond Kiss*. Burns's muse is also commemorated by a tea-

room, Clarinda's, a little further down. Just on the right side of twee, with patterned plates on the wall and flowers on the tables, it provides the only chance of a light meal at this end of the Canongate.

There are some attractive houses near the gates of Holyrood, most obviously two well-kept, gleaming white houses, Canongate Manse and Whiteford House, now a Scottish war veterans' residence. White Horse Close is pretty, too, the gabled building at the end was once the inn from

Murder and mayhem on the Mile

Descending from either side of the Royal Mile are 61 closes and wynds: narrow, steeply sloping passageways with houses towering six or even ten storeys above. The word 'close' refers to an alley that is open only at one end and could be closed at night and is still used today to refer to the central stairwell in tenements; a 'wynd' is an alley which is open at both ends. During the Middle Ages, Edinburgh was one of the most overcrowded cities in Europe and these alleys were the most densely populated and sordid areas of all. Walking tours through and under these medieval closes combine stories of historical brutality with tales of ghosts and the supernatural.

Mary King's Close, the historically most terrifying and supernaturally most potent of Edinburgh's closes, is now buried under the City Chambers, inaccessible except via the trip operated by Mercat Walking Tours. The story of the close is horrific. All the street's residents were killed during an epidemic of the Black Death. What is most shocking is that the City Fathers walled off the close in an failed attempt to quarantine the plague, denying everyone who lived there both food and water. It is difficult for the guide's stories to compete with the unimaginable terror of the past.

Less weighed down by such a single tragedy, other tours highlight the routine tortures, murders and witch hunts of medieval Edinburgh. The walks operated by **Mercat Walking Tours** and **Robin's Ghost and History Tour** mix tales of the supernatural with local history and offer the opportunity to descend into the buried vaults and streets that run beneath the city. The Mercat tour of the vaults doesn't takes itself, or the ghost stories, too seriously and provides a good insight into the history of the area. The Robin's tour is more detached from the history of the Middle Ages and is not as interesting or scary.

The **Witchery Murder and Mystery Tour**, with your guide Adam Lyal (deceased), doesn't go underground and is more in the tradition of pantomime than a history lecture. But the guide works the crowd effectively, drawing shrieks and giggles if not real fright. An overemployed extra ambushes the tour at various points, dressed as a mad monk or medieval harridan, which is a bit naff although this trip down the Cowgate after dark does suggest that the shady world of Burke and Hare could still exist in contemporary Edinburgh.

Mercat Walking Tours
16A, Cockburn Street, City Chambers, EH1 (661 4541). 1, 6, 34, 35 buses. **Open** *office* 9.30am-9pm daily; *tours* Mary King's Close, eight tours a day, prior booking only; Royal Mile Walk 11am, 2pm daily; Vaults Tour 11am-4pm on the hour daily. All tours meet at the Mercat Cross, St Giles' Cathedral, High Street. **Tickets** Mary King's Close £5/£4 concs; Royal Mile Walk £5/£4 concs; Vaults Tour £4/£3.50 concs. **No credit cards. Map 9 C2**
e-mail: des@mercat-tours.co.uk.
http://www.mercat-tours.co.uk

Robin's Ghost and History Tour
66 Willowbrae Road, EH8 (661 0125). 43, 44, 75 buses. **Open** *phone* 24-hours daily; *tours* Dr Jekyll's Ghost Tour, Apr-Nov, 25 Dec-4 Jan 9pm daily; Ghost and Witches Tour 7pm daily; Grand Tour 10am, 7pm daily; Midnight Ghost Tour (groups of 20+) 11pm daily; Royal Mile 11am daily. All tours meet at the Tourist Information Centre on Princes Street. **Tickets** Dr Jekyll's Ghost Tour £5/£4 concs; Ghost and Witches Tour £5/£4 concs; Grand Tour £5/£4 concs; Midnight Ghost Tour £5 (no concs); Royal Mile £4/£2-£3 concs. **No credit cards. Map 8 D2**

Witchery Tours
352 Castlehill, Royal Mile, EH1 (225 6745). 1, 6, 34, 35 buses. **Open** *office* 10am-6pm daily; *tours* (advance bookings only) Ghost and Gore Tour May-Sept 7pm, 8pm daily; Murder and Mystery Tour 9pm, 10pm. All tours meet outside the Witchery Restaurant, Castlehill. **Tickets** Ghost and Gore Tour £7/£4 child; Murder and Mystery Tour £7 (no concs). **Credit** MC, V. **Map 9 A2**
e-mail lyal@witcherytours.demon.co.uk
http://www.clan.com-edinburgh-witchery

where the stage coach to London left. In 1745 it was called into service as the officers' quarters of Prince Charles Edward Stuart's army.

At the bottom of the Royal Mile stands the Palace of Holyroodhouse, originally built by James IV to be near the Abbey, with various additions and refurbishments being made by subsequent monarchs. Despite being burned and looted by Henry VIII's army in 1544, and further damaged in 1650 when Cromwell's army used it as a barracks and accidentally burned down the south wing, its finished form radiates a combination of solidity and elegance. The purpose of the strange, squat building just inside the fence by the main road is unknown. It might have been a bathhouse, or perhaps a doocot (where 'doos' or pigeons nest).

Holyrood Abbey, now an irreparable ruin, was founded by David I in 1128. It was sacked by Edward II in 1322, damaged in 1544 and 1570 with the loss of the choir and transepts and violated further by a Presbyterian mob in 1688.

From the gates of Holyroodhouse the road heads towards Arthur's Seat. The block on the right of the corner with Holyrood Road is an old brewery site that has been bought as the site of the new Scottish Parliament scheduled for completion in mid-2001. Directly opposite is the two-and-a-half-acre site on which the Dynamic Earth centre is taking shape. Scheduled to open in May 1999, the construction is being funded by the Millennium Project and designed by architect Sir Michael Hopkins. It will tell the story of the planet utilising state-of-the-art special effects and stand on the site where James Hutton (1726-97), 'the father of geology', lived and worked. Past the plain but striking Queensberry House Hospital and the new premises of Scotsman Publications is the sprawling Moray House Teacher Training College – unlovely concrete blocks, for the most part, stained by the weather like the modern homes further up the road. At the top of the long, rather depressing haul that is Holyrood Road lies the junction with the Pleasance. Straight ahead runs the Cowgate with St Cecelia's Hall past Blackfriar's Street on the right. Turning right up St Mary's Street leads back up to the Netherbow. If you need refreshment before going on, the woody and homely **Holyrood Tavern** is a typical Old Town pub.

Camera Obscura

Castlehill, EH1 (226 3709). 1, 6 buses. **Open** *Nov-Mar* 10am-5pm daily; *Apr-Oct* 9.30am-5.30pm Mon-Fri; 10am-6pm Sat, Sun. **Admission** £3.85 adult; £1.95 child; group discounts. **Credit** JCB, MC, £TC, V. **Map 9 A2**
It's all done with mirrors in this attraction at the top of the Royal Mile, created by optician Maria Short in the 1850s. The main event is a 20-minute show in the domed hut on the roof. Images of the surrounding area — and from this high up that's quite a big area – are reflected and refracted on to a white disk in the middle of the small, darkened room. As the lenses turn the circle, the guide will invite kids to 'pick up' people and buses on pieces of paper, which is quite amusing but ultimately a bit twee. The hologram exhibition on the way up is extensive and well presented. It is worth leaving

time to go out on the roof afterwards as the binoculars give excellent views over the New Town and Calton Hill. It is not, however, worth visiting on a cloudy day as the camera is dependent on natural light for the strength of the image.

Edinburgh Old Town Weaving Company

555 Castlehill, EH1 (226 1555). 1, 6, 34, 35 buses. **Open** *exhibition* 9.30am-5.30pm daily; *shop* 9am-6pm Mon-Sat; 10am-6pm Sun. **Admission** £3 adult; £1.50 child; £2 concs; £8 family, group discounts (10+). **Credit** AmEx, MC, £TC V. **Map 9 A2**
It's not quite loud enough to need earmuffs, but this noisy attraction houses working tartan looms on which visitors can try their hand at weaving. There's also a history of tartan exhibition. The large shop sells the products created on the looms and visitors can find out which tartan they should be wearing themselves.

St Giles' Cathedral

Royal Mile, EH1 (225 4363). High St buses. **Open** *Easter-mid Sept* 9am-7pm Mon-Fri; 9am-5pm Sat; 1-5pm Sun; *mid-Sept-Easter* 9-5pm Mon-Fri; 9am-5pm Sat; 1-5pm Sun. **Services** 8am (Holy communion), noon (daily, service) weekdays; 8am, 10am, 11.30am, 6pm (recital of music), 8pm (evening service) Sunday. **Admission** by donation. **Credit** JCB, MC, £TC, V. **Map 9 B2**
There has been a church on the site of St Giles' Cathedral since 854. The oldest remnants are the four pillars surrounding the Holy Table in the centre, which date from around 1120. The ornate crown spire they support was completed in 1495. St Giles' suffered the usual destruction wrought by the English armies and the Reformation. After the dust had settled John Knox (1505-72) spent 12 years as its parish minister. Charles I made it a cathedral in 1633, and it retained its status as a Presbyterian cathedral even after bishops were banished in the 'Glorious Revolution' of 1688. Inside, a great vaulted ceiling shelters a medieval interior dominated by the banners and plaques of many Scottish regiments. The main entrance takes visitors past the West Porch screen, originally designed as a royal pew for Queen Victoria. The dazzling West Window is by Icelandic stained-glass artist Leifur Breidfjord and was dedicated to Robert Burns's memory in 1984. The organ is an even more recent addition, from 1992, with a glass back revealing the workings. The Knights of the Thistle have their own chapel, an intimate panelled room with intricate wooden carvings of thistles, roses and shamrocks, divided into Knights' stalls.

Scottish Poetry Library

Tweeddale Court, 14 High Street, EH1 (557 2876). 1, 6, Bridges Buses. **Open** noon-6pm Mon-Wed, Fri; 2-8pm Thur; 11am-5pm Sat. **Admission** free; £1 (day use of members' room). **Membership** £10 (annual). **No credit cards. Map 9 D2**
The emphasis of the library's extensive collection is on twentieth-century poetry, written in Scotland in Scots, Gaelic or English. It also has a good collection of older Scottish poetry, and contemporary work from around the world. Everyone is welcome to peruse the library and it has a computer for generating specialist lists and bibliographies.

Tron Kirk & Old Town Information Centre

High Street, EH1 (225 1637). 1, 6, Bridges buses. **Open** *June-Sept* 10am-7pm daily; *Oct-Easter* closed; *Easter-May* 10am-5pm daily. **Admission** free, donations welcome. **No credit cards. Map 9 C2**
The Tron Kirk was completed in 1648 and reduced in size to accomodate the South Bridge in 1785. The current steeple was built after the original was destroyed in the fire known as the 'great conflagration' of 1824. The building is now owned by the City Council and houses an informative exhibit about the development of the Old Town which includes excavated remains of Marlin's Wynd – an early 1600s alley which was demolished to make way for the Kirk.

The New Town

The architectural visions of James Craig, William Playfair and Robert Adam combine to give the New Town its grandiose air of Georgian splendour.

The New Town originally described the late-eighteenth-century development of Princes, George and Queen Streets. Today, the name loosely describes a succession of predominantly nineteenth-century 'new towns' running north of Princes Street. Built as gracious, upmarket residential alternatives to the cramped Old Town, the New Town was consciously out to impress. Its wide streets, grassy squares and classical style of architecture contrast sharply with the mood and look of the Old Town. Shops and offices now occupy the original New Town but further north the quiet, residential streets have changed little over the centuries. This area of Edinburgh is regarded as one of the best examples of romantic classicism in the world; its well-ordered streets and circuses are a delight to wander round.

Princes Street

Princes Street is where the people of Edinburgh shop. At nearly a mile long, it provides a grand dividing line between the Old and New Towns and combines a glimpse of everyday Edinburgh life with some spectacular views. Shops and department stores look south across Princes Street Gardens with the drama of **Edinburgh Castle**, the jagged skyline of the Old Town and the brooding presence of Salisbury Crags, Arthur's Seat and Calton Hill giving a stunning vista.

Princes Street Gardens lie in the ravine running between the foot of Castle Rock and the ridge of the Old Town. An act of parliament in 1816 prevented the site's commercial development after the Nor' Loch was drained. Today, it is a well-clipped, rolling swathe of grass crossed with bench-lined paths and an ideal venue for a rest or stroll. Waverley Station lies at the end of the east garden while, at the far end of the west garden, is the Victorian Gothic St John's Church.

Statues of numerous famous city residents edge the gardens. At the west end is Sir James Young Simpson, the Victorian pioneer of the use of chlo-

*Clear lines and simple proportions are one face of **Princes Street's** architectural chaos.*

roform in childbirth who was frequently found self-anaesthetised on the floor of his lab. Allegedly. He stands opposite the coolly classical 1930s building that houses Fraser's department store, the first of Princes Street's architecturally inconsistent parade of shops. The broadcaster Moray McLaren famously lambasted the street as 'one of the most chaotically tasteless streets in the United Kingdom'. Originally laid out in the 1780s to form the southern boundary of the New Town, it is now an endearing mishmash of overdressed Victoriana department stores and more minimalist twentieth-century additions. Until recently, town planners and style purists viewed Princes Street as Edinburgh's architectural Achilles heel. There have been many proposals to implement stylish homogeneity, including a 1938 rebuild in glass and steel and, in 1958, a series of high-level pedestrian walkways linking each building. Today's mutterings concern a shopping mall below street level, but plans to cut back traffic and increase the street's pedestrian zones have, however, come to positive fruition.

BOTTOM OF THE MOUND

On the corner of Princes Street and the Mound, the statue of the wig-maker turned poet, Allan Ramsey, stands over a floral clock, which dates from 1903.

Although it is usually fairly quiet, the flat, cobbled expanse known simply as the 'bottom of the Mound' is transformed into a hive of activity come the Festival. Clothes stalls, performance artists and musicians jostle for space and attract huge crowds. The impressive **National Gallery** and the **Royal Scottish Academy**, both designed by William Playfair, the nineteenth-century architect behind many of Edinburgh's classical revival buildings, provide a grand backdrop. The National Gallery houses a collection of early Italian, Renaissance and European art, along with works by nineteenth and early-twentieth-century Scottish artists. The neighbouring Royal Scottish Academy, a venue for temporary art exhibitions, is topped by sphinxes and an incongruous statue of the young Queen Victoria. Originally this was displayed at street level, but Victoria was displeased with her chubby appearance and demanded its roof-top elevation to avoid the close scrutiny of her subjects.

Jenners, the world's oldest privately owned department store, commands a corner position on Princes Street and St Andrew Street. Founded in 1838 by two Leith drapers, it was extravagantly rebuilt in 1893 after a fire destroyed the original building. An estimated 25,000 people crowded the streets for the unveiling of its elaborately carved, statue-encrusted frontage, which was inspired by the façade of Oxford's Bodleian Library. Just across St Andrew Street stands Scotland's first

steel-framed store, built in 1906, and today housing Burton's. It is surmounted by a group of gilded figures perched on a small belvedere and wrestling with an open-work sphere.

Gothic excess reaches new heights in the **Scott Monument**, a 200 foot (61 metre) high memorial to Sir Walter Scott: the prolific nineteenth-century author and promoter of Scotland's romantic past. Dubbed the city's 'medieval space rocket', it stands on the corner of Waverley Bridge, named after Scott's Waverley novels, and Princes Street. Dominating the skyline, it was originally to have been placed in the less public, residential enclave of Charlotte Square. John Ruskin, the nineteenth-century art critic known for his cutting ripostes, likened it to a misplaced church spire. An advocate of Scottish national dress, Scott is appropriately wearing a rustic shepherd's plaid. His dog, Maida, sits at his feet. Somewhat overshadowed by this Gothic extravagance is a diminutive statue of the Scots-born Victorian missionary and explorer, David Livingstone.

Princes Street ends with the **Balmoral Hotel**, a huge late-Victorian edifice. Its clock usually runs three minutes fast to hurry passengers to Waverley Station just below – except over Hogmanay. Facing the hotel and North Bridge is an exercise in classical restraint: the regal **Register House** (*see below*), built in 1774 by Robert Adam, the key member of the famous Adam dynasty of architects. In front is a statue of the Duke of Wellington, hero of the Battle of Waterloo. Looking ahead, along Waterloo Place, is a good view of Calton Hill crowned by the National Monument and the **Nelson Monument**.

Round the corner, on Leith Street, there is a small explosion of 1960s architectural brutalism in the form of the St James Shopping Centre, built on the site of an eighteenth-century square. Further down, with views back up to Calton Hill, is Picardy Place. Once home to a colony of Protestant French silk weavers, today it is a congested roundabout that is given a bit of light relief by outsize sculptures of a foot and a grasshopper by the Leith-born artist Sir Eduardo Paolozzi, which lie in front of the Roman Catholic cathedral of St Mary's.

George Street

The wide and grand George Street forms the backbone of the first New Town. The first large-scale development outside the Old Town, the New Town was designed by the winner of a 1766 architectural competition, an ambitious 21-year-old

Fan lights and brass knockers - the ruthless formality reaches right down to the smallest architectural details in the New Town.

MUSEUMS OF THE ROYAL MILE
a walk through history

1 *The Writers' Museum*
Treasure-house of items relating to
Robert Burns, Sir Walter Scott and
Robert Louis Stevenson.

2 *City Art Centre*
Exciting and
innovative temporary
exhibitions.

3 *Museum of Childhood*
Childhood
memories
galore - from
cuddly toys to
castor oil!

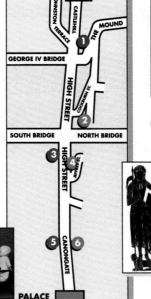

CASTLE
JOHNSTON TERRACE
CASTLEHILL
THE MOUND
GEORGE IV BRIDGE
HIGH STREET
COCKBURN ST.
SOUTH BRIDGE
NORTH BRIDGE
HIGH STREET
ST MARY'S ST
CANONGATE
PALACE

4 *Brass Rubbing Centre*
Try your hand
at brass rubbing
- no experience
needed.

5 *Huntly House Museum*
Packed with collections relating to
Edinburgh's past - social history,
silver, glass,
pottery, shop
signs.

6 *The People's Story*
Tells the story of the
ordinary people of
Edinburgh, from the
18th century to the
present day.

·EDINBVRGH·
THE CITY OF EDINBURGH COUNCIL

Oh what a Circus, Oh what a New Town - three of **Moray Place's** *12 sides. See page 52.*

architect called James Craig. The layout of three parallel roads – Princes, George and Queen Streets – and two squares replaced Craig's earlier design of radial roads, that was inspired by the Union Jack – a symbol which was a bit too highly charged for the Scots after the 1707 Act of Union. Craig was obviously keen for royal approval. He dedicated his final plan to George III, who in turn had an influence on the names of the streets. George Street is named after the monarch and Princes Street after his sons. The original name of St Giles was dropped as it reminded the King of a sleazy quarter of London. The plans are on view in **Huntly House** on the Canongate.

FINANCIAL HEART

Today, George Street is home to smart shops and businesses. At its eastern end is St Andrew Square, named after Scotland's patron saint. In its centre stands the Melville Monument. A 135 foot (41 metre) Doric column inspired by Rome's Trajan Column, it is topped by a statue of Henry Dundas, 1st Earl of Melville, who was a notorious eighteenth-century political wheeler dealer. The square has long been the financial heart of Edinburgh.

The Royal Bank of Scotland headquarters are in a former mansion on the east side of the square.

The mansion was built in 1772 for Sir Laurence Dundas on the site that, in Craig's plan, was reserved for St Andrew's Church. Set back from the square, its private lawn is a rare sight in the New Town and a mark of Sir Laurence's political muscle overruling the council's planning orders. Inside the bank, the sumptuously decorated iron dome of the Telling Room (1860) is open during banking hours.

Next door is an outlandishly loud pseudo-palazzo with rooftop statues, which was once the British Linen Bank. Just off the square in West Register Street is the **Café Royal**, an extravagantly dressed, turn-of-the-century oyster bar with murals of, among others, the inventors Michael Faraday and James Watt.

Back through St Andrew Square, on George Street, is the 1940s green and black, former Guardian Royal Exchange office. Scandinavian in tone, its vast front door is elaborately carved and flanked by columns and bronze figures. To its left is the **Dome**, a former bank and now a vast drinking venue. Epitomising the grandiose excess of Edinburgh's nineteenth-century banks, its richly decorated domed interior is also worth taking a look at. It may have prompted John Ruskin's 1853 critical onslaught. Commenting on the city's liberal use of classical columns, Ruskin declared:

St Stephen's seen from Queen Street – Playfair's finest New Town church.

Roots Mon!

Register House and West Register House are not only architecturally splendid, they are both working buildings and, together with New Register House and the Edinburgh Room of the Central Library, hold many documents that are useful for anyone wanting to find out more about their Scottish antecedents.

The Scottish Record Office (SRO) in Register House holds the greatest wealth of general documents, with an overflow in West Register House. The General Register Office for Scotland (GRO) in New Register House holds old parish registers (pre-1855), statutory registers of births, marriages and death, (from 1855) and census returns (1851-91). These are all indexed on a computer database. Only a few registers of emigrants are held in Scotland. The central register for emigrants is kept at the Public Record Office at Kew in London.

Searching the records is an absorbing process, but it is not quick – come armed with as much information from relatives as possible. The SRO, GRO and the Central Library have leaflets that will help and there are staff who will give advice at the front desks of the various offices of the SRO. The Scottish Room of the Central Library (downstairs from the Edinburgh Room) also has books on different families and on how to start the search.

Scottish Record Office
HM General Register House, 2 Princes Street, EH1 (535 1314). Princes St buses. **Open** 9am-4.30pm Mon-Fri. **Admission** free. **Map 8 D1**
The SRO contains a veritable cornucopia of documents: wills; sasines (property records); taxation records; church records and burgh records. The book *Tracing Scottish Local History* (HMSO) is a detailed guide to the records in the SRO and how to use them.

General Register Office for Scotland
New Register House, West Register Street, EH1 (334 0380). Princes St buses. **Admission** free. **Map 8 D1**
The GRO provides access to the registers of official births deaths and marriages, as well as old parish registers. Charges are made for searching and having copies made.

West Search Room
West Register House, Charlotte Square, EH2 (535 1314). George St buses. **Open** 9am-4.30pm Mon-Fri. **Admission** free. **Map 8 A1**
The WSR is an overflow for the SRO and contains maps and plans, records of government departments and microfilm records. It also has a small exhibition of documents illustrating 800 years of Scottish history.

The Edinburgh Room
Central Library, George IV Bridge, EH1 (225 5584). George IV Bridge buses. **Open** 10am-8pm Mon-Thur; 10am-5pm Fri; 9am-1pm Sat. **Admission** free. **Map 9 B3**
The Edinburgh Room contains local records and newspapers as well as a wealth of research material on local events such as the Edinburgh International Festival. The Scottish Room, downstairs, is also a useful resource.

'Your decorations are just as monotonous as your simplicities.' Opposite is the displaced St Andrew's Church, built in 1787.

ARCHITECTURAL PUN
A flamboyant-looking statue of George IV stands at the junction with Hanover Street, erected to mark his visit to Edinburgh in 1822. This is a good spot for views north down Hanover Street to the Firth of Forth and Fife. To the south you get the full impact of the Royal Scottish Academy and, beyond that, on the Mound, the Assembly Hall and New College. The Assembly Hall and New College is built on a direct axis with Tolbooth St John's from which, at this angle, it appears to borrow the latter's imposing spire. This architectural pun was no accident on the part of its designer, William Playfair and would have been well understood by his contemporaries: Tolbooth St John's was built between 1842 and 1844 as the Assembly Hall for the Church of Scotland but, following the Disruption of 1843, the Church split and Playfair designed the Assembly Hall and New College for the newly formed Free Church.

Further along George Street, the Assembly Rooms were built by public subscription in 1787 and became a favoured haunt of Edinburgh's Regency partying set. During the Festival, they are home to one of the Fringe's largest venues. This was a popular quarter for literary types in the nineteenth century. The poet Shelley and his first wife Harriet Westbrook honeymooned at 84 George Street, above today's Victoria Wine shop, and Sir Walter Scott lived around the corner at 39 North Castle Street. At 45 George Street (today Justerini and Brooks), the influential literary journal, *Blackwood's Magazine* (Henry James and Oscar Wilde were among its contributors), had its headquarters. More recently, **Milne's Bar** on the corner of Hanover and Rose Streets, was a popular 1960s hangout for a generation of Scots writers such as Norman McCraig and Sorley McLean.

Charlotte Square

Concluding George Street is Charlotte Square. Named after George III's wife, Queen Charlotte, it was designed by Robert Adam in the 1790s as one of Edinburgh's classiest residential enclaves. Stately terraced townhouses ornamented with sphinxes and pediments line the square. **Georgian House**, 7 Charlotte Square, offers the chance to look at an original interior. A monument to Prince Albert, husband of Queen Victoria, sits in the central grass square overlooked by **West Register House** (*see box:* **Roots Mon!**), a grandly domed and porticoed affair originally built as St George's Church. The square has been home to numerous illustrious residents over the centuries, the most notable being Alexander Graham Bell, the inventor of the telephone, who was born in 1847 at 16 South Charlotte Street.

Just off Charlotte Square is Young Street. One of an ordered network of narrow streets that runs along either side of George Street, it gives a fuller picture of Craig's New Town plan. Tucked away from the grander streets, this is where the less financially fortunate lived. To the north of Young Street, Queen Street and Queen Street Gardens run parallel to George Street. The gardens were created as a stretch of disciplined rural-ness and remain, like all New Town gardens, accessible only to residents. The townhouse at 8 Queen Street was built by Robert Adam, next door is Thomas Hamilton's Royal College of Physicians.

The **National Portrait Gallery**, a confident, late-nineteenth-century imitation of the Gothic-cum-medieval look, is at the east end of Queen Street. The entrance foyer, decorated with murals recounting Scotland's history, is impressive. Appropriately, Sir Henry Raeburn lived over the way at 32 York Place. He was portrait artist to Edinburgh's Enlightenment luminaries, and painted one of Scotland's most ubiquitous cultural exports, the *Reverend Walker Skating*.

Dundas Street & environs

A gridiron of streets continues north from Queen Street down the hill to the Water of Leith. These are lined with solid, well-proportioned sandstone residences turned slate grey with age. The area around Dundas Street is considered to be the heart of today's New Town, but it was constructed after the first eighteenth-century new town and is one of six developments built in the early nineteenth century as speculative ventures on the part of the landowners. Scottish property laws allowed landowners to stipulate architectural style, hence the New Town's cohesive classical formality. Resolutely residential and exclusive, the New Town wasn't designed to attract outsiders or hoi polloi from the Old Town. Apart from churches, there were originally no public buildings, squares or markets: only in recent decades have shops and restaurants opened along its main roads. There is still a classy air to the area, but it is now home to a wider social mix. The best approach to exploring this part of the New Town is simply to follow your feet as it is nearly impossible to get completely lost.

The New Town has been home to many famous people, who are often remembered on the stone-carved inscriptions on the front of the buildings where they resided. Robert Louis Stevenson lived just below Queen Street Gardens at 17 Heriot Row. It is said that as a sickly child he looked on to the gardens and found inspiration for his novel *Treasure Island*. As a young bohemian in his signature black velvet jacket, he bypassed the elegance of the New Town, preferring the Old Town and its more rough-and-ready drinking haunts.

Dundas Street contains a number of private art galleries and the New Town Conservation Centre (13A Dundas Street, 557 5222). Its small library is open to the public (call for opening hours) and contains much information on the New Town and its architecture. Cutting across Dundas Street is Great King Street. Built in 1804, it is a brilliant declaration of the classical New Town-look. Fanlights, windows and even chimney stacks are symmetrically arranged to give maximum impact to the architectural grandeur. Another famous New Town resident, JM Barrie, the author of *Peter Pan*, lodged as a student at 3 Great King Street.

Just beyond lies Drummond Place, named after George Drummond, six-times Lord Provost and driving force behind the building of the first New Town. Built in the shape of a horseshoe with a central garden and cobbled roads, it sums up the New Town's ethos for urban living: smart tenement buildings with ample front doors and high ceilings (architects consciously designed them to look like upmarket houses) overlook a spacious oasis of greenery. Doubtless finding pleasure in all this was Compton Mackenzie. The author of the famous Scottish tale *Whisky Galore* lived at 31 Drummond Place.

The Moray Estate is one of the grandest of the New Town's residential quarters. It lies to the west of Howe Street and is best approached from Heriot Row. Built in 1822 on land belonging to the Earl of Moray, this development is formed by a succession of linked crescents. The architectural climax comes in Moray Place. An overbearing, 12-sided circus, punctuated by sturdy columns set into the façade, this is New Town classical formality at its proudest.

Scott Monument

East Princes Street Gardens, EH2 (529 4068). Princes St buses. Closed for restoration until 1999.
This over-elaborate and ornate counterpoint to the austerity of most of Edinburgh's architecture is a fitting memorial to the man who orchestrated George IV's celebrated tartanising visit to Edinburgh in 1822. It was designed by George Meikle Kemp and completed in 1840, 14 years after Sir Walter Scott's death. Although closed for restoration work until 1999, at 200ft (61m) it is a city-centre landmark.

Stockbridge

Village life in the heart of the city.

At first glance Stockbridge appears unremarkable. The area, which started life as an outlying village, clustered round the old wooden Stock Bridge over the Water of Leith to the north-west of the Old Town, today joins seamlessly to the city. Less architecturally conformist than many of Edinburgh's suburbs, Stockbridge retains an air of a self-contained township with its turn-of-the-century tenemented streets, genteel terraces and occasional villas. Historically it was a centre of small-scale industry when mills and tanneries were built along the banks of the Water of Leith back in the early eighteenth century. Later came breweries and filth. Downhill from the New Town, the river soon became an open sewer and general rubbish tip. Today, however, the river has been cleaned up and the Water of Leith walkway is one of Edinburgh's quiet and scenic secrets.

St Stephen Street & environs

In the late 1960s and early 1970s, cheap rented accommodation turned Stockbridge into a bohemian and student heartland. Recent gentrification has blunted the groovy edge but many second-hand shops still line Stockbridge's main shopping area of Deanhaugh Street and Raeburn Place. St Stephen Street, just south of the bridge, was once home to Nico (of Velvet Underground fame) and a wealth of junk-cum-antique shops, few of which remain. On the corner is the **Bailie Bar**, a cosy drinking hole that has several photographs from the time. Further along are Regency-style shops and a marooned old gateway that is the last vestige of Stockbridge's meat and vegetable market. It was built in 1826 after a public campaign lead by one Captain Carnegie and was a coup for local shoppers. Town officials had hoped that Stockbridge, like neighbouring New Town, would remain a market-free zone.

On the other side of Kerr Street and just up Gloucester Street is Duncan's Land, one of the area's oldest buildings. Now a restaurant, the sturdy stone and rubble house dates from the late 1790s. It was the birthplace, in 1796, of David Roberts, the painter of Middle Eastern souks and Pharaonic temples known for his penchant for dressing up as a sheik. The carved lintel, inscribed

*Ann of Grecian gables – Ann Street in the **Raeburn Estate** page 54.*

'Fear Only God 1650', is in fact 'borrowed' from an earlier building. Opposite Duncan's Land, a mass of modern flats stands on the site of a series of streets demolished in the name of slum tenement clearances in the 1960s and 1970s.

Running off Kerr Street and just before Stock Bridge, which dates from 1900, is Hamilton Place. Along it, past the **Theatre Workshop** and Saxe-Coburg Street, is the low-slung, neo-classical Edinburgh Academy on Henderson Row. Built in 1824, it was the fittingly austere location for the film *The Prime of Miss Jean Brodie*. Down Saxe-Coburg Street itself lies the quaint 1820s square Saxe-Coburg Place.

Down Gabriel's Road (the small lane in the corner of the Place) and across Glenogle Road are what are locally known as 'the colonies'. The first of a series of artisan dwellings built by the Edinburgh Co-operative Building Company from the 1860s onwards, they defy Edinburgh's usual preference for tenements. Eleven narrow streets (named after members and supporters of the co-operative) are lined with two-storey, stone terraces. What makes them unusual is their 'double sidedness'. The entrance to the upper level is from external steps that run from one street, with access to the ground floor from the opposite side.

Across the bridge at the end of Glenogle Road and right, along Arboretum Place, is the **Royal Botanic Garden** (*see below*).

Healthy waters at **St Bernard's Well**.

The Raeburn Estate

Just off Deanhaugh Street at the top of Leslie Place lies the Raeburn Estate. An early-nineteenth-century speculative property development by the artist Sir Henry Raeburn, it seduced the moneyed classes to move to Stockbridge. Less triumphal in scale than the New Town, St Bernard's Crescent is nonetheless an architectural heavyweight with thick Grecian columns and vast front doors. Over the way is the far more delicate Danube Street, with wrought iron balconies and rooftop balustrades. Behind this show of architectural propriety, Dora Noyce ran a brothel up until the 1980s. Known for serving liquid refreshment from a silver teapot, the infamous Mrs Noyce described her establishment as 'more of a YMCA with extras'.

Overlooking the Water of Leith is Dean Terrace, which rises up to Ann Street. Unassuming and bijoux, Ann Street is today one of Edinburgh's most exclusive addresses. Named after Raeburn's wife, the proportions are dolls' house-like compared to the lofty heights of the New Town. There is a cottage-garden ambience to the street, with each terraced house fronted by a small garden. Many famous residents have found refuge here, including Thomas de Quincey, the notorious nineteenth-century drug-taker and author of *The Confessions of an English Opium Eater*.

The Dean

To the west of Ann Street is the one-time Dean estate. John Learmonth bought the estate with an eye to financial gain in 1825. As Edinburgh's Lord Provost, Learmonth negotiated the building of Dean Bridge to cross the Water of Leith and link the land to the city. Not entirely successful on the money-making front, thanks to a saturated mid-nineteenth-century property market, Learmonth's development fell short of his aspirations. Later, rows of tenements with bay windows were added. They continue to stand proud along the east of Queensferry Road.

Further along Queensferry Road, what looks like a castle imported from a Disneyesque landscape can be seen looking north along Learmonth Avenue. This is Fettes College, a private school for boys built in the 1860s. A flamboyant coupling of the French chateau and Scots Baronial styles, it is topped by a soaring clock tower. Prime Minister Tony Blair was educated here, as was James Bond. According to espionage fiction, Bond was sent to Fettes after an 'incident' with a maid at his former school, Eton College.

Back on Queensferry Road is Stewart's Melville College. Another architectural flight of fancy, this is an 1848 hybrid of Renaissance and Jacobean styles marched out in a sea of leaded domes. It is one of Edinburgh's many so-called 'pauper palaces', funded by wealthy benefactors to school and house poor, often orphaned, children. Just around the corner, off Dean Path, is Dean Cemetery. Laid out in 1845, among its famous dead are architect William Playfair, pioneering photographer David Octavius Hill and the man who inspired Conan Doyle's Sherlock Holmes, Dr Joseph Bell. The tombs are among the most magnificent and bombastic in Edinburgh, built for men who wanted knew how they wanted to be rememberd. From an artistic point of view, it is fascinating to see the changes in the way that Celtic knots and flourishes have been incorporated.

The Water of Leith

From its source in the Pentland Hills, which lie south-west of Edinburgh, the Water of Leith travels 21 miles (33 kilometers) before emptying into the Firth of Forth at Leith. It provided power for the many mills that grew up along its banks. The Water of Leith Walkway Trust, founded in 1976, has laid out pedestrian routes along the banks that make a peaceful escape route from the city to more rural retreats beyond.

The Stock Bridge is a good point to join the Water of Leith. From the stairway on the northeast end, the path leads downriver towards the Royal Botanic Garden. Going upriver along Saunders Street, the path goes past Dean Village to the **National Gallery of Modern Art** and, beyond that, to Roseburn. At the end of Saunders Street, the path is at its most dramatic as it enters a valley between the New Town and the private Dean Gardens to the north. Along the walkway is a neo-classical circular temple, St Bernard's Well. The story goes that three schoolboys discovered a mineral water spring in 1760. Cashing in on the craze for 'taking the waters', in 1788 Lord Gardenstone commissioned architect Alexander Nasmyth to build a temple to replace an earlier well-house. The pump room (occasionally opened to the public) is richly decorated in mosaics. Above, standing beneath the temple's dome, is a statue of Hygeia, the goddess of health. Further along the walkway, there are epic views of Dean Bridge, built in the 1820s by engineer Thomas Telford. To the north of the bridge stands Holy Trinity Church, built in an 1830s reproduction of the English Perpendicular style.

As the walkway passes under Dean Bridge and rises along Miller Row to Old Dean Bridge it enters Dean Village. Originally called the Village of the Water of Leith, mills have clustered here since the fifteenth century. The Incorporation of Baxters (bakers) ran 11 water mills here, supplying milled meal to the whole of Edinburgh. Today, Dean Village is faintly reminiscent of a Bavarian township with gabled houses staggered along a deep

gorge. It is a surprisingly quiet and secluded spot considering its proximity to the city centre. Bell's Brae (brae is Gaelic for upper part) runs steeply up to Dean Bridge. Formerly the main road running north out of Edinburgh, the Brae is still lined with a rich agglomeration of seventeenth century stone buildings. Opposite Old Dean Bridge is Baxter's Tolbooth, which was given an unappealing makeover in the 1970s. Still visible, however, is a stone carved with wheat sheaves and bakers' shovels with the inscription 'God's Providence Is Our Inheritance', dating from 1675. Just beyond the bridge is West Mill, now converted into flats, and Well Court (1884), which was built as artisan housing in an act of Victorian philanthropy by John Ritchie Findlay, proprietor of *The Scotsman*, whose own home overlooked the village.

The Water of Leith walkway continues just above Well Court, following the river through shady nooks and past weirs to pass under Belford Bridge. Here, steps lead up to Belford Road and a five-minute walk to the National Gallery of Modern Art. Alternatively, about a quarter of mile (400 metre) beyond, a steep path winds up to the rear of the gallery. Looking back across the river there is a splendid view of Donaldson's School for the Deaf. Designed by William Playfair in the 1840s, its turrets and ornate grandeur appealed to Queen Victoria, who is said to have suggested taking it up as a residence rather than the **Palace of Holyroodhouse**. The Gallery of Modern Art is another of Edinburgh's pauper palaces, this time in neo-classical style. It looks out across Belford Road, on to yet another pauper palace, the Dean, built by Thomas Hamilton in 1833. Usually one for the severe classical repertoire, here Hamilton loosened his architectural style and opted for showy roof-top pavilions.

Royal Botanic Garden

Inverleith Row, EH3 (552 7171). 8(A), 9(A), 19, 23, 27, 37 buses. **Open** *Apr-Aug* 9.30am-7pm daily; *Sept* 9.30am-6pm daily; *Oct* 9.30am-5pm daily; *Nov-Jan* 9.30am-4pm daily; *Feb* 9.30am-5pm daily; *Mar* 9.30am-6pm daily. **Admission** free, but suggested donation of £2.50 to Glasshouse Experience. **Credit** *shop* V, £TC. **Map 4 D2**
One of only two Royal Botanic Gardens in Britain (the other is London's Kew). Edinburgh's first botanic garden was founded as a Physic Garden in 1670 next to the Palace of Holyroodhouse. The garden then occupied grounds by the Nor' Loch and on Leith Walk, before moving to its present site in 1823. Today, its 72 acres (28 hectares) make one of the most peaceful places in the city. It is home to over 2,000 specimens of trees, a rock garden, herbaceous borders and the recently landscaped Pringle Chinese Collection. The 'Glasshouse Experience' belies a necessary move towards commercialisation and houses a wide collection of plants, from the most humid to arid climes, in three separate glasshouses, including the impressive Victorian Palm House. From the central rise of the garden, in front of **Inverleith House** and the **Terrace Café**, is one of the best panoramic views of Edinburgh, looking up to the Castle, Calton Hill and, on a fine day, beyond to the Pentland Hills and the Lammermuirs.
Disabled: access; toilets.

Calton Hill

Edinburgh's Athenian crown with its Doric columns and monuments provides an accessible vantage point.

Calton Hill is, along with Arthur's Seat and Castle Rock, one of best places from which to view Edinburgh. The top of **Nelson's Monument** (*see below*) affords the viewer a sense of the bulk and anarchy of the Old Town to the south; the formality of the New Town to the north-west; and the modern chaos of Granton's gas towers and Leith's Docks to the north. Almost all of Scotland's capital is in view as it sweeps down from the Pentland hills to the Firth of Forth. On a clear day, the views over the Forth to Fife and east towards North Berwick are also splendid.

The hill is a favoured and atmospheric spot. When a sunny summer afternoon turns chill and the sea mist, known locally as a 'haar', sweeps up from the Forth, the view of mist-torn chimneys and tenements creates an impression of what Edinburgh was like when it was called 'Auld Reekie' – although the smoking chimneys are long gone with the advent of Clean Air Acts. This is a hill on the edge of old Edinburgh, the site of the **City Observatory** (*see below*) from which science regimented time. And also the site of the modern Beltane celebrations when pagan ritual still marks the passage of time.

Waterloo Place

Most visitors approach the hill from the west: along Princes Street or across North Bridge. Looking up, it is easy to understand why Edinburgh retains the accolade of the 'Athens of the North'. What is rather more strange is that the name came first – from the city's position on the grand tours of the late eighteenth century and its relationship with imperial, 'Roman' London. The classical-styled architecture followed to justify and immortalise the phrase.

Turning the corner into Waterloo Place brings exposure to the full impact of the nineteenth century neo-classical architectural regime. Some call it balanced and perfectly proportioned. Others find it stultifying in its grey formality – small wonder that, until recently, Edinburgh had a reputation for dour rectitude. A glimpse at what has replaced the rectitude, or rather what lies underneath its upright moral fibre, is visible down to the left from Regent Bridge. Just by the **St James Oyster Bar** is where Renton ran into a car in the opening scenes of the film *Trainspotting*.

A few yards further along, Waterloo Place bisects the Old Calton graveyard. The steps to the right lead up to the largest part of the cemetery, the last resting place of many of the main figures of the Enlightenment. The two most imposing memorials are Robert Adam's tower for the philosopher and historian David Hume and the obelisk to the political reformers of 1793-4 who were transported for having the audacity to demand the vote for the Scots. A plaque at the entrance lists some further inhabitants of note. The cemetery is worth a wander if you have time. The back of the tombs at the far, left-hand end of the cemetery give a fine and less obvious view of Edinburgh Castle than the one from the top of Calton Hill, as well as the **Venue** nightclub immediately below. The rather Gothic building backing on to that corner of the graveyard is the old Governor's House of the Calton Gaol: it is the first piece of turreted architecture visible from the East Coast trains into Waverley Station and is often, quite vocally and amusingly to those in the know, mistaken for the Castle itself.

The cemetery was divided in 1815, when Princes Street was extended and the North Bridge built. Before then, access to the hill had been up the steep road which is itself known, slightly confusingly, as Calton Hill and that now runs from the end of Waterloo Place down to Leith Street. Rock House, set back above the road on the north side, is one of the only houses in Edinburgh to have good views both north and south and was home to a succession of photographers from the 1830s up until 1945. If you're in need of a bit of sustenance, now is the time to get it, as the only food available on top of the hill is from an itinerant burger van. Café 1818 is a suitable stop.

The most direct route up Calton Hill from here is via the steps at the end of Waterloo Place. Once up the first set of steps, either go straight ahead and meander up the side of the hill or, if you've more energy, take the steep steps to the right.

Regent Road

Before the final assault on the hill, Regent Road, leading straight on from Waterloo Place, has a few sights to offer. The big building on the right is St Andrew's House, which was built on the site of Calton Gaol. A fine example of modernist, 1930s

*It's a Blockbuster! – **Playfair's Monument** to his uncle, Professor John Playfair. Page 58.*

architecture, its formality and presence make it a suitable home to the civil service. The first part of the gaol was built in 1791-5. A new prison building and the Governor's House, designed by Archibald Elliot, were added in 1815. Even then, the Governor's House was considered in bad taste. Not so the public executions that took place on the prison roof, in full view of the crowds on Calton Hill, until 1864.

On the left of the road, just before the turning that is the vehicular access to Calton Hill, the tarmac on the pavement has been scorched and burned. This is a result of the braziers that kept the members of the Vigil for a Scottish Parliament warm during the long cold nights between 1992 and 1997. It seemed an auspicious site for the Vigil, next door to the Royal High School, which everyone thought would house the new Scottish Parliament as it had been converted into a debating chamber before the failed referendum for a Scottish Assembly in 1976. However, after the 'yes-yes' vote of autumn 1997, the government said 'no-no' to the Royal High School and chose a site down the hill, opposite Holyrood House.

The Royal High School, designed by Thomas Hamilton and modelled on the Temple of Theseus in Athens, was completed in 1829. It is the most extensive of the neo-classical buildings of that time, with a massive Doric central block and pillared wings Because of its monumental size, it is difficult to get a proper perspective, even when walking past on the other side of Regent Road, so it's best to notice the detail here and contemplate its grandeur from one of the closes at the lower end of the Royal Mile. The view down to Holyrood, the Canongate Churchyard and up to the Castle are worth straying this far for. While the Royal High School's architecture is appropriate for its function, Hamilton's Robert Burns Memorial, just across the road, is completely out of tune with its purpose. The large collection of Burns relics, which were once displayed there, can be seen in the **Writer's Museum**. The paths on the right lead down to Calton Road and provide a suitable shortcut to Holyrood if you're not going back up the hill. A few steps past the Burns Memorial is the entrance to the New Calton graveyard, which is large but not overly fascinating.

Arriving, slightly puffed, at the top of the steps up the hill, you're confronted by a large cannon. This rather magnificent beast is Portuguese in origin and provides a suitably phallic accompaniment to many a wedding photograph, with Nelson's Monument thrusting boldly in the background.

Nearby, the set of 12 Doric columns that form the National Monument to those who lost their lives in the Napoleonic Wars were erected in the 1820s. Although it is generally regarded with affection nowadays, it was dubbed 'Edinburgh's Disgrace' when the original plans to build a replica of the Parthenon were thwarted because only half the £42,000 required was raised by public donation.

The building in the walled grounds is the City Observatory (William Playfair, 1818), which is based on the Temple of the Winds in Athens. The original City Observatory (James Craig, 1792) is the three-story Gothic tower on the south-western corner of the walls although it was never put to the use for which it was designed. In the opposite corner to this is a disused astronomical dome, which today houses the **Edinburgh Experience** (*see below*). This 'three-dimensional trip through the history of Edinburgh' is actually rather good. The commentary is lively and informative and, although a bit long in the tooth, the pictures are well chosen. Incorporated into the south-eastern wall of the observatory is Playfair's monument to his uncle, Professor John Playfair.

The circular building to the south-west of the observatory is another Playfair copy. It is a monument to the philosopher Dugald Steward and based on the monument to Lysicrates on the Acropolis at Athens. Looking west from this monument, the modern monstrosity in the foreground is the **St James Centre**, which is, at least, grey.

Although Calton Hill has plenty of open space to wander round, rest upon and enjoy the views from, the Regent Gardens to the east are private and belong to the residents of the Regent, Carlton and Royal Terraces. These New Town terraces are unique in that they follow the contours of the hill and not a grid pattern. They are regarded as being particularly fine examples of the New Town architectural style.

Although not part of Calton Hill, Broughton is an easy walk from here. There is a gate at the north side of the hill on Royal Terrace by the Greenside Church – referred to by Robert Louis Stevenson as 'the church on the hill'. After negotiating the fumes and cars of Leith Walk and Picardy Place, Broughton Street is a bustling and lively community with plenty of good bars, cafés and restaurants for the weary. At the bottom of Broughton Street, across the roundabout, is Mansfield Church with walls covered in murals by Phoebe Traquair.

Timepiece

The **City Observatory** has played an important role in Edinburgh's history. Merchant ships relied on it as an accurate chronometer to be able to ascertain their position from the position of the stars.

Inside the observatory is the Politician's Clock – so called because it has two faces. The first, facing into the observatory, was used to set the time at night according to the stars. The second faced out so that ships' captains could set their timepieces, which they had carried all the way up from Leith Docks.

In 1852, another timepiece was placed on top of the Nelson Monument. This is a large white ball that is raised to the cross on the white mast from where it drops at 1pm each day, except when it is too misty or the wind is too high. This meant that chronometers no longer had to be hauled all the way up from Leith. In 1861, a steel wire over 4,000 feet (1,220 metres) long was attached between the monument and the Castle to facilitate the firing of the 1pm gun that still shocks the unwary to this day.

The church has been bought by the Mansfield Traquair Trust and the murals are being restored for public display. The church's vaults are home to the excellent club **Café Graffiti**.

The Edinburgh Experience

City Observatory, Calton Hill, EH7 (556 4365). Princes St buses. **Open** *Apr-Oct* 10.30am-5pm daily; *Nov-Mar* closed. **Admission** £2 adult; £1.20 concs; £6 family; group discounts on request. **Credit** MC, £$TC, V. **Map 4 G4**

One of the telescope domes of the City Observatory has been converted into a theatre for this 20-minute, 3-D slide show. The slides are startlingly vivid and the soundtrack makes good use of irony to tell the standard Edinburgh anecdotes rather more sharply than you will hear them elsewhere. Unfortunately, vandalism has forced the closure of the shutters in the City Observatory itself, so you can't see the rather fine Politician's Clock unless you join one of the free stargazing sessions that happen every Friday evening, organised by the Astronomical Society of Edinburgh.

Disabled: access with assistance.

Nelson Monument

Calton Hill, EH7 (556 2716). Princes St buses. **Open** *Apr-Oct* 1-6pm Mon; 10am-6pm Tue-Sat; *Oct-Mar* 10am-3pm Mon-Sat. **Admission** £2. **No credit cards. Map 4 G4**

The view from the top of this monument, designed in the shape of Nelson's telescope by Robert Burn in 1807, is worth the entry price. Also, invest in the photocopied brochure to help work out what you are looking at. The ball on the top falls each day at 1pm, as it has since it was a time signal to shipping in Leith Docks. Be warned that, with 143 steps, it is quite a climb to the top, the door up there is only 17in (42cm) wide and the parapet is sturdy but not very high.

Arthur's Seat & Duddingston

Edinburgh's very own diminutive Highland hill gives the city a rugged heart.

No other European city has such a mass of splendidly rugged landscape at its heart as Edinburgh has in the extinct volcano, Arthur's Seat. Looming sternly out of Holyrood Park, it hasn't erupted for more than 350 million years, but the lava flows that shaped the local geology are still clearly visible. Although people tend to think its name refers to King Arthur, the name is more likely to be a corruption of 'Archer's Seat'. The 650-acre (260-hectare) Holyrood Park surrounding it, now a public park, was first used around 9,000 years ago, for hunting. Terraces, known in Scotland as runrigs, were developed by farmers on the lower slopes and can still be seen on the eastern slopes. From the twelfth century onwards it was used as a hunting ground by Scottish kings, becoming a royal park in the sixteenth century.

The 823-foot (250 metre) peak and the neighbouring Whinney Hill, lower by 250-feet (76 metres), are encircled by Queen's Drive, which has entrances off Holyrood Road, London Road and the top of Dalkeith Road. It can also be approached from the other side via Duddingston Road West.

The face Arthur's Seat presents to the Old Town is the dark, forbidding curve of Salisbury Crags. A path, called the Radical Road, runs directly below the rockface. From the road, some of the features that nudged James Hutton towards his invention of the modern discipline of geology are visible in the rocks.

Turning left at the Holyrood Palace entrance to the park, Queen's Drive passes St Margaret's Loch, with the ruined St Anthony's Chapel perched above it. Just before the loch, there is a grille set into the wall on the right. This is St Margaret's Well, the surround of which originally stood near Restalrig Church where, during the plague years, a spring was relied upon as a source of clean water. The surround was removed in 1860 to make way for a railway depot and put here, where there was already a natural spring.

Past St Margaret's Well is the starting point for a path that divides at the beginning of the valley known as Hunter's bog. Going to the right leads up to the top of Salisbury Crags, straight ahead the valley rises to a twisting and steep path (with steps) to the summit, while the paths to the left go up through the Dasses, also to the peak of Arthur's Seat. Although all the paths can give the feeling of being in the heart of the countryside, the approaches to the peak are steep in places. The peak is most easily approached from the car park beside Dunsapie Loch on the east side, past Whinney Hill. It's at a fairly easy gradient and not too strenuous a walk. Once on the summit the views, of Edinburgh sprawling below, over the Firth of Forth, into Fife, and south into the Borders, are easily worth the effort.

Duddingston

From the north-east end of Dunsapie Loch a steep path leads down into Duddingston. Alternatively, continue along Queen's Drive to the bottom of the hill, where it joins Holyrood Park Road, and turn left down towards Duddingston, passing beneath the rock formations named Lion's Haunch and Samson's Ribs.

The name Duddingston is said to come from a Gaelic word meaning 'the house on the sunny side of the hill'. The area has been settled since the twelfth century, but artifacts from the late Bronze Age have also been found there. The chief occupations of the parishioners of Duddingston were farming (the soil is very fertile and the area was once intensively farmed) and weaving (they produced a coarse flaxen material known as 'Duddingston hardings'). Producing and selling salt was another mainstay.

Duddingston Village is tiny, consisting mainly of the Causeway and Old Church Road, set back off the main road of Duddingston Road West. The village and its surrounding green belt was declared a conservation area in 1975, and it remains a little slice of countryside in the midst of a big city.

Duddingston Loch has provided modern Edinburgh with one of its favourite symbols, and one that is practically an unofficial logo for the city: the wry painting of *Reverend Robert Walker*

Skating on Duddingston Loch by Sir Henry Raeburn (1756-1823). Accounts from the last century describe the loch as swarming with multitudes of skaters whenever it froze. The loch is also virtually synonymous with the sport of curling. Edinburgh devotees of 'the roaring game' migrated to Duddingston in 1795 when their traditional ground of the Nor' Loch below Edinburgh Castle had been drained and its replacement at Canonmills was met with indifference. The club attracted many eminent citizens, and every frosty day the magistrates led a procession to the loch 'with great pomp and circumstance'. Rules formulated at Duddingston were adopted by curlers all over the country.

Even without its capacity to freeze over, the loch has always been a popular spot for its sheer natural beauty. It is just over 550 yards (500 metres) long and less than 270 yards (250 metres) at its widest point. The waterside outside Duddingston Village is usually crowded with ducks, geese and swans padding around on the lookout for bread. It is a bird sanctuary too: there is a heronry in the trees at the western end and bitterns have been seen in the reedbeds there. The best views of the loch, for ornithological purposes, are from the slopes above Queen's Drive.

The small octagonal building at the edge of the loch is Thomson's Tower, named after Reverend John Thomson (1778-1840), the most famous of the parish's ministers, who gave rise to the enduring Scots phrase 'Jock Tamson's bairns'. Sir Walter Scott, a friend of Thomson's, frequently visited him and wrote part of *The Heart of Midlothian* in this stunted, turret-like construction at the foot of the Manse's garden. The well-connected Reverend Thomson, a landscape painter, also played host to JMW Turner at the Manse.

Duddingston Kirk dates from 1124 and has a Norman arch separating the chancel and the nave. The north aisle was added in 1631, and many alterations have been made to the building, such as the enlarging of the windows, which destroyed many of the original features. The carvings around the church, especially around the south doorway, are rough and ready but fascinating, and the image of a fullydressed Christ on the cross suggested to some scholars that the original church was actually the work of Saxons. The little tower, on the left of the church gates and now called Session House, was a watchtower. At the height of 'resurrectionist' activity, the graveyard had to be guarded to prevent bodies being stolen and sold to anatomists for dissection.

On the right-hand side of the gates is the 'loupin-on stone', a stepped platform to help horsemen

Climb every mountain – **Arthur's Seat** *with* **St Margaret's Loch** *and* **St Anthony's Chapel** *in the foreground. Page 59.*

mount. A punishment appliance called 'the jougs' (from the word yoke), an iron collar in which wrongdoers were clamped, is attached to the wall behind. Common to most parishes at one time, the Duddingston jougs are now almost unique in having survived in their original place.

Across the road is the west entrance to the Causeway, Duddingston Village's main street. The Causeway is a narrow road folded into three, with Arthur's Seat looming above the roofs of the big houses set back from the road.

Over the wall from Duddingston Kirk lies **Dr Neil's Garden** (*see below*), a rock garden specialising in Alpine plants and trees. It is only open to the public for a couple of weekends a year.

Duddingston was a place where weary travellers would dismount and seek rest and refreshment. The **Sheep Heid Inn** on the Causeway is one of the oldest public houses in Scotland and a favourite of James VI and I. In 1580, he presented the landlord with a ram's head, unfortunately now stolen. The inn has retained all its charm. Shelves abound with books, trophies and knick-knacks and the walls are adorned with a mass of pictures. There is a beer garden outside, overlooked by an indoor terrace.

Duddingston is proud of the fact that Bonnie Prince Charlie slept there on 19 September 1745, when he held a Council of War before the Battle of Prestonpans and stayed close to his forces rather than head back to Holyrood Palace for the night. Where he actually slept has been the subject of much conjecture – it was finally decided the white, pebble-dashed cottage at the end of the Causeway was where he stayed.

On Duddingston Road is the main attraction of the area for some, Duddingston Golf Course, which celebrated its centenary in 1995. It's in the grounds of the neo-classical Mansion House, with Corinthian portico, built in 1768 by Sir William Chambers as a bachelor pad. The Mansion House is currently occupied by a firm of architects and signposted by some rather unwelcoming 'private road' signs, but it's worth a glimpse through the trees, as is the folly known as the Temple, at the sixteenth tee, which gave the club its logo.

Over the main road from the entrance leading to the clubhouse is the Innocent Railway walkway and cycle track. The path sadly doesn't afford any views of the Bawsinch Nature Reserve over the wall, or Prestonfield Golf Course on the other side, but does lead back to the Salisbury Crags end of Holyrood Park.

Dr Neil's Garden

1 Wolseley Gardens, EH8 (659 6545). London Rd buses. **Open** weekends in May, June, Aug.
Details of open weekends can be obtained from the Tourist Information Centre or Scotland's Garden Scheme, 31 Castle Terrace, EH1 (229 1870/fax 229 0443). Group visits to the garden and the old village kirk (with light refreshments provided) can be arranged by calling Dr Neil's direct.

The Southside

South of the Old Town, the former gathering grounds for Scotland's great armies now attract willing suburban conscripts to their green spaces and historic sites.

Edinburgh's Southside is the great swathe of land that stretches from the Cowgate south to Blackford Hill between Newington, to the east, and Morningside, to the west. It contains beautiful green spaces, academic institutions, streets and buildings where the narrative of Scottish history is apparent to even the most casual passer-by. At times it seems as if the visitor is spoiled for choice when it comes to recreational and cultural nourishment. Odd, then, how the most popular attraction of all is a dead dog.

Greyfriars

The mystery of **Greyfriars Kirk** (*see below*), opposite Chambers Street at the south end of George IV Bridge, has nothing to do with ghostly grey friars or how an estimated 80,000 corpses have been squeezed into the kirkyard. The central conundrum is the interest in a certain shaggy hound who turned up his toes in 1872.

Bobby was the loyal mutt who lived by his late master's grave for 14 years and was an object of affection for many. But when he died, the minister at the time waited until cover of darkness to plant the pooch in the only unconsecrated plot left available. After all, a dumb animal could not be left lying in sacred soil. The misleading notice in the kirkyard says Bobby 'was buried nearby' his master. The minister had a better handle on the great scheme of things than many visitors since.

Greyfriars Kirkyard has played a pivotal role in the history of Scotland. It is where the National Covenant was signed in 1638 and where the bodies of executed Covenanters were buried alongside common criminals. They, and the survivors of the Battle of Bothwell Brig (1679), were kept in the Covenanters' Prison under desperate conditions for five months. Martyrs' Monument, with its chilling inscription 'Halt passenger, take heed of what you do see, This tomb doth shew for what some men did die', is their memorial.

The statue of Bobby the dog apart, Greyfriars Kirk pulls off the trick of being simple but not austere. Formerly the site of a Franciscan friary, it dates from 1620 but was severely damaged, then rebuilt, after a fire in 1845. In the kirkyard, there are hardly any modern buildings within sight to break the historical spell, apart from the Museum of Scotland extension to the **Royal Museum**. **George Heriot's School** (1628; *see below*), which owes its existence to a legacy from Heriot, goldsmith and jeweller to the court of James I, adds to the atmosphere, as does a portion of the Flodden Wall. This was the defence structure built around Edinburgh in 1513 after the Battle of Flodden, in anticipation of the arrival of the English armies. Wandering around the kirkyard when there's a 'haar' provides a palpable time-slip effect.

Down Candlemaker Row, then right along the Cowgate, one of the first buildings on the right is the Magdalen Chapel. Now the headquarters of the **Scottish Reformation Society** (*see below*), this former church dates from 1547 (steeple added 1626) and is home to the only surviving pre-Reformation stained glass in Scotland. Sadly, the glass in question – four fading rounds that were inserted in 1553 – is a bit of a disappointment. More interesting are the 'brods' (receipts for gifts of money or goods to the chapel, dating from the sixteenth to the nineteenth centuries) that wrap round the walls like a frieze and the Deacon's Chair (1708). It is claimed that the chapel is where the first General Assembly of the Church of Scotland was held in 1578 and, in the bloody days of the late seventeenth century, it served as a mortuary for those executed Covenanters whose bodies were buried at Greyfriars.

Grassmarket

There has been a market in the Grassmarket since at least 1477 – a 1977 plaque on a rock there commemorates the five hundredth anniversary of the date it received its Charter from James III. Down King's Stables Road at the Grassmarket's northwest corner, gardens provided the raw material for a vegetable market from the twelfth century while the Grassmarket itself held livestock sales. King's Stables Road was the site of a medieval tournament ground, begun when England's Edward III

Revelling in the perpendicular – full-on Victorian museum chic in the main hall of the **Royal museum of Scotland.**

occupied the Castle in the 1330s, and finished by David II when Scotland regained the Castle.

But the Grassmarket also has a darker history. It was a frequent venue for executions, the most famous being the Porteous lynching (1736), given literary form in Sir Walter Scott's *The Heart of Midlothian*. John Porteous was an unpopular captain of the town guard. On 14 April 1736, he was in charge of the execution of two smugglers in the Grassmarket. Sensing trouble, he sealed off the area with guardsmen but went ahead with the hanging. The mob threw stones, Porteous ordered his men to open fire: three in the crowd were killed and a dozen wounded. Porteous was tried for murder and found guilty. He was to be hanged on 20 July, but a royal warrant from Queen Caroline reprieved him. Not for long, though. A mob broke into the Old Tolbooth on the Royal Mile on 19 July, dragged Porteous down to the Grassmarket and hung him. He was buried in Greyfriars, and there's still an entrance called Porteous Pend at the southwest corner of the Grassmarket, next to Mary Mallinson Antiques. On the north side of the Grassmarket, now a row of pubs and restaurants, the **White Hart Inn** (*see below*) is where Robert Burns supposedly wrote *Ae Fond Kiss* and the protagonist in Iain Banks's *Complicity* gets some hints about the whereabouts of a dismembered body.

The street leaving the Grassmarket on the way to Lothian Road is West Port, former home to murderers Burke and Hare who sold their victims to university anatomists (1827-8). At the bottom of West Port, opposite the Fiddlers Pub, is the Vennel: a steep lane leading up to Lauriston Place that runs along one of the best-preserved sections of the Flodden Wall. At the top of West Port, at the junction of High Riggs and East Fountainbridge, is Main Point. At one time this was a key exit from Edinburgh with roads leading to Glasgow, Stirling and the south-west. In 1770, a rather pleasant house was built on the site, now surrounded by tenements and more modern buildings. But back then it took the common name given to any residence at an apex – a gusset house. This particular gusset house looks a little shabby these days and its ground floor is occupied by the far from reputable Burke and Hare pub.

Edinburgh University

Younger than the universities of St Andrews or Glasgow, Edinburgh University dates from 1582. Old College, now its central focus, occupies the original site. It was built by Robert Adam, who started the work in 1789, and William Playfair, who finished it after the interruption of the Napoleonic Wars. Rowand Anderson added the landmark dome in 1883. Certain areas of Old College are accessible to the public, notably the Playfair Library (where guided tours in summer

show off one of the city's finest classical interiors) and the old Upper Museum (now part of the **Talbot Rice Gallery**). The Upper Museum features a table from Napoleon's lodgings on St Helena with a cigar burn made, allegedly, by the Corsican snowbird himself. For details of how to join these tours contact the **University of Edinburgh Centre** (*see below*).

Next door to Old College, on Chambers Street, is the Royal Museum of Scotland, designed by Captain Francis Fowke and completed in 1888.

For even older buildings that are now part of the University, enthusiasts can go hunting down the bottom of Infirmary Street, off South Bridge. Through the gates at the foot of the street are the Old High School (1777) and Old Surgeon's Hall (1697). Adjacent are Victorian premises that once housed the wards of the Royal Infirmary where Joseph Lister discovered the benefits of antiseptic surgery. 'New' Surgeon's Hall was built in 1832 on Nicolson Street, a stone's throw from Old College. This building is home to the Royal College of Surgeons of Edinburgh and was another William Playfair design. Access is limited but can be gained via the **Sir Jules Thorn Exhibition of the History of Surgery** and the **Playfair Pathology Museum**, whose anatomy displays are not for the weak of stomach.

Not all University of Edinburgh buildings are as historically rich. The arts and social science campus at George Square is home to a phalanx of ugly 1960s blocks, whose erection caused quite a fuss as most of the eighteenth-century square was demolished to make room for them. The original tenements on the west side give a hint of what it was like when Sir Walter Scott spent his early years there (at No.25).

Just to the north and east of George Square, the empty block now used as a car park marks the old area of Bristo, which was also demolished to make way for university buildings. Facing Bristo Square – a favourite spot for skateboarders – are Teviot Row Student Union, the rather pompous McEwan Hall (1897), which was gifted to the university by local brewing magnate Sir William McEwan and is used for ceremonial occasions, and the classical Reid Concert Hall, which houses the **Edinburgh University Collection of Historic Musical Instruments**. Conveniently nearby, in West Nicolson Street, is **Peartree House**, a seventeenth-century building that is now a pub with a capacious beer garden.

Burgh Muir

South Edinburgh is covered with green spaces, notably the Meadows, Blackford Hill and the Braid Hills. But before the late eighteenth-century population explosion that saw Edinburgh expand beyond the Old Town, the whole area south of

School's out for summer – a studious day on **The Meadows**.

North Meadow Walk was open country. The Meadows' Burgh Loch supplied the city's (somewhat brackish) water. At times of low rainfall, the water level dropped, turning the loch into a swamp. A piped supply was started from Comiston in 1676 and Burgh Loch was drained, eventually leaving the Meadows as they appear now – a great big sports park. It's easy to pick up casual games of football there on Sunday afternoons and local running shop Run & Become organises races during the summer on the Sri Chimnoy Mile, a totally flat course one mile round.

In 1886 the Meadows was the site of the ambitious International Exhibition of Industry, which was housed in a huge temporary structure at the western end. It did, however, leave the city several permanent souvenirs including the whale jawbones at Jawbone Walk on Melville Drive, which were a gift from the Zetland and Fair Isle Knitting Stand, and the memorial pillars where Melville Drive joins Brougham Place. Down Causewayside from the east end of the Meadows is a refurbished garage that was designed in the 1930s International modern style by Sir Basil Spence.

Beyond the old Burgh Loch of the Meadows lay the Burgh Muir, or town heath, given to Edinburgh in 1128 by David I. Merchiston Castle lay at the western edge of this open countryside that sprawled south towards the Pentlands. But the heath's days were numbered: while the upper classes moved north out of the Old Town in the early nineteenth century, the middle classes moved south to build the suburbs of Bruntsfield, Marchmont, Morningside and the Grange on its grassy reaches. Ironically, in the sixteenth and seventeenth centuries (and possibly as far back as the 1400s, when the plague first came to Scotland), the Burgh Muir was where the dying victims of epidemics would be banished to expire. Its other role was as a rallying ground for Scots armies. The royal standard was pitched in the Bore Stone (a rock with a hole in it) on the Burgh Muir, then carried off at the head of the army. This lasthappened before the Scottish defeat at Flodden (1513). The Bore Stone is now displayed on a plinth on Morningside Road by the old church at the corner of Newbattle Terrace. It was fixed there in 1852 by Sir John Stuart Forbes, who claimed he had rescued it from the indignity of lying prone in a field.

Marchmont was built between 1876 and 1914 in Scottish baronial style. The cobbled sweep of Warrander Park Road gives a general idea, although the area now has a student ghetto flavour. Nearby, and incorporated into James Gillespie's High School, is Bruntsfield House, a sixteenth-century landmark on the old Burgh Muir.

Grange Cemetery on Beaufort Road is the city's neatest burial ground. Both Thomas Chalmers and Thomas Guthrie, who helped found the Free Kirk in 1843, are here. One imagines that neither would have approved of the fictional goings-on at St Trinian's, the louche school for girls created by cartoonist Ronald Searle and immortalised in a series of 1960s films, inspired by a pair of schoolgirls from the real St Trinnean's at neighbouring Palmerston Road (a short-lived establishment at No.10 that opened in 1922, moved over to Dalkeith Road, then closed in 1946).

Out on their own

Sitting cheek by jowl with one of the city's shabbiest housing schemes are the impressive remains of the fourteenth century **Craigmillar Castle** (*see below*). An L-shaped tower house, surrounded by a later curtain wall, it was razed by the Earl of Hertford after the English invasion of 1544, but later refurbished. The castle was a favourite spot for Mary, Queen of Scots, who retreated there after the murder of her favourite, David Rizzio, in 1566. Because of the large number of French in Mary's court who took up residence in the surrounding area, the region immediately to the south of the castle became known as 'Little France'. The approach from Niddrie Mains Road through the housing estates of Niddrie and Craigmillar reveals a side of Edinburgh that most visitors don't see.

At the south-western extreme of the Burgh Muir another act of academic vandalism was perpetrated in the 1960s, this time by Napier College of Commerce and Technology (now Napier University) when it constructed its appalling Colinton Road campus around Merchiston Castle. The fifteenth-century L-plan tower house once had such features as a moat and a secret passage. Early in its history it fell into the hands of the Napier family, of whom John Napier (1550-1617) – mathematician and inventor of logarithms – is the most celebrated scion. In the 1830s, Merchiston Castle became a school, but a century later it fell into disuse, until Napier College took it over.

Blackford

Sitting on top of Blackford Hill like a twin teacake tribute to Victorian empiricism is the **Royal Observatory**. It took over the work of the observatory on Calton Hill when light pollution there became too great in the late nineteenth century. When the new building was completed in 1895 it was well outside the city boundary. It has a well-designed visitor's centre that allows access to the flat roof between the domes from where there is an excellent view of the city's northern aspect (there are a couple of small telescopes for anyone who wants a close-up). Every Friday night during the

winter, weather permitting, there's a public observing session with a six-inch refracting telescope.

Blackford Hill itself makes for a good Sunday afternoon stroll and, down on its south side, is the Hermitage of Braid, a gentler walk by the Braid Burn. A late-eighteenth-century villa in the middle of the Hermitage acts as a countryside information centre and has a rudimentary tearoom in its basement. Herons have been sighted hereabouts – it's the kind of bucolic vale where you can forget you're in a city. Farther south still lie the Braid Hills, with two golf courses and yet another great view of Edinburgh and beyond (on a clear day you can see Ben Lomond). Access is either via Braid Hills Drive or left off Braid Road heading south on the way to the suburb of Buckstone. Turn the other way down Braid Road, heading back to Morningside, and you pass the spot where the last public execution for highway robbery took place in Edinburgh. In December 1814, two men mugged a man delivering a horse to the city from the Borders. They said all they got was four pence. The victim said he lost £5, bread and a spleuchan (tobacco pouch). The sad pair were strung up outside where 66 Braid Road now stands – in the roadway, all that's visible are two recessed squares where the gibbet was fixed. Stick around for any length of time absorbing the atmosphere and curtains twitch: they keep a tight grip on their spleuchans in these parts still.

Craigmillar Castle
Craigmillar Castle Road, off Old Dalkeith Road, EH16 (661 4445). Open Apr-Sept 9.30am-6.30pm daily; Oct-Mar 9.30am-4.30pm Mon-Wed, Sat; 2-4.30pm Sun. Admission £1.80; £1.30 concs; 75p children.
A substantial and atmospheric ruin now managed by Historic Scotland.

George Heriot's School
Lauriston Place, EH3 (229 7263/fax 229 6363). 23, 27, 28, 45, 47 buses. Open June, July, first 2 weeks Aug. Ring to book and to confirm dates. Admission free. Map 6 F6
School prefects give historical tours of this fine seventeenth-century building, which was used in its early days as a military hospital for Cromwell's troops.

Greyfriars Kirk
2 Greyfriars Place, Candlemaker Row, EH1 (visitors' centre 226 5429/fax 225 1900). George St buses. Open Easter-end Oct 10.30am-4.30pm Mon-Fri; 10.30am-2.30pm Sat. Admission free. Map 9 B3

Scottish Reformation Society
The Magdalen Chapel, 41 Cowgate, EH1 (220 1450). 2, 12, George IV Bridge buses. Open 9.30am-4pm Mon-Fri; Admission free. Map 9 B3

University of Edinburgh Centre
7-11 Nicolson Street, EH8 (650 2252/fax 650 2253). Bridges buses. Open 9am-5pm Mon-Fri. Map 7 G6

The White Hart Inn
34 Grassmarket, EH1 (226 2688). 2, 12, George IV Bridge buses. Open 11am-midnight Mon-Wed; 11-1am Thur-Sat; 12.30-11pm Sun. Map 9 A3

The Western Rim

Way out west, where the canal meets the setting sun, the tourist trail peters out but there are still sights to be seen.

Ask an Edinburgh native about the Western Rim and you'll get a blank look. It doesn't exist. Although other parts of the city are well known and well defined, there's a great swathe of Edinburgh starting at Lothian Road and working out west that is often neglected by visitors. Much of it is residential, but this area contrasts some of the old economic engines of the city (like brewing or railways) with the new (particularly finance). There are also reminders of Edinburgh life that pre-date the last millennium.

Lothian Road

At the foot of Lothian Road, there are two churches. The obvious and slightly squat one is St John's, a great Episcopalian theme park with assorted shops in the basement.

Consecrated in 1818, its stained glass is reckoned to be the finest collection under one roof in the whole of Scotland. Technically fine that is, as its relentless, nineteenth-century worthiness does overwhelm. The window best suited to contemporary tastes is in the chapel (built in 1935). It is a muted, blue and purple affair with Christ praying by the Sea of Galilee.

Next door is St Cuthbert's, named after a Northumbrian who beat the drum for early Christianity. He died in 687 and, according to legend, a church was built on this site soon after. According to the history books, however, the first recorded church on the site was built in the twelfth century when David I granted lands for the purpose. Its colourful history includes getting caught up in various sieges of Edinburgh Castle; it was occupied by Cromwell's troops in 1650, then Bonnie Prince Charlie's in 1745. Not surprisingly, the building has gone through many incarnations: the current one only dates to 1894, although the steeple was built in 1789. The graveyard provides a shady retreat in the heart of the city for the footsore tourist. Other inhabitants include artist Alexander Nasmyth (who painted the famous portrait of Robert Burns), the logarithm inventor John Napier and the city's

Skateboard finance – the **Exchange,** *page 68.*

original drugs writer, Thomas de Quincey. He penned *Confessions of an English Opium Eater* in 1822, beating Irvine Welsh to the punch by around 170 years.

Inside, St Cuthbert's has a large frieze behind the apse based on Leonardo's *Last Supper*. Other assorted artwork and one of its stained-glass windows was commissioned from Tiffany's in New York. All very un-Presbyterian.

Opposite the churches is the secular temple to expensive overnighting, the **Caledonian Hotel**. This great, red-stone edifice was frowned upon by natives when it appeared in 1903 as something more suited to vulgarian Glasgow. Originally a

*Alimentary my dear McEwan – the **Union Canal** with the **Fountain Brewery** to the right.*

railway hotel, its adjacent station closed in 1965, although the frieze over the former station entrance survives in the foyer by the hotel bistro.

Lothian Road itself, which dates to the 1780s, was a favourite haunt of the young Robert Louis Stevenson, escaping the bourgeois claustrophobia of his New Town home.

Haymarket

The Western Rim was once a bucolic stretch of farms and small hamlets with the area in immediate proximity to the Castle being given over to market gardens from the twelfth century at the latest. Such rural peace hardly seems credible given the riot of tenements and late-twentieth-century developments that are crammed into the area now, but seek out some of the older buildings and the picture slowly emerges.

Down Distillery Lane, for instance, off Dalry Road at Haymarket, there's a beautiful eighteenth-century mansion called Easter Dalry House (now an office) – Haymarket Station is in what used to be its garden. Further out along Dalry Road, on Orwell Place, is Dalry House – a survivor from the early seventeenth century. Hidden away in a residential warren, it is hard to imagine this beige-harled effort as an old Scots manor in extensive grounds. Although the height of respectability these days (it is run by Age Concern), former

owner John Chiesley wasn't quite as douce. He was executed for murder in 1689, then buried in the back garden.

Way out west, at the end of Gorgie Road behind the Shell petrol station, is Stenhouse Mansion. This three-storey block was built in 1623 and would once have stood obvious in a meander of the Water of Leith. Now, it is so well hidden that few locals even know it's there. Run as a conservation and restoration centre by Historic Scotland (668 8600), the motto above the door reads, 'Blisit be God for all his giftis', a grace from the days when the master of the house, Patrick Eleis, could have looked back at the Castle, two-and-a-half miles (four kilometres) away over open land.

The Exchange

In the last few years, the area around the West Approach Road and Lothian Road has seen a £350-million construction extravaganza described by the city's public relations team as Edinburgh's most important since the New Town.

First on the scene, in 1985 and before a formal development strategy had been hatched, was the almost Romanian façade (Ceauçescu era) of the **Sheraton Grand Hotel**. In 1988, the city council launched a plan to promote the area as the Exchange, a new financial district. Investment managers Baillie Gifford sited Rutland Court, with its mirror-shades chic, on the West Approach Road in 1991, but the heart of the new area was to be the emblematic **Edinburgh International Conference Centre**. Designed by Terry Farrell, this opened on Morrison Street in 1995 and resembles an ambitious upturned engine part.

Soon the big names were moving in. Scotland's largest company, Standard Life, opted for new headquarters on Lothian Road, in 1997, while the Clydesdale Bank erected its Plaza on the other side of the West Approach Road. The overall effect is reminiscent of London's Broadgate but with less Gordon Gecko sociopathy. The Standard Life building, by the Michael Laird Partnership, made an attempt at incorporating more creative elements, courtesy of sculptor John Maine (gates, entrance) and artist Jane Kelly (lights, railings). But the latest arrival, on the corner of Morrison Street and Semple Street beats them all for sheer verve. The Scottish Widows headquarters by Glasgow's Building Design Partnership, completed in 1998, has a main crescent block that begs to house something more interesting than a pensions management company. But that's what generates the cash to pay for this kind of architecture in contemporary Edinburgh.

Canal dreams

Before the railways made an impact on the city, the last word in nineteenth-century transport was the Union Canal. The combined efforts of French stonemasons and Irish navvies helped build the waterway, which was completed in 1822 and ran from Lothian Road to Camelon near Falkirk where it linked up with the Forth & Clyde Canal to Glasgow. In from West Lothian came passengers, coal and building materials; out from the city went merchants' goods, horse manure and more passengers, although not always in the same barge.

The original terminus of Port Hopetoun was at the site of Lothian House on Lothian Road, now home to the **ABC Film Centre**. A close scrutiny reveals decorative elements commemorating canal life. But as railways captured the zeitgeist of the age – and the Edinburgh and Glasgow Railway Company bought up the waterway in 1848 – the canal was allowed to decay and commercial traffic died out after the 1860s. Port Hopetoun was drained and built upon in 1922, while the canal itself was officially mothballed in the 1960s, with parts being built over. The canal now ends at Fountainbridge and can be reached via Gilmore Park, next door to the Fountain Brewery where the old Leamington Lift Bridge now sits.

The canal towpath is now an alternative, if down-at-heel, route out of the city centre for joggers, walkers and cyclists. It provides intriguing glimpses of industrial relics on its way past Polwarth and Colinton to the aqueduct at Slateford. The only traffic on the canal itself is from rowing boats and waterfowl. Eco-friendly recreational water transport is *en vogue*, however, and the Millennium Link, a project to reopen both the Union and the Forth & Clyde Canals, will create a continuous waterway between Edinburgh and Glasgow once again. Although there's no completion date set, most of the money is in place.

Small beer

At the height of the nineteenth-century beer frenzy, Edinburgh had over 40 breweries – now there are just two. The biggest is the Fountain Brewery on Fountainbridge (no visitors), part of Scottish & Newcastle's empire and a manufacturing centre for two million barrels of iconic fizz each year, including McEwan's Export, McEwan's Lager and Younger's Tartan Special. It is also responsible for the pungent smell of yeast that hangs over west Edinburgh from time to time.

Further out in Slateford Road, the Caledonian Brewery is a modern success story. Formerly owned by English brewer Vaux, it was to be closed in 1987 but was saved by a local management buyout. The business focused on real ales and now its Caledonian 80/- and Deuchars IPA pick up awards. Caledonian's Victorian red-brick buildings host ceilidhs on Saturday nights and there's an annual beer festival (*see chapter* **Edinburgh by Season**).

Dalry

On the corner of Angle Park Terrace and Henderson Terrace is a famous Edinburgh institution: The **Athletic Arms**, popularly known as the Diggers, which has served the best pint of McEwan's 80/- in the city since formica was modern and Eric Clapton was cutting edge. The unremarkable Dalry Cemetery next door is where the pub nickname comes from as the gravediggers used to pop in after work. A little further out at the start of Slateford Road is North Merchiston Cemetery, left to decay during years of private ownership although now being cleaned up by the local authority. There's something particularly affecting about the unkempt North Merchiston with its sprinkling of simple headstones for young men who died in World Wars I and II. The overall impact is far greater and more melancholic than at neighbouring Dalry.

Just off the western end of Gorgie Road sits the architectural mishmash of Saughton Prison, Edinburgh's lock-up since 1919. Its ghoulish claim to fame is as the site of the city's most recent execution. A total of four men have been dispatched at Saughton. The last to go, George Alexander Robertson, was found guilty of murder and hanged in June 1954. His and the three other bodies lie buried inside the precincts of the gaol.

Leith

The birthplace of golf – maybe. Just don't call it Edinburgh's docks.

Leith was for centuries the main port in Scotland and an important centre for shipbuilding. Although Leith and Edinburgh's histories are inextricably linked, the people of Leith have always felt a sense of separateness from Edinburgh and traditionally cast themselves as tenacious underdogs, ready to correct anyone who assumes they're 'from Edinburgh'.

The bad feeling can be traced back to 1329 when Robert the Bruce included Leith in his Charter to Edinburgh. This gave the city control over the harbour to the extent that the captain of a ship berthed at Leith could not unload any cargo until the correct taxes had been paid three miles (five kilometres) inland at the Edinburgh Tolbooth. In a further Charter of 1428, James I gave Edinburgh the right to exact tolls from boats entering the port. Edinburgh controlled all Leith's foreign trade until 1833 – and the resentment became bitter. There were, however, a few years of separation. When the first modern docks were laid out in the early 1800s their cost was so large that Edinburgh had to declare itself bankrupt. The docks were effectively nationalised in 1825. In 1833, an Act of Parliament gave Leith its independence as a parliamentary burgh. But the town never managed to generate enough income to sustain itself and amalgamation became increasingly likely after World War I. Not that it was popular with Leithers: in 1919 a last-ditch, toothless 'referendum' was carried out in which Leithers voted 29,891 to 5,357 against amalgamation. But financial constraints were against them, and Edinburgh and Leith were merged in 1920.

Politics aside, Edinburgh and Leith have physically merged into one along Leith Walk, the mile-long thoroughfare that links the two. The Boundary Bar (379 Leith Walk; 554 2296) opposite Pilrig Church marks the point where Edinburgh and Leith join and the dividing line cuts through the middle of the bar. Legend has it that the resentment felt by Leithers was so deeply ingrained that drinkers on the Leith side used to refuse to cross to the other side of the bar at closing time to take advantage of Edinburgh's later opening times.

Entering Leith down Leith Walk from Edinburgh city centre brings you straight to the Kirkgate. The historic hub of the town has been torn down and replaced with this faceless shopping arcade backing on to high-rise flats. In Leith, you're never far from a town planner's bungle.

Diagonally across from the Kirkgate are the supermarket Scotmid and the aquatic playground **Waterworld** (*see below*). They stand on the site once occupied by Leith Central Station. Although it is now demolished, the abandoned station was part of the inspiration for *Trainspotting*. The hard drugs scene of the 1980s, as featured in Irvine Welsh's novel, threatened to tar Leith's reputation permanently, but the town's continuing regeneration is helping it to shake off its image as a junkie-ridden town in permanent industrial decline. The conversion of bonded warehouses into loft space is only the latest stage of a transformation that has also seen the advent of designer bars and cafés along the shorefront. But don't bother looking for any landmarks from the *Trainspotting* film here, or anywhere else in Leith because all but a few scenes were filmed in Glasgow.

Leith Links

To the east of the Kirkgate, at the foot of Easter Road, lie the green spaces of Leith Links. As Leith's traditional common land the Links has been used for everything from cattle-grazing to archery contests. The Links also has a strong claim to be the home of golf, although the game has been prohibited there since 1907. While it is reported that, in 1593, the golf course on the Links was second only to St Andrews' in seniority, the game's first set of rules was formulated in Leith. The Links also has more tragic associations. In 1560, the English army dug in there and raised artillery to besiege the town. Two of the gun emplacements, Giant's Brae and Lady Fyfe's Brae, can still be seen as grassy mounds. Nowadays, the Links is mainly used for dog-walking, weekend football games and as the venue for visiting fairs.

Down Constitution Street, towards Bernard Street and the Shore, is South Leith Parish Church which was rebuilt after being destroyed by cannon fire in the 1560 siege. Subtle ornaments to the architecture begin to reflect the maritime nature of the area and, among such fine pubs as Home's and Noble's (with beautiful stained-glass windows), the **Port O'Leith** has a true maritime atmosphere. Inside this cosy local are a huge array of flags and memorabilia, left to the bar by grateful seamen.

On the waterfront: **The Shore**, *Leith (page 72).*

Signs of civic prosperity are visible in buildings like Leith Assembly Rooms and, round the corner in Bernard Street, the elegant, domed Old Leith Bank. The more upmarket of the new businesses that flooded into Leith during its regeneration in the 1980s are concentrated around here, Leith's financial centre. For refreshment, the Carrier's Quarters pub (42 Bernard Street, 554 4166), built in 1785 and barely changed since then, is a marvellous haven, particularly on winter nights.

The Shore

The Shore, the street overlooking the Water of Leith, is where the regeneration is most apparent. The area has been lovingly restored with new and appropriate buildings added. It boasts a run of fine bars and restaurants. Between the bright and airy Raj Indian restaurant (88-91 Henderson Street; 553 3980) at the junction of the Shore and Henderson Street, and **Malmaison**, a breathtakingly restored seamen's mission, there are ample opportunities for good dining.

The **King's Wark** pub on the corner of the Shore and Bernard Street is the only remnant of James I's 'wark'. This was a storage point for cargo destined for royal use, which was begun around 1428, when James extended the port, and added to by subsequent monarchs until, at one time, it covered several blocks.

In the streets between the Shore and Constitution Street you can imagine the haphazard tangle of narrow alleys from centuries past, despite the smart new apartment blocks and business premises that thrive there now. Historically, the most notable building is Provost Lamb's House, which is of uncertain age but great character. The Shore comes into its own on summer evenings when al fresco drinking, normally anathema to Scots, seems perfectly natural.

The docks are still working commercially and access to some areas is limited. Signs indicate which parts these are, so it is easy to wander around, although it is quite a distance from one end to the other. The Tall Ships Race, which docked at Leith in 1996, gave the first real indication of the potential of the area for major events as thousands came to see the ocean-going sailing vessels. Now, the **Royal Yacht Britannia** has found a berth at Leith.

Although no dock area is a sensible place to go wandering at pub closing time on a Friday or Saturday, Leith is less threatening than Lothian Road or Rose Street up in the centre of Edinburgh at those times. Strangers to Leith should, however, exercise discretion when choosing their pubs and try to remain on the main thoroughfares later in the evening. Women on their own should certainly avoid Coburg Street and Coalhill at night lest they attract the attention of kerb-crawlers.

North and south

Historically, Leith was split by the Water of Leith. The area to the west of the river mouth is called North Leith and to the east is South Leith. The river was described by Robert Louis Stevenson as 'that dirty Water of Leith'. Its reputation was well deserved but it has been cleaned up over the last 25 years. The Water of Leith walkway, which starts at the northern end of the Sandport Place Bridge, follows the riverbank up to the heart of Edinburgh and is one of the best walks in the city.

Even if it is the centre of Leith's red-light district, Coburg Street, which connects the Shore with Ferry Road and runs parallel with the Water of Leith, is worth passing through in the daylight. Points of interest include the Dutch-style steeple of the ruined Old St Ninian's Church and the old North Leith Churchyard. A detour into Couper Street, opposite, brings you to **EASY** (Edinburgh Architectural Salvage Yard), an Aladdin's cave of old fireplaces, pews, doors and other flotsam.

Straight over the bridge from Bernard Street, past the grand columns of Custom House and down Dock Place, lies the **Waterfront Wine Bar & Bistro**. It was one of the first attempts to lure solvent professionals to the area. It now has a branch of the popular Pierre Victoire chain of restaurants and a trendy, over-designed café-bar, Sirius (Dock Place; 555 3344), for company.

Round the corner, on Commercial Street, the developments have been far more dramatic. A row of bonded warehouses running almost the entire length of the street is being cleaned up and renovated to be apartments and restaurants. Facing them, across the quayside, is the imposing piece of post-modern architecture that houses the new Scottish Office, a sight impressive enough to make demands for the Scottish Parliament to be sited in Leith appear eminently reasonable. There is still plenty of space down at the docks, and plans are under way for a ferry terminal that will link Leith to Europe once more.

North Leith is best approached via Great Junction Street, a busy street of grocers, downmarket clothing shops, funeral directors and a couple of grim indoor markets. During shopping hours, it's usually thronging with senior citizens. Many of Leith's younger residents have been rehoused in outlying housing schemes.

One of the few sights off Great Junction Street is Junction Place's **Victoria Baths** (*see below*), opened in 1896. Left, down Bangor Street, is **Leith Mills**, where Scottish gifts, knitwear, golfing paraphernalia, a Clan Tartan centre and a café are all crammed into a warehouse space.

Over Junction Bridge, the corner of Ferry Road and North Junction Street is overlooked by a gable-end mural depicting the history of Leith. Symbolised as the final piece of a jigsaw – and the

*The po-modern industrial architecture of the **Scottish Office** dominates Commercial Quay.*

target of some mud-slinging by local kids – a Sikh is pictured reaching to take the outstretched hand of the community. Most of the Sikhs in Edinburgh live in Leith, and their temple is in a converted church just back over the bridge and down Mill Lane towards the Shore. To the left of the mural are two grand but unfussy buildings, Leith Library and Leith Theatre, opened in 1932 and a superb example of economical design, with the theatre's portico following the curve of the library's semicircular reading room. Straight ahead is North Junction Street, where Leith School of Art inhabits the oldest Norwegian seamen's church outside Norway, a small Lutheran kirk from 1868.

The spire of North Leith Parish Church on Madeira Street, its impressive classical columns tucked away off the main road, marks the area where Leith Fort once stood. In 1779, John Paul Jones sailed up to Leith on a ship donated by the French and demanded £20,000 in compensation for British atrocities in America. A sudden storm forced him to cancel his plans, but the scare prompted the building of a fort housing 100 men, who, until its completion in 1809, were permanently encamped on the Links. Only guardhouses and parts of the wall remain, and on its site are the forbidding blocks of flats that inherited the name.

Following the shoreline west along Lindsay Road, past the gleaming white silos of Chancelot Mill, leads to the old fishing village of Newhaven. Much of the original village has been pulled down, but there are still some original fishermen's cot-

tages in the streets near the shore. Up until this century, Newhaven was a very insular community, thought to have descended from the intermarriage of locals and the craftsmen brought over from France, Scandinavia, Spain and Portugal by James III to build ships. Newhaven became famous for its sturdy and colourfully dressed fishwives who used to carry their creels full of fresh fish up to Edinburgh to sell every morning.

The once-flourishing Fishmarket, built in 1896, now uses only a fraction of the space that it once took up. The long, red building has become home to a branch of Harry Ramsden's fish and chip shop and the **Newhaven Heritage Museum**. Although small, this is a vibrant community museum, renowned for its child-friendly exhibits that has recordings of local residents recalling their working lives in the early twentieth century and is also a bit of a hang-out for the older generation – who are more than happy to regale the interested visitor with stories.

Leith Victoria Swimming Pool
Junction Place, Leith EH6 (555 4728). Great Junction St buses. **Open** *Phone for times.* **Tickets** £1.40 adults; 85p children. **No credit cards. Map 2 Leith**

Leith Waterworld
377 Easter Road, Leith, EH6 (555 6000). 1, 6, 24(A) buses. **Open** *school holidays* 10am-5pm daily. *All other times* 10.30am-5.30pm Wed; 10am-5.30pm Thur-Sun. **Closed** Mon,Tue. **Tickets** £2.30 adult; £1.40 under-18s; £5.50 family; £1.40-£1.80 concs. **No credit cards. Map 2 Leith**

Museums

Edinburgh may be well preserved, but it is far from becoming a living museum. The real museums provide a coherent and vibrant picture of a city at the heart of the Scottish nation.

First impressions count. But despite the outward appearance of creeping tartanisation, behind the scenes, in the museums, Edinburgh has managed to retain historical credibility while creating modern exhibitions that enhance the pleasures of walking round the city centre. And, for the most part, without going down the Disney route of turning an experience into an 'Experience'. However, it remains to be seen whether the geological Dynamic Earth exhibition, due to open in May 1999 and billed as 'the journey of a lifetime, 4,500 million years in the making', will fall into the former or the latter camp.

The museums and attractions that line the Royal Mile all add their own flavours to the city's history and help to put some dramatic flesh on the bare bones of the Old Town's walls and wynds. The long-awaited Museum of Scotland extension to the **Royal Museum**, on Chambers Street, adds another perspective to this venerable Victorian institution and, it is hoped, will increase the number of visitors to the level it was prior to the imposition of an entry charge. Dotted around the city are the hidden, charming museums that few visitors, let alone Edinburgh residents, ever see. To seek them out is to create a rather different impression to the view from the top of the tourist bus.

Brass Rubbing Centre

Trinity Apse, Chalmers Close, The Royal Mile, EH1 (556 4364). 1, 6, Bridges buses. **Open** 10am-5pm Mon-Sat; *Festival* 10-5pm Sun. **Admission** free. **Credit** £TC. **Map 9 D2**
Housed in an airy church just up from **John Knox House Museum** (*see below*), the centre demonstrates that, although brass rubbing might be a good kid's activity, it has an artistic side, too, particularly when Celtic knots are concerned. Cheery, friendly staff and good schematic guides show how to do it. Rubbings cost from 90p according to size.

Castle Museums

Edinburgh Castle, Castlehill, EH1 (enquiries 668 8800/ticket office 225 1012). 1, 6, 34, 35 buses. **Open** *Apr-Sept* 9.30am-6pm daily; *Oct-Mar* 9.30am-5pm daily. **Admission** £6 adult; £4.50 concs; £1.50 under-16s. **Credit** AmEx, DC, MC, V, £TC. **Map 9 A2**
Edinburgh Castle is a fascinating hotchpotch of buildings built between the twelfth century and the present day. A visit can easily last anything from two hours to a whole afternoon and suits all age groups. The amount of walking and cobbled pathways make sensible shoes advisable. A guided tour and a taped audio guide – in one of six languages – is included in the entry price. The tour guides are very friendly and happy to answer questions or have their photo taken with

visitors. The audio guide is recommended and its soundtrack, including gunfire and spooky music, helps the imagination along, although it is advisable to ask how use it, as it can be confusing. Crown Square is the Castle's main courtyard and location of various sights: the Palace houses the Honours of Scotland, Scotland's Crown Jewels; its cramped, dimly lit corridors are atmospheric but not for the claustrophobic. Next to the Palace, the Great Hall is a vast ceremonial hall packed with swords and suits of armour, and the Scottish National War Memorial opposite is a moving tribute to the victims of war where those of Scottish ancestry can look for names of relatives in the books of remembrance. The Castle is paradise for anyone interested in military history. Various regimental museums house regimented but attractive displays of weapons, uniforms and medals. There's also the ancient chapel of St Margaret, a dog cemetery, and dungeons housing Mon's Meg – a giant 500-year-old cannon. Weather permitting, the museum weary can wander along the battlements and admire the views. There is a beautifully designed but overpriced café and lots of gift shops crammed with tartan kitsch.
Disabled: access; courtesy vehicle; toilets.

Edinburgh University Collection of Historic Musical Instruments

Reid Concert Hall, Bristo Square, EH8 (650 2423). George IV Bridge buses. **Open** 3-5pm Wed; 10am-1pm Sat; *Festival* 2-5pm Mon-Fri. **Admission** free. **No credit cards. Map 6 F6**
The University's collection of musical instruments is over 1,000 strong and shows how the design of individual instruments has evolved. It includes a few choice oddities such as a clarinet-cum-walking-stick, as well as a good selection of bagpipes. Not always open as advertised, so phone first.

Georgian House

7 Charlotte Square, EH2 (226 3318 phone & fax). George St buses. **Open** *Apr-Oct* 10am-5pm Mon-Sat, 2-5pm Sun. **Admission** £4.20 adult; £2.80 concs; £11.20 family; group discounts on request. **Credit** £TC. **Map 8 A1**
The National Trust for Scotland has refurbished this prestigious, Robert Adam-designed New Town residence to the sumptuous glory it would have shown when rich businessman John Lamont lived here in the early nineteenth century. The rooms, from drawing room to kitchen, contain period furnishings, right down to the newspapers. With a guide in each room to relate all the anecdotes about lifestyle and furnishings, there's no need for glass cases and everything can be looked at right up close – so long as you don't touch.

Gladstone's Land

477B Lawnmarket, EH1 (226 5856/fax 226 4851) 1, 6, 34, 35 buses. **Open** *Apr-Oct* 10am-5pm Mon-Sat; 2-5pm

The ruins of Holyrood Abbey, founded in 1128, are in the grounds of the **Palace of Holyroodhouse.** *Page 77.*

Sun. **Admission** £3 adult; £2 concs; £8 family; group discounts. **Credit** £TC. **Map 9 B2**
The sort of dwelling that Lamont (*see above*) left behind when he moved to the New Town. This National Trust for Scotland property is kept in the style the former owner, Thomas Gledstane, would have had it in the seventeenth century. The NTS style of display is not really suited to such confined rooms, but the guides are useful and help make this an essential stop in any tour of the Royal Mile that hopes to get under the un-soaped skin of historic Edinburgh.

Huntly House

142-146 Canongate, The Royal Mile, EH8 (529 4143/fax 557 3346). 1, 6, Bridges buses. **Open** 10am-5pm Mon-Sat; *Festival* 2-5pm Sun. **Admission** free. **No credit cards. Map 7 A5**
A packed, old-fashioned museum in three original tenements opposite the Canongate Tolbooth. There's too much to see for many of the displays to be more than crammed glass cases, but with the guidebook they help form a rounded picture of Edinburgh as it developed from Roman times, through the building of the New Town, to the nineteenth century. However, it is the tenements themselves, united into a single block in 1570, that are the real museum here. Corners that would once have been whole rooms, have been furbished and laid out as they would have been in the past. The building's structure is also fascinatingly visible and there are some real oddities in the collections – the eclectic nature of which is indicated by the inclusion of the National Covenant and Greyfriars Bobby's collar and feeding bowl.

John Knox House Museum

43 High Street, EH1 (556 9579/fax 556 7478). 1, 6, Bridges buses. **Open** 10am-4.30pm Mon-Sat. **Admission** £1.95 adult; £1.50 concs; 75p children. **Credit** MC, V, £TC. **Map 9 D2**
Although it is only probable that the religious reformer John Knox died here in 1572, the belief that he did has been enough to stop one of Edinburgh's oldest residences, built in 1450, from being razed. The house now holds a detailed exhibition of the Scottish Reformation, complete with an audio re-enactment of Knox's debate with the Catholic Mary, Queen of Scots. With such a complex topic, the displays are by necessity very wordy and the house itself is not shown to its best advantage. But the trick of contrasting Knox with royalist James Mossman (who certainly did live here and who made the Scottish Crown on view in the Castle) works well.

Lauriston Castle

Cramond Road South, Davidsons Mains, EH4 (336 2060). 40, 80B buses. **Open** *Apr-Oct* 11am-5pm Mon-Thur; 2-4pm Sat-Sun; *Nov-Mar* 2-4pm Sat-Sun. **Admission** £4 adult; £3 concs. **Credit** AmEx, MC, V, £TC.
Set in large, reasonably well-kept grounds on the way to Cramond, this sixteenth-century fortified house was left to the nation by William Reid, an enthusiastic antiques collector who furnished it throughout with Edwardian period furniture. Viewing of the house with its exquisite and unique interiors is by guided tours only – these are usually hourly so phone first or spend the time wandering around the grounds and watching the Edinburgh croquet club in full dastardly action on the lawn while you wait.
Disabled: partial access; toilets.

Museum of Childhood

42 High Street, EH1 (529 4142/fax 558 3103). 1, 6, Bridges buses. **Open** 10am-5pm Mon-Sat; *Festival* 2-5pm Sun. **Admission** free. **Credit** *shop* MC, V, £TC. **Map 9 D2**
Don't think yourself too old for this one. This High Street

Typical tenement **– Gladstone's Land** *has been restored to the condition it would have been in the seventeenth century. Page 74.*

museum, founded by local councillor Patrick Murray in 1955, is about childhood and not a venue for children. Its small rooms and winding staircases are packed with centuries of toys, schoolbooks and kids' paraphernalia. So packed that it needs taking slowly to appreciate the masses of tiny objects in dolls' houses, toy circuses and train sets. Some of it is quite recent and frequently evokes a heartfelt 'I had one of those!' from misty-eyed visitors. Occasional temporary exhibitions and a good shop.
Disabled: access; toilets.

Newhaven Heritage Museum

24 Pier Place, Newhaven, EH6 (551 4165). 7, 11, 16, 17, 22, 25 buses. **Open** noon-5pm daily. **Admission** free. **No credit cards.**
What this one-room museum lacks in size it makes up for in vitality. It needs to as it's just a hike from the middle of town – next door to Harry Ramsden's fish and chip shop, east of Leith on the Forth shore – but one the fishwives made every day loaded down with their creels of fish to sell door-to-door round the city. The Newhaven living history project has done its job well and the recorded memories are vibrant and telling, although the accents might prove difficult to non-locals. The wordy exhibits are child-friendly.
Disabled: access.

The Palace of Holyroodhouse

Holyrood Road, EH8 (556 1096). 1, 6, 60 buses. **Open** *Apr-Oct* 9.30am-5.15pm daily; *Nov-Mar* 9.30am-3.45pm daily. **Admission** £5.30 adult; £3.70 OAPs; £2.60 under-17s; £13 family; group discounts. **Credit** AmEx, JCB, MC, V, £TC. **Map 7 J5**
Originally built by James IV with refurbishments being made by subsequent monarchs, the Palace was frequently used by Queen Victoria when travelling to or from Balmoral, a tradition kept up by the present Queen, who frequently stays. When she is in residence, the Palace is closed to the public, but when it is open, the furniture, tapestries, paintings and objets d'art from several centuries are on display, as are the private apartments and lavishly decked-out bed of Mary, Queen of Scots. The memory of Mary is indelibly associated with the Palace. In 1576, six months pregnant, she watched as four Scottish noblemen murdered her secretary David Rizzio with the consent of her husband, Lord Darnley, who wanted to kill the baby she was carrying. She fled to Edinburgh Castle and there gave birth to her child, James VI. The Great Gallery alone would make a visit worthwhile. It's 150ft (45m) long and is decked out with more than a 100 bizarre portraits by Dutch artist Jacob de Wit, who was under contract to Charles II. The King wanted 2,000 years' worth of his ancestors painted and de Wit complied, creating a host of imaginary monarchs and giving every single one, real or fabled, Charles II's protuberant nose. In this room, for a month in 1745, Prince Charles Edward Stuart held dances that captivated Edinburgh society.
Disabled: restricted access.

The People's Story

163 Canongate, EH8 (529 4057/fax 557 3346). 1, 6, Bridges buses. **Open** 10am-5pm Mon-Sat; *Festival* 2-5pm Sun. **Admission** free. **Credit** *shop* £TC. **Map 7 H5**
This intelligently organised museum focuses on the lives of the people of Edinburgh from the late eighteenth century to the present day. Many of the artefacts and documents stem from the organisation of labour, while the tableaux illustrate the common people's living and working conditions. Use of authentic smells and tape loops enhance the experience. The Tolbooth, built in 1591, was much used as the Canongate's jail, so the law and disorder section seems particularly appropriate. The video show in the top room gives the whole a good perspective, while the guidebook contains some fascinating living history anecdotes.
Disabled: access; toilets.

Playfair Pathology Museum

Royal College of Surgeons, 18 Nicolson Street, EH8 (527 1649/fax 557 6406). Bridges buses. **Open** viewing by appointment only. **Admission** free. **No credit cards.** **Map 7 G6**

Named after the architect of the building not the contents, the museum is housed in Playfair's magnificent and well-preserved Royal College of Surgeons, opened in 1832. The collection is also well preserved – mostly in formaldehyde – and is a complement to the adjacent Sir Jules Thorn Exhibition. It is a working museum for the study of pathology, so the specimens – grouped according to the parts of the human body – are there to display disease, abnormalities and deformities. Close perusal by the lay person with a sense of imagination is quite distressing. Viewing is by booking well in advance only and in groups of at least ten. The guide is chosen according to the knowledge of the visitors.

Police Information Centre

188 High Street, EH1 (226 6966/fax 225 5990). 1, 6, Bridges buses. **Open** Sept-Oct, Mar-Apr 10am-8pm daily; *May-Aug* 10am-10pm daily; *Nov-Feb* 10am-6pm daily. **Admission** free. **No credit cards.** **Map 9 C2**

Even the police have turned their fully functional information centre into a museum. Not that there's much to see: a bit of history of policing in Edinburgh and a couple of cases with memorabilia. But that does include one artefact covered in the cured skin of executed serial killer William Burke.

Royal Museum

Chambers Street, EH1 (225 7534/fax 220 4819). Bridges or George IV Bridge buses. **Open** 10am-5pm Mon, Wed-Sat; 10am-8pm Tue; noon-5pm Sun. **Admission** £3 adult (£5 annual season ticket); £1.50 concs (£2.50 annual season ticket); £9 family annual season ticket; free under-18s. Free admission 4.30-8pm Tue. Audio and guided tours available. **Credit** *shop* MC, V, £TC. **Map 9 B3**

A few minutes' walk south of the High Street, this spacious museum boasts lofty Victorian galleries, a beautiful atrium and a brand new extension opening in late 1998. All the favourites of the Victorian museum-makers are here with more besides: geology, anthropology, fossils, taxonomy, costumes, Chinese art and industry are all well represented and displayed. Some areas, such as the stuffed animals, are of the traditional improve-your-mind Victorian variety, but others, like the interactive shark display, are innovative. The new building, the National Museum of Scotland, which is dedicated to the history of the people of Scotland, shows promise. The temporary exhibitions and frequent lectures are usually excellent. The perfect place for wet weather.
Disabled: access; toilets.

The Royal Observatory

Blackford Hill, EH9 (information line 668 8100/visitor's centre 668 8405). 38, 40, 41(A) buses. **Open** *information line* 2-4pm Mon-Fri; *visitor's centre* 10am-5pm Mon-Sat; noon-5pm Sun; group visits by arrangement. **Admission** £2.50 adult; £1.50 child/concs; £1 disabled. **Credit** MC, V.

When light pollution became too strong on Calton Hill, the Royal Observatory was moved south of the city to Blackford Hill. Today, the city has grown out to meet the Observatory, which gives picturesque views of Edinburgh from the south. Although there are telescope sessions on winter Friday evenings – weather permitting – it is not a working observatory but an important centre for the scientists who carry out research around the world using the UK's telescopes. The extensive visitor centre exhibitions are excellent, however, and will intrigue even those with only a faint interest in science for hours. Basic astronomical science is clearly explained, the history of astronomy in Edinburgh intriguingly told and the universe beautifully illustrated.
Disabled: partial access.

Royal Yacht Britannia

Western Harbour, Leith Docks (554 4343). 10A, 16, 22A, 32 buses. **Open** 10am-5pm daily. **Admission** £6.

HMY *Britannia* will be open to the public from September 1998. She will be berthed at Western Harbour until the purpose-built Ocean Terminal is completed in 2000.

Russell Collection of Early Keyboard Instruments

St Cecilia's Hall, Cowgate, EH1 (museum 650 2805/2806/faculty 650 2427). Bridges buses. **Open** 2-5pm Wed; 2-5pm Sat (except public & university holidays); *Festival* 10.30am-12.30pm Mon-Sat. **Admission** £3 adult; £2 concs; group rates on request from curator. **No credit cards.** **Map 9 C3**

This important collection of 51 harpsichords, spinets and virginals – which produce a note by plucking the strings – and clavichords and early pianos – which strike the strings – forms a living museum for restoration, the study of keyboard organology and performance practice. The instruments date from the mid-sixteenth century and many are beautifully painted works of artistic as well as technical merit. The elliptical and serenely decorated St Cecilia's Hall (1763, Robert Mylne) is Scotland's oldest purpose-built concert hall and is still in use – occasionally for concerts using the Russell Collection.

Scotch Whisky Heritage Centre

354 Castlehill, The Royal Mile, EH1 (220 0441/fax 220 6288).1, 6 buses. **Open** Apr-Sept 9.30am-6.30pm daily; Oct-Mar 10am-6pm daily. **Admission** £4.95 adult; £3.50 concs; £2.50 under-18s; £12 family; groups of over 10 people receive 10% discount. **Credit** AmEx, DC, JCB, MC, V, £TC. **Map 9 A2**

A blatantly tourist-oriented attraction with guides who take the visitor through rooms illustrating the processes by which the Scottish national drink is made, followed by a ghost train-like tour through various tableaux on the history of distilling and ending up with a free dram in the tasting bar. It is well thought-through, but a bit too long. The shop has some good blends but is distinctly lacking in single malts – best buy them further down the High Street.
Disabled: access; toilets.

Sir Jules Thorn Exhibition of the History of Surgery/Dental Museum

9 Hill Square, EH8 (527 1649/fax 557 6406). Bridges buses. **Open** 2-4pm Mon-Fri. **Admission** free. **No credit cards.** **Map 7 G6**

Tucked away in the square behind Surgeons Hall, this hidden treasure of Edinburgh's museums tells the history of surgery in Edinburgh since 1505 when the Barber Surgeons were granted a Charter. In providing the links between the growth of Edinburgh and increases in medical knowledge of its surgeons and anatomists the exhibition manages to say a lot about both city and profession. There's a lot to read, but the exhibits are well displayed – if occasionally, out of necessity, on the macabre side. The floor above Sir Jules Thorn's Exhibition is dedicated to modern surgical practice. The Dental Museum takes up an adjoining room and, although not so well laid out, provides telling insights to the history of dentistry for anyone prepared to read between the lines.

The Writer's Museum

Lady Stairs House, Lawnmarket, The Royal Mile, EH1 (529 4901/fax 220 5057). 1, 6, 34, 35 buses. **Open** 10am-5pm Mon-Sat; *Festival* noon-5pm Sun. **Admission** free. **No credit cards.** **Map 9 B2**

Lady Stair's House, built in 1622, provides a suitable Old Town environment to contemplate the combined literary might of Robert Burns, Sir Walter Scott and Robert Louis Stevenson. The exhibits are skewed towards memorabilia – Scott's chess set, Burns' snuff box and the like – but the museum provides a suitable atmosphere to contemplate the greats of Scottish literature.

Art Galleries

With a lively contemporary art scene developing in the city, Edinburgh's gallery spaces are looking brighter and hanging better than they have for a long time.

Edinburgh's art scene has undergone something of a make-over during the last few years. Although the city boasts a superb collection of art through the ages, found in the august National Gallery, its contemporary art front was once far from lively. Glasgow eclipsed the capital with its robust reputation as a hotbed of young talent, while Edinburgh seemed to be resting on its conservative laurels. Glasgow School of Art continues to be home to a vibrant band of young artists, including Turner Prize-winner Douglas Gordon and the shortlisted Christine Borland. Yet Edinburgh's galleries are entering a new era of greater internationalism. Artists based around Scotland who are already recognised on the international circuit are now receiving more fulsome coverage in the capital's galleries and there is a move away from lingering parochialism.

The part of the Old Town above Market Street has been dubbed the 'gallery quarter' with art spaces such as the Collective, the Fruitmarket and Stills injecting a buzz into the scene. The capital is now demonstrating an interest beyond the archetypal Scottish landscape. Likewise the 'Young British Artist' (YBA) phenomenon that is popularly seen to orbit London is alive and kicking in Scotland. The likes of Nathan Coley, Roderick

Buchanan, Dalziel and Scullion, Edward Stewart and Stephanie Smith form part of a wave of vibrant Scotland-based artists whose work is now being championed in Edinburgh. Resident Callum Innes, who was shortlisted for the Turner Prize in 1996, had an acclaimed solo show at the city's Inverleith House in the Royal Botanic Garden.

Adding further fuel to Edinburgh's art scene is the fact that the British Art Show, which is the touring vehicle for the country's hottest artists, is to kick off in Edinburgh in 2000.

Meanwhile, the Dean Gallery is to open across the road from the National Gallery of Modern Art in spring 1999 to exhibit works from the NGMA's surrealism and Dada collection alongside temporary shows of contemporary art. The Dean, built by Greek revivalist Thomas Hamilton in the 1830s, is being converted into a two-level gallery by British architect Terry Farrell with funding from the National Heritage Fund. It will also house work gifted by Sir Eduardo Paolozzi, the Leith-born artist famed for his collages and sculpture.

Elsewhere, most of the large national galleries have more paintings in their vaults than on display and art lovers wishing to see these hidden treasures can request to be taken down and shown their desired masterpiece (624 6200).

Playfair's temple – the **National Gallery of Scotland** *houses a superb collection. Page 182.*

Bellevue Gallery

4 Bellevue Crescent, EH3 (557 1663). 7A, 8(A), 9(A), 39 buses. **Open** noon-6pm Wed-Sun. **Closed** mid-end Sept. **Credit** MC, V. **Map 3 F3**

Situated just beyond Broughton Street is this privately owned gallery that fills the ground floor of a converted New Town terraced house. An expanse of polished floors and bright white walls, it is one of Edinburgh's rare commercial galleries specialising solely in contemporary art. Hosting both solo and group shows by newcomers and established artists alike, it is a space with a future.

Bourne Fine Art

6 Dundas Street, EH3 (557 4050). 19A, 23, 27, 37, 47 buses. Festival 10am-6pm Sat. **No credit cards**. **Map 3 F4**

Dundas Street, one of the New Town's busiest thoroughfares, is home to many of Edinburgh's commercial, upmarket galleries. One of the grandest is Bourne Fine Art with its bowed-window façade. Specialising in traditional Scottish landscapes and portraiture by artists from the 1700s through to the 1950s, the gallery's line-up of artists includes luminaries such as Sir David Wilkie, Sir William MacTaggart, JD Cadell and a host of lesser-known artists. Recently the gallery has been moved to the occasional show of work by contemporary artists.

National Portrait Gallery. *See page 83.*

City Art Centre

2 Market Street, EH1 (529 3993). Princes St buses, then 5 min walk. **Open** 10am-5pm Mon-Sat; *Festival* ring to confirm opening hours. **Admission** £4 adult; £2.50 concs; £10 family; group discounts. **Credit** MC, V. **Map 9 C1**

Built as offices for *The Scotsman* newspaper towards the end of the nineteenth century, this six-storey building was converted into the City Art Centre in 1979. Described as the 'Ford Cortina of art galleries' in as much as it puts on exhibitions for all the family, the gallery has a mixed repertoire of exhibitions. Funded by the City of Edinburgh Council, shows range from family blockbusters like Star Trek to exhibitions of Chinese artefacts and contemporary photography. It frequently hosts temporary exhibitions drawn from the city's collection of nineteenth and twentieth-century Scottish art, although the bulk of this is in semi-permanent storage. Cultural consumerism is encouraged in the gallery's shop and relaxation in the ground-floor licensed café.
http: www.cac.org.uk

Collective Gallery

22-28 Cockburn Street, EH1 (220 1260). 1, 6, Bridges buses. **Open** 11am-5.30pm Tue-Thur, Sat; 11am-5pm Fri; *Festival* 2-5pm Sun. **Admission** free. **Credit** AmEx, MC, V, £TC. **Map 9 C2**

Situated in Edinburgh's 'gallery triangle', the Collective is one of the city's most vibrant exhibition spaces. Established in 1984, it is known for showcasing work by the most dynamic artists on Scotland's art scene. Besides trumpeting local talent, the artist-run gallery has a track record for guest-curated shows that bring together established artists from further afield, including London-based YBAs. A three-roomed space, the shows are not consistently strong but there is always a sense of adventure on entering the gallery to confront a video work or a sculptural agglomeration. The small Project Room has likewise carved itself a niche as a space to be reckoned with. Hosting a programme of often debut, solo shows, here you get to glimpse at who might be who in contemporary Scottish art.
Disabled: access with assistance.

Edinburgh College of Art

Lauriston Place, EH3 (221 6032). 23, 27, 28, 37, 45, 47 buses. **Open** 10am-8pm Mon-Thur; 10am-6pm Fri; 10am-2pm Sat. **Admission** free. **No credit cards**. **Map 6 E6**

South of the Castle is Edinburgh College of Art, which operates a year-round programme of exhibitions. For many, the highlight is the annual degree shows in June when the public can eye-up (and purchase) future art stars. The college puts on regular shows by artists from all over the world, taking in everything from photography to installations.
Disabled: access; toilets.
http: www.eca.ac.uk

Edinburgh Printmakers Workshop & Gallery

23 Union Street, EH1 (557 2479). Leith Walk buses, then 5-min walk. **Open** 10am-6pm Tue-Sat. **Admission** free. **Credit** AmEx, JCB, MC, £TC, V. **Map 4 G3**

Scotland has long been known for its strong printmaking tradition, and the Printmakers Workshop is probably the country's leading gallery dedicated to exhibiting work by contemporary printmakers. Founded in 1967, the gallery adjoins the Printmakers Workshop, so while perusing the latest screen prints, lithographs and etchings it's possible to witness work in action from the gallery window, which overlooks the workshop.
e-mail: printmakers@ednet.co.uk

Fruitmarket Gallery

45 Market Street, EH1 (225 2383). Princes St buses, then 5-min walk. **Open** 11am-6pm Mon-Sat; noon-5pm Sun. **Admission** free. **Credit** *shop* AmEx, V. **Map 9 C1**

Heroes and (some) heroines in this frieze at the **National Portrait Gallery**. *See page 83.*

Next door to Waverley Station, this one-time fruitmarket was given a major overhaul in 1992 by the high-profile Edinburgh architect Richard Murphy. A two-level rectangular, glass-fronted space, it is billed as Scotland's top contemporary art gallery, through receiving the highest gallery grant from the Scottish Arts Council. As well as hosting touring shows – frequently from Oxford's Museum of Modern Art and including exhibitions by Marina Abramovic and Yoko Ono – the Fruitmarket curates its own programme of exhibitions. Scotland-based artists with international reputations, such as Alison Watt and the collaborating duo Stephanie Smith and Edward Stewart, have shown in the space along with a diverse range of artists from further afield. Over the years the Fruitmarket has also established a tradition of bringing to Britain, often for the first time, work by artists from beyond the Western world, including a hugely popular show of paintings by artists from China. The gallery operates a strong programme of artist talks and events; the lower floor is partially given over to a stylish café and a well-stocked bookshop that sells everything from exhibition catalogues through to philosophical treatises.
e-mail info@fruitmarket.co.uk

Ingleby Gallery
6 Carlton Terrace, EH7 (556 4441). London Road buses.
Open 10am-6pm Wed-Sat. Festival 10am-6pm Mon-Sat.
Credit MC, V. **Map 4 J4**
Housed in one of William Playfair's grand townhouses that look out on to the **Palace of Holyroodhouse** and Arthur's Seat is the Ingleby Gallery. Doubling up as a family home as well as a gallery, here it is possible to look at art while slumped on a sofa, in a space that has consciously moved away from the 'white cube' look. One of Edinburgh's few commercial galleries that specialises in contemporary art, the range of work extends from established British greats

like Howard Hodgkin, Andy Goldsworthy and Callum Innes through to lesser-known artists. Ceramics and sculpture also feature in the gallery's rolling programme of exhibitions. *Disabled: access; toilets.*

Ink Tank
28 St Stephen Street, EH3 (226 5449). 20, 28, 80(A/B) buses. **Open** 9am-6pm Mon-Fri; weekends by appointment. **No credit cards. Map 3 D3**
Doubling up as a graphic design business, Ink Tank is a tiny gallery situated to the north of Princes Street in Stockbridge. Setting out to promote innovative work by both recent art graduates and more established artists, this is the place to witness the crossover between art and design.
e-mail: inktank@ednet.co.uk

Inverleith House
Royal Botanic Garden, Inverleith Row, EH3 (552 7171).
Open 10am-5pm Wed-Sun; call to confirm hours, as they are subject to change. **Admission** free. **No credit cards. Map 3 D2**
Situated slap in the middle of the Royal Botanic Garden, Inverleith House enjoys a degree of splendid isolation from the city-centre art scene. Yet, it is one of Edinburgh's finest gallery spaces, with a strong and zappy exhibitions programme. Worth the venture, if only to check out the art along with the herbaceous borders. A sturdy but stately stone mansion with brilliant views of Edinburgh's skyline, Inverleith House dates back to the late eighteenth century. It was converted to a gallery in 1960 and, up until 1984, was home to the **National Gallery of Modern Art** (*see below*). Now run by the Royal Botanic Garden, the shows make frequent reference to the natural world but are not confined to exhibitions of botanical prints. Callum Innes has shown here along with Myron Stout, Susan Derges and the famed brick-

*Give me Moore – the austere **National Gallery of Modern Art** is bright and airy inside.*

layer Carl Andre. As well as showing work by international artists, Inverleith House keeps a sharp eye on local, up-and-coming artists, by curating group shows of home-grown talent and hosting the Absolut Scottish Open.
http: www.rbge.org.uk/inverleith-house/

The Leith Gallery
65 The Shore, EH6 (553 5255). 1, 6, 10A, 32, 52 buses. **Open** 11am-6pm Mon-Fri, 11am-4pm Sat; *Festival* 11am-6pm Mon-Sat. **Admission** free. **Credit** AmEx, MC, V. **Map 2 Leith**
A successful commercial gallery overlooking Leith harbour and specialising in contemporary Scottish art. With no aspirations towards championing the avant-garde, here you find landscapes, stilllifes and slightly saucy beach scenes by a diverse range of Scotland-based artists.
e-mail: info@the.leithgallery.co.uk
http: www.the-leith-gallery.co.uk

Matthew Architecture Gallery
20 Chambers Street, EH1 (650 2342). Bridges or George IV Bridge buses. **Open** *exhibitions* 10am-4.30pm Mon-Fri; can vary, call to confirm. **Admission** free. **No credit cards. Map 9 C3**
Housed in the University of Edinburgh's School of Architecture, this one-time student common room has fast become Scotland's leading architectural gallery. Opened in 1992, the gallery, named after a former professor, Sir Robert Matthew, showcases work by top Scottish architectural practices and touring shows from all over the world. The gallery has also successfully ventured into solo shows by international names such as Siah Armajani and Per Kirkeby.
e-mail: matthew.gallery@ed.ac.uk

National Gallery of Modern Art
Belford Road, EH4 (624 6200). 13 bus. **Open** 10am-5pm Mon-Sat; 2-5pm Sun. **Admission** free except for special loan exhibitions. **Credit** *shop* AmEx, MC, V, £TC. **Map 5 A5**
Since 1984 Scotland's national collection of modern art has been housed in what was once John Watson's School. An

imposing, nineteenth-century neo-classical edifice set in parkland, dotted with sculptures by Paolozzi, Henry Moore and Dan Graham, the gallery makes an ideal day-trip destination. The gallery can be approached from the pleasant Water of Leith walkway, which meanders through Stockbridge and Dean Village. The ambitious could even take in **Inverleith House** (*see above*), which can also be reached from the Water of Leith approximately 2 miles (3km) downstream. Any external hints at austerity are kicked aside by the bright and airy galleries. Works from a permanent collection of twentieth-century Scottish art are regularly rotated around the downstairs galleries. Although not so strong on the work of the most contemporary of bright young things in the Scottish scene, the collection is hot on works by the older generation of artists, particularly the so-called 1980s Glasgow Boys – Peter Howson, Steven Campbell, Adrian Wiszniewski and Ken Currie. The upstairs galleries are given over to international art. Big names from fauvism, surrealism and abstract expressionism such as Matisse, Magritte, Picasso and Pollock feature along with British greats like Bacon and Helen Chadwick. The permanent collection is also augmented by touring exhibitions.
Disabled access; toilets.
e-mail: pressinf@natgalscot.ac.uk

National Gallery of Scotland
The Mound, EH2 (624 6200). Princes St buses. **Open** 10am-5pm Mon-Sat; 2-5pm Sun. **Admission** free except for special loan exhibitions. **Credit** *shop* AmEx, MC, V, £TC. **Map 8 C2**
One of the city's landmark classical revival buildings, the National Gallery was built in 1848 by the prolific Edinburgh architect William Playfair. Originally housing both the **Royal Scottish Academy** (*see below*) and the National Gallery, it became the latter's exclusive home in 1911. Sumptuously decorated in 'stately home' style, a succession of galleries is bedecked with a rich collection of paintings, sculpture and furniture. From early Florentine and Northern and Italian Renaissance art – including Raphael's Bridgewater *Madonna* and Hugo van der Goes' *Trinity Panel* – the collection courses through the centuries. Poussin's

Seven Sacraments is a high point, as are Rubens *The Feast of Herod* and Joshua Reynolds' *The Ladies Waldegrave*. Canova's *Three Graces* has pride of place until 1999 when it returns for a stint in London's Victoria and Albert Museum. In 1994, much media attention was given to the marble statue's possible departure from Britain, a joint purchase by the V&A and the National Gallery saving it for the nation. French art is well represented by Watteau, Chardin and those key-players of Impressionism Monet and Pissarro. A lower gallery, built in the 1970s, is given over to Scottish art and luminaries such as Wilkie and Raeburn, painter of the so-called *Skating Minister*. Otherwise known as the *Rev Walker Skating on Duddingston Loch*, the vicar is one of the gallery's big cultural exports and is found on everything from fridge magnets to chocolates on sale in the gallery shop.
Disabled: access; toilets.

National Portrait Gallery

1 Queen Street, EH2 (624 6200). 23, 27, 37, 47 buses. **Open** 10am-5pm Mon-Sat; 2-5pm Sun. **Admission** free. **Credit** *shop* AmEx, MC, V, £TC. **Map 3 F4**
Housed in an elaborately pinnacled, Gothic revival edifice, the Portrait Gallery is a must for those wanting to get to grips with Scotland's history or check out its more contemporary heroes and heroines. The foyer is decorated with murals detailing momentous moments in Scottish history, while paintings of kings and queens, including the tragic figure of Mary, Queen of Scots and Bonny Prince Charlie, give a brilliant visual guide to the rise and fall of the Scottish monarchy. The upper galleries are filled with portraits of statuesque, tartan-dressed lairds and ladies. A further gallery is devoted to twentieth century achievers including designer Jean Muir, dancer Moira Shearer and writer Irvine Welsh. A downstairs gallery hosts small temporary shows of work by contemporary artists, while one upstairs gallery is becoming increasingly strong on contemporary photography shows by international names such as Eve Arnold and the Kobal Photographic Portrait Award.

Open Eye Gallery

75-79 Cumberland Street, EH3 (557 1020). 23, 27, 37, 47 buses. **Open** 10am-6pm Mon-Fri; 10am-4pm Sat. **Admission** free. **No credit cards. Map 3 E3**
Situated on one of the New Town's quiet streets, the Open Eye has earned a reputation as a vibrant commercial gallery and has been going strong since 1980. Exhibitions change every three weeks and feature artists drawn from Scotland and further afield. Paintings jostle for attention alongside ceramics, jewellery and sculpture. From beach scenes through to street scenes, the paintings tend away from the cutting edge, while the jewellery and ceramics are often a sure step away from high-street conventionality.

Patriothall/WASP Gallery

Patriothall Studios, off 48 Hamilton Place, EH3 (225 1289). 20, 28, 80(A/B) buses. **Open** noon-5pm Mon-Fri; noon-6pm Sat-Sun. **Admission** free. **No credit cards. Map 3 D3**
Slightly off the beaten track, to the north of the city centre in Stockbridge, is Patriothall Gallery. As an informal exhibition space, the shows predominantly feature work by the artists based in the 60 or so studios found under the same roof. More often than not featuring work for sale, this is the place to take a look at young talent and consider making a purchase.

Portfolio Gallery

43 Candlemaker Row, EH1 (220 1911). George IV Bridge buses. **Open** noon-5.30pm Tue-Sat. **Admission** free. **No credit cards. Map 9 B3**
Somewhat tucked away just off Grassmarket and overlooking Greyfriars cemetery is Scotland's leading photography and photography-related gallery. A two-level, small-scale, bright white space, Portfolio has been up and running since 1988. The emphasis is resolutely on the contemporary, and

the notorious photographer of dead flesh Andres Serrano has shown in the space along with Helen Chadwick and Avi Holtzman. The gallery also produces a quarterly catalogue of contemporary photography in Britain, entitled *Portfolio*.

Royal Scottish Academy

The Mound, EH2 (225 6671). Princes St buses. **Open** 10am-5pm Mon-Sat; 2-5pm Sun. **Admission** free to most exhibitions. **Credit** *shop* MC, V, £TC. **Map 8 C2**
Grandly lording it over Princes Street is the Royal Scottish Academy. Built to house the Society of Antiquaries and the Royal Society, the robustly neo-classical building was designed by William Playfair in the 1830s. Converted in 1911 to the headquarters of the Royal Scottish Academy, today it also fills the role of a large-scale temporary exhibitions space. The year is mapped out by annual shows of work by members of the Royal Scottish Society of Watercolourists, the Society of Scottish Artists and the Royal Scottish Academy itself. More gutsy shows are delivered by yearly exhibitions of student art. During the summer, the RSA's neighbour, the National Gallery (*see above*), frequently fills the gallery with one of its big Festival exhibitions.

Scottish Gallery

16 Dundas Street, EH3 (558 1200). 23, 27, 37, 47 buses. **Open** 10am-6pm Mon-Fri; 10am-4pm Sat. **Admission** free. **Credit** AmEx, JCB, MC, £TC. **Map 3 E4**
With a history dating back to 1842, the Scottish Gallery is Scotland's oldest commercial gallery. Situated on Dundas Street, the heart of Edinburgh's commercial gallery quarter, over the years the gallery has shown work by many of the country's leading artists. Today the emphasis is on contemporary and fairly established artists. A downstairs gallery is given over to ceramics and jewellery made by some of the country's most exciting designers.
e-mail: mail@scottish-gallery.co.uk

Stills Gallery

23 Cockburn Street, EH1 (622 6200). 1, 6, Bridges buses. **Open** 10am-6pm Tue-Sat; *Festival* 10am-8pm Tue-Sat, noon-6pm Sun-Mon. **Admission** free. **Credit** JCB, MC, V. **Map 9 C2**
Since opening in the late 1970s, Stills has evolved from a primarily photographic space into one of the city's most dynamic contemporary art venues. Revamped and enlarged in 1997 by Edinburgh architects Reiach and Hall in collaboration with Glasgow artist Nathan Coley, the gallery is today a clean-cut, concrete-floored rectangular space. Within the Stills complex there are a mezzanine café, which frequently puts on small exhibitions, digital imagery labs and a small bookshop. The widening of the exhibitions policy has enabled Stills to bring some exciting artists – such as Cornelia Parker, Joel-Peter Witkin and Tracey Emin – to Scotland and hence present some of the sharpest contemporary art shows in Edinburgh.
Disabled: access.
e-mail: info@stills.demon.co.uk

Talbot Rice Gallery

Old College, South Bridge, EH8 (650 2211). Bridges buses. **Open** 10am-5pm Mon-Sat. **Admission** free. **No credit cards. Map 7 G6**
Situated just off William Playfair's grand and stately Old Quad, which was built for the University of Edinburgh in the early years of the nineteenth century, is, by comparison, the young addition of the Talbot Rice Gallery. Opened in 1975, it is named after the university's Watson Gordon Professor of Fine Art, the late David Talbot-Rice, famed for his writings on Islamic art. Although housing the university's Torrie Collection, consisting of Dutch and Italian old masters, the greatest part of the gallery is given over to temporary exhibitions. A vast and lofty space with balcony galleries, exhibitions range from solo shows of established Scottish artists to group shows of recent graduates.

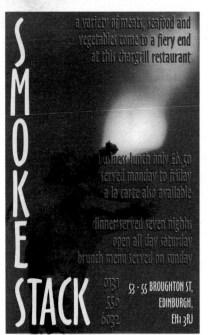

S
M
O
K
E
STACK

a variety of meats, seafood and vegetables come to a fiery end at this chargrill restaurant

business lunch only £6.50 served monday to friday a la carte also available

dinner served seven nights open all day saturday brunch menu served on sunday

0131 556 6032

53 - 55 BROUGHTON ST, EDINBURGH, EH1 3RJ

the basement

freshly prepared food at very reasonable prices served from 12 till 10 p.m seven days

0131 557 0097

10a-12a broughton street, edinburgh, eh1 3rh

montpeliers 159–161 bruntsfield place 0131 229 3115

A high quality, stylish, traditional bar and bistro, authentic and full of character. A place where customers can relax in informal, comfortable surroundings and simply enjoy the passage of time.

indigo yard 7 charlotte lane 0131 220 5603

Efficient and smart, without being intimidating, Indigo yard has fast gained a reputation as Edinburgh's premier bar/restaurant. High quality food and drinks are available all day.

iguana 41 lothian street 0131 220 4288

Iguana is a relatively new urban cafe bar with a continental feel and a highly individual style which has proved popular with young professionals and students alike.

indigo (yard)

Sleeping, Eating & Shopping

Accommodation

From the bonnie bunks of Bruntsfield to Malmaison's designer delights, Edinburgh has got enough beds to sleep a small town. And more.

The Balmoral – *Trusthouse Forte's flagship hotel dominates the east end of Princes Street.*

Edinburgh is undergoing something of a renaissance in accommodation. With the onset of the Scottish Assembly, an increasing number of festivals and several new attractions under construction, tourism has become a year-round trade. Consequently, the industry has recognised the need for high standards of service as establishments compete for guests. All manner of modern requests can now be met, while traditional Scottish hospitality is as strong and friendly as it ever was.

The plethora of deluxe hotels reflects the growing number of international holiday-makers and business visitors coming to the capital, while the explosion in budget accommodation is shaking up the complacency that is occasionally displayed in that part of the market.

Although there are some 18,500 beds for hire in the city, from Easter to September finding the right room at the right price can be a problem unless you book ahead. At peak times – Hogmanay and August (during the Festival) – it is very difficult.

Prices fluctuate according to demand and many hotels offer weekend or midweek special deals out of season that provide great value.

Edinburgh and Lothian Tourist Board
3 Princes Street, EH2 (473 3800/credit-card line 333 2167). Princes St buses. **Open** 9am-7pm Mon-Fri. **Credit** MC, V. **Booking fee** £4 plus 10% deposit. **Map 8 D2**
Will make reservations across the city from its offices in the top floor of the Waverley shopping centre or via the credit-card line. The brochure contains a list of all members and grades accommodation using a star rating system – based on the standard of furnishings and overall quality of the welcome. An information sheet on disabled accommodation is also available.

Deluxe

The Balmoral
1 Princes Street, EH2 (556 2414/fax 557 3747). Princes St buses. **Rooms** 184 (all en suite). **Rates** *single* £160; *double* £195; *suite* £330. **Credit** AmEx, DC, JCB, MC, £$TC, V. **Map 8 D2**
This landmark Edwardian building beside the Waverley Rail Station dominates the east end of Princes Street. It was

recently taken over by the Trusthouse Forte group, which has made it its flagship hotel and is refurbishing it. The results, so far, are impressive. From the majestic marble reception to the two cosmopolitan restaurants and large suites, it is a hotel with its feet firmly in the late 1990s but its heart in the 1890s. South- and west-facing rooms have superb views of the Castle and Old Town, while every bedroom has been refurbished to a high standard. The Palm Court café serves afternoon tea in a convivial atmosphere with harp music piped from above. By contrast, the NB sports-themed pub has live music at the weekends and a bustling feel. The Lobby bar, open only in the evenings, is redolent of a gentleman's club with its cigars and single malts. Chef Martin Wishart, trained by Marco Pierre White, has transformed the cuisine on offer in Hadrian's Brasserie, while the No 1 gourmet restaurant downstairs deservedly holds a Michelin star for the high-quality fare produced by chef Jeff Bland.

Hotel services *Air-conditioning. Babysitting. Bar (2). Beauty salon. Business services. Concierge. Conference facilities. Currency exchange. Disabled: access; toilets. Fax. Gym. Laundry. Multilingual staff. No-smoking rooms. Restaurant (2). Swimming pool.* **Room services** *Hairdryer. Minibar. Modem line. Radio. Room service (24 hours). Rooms adapted for disabled (2). Safe.*

The Caledonian

Princes Street, EH1(459 9988/fax 225 6632). Princes St buses. **Rooms** 246. **Rates** *single £147; double £220; suite £345.* **Credit** AmEx, JCB, MC, £$TC, V. **Map 8 A2**

This red sandstone building, built as a station house in 1903 by the Caledonian Railway Company (the rail tracks still lie under the hotel), stands tall at the West End corner of Princes Street. The sense of a bygone Edwardian era is maintained throughout: huge arched corridors lead past grand staircases with stained-glass windows depicting Scottish towns along the rail route. Rooms are large with mosaic bathrooms. The high standard of service has made it a favourite of such auspicious guests as Sean Connery and Nelson Mandela. La Pompadour restaurant on the first floor is the place for Gallic fine dining, while Carriages brasserie, in the former ticket hall, has won awards for its afternoon teas. The meeting rooms are definitely worth a peek for their stunning wall murals. The pervasive mood throughout is one of authentic Scottish tradition.

Hotel services *Babysitting. Bar. Beauty salon. Business facilities. Concierge. Currency exchange. Disabled: access; toilets. Fax. Gym. Laundry. Multilingual staff. No-smoking rooms. Restaurant. Safe. Swimming pool.* **Room services** *Hairdryer. Minibar. Modem line (30). Radio. Room service (24 hours). Rooms adapted for disabled (2).*

The Howard

34 Great King Street, New Town, EH3 (557 3500/fax 557 6515). 23, 27, 37, 47 buses. **Rooms** 15 (all en suite). **Rates** *single £125; double £195; suite £275.* **Credit** AmEx. **Map 3 E3**

This discreet terrace residence only reveals its identity through the brass plaque on the door and combines Georgian style and architecture with contemporary comfort and luxury. The breakfast room overlooks the cobbled street and contains original nineteenth-century murals, some of which are so fragile they have been papered over to preserve them. The bedroom suites either have a Roman theme or four-poster bed, large bathrooms and state-of-the-art showers with steam jets. Sir Cliff Richard gave an impromptu performance here when he stayed.

Hotel services *Babysitting. Bar. Conference facilities (35 people). Currency exchange. Fax. Laundry. Multilingual staff. Parking (free). Pets by arrangement. Restaurant. Safe.* **Room services** *Hairdryer. Room service (24 hours). Satellite TV.*
e-mail: reserve@thehoward.com
http: www.thehoward.com

Sheraton Grand Hotel

1 Festival Square, EH3 (229 9131/fax 228 4510). Bruntsfield buses. **Rooms** 261 (all en suite). **Rates** *single £155-£220; double £195-£260; suite £280-£320.* **Credit** AmEx, DC, JCB, MC, £$TC, V. **Map 8 A3**

This imposing concrete hotel block next to the Edinburgh International Conference Centre is always swarming with business delegates. It has been modified recently to create a more 'Scottish' ambience – the staff now wear tartan uniforms. The accommodation is modern and the mood brisk – but the feeling that you could be anywhere in the world still remains. Marble, chandeliers and American cherrywood panelling abound in the large reception, where coolly efficient international staff bustle officiously. All rooms have the same décor, double glazing and air-conditioning. Some of the suites on the east side face the Castle and all have separate lounges and king-size beds. The Terrace conservatory restaurant overlooks the paved square and your food is stir-fried or grilled in front of you in the central cooking area. The adjacent Grill Room holds three AA stars and the French chef uses only fresh Scottish produce.

Hotel services *Babysitting. Bar (2). Business services. Conference facilities. Currency exchange. Disabled: access; toilets. Fax. Gym. Laundry. Multilingual staff. No-smoking rooms. Parking (free). Patio. Restaurant (2). Swimming pool.* **Room services** *Hairdryer. Minibar. Modem line. Radio. Rooms adapted for disabled (4). Safe. Smart rooms (28 with fully equipped office facilities).*
http: www.sheratongrand.co.uk

Expensive (£90 upward)

Albany Hotel

39-43 Albany Street, New Town, EH1 (556 0397/fax 557 6633). 7A, 8, 9, 19, 39 buses. **Rooms** 21. **Rates** *single £75-£85; double £125-£190.* **Credit** AmEx, JCB, MC, £TC, V. **Map 3 F4**

This three-storey Georgian terrace townhouse is only a five-minute walk from Princes Street, yet sits in a quiet New Town street. It has been refurbished in an understated way in keeping with the original features of the house. Its location, personal service and intimate atmosphere make it a popular choice for business people and tourists.

Hotel services *Babysitting. Bar. Children: cots; reduced rate. Garden. Ironing facilities. Laundry. Pets by prior arrangement. Restaurant.* **Room services** *Hairdryer. Minibar (13). Modem line. Satellite TV. Tea/coffee. Telephone. Trouser press.*

Bank Hotel

1 South Bridge, EH1 (556 9043/fax 558 1362). Bridges buses. **Rooms** 9 (all en suite). **Rates** *single £50-£90; double/twin £100-£150; family £120-£150.* **Credit** MC, £TC, V. **Map 9 C2**

Rooms above Logie Baird's Bar at the intersection of the Royal Mile and Bridges in the historic Old Town. The mood is Gaelic with wood panelling, dark tartan and mustard-coloured hallways, but its surprising subtle works. Each bedroom is themed around a famous Scot. The huge bathrooms, with views of the impressive architecture that surrounds the building, do not fully justify the price of what are, after all, rooms above a pub.

Hotel services *Bar. Business services. Concierge. Fax. Garden. Laundry. Multilingual staff. Pets by arrangement. Restaurant. Safe.* **Room services** *Ironing facilities. Modem line. Satellite TV. Tea/coffee.*

The Bonham

35 Drumsheugh Gardens, West End, EH3 (226 6050/fax 226 6080/central reservations 623 6060). George St buses. **Rooms** 50. **Rates** (B&B) *single £115-£120; double/twin £150-£170; suite £235-£255.* **Credit** AmEx, DC, JCB, MC, £$TC, V. **Map 5 C5**

The Caledonian – *a favourite of the stars.*

This recently opened hotel (sister to the Howard and Channings) offers a contemporary blend of comfortable, light minimalism without being Starck. Neutral colours with some bright splashes and art deco furniture complement the high ceilings and cornices of the original Victorian building. Low lighting adds to the relaxed ambience; the vertical steel cable light (designed by Johnathon Speirs) on the stairwell makes an interesting feature. The bedrooms at the rear of the building afford panoramic views across the Firth of Forth.
Hotel services *Babysitting. Bar service. Business services. Concierge. Conference facilities (50 people). Currency exchange. Disabled: access; toilets. Fax. Flotation tank. Laundry. Multilingual staff. No-smoking rooms. Reflexology. Restaurant. Safe.* **Room services** *Hairdryer. Ironing facilities. Minibar. Modem line. Radio. Room service (24 hours). Rooms adapted for disabled (1). Tea/coffee. Voicemail.*
e-mail: reserve@thebonham.com
http: www.thebonham.com

Channings
12-16 South Learmonth Gardens, West End, EH4 (315 2226/fax 332 9631/central reservations 332 3232). George St buses. **Rooms** 48. **Rates** *(B&B) single* £105-£110; *double/twin* £130-£155; *suite* £220-£225. **Credit** AmEx, DC, JCB, MC, £$TC, V. **Map 2 B4**
A cosy, terraced five-house conversion that retains the atmosphere of an ornate Edwardian home. Located on the western outskirts of town, it is convenient for the airport. Open fires, antique prints and books in the lounges add to the hushed intimacy. The staff pride themselves on their attentive service. Rooms are individually decorated; the best face out front over the West End houses to Tony Blair's old school, Fettes. The basement brasserie restaurant, though quite dark, is popular with locals.
Hotel services *Babysitting. Bar. Business services. Conference facilities (35 people). Currency exchange. Disabled: access with assistance. Fax. Laundry. Multilingual staff. No-smoking rooms. Parking (free). Patio. Restaurant. Safe.* **Room services** *Hairdryer. Ironing facilities. Modem line. Radio. Room service (24 hours). Rooms adapted for disabled (1). Tea/coffee. Trouser press. Voicemail.*
e-mail: reserve@channings.co.uk
http: www.channings.co.uk

Crowne Plaza Edinburgh
80 High Street, Royal Mile, EH1 (557 9797/fax 557 9789). 1, 6, Bridges buses. **Rooms** 238 (all en suite). **Rates** *single* £115-£165; *double* £140-£190; *suite* £250-£300. **Credit** AmEx, DC, JCB, MC, £$TC, V. **Map 9 D2**
This turreted hotel may look like one of the original stone buildings on the Royal Mile but it was built at the beginning of the 1990s. Bustling and modern within, it provides all of the benefits associated with this American chain. The hotel is large – its imminent extension will make it the largest in

Scotland – and all of the rooms have recently been refurbished. The rock group Oasis stayed but didn't feel moved to throw any televisions through the windows. The Great Scottish Hall occasionally hosts ceilidhs and there's regular live music in the Piano Bar downstairs. Advocates restaurant, which overlooks the cobbled High Street, has an à la carte menu, while Carrubers bistro serves light lunches.
Hotel services *Bar. Business services. Concierge. Conference facilities (220 people). Currency exchange. Disabled: access; toilets. Fax. Gym. Laundry. Multilingual staff. No-smoking rooms. Restaurant. Safe. Swimming pool.* **Room services** *Hairdryer. Minibar. Modem line. Room service (24 hours). Rooms adapted for disabled (3). Satellite TV. Tea/coffee. Trouser press.*

The George Intercontinental Hotel
19-21 George Street, EH2 (225 1251/fax 226 5644). George St buses. **Rooms** 195 (all en suite). **Rates** *single* £158; *double* £175; *suite* £420-£585. **Credit** AmEx, DC, JCB, MC, £$TC, V. **Map 8 C2**
Conveniently located on Edinburgh's smartest street in the town centre. Designed by George Adam in 1775, the building's best feature is his trademark domed cupola in the roof of the opulent Carvers restaurant (renowned for its Sunday roasts). The east-wing bedrooms are aimed at the corporate guest, while the west wing has a softer 'classic country' style. The place is mobbed by the shoulder-pad set during the television festival in August. Le Chambertin restaurant has two AA stars and is a favourite for business lunches.
e-mail: edinburgh@interconti.com
Hotel services *Babysitting. Bar (2). Business services. Concierge. Conference facilities (200 people). Currency exchange. Disabled: access. Fax. Gym: free access to nearby health club. Laundry. Multilingual staff. No-smoking rooms. Parking (free). Restaurant (2). Safe.* **Room services** *Business rooms (10 with fully equipped office facilities). Hairdryer. Minibar. Modem line. Radio. Room service (24 hours). Rooms adapted for disabled (3).*

Malmaison
1 Tower Place, Leith, EH6 (555 6868/fax 468 5002). 1, 6, 10A, 32, 52 buses, then 2-min walk. **Rooms** 60 (all en suite). **Rates** *single/double* £90-£125; *suite* £135. **Credit** AmEx, DC, MC, £TC, V. **Map 2 Leith**
This ex-seaman's mission on the Leith dockside, which dates from 1881, has been transformed by designer Amanda Rosa. The subtle style and sexy sophistication of this award winning hotel have helped to breathe new life into Edinburgh's hotel trade by setting a new standard in chic, sleek décor at affordable prices. All bedrooms are decorated in either checks or wide stripes; the muted palette of coffee and cream through to navy and olive is stunningly effective. The best rooms are the suites at the front of the building and the four-poster rooms. The detail is everything, from the custom-made aromatherapy toiletries in the bathrooms to the CD choice in reception. The brasserie's chef, Lawrence Robertson, has won a loyal following for his wholesome, uncomplicated French-style food and the adjacent café serves vegetarian food throughout the day. Thoroughly recommended for its comfortable style and value for money.
Hotel services *Babysitting. Business services. Café-bar. Conference facilities (35 people). Disabled: access; toilets. Laundry (Mon-Fri). Multilingual staff. Parking (free). Patio. Pets by arrangement. Restaurant. Safe.* **Room services** *Arran Aromatic toiletries. CD players. Hairdryer. Minibar. Radio. Room service (full 7am-11pm; limited 11pm-7am). Rooms adapted for disabled (2). Tea/coffee. Trouser press.*

The Point
34 Bread Street, Tollcross, EH3 (221 5555/fax 221 9929). Bruntsfield buses, then 5-min walk. **Rooms** 95 (all en suite). **Rates** *single* £70-£75; *double/twin* £90-£95; *suite* £150. **Credit** AmEx, DC, MC, £TC, V. **Map 6 D6**

THE ACTIVE ISSUE NO.172

£2.50 US$6

i-Deas,fashion,clubs,music,people

steady...

Subscribe now to i-D to receive 12 issues
full of the latest i-Deas, fashion, clubs, music and people.

Owned and designed by architect Andrew Doolan, this hotel is state-of-the-art metropolitan minimalism. Clean lines, sweeping curved walls and blocks of soft colour (a painter is in residence for touch-ups) give a feeling of fluidity and space. The coloured lighting adds to the soothing aura, while the white bedrooms with their black leather furniture and low-level beds swathed in white linen are oriental in their understated simplicity. The executive suites are huge, as are all of the bathrooms; some have square Jacuzzis, which are lit internally and have a white leather headrest at each end. Environmentally friendly sensor heating clicks on as you enter the rooms, and some at the front of the hotel have Castle views. The ground-floor restaurant offers quality bistro dining for just £9.99. The glass-fronted Monboddo bar is the place to see and be seen in (don't bother with the food, though). A rooftop glass penthouse is planned.
Hotel services *Babysitting. Bar. Business services. Children: cots; reduced rate. Currency exchange. Disabled: access; toilets. Fax. Laundry. Multilingual staff. No-smoking rooms. Pets by arrangement. Restaurant. Safe.* **Room services** *CD player. Hairdryer. Modem line. Radio. Room service (11am-11pm). Rooms adapted for disabled (2). Tea/coffee.*

Prestonfield House Hotel

Priestfield Road, EH16 (668 3346/fax 668 3976). 2, 12, 14, 21, 38 buses. **Rooms** 31 (28 en suite). **Rates** (B&B) single/double occupancy £125-£180. **Credit** AmEx, DC, JCB, MC, £$TC, V.
Built in 1687 and former home to the Lord Provost, this country house is surrounded by parkland and nestles below Arthur's Seat. The heavy cornicing and plasterwork on the ceilings (allegedly by the craftsmen who worked on Holyrood Palace) give the house its Jacobean character. Recently extended to incorporate additional bedrooms, the new wing's contemporary comfort is very much in keeping with the atmosphere of the house. Access to the adjacent 18-hole golf course adds to the uniqueness of staying in a spacious, peaceful manor house with the city on your doorstep.
Hotel services *Babysitting. Bar. Conference facilities (60 people). Currency exchange. Disabled: access; toilets. Fax. Garden. Laundry. Multilingual staff. No-smoking rooms. Parking (free). Restaurant. Safe.* **Room services** *Hairdryer. Ironing facilities. Modem line. Radio. Room service (24 hours). Rooms adapted for disabled (2). Satellite TV. Tea/coffee.*

Royal Terrace Hotel

18 Royal Terrace, EH7 (557 3222/fax 557 5334). London Road buses. **Rooms** 94. **Rates** *single* £120-£132; *double* £160-£205; *suite* £250. **Credit** AmEx, DC, MC, £$TC, V. **Map 4 H4**
Designed by William Playfair in 1822, this quiet terrace sits beneath Calton Hill with views from the front towards Leith. The Georgian opulence (now a little faded) is echoed in the swags and flounces of the soft furnishings and chandeliers, while a contemporary touch in the form of a small gym and pool has been added in the basement. The courtyard garden is popular in the summer months with its life-size chess board and fountain. Rooms on the top floor are small due to the sloped attic ceilings.
Hotel services *Babysitting. Bar. Business services. Concierge. Conference facilities. Currency exchange. Fax. Garden. Gym. Restaurant (2). Swimming pool.* **Room services** *Hairdryer. Radio. Room service (24 hours).*

Hotels & guesthouses

Those recommended here are only a sample – in some residential areas on the outskirts of town every second house is a guesthouse. Different areas are convenient for different reasons: Pilrig is

close to the Playhouse Theatre; Murrayfield is handy for the rugby stadium and EICC; Newington, Bruntsfield and the Meadows are close to the Royal Infirmary hospital and University; and Portobello is beside the A1 dual carriageway.

17 Abercromby Place

17 Abercromby Place, New Town, EH3 (557 8036/fax 558 3453). 23, 27, 37, 47 buses. **Rooms** 9 (all en suite). **Rates** (B&B) *single* £45; *double* £90. **Credit** MC, £TC, V. **Map 3 E4**
The whole concept of townhouse hotels is at its apotheosis in Edinburgh. The Georgian New Town retains all its original aspects of architecture, atmosphere and aloof gentility – which naturally rubs off on these establishments. The Lloyd family's townhouse is one of the best. Formerly the home of the distinguished architect William Playfair, it is located on one of the New Town's most sought-after cobbled streets, opposite Queen Street gardens. Five stunning floors retain their original features and display the family's impressive collection of antiques, oil paintings and tapestries. The rooms are large with bay windows to enjoy the views of the Forth estuary and Fife hills. No smoking throughout.
Hotel services *Business services. Conference facilities. Evening meals by arrangement. Fax. Parking (free). Pets by arrangement.* **Room services** *Hairdryer. Modem line. Patio. Tea/coffee.*

Apex International Hotel

31-35 Grassmarket, EH1 (300 3456/fax 220 5345). Haymarket rail, then 2 bus. **Rooms** 175 (all en suite). **Map 9 A3**

Apex European Hotel

90 Haymarket Terrace, EH12 (474 3456/fax 474 3400). Haymarket Station rail. **Rooms** 68 (all en suite).
For both **Rates** *standard room only* £64.95-£79.95. **Credit** AmEx, DC, MC, £TC, V. **Map 5 B6**
The Edinburgh-based Apex has put a spin on the concept of budget hotels – providing the standard accommodation at a basic rate while managing to inject some style and individuality into the affair. The Grassmarket branch in the heart of the Old Town, with its sleek grass façade, has a fine view of the side of the Castle from its top-floor restaurant. The rooms with two double beds are fantastic value for groups and very popular. The West End branch is convenient for Haymarket Station. The street-level restaurant, Tabu, serves a three-course, table d'hôte menu for just £9.99.
Hotel services *Babysitting. Bar. Business services. Children: cots; reduced rates. Conference facilities (225). Disabled: access; toilets. Fax. Gym. Laundry. Multilingual staff. No-smoking rooms. Parking (free). Patio. Restaurant. Safe.* **Room services** *Hairdryer. Modem line. Radio. Room service (24 hours). Rooms adapted for disabled (6). Satellite TV. Tea/coffee. Trouser press.*
e-mail: information@apexhotels.co.uk
http: www.apexhotels.co.uk

Bar Java

48-50 Constitution Street, Leith, EH6 (467 7527/fax 467 7528). 16, 22A, 34 buses. **Rooms** 10. **Rates** (B&B) *single/double* £20 per person. **Credit** AmEx, JCB, MC, £TC, V. **Map 2 Leith**
Near the rejuvenated Leith dock area and popular choice with Festival and Hogmanay performers. Ten rooms, each named after an island, sit above a funky bar. A beer garden out the back and interesting locals inside provide some character. Snacks and a wide variety of flavoured teas, coffees and smoothies are available all day. A great brunch is available on Sundays.
Hotel services *Babysitting. Bar. Café. Disabled: access. Garden. Multilingual staff. Parking (free). Safe. TV/VCR lounge.* **Room services** *Radio.*

Malmaison – *setting new standards in sophisticated style for hotels. Page 89.*

Balfour Guest House

92 Pilrig Street, EH6 (554 2106/fax 478 2600). Leith Walk buses. **Rooms** 24 (5 fully en suite; 14 with shower). **Rates** *single £25; twin en suite £46;* group rates by arrangement. **No credit cards. Map 4 H1**

Isabel and Richard Cowe's large Georgian house is often full of visiting school parties enjoying their friendly hospitality. For groups, dinner can be provided in the basement dining room and packed lunches can be supplied on request, too. The rooms are all reasonably furnished. The central location with free parking makes this a popular choice for groups. **Hotel services** *Disabled: access and room by prior arrangement. Parking (free). Payphone. Safe. TV lounge.* **Room services** *Clock/radio. Tea/coffee.*

Claremont Hotel

14-15 Claremont Crescent, Broughton, EH7 (556 1487/fax 556 7077). 7A, 8, 9, 19, 39 bus. **Rooms** 23 (all en suite). **Rates** (B&B) *single £25-35; double/twin £22-£30;* under-12s free; 12-16 half price. **Credit** AmEx, MC, £TC, V. **Map 3 F2**

Two, huge Georgian houses knocked into one. The reception area is sparse and the rooms are clean, comfortable and very large with views of Arthur's Seat or the Forth. The place is a hive of activity with quiz nights in the public bar and a disco downstairs. Full Scottish breakfast and evening meals are available, too. Close to Broughton Street. Parking at rear. **Hotel services** *Bar (2). Bar suppers (Mon-Thur). Garden. No-smoking rooms. Parking (free). Payphone. Pets by arrangement. Safe.* **Room services** *Tea/coffee. TV.*

Frederick House Hotel

42 Frederick Street, EH2 (226 1999/fax 624 7064). 20, 28, 80 buses. **Rooms** 45 (all en suite). **Rates** (B&B) *single £35-£70; double/twin £45-£95; suite £120-£180; family* (sleeps 4) *£90-£140.* **Credit** AmEx, DC, JCB, MC, £$TC, V. **Map 8 B1**

Slap bang in the centre of town, this hotel is well placed near George Square Bus Station and Waverley Rail Station. The 'B' listed building has been transformed from offices into five floors of bedrooms in patterned greens, gold and rouge; the best rooms are at the front of the hotel and the Skyline suite has views to the Forth. Breakfast is taken in the Café Rouge brasserie opposite (included in the tariff). **Hotel services** *Babysitting. Business services. Fax. Lift. Multilingual staff. Safe.* **Room services** *Hairdryer. Modem line. Radio. Satellite TV. Tea/coffee. Trouser press.*

Greenside Hotel

9 Royal Terrace, EH7 (557 0022/0121/fax 557 0022). Leith Walk buses, then 5-min walk. **Rooms** 15 (all en suite). **Rates** (B&B) *single £35-£50; double £45-£80; family £75-£120.* **Credit** AmEx, DC, JCB, MC, £TC, V. **Map 4 M4**

Ailsa Craig Hotel

24 Royal Terrace, EH7 (557 1022/fax 556 6055). Leith Walk buses, then 5-min walk. **Rates/credit** as Greenside Hotel (*above*). **Map 4 M4**

Two hotels, identically furnished with comfortable, large beds in the huge rooms with their original Georgian features. Some have views toward the Forth and all enjoy the quiet of this residential crescent. The Ailsa Craig has the largest rooms: some fitted with five beds. Both are popular with people in town to see a show at the Playhouse Theatre nearby. **Hotel services** *Bar. Garden. Lunch/evening meals by arrangement.* **Room services** *Hairdryer. Modem line. Radio. Tea/coffee. Trouser press.*

Grosvenor Gardens Hotel

1 Grosvenor Gardens, Haymarket, EH12 (313 3415/fax 346 8732). Haymarket rail or buses. **Rooms** 8 (all en suite). **Rates** (B&B) *single £30-£50; double/twin £60-£100.* **Credit** MC, £TC, V. **Map 5 B6**

Tucked away in a quiet cul-de-sac, this hotel is sumptuously swathed in cream, gold and pink colours. The large bedrooms have high ceilings and bay windows, but the en suite bathrooms are small. The place is kept immaculately and the mood is one of tranquillity and style. **Hotel services** *No-smoking rooms. Safe.* **Room services** *Radio. Hairdryer. Tea/coffee.*

Hotel Ibis

6 Hunter Square, EH1 (240 7000/fax 240 7007).
Waverley rail, then 5-min walk, or Bridges buses. **Rooms**
97 (all en suite). **Rates** *single/double* £55. **Credit** AmEx,
DC, MC, £TC, V. **Map 9 E2**
The international chain has a reputation for efficiency and
good value, but the downside to this is a certain bland
anonymity. This branch opened in early 1998 and the box-like
rooms still reeked of paint when we visited, while the reception staff struggled to introduce a warm welcome to the TV-
dominated entrance area. Still, it is bang in the centre of town
and if you are here on business, you might find it a pleasing
launching pad.
Hotel services *Bar. Disabled: access; toilets. Fax.
Laundry. Multilingual staff. No-smoking rooms. Pets by
arrangement. Restaurant. Safety deposit boxes.* **Room
services** *Rooms adapted for disabled (6).*

Minto Hotel

*16-18 Minto Street, Newington, EH9 (668 1234/fax 662
4870). Bridges buses.* **Rooms** 23 (all en suite). **Rates**
single £50-£60; *double/twin* £70-£95; *family* £95-£120.
Credit AmEx, DC, MC, £TC, V.
A cheap stopover for groups. There's always a wedding or
party happening in the function suite; a piper calls every
Saturday to pipe in the happy couple during the summer
months. Heavily patterned in pinks and blues, the Minto is
fairly basic but comfortable. The warmth of the welcome is
what makes regulars return.
Hotel services *Baby-listening. Bar. Disabled: access;
toilets. Fax. Laundry. Lounge. Parking (free). Safe.* **Room
services** *Hairdryer. Modem line. Room service (11am-
10pm). Tea/coffee.*

Parliament House Hotel

*15 Calton Hill, EH1 (478 4000/fax 478 4001). 26, 85,
86, Princes St buses.* **Rooms** 53 (all en suite). **Rates**
single £70; *double/twin* £100; *family* (sleeps 4) £120; *suite*
£170. **Credit** AmEx, DC, MC, £TC, V. **Map 4 G4**
Tucked away beside Calton Hill opposite the St James shopping centre, this hotel was named before it was decided to
site the Scottish Parliament at Holyrood – not at the Royal
High School. Bedrooms only: continental breakfast is served
in your room and there is no bar. The rooms are medium
sized with basic furnishings and busy, navy patterned wall-
paper. The rooms at the front of the hotel have the best views
across to Leith and the Forth.
Hotel services *Disabled: access. Multilingual staff.*
Room services *Rooms adapted for disabled (2).
Tea/coffee. Trouser press.*

Thain Inn

*123 Grove Street, Fountainbridge, EH3 (0800 212
570/229 9231/fax 229 9250). 1, 6, 28, 34, 35 buses.*
Rooms 22 (all en suite). **Rates** *single/double/twin* £20-£30
per person. **Credit** AmEx, DC, MC, £TC, V. **Map 5 C7**
Owned by the Herald House hotel opposite (guests can use
the bar and restaurant), this small block of bedrooms is like
a university hall of residence. The rooms are very basic with
breeze-block walls and electric heaters, but they do have a
microwave, fridge and tiny dining table, making them popular with the independent traveller.
Hotel services *Disabled: access. Lift.* **Room services**
*Microwave. Radio. Refrigerator. Rooms adapted for
disabled (2). Tea/coffee. TV.*

The Town House

*65 Gilmore Place, Tollcross, EH3 (229 1985). 10(A), 27,
47 buses.* **Rooms** 5 (all en suite). **Rates** (B&B) £25-£35.
Credit £TC. **Map 6 D7**
This detached Victorian house sits next to a church on a busy
route into town. It's close to the major theatres and a popular Festival stopover. Spread over three floors, the house is
very comfortable and run with pride by the amiable Susan

Virtue. Everywhere is clean and well maintained, although
the bathrooms tend to be a little small.
Hotel services *Completely no smoking. Lounge. Parking
(free). Tea/coffee.* **Room services** *Hairdryer. TV.*

Travel Inn

*1 Morrison Street Link, Haymarket, EH3 (228 9819/fax
228 9836). Haymarket rail or buses.* **Rooms** 128. **Rates**
£38 per room. **Credit** AmEx, DC, MC, £$TC, V. **Map 5
B6**
This colossal branch of Britain's largest budget hotel chain
boasts one of the cheapest room rates in town. All rooms can
squeeze in two adults and two kids and are exactly the same
– right down to the light switches. The financial incentive
obviously works because, despite being little more than a
faceless, classless and bland slumber land, it boasts a year-
round occupancy rate of 97%. The ground-floor restaurant
is open all day and carries through the formula with its informal catering and atmosphere. There is a car park at the rear,
which is due to be incorporated into an extension in May
1999. No room service or phones.
Hotel services *Bar. Currency exchange. Disabled:
access. Fax. Laundry. Multilingual staff. No-smoking
rooms. Restaurant.*

Disabled facilities

Many hotels have disabled rooms and access; the
Tourist Board will send you a list if you contact
them. Other advice is available from **Disability
Scotland** and the **Lothian Coalition of
Disabled People** (*see chapter* **Directory**).
  Holiday accommodation solely for the disabled
and their carers is provided by:

Trefoil House

*Gogarbank, EH12 (339 3148/fax 317 7271). SMT 37
bus.* **Rooms** 10 (4 en suite). **Rates** (full weekly board)
single £230 guest; £213 carer; per night £42. Other rates
on request. **Credit** £TC.
Services *Bar. Conference facilities (100 people). Dining
room. Disabled: access; toilets. Fax. Garden. Laundry.
Lift. No-smoking rooms. Pets: guide dogs only. Safe.
Swimming pool.*

Private apartments

Renting a flat is a popular form of accommodation
during the Festival and Hogmanay – so, as always,
it's best to book early. Alternatively look in the
Thursday property section of *The Scotsman*.

Canon Court Apartments *20 Canonmills, EH3 (474
7000/fax 474 7001). 7A, 8(A), 9(A), 19, 23 buses.* **Open**
8am-8pm Mon-Fri; 8am-2.30pm Sat. **Flats** 27. **Rates** *per
night* £59-£128. **Credit** AmEx, MC, £TC, V. **Map 3 E2**

Glen House Apartments *22 Glen Street, EH3 (228
4043/fax 229 8873). Bruntsfield buses, then 5-min
walk.* **Open** 9am-5.30pm Mon-Fri. **Rooms** 60. **Rates**
weekly £160-£700. **Credit** AmEx, DC, JCB, MC, £TC, V.
Map 6 E7

Colin Hepburn *3 Abercorn Terrace, Portobello, EH15
(669 1044 phone & fax). 15, 20, 26, 66, 84, 85, 86
buses.* **Open** 9am-10pm daily. **Rooms** 21. **Rates** *weekly*
£135-£350. **Credit** MC, £TC, V.

Brian Mathieson *2 Learmonth Terrace, EH4 (332
0717/226 6512/fax 226 6513. George St buses.* **Open**
9am-11pm daily. **Rooms** 5 apartments. **Rates** *weekly*
£200-£700. **Credit** £TC. **Map 2 B4**

Agencies

Factotum *40A Howe Street, EH3 (220 1838/fax 220 4342). 20, 28, 80(A,B) buses.* **Open** 9am-5.30pm Mon-Fri. **No credit cards. Map 3 D4**
e-mail: factotum@easynet.co.uk
http: www.factotum.co.uk

Festival Flats *3 Linkylea Cottages, Gifford, East Lothian, EH41 (01620 810 620/fax 01620 810 619).* **Open** 9am-5pm Mon-Fri. **No credit cards.**

Greyfriars Property Services *29-30 George IV Bridge, EH1 (220 6009/fax 220 6008). George IV Bridge buses.* **Open** 9.30am-12.30pm, 1.30-5.30pm Mon-Fri (*summer* 9am-noon Sat). **No credit cards. Map 9 B3**
e-mail: david@greyprop.co.uk

Mackay's Agency *30 Frederick Street, EH2 (225 3539/fax 226 5284). Princes St buses.* **Open** *office* 9am-5.30pm Mon-Fri; 9am-4pm Sat; 10am-3pm Sun. Phone enquiries 9am-8pm Mon-Fri. **Credit** MC, £TC, V. **Map 8 B1**

Seasonal lets

Universities let out their halls of residence during student holidays. They can be out of town, but are a useful form of basic accommodation.

Carberry Tower Conference Centre *Musselburgh, EH21 (665 3135/fax 653 2930).* **Beds** 90. **Rates** from £33.40 (B&B).

Edinburgh University Accommodation Service *Vacation Lets Office, 30 Buccleuch Place, EH8 (650 4669/fax 650 6867).* Call for locations and rates. **Map 7 G7**

Fet-Lor Youth Club *122 Crewe Road South, EH4 (332 4506).* **Beds** 36. **Rates** *single* £40; *twin* £60. Available during Festival.

Heriot Watt Conference Office *Riccarton, EH14 (451 3669/fax 451 3199).* B&B accommodation.
e-mail: ecc@hw.ac.uk

Napier University *Conference and Letting Services, 219 Colinton Road, EH14 (455 4331/fax 455 4411).* Locations south of town.
e-mail: vacation.lets@napier.ac.uk

Queen Margaret College *Hospitality Services Department, Clerwood Terrace, EH12 (317 3310/fax 317 3256).* West of city centre.

Hostels

Scottish Youth Hostel Association

7 Glebe Crescent, Stirling FK8 2JA. (01786 891 400/fax 01786 891 336). **Open** 9am-5pm Mon-Fri.
The SYHA will provide information on accommodation in its hostels around Scotland; to stay in them you must be a member. There are a number of independent hostels around town, but they get very busy. Check about curfews when booking.
e mail: groups@syha.org.uk
http: www.syha.or.uk

Edinburgh Backpackers Hostel *65 Cockburn Street, EH1 (reception 220 1717/fax 220 5143/advanced reservations 221 0022/fax 539 8695). Waverley rail, then 5-min walk or Bridges buses.* **Beds** *dorm* 115; *double* 3; *twin* 1. **Reception open** 24-hours daily; *central reservations* 9am-5.30pm Mon-Fri. **Rates** *dorm (low season)* £10; *July* £11.50; *Aug, 27 Dec-1 Jan* £12.50; *double/twin (low season)* £35; *Aug, 27 Dec-1 Jan* £40. **Credit** MC, £TC, V. **Map 9 C2**

Bruntsfield Youth Hostel *7 Bruntsfield Crescent, EH10 (447 2994/fax 452 8588). Bruntsfield buses.* **Beds** 150. **Reception open** 7am-11pm daily. Curfew 2am. **Rates** £8.60 SYHA members; £10.10 non-members. **Credit** JCB, MC, £TC, V.

Castle Rock Hostel *15 Johnston Terrace, EH1 (225 9666/fax 226 5078). 1, 6, 34, 35 buses.* **Beds** 198. **Reception open** 24 hours daily. No curfew. **Rates** *night* £10. **Credit** MC, £TC, V. **Map 9 A2**

Edinburgh Central SYHA *Robertson's Close/College Wynd, Cowgate, EH1 (337 1120). Bridges buses, then 10-min walk.* **Beds** 121. **Reception open** 7am-2am daily. Curfew 2am. **Rates** *night* £11.50. **Credit** MC, £TC, V. **Open** June-Sept. **Map 9 C3**

Eglington Youth Hostel *18 Eglinton Crescent, EH12 (337 1120/fax 313 2053). Haymarket rail or buses, then 10-min walk.* **Beds** 165. **Reception open** 7am-midnight daily. Curfew 2am. **Rates** (B&B) SYHA members *low season* £11.50, *July-Aug* £12.50; non-members *low season* £13, *July-Aug* £14. **Credit** MC, £TC, V. **Map 5 B6**

High Street Hostel *8 Blackfriars Street, EH1 (557 3984/fax 556 2981). Bridges buses, then 2-min walk.* **Beds** 140. **Reception open** 24 hours daily. **Rates** *night* £9.90 (credit-card surcharge 30p); *weekly* £59.40 (seventh night free). **Credit** AmEx, JCB, MC, £TC, V. **Map 9 D2**
e-mail: 101357.553@compuserve.com

Princes Street East Youth Hostel *5 West Register Street, EH2 (556 6894/fax 558 9133). Princes St buses.* **Beds** 114. **Reception open** 24 hours daily. **Rates** *night* £9.50. **Credit** MC, £TC, V. **Map 8 D1**

Princes Street Backpackers *3-4 Queensferry Street, West End, EH2 (226 2939). Princes St buses.* **Beds** 300. **Reception open** 24-hours daily. **Rates** *night* £10-£13; *weekly* £50. **Credit** MC, £TC, V. **Map 5 C5**
e-mail: princes.west@cableinet.co.uk

Royal Mile Backpackers *105 High Street, EH1 (557 6120/fax 556 2981). Bridges buses, then 5-min walk.* **Beds** 38. **Reception open** 7-3am daily; 24-hour access. **Rates** *night* £9.90 (credit-card surcharge of 30p). **Credit** AmEx, MC, £TC, V. **Map 9 C2**
e-mail: 101357.553@compuserve.com

Camping and caravanning

Edinburgh Caravan Club Site *Marine Drive, Silverknowes, EH4 (312 6874). 8A, 9A, 14A buses (May-Sept only).* **Reception open** 8am-8pm daily. **Rates** *tent* £3 pitch, £4 adult; *caravan* £6 pitch, £4 adult, £1.20 children, £1.45 electrical link. **Parking** *cars* £1.50; *m/bike* 50p. **Credit** MC, V.

Mortonhall Caravan Park *Frogston Road East, EH16 (664 1533). 7, 11 buses.* **Reception open** 8am-10pm daily. **Rates** *pitch & 2 adults* £8-£12.50; £1 extra adult. **Credit** AmEx, JCB, MC, £TC, V.

Short notice

Festival Beds

38 Moray Place, EH3 (225 1101/fax 623 7123). Haymarket buses, then 10-min walk. **Open** 9am-5.30pm Mon-Fri.
If you arrive when the Festival is in full swing and you have no place to stay, then this is the place to contact for bed and breakfast in a private house; about 80 properties contribute. During the Festival in August 1997 there was only a 50% occupancy rate, even though some visitors were seen sleeping on the streets, which is not recommended, even in the summer.

Pubs & Bars

'Leeze me on Drink! it gies us mair
Than either School or Colledge:
It kindles Wit, it waukens Lear,
It pans us fou o'Knowledge.'

Scotland's reputation as a land of hardened drinkers is one it seems keen to cultivate. From the poems of Burns – *The Holy Fair* is quoted above – to the early comedy of Billy Connolly, the boozer, whether of claret, hot toddy, pints of heavy or nips of whisky, has been seen as a purveyor of positivity. Edinburgh's pub philosophers might not have the international reputation of their Dublin counterparts, but you won't have to look far to find a knot of intellectual types who will happily remind you of the role of Milnes Bar in the Scottish Renaissance. So too will the guides on the **Literary Pub Tour** (*see below*), which visits a few of the bars made famous by the likes of Burns, Stevenson and Scott.

Edinburgh has always provided the full range of darkened drinking dens and high-class watering holes. Nowadays the watchword is 'cosmopolitan' as the emphasis has shifted out of the dens and into the palaces: the style bar, once the preserve of Glasgow's fashion junkies, has arrived in Edinburgh with a vengeance. Recent years have seen a veritable explosion of wildly coloured and equally wildly populated bars where the emphasis is on the chic, the stylish and the attraction of beautiful people like moths to a light. Of course, the dens are still there: down Leith way, around the Grassmarket and in the outer reaches of the city. But if you do happen into the kind of unsavoury establishment where ordering a half-pint is considered a slight on the proprietor's honour, the chances are next door there'll be an orange and blue-hued bistro bar with a peach vodka happy hour.

The opening times given are year round. During the Festival many city-centre establishments stay open until 3am.

Literary Pub Tour
starts from the Beehive Inn, 18 Grassmarket, EH1 (225 7171). 2, 12 buses. **Runs** *Apr-June, Sept, Oct* 7.30pm Thur-Sun; *July/Aug* 6pm, 8.30pm daily; *Nov-Mar* 7.30pm Fri.* **Tickets** £6 (£5 concs).

Abbotsford
3 Rose Street, EH2 (225 5276). Princes Street buses. **Open** 11am-11pm daily. **Food served** 10am-2.15pm; 6pm-10pm daily. **Map 8 C1**
Although mostly used as a local, the Abbotsford is much in demand from those looking for a pint before heading for a train at Waverley Station. Its circular bar and Victorian

décor are among the best in the city. The upstairs restaurant serves healthy Scottish food that begs to be washed down with one of the many real ales on offer.

The Antiquary
72-78 St Stephen Street, EH3 (225 2858). 20, 28, 80(A/B) buses. **Open** 11.30am-12.30am Mon-Wed; 11.30am-1am Thur-Sat; 11am-midnight Sun. **Food served** 11.30am-2pm Mon-Sat; 11.30-2.30pm Sun. **Map 3 D3**
One of St Stephen Street's longest-established bars, which has maintained a bohemian atmosphere while others have opted for trendy refurbishment. Attracting a very mixed crowd – including students and locals – the bar nonetheless has a warm atmosphere. Lunch is served from a simple and reasonably priced menu. Sunday brunch, popular with the hungry and hungover, is served until 3.30pm.

Athletic Arms
1-3 Angle Park Terrace, EH11 (337 3822). 4, 28, 34, 43, 44, 66(A) buses. **Open** 11am-midnight Mon-Sat; 12.30-6pm Sun. **Map 5 A8**
The location, near two of the city's prime sporting arenas, Tynecastle Park and Murrayfield Stadium, sets the theme for both the clientele and the banter. And the position next door to Dalry graveyard provides its nickname of the Diggers. A friendly mix of locals, students and real ale fans are drawn to the highly efficient service and one of the best pints of McEwans 80/- in town.

The Auld Toll Bar
37/39 Leven Street, EH3 (229 1010). Bruntsfield buses. **Open** 11am-11.30pm Tue-Thur; 11am-midnight Fri, Sat; 12.30-11pm Sun; 11am-11pm Mon. **Food served** 11am-11.30pm daily; from 12.30pm Sun. **Map 6 D7**
A favourite with residents of Tollcross and Bruntsfield, this comes across as an old man's pub – basic interior, sport on the telly and no-nonsense grub – but is far more friendly than that. The garden at the back is surprisingly secluded and perfect for balmy summer evenings.

The Bailie Bar
2-4 St Stephen Street, EH3 (225 4673). 20, 28, 80(A/B) buses. **Open** 11am-midnight Mon-Sat; 12.30-11pm Sun. **Food served** 11am-5pm Mon-Fri; 11am-6pm Sat; 12.30-6pm Sun. **Map 3 D3**
A favourite meeting place for Stockbridge residents before a night up the town, this friendly bar has a laid-back, unpretentious atmosphere. The food goes far beyond the expectations of traditional pub grub without breaking the bank.

Bannerman's
212 Cowgate, EH1 (556 3254). Bridges buses. **Open** noon-1am Mon-Sat; 11am-midnight Sun. **Food served** noon-3pm Mon-Fri; 11am-4pm Sun. **Map 9 C3**
A large but cosy vaulted pub in the heart of the Old Town that attracts rugby-playing students and an older crowd with its relaxed, living-room atmosphere and wide range of ales and whiskies. Sunday breakfasts are very popular. Local bands play twice a week – jazz or soul (Wed) and rock (Sat).

Ease into a front row seat at the **Café Royal Bistro Bar**.

The Bare Story

253-255 Cowgate, EH1 (556 3953). Bridges buses.
Open 4.30pm-1am daily. **Map 9 C3**
Part of the Oyster Bar chain (check the anagram), this unfussy pub prides itself on being down to earth and unpretentious. There's a good deal here for everyone – not just the students who make up much of the young, lively clientele. DJs play every Sunday for those who don't want the weekend to end. All major sporting events are shown on the TV, as well as *The Simpsons* nightly (except Saturday).

Bar Kohl

54 George IV Bridge, EH1 (225 6936). George IV Bridge buses. **Open** 11am-1am Mon-Sat. **Food served** 11am-2.30pm Mon-Sat. **Map 9 B2**
Serving much more than style, Bar Kohl claims to be the first vodka bar established in Britain. But besides the 250 types of vodka, there's an extensive selection of other spirits and bottled beers, as well as Budweiser on draught. American deli-style food is served. With a hip hop/swing soundtrack, imported direct from record companies in California, this unique, family-run premises is busy over the weekend with clubbers.

Barony Bar

81-85 Broughton Street, EH1 (557 0546). 7A, 8(A), 9(A), 19, 39 buses. **Open** 11am-midnight Mon-Thur; 11am-12.30am Fri, Sat; 12.30-11pm Sun. **Food served** 11am-9pm daily; from 12.30pm Sun.
An open-plan pub in the traditional theme – tiled walls, lots of wood and a roaring open fire. Popular with a wide range of locals, students and professionals, it provides a good range of cask ales as well as Beck's on draught. Traditional pub food is served and a good range of pies is still on sale after the kitchen closes.

Baroque

39-41 Broughton Street, EH1 (557 0627). 7A, 8(A), 9(A), 19, 39 buses. **Open** 10am-1am Mon-Sat; noon-1am Sun. **Food served** 11am-7pm Mon-Sat; noon-7pm Sun.
Map 3 F3

Not a venue you are likely to miss, with its bold, primary-coloured walls and contrasting furniture. The décor, supposedly based on the design work of Barcelona's Gaudi, is a curious mixture of colours and styles. The huge windows create an airy atmosphere in the summer. Take advantage of the large TV screen to watch major sporting events while munching your way through plates of nachos and melting cheese. Like most of Broughton Street's bars, Baroque becomes extremely busy at the weekends.

Bar Sirius

7-10 Dock Place, EH6 (555 3344). 10A, 16, 22A, 32, 52, 88(A) buses. **Open** 11am-midnight Mon-Wed; 11.30am-1am Thur-Sat; 11.30-1am Sun. **Food served** 11.30-midnight daily. **Map 2 LEITH**
Situated by the shore in Leith, this designer bar attracts a young, trendy clientele with its stylish décor and good music. The happy hour on Fridays (4.30-7.30pm) is popular: doubles for the price of singles, £1 a pint and other specials.

The Basement

10A-12A Broughton Street, EH1 (557 0097). 7A, 8(A), 9(A), 19, 39 buses. **Open** noon-1am daily. Food served noon-10pm daily. **Map 3 F3**
A popular basement bar with the local style merchants and anyone who wants good food in a cosy but lively environment. Wrought iron décor by Alex Wright of Wreckage offsets the staff's geek-chic Hawaiian shirts. The weekend Mexican menu is popular, so booking ahead is advised.

Bennet's Bar

8 Leven Street, EH3 (229 5143). Bruntsfield buses. **Open** 11am-11.30pm Mon-Wed; 11am-12.30am Thur-Sat; 7-11pm Sun. **Food served** noon-2pm Mon-Sat. **Map 6 D7**
The tiled and mirrored walls and a fantastic carved wooden gantry give this traditional bar a friendly Victorian feel. Next door to the King's Theatre, it attracts theatre-goers (and sometimes stars of the show) as well as regulars and people meeting up before dinner. There is no music, just a lot of chat, well-kept beers, over 100 malt whiskies and homemade food.

Bert's Bar

*2-4 Raeburn Place, EH4 (332 6345). 20, 28, 80(A/B)
buses.* **Open** 11am-midnight Mon-Thur; 11am-1am Fri,
Sat; 12.30-11pm Sun. **Food served** 11am-midnight; from
12.30pm Sun. **Map 2 C3**
Bert's themed Victorian minimalism attracts suited accoun-
tant types on their way home from work in the New Town,
but the friendly, laid-back atmosphere also draws a young
crowd at night. The William Street branch is a welcome shelter for weary West End shoppers.
Branch: 29-31 William Street, EH3 (225 5748).

Biddy Mulligan's

94-96 Grassmarket, EH1 (220 1246). 2, 12 buses. **Open**
9am-1am daily. **Food served** 9am-8pm daily. **Map 9 A3**
Reputed to be one of the busiest pubs in Edinburgh, Biddy's
is an Irish pub with crowded nights and a feel-good atmosphere. Irish bands play every Thursday and Sunday night
and it's the place to watch Irish football on the television.
Popular with students.

Black Bo's

57-61 Blackfriars Street, EH1 (557 6136). Bridges buses.
Open 4pm-1am Mon-Sat; 6pm-1am Sun. **Map 9 D2**
A down-to-earth but colourful bar that attracts a hip, happening and young (or young at heart) crowd. Early evenings
tend to be mellow, but late at night it fairly hums with life.
Food is not served in the bar but the same management runs
a restaurant next door. Background music is mainly hip hop
and DJs play most evenings.

Blue Bar Café

10 Cambridge Street, EH1 (221 1222). Bruntsfield buses.
Open noon-midnight daily. **Food served** noon-11pm
daily. **Map 8 A3**
Minimalist, airy and stylish, Blue introduced itself as one of
Scotland's most refreshing style bars when it opened in July
1997. Set above its big sister the Atrium (*see chapter
Restaurants*), just off Lothian Road, it draws a young,
funky clientele for drinks and a range of contemporary food.
The stock of 57 varieties of whisky includes some rare
Cadenheads cask-strength malts.

Bow Bar

80 West Bow, EH1 (226 7667). George IV Bridge buses.
Open 11am-11.30pm Mon-Sat; 2-11pm Sun. **Map 9 A3**
Close to the Grassmarket but not overrun with students, this
is a civilised, down-to-earth bar. Specialising in cask ales, it
also boasts a collection of 135 malt whiskies and has a quiet
traditional feel. Pies are served noon-4pm. Appeals to the
older spectrum of professionals and real ale enthusiasts.

Brecks Bar

110-114 Rose Street, EH2 (225 3297). Princes St buses.
Open 10am-midnight Mon-Fri; 11am-1am Sat; 12.30-
midnight Sun. **Food served** noon-9.30pm daily; from
12.30 Sun. **Map 8 B1**
With its impressive circular bar, Brecks provides a fine
escape from the hazards of buskers and shoppers on Rose
Street. The large dining area at the back has ridiculously
comfortable sofas, and there is no rule against just taking
your drink there.

Burns Alehouse

*7 Bernard Street, Leith, EH6 (554 7515). 10A, 16, 22A, 32,
52, 88(A) buses.* **Open** 11am-11pm Mon-Sat; 11am-5pm Sun.
Food served noon-2pm, 6-9pm Mon-Sat. **Map 2 LEITH**
Formerly the Cavern bar, this traditional premises in the
heart of Leith has been kept in the family and has recently
been overhauled and renamed. It offers an inviting environment for beers and a range of other drinks, while the bistro
menu – centred on the German speciality of rosti potatoes,
with an imaginative range of accompaniments – can be
served in the bar if customers prefer.

Café Kudos

23 Greenside Place, EH1 (558 1270). Leith Walk buses.
Open noon-1am daily. **Food served** noon-6pm daily.
Map 4 G4
Attracting pre-show drinkers for the next door Playhouse
and a strong gay crowd, the relaxed atmosphere and surroundings make this an ideal venue for a pre-club or pre dinner drink. The décor is unusual yet low-key with artwork
displayed on the walls. Serves coffee as well as a large choice
of draught beers and alco-pops.

Café Royal Bistro Bar

*17 West Register Street, EH2 (556 2549). Princes St
buses.* **Open** 10am-1am daily. **Food served** 11am-
5.30pm Mon-Fri. **Map 8 D1**
A smart but casual and relaxed environment for a drink,
coffee, lunch or afternoon snack from the inexpensive and
internationally influenced menu. The drinks promotions
(5-7.30pm Mon-Sun) attract workers from nearby offices.
The bar draws a strong contingent of rugby fans when
there's a match on the big screen and tourists through the
summer.

Café Royal Circle Bar

*19 West Register Street, EH2 (556 1884). Princes St
buses.* **Open** 11am-11pm Mon-Wed; 11am-midnight
Thur; 11am-1am Fri, Sat; 11am-11pm Sun. **Map 8 D1**
This expansive, luxurious heritage-listed interior, complete
with Royal Doulton tiles, has an island bar well stocked with
a selection of fine malt whiskies. It gets busy after 5pm and
on weekends.

The Caledonian Ale House & Bistro

*1 Haymarket Terrace, EH12 (337 1006). Haymarket rail
or buses.* **Open** 11am-midnight Mon-Wed; 11am-1am
Thur-Sat; 11am-midnight Sun. **Food served** noon-
9.30pm daily. **Map 5 B6**
The bottom floor of the Caledonian Ale House is lively
and bustling, with mirrored, tiled and wood-panelled
walls. Upstairs is the bistro, which is rather more quiet
and intimate. Popular mostly with office workers, except
when sport is shown on the big screen and a more varied
crowd appears.

The Caley Sample Room

*58 Angle Park Terrace, EH11 (337 7204). 4, 28, 34, 43,
44, 66(A) buses.* **Open** 11am-midnight Mon-Thur; 11am-
1am Fri, Sat; 12.30pm-midnight Sun. **Food served** noon-
2.30pm daily; from 12.30pm Sun. **Map 5 A8**
This big, warm, open bar sells all the real ales brewed in the
nearby Caledonian Brewery together with a good selection
of guest ales and good old-fashioned pub grub (with discounts for OAPs). Big screen televisions show sporting
events and the pub is ideally placed for a tipple after the
match, whether at Tynecastle or Murrayfield.

Cameo Bar

38 Home Street, EH3 (228 4141). Bruntsfield buses.
Open 12.30pm-11am Mon-Wed; 12.30pm-1am Thur-Sun.
Map 6 D6
A neat and cleanly designed bar serves as a pre-film watering hole for patrons of the Cameo and a comfortable place to
meet for a chat. The walls act as an art gallery for small, local
exhibitions and the continental atmosphere is further
enhanced by good coffee and papers to read.

Canny Man's

*237 Morningside Road, EH10 (447 1484). Bruntsfield
buses.* **Open** noon-midnight Mon-Sat; 12.30-11pm Sun.
Food served noon-3.30pm daily; from 12.30pm Sun.
One of the city's most famous hostelries, the bar, also
known as the Volunteer Arms, is a maze of alcoves. Once
popular with students and locals, it has become somewhat
exclusive of late, a little pricey and jealous of its privacy.

Shaking up an early cocktail, before the storm hits **The Dome** (page 100). This former banking

Carwash

11-13 North Bank Street, EH1 (220 0054). George IV Bridge buses. **Open** noon-1am Mon-Sat; 6pm-1am Sun. **Food served** noon-6pm Mon-Sat. **Map 9 B2**

This stylishly created retro pub is adorned with pictures of cult '70s icons and kitsch objects of desire. The red, purple and green walls encourage a party atmosphere that draws in young clubbers at night and shoppers and locals through the day. Cocktails are the house speciality, available by the glass and in two- or three-pint pitchers. The cocktail happy hour (4-8pm daily) is a winner. Upstairs, there's a pool table and table-football.

Cas Rock

104 West Port, EH1 (229 4341). 2, 12, 28 buses. **Open** noon-1am Mon-Sat; 12.30pm-midnight Sun. **Map 6 E6**

An open, spacious pub in a modern block, that is firmly based around indie and punk music. The jukebox selection is spot on and live bands play three or four times a week. *See chapter* **Music: Rock**.

Cask & Barrel

115 Broughton Street, EH1 (556 3132). 7A, 8(A), 9(A), 19, 39 buses. **Open** 11am-11pm Sun-Tue; 11-1am Wed-Sat. **Food served** noon-2pm daily. **Map 3 F3**

A no-nonsense beer-drinkers' pub. The fine guest ales complement a full quota of local brews and help make this stand apart from the Broughton Street style-mafia's haunts. No music, but plenty of chat from the sporty types and a handy spot for meeting before going on to Café Graffiti (*see chap-*

ter **Nightlife)**. Gets rowdy at weekends, especially when Scotland are playing at home at Murrayfield.

Catwalk Café

2 Picardy Place, EH1 (478 7771). Leith Walk buses. **Open** 10am-1am, **food served** 10am-7pm, daily. **Map 4 G4**

Since opening in 1997, this chic addition to the Broughton Street scene has made quite an impression and hosted several fashion shoots. The interior is minimalist but full of style. The food has a continental influence and there is a wide variety of teas offered as thirst-quenchers. DJs play every night, with Thursday an open-decks night. At its best in summer when the glass wall at the front slides back to let in the sun and open it out to the street.

Cellar No. 1

1A Chambers Street, EH1 (220 4298). Bridges or George IV Bridge buses. **Open** noon-1am Mon-Wed; noon-3am Thur-Sat; 6pm-1am Sun. **Food served** noon-10pm Mon-Sat; 6-10pm Sun. **Map 9 C3**

This cosy basement bar draws in professionals and students with its regular live jazz and gypsy guitar nights. There is a wide range of wines, available by the glass and the bottle, plus an assortment of draught and bottled beers. Prints of musicians and wine labels set the tone.

WJ Christie's

27 West Port, EH1 (229 4553). 2, 12, 28 buses. **Open** noon-1am Mon-Sat; 12.30pm-1am Sun. **Map 6 E6**

This informal and lively pub is a favourite with locals and stu-

hall is a quiet place for a relaxing drink by day, but come Saturday night it gets heaving.

dents from the nearby Edinburgh Art College. 'The downstairs bar features a different event every evening; busiest and most popular is the comedy on Thursdays and Sundays.

City Café
19 Blair Street, EH1 (220 0127). Bridges buses. **Open** 11am-1am daily. **Food served** 11am-10pm daily. **Map 9 C2**
Still one of Edinburgh's most fashionable bars, the City Café attracts a mixed but mostly young clientele. Pre-clubbers rub shoulders with pool players in this 1950s-style chic hangout. The atmosphere is relaxed yet bustling and it gets very busy at weekends. There is a large selection of imported beers and a good choice of pitchers and cocktails. The sweet-toothed can get stuck into the confectionery selection.

Clark's Bar
142 Dundas Street, EH3 (556 1067). 19A, 23, 27, 37, 47 buses. **Open** 11am-11pm Mon-Wed; 11am-11.30pm Thur-Sat; 12.30pm-11am Sun. **Map 3 F3**
A New Town institution loved by locals and appreciated by strangers who drop in on their way down to Stockbridge and Canonmills. Just the place for a good, clear pint in traditional surroundings with comfy leather settees. Gets busy when there's a big match on.

The Clans
19-21 George Street, EH2 (225 1251). George St buses. **Open** 11am-1am Mon-Sat; noon-11pm Sun. **Food served** 11am-10pm Mon-Sat; from noon Sun. **Map 8 C1**

The bar of the George Intercontinental Hotel has a Scottish feel with coats of arms and tartans framed and mounted among the stags' heads on the dark blue walls. It becomes 'network central' during the Television Festival in August.

The Conan Doyle
71-73 York Place, EH1 (524 0031). Leith Walk buses. **Open** 11am-midnight Mon-Thur; 11am-1am Fri, Sat; 1pm-midnight Sun. **Food served** noon-10pm Mon-Thur; noon-3pm Fri; noon-6pm Sat; 1-7pm Sun. **Map 3 F4**
Convenient for the bus station, at the Broughton Street end of York Place. Named after one of Edinburgh's famous authors, it is also a bit like sitting in Sherlock Holmes's lounge. The meals are basic but substantial.

The Cumberland Bar
1 Cumberland Street, EH3 (558 3134). 19A, 23, 27, 37, 47 buses. **Open** noon-11.30pm Mon-Wed; noon-midnight Thur-Sat; *summer* 12.30-11pm Sun. **Food served** noon-2pm Mon-Sat; 12.30-2pm Sun. **Map 3 E3**
A shrine to real ale. Numerous polished pumps take pride of place on the bar and there are some 130 whiskies behind it. Vintage tobacco and drink advertisements reinforce the feeling of comfortable nostalgia. There's no music and neither children nor pets are allowed into the bar, making the Cumberland a quiet, if somewhat clubby, haven during the day.

Doin' the Mile in right royal style

At 1,984 yards, the Royal Mile is actually an old Scots mile, not one of the newfangled variety with 1,760 yards. And, apart from having its head on the Castle Rock and its tail in the Queen's Holyrood Palace, it is not particularly regal. But who cares when it compliments the best sightseeing in Europe with a regular series of pit stops for the parched tourist? This is the sort of drinkers' paradise that, while retaining an emphasis on the traditional, is not afraid to open itself up to the modern and trendy.

Starting at the Castle, it's downhill all the way – which makes the going easier for the merry traveller. The first stop is the **Ensign Ewart**, an alcove-friendly bar named after a hero of Waterloo whose memorial can be seen on the north side of the Castle Esplanade. The **Jolly Judge**, situated just off the Lawnmarket in a seventeenth-century close, is a popular haunt for tourists and locals, serving well-kept traditional ale and acting as part of the Literary Tour. Both have regular live folk music. On the corner of Lawnmarket and the Mound, **Deacon Brodie's Tavern** keeps the traditional vein going and positively throbs during the summer. It is a recognised meeting point for many locals.

Past Parliament Square, where it is customary to spit for luck on the Heart of Midlothian, are the **Covenanter** and **Valentine's**. Neither flashy nor dull, functional is the best description of them and that includes the food. The **Filling Station**, opposite, is all themed up with nowhere to go with its American motor motifs and rowdy, Friday night clientele. On the corner of Cockburn Street is **EH1**. This stylish café bar, with its designer interior, DJs (Thur-Sun, from 9pm) and cocktail-friendly atmosphere, came as something of a culture shock when it first appeared on the Mile. But it's popular with lunching office workers, passing tourists and weekend clubbers.

Just over the crossroads with North Bridge is **Logie Baird's Bar**, part of the Bank Hotel and

themed with famous characters from Scotland's history, whose portraits and works line the walls. It serves Scottish cuisine to tourists during the day but seems to have attracted a boisterous crowd in the evening – although peace is to be had in the quiet area upstairs.

Across the road opposite the Crown Plaza is a trio of standard, traditional, tartan-carpeted public houses. The **Mitre**, the **Royal Mile** and **Jocks.** All serve fine food and ales in a friendly atmosphere, which is all a good pub really needs.

At the bottom of the High Street, on the crossroads with Jeffrey Street and St Mary's Street, are the **Tass** and the **World's End**. The former, on the left facing down hill, has a huge stuffed Rabbie Burns dummy overlooking plain but amiable surroundings and forced to endure the jazz on Tuesdays. The latter has a warmer, more tartan feel with great quiz nights, a reasonable whisky selection and well-kept real ales.

The last watering holes of the Mile are to be found on the Canongate. The small **White Horse** is fine for those wanting to complete their Royal Mile collection but hardly memorable otherwise, while the brown-exteriored **Jenny Ha's** (no kids allowed here) is in the modern tradition of low ceilings, dense smoke, pool table and fizzy beer. The homely **Tolbooth** is sandwiched between tearooms, a tattoo parlour and several shops on the Scottish heritage trail. Finally, the **Canon's Gait** is an excellent way to round off the Royal Mile pub trail. It has good live music in the basement (evenings Fri-Sun), great grub (noon-2.30pm, Mon-Sat), a good whisky selection, Old Town décor and snug surroundings. Anyone who has managed to get this far can return home with the proud boast that they have drunk in everything the Royal Mile has to offer.
Canon's Gait, *232 Canongate, EH1 (556 4481).*
Open noon-11.30pm Mon-Wed; noon-1am Thur-Sat; 12.30pm-1am Sun.
Deacon Brodie's Tavern, *435 Lawnmarket, EH1 (225 6531).* Open 10am-1am Mon-Sat; 12.30pm-1am

---

The Dome
14 George Street, EH2(624 8624). George St buses.
Open 10am-1am daily. **Food served** noon-11pm daily. **Map 8 C1**
This fine former banking hall is buzzing and stylish, with a highly groomed and voluble clientele making themselves at home under the 80ft carved dome ceiling. The place recently won an award for the best house wine in Scotland. The emphasis is on customer care so expect quick, friendly service from the island bar. Because it is a listed building, the front stairs cannot be altered to accommodate wheelchair users, but door staff are happy to lend a hand; the premises does have disabled toilets.

Dr Watt's Library
3 Robertson's Close, EH1 (557 3768). Bridges buses.
Open noon-1am daily. **Food served** *summer* noon-7pm daily; *otherwise* noon-3pm daily. **Map 9 D3**
Best described as a 'party pub'. Usually packed full of students, it holds a 1970s-themed club night every third Friday. Specialises in burgers, baguettes and test-tube shooters – flavoured spirits that are just a little too easy to knock back.

The Doric Tavern & McGuffie's Bar
15-16 Market Street, EH1 (225 1084). Princes St buses, then 5-min walk. **Open** Doric Tavern noon-1am Mon-Sat.

Sun. **Food served** noon-10pm daily; from
12.30pm Sun.
EH1 Bar and Brasserie, *197 High Street, EH1
(220 5277).* Open 9.30am-1am daily. Food served
9.30am-1am daily.
Ensign Ewart, *521 Lawnmarket, EH1 (225
7440).* Open 9.30am-11.30pm Mon-Thur; 9.30am-
midnight Fri-Sat; 12.30pm-midnight Sun. Food
served 9.30am-11.30pm; from 12.30pm Sun.
The Filling Station, *235 High Street, EH1 (226
2488).* Open noon-midnight Mon-Thur; noon-1am
Fri-Sat; 12.30-11pm Sun.
Jenny Ha's Bar, *67 Canongate, EH8 (556 2101).*
Open 11am-11pm Mon-Wed; 11am-midnight Thur-
Sat; 12.30-11pm Sun. Food served 11am-4pm Mon-
Sat; 12.30-4pm Sun.
Jock's, *119 High Street, EH1 (524 0020).* Open
11am-11pm Sun-Thur; 11am-1am Fri, Sat. Food
served noon-9pm Mon-Sat.
The Jolly Judge, *7A James Court, EH1 (225
2669). 1, 6, 34, 35 buses.* Open 11am-11pm Mon-
Wed; 11am-midnight Thur-Sat; 12.30-11pm Sun.
Food served noon-2pm daily; from 12.30pm Sun.
Logie Baird's Bar, *Bank Hotel, 1 South Bridge,
EH1 (556 9043). Bridges buses.* Open 9am-1am
daily. Food served 9am-9pm daily.
The Mitre, *133 High Street, EH1 (524 0071).*
Open 11am-midnight Mon-Thur; 11am-1am Fri-Sat;
12.30pm-11pm Sun. Bar food until 9pm Sun-Thur;
until 7pm Sat; until 3pm Fri.
Royal Mile Tavern, *127 High Street, EH1 (556
8274).* Open 9am-midnight Sun-Thur; 9am-1am Fri,
Sat. Food served noon-9.30pm daily; snacks
thereafter.
The Tass, *1 High Street, EH1 (556 6338).* Open
11am-1am Thur-Sat; 11am-midnight Sun-Wed. Food
served noon-7pm daily.
Tolbooth Tavern, *167 Canongate, EH8 (556
5348).* Open 8am-11pm Mon-Thur; 8am-1am Fri;
8am-12.45am Sat; 12.30-11pm Sun. **Food served**
noon-2pm daily.
Valentine's & Covenanter Bar, *154-160 High
Street, EH1 (225 7064).* Open 11am-11pm Sun-Thur;
11am-1am Fri, Sat. Food served 11am-11pm daily.
The White Horse Bar, *266 Canongate, EH8
(556 3403).* Open 11am-11pm Mon-Fri; 11am-
midnight Sat; 12.30-11pm Sun.
The World's End, *4 High Street, EH1 (556
3628).* Open 11am-1am Mon-Sat; 12.30-11pm Sun.
Food served *summer* 12.30-6pm Sun; noon-8pm
Mon-Sat; otherwise noon-3pm Mon-Wed; noon-3pm,
5-8pm Thur; noon-8pm Fri, Sat.

McGuffie's Bar 11am-1am Mon-Thur; 10am-1am Fri, Sat.
Closed Sun (except during the Festival). **Food served**
noon-6pm Mon-Sat. **Map 9 C1**
The Doric Tavern upstairs has a homely, hidden-away feel
and serves an excellent bistro menu in the larger of its two
rooms; the smaller is a laid-back talking shop that becomes
very busy in the evenings. A favourite with journalists from
the nearby *Scotsman* building and a popular haunt for many
of Edinburgh's arty intelligentsia. Downstairs, McGuffie's
Bar has a more down-to-earth atmosphere and serves traditional pub grub. McGuffie's attracts office workers and –
because of their position close to Waverley Station – both
bars are favoured by commuters.

The Drum & Monkey
*80 Queen Street, EH2 (538 8111). Princes St buses, then
5-min walk.* **Open** 11am-midnight Mon-Wed; 11am-1am
Thur-Sat. **Closed** Sun. **Food served** noon-9pm daily.
Map 3 E4
This bar is plush without being intimidating, looks and feels
like a gentleman's club, but serves a cracking good Bloody
Mary to the mainly office worker crowd. The food upstairs is
more upmarket than the more traditional fare served in the
Cellars Bistro downstairs. There's a private dining area that can
be reserved for parties of between eight and 14 people. A jazz
band plays every Saturday afternoon, when it gets very busy.

Festival Theatre Bar
13-29 Nicolson Street, EH8 (662 1112). Bridges buses.
Open 10am-6pm daily. **Food served** 10am-6pm daily.
Map 7 G6
A lovely place to sit and watch the world go by through the
plate glass front of the theatre. Great on a sunny day but a
little cold and clinical in winter. The café serves unbeatable
(and huge!) scones and reasonable light lunches and snacks
during the bar opening hours. Beware of interval crowds
and, surprisingly for a theatre, rancid house white wine.
No-smoking bar.

Fibber Magee's
*24 Howe Street, EH3 (220 2376). 20, 28, 80(A/B)
buses.* **Open** 11am-1am Mon-Fri; 10am-1am Sat, Sun.
Food served noon-6pm Mon-Fri; 10am-6pm Sat, Sun.
Map 3 D4
This Irish pub with a difference offers relaxed days and lively nights in a mixed crowd. Spread over two bars, it is dark
but colourful and lanterns leaning over the bar area add a
nice touch. Fibber's opens at 10am at weekends to meet
demand for breakfasts. A snack menu comes into effect after
6pm right through until closing time.

The Filmhouse Bar
88 Lothian Road, EH3 (228 2688). Bruntsfield buses.
Open 10am-11.30pm Sun-Thur; 10am-12.30am Fri, Sat.
Food served noon-10pm daily. **Map 8 A3**
A large and comfortable café bar ideal whether you are meet-
ing friends before a film or simply want a quiet drink alone.
A non-smoking area acts as a small gallery space for pho-
tographic exhibitions. The bar is a magnet for film buffs on
Sunday evenings when the specialised film quiz sorts out the
Tarantinos from the Edward Wood Juniors.

Finnegan's Wake
*9B Victoria Street, EH1 (226 3816). George IV Bridge
buses.* **Open** noon-1am Mon-Sat; 12.30pm-1am Sun. **Food
served** noon-9pm daily; from 12.30pm Sun. **Map 9 B2**
The chance to become immersed in Ireland without leaving
the country. Plastered with Irish memorabilia – including a
phonebox and more than a couple of signposts – it offers a
range of Irish beers and whiskies. A live band plays 'traditional Irish music, with a bit of everything thrown in' every
night from 10pm. Often busy and always lively.

Footlights & Firkin
7 Spittal Street, EH3 (229 8368). Bruntsfield buses. **Open**
11am-1am Mon-Sat; 12.30pm-1am Sun. **Food served**
noon-7pm daily; *snacks* 7pm-1am daily. **Map 8 A3**
Like all Firkin pubs, the Footlights & Firkin is down-to-
earth. Dogbolter, the award-winning house ale, is standard
in every Firkin pub, but Bill Clinton's Love Potion is
exclusive to the Footlights. There are lots of arcade games
but the pride and joy really has to be the table-football, complete with floodlights.

Granary Bar
*Hilton National Hotel, 69 Belford Road, EH4 (332 2545).
13 bus.* **Open** noon-midnight Sun-Thur; noon-1am Fri,
Sat. **Food served** noon-10pm daily. **Map 5 A5**

Volunteer for **Canny Man's,** *page 97.*

Unlike many hotel bars this has the atmosphere of a welcoming local. Housed in a nineteenth-century mill building overlooking the Water of Leith, the Granary presents itself like a traditional British pub, right down to the quiz nights on Tuesdays and Sundays. There's live music on Fridays.

The Green Tree
182-184 Cowgate, EH1 (225 1294). Bridges buses. **Open** 11am-1am Mon-Sat; 12.30pm-1am Sun. **Map 9 C3**
One of the few beer gardens in Edinburgh that, come a sunny day, becomes packed with a young crowd trying to overcome the curse of the pale skin. Indoors, the bar is warm and welcoming all year round. In winter an open fire lifts hearts almost as much as the drinks from the island bar. A restaurant is due to be added in October 1998.

Greyfriars Bobby
34A Candlemaker Row, EH1 (225 8328). George IV Bridge buses. **Open** 11am-1am Mon-Sat; 12.30pm-1am Sun. **Food served** 11am-midnight daily; from 12.30pm Sun. **Map 9 B3**
Named after Edinburgh's legendarily faithful terrier, this is a lively and busy traditional pub attracting students, locals and tourists. The reasonably priced menu changes daily, is available all day and is discounted for students.

Henry's Cellar Bar
8-16A Morrison Street, EH3 (221 1288). Bruntsfield buses. **Open** noon-3am daily. **Map 5 C6**
Dark and cosy with a distinctly bohemian feel. Snacks are provided at the bar from the adjoining restaurant (until 11pm) where the speciality is dim sum – Chinese dumplings. Bands play every night of the week and the clientele varies with the bands. At weekends a student-led crowd gets down to the hip hop/soul/jazz fusion while an older crowd dominates during the rest of the week. *See chapter* **Nightlife.**

Hogshead Ale House
30-32 Bread Street, EH3 (221 0575). Bruntsfield buses. **Open** 11am-1am daily. **Food served** noon-9pm daily. **Map 8 A3**
This huge bar appears as if a very large country pub had dropped into the city centre and serves a regularly changing choice of up to 14 cask ales. Very busy, so although the music is kept at a discreet level it's very noisy. The pub grub is a cut above the average.

Holyrood Tavern
9A Holyrood Road, EH8 (556 5044). 60 bus. **Open** noon-12.45am daily. **Food served** noon-2pm, 5-8.30pm, Mon-Fri; noon-5.30pm Sat, Sun. **Map 7 H5**
A fun pub with big comfy, if threadbare, couches. A piano and the front of a car are its prime oddities. Situated between the Royal Mile and the Pleasance Theatre, it gets very hectic during the Festival period. Pies, burgers and nachos are served in healthy proportions.

Iguana
41 Lothian Street, EH1 (220 4288). George IV Bridge buses. **Open** 9am-1am daily. **Food served** 9am-10pm daily. **Map 6 F6**
This cool style bar is geared towards a young, vibrant crowd. From morning to night, hip students and sharp professionals sit chatting, sipping coffees, drinking beers and working their way through the Mediterranean-influenced menu. Very popular as a pre-club venue, it hosts DJs on Friday and Saturday nights. On the first Friday of the month, a pre-club party begins here then continues at the Honeycomb (*see chapter* **Nightlife**).

Indigo (yard)
7 Charlotte Lane, EH2 (220 5603). George St buses. **Open** 8.30am-1am, **food served** 8.30am-1am, daily. **Map 5 C5**
Indigo (yard) has taken the feel of drinking and eating in the fresh air and transported it inside. A huge glass canopy covers what used to be a courtyard and has transformed the exterior into an interior. Bohemian students mix with business people and trendy professionals for cappuccino, hot chocolate, beers, wines, shooters and pitchers of cocktails.

International Bar
15 Brougham Place, EH3 (229 6815). 24, Bruntsfield buses. **Open** 9am-1am Mon-Sat; 12.30pm-1am Sun. **Map 6 E7**
A basic, traditional bar that attracts business people, students and locals with its relaxed atmosphere. Drinks are cheap compared to other places in the area and the IB lays claim to 'the best pint of Guinness in town' because the management looks after it so well. Snacks served all day.

The Junction Bar
24-26 West Preston Street, EH8 (667 3010). Bridges buses. **Open** 11am-1am Mon-Sat; 12.30pm-1am Sun. **Food served** 11am-12.45am daily; from 12.30pm Sun. **Map 7 H7**
A favourite with students (especially trainee vets from the nearby college known as the Dick Vet), this two-roomed pub has blackboards on the walls showing what food is on offer. All major sporting events are shown on television.

The Kenilworth
152 Rose Street, EH2 (226 4385). Princes St buses. **Open** 10am-11pm Mon-Thur; 9am-12.45am Fri, Sat; 12.30-11pm Sun. **Food served** as opening hours. **Map 8 B1**
Housed in a beautiful listed building with tiled walls, an Edwardian ceiling and stained-glass windows, this has something for everyone – students and OAPs have the advantage of discounted meals, shoppers come in to escape from the crowds and the pub is also child-friendly with a special family room at the back.

King's Bar
Bruntsfield Hotel, 69-74 Bruntsfield Place, EH10 (229 1393). Bruntsfield buses. **Open** 11am-12.30pm Mon-Wed; 11am-1am Thur, Fri; 11am-1am Sat, Sun. **Food served** noon-2.30pm, 5.30-9pm daily. **Map 6 D8**
Busy, friendly and cosy with big comfortable chairs, the low-ceilinged basement bar of the Bruntsfield Hotel attracts a very mixed crowd of students, business people and locals. Draught beers, including Caledonian 80/- and Deuchar's IPA, feature in the happy hours (5-7pm Mon-Sat).

King's Wark
36 The Shore, EH6 (554 9260). 1, 6, 10A, 32, 52 buses. **Open** noon-11pm Mon-Thur; noon-midnight Fri, Sat; 11am-11pm Sun. **Food served** noon-10pm daily. **Map 2 LEITH**
The traditional and relaxing atmosphere at the King's Wark appeals to a mixed, somewhat mature clientele. Perfectly placed overlooking Leith Shore, it has kept a maritime theme.

The Kitchen
235 Cowgate, EH1 (225 5413). Bridges buses. **Open** 10.30pm-3am Mon-Thur, Sun; 10pm-3am Fri, Sat. **Map 9 C3**

This pub/club with original décor is geared towards students and young locals. The policy is 'anything goes', there are no dress codes and the emphasis is on fun. Popular with people who don't have a girlfriend/boyfriend/snog. Yet.

Last Drop Tavern

74-78 Grassmarket, EH1 (225 4851). 2, 12 buses. **Open** 11am-1am Mon-Sat; 12.30pm-1am Sun. **Food served** noon-6.30pm; snacks until close. **Map 9 A3**
Not a reference to its lack of ale but to the gallows that were once situated close by. The sort of place where the staff wear T-shirts to that effect. The pub fare is basic and cheap, which partially explains the abundance of students. Very busy indeed at weekends.

Leith Oyster Bar

10 Burgess Street, EH6 (554 6294). 1, 6, 10A, 32, 52 buses. **Open** noon-1am daily. **Food served** noon-10pm daily. **Map 2 LEITH**
This Leith waterfront member of the Oyster Bar chain attracts a wide-ranging clientele. The interior is warm and inviting, with paintings of the surrounding area in muted green on the walls and photos of old Leith. Oysters are popular, as are the nachos. There is also a good range of wine and real ales.

The Livingroom

235 Cowgate, EH1 (225 4628). Bridges buses. **Open** 11am-1am daily. **Food served** 11am-6pm daily. **Map 9 C3**
Decorated as a large, old living room, this Gothic-looking pub offers a wide selection of cocktails. On Thursday, Friday and Saturday nights, regular DJs play a mix of soul, hip hop and funk. Students – attracted by special food and drink offers – make up most of the clientele.

Maggie Dickson's

92 Grassmarket, EH1 (225 6601). 2, 12 buses. **Open** 11am-1am daily. **Food served** 11am-6pm daily. **Map 9 A3**
The number of Irish bars in Edinburgh is still growing, but this member of the old guard remains as popular as ever. Traditional bar food is served, with discounts for punters whose loyal patronage means it's often standing-room only at weekends. Platters on offer from 7pm 'til closing. Monday is quiz night. Every night seems to be party night.

Maison Hector

47 Deanhaugh Street, EH3 (332 5328). 20, 28, 80(A/B) buses. **Open** 11am-midnight Mon-Wed; 11am-1am Thur, Fri; 10.30am-1am Sat; 10.30am-midnight Sun. **Food served** until 10pm daily. **Map 2 C3**
Situated in the bo ho bounds of Stockbridge, this tastefully trendy, brightly hued bar/restaurant is a great escape from the frenzy of the shops outside. Stocks a huge selection of coffees, teas, smoothies, fruit crushes and milkshakes or, if something a bit stronger is required, there are 14 different bottled beers, including a good Czech contingent. The freshly made Margaritas stand out in the extensive cocktail list.

Malmaison Café Bar

1 Tower Place, EH6 (555 6969). 10A, 16, 22A, 32, 52, 88(A) buses. **Open** 10am-3am daily. **Food served** 10am-10pm daily.
Situated in the chic, contemporary environs of Malmaison Hotel, this bar attracts celebrity residents and quaffers from Leith's revamped residential and commercial developments, all of whom enjoy the sophisticated but relaxed atmosphere. Well-stocked bar with good food menu, but both wines and food can also be conjured up from the hotel's brasserie for consumption in the bar area.

The Malt Shovel

11-15 Cockburn Street, EH1 (225 6843). Princes St or Bridges buses, then 5-min walk. **Open** 11am-12.30am

Sun-Thur; 11am-1am Fri, Sat. **Food served** noon-6pm daily. **Map 9 C2**
Ideally located for a quick drink on the way to or from Waverley Station, this is a traditional pub with a welcoming air. Behind the bar, cask ales and over 100 malts feature.

The Maltings

81-85 St Leonard's Street, EH8 (667 5946). Bridges buses, then 5-min walk. **Open** noon-1am Mon-Sat; 12.30pm-1am Sun. **Map 7 H7**
Close to the student residence at Pollock Halls and the head-quarters of Scottish Widows, the Maltings is also good for a spot of sinful drinking after a virtuous visit to the Commonwealth Pool. A sizeable establishment, it nonetheless fills its nooks and crannies to capacity. Five real ales reside behind the bar, and promotions feature every evening.

Mathers

25 Broughton Street, EH1 (556 6754). 7A, 8(A), 9(A), 19, 39 buses. **Open** 11am-midnight Mon-Thur; 11am-1am Fri, Sat; 12.30-midnight Sun. **Food served** until 3pm; 4pm Sun. **Map 3 F3**
An antidote to Broughton Street's style explosion, Mathers is a split-level bar with a traditional feel, attracting an older mixed crowd. The compact but well-stocked bar offers a good range of beers and lagers. Televised sport is a regular feature, and the ladies' boasts what must be the loftiest toilet in town.

Maxies Bistro

32B West Nicolson Street, EH8 (667 0845). Bridges buses. **Open** 11am-midnight Mon-Thur; 11am-1am Fri, Sat. **Closed** Sun. **Food served** noon-3pm, 5-11pm, Mon-Sat. **Map 7 G6**
An expansive cellar bar with a civilised air, Maxies has an extensive wine list that concentrates on the New World, although European vintages are well represented. Small glasses start at £1.50 and large glasses, which hold a third of a bottle, are priced from £2.80. Good bistro food is served.

Milne's Bar

35 Hanover Street, EH2 (225 6738). Princes St buses. **Open** 11am-midnight Mon-Thur; 11am-1am Fri, Sat; 12.30-midnight Sun. **Food served** 11am-midnight daily; from 12.30pm Sun. **Map 8 C1**
An atmospheric pub on three levels with dark wood interior and plenty of cosy nooks. Infused with literary history as the place where the members of the 'Scottish Renaissance' used to drink. Despite its size, it gets incredibly busy at weekends. An impressive array of cask ales, good quiz machines and value-for-money meals.

Monboddo

The Point Hotel, 32 Bread Street, EH3 (221 5555). Bruntsfield buses. **Open** 10am-midnight Sun-Thur; 10am-1am Fri, Sat. **Food served** 10am-10pm Sun-Thur; 10am-5pm Fri; 10am-8pm Sat. **Map 8 A3**
This bar and grill is the latest addition to the contemporary chic of the Point Hotel. The surroundings epitomise minimalist elegance – all sleek curves, modern art and chrome – and have attracted a similar clientele to a suitable beverage list. The food is reasonably priced but minimal.

Montpeliers

159 Bruntsfield Place, EH10 (229 3115). Bruntsfield buses. **Open** 11am-1am Mon-Sat; 9pm-1am Sun. **Food served** breakfast/lunch 9am-6pm; dinner 6-10pm; supper 10pm-close. **Map 6 D8**
Bringing a bold splash of style to Bruntsfield, Montpeliers has a continental atmosphere and offers al fresco drinking in the summer. Twelve wines, at £1.95 per small glass or £2.95 per large glass (one third of a bottle), jostle for space with champagnes and other drinks. The unpretentious but imaginative menu includes a good vegetarian selection.

NB's

The Balmoral Hotel, 1 Princes Street, EH1 (556 2414).
Princes St buses. **Open** 11am-midnight Mon-Thur; 11am-
1am Fri, Sat; noon-midnight Sun. **Food served** noon-
2.30pm daily. **Map 8 D2**
This smart watering hole, housed in one of Edinburgh's top
hotels, has a relaxed air and attracts a happy mix of revellers,
sports fans and weary shoppers. Live music Thur-Sat.

Negociants

45-47 Lothian Street, EH1 (225 6313). George IV Bridge
buses. **Open** 9am-3am daily. **Food served** 9am-2.30am
daily. **Map 6 E6**
The waiting service at this traditional bar, where an impressive selection of foreign bottled beers and cocktails adds to
the usual array of draught beers, wines and spirits, puts the
accent on waiting rather than service. During the day, it's a
relaxed spot for coffees, hot chocs and pastries. In the summer months tables and chairs are set up on the pavement.

O'Neill's

99 Hanover Street, EH2 (225 0911). Princes St buses,
then 5-min walk. **Open** 11am-midnight Mon-Thur; 11am-
1am Fri, Sat; 12.30pm-midnight Sun. **Food served** noon-
6pm daily; from 12.30pm Sun. **Map 8 C1**
There's a lot going on at this branch of the Irish-themed chain
with regular promotions, a happy hour (3-7pm), live music
(Fri, Sat), 15 Irish whiskies, pocheen and Rumplemintze, a
100° proof peppermint liqueur.

The Old Fire Station

52 West Port, EH1 (228 4543). 2, 12, 28 buses. **Open**
11am-1am daily. **Food served** 11am-3pm, 7pm-1am
Mon-Fri; 11am-1am Sat, Sun. **Map 8 A3**
Part of the Eerie Pub Company, this popular student hangout is ghoulishly decked out and serves plenty of spirits and
unnervingly named cocktails.

The Outhouse

12A Broughton Street Lane, EH1 (557 6668). 7A, 8(A),
9(A), 19, 39 buses. **Open** noon-1am Mon-Sat; 12.30pm-
1am Sun. **Food served** 12.30-4pm daily. **Map 3 E3**
Although students and pre-clubbers love this stylish bar, its
lack of pretension makes it a comfortable watering hole for all-
comers. Downstairs, blond wood and minimalist furnishings
lead to the beer garden and boule court, while the loft-like
upstairs bar is dotted with squishy 'pods'. The bar serves all
the style-bar staples and a good range of pitchers and shooters.

Peartree House

38 West Nicolson Street, EH8 (667 7533). Bridges buses.
Open 11am-midnight Mon-Thur; 11am-1am Fri, Sat;
12.30pm-midnight Sun. **Food served** noon-2.30pm Mon-
Sat; 12.30-2.30pm Sun. **Map 7 G6**
A favourite with students and their sozzled tutors, this long-
established traditional bar gets jam-packed at weekends.
The buffet lunch is good value at £3 a plate, but what makes
this pub worth a visit is its beer garden. There's a quiz on
Monday nights and regular live music.

Penny Black

17 West Register Street, EH2 (556 1106). Bridges buses.
Open 5am-6.30pm Mon-Thur; 5am-10.30pm Fri, Sat.
Closed Sun. **Map 8 D1**
No frills, no food, no frolicking DJs. At the Penny Black, a spot
of television is as fancy as it gets. But check out those opening
hours. Popular with postmen, doormen and the generally nocturnal – who otherwise have to head down Leith Walk for a pre-
breakfast tipple – the Penny Black is a city-centre institution.

Phoenix Bar

46 Broughton Street, EH1 (557 0234). 7A, 8(A), 9(A),
19, 39 buses. **Open** 8am-1am Mon-Sat; 12.30pm-1am
Sun. **Map 3 F3**

This down-to-earth boozer is an oasis of cheap drink and
Trainspotting-style locals in the heart of trendy Broughton
Street. The go-go girls are long departed but the ceiling to
floor mirrors remain. Open late, big screen sports and an
excellent quiz on Sunday nights.

Physician & Firkin

58 Dalkeith Road, EH16 (662 4746). Bridges buses, then
10-min walk. **Open** 11am-1am daily. **Food served**
11am-10pm daily. **Map 7 J8**
Like many Firkins, the Physician brews on the premises
(brewery tours are available), offering three house ales and
two guests (some of which are quite unusual). In the summer, partake in the beer garden barbecue. Board games are
available, but the outsized versions of Connect 4, Battleships
and Jenga are much more fun. Johnny's Quiz Night is on
Mondays, and there is a DJ on Friday nights.

Port O'Leith

58 Constitution Street, EH6 (554 3568). 16, 22A, 34
buses. **Open** 9am-12.45am Mon-Sat; 12.30pm-12.45am
Sun. **Map 2 LEITH**
Leith may be going upmarket, but the Port O'Leith remains
friendly, down-to-earth and welcoming. Loyal regulars happily rub shoulders with visiting sailors, passers-by and artisans. Comfortable and fuss-free, with a straightforward
drinks list. Snacks available all day.

Queen Street Oyster Bar

16A Queen Street, EH2 (226 2530). Princes St buses,
then 5-min walk. **Open** noon-1am Mon-Sat; 12.30pm-1am
Sun. **Food served** noon-10pm daily; from 12.30pm Sun.
Map 3 E4
A stone-walled, warmly lit basement bar close to the BBC,
this is a small, intimate establishment that quickly fills with
a professional crowd. Belgian and Czech beers, wines and
the occasional cocktail are dispensed from the bar.

The Rat & Parrot

28 Shandwick Place, EH2 (226 4579). Haymarket buses
or rail. **Open** 8am-1am Mon-Sat; 10am-1am Sun. **Food**
served 10am-10pm daily. **Map 5 C6**
This large West End bar pulls in business people during the
day and a younger crowd at night. There is a wide selection
of bottled beers, pitchers and cocktails – including the secret
blend of the house speciality: Pure Fetish. The extensive bar
menu includes snacks and main dishes.

Rose Street Brewery

55 Rose Street, EH2 (220 1227). Princes St buses. **Open**
11am-midnight Mon-Thur; 11am-1am Fri, Sat; 12.30-9pm
Sun. **Food served** 11am-9pm Mon-Sat; 12.30-9pm Sun.
Map 8 B1
A good-looking pub that attracts a mixed clientele and
brews its own 80/- and 90/- ales on the premises (book in
advance for the brewery tours). In addition, a comprehensive range of malt whiskies are to be found behind the bar.
Traditional bar meals served until 9pm, with snacks thereafter until closing time.

Route 66

6 Baxter's Place, Leith Walk, EH1 (524 0061). Leith
Walk buses. **Open** 12.30pm-1.30am Mon-Sat; 3pm-1.30am
Sun. **Food served** 12.30-7pm Mon-Sat; 3-7pm Sun. **Map**
4 G3
A focal point of Edinburgh's 'pink triangle', this friendly joint
has a reasonably priced menu courtesy of ex-Blue Moon Café
staff. These days, you can get your kicks at Route 66 playing pool on the new table.

The Royal Oak

1 Infirmary Street, EH1 (557 2976). Bridges buses.
Open 9am-2am Mon-Sat; 12.30pm-2am Sun. **Map 9**
D3

On the pish

Scottish drinking culture, like drinking cultures the world over, has its own peculiarities and vocabulary. Don't be too put off by the gallus locals, the pub is the place for forthright discussion – although it might be wise to have a wee peek at the local vocabulary box (*see chapter* **Directory**) before you get down the 'howff'. This is an old Scots word, which probably derives from the Dutch 'hof' for courtyard or enclosed place, and can be used to refer to any regular meeting place, but which is most commonly used to refer to a pub. Although it is occasionally written it has become archaic in everyday use – a bit like the word 'tavern' in English.

For anyone who likes their beer, a pint of 80 shilling is a necessary experience while in Edinburgh. Preferably a pint from one of the local breweries, Caledonian or Belhaven. While at the bar, you might hear someone asking for a pint of heavy and feel tempted to ask for one yourself, but apart from the thrill of the request, the fizzy, chemical-heavy refreshment, which is slightly less alcoholic than Export (the other generic fizzy beer) and most akin to an English bitter, does not come recommended. Real ale in Scotland is sold as 70, 80 and 90 shilling, a reference to the amount of duty paid on a barrel of beer, according to its strength, back in the days when the currency was pounds, shillings and pence. Seventy shilling (70/-) is a light, thirst-quenching brew of low alcoholic content, 80/- is a standard strength pint while 90/- is the sort of beer to linger over unless you fancy finishing the evening in the gutter.

In which case you will be guttered. Or pished. Or oot yer faced. Or skunnered. Or ready for the next pub and a nippy sweety, a wee toddy or a drop of the hard stuff. In which case a whisky is what you'll be after. In Edinburgh it'll be a nip – but in Glasgow it's more likely to be a dram – and at this point the delights of the 'water of life' (*uisge beatha* in Gaelic) should come singing to your lips. Most brands are a blended mix of grain and malt whiskies, but the uniqueness of each distillery's products has become recognised in recent years and the best bars offer the delights of a single (cask-strength if you're lucky) malt – for a price.

If your session has been a success, it should now be morning and time for a bottle of Scotland's other drink: Irn Bru. This sweet, bubble gum-flavoured fizzy drink is the perfect hangover cure.

Under the same management for the past 20 years, this traditional pub is known world wide for its unplugged folk music. Sessions kick off around 9.30pm, seven days a week. Singarounds are the Oak's particular speciality. Over 50 malts and a good selection of cask ales grace the bar.

Russian Vodka Bar Kalinka
65 Henderson Street, EH6 (467 7053). 1, 6, 10A, 32, 52, 88 buses. **Open** 5-11.30pm Mon-Wed; 10am-11.30pm Thur; 10am-1.30am Fri; 10am-1am Sat; 12.30-11.30pm Sun. **Food served** during opening hours on Fri, Sat, Sun. **Map 2 LEITH**
What might, at a glance, appear to be an old-school Leith bar, turns, with a second look, into a formidably Russian hostelry. And with a genuine Russian princess providing the music on Sunday afternoons, it's more than a theme. Good Russian menu served during the day.

Ryan's
2 Hope Street, EH2 (226 6669). Princes St or George St buses. **Open** 11am-1am Mon-Sat; 12.30pm-1am Sun (bar only). **Food served** until 10pm daily. **Map 8 A1**

St James Oyster Bar
2 Calton Road, EH8 (557 2925). Leith Walk buses. **Open** noon-1am daily. **Food served** noon-10pm daily. **Map 4 G4**
Close to Waverley Station and the Playhouse, this is the Oyster Bar chain's largest outpost. But it is as a rambling, dark alcoved, pre-gig hangout for The Venue that it is best used. Quiz night on Sundays. The food has a Mexican slant, to be washed down with the fine real ales.

Sandy Bell's
25 Forrest Road, EH1 (225 2751). George IV Bridge buses. **Open** 11am-12.30am Mon-Sat; 12.30-11pm Sun. **Map 6 F6**
Close to the university, Sandy Bell's is a down-to-earth, traditional pub. Real ales and malts refresh an unpretentious crowd, and the pub has a legendary status among folk music circles, with live music on a regular basis.

Scruffy Murphy's
49-50 George IV Bridge, EH1 (225 1681). George IV Bridge buses. **Open** 11am-1am Mon-Sat; 12.30pm-1am Sun. **Food served** 11am-midnight Mon-Sat; 12.30pm-midnight Sun. **Map 9 B3**
Well-worn wood and comfortable seating give this Irish theme bar the lived-in feel of a Dublin pub. Irish bar meals are served all day. Live music features most evenings.

The Sheep Heid Inn
43 The Causeway, Duddingston, EH15 (656 6952). 42, 46 buses. **Open** 11am-11pm Mon-Thur; 11am-midnight Fri, Sat; 12.30-11pm Sun. **Food served** until 9pm daily.
Away from the bustle of the city centre, this historic pub is worth travelling to visit. Boasting a great skittle alley (£40 hire per evening; £10 per hour in the afternoon), the beer garden is also popular in summer. Fresh and hearty home-cooked food is served until 9pm, and on Sunday roasts are served all day in the upstairs bistro.

Southside Steamie

72-74 Newington Road, EH9 (667 9019). Bridges buses.
Open 11.30am-1am Mon-Sat; 12.30pm-1am Sun. **Food served** until midnight daily.
Popular with students, this bright and bold Southside bar is increasingly attracting a broader clientele who also enjoy the daily promotions (4.30-7pm every day). Quiz night is Monday. Food is no-nonsense and sustaining.

The Standing Order

62-66 George Street, EH2 (225 4460). George St or Princes St buses. **Open** 11am-1am Mon-Sat; 12.30pm-1am Sun. **Food served** until 10pm daily. **Map 8 B1**
Edinburgh's branch of the Great British Wetherspoons Experience. Which means a grand, spacious bar housed in a former bank building, affordable pub grub, modestly priced, well-kept beer and no-smoking areas. Formulaic, but fine.

Traverse Theatre Bar

14 Cambridge Street, EH1 (228 5383). Bruntsfield buses. **Open** 10.30am-11pm Mon; 10.30am-midnight Tue-Thur; 10.30am-1am Fri, Sat; 6.30pm-midnight Sun. **Food served** noon-8pm Sun-Thur; noon-midnight Fri, Sat. **Map 8 A3**
This spacious, well-designed, modern bar pulls in a far wider clientele than the core group of theatre goers. Students, trendies and would-be trendies make it their haunt of an evening, attracted by the wide selection of draught beers and lagers, spirits promotions and cracking (but not intrusive) background music. Workers from the surrounding offices, parents (it has a children's licence to 8pm) and shoppers make use of the reasonably priced lunchtime menu; decidedly different bar snacks are available in the evenings, too.

Tron Ceilidh House

9 Hunter Square, EH1 (226 0931). Bridges buses. **Open** 11am-midnight Mon-Thur; 11am-1am Fri; 12.30pm-midnight Sun. **Food served** noon-11pm daily; from 12.30pm Sun. **Map 9 C2**
A sprawling bar on four levels, featuring live jazz and folk six nights a week, often augmented by informal sessions. Caledonian ales and malt whiskies are well represented behind the bar. An imaginative menu mixes traditional Scottish dishes with Cajun and Creole creations, while the upper level is dedicated to Satchmo's Jazz Café.

Uluru

133 Lothian Road, EH3 (228 5407). Bruntsfield buses. **Open** 8am-midnight Mon-Thur; 8am-1am Fri; 10am-1am Sat; 10.30am-midnight Sun. **Food served** as opening hours. **Map 8 A3**
This new bar/café on Lothian Road is popular with business people and locals. The warm yellow interior and polished wood floors create a spacious environment that is stylish yet relaxed while the all-day menu offers a moderately upmarket selection.

The Waterfront Wine Bar & Bistro

1C Dock Place, EH6 (554 7427). 10A, 16, 22A, 32, 52, 88(A) buses. **Open** noon-11pm Mon-Thur; noon-midnight Fri, Sat; 12.30-11pm Sun. **Food served** until 9.30pm daily. **Map 2 LEITH**
This traditional bar situated by the shore in Leith appeals to a mixed but largely mature clientele. The dockside al fresco eating and drinking in summer and open fires in winter create a relaxed atmosphere. There are also a number of speciality ales and a selection of imported beers on offer.

The Watershed

44 St Stephen Street, EH3 (220 3774). 20, 28, 80(A/B) buses. **Open** 10am-12.30pm Sun-Thur; 10am-1am Fri, Sat. **Food served** 10am-7pm Mon-Sat; 10am-5pm Sun. **Map 3 D3**
This stylish basement bar-cum-bistro in the heart of trendy Stockbridge attracts a predominantly student and pre-club crowd at weekends, with a more eclectic crowd during the

Cas Rock, *for towering sounds. Page 98.*

week. Games are available behind the bar, where a reasonable selection of malts, wines and vodkas vies for space alongside pitchers.

West End Oyster Bar

28 West Maitland Street, EH12 (225 3861). Haymarket buses. **Open** noon-1am Mon-Sat; 12.30pm-1am Sun. **Food served** noon-10pm daily; from 12.30pm Sun. **Map 5 B6**
An unpretentious bar occupying a ground floor and basement near Haymarket Station. Food includes oysters and Mexican-style chilli and nachos. Behind the bar, three real ales and coffees are joined by a £6.50 deal on a bottle of sparkling Cava. The table-football has attracted its own singles and doubles ladder, live music is presented at weekends, and major sporting events are shown on the giant screen.

Whighams Wine Cellar

13 Hope Street, EH2 (225 8674). Princes St or George St buses. **Open** noon-midnight Mon-Thur; noon-1am Fri, Sat. **Closed** Sun. **Food served** noon-10pm Mon-Thur; noon-9pm Fri, Sat. **Map 8 A1**
This atmospheric, candle-lit cellar bar is a popular spot for the business community during the day and after work; later in the evening a mature clientele arrives. Alongside draught and bottled beers and a range of whiskies and other spirits, Whighams boasts a selection of wines rivalled by few bars in Edinburgh. There's a choice of over 100 bottles, starting from the house Cabernet Sauvignon at £7.95.

Whistle Binkies

6 Niddry Street, EH1 (557 5114). Bridges buses. **Open** 5pm-3am Mon-Sat; 7pm-3am Sun. **Map 9 D2**
Live music seven nights a week is just one attraction of this Scottish bar, generous closing times being another. Simply furnished and cosy, Whistle Binkies is centrally located but tucked awa; numerous little rooms and great beer add atmosphere.

Shopping & Services

Take the tartan tourist-trap tack test and pass on by to shopping heaven and Edinburgh's sartorially elegant side.

The traditional charm of shopping in Edinburgh has been threatened over the past couple of decades by the arrival of national chainstores and out-of-town shopping malls. Yet, largely because of the city's idiosyncratic character, city-centre shopping has survived. A myriad of specialist and independent outlets sell everything from candles to curios in an atmosphere that can encompass the cosmopolitan, the quaint and the laid-back in the turning of an Old Town corner. There's no need to rush around, shopping 'til you're dropping. Do as the Edinburghers do, and just wander.

Princes Street is the shopping heart of the capital. Once dominated by family-run institutions, of which **Jenners** (*see box* **The grand old man of Princes Street**) is the only one remaining, it is now home to a mixture of upmarket and high-street names that spill over into the surrounding streets. The stores are on the north side of the street, giving shoppers fantastic views of the Castle and Old Town. It's a pleasant place to shop, as long as it isn't a Saturday afternoon, when it seems the entire city makes its consumer pilgrimage there. George Street, two blocks to the north, offers an elegant respite from the hubbub with an eclectic and reassuringly expensive range of shops.

Even when the shops look quaintly old-fashioned, they are far from fuddy-duddy. In particular, Edinburgh is a mecca for the antique or second-hand aficionado, with Thistle Street, Broughton Street, Victoria Street and Causewayside all home to clusters of fascinating and funky junk shops. Veer off the Rose Street and Royal Mile tourist trails of tacky souvenirs and there are plenty of unusual gift opportunities, especially in Cockburn Street and the Grassmarket.

Much of the enjoyment of Edinburgh's cosy consumer culture is down to the persistence of its many villages. Areas such as Morningside, Tollcross and Stockbridge are self-contained. Residents still do their daily shopping locally and each area has its own grocer, florist, chemist and post office. Butchers and fishmongers also continue to survive, despite the continued growth of

vegetarianism. Look out for the gorgeous art deco façades of fishmongers such as John Croan (270 Canongate) and W Brown (55 Elm Row).

The adoption of flexible opening hours has encouraged the city's relaxed attitude to consumerism. Most shops are usually open from 9am to 6pm. In recent years, many shops have started to stay open late on Thursdays. And, amid much clerical consternation, many shops also open on Sundays, although usually only from noon.

Antiques

Byzantium
9 Victoria Street, Old Town, EH2 (225 1768). George IV Bridge buses. **Open** 10am-5.30pm Mon-Sat (*Christmas & Festival only* noon-5pm Sun). **Credit** varies. **Map 9 B2**
Unusual antiques and jewellery fill this large shopping centre, with around 15 outlets on two floors.

Causewayside
Southside. 42, 46, Bridges buses. **Map 7 H8**
A string of antique shops along this street form a genteel fleamarket with lots of intriguing curios among the assorted furniture, crockery and other antiques – mainly pre-1950s.

Edinburgh Architectural Salvage Yard
Unit 6, Couper Street, Leith, EH6 (554 7077/fax 554 3070). Leith Walk buses. **Open** 9am-5pm Mon-Sat. **Credit** JCB, MC, £TC, V. **Map 2 Leith**
Not the place to find a pocket-size souvenir, but this tiered warehouse of larger period furnishings is fascinating to wander around. Church pews, Victorian rolltop baths and sundials are among the curiosities on offer. The series of gangways connecting the various areas make it feel like you're navigating a ship's cargo hold.

Just Junk
87 Broughton Street, EH1 (557 4385). 8, 9, 19, 39 buses. **Open** 10.30am-6.30pm Tue-Sat; noon-4pm Sun. **Credit** MC, £TC, V. **Map 3 F3**
Mainly stocks 1950s and 1960s furniture, bric-a-brac and clothes. The ever-changing window display often has at least one amazing oddity worth investigating.

Kookie Hill
5 East Fountainbridge, Tollcross, EH3 (229 7920). 23, 24, Bruntsfield buses. **Open** 11am-5.30pm Tue-Sat. **Credit** £TC. **Map 6 D6**
Offbeat household collectibles and classic kitsch fill this small, colourful shop near Tollcross – where even the counter is actually a chic cocktail cabinet. The place to come for a pineapple ice bucket or Elvis sunglasses.

Utilities

34 Broughton Street, EH1 (557 6353). 8, 9, 19, 39
buses. **Open** 11am-6pm Mon-Sat. **No credit cards.**
Map 3 F3
Squeeze past the furniture and knick-knacks piled higgledy-piggledy both inside and outside and you'll find some real treasures among the clutter, especially the dolls' houses, unusual glassware and lamps. Enchanting and alluring, this shop is difficult to get into and even harder to leave.

Auctions

Christie's Scotland
*5 Wemyss Place, EH3 (225 4756/fax 225 1723). George
Street buses.* **Open** 9am-1pm, 2-5pm Mon-Fri. **No credit
cards. Map 3 D4**
Antiques and paintings are auctioned at various times, usually listed in the window. Christie's also offers free auction estimates and advice on probate and insurance valuations.

Lyon & Turnbull
*51 George Street, EH2 (225 4627/fax 225 2177). George
Street buses.* **Open** 9am-5pm Mon-Fri; 9am-1pm Sat. **No
credit cards. Map 8 C1**
Regular Saturday morning sales of art, antiques and household goods have been held at this city-centre auction house since 1826. House-clearance auctions take place in the lanes – off Thistle Street – during the week. Viewing is on the morning of the sale and all auctions start at 11am.

Arts & entertainment

Books

Keep a keen eye out for the regular 'Meet the Author' events at Waterstone's and James Thin, advertised in the window displays and *The List* magazine. Thin's events are usually free and not ticketed. Those at Waterstone's tend to be ticketed at about £2 (often redeemable against a copy of the tome in question): book ahead – especially for better-known authors.

Bauermeister Booksellers
*19 George IV Bridge, EH1 (226 5561/fax 220 0679).
George IV Bridge buses.* **Open** 9am-8pm Mon-Fri; 9am-5.30pm Sat; noon-5pm Sun. **Credit** AmEx, DC, MC, £TC,
V. **Map 9 B2**
Located just off the Royal Mile, this two-floor store is good for tourist guides, maps, magazines and educational titles as well as cut-price fiction titles.
e-mail: bauerbooks@cix.co.uk

Beyond Words
*42-44 Cockburn Street, EH1 (226 6636/fax 226 6676).
1, 6, 34, 35, Bridges buses.* **Open** 10am-8pm Tue-Sat;
noon-5pm Sun-Mon. **Credit** MC, V. **Map 9 C2**
Tranquil shop specialising in photography books. A discreet bench running round the foot of all the shelves invites visitors to browse at leisure. Useful for finding more interesting visual mementoes of Scotland than the usual tourist titles.

The Cook's Bookshop
*118 West Bow, EH1 (226 4445/fax 226 4449). 2, 12,
George IV Bridge buses.* **Open** 10am-5pm Mon-Fri;
10.30am-5pm Sat. **Credit** AmEx, MC, V. **Map 9 A3**
Owned by celebrity cook Clarissa Dickson-Wright, this snug nook is more like someone's kitchen and is dominated by two old-fashioned fireplaces and offers a wide selection of new and second-hand cookery titles.

Deadhead Comics
*27 Candlemaker Row, EH1 (226 2774). George IV
Bridge buses.* **Open** 10am-6pm Mon-Sat; 12.30-5.30pm
Sun. **Credit** JCB, MC, £TC, V. **Map 9 B3**
Luminous yellow on the outside and yet curiously dark inside, this friendly comic shop has helpful staff and a vast range of Marvel, DC and independent titles, plus fantasy cardgames and role-playing figures.

McNaughtan's
*3A Haddington Place, EH7 (556 5897/fax 556 8220).
Leith Walk buses.* **Open** 9.30am-5.30pm Tue-Sat. **Credit**
MC, £TC, V. **Map 4 G3**
A library-like shop at the top of Leith Walk with towering oak bookcases full of second-hand literary treasures. Browsers are welcome. There's a handy colour-coded guide to the shop's layout just inside the door.

Tills Bookshop
*1 Hope Park Crescent (Buccleuch Street), EH8 (667
0895). 40, 41, 42, 46 buses.* **Open** noon-7.30pm Mon-Fri;
11am-6pm Sat; noon-5.30pm Sun. **Credit** £TC. **Map 7
G7**
Small, friendly booksellers with a well-priced selection of books and a cool range of old film posters.

James Thin
53-59 South Bridge, EH1 (556 6743). Bridges buses.
Open 9am-10pm Mon-Fri; 9am-5.30pm Sat; 11am-5pm
Sun. **Credit** AmEx, MC, £TC, V **Map 9 C3**
Opened in 1848, this traditional-looking Scottish bookshop has some cult surprises among its comprehensive range of titles. The huge, four-floor South Bridge branch also has an impressive and reasonably-priced second-hand book section.
Branches are too numerous to list here. Check the telephone directory for your nearest.

Waterstone's
*128 Princes Street, West End, EH2 (226 2666/fax 226
4689). Princes St buses.* **Open** 9.30am-9pm Mon-Fri;
9.30am-8pm Sat; 11am-6pm Sun. **Credit** AmEx, DC, MC,
£TC, V. **Map 8 A2**
A large store with a vast range of titles laid out in three well-organised and spacious floors. The West End Princes Street branch is also home to a Seattle Coffee Company café, which offers fine views of Princes Street gardens and the Castle.
Branches: 13-14 Princes Street, East End, EH1 (556
3034); 83 George Street, EH2 (225 3436).

Word Power
*43 West Nicolson Street, Southside, EH8 (662 9112).
Bridges buses.* **Open** 10am-6pm Mon-Fri; 10.30am-6pm Sat
(Dec noon-4pm Sun). **Credit** AmEx, MC, V. **Map 7 G6**
A relatively new shop, but already established as a vibrant centre for the capital's alternative writing scene. An excellent range of radical, women's and gay books and magazines are crammed into a small but bright space. Hosts the radical book fair every year around the middle of May.

West Port Books
145 West Port, EH1 (229 4431). 2, 12, 28 buses. **Open**
10.30am-5.30pm Mon-Wed; 11.15am-5.30pm Thur-Sat.
Credit MC, £TC, V. **Map 6 E6**
The rooms in this labyrinthine shop near the Grassmarket are overflowing with an eclectic range of second-hand and remaindered books, classical records and sheet music.
e-mail: westport@compuserve.com

Music & video

Alphabet Video
22 Marchmont Road, EH9 (229 5136). 24, 40, 41 buses.
Open 2-10pm daily. **No credit cards. Map 6 F8**

Wonderfully idiosyncratic video shop well worth the hike across the Meadows, with an excellent range of new, old, mainstream and independent films from £1 for two-day hire. To hire films you'll need two pieces of ID with your name and address on them to become a member of the video club (£5 membership charge). With Mark Alphabet's willingness to find any rare films for you, and a stock of over 4,000 titles, you need go nowhere else. Beautiful tropical fish add to the pleasure of browsing.

Avalanche

31A Dundas Street, EH3 (556 9955 phone & fax). 23, 27, 37, 47 buses. **Open** 10am-6pm Mon-Sat. **Credit** MC, V. **Map 3 E3**
Kevin Buckle's distinctly individual shop – opened in 1983 – is now a Scottish indie institution, with an eclectic budget range of new and second-hand vinyl and CDs. Especially good for more obscure finds – there's even a category devoted to New Zealand bands.
Branches: 28 Lady Lawson Street, EH3 (228 1939); 17 West Nicolson Street, EH8 (668 2374).

Blackfriars Folk Music Shop

49 Blackfriars Street, EH1 (557 3090 phone & fax). 1, 6, Bridges buses. **Open** 9.30am-5.30pm Mon-Sat. **Credit** AmEx, MC, £TC, V. **Map 9 D2**
Cosy bagpipe and folk music centre, with wide selection of recordings and magazines, plus traditional instruments such as the fiddle, bodhran and, of course, the pipes.
e-mail: scotfolk@compuserve.com
http: www.scotfolk.home.ml.org

Fopp

55 Cockburn Street, EH1 (220 0133/fax 220 3781). 1, 6, 34, 35, Bridges buses. **Open** 9.30am-7pm Mon-Sat; 11am-6pm Sun. **Credit** AmEx, DC, JCB, MC, £TC, V. **Map 9 C2**
Just off the Royal Mile, part of a national independent chain with a reputation for indie and dance vinyl and CDs, but also good for jazz, soul and ska sounds with many special offers among the two floors of well-organised stock.

Record Shak

69 Clerk Street, EH8 (667 7144). Bridges buses. **Open** 10am-6pm Mon-Sat. **Credit** AmEx, MC, £TC, V. **Map 7 G7**
Stocks a wide range of second-hand vinyl and CDs including 1960s/70s rock and pop, jazz and country.

Ripping Music & Tickets

91 South Bridge, EH1 (226 7010/fax 226 1469). Bridges buses. **Open** 9.30am-6.30pm Mon-Fri; 9am-7pm Thur; 9am-6pm Sat; noon-5.30pm Sun. **No credit cards. Map 9 C3**
Sells tickets for rock 'n' pop gigs. See *The List* for events.

Über-Disko

36 Cockburn Street, EH1 (226 2134). 1, 6, Bridges buses. **Open** 9.30am-6pm Mon-Sat (*Festival & Dec* open until 7pm; 11am-5pm Sun). **Credit** AmEx, JCB, MC, £TC, V. **Map 9 C2**
Formerly known as 23rd Precinct, this small, sparse dance shop specialises in house and techno sounds.

Underground Solushun

9 Cockburn Street, EH1 (226 2242/fax 220 5221). 1, 6, Bridges buses. **Open** 10am-6pm Mon-Wed, Sat; 10am-7pm Thur-Fri; noon-5pm Sun. **Credit** JCB, MC, £TC, V. **Map 9 C2**
The best outlet for vinyl dance imports, with a massive selection of house, garage, techno and jungle sounds in a non-intimidating atmosphere. The friendly staff are happy to answer questions, play your choices and offer you tips for a hot night's clubbing.

Virgin Megastore

124-125 Princes Street, EH2 (220 2230/fax 220 1757). Princes Street buses. **Open** 9am-6.30pm Mon; 9.30am-6pm Tue; 9am-6pm Wed; 9am-8pm Thur; 9am-6pm Fri-Sat; 11am-6pm Sun. **Credit** AmEx, MC, £TC, V. **Map 8 A2**
Three floors of mainly mainstream records, CDs, videos and games slap bang in the centre of town. The largest selection in the city, but also the most expensive. Also a ticket centre for gigs and events in both Edinburgh and Glasgow.

Sport & outdoor

Blacks Outdoor Leisure

13-14 Elm Row, EH7 (556 3491). Leith Walk buses. **Open** 9am-5.30pm Mon-Fri; 9.30am-7pm Thur; 9am-5.30pm Sat (*Dec* noon-5pm Sun). **Credit** AmEx, DC, MC, £TC, V. **Map 4 G3**
Stocks a fine selection of rucksacks, clothes and equipment for those who want to stand out from the crowd. Good tent department upstairs.
Branch: 24 Frederick Street, EH2 (225 8686).

Millets

12 Frederick Street, EH2 (220 1551). Princes Street buses. **Open** 9am-5.30pm Mon-Wed, Fri-Sat; 9am-6.30pm Thur (*Festival & Dec* 11am-5pm Sun). **Credit** AmEx, JCB, MC, £TC, V. **Map 8 B1**
City-centre outlet with an excellent range of budget-priced outdoor gear on two floors. The range of tents is unbeatable.

Graham Tiso

115-123 Rose Street, EH2 (225 9486/fax 220 2029). Princes Street buses. **Open** 9.30am-5.30pm Mon, Wed, Fri, Sat; 10am-5.30pm Tue; 9.30am-7.30pm Thur; noon-5pm Sun. **Credit** JCB, MC, £TC, V. **Map 8 B1**
Well-stocked sports shop hidden behind Princes Street.

Toys & games

Aha Ha Ha

99 West Bow, EH1 (220 5252). 2, 12, George IV Bridge buses. **Open** 10am-6pm Mon-Sat (*Festival & Dec* noon-4pm Sun). **Credit** AmEx, JCB, MC, £TC, V. **Map 9 A3**
Cheap and definitely cheerful shop – instantly recognisable by the massive Groucho moustache and glasses over the door – with a huge range of jokes, novelties and disguises and an appealing selection of trashy wigs.

Balloon & Party Shop

3 Viewforth Gardens, EH10 (229 9686 phone & fax). Bruntsfield buses. **Open** 10am-5.30pm Mon-Sat. **Credit** AmEx, MC, £TC, V.
Unassuming small outlet selling banners, balloons of all kinds and party accessories. Decoration service available.

Early Learning Centre

67-83 Shandwick Place, EH2 (228 3244). Haymarket buses. **Open** 9am-5.30pm Mon-Sat. **Credit** MC, £TC, V. **Map 5 C5**
Stocks a range of well-priced, safe educational toys, games and playsets with plenty of toys on hand to try out. Especially good for children's art equipment.
Branches: 61 St James Centre, EH1 (558 1330); Gyle Shopping Centre, South Gyle Broadway, EH12 (538 7172).

Games Workshop

136 High Street, EH1 (220 6540). 1, 6, Bridges buses. **Open** 10am-6pm Mon-Tue; 10am-8pm Wed-Thur; 10am-6pm Fri-Sat; 11am-5pm Sun (*Dec* open from 9am). **Credit** MC, £TC, V. **Map 9 D2**
War-gaming figures and accessories plus regular workshops and battle enactments on their table-top fantasy kingdom.

Cruise *on down for designer delights.*

Monkey Business

167 Morrison Street, EH3 (228 6636). Haymarket buses, then 5-min walk. **Open** 9.30am-5pm Mon-Sat. **No credit cards.** **Map 5 C6**
Bouncy castles available to hire from £50 per day with free delivery, set-up and collection. The shop also has fancy dress hire, fireworks, balloon displays, jokes, novelties, wigs and masks.

Mulberry Bush

77 Morningside Road, EH10 (447 5145). Bruntsfield buses. **Open** 9.30am-12.30pm, 1.30-5pm Mon-Sat (early closing Wed 3.45pm). **Credit** £TC.
Homely, long and narrow suburban shop, south of the city centre, with educational toys and folk crafts – including a beautiful range of handcrafted wooden toys.

Toys Galore

193 Morningside Road, EH10 (447 1006/fax 447 9200). Bruntsfield buses. **Open** 9am-5.30pm Mon-Sat (Jan & Feb 9am-5pm). **Credit** AmEx, MC, £TC, V.
Choc-a-bloc with top toy names at pocket-money prices.

Wonderland

97 Lothian Road, EH3 (229 6428/fax 229 7625). Bruntsfield buses. **Open** 9.30am-6pm Mon-Fri; 9am-6pm Sat (Dec noon-5pm Sun). **Credit** AmEx, MC, £TC, V. **Map 8 A3**
A paradise for kids of all ages with a breathtaking range of classic, horror and sci-fi models.

Department stores

Princes Street is home to most of the major department stores with branches of Debenhams, Frasers,

Marks & Spencer, Bhs and Boots. But the mammoth John Lewis store which is accessible from within the St James Centre or from Leith Street is – along with Jenners (*see box* **Grand old man of Princes Street**) – probably the best of these, with an impressive array of goods on several floors. This is where locals go for everything from a new lamp to a replacement garlic press.

Bhs

64 Princes Street, EH2 (226 2621). Princes Street buses. **Open** 9am-5.30pm Mon-Wed; 9am-8pm Thur; 9am-6pm Fri-Sat; 11am-5pm Sun. **Credit** AmEx, MC, £$TC, V. **Map 8 C2**

Debenhams

109-112 Princes Street, EH2 (225 1320/fax 220 0715). Princes St buses. **Open** 9.30am-6pm Mon-Wed; 9.30am-8pm Thur; 9.30am-7pm Fri; 9am-6pm Sat; noon-5pm Sun (hours vary according to season). **Credit** AmEx, DC, MC, $£TC, V. **Map 8 B2**

Frasers

145 Princes Street, EH2 (225 2472). Princes St buses. **Open** 9am-5.30pm Mon-Wed, Fri; 9am-7.30pm Thur; 9am-6pm Sat; 11am-5.30pm Sun. **Credit** AmEx, MC, £TC, V. **Map 8 A2**

John Lewis

69 St James Centre, EH1 (556 9121/fax 550 3000). Princes St buses. **Open** 9am-5.30pm Tue, Wed, Fri; 9am-7.30pm Thur; 9am-6pm Sat (hours vary during Dec). **Credit** AmEx, SC, £TC. **Map 4 G4**

Marks & Spencer

54 Princes Street, EH2 (225 2301/fax 459 7802). Princes St buses. **Open** 9.30am-5.30pm Mon-Wed; 9am-8am Thur; 9am-7pm Fri; 8.30am-6pm Sat; noon-5pm Sun. **Credit** SC. **Map 8 C2**
Branches: Menswear Store, 104 Princes Street, EH2 (225 5765); 21 Gyle Avenue, EH12 (317 1333/fax 317 1444).

Fashion

Big Ideas

96 West Bow, Grassmarket, EH1 (226 2532). 2, 12, George IV Bridge buses. **Open** 10am-5.30pm Mon-Sat. **Credit** AmEx, MC, £TC, V. **Map 9 A3**
Sizes from 14 up are catered for in this centrally located women's outlet. Its range of upmarket, continental labels offers refreshingly bright and eye-catching styles for daytime and evening wear.

Corniche

2 Jeffrey Street, EH1 (556 3707). 1, 6, Bridges buses. **Open** 10am-5.30pm Mon-Sat (Festival & Dec noon-4pm Sun). **Credit** AmEx, JCB, MC, £TC, V. **Map 9 D2**
Offers a select range of women's clothes by designers such as Moschino, Anna Sui and Thierry Mugler, with regular end-of-line bargains.

Cruise

14 St Mary's Street, EH1 (556 2532/fax 557 5894). 1, 6, Bridges buses. **Open** 10am-6pm Mon-Wed, Fri; 10am-7pm Thur; 9am-6pm Sat; 1-5pm Sun. **Credit** AmEx, DC, MC, £TC, V. **Map 9 D2**
Established outlet with a select range of labels such as Joseph Tricot and Jasper Conran. The minimalist, whitewashed surroundings and pampered service are obviously designed to offset potential heart attacks at the high prices.
Branch: 94 George Street, EH1 (226 3524).

Cult Clothing

7-9 North Bridge, EH1 (556 5003). Bridges buses. **Open** 9.30am-6pm Mon-Wed, Fri, Sat; 10am-7pm Thur; noon-5pm Sun. **Credit** AmEx, MC, £TC, V. **Map 9 C2**
Edinburgh was running a poor second to Glasgow for clubwear until the recent opening of this massive, central retailer, which specialises in labels such as Mambo and Airwalk. Such de rigeur hipness doesn't necessarily come with a sky-high price tag either, with combat trousers averaging around £20 and psychedelic-style dresses from £30.

Kool

22 Victoria Street, EH1 (225 4413/fax 220 4192). 2, 12, George IV Bridge buses. **Open** 10am-6pm Mon-Sat. **Credit** MC, V. **Map 9 B2**
A tiny outlet, but unmissable with its outrageously shiny, holographic interior décor. The clothes are equally funky, and mostly from small independent labels. The kind of place to buy a treat rather than a bargain.

Pie in the Sky

21 Cockburn Street, EH1 (220 1477/fax 225 4080). 1, 6, 34, 35, Bridges buses. **Open** 9.30am-6pm Mon-Wed, Fri; 9.30am-7pm Thur; 9.30am-6pm Sat (*May-Dec* noon-5pm Sun). **Credit** AmEx, MC, £TC, V. **Map 9 C2**
Well-established student haunt close to Waverley Station selling cheap tie-dye and day-glo clubbing gear with all the accessories.

Wacky Enterprises

24 Victoria Street, EH1 (225 7180/fax 220 4192). 2, 12, George IV Bridge buses. **Open** 10am-5.30pm Mon-Wed, Fri; 10am-6pm Thur; 10am-6pm Sat (*Festival & Dec* noon-5pm Sun). **Credit** JCB, MC, £TC, V. **Map 9 B2**
Lots of colourful hippie dresses, tops, trousers and off-kilter bedroom accessories on two packed floors.

Children

New & Junior Profile

88-92 Raeburn Place, Stockbridge, EH4 (332 7928). 20, 28, 80 buses. **Open** 9am-5.30pm Mon-Sat. **Credit** JCB, MC, £TC, V. **Map 2 C3**
Pretty and practical clothes in bright colours and folksy designs. Mid-range prices.

Shoos

8 Teviot Place, EH1 (220 4626). George IV Bridge buses. **Open** 9.30am-5.30pm Mon-Fri; 9am-5.30pm Sat. **Credit** MC, £TC, V. **Map 6 F6**
Small shop specialising in Start-Rite shoes.

Topsy Turvy

18 William Street, EH3 (225 2643). Haymarket buses. **Open** 10am-5pm Mon; 9.30am-5.30pm Tue-Sat. **Credit** AmEx, MC, V. **Map 5 C6**
A cosy West End outlet with tots-to-teens designer clothes from Germany, France and Holland.

Cleaning & repair

Kleen Cleaners

10 St Mary's Street, EH1 (556 4337). 1, 6, Bridges buses. **Open** 8.30am-6pm Mon-Fri; 10am-1pm Sat. **No credit cards. Map 9 D2**
Dry cleaning, plus speedy repairs and alterations.

Canonmills Launderette

7-8 Huntly Street, EH3 (556 3199). 7A, 8, 19, 23, 27, 37, 47 buses. **Open** 8am-8pm Mon-Fri; 8am-5pm Sat, Sun. **Credit** MC, £TC, V. **Map 3 G2**
Same-day dry-cleaning service for items that arrive before noon. Prices from £3 to £5 per item. A wash costs £1.90.

Dress hire

No. 19

19 Grassmarket, EH1 (225 7391). 2, 12 buses. **Open** 11am-5pm Mon-Sat. **Credit** AmEx, DC, MC, £TC, V. **Map 9 A3**
Good selection of fancy evening dresses available, all one-offs and made on the premises with three-day hire from £55.

Highland Laddie

6 Hutchison Terrace, EH14 (455 7505). Slateford rail. **Open** 9.30am-5pm Mon-Sat. **No credit cards.**
Tartan for men and children with good, old-fashioned service and attention to detail. Costs £48 for a full outfit, jacket, waistcoat and shoes; £30-£40 for children's outfits. *e-mail: highlandlad@cableinet.co.uk*

McCalls of the Royal Mile

11 High Street, EH1 (557 3979/fax 557 8546/freephone 0800 056 3056). 1, 6, 34, 35 buses. **Open** 9am-5.30pm Mon-Wed, Fri, Sat; 9am-7.30pm Thur; noon-4pm Sun. **Credit** AmEx, JCB, MC, £TC, V. **Map 9 C2**
Hires out Highland dress for children with a toybox available to amuse them while you wait. Set price of £28.50 for everything bar the shirt and insurance.

Hairdressers

Woods the Barbers

12 Drummond Street, EH8 (556 6716). Bridges buses. **Open** 8.30am-5pm Mon, Tue, Thur, Fri; 9am-1pm Wed; 8.30am-4pm Sat. **No credit cards. Map 7 G6**
Classic barbers in the south of the city that is great for a quick cut – £4 for a short back and sides.

Cheynes

46 George Street, EH2 (220 0777). George St buses. **Open** 9am-5.15pm Mon-Wed, Fri; 9am-6.40pm Thur; 9am-3.40pm Sat. **Credit** MC, V. **Map 8 C2**
Popular Edinburgh chain of hairdressers for men and women, renowned for quality haircuts, perms and colourings. Prices start from around £15. Appointments necessary. **Branches** are too numerous to list here. Check the telephone directory for your nearest.

Patersons SA

129 Lothian Road, EH3 (228 5252 phone & fax). Bruntsfield buses. **Open** 9am-6pm Mon-Fri; 10.30am-7.30pm Thur, 9am-4.30pm Sat. **Credit** AmEx, MC, V. **Map 8 A3**
Bright, comfortable and gay-friendly hairdressers, so popular it had to open up another branch around the corner. Haircut prices start from £20.
Branch: 6-8 Bread Street, EH3 (229 5151).

Fetish

Leather & Lace

8 Drummond Street, EH8 (557 9413). Bridges buses. **Open** 10am-9pm Mon-Sat; noon-9pm Sun. **Credit** JCB, MC, V. **Map 7 G6**
Home to a wide range of toys and equipment for those with an ever-active imagination to match their ever-active bedroom lives. If the knotty problem of restraint comes up, the friendly staff can point you in the right direction. Expansive video section.
Mail order.

Whiplash Trash

53 Cockburn Street, EH1 (226 1005). 1, 6, 34, 35, Bridges buses. **Open** 10.30am-5.30pm Mon-Wed, Fri, Sat; 10.30am-6pm Thur. **No credit cards. Map 9 C2**
Good range of PVC, leather and rubber gear.

New age enlightenment

Perhaps it's the laid-back feel of the city, perhaps it's the wide open spaces, but, for whatever reason, Edinburgh attracts alternative spirits of all kinds – especially in the summer – and while New Age lifestyles are not necessarily more popular than elsewhere, they are certainly well catered for here.

Napiers Dispensary
1 Teviot Place, EH1 (225 5542/fax 220 3981). George IV Bridge buses. **Open** 10am-5.30pm Mon; 9am-5.30pm Tue-Sat. **Credit** MC, £TC, V. **Map 6 F6**
Established in 1860, this respected medical herbalist is well stocked with homeopathic medicines and books, vitamin supplements, organic and ecological toiletries, essential oils, herbal teas and Bach flower remedies. The staff are informed and helpful, while the clinic next door offers a range of services from acupuncture and homeopathy to psychotherapy and osteopathy, as well as herbal treatments.
Branches: Napiers Clinic, 18 Bristo Place, EH1 (225 5542); 35 Hamilton Place, EH3 (315 2130).

Body & Soul Bookshop
52 Hamilton Place, Stockbridge, EH3 (226 3066 phone & fax). 20, 28, 80 buses. **Open** 10am-6pm Mon-Sat (*Dec* open Sun). **Credit** AmEx, DC, MC, £TC, V. **Map 3 D3**
Relaxed, scented and pleasant shop with an interesting range of books, magazines, CDs and gifts related to alternative health, New Age spirituality and gay and lesbian lifestyles.

Crystal Clear
52 Cockburn Street, EH1 (226 7888/fax 225 4080). 1, 6, 34, 35, Bridges buses. **Open** 9.30am-6pm Mon-Wed, Fri, Sat; 9.30am-7pm Thur; noon-5pm. **Credit** JCB, MC, £TC, V. **Map 9 C2**
Tiny but atmospheric shop packed with intriguing books and crystals, Buddhist singing bowls, wind chimes and relaxation tapes. Owner Thom McCarthy has done it all, from running a shopping empire to living in a monastery for ten years and now back to running a shop – albeit spiritual – and is usually around to offer friendly and knowledgeable advice.

The Edinburgh Floatarium
29 North West Circus Place, New Town, EH3 (225 3350/fax 225 3351). 20, 28, 80 buses. **Open** 9am-8pm Mon-Fri; 9am-6pm Sat; 9.30am-4pm Sun. **Credit** JCB, MC, £TC, V. **Map 3 D4**
The sea salt floats are the main attraction here, among various beauty and health treatments. The shop at the front also sells a wide selection of New Age books, crystals and gifts.

The Whole Works
Jackson's Close, 209 Royal Mile, EH1 (225 8092). 1, 6, 34, 35, Bridges buses. **Open** 9am-8pm Mon-Fri; 9am-5pm Sat. **No credit cards**. **Map 9 C2**
Stress management, counselling, acupuncture, aromatherapy, dreamwork, homeopathy and reflexology are just some of the treatments on offer at this alternative therapy centre.

Helios Fountain
7 Grassmarket, EH1 (229 7884/622 7173). 2, 12 buses. **Open** 10am-6pm Mon-Sat; noon-4pm Sun. **Credit** MC, £TC, V. **Map 9 A3**
This homely shop has a café at the back, and a mini-bookshop at the front with a good range of vegetarian and vegan cookery titles, plus incense, Celtic jewellery, crafts, trinkets and a huge selection of beads for necklaces or bracelets.

Jewellery

Joseph Bonnar
72 Thistle Street, EH2 (226 2811/fax 225 9438). George St buses. **Open** 10.30am-5pm Mon-Sat. **Credit** JCB, MC, £TC, V. **Map 8 C1**
Renowned antique jeweller with an extensive selection. Prices start from around £50 up to £20,000.

Scottish Gems
24 High Street, EH1 (557 5731). 1, 6, 34, 35 buses. **Open** 10am-5.30pm Mon-Sat; *Jun-Aug* 10am-6pm Mon-Sat; *Dec* noon-4pm Sun. **Credit** AmEx, DC, JCB, MC, £TC, V. **Map 9 B2**
Amid the twee décor, there is a range of modern Scottish jewellery – including Celtic wedding rings – with reasonable prices starting from £20 for rings.
Branch: 162 Morningside Road, EH10 (447 5579).

Second-hand

WM Armstrong & Son
83 Grassmarket, EH1 (220 5557). 2, 12, George IV Bridge buses. **Open** 10am-5.30pm Mon-Sat. **Credit** MC, V. **Map 9 A3**
The oldest second-hand shop in the capital, originally set up as a gentlemen's outfitter in the Cowgate in 1840, now known for its amazing range of retrowear. New stock arrives daily and prices are reasonable, starting from £15 for evening dresses, £10 for jeans, and £15 for a leather jacket. Look out also for its Rusty Zip shop, which sometimes offers spontaneous, half-price, one-day sales.
Branches: 313 Cowgate, EH1 (556 5977); Rusty Zip, 14 Teviot Place, EH1 (226 4634).

Herman Brown
151 West Port, EH1 (228 2589). 2, 12, 28 buses. **Open** 11.30am-6pm Mon-Sat. **Credit** AmEx, MC, V. **Map 6 E6**
Unusually kitsch bric-a-brac and lamps are as much of a feature as the well-made clothes in this classy retro shop. Prices start at around £3 for tops and under £10 for dresses but can get rather more for period dresses. There's also an eye-catching range of quirky jewellery and a good selection of bags and accessories.

Flip of Hollywood
59-61 South Bridge, EH1 (556 4966/fax 557 6924). Bridges buses. **Open** 9.30am-5.30pm Mon-Wed; 9.30am-5.45pm Thur-Sat (*Festival* noon-5pm Sun). **Credit** JCB, MC, £TC, V. **Map 9 C3**
One of the national chain of American clothing shops. Has seen better days, but it's worth checking out for the extensive range of well-priced jeans, cords and shirts.

Gourmet's delight

Scotland is home to a well-established and vibrant Italian community and Valvona & Crolla is where they go for supplies. The 'gourmet's delight of the north', as it is otherwise known, is a long, narrow Italian food shop famed for its mouthwatering range of Mediterranean delicacies packed into rows and rows of shelves that touch the ceiling.

Ralph Valvona started importing food from Italy for the growing Italian immigrant community in the 1870s, and formed the company in 1934 with Alfonso Crolla (grandfather of the current generation of owners – Victor and Philip Contini, who run the business with Philip's wife Maria). Over the past 60-odd years they've been successfully educating Scots in all things Italian as the Mediterranean diet has become increasingly popular. In recent years they've risen to the challenge of the big supermarkets by going upmarket, concentrating on the quality and source of their ingredients, but the prices have remained reasonable.

The key to their success is specialisation: importing fresh mozzarella from Naples; gathering a library of olive oils; and selling boxes of plump Sicilian tomatoes and fresh wild fungi all year round. Their new café, hidden at the back of the store (*see chapter* **Bistros & Cafés**), allows you to sample the succulent wares and understand just how Valvona & Crolla have earned their reputation.

Valvona & Crolla
19 Elm Row, EH7 (556 6066/fax 556 1668). Leith Walk buses. **Open** 8am-6pm Mon-Wed; 8am-7.30pm Thur-Fri; 8am-6pm Sat. **Credit** AmEx, MC, £TC, V. **Map 4 G3**

15 The Grassmarket
15 Grassmarket, EH1 (226 3087). 2, 12, George IV Bridge buses. **Open** noon-6pm Mon-Fri; 10.30am-5.30pm Sat (*Festival* noon-8pm Mon-Sat; 2-6pm Sun). **No credit cards. Map 9 A3**
Small cavern-like shop with period lace, linen and velvet curtains, plus pre-1950s men's suits, tweed jackets and an impressive selection of trilby hats.

Shoes

Schuh
6 Frederick Street, EH2 (220 0290). Princes Street buses. **Open** 9am-6pm Mon-Wed; 9am-8pm Thur; 9am-8pm Fri, Sat; noon-5pm Sun. **Credit** AmEx, MC, £TC, V. **Map 8 B1**

This popular, 15-year-old Scottish chain has a fantastic range of own-make and brand-name shoes, boots and trainers, including many outrageous styles in their large central outlet. This is the place to go if you need a pair of purple velvet, 16-hole Docs or red, patent leather thigh high boots. Look out for its winter and summer sales.
Branch: 32 North Bridge, EH1 (225 6552).

Barnets Shoes
7 High Street, EH1 (556 3577 phone & fax). 1, 6, Bridges buses. **Open** 9am-5pm Mon-Sat. **Credit** AmEx, JCB, MC, £TC, V. **Map 9 C2**
Small and low-key, this is an unassuming purveyor of high-quality workwear and outdoor shoes and boots at budget prices. Possibly the ultimate recommendation is that this is where the local traffic wardens shop for their shoes.

Specialist

Edinburgh Woollen Mill
453 Lawnmarket, High Street, EH1 (225 1525). 1, 6, 34, 35 buses. **Open** *Sept-May* 9am-5.30pm Mon-Sat; 11am-4pm Sun; *Jun-Aug* 9am-8pm Mon-Fri; 9am-6pm Sat; 11am-5pm. **Credit** AmEx, MC, £$TC, V. **Map 9 B2**
Well-established woollen-wear outlet, with branches scattered around the city, selling good-quality traditional clothes, shawls, rugs and scarves at affordable prices.
Branches: 62 Princes Street, EH2 (225 4966); 139 Princes Street, EH2 (226 3840).

John Morrison Kiltmakers
461 Lawnmarket, High Street, EH1 (225 8149/fax 226 5472). 1, 6, 34, 35 buses. **Open** 9am-5.30pm Mon-Fri; 9am-5pm Sat; 11am-5pm Sun *(Festival & Dec* 9am-9pm Mon-Sat). **Credit** AmEx, DC, JCB, MC, £TC, V. **Map 9 B2**
Traditional outfitter who believes in old-fashioned service. Prince Charlie kilts from £250, vest from £230, shoes from £104, sporrans from £60.

Kate's Costumes
Unit 26, Castle Brae Business Centre, Peffer Place, Peffermill, EH16 (652 0306). 2, 12, 14, 42, 46 buses. **Open** 10am-4pm daily, or telephone for an appointment. **No credit cards.**
Kate has thousands of costumes in stock at her airy, out of town establishment, but if she hasn't got the one you need, she and her two veteran costumier partners can design and make it, whatever the period or theme. Hire prices start at £10 for three days, while a tailored one-off costs from £25 unless you want to keep it after the party.

Kinloch Anderson
Commercial Street/Dock Street, Leith, EH6 (555 1390/fax 555 1392). 10, 16, 22, 32, 52, 88 buses. **Open** *mid Oct-mid Apr* 9am-5pm Mon-Sat; *mid Apr-mid Oct* 9am-5.30pm Mon-Sat. **Credit** AmEx, DC, JCB, MC, £$TC, V. **Map 2 Leith**
Well-established makers and retailers of Highland dress since 1868. This somewhat spartan retail shop, deep in the heart of Leith, is low on atmosphere but offers a full range of traditional tartan clothes and kilts at reasonable prices.

Leith Mills
70-74 Bangor Road, Leith, EH6 (553 5100/fax 553 4415). Great Junction St buses. **Open** *Jun-Oct* 9am-5.30pm Mon-Sat; 10am-5pm Sun; *Nov-May* 10am-5pm Mon-Sat; 10am-4pm Sun. **Credit** AmEx, MC, £$TC, V. **Map 2 Leith**
After the Clan Tartan Centre has tracked down the appropriate tartan for your surname on its computerised archive of over 50,000 names, renowned tailors James Pringle Weavers – within the same building – can fit you out in full Highland dress from upwards of £500.

Tattoos & body piercing

Tribe Body Manipulations
248 Canongate, EH6 (558 9460). 1, 6, Bridges buses. **Open** noon-6pm Mon-Sat. **No credit cards**. **Map 7 G5**
Alternative tattoos and piercing – of everything imaginable – in a small, friendly shop. Prices start from £20. Concession holders are eligible for a 20% discount on Wednesdays. Wide range of original body jewellery.

Bill's Tattoo Studio
72 Elm Row, EH7 (556 5954). Leith Walk buses. **Open** 9am-6pm Mon, Tue; 9am-6pm Thur, Fri; 8am-6pm Sat. **No credit cards.** **Map 4 G3**
Well-established, traditional tattoo parlour with piercing,

Millenary mamma at **Kate's Costumes**.

too. Bill might appear a bit abrasive at first, but he won't let you walk out with anything you'll regret later. Prices start from £15 for both tattoos and piercing.

Household

James Gray & Son
89 George Street, EH2 (225 7381/fax 220 4210). George St buses. **Open** 9am-5.30pm Mon-Sat *(Dec* 11am-5pm Sun). **Credit** £TC. **Map 8 B1**
Traditional city-centre ironmongers and hardware shop with an extensive range of quality goods for the home and garden – although not exactly the cheapest around, expect to pay about 20% more than anywhere else.

Habitat
32 Shandwick Place, EH2 (225 9151/fax 220 3737). Haymarket buses. **Open** 9am-5.30pm Mon-Wed; 9am-7pm Thur; 9am-5.30pm Fri; 9am-6pm Sat; 11.30am-5.30pm Sun (extended hours during Dec). **Credit** AmEx, MC, £TC, V. **Map 5 C5**
Popular household chain store with affordable, attractive furnishings and furniture on three laidback, roomy floors at the west end of Princes Street.

Inhouse
28 Howe Street, EH3 (225 2888/fax 220 6632). 20, 28, 80 buses. **Open** 9.30am-6pm Mon-Wed; 10am-7pm Thur; 9.30am-6pm Fri; 9.30am-5.30pm Sat *(Festival* noon-5pm Sun). **Credit** MC, £TC, V. **Map 3 D4**
Two floors of designer names and high-street brands, with delightful trinkets to catch the eye at every turn. Upstairs is mainly larger furniture – £400 for a chair – downstairs is the real Santa's grotto, ideal for practical but unusual household furnishings.

Lakeland
52 George Street, EH2 (220 3947/fax 220 3962). George St buses. **Open** 9am-5.30pm Mon-Wed, Fri, Sat; 9.30am-5.30pm Thur *(Festival & Dec* open until 7pm Mon-Sat; *Dec* noon-5pm Sun). **Credit** MC, £TC, V. **Map 8 B1**
Two floors of every kitchen accessory you could ever need, and many more eccentric inventions you'd probably never have thought of – and which you'll probably never use. A mini-hoover for crumbs, anyone?

Ware On Earth
15 Howe Street, EH3 (558 1276). 20, 28, 80 buses. **Open** 10am-6pm Mon-Wed, Fri; 10am-7pm Thur; 9.30am-5.30pm Sat *(Dec* noon-4pm Sun). **Credit** AmEx, JCB, MC, £$TC, V. **Map 3 D4**
Bright, rustic shop on the way down to Scotckbridge with a wide range of colourful, handpainted ceramics laid out on pine kitchen furniture.

Food & drink

Delicatessens

Margiotta
*77 Warrender Park Road, EH9 (229 2869). 24(A), 40,
41(A) buses.* **Open** 7.30am-10pm Mon-Sat; 8am-9pm Sun.
Credit MC, V. **Map 6 E8**
It's not cheap – everything's at least 20% more expensive
than elsewhere – but with branches throughout the Old and
New Towns this well-stocked deli is extremely handy when
you're caught without some red pesto at 8pm.
Branches are too numerous to list here. Check the
telephone directory for your nearest.

Peckhams
*155-159 Bruntsfield Place, EH10 (229 7054). Bruntsfield
buses.* **Open** 8am-midnight Mon-Sat; 9am-midnight Sun.
Credit MC, V. **Map 6 D8**
Huge grocers, south-west of the centre, with shelves up to
the ceiling full of tempting luxuries. The place to go for exotic sweet and savoury delicacies and beverages.
Branch: Unit 12, Waverley Rail Station, EH1 (557 9050).

Drink

Better Beverage Company
*43 William Street, EH3 (538 7180/fax 226 6617).
Haymarket buses, then 5-min walk.* **Open** 10am-6pm
Mon-Fri; 10am-5pm Sat. **Credit** £TC. **Map 5 C6**
Even if you don't like coffee, the mouthwatering range of
beans in this unassuming Aladdin's cupboard of caffeine will
make you wish you did.

Oddbins
*223 High Street, EH1 (220 3516). 1, 6, 34, 35, Bridges
buses.* **Open** 11am-9pm Mon-Thur; 11am-10pm Fri, Sat;
12.30-8pm Sun. **Credit** AmEx, JCB, MC, £TC, V.
Map 9 C2
Best of the chain liquor retailers, with eager assistants, a
huge range of beers, wines and liqueurs, plus more
whiskies (including the occasional cask-strength single
malt) to fill a glass with than any of its English branches.
Keep an eye on the sandwich boards outside for details of
tastings.
Branches are too numerous to list here. Check the
telephone directory for your nearest.

Peter Green & Co
*37A-B Warrender Park Road, EH9 (229 5925). 24 (A),
40, 41A buses.* **Open** 9.30am-6.30pm Mon-Thur; 9.30am-
7.30pm Fri; 9.30am-7pm Sat. **Credit** MC, £TC, V. **Map 6
F8**
Diverse selection of wines and over 100 whiskies.

Royal Mile Whiskies
*379 High Street, EH1 (225 3383/fax 226 2772). High St
buses.* **Open** 10am-10pm Mon-Sat; noon-10pm Sun.
Credit AmEx, MC, £TC, V. **Map 9 D2**
Traditional façade and classic range of whiskies inside, with
over 300 varieties available to tantalise the tastebuds.
e-mail: whiskies@demon.co.uk

Scotch Malt Whisky Society
*The Vaults, 87 Giles Street, Leith, EH6 (554 3451/fax
553 1003). Great Junction St buses.* **Open** 10am-5pm
Mon-Wed; 10am-11pm Thur, Fri; 11am-2.30pm, 5-11pm
Sat. **Credit** AmEx, MC, V. **Map 2 Leith**
Unique malt whiskies, bottled direct from single casks, are
available to members only. If you're a bit of a whisky con-
noisseur, forget the commercial malts, phone for a tasting
programme and join the Society. Your tastebuds' pleasure
will more than compensate for the membership fee of £50

for the first year (which includes a bottle of whisky) and £20
per year thereafter.

Scotch Whisky Heritage Centre
*354 Castlehill, The Royal Mile, EH1 (220 0441/fax 220
6288). High Stbuses.* **Open** 10am-6pm Mon-Sun (licensed
from 12.30pm on Sundays). **Credit** AmEx, DC, JCB, MC,
£TC, V. **Map 9 A2**
Try before you buy from the fascinating range at the whisky
centre's friendly bar and gift shop – open to all, whether you
want to go on the accompanying tour (*see chapter*
Sightseeing) or not.

Ethnic

Lupe Pintos Deli
*24 Leven Street, EH3 (228 6241/fax 228 2390).
Bruntsfield buses.* **Open** 10am-6pm Mon-Sat. **No credit
cards.** **Map 6 D7**
Every inch of available space in this small shop is crammed
with Mexican, Spanish and Caribbean products. Whether
you want authentic salsa, American marshmallow Fluff or
a string of chillies, they're all here. If they're not, you can be
sure the dedicated staff will try to get them in.

Pat's Chung Ying Chinese Supermarket
199-201 Leith Walk, EH6 (554 0358). Leith Walk buses.
Open 10am-6pm daily. **Credit** MC, £TC, V. **Map 4 H2**
An exquisite smorgasbord of Chinese foods – frozen, fresh
and packaged – are available in this vast, modern shop.

Specialists

Mr Boni's
*4 Lochrin Buildings, EH3 (229 5319/fax 229 0173).
Bruntsfield buses.* **Open** 10.30am-10.30pm Mon-Wed;
10.30am-11pm Thur; 10.30am-midnight Fri, Sat; noon-
10.30pm Sun. **Credit** AmEx, MC, £TC, V. **Map 6 D7**
This family-run, ice-cream institution opened 75 years ago
and Mr Boni – the grandson of the founder – still thinks up
recipes to add to the rota of 300 imaginative flavours. Pooh
Bear Crunch is a bestseller. All made from fresh, natural
ingredients.

Casey's Confectioners
*52 St Mary's Street, EH1 (556 6082). 1, 6, Bridges
buses.* **Open** 9am-5.30pm Mon, Fri; 9.30am-5.30pm Sat.
No credit cards. **Map 9 D2**
This old-fashioned sweet shop has – happily – hardly
changed since it first opened in 1954 (apart from the prices)
and retains its picture-postcard, art deco exterior. Inside
there are racks of colourfully filled jars of their own, handmade range of mouthwatering sweets fill the otherwise spartan surroundings. Go on, get a 50p bag of Berwick Cockles
and saunter up the Pleasance.

Crombies of Edinburgh
*97-101 Broughton Street, EH1 (557 0111/fax 556
3920). 7A, 8, 9, 19, 39 buses.* **Open** 8am-6pm Mon-
Thur; 8am-7pm Fri; 8am-5pm Sat. **Credit** JCB, MC, £TC,
V. **Map 3 F3**
Sells top quality quality meats from local farms. But their
extensive and inventive range of pies and sausages are what
gets the queues reaching out of the door. Try the venison,
wild boar and apple sausage in your Sunday fry up and
you'll taste why.

Eddie's Seafood Market
7 Roseneath Street, EH9 (229 4207). 24, 40, 41 buses.
Open 9am-6pm Mon-Sat. **No credit cards.** **Map 6 F8**
This large, bright minimalist shop not only has the bustle
and noise of a real market – courtesy of the ever-vocal all-
Chinese staff – but also a wide and well-priced range of fish.

Aye for a bargain

When it comes to places for finding bargains, Edinburgh doesn't have anywhere matching the mammoth splendour of Glasgow's Barras market. But, along with the many antique and second-hand shops, the city has other, less obvious, bargain basements for those who are willing to make the effort.

Charity shops
Opening hours 10am-4pm.
Car boot sales have depleted the bargains to be had in charity shops severely in the past few years, as people put their junk on sale rather than donate it to their local charity shop. But perhaps because most of the takings from each shop still go to a worthwhile cause, they continue to thrive, and many cheap curiosities can still be found, especially in bric-a-brac and books. Several charity shops can usually be found on the high street of any of the capital's villages. However, a few are notoriously well endowed: Stockbridge (Raeburn Place, Deanhaugh Street and Hamilton Place); Morningside (Between Church Hill and the **Canny Mans** pub); Leith Walk (from McDonald Road down into the Kirkgate in Leith); and from Nicolson Street(West Richmond Street) to Newington. Check the *Yellow Pages* for specific addresses.

Greenside Place Car Boot Sale
Level 2 in car park off Leith Street, EH1 (339 8085). Leith Walk buses. **Open** 10am-2pm Sun. **No credit cards. Map 4 G4**
With room for up to 300 car boot stalls – most run by ordinary folk clearing out their attic – this is a mecca for bargain hunters, the kind of place where you really could find an antique vase worth thousands for only £1 among the bric-a-brac, antiques and junk on offer. Haggling is acceptable, although by no means always expected. Keen bargain hunters arrive when the stalls start setting up around 9.30am. By 10.30am the car park is usually heaving with punters. But if you can't get up quite that early on a Sunday morning, the last hour is a good time to get cut-price bargains from what's left. The car boot sale is not dangerous, but, like any other place with crowds, look out for pickpockets and keep your valuables close at hand.

Ingliston Market
Off Glasgow Road (A8), Edinburgh West, past Edinburgh Airport. Scottish Citylink service 900/902 to Glasgow; SMT 16 (platform A) buses, both from St Andrews Bus Station. **Open** 10am-4pm Sun. **Credit** varies.
Probably the nearest Edinburgh has to a Barras set-up, with around 100 traders selling mostly clothes, household and electrical goods and hippie paraphernalia on an outdoor field, plus a car boot sale alongside with anything from 20 to 200 cars depending on the weather. If you want a cheap fleece, novelty clock or lighter, then this place will offer the best prices, although check the quality first

Meadows Fair
Usually first weekend in June, check local press for details. **Open** 10am-6pm Sat; noon-5pm Sun. **Credit** varies. **Map 6 F7**
A two-day festival on the Meadows. Hundreds of stalls sell anything from antiques to home-made arts and crafts, clothes, books, records and plain junk. If the weather is good, it can be a gorgeous, leisurely day out with many bargains to be found, as well as activities for kids, live music, all manner of food stalls and fairground rides.

New Street Indoor Sunday Market
Waverley Car Park, New Street, EH8 (339 8085). 1, 6 buses. **Open** 10am-4pm Sun. **No credit cards. Map 7 G5**
More traders than cars, unless Greenside is full, when the spillover to here can make Sunday morning bargain hunting something of a marathon.

Sam Burn's Junkyard
Take the main road to Prestonpans (if you get to Prestonpans you've missed it – keep your eyes peeled for the easy-to-miss sign indicating where to turn off). **Open** 10am-5pm Mon-Fri.
There's every possibility of finding a gorgeous 1950s dress or a classic Hammond organ for only a few pounds here. But what state your bargain will be in depends on the weather as most of the stuff – which comes from house clearances – is piled higgledy-piggledy outside in huge piles. As extreme as bargain hunting gets.

S Luca
32 High Street, Musselburgh, EH21 (665 2237/fax 653 3828). 15(A), 43, 44 buses. **Open** 9am-10pm Mon-Sat; 10.30am-10pm Sun. **Credit** MC, £TC, V.
Established in 1908, this traditional ice-cream parlour, only 15 minutes by car from the city centre, is ideal for picking up a creamy cone on a daytrip to the countryside.

MacSweens of Edinburgh
118 Bruntsfield Place, EH10 (229 9141). Bruntsfield buses. **Open** 9.30am-5.30pm Tue-Fri; 9.30am-4.30pm Sat. **Credit** MC, V. **Map 6 D8**
So dedicated are the MacSweens to their haggis that every single batch is tasted by one of the family. Vegetarian haggis are also available.

Iain Mellis: Cheesemonger
30A Victoria Street, EH1 (226 6215). 2, 12, George IV Bridge buses. **Open** 9.30am-5.45pm Mon-Fri; 9.30am-5.30pm Sat. **Credit** MC, £TC, V. **Map 9 B2**

Only the most olfactorily-challenged of passers-by could miss the pungent odour from this small, galley-shaped cheesemonger a mere step from the Royal Mile. Try a slice of gubbeen.
Branch: 205 Bruntsfield Place, EH10 (447 8889).

Health & vegetarian

Holland & Barrett
18 Nicolson Street, EH8 (667 6002). Bridges buses. **Open** 9am-5.30pm Mon-Sat. **Credit** AmEx, MC, £TC, V. **Map 7 G6**
Good for basic vegetarian supplies and health supplements.

Nature's Gate
83 Clerk Street, EH8 (668 2067 phone & fax). Bridges buses. **Open** 10am-7pm Mon-Sat; noon-4pm Sun. **Credit** JCB, MC, £TC, V. **Map 7 G7**
Wide range of vegetarian and vegan foods with an impressive selection of organic wines and beers to top it all off.

The grand old man of Princes Street

The ideal place to study Morningside matrons, the pukka ladies of Edinburgh south, is either in the posh tearooms of Jenners, 'the grand old man of Princes Street', or from the hushed balconies of its shopping hall. The world's oldest independent store is also known as the Harrods of Scotland. Thankfully, the prices are far less painful, but it is just as classy. Internationally renowned for its character, quality and old-fashioned efficient service, it's no wonder that the Sultan of Brunei and our own royal family are among Jenners' regular customers.

Visually striking, the current building dates from 1895 – the original store was gutted by fire three years earlier – and the female figures carved into the columns are a homage to the loyalty of Jenners' lady customers, which is where the Morningside matrons come in again, for they are cultural descendants, if not actual relatives, of those early Jenners enthusiasts.

Country customers used to come up to Edinburgh just to spend the entire day in Jenners and it's still perfectly possible – and delightful – to wander around the labyrinthian six floors of this stately store for hours on end, such is the range of items available. It's virtually a small village, with a hairdressers, beauty salon, photographic studio, ATM machine and posting facilities, as well as departments willing and able to fit you and your home out from top to bottom. The extensive haberdashery section and the playground of a toy department are both unbeatable in Edinburgh.

Meanwhile, the cosy foodhall is replete with all the exquisite Scottish goodies you'd expect, including the Jenners range of shortbreads, marmalades and biscuits in its own characteristic packaging, as well as unexpected bargain treats. This is the only place in the city where you'll find such succulent Dijon mustard at such a cheap

Real Foods
37 Broughton Street, EH1 (557 1911/fax 558 3530).
7A, 8, 9, 19, 39 buses. **Open** 9am-6pm Mon-Wed, Fri;
9am-7pm Thur; 9am-5.30pm Sat; 11am-5pm Sun. **Credit**
JCB, MC, V. **Map 3 F3**
A veritable one-stop supermarket for the vegetarian and vegan, even if the prices aren't always cheap.
Branch: 8 Brougham Street, EH3 (228 1201).

24-hour grocers

Alldays
91-93 Nicolson Street, EH8 (667 7481). Bridges buses.
Open 24 hours daily. **Credit** MC, V. **Map 7 G6**
Stock a wide range of food, drink and late night munchies.
Branches: 126 Marchmont Road, EH9 (447 0353); 127-129 Corstorphine Road, EH12 (337 1039).

Costcutter
125 Lothian Road, EH3 (622 7191). Bruntsfield buses.
Open 24-hours daily. **Credit** MC, V. **Map 8 A3**
Stocks a basic range of grocery and household supplies.

Sainsbury's
185 Craigleith Road, Blackhall, EH4 (332 0704). 38, 80 buses. **Open** 8am-8pm Mon-Thur; 8am-10pm Fri, Sat.
Credit AmEx, MC, £TC, V.
Supermarket with an extensive range of quality produce and household supplies, which also has a coffee shop, 3 ATMs, Supasnaps, Sketchley dry cleaners, free parking and assistance for people with mobility difficulties.

Vegetables

Argyle Place
Marchmont, EH9. 24, 40, 41 buses. **Map 6 F8**
A busy strip of fruit and vegetable shops on the south side of the city where locals come for the cheap produce.

Specialist & gifts

Aitken Dott & Son/Miller Graphics
36 North Bridge, EH1 (225 1006/fax 225 8528). Bridges buses. **Open** 9am-5pm Mon-Wed; 9am-7pm Thur; 10am-5pm Sat. **Credit** AmEx, MC, £TC, V. **Map 9 C2**
Centrally located professional suppliers. Split into two parts, the basement specialises in paper and card of all shades, sizes and weights as well as printing facilities. Upstairs is a wide selection of paints, pens, gift cards and stationery.
e-mail: millersgraphics@btinternet.com

Afrika Plus
28 Lochrin Buildings, EH3 (229 7771/fax 622 7139).
Bruntsfield buses. **Open** 9am-5.30pm Mon-Fri; 10am-6pm Sat; 11am-5pm Sun. **Credit** MC, £TC, V. **Map 6 D7**
Tucked away in a Tollcross sidestreet lie unusual West African handicrafts, musical instruments, jewellery and food in this small outlet.

All Things Scottish
9 Upper Bow, EH1 (no telephone). High St buses. **Open** 9am-6pm daily. **Credit** AmEx, DC, JCB, MC, $£TC, V. **Map 9 A2**
This tiny outlet ,right at the top of the Royal Mile scores highly on the tartan tat, tackiness meter with such twee items as fridge magnets featuring teddy bears as pipers as well as the obligatory whisky flavoured condoms. Gets big bonus points for the scary, life-size model piper which dominates the window display.

Robert Cresser
40 Victoria Street, EH1 (225 2181 phone & fax). George IV Bridge buses. **Open** 9.30am-5pm Mon-Sat (*Festival* open until 6.30pm). **No credit cards**. **Map 9 B2**
Generations of Edinburgh families have bought their brushes and brooms here since it was first established in 1873. The dark Dickensian interior and product list have barely changed in over a century.

price. And don't leave the store without visiting the small but perfectly formed wig department, with styles for every mood and whim, from rock star outlandishness to sleek bobs and tight perms – and prices start at only £60 each.

Jenners
48 Princes Street, EH2 (225 2442/fax 220 0327). *Princes St buses.* **Open** 9am-5.30pm Mon, Wed, Fri, Sat; 9.30am-5.30pm Tue; 9am-7.30pm Thur (hours vary according to season). **Credit** AmEx, DC, MC, £TC, V. **Map 8 D2**

Digger
35 West Nicolson Street, EH8 (668 1802 phone & fax). *Bridges buses.* **Open** 10am-6pm Mon-Sat. **Credit** AmEx, JCB, MC, V, £TC. **Map 7 G6**
Small, colourful shop briming over with well-priced crafts and possible presents.

Eden
37-39 Cockburn Street, EH1 (220 3372). 1, 6, 34, 35, Bridges buses. **Open** 9.30am-6pm Mon-Wed, Fri, Sat; 9.30am-7pm Thur; *May-Dec* noon-5pm Sun. **No credit cards. Map 9 C2**
Stocks a mixture of ethnic wooden crafts and textiles together with such brightly coloured oddities as inflatable chairs and furry personal organisers.

Edinburgh Candle Shop
42 Candlemaker Row, EH1 (225 9646 phone & fax). *George IV Bridge buses.* **Open** 10am-6pm Mon-Fri; 10am-5.30pm Sat (*Festival & Dec* open until 8pm). **Credit** AmEx, MC, V. **Map 9 B3**

Tiny-tot's totty at the tacky tartan tat test.

All shapes, sizes, colours and scents of candles for every occasion are crammed into this tiny shop.

Judith Glue: Designer knitwear & crafts
64 High Street, EH1 (556 5443 phone & fax). 1, 6, Bridges buses. **Open** 9.30am-6pm Mon-Sat; 10.30am-6pm Sun. **Credit** £TC. **Map 9 C2**
Orkney-based knitwear designer who also sells Scottish crafts including jewellery, ceramics, stationery and food produce. Her interiors shop, just along the street, concentrates on funky furnishings for the home.
Branch: 60 High Street, EH1.

Paper Tiger
53 Lothian Road, EH1 (228 2790). Bruntsfield buses. **Open** 9.30am-6pm Mon-Wed, Fri; 9.30am-6.30pm Thur; 9.30am-5.30pm Sat (*Festival & Dec* 9am-6.30pm Mon-Sat; noon-5pm Sun). **Credit** JCB, MC, £TC, V. **Map 8 A3**
Stocks funky designs of cards, envelopes, wrapping paper, diaries and notebooks.
Branch: 16 Stafford Street, EH3 (226 2390).

The Pipe Shop
92 Leith Walk, EH6 (553 3561/fax 555 2591). Leith Walk buses. **Open** 8.45am-6pm Mon-Sat. **Credit** AmEx, JCB, MC, £TC, V. **Map 4 J1**
A well-established and down-to-earth puffer's paradise – worth the trek down to the foot of Leith Walk – with a splendid selection of pipes, cigarettes and tobaccos.
http:/www.thepipeshop.com.uk

Mr Wood's Fossils
5 Cowgatehead, Grassmarket, EH1 (220 1344). 2, 12, George IV Bridge buses. **Open** 10am-5.30pm Mon-Sat. **Credit** AmEx, JCB, MC, £TC, V. **Map 9 A3**
Don't be put off by the expensive rarities in the window – inside this low-key treasure trove of archaeological oddities the prices start at under £1 with some of the beautifully cut and polished fossils at very reasonable prices. The ancient bison's legs will cost a bit more.

Return to Sender
*34 Cockburn Street, EH1 (622 7318). 1, 6, Bridges
buses.* **Open** 9.30am-6pm Mon-Wed, Fri-Sat; 9.30am-7pm
Thur *(Festival & Dec* noon-5pm Sun). **Credit** AmEx, DC,
MC, £TC, V. **Map 9 C2**
Home to an eclectic selection of postcards ranging from the
Simpsons to saucy 3D winking ladies. Prices start from 45p.

Round the World
*82 West Bow, EH1 (225 7086/fax 220 6412). 2, 12,
George IV Bridge buses.* **Open** 10am-6pm Mon-Sat.
Credit JCB, MC, £TC, V. **Map 9 A3**
Trendy designer items and joke novelties abound in these
sleek, modern emporia of hipness.
Branches: 15 NW Circus Place, EH3 (225 7800); Gyle
Shopping Centre, South Gyle Broadway, EH12 (538 8889).

Scottish Crafts
*328 Lawnmarket, High St, EH1 (225 4152/fax 220
3741). 1, 6, 34, 35 buses.* **Open** *(Festival* 9am-10pm Mon-Sun). **Credit** AmEx, DC, JCB,
MC, £TC, V. **Map 9 B2**
Amidst the overabundance of tartan kitsch at the top of the
Royal Mile, this shop tops the tackometer. Everything cheesy
the tourist could want – the clan fridge magnets and Mad
Hatter-style tartan hats stand out.
e-mail: scottishcrafts@cableinet.co.uk

Slocombe & Humphreys
*26 St Mary's Street, EH1 (558 9558 phone & fax). 1, 6,
Bridges buses.* **Open** 10am-6pm Mon-Wed, Fri, Sat;
10am-7.30pm Thur *(Festival & Dec* noon-5pm Sun).
Credit AmEx, JCB, MC, £TC, V. **Map 9 D2**
Modern handmade crafts and decorations by various artists,
from the kitsch to the beautiful.

Studio One
*10-16 Stafford Street, EH3 (226 5812/fax 226 6582).
Haymarket buses.* **Open** 9.30am-6pm Mon-Wed, Fri;
9.30am-6.30pm Thur; 9.30am-5.30pm Sat; noon-5pm Sun.
Credit JCB, MC, £TC, V. **Map 5 C5**
Popular basement shop filled with ethnic and trendy gifts
and household furnishings. The children's nook is good for
pocket-money curiosities and novelties. The Morningside
branch is a cook's paradise with a good range of quality
kitchen utensils and crockery.
Branch: 71 Morningside Road, EH10 (447 0452)

George Waterston & Sons
*35 George Street, EH2 (225 5690/fax 220 1479). George
St buses.* **Open** 9am-5.30pm Mon-Wed, Fri, Sat; 9am-
6.30pm Thur *(Dec* open half-hour later; *Festival & Dec*
noon-5pm Sun). **Credit** JCB, MC, £TC, V. **Map 8 B1**
Centrally located veteran stationer, established 1752, with
wide range of cards and writing supplies in a split-level shop,
plus excellent facilities for printing personalised stationery.

Wind Things
*11 Cowgatehead, Grassmarket, EH1 (622 7032 phone &
fax). 2, 12 buses.* **Open** 10am-5.30pm Mon-Sat *(Festival
& Dec* 10am-5.30pm daily). **Credit** AmEx, JCB, MC, £TC,
V. **Map 9 A3**
Every kind of kite from old-fashioned boxes to Chinese drag-
ons hang from the ceiling. Circus props such as plate-spin-
ning equipment, unicycles, juggling knives and practical
guides fill out this bright, modern shop.

White Dove
140 High Street, EH1 (220 1566). 1, 6 buses. **Open**
10am-6pm Mon-Sat; 11am-6pm Sun. **Credit** AmEx, DC,
JCB, MC, £TC, V. **Map 9 C2**
Among the wizard and troll fantasy figures are many ideal
tartan kitsch gifts. You won't want to leave Edinburgh without one of this shop's creepy, porcelain piper dolls.

One-stop shopping

The Gyle Centre
*South Gyle Broadway, EH12 (539 8828/fax 539 8999).
South Gyle rail, then 58 bus.* **Open** 8am-10pm Mon-Fri;
8am-8pm Sat; 9am-7pm Sun. **Credit** varies.
Huge complex of chainstores on the outskirts of the city.

St James Centre
*St James Centre, Leith Street, EH1 (557 0050). Princes
St buses.* **Open** 7.30am-6.30pm Mon-Wed, Fri, Sat;
7.30am-8.30pm Thur; noon-5pm Sun. **Credit** varies. **Map
4 G4**
A dreary, grey fortress behind the east end of Princes Street
housing a range of shops, including the mighty John Lewis.

Waverley Market
*Princes Street, East End, EH1 (557 3759/fax 557 9179).
Princes St buses.* **Open** 8.30am-6pm Mon-Wed, Fri, Sat;
8.30am-7pm Thur; 11am-5pm Sun *(Festival & Dec* open
later). **Credit** varies. **Map 8 D2**
Opened on the site of the old fruit and vegetable market in
1984, Waverley has a horrible, crude concrete exterior, but
inside there are two floors of upmarket, independent outlets
selling clothes and gifts.

Services

Chemists

Boots the Chemist
*101-103 Princes Street, EH2 (225 8331). Princes St
buses.* **Open** 9am-6pm Mon-Wed, Fri, Sat; 9am-7.30pm
Thur; *summer* noon-5pm, *winter* 1-5pm Sun. **Credit**
AmEx, MC, £$TC, V. **Map 8 B2**
The largest store is on Princes Street.
Branches are too numerous to list here. Check the
telephone directory for your nearest.

Electronic supplies

Tandy
25 Shandwick Place, EH2 (228 4360). Haymarket buses.
Open 9am-6pm Mon-Sat; 9am-7.30pm Thur; noon-5pm
Sun. **Credit** MC, V. **Map 5 C5**
Centrally located suppliers of electronic equipment, acces-
sories and parts, with an extensive, well-priced range.
Branch: 27 North Bridge, EH1 (556 0301).

Faxing

Alva Business Centre
*Alva House, 82 Great King Street, EH2 (557 2222). 23,
27, 37, 47 buses.* **Open** 9am-5pm Mon-Fri. **No credit
cards. Map 3 F3**
Faxing – at £2 per page – is only one of the many services
offered at this professional West End company. Others
include rented offices – albeit from £300 per month – word-
processing and translating.

Florists

Clare Florist
*Unit 4, Waverley Steps, EH1 (556 6622/fax 556 7844).
Princes St buses.* **Open** 9am-6pm Mon-Sat. **Credit**
AmEx, JCB, MC, V. **Map 8 D2**
A good selection of classic blooms are available from
various branches, the most central of which is just beside
the train station.
Branch: Jenners, Rose Street entrance (225 7145).

Narcissus

50A Broughton Street, EH1 (478 7447 phone & fax).
7A, 8, 9, 19, 39 buses. **Open** 10am-6pm Mon-Sat; 11am-5pm Sun. **Credit** AmEx, JCB, MC, £TC, V. **Map 3 F3**
Select range of simple but exotic blooms and plants, including impressively tall cacti, all at reasonable prices in a small, low-key shop. Full range of services including international and national deliveries.

Foreign newspapers

International Newsagents

351 High Street, EH1 (225 4827). 1, 6, 34, 35 buses.
Open 6am-6pm Mon-Fri; 7am-6pm Sat; 9am-4pm Sun
(Festival 6-2am Mon-Fri). **No credit cards. Map 9 C2**
Stocks French, Spanish, German and American dailies, plus an extensive range of European magazines.

Internet & e-mail

Cyberia

88 Hanover Street, EH2 (220 4403/fax 220 4405).
Princes St buses. **Open** 10am-10pm Mon-Sat; 11am-8pm Sun. **Credit** £TC. **Map 8 C1**
Spacious Internet café with coffee, snacks and a licensed bar. Surfing costs £2.50 per half-hour (£2 concs) and e-mail accounts start at £12 per month. The public e-mail drop-box facility means friends can send you messages via Cyberia's e-mail address. Your mail will be kept on a list displayed in the café for two weeks; collection costs 50p per mail.
e-mail: edinburgh@cybersurf.co.uk
http: www.cybersurf.co.uk
http: www.dewars.cybersurf.co.uk (web camera)

Web 13

13 Bread Street, EH3 (229 8883/fax 229 9899).
Bruntsfield buses. **Open** 9am-10pm Mon-Fri; 9am-6pm Sat; noon-6pm Sun. **No credit cards. Map 8 A3**
Accessible and friendly cyber-café in the financial district. Offers the full range of internet and web training. Surfing costs from £2.50 per half-hour (£2 concs) and e-mail accounts are from £20 for six months. The all-day café has an extensive and cheap menu.
e-mail: ian@web13.co.uk
http: www.web13.co.uk

Locksmiths

City Locksmiths

5-3 Dorset Place, EH11 (Freephone 0500 88 99 41/0800 980 8141). 10, 27 buses. **Open** 24 hours daily. **Credit** AmEx, JCB, MC, £TC, V. **Map 5 C7**
City-centre locksmiths with a 24-hour service.

Mobile phones

Carphone Warehouse

80A Princes Street, EH2 (226 3155/fax 225 8526).
Princes St buses. **Open** 9am-5.30pm Mon-Fri; 9am-7pm Thur; 9am-6pm Sat; 11am-5pm Sun. **Credit** AmEx, MC, V. **Map 8 A2**
Vast, well-priced selection of mobile phones and pagers.
Branches: 62 Haymarket Terrace, EH12 (337 6771); 24 Dalziel Place, London Road, EH7 (661 7005).

Opticians

Dollond & Aitchison

50 St James Centre, EH1 (558 1149). Princes Street buses. **Open** 9am-5.30pm Mon-Sat; 9am-7pm Thur. **Credit** AmEx, JCB, MC, V. **Map 4 G4**

Wide range of quality frames. Most repairs can be done on the premises on the same day.
Branches: 56 Newington Road, EH9 (667 6442); 13 Queensferry Street, EH2 (225 2117).

Vision Express

Units 12-14, St James Centre, EH1 (556 5656/fax 556 3555). **Open** 9am-5.30pm Mon,Wed, Fri, Sat; 10am-5.30pm Tue; 9am-7pm Thur; noon-5pm Sun. **Credit** MC, £TC, V. **Map 4 G4**
Huge selection of spectacles to choose from, most ready within an hour. Prices from £40 for single-vision lenses.

Photocopying

Most newsagents, independent chemists and art shops offer cheap – although not necessarily good quality – photocopying facilities from 4p for an A4 copy. Look out for the yellow and black signs hanging outside shops.

Photo-processing

There are numerous branches of photo-processing shops such as Supasnaps around the city, but chemists are generally cheaper and offer all the same facilities, including one-hour processing, although this service normally carries a premium.

SupaSnaps

94-96 South Bridge, EH1 (225 9250). Bridges buses.
Open 9am-5.30pm Mon-Sat. **Credit** AmEx, MC, £TC, V. **Map 8 D3**

Travel

Campus Travel

53 Forrest Road, EH1 (668 3303/fax 225 8572/telesales 668 3303). George IV Bridge buses. **Open** 9am-5pm Mon-Sat; 9.30am-5pm Wed. **Credit** AmEx, MC, £TC, V. **Map 6 F6**
Popular Southside student and youth travel agent. Excellent for adventure travel, but be prepared to wait a while to be served – there's rarely a quiet period in the day.

Edinburgh Travel Centre

92 South Clerk Street, EH8 (667 9488). Bridges buses.
Open 9am-5.30pm Mon-Fri; 10am-1pm Sat. **Credit** AmEx, MC, £TC, V. **Map 7 H7**
Specialises in student and youth travel, but also provides a reliable and well-informed source of information for travellers of all ages.
Branch: 3 Bristo Square, EH1 (668 2221).

Go Blue Banana

12 High Street, EH1 (556 2000/fax 558 8400). 1, 6, Bridges buses. **Open** 9am-5pm Mon-Sat; 10am-4pm Sun. **Credit** JCB, MC, £TC, V. **Map 9 C2**
Organises a range of budget tours of the Scottish Highlands – including a jump-on, jump-off bus that allows you to plan your own itinerary. Prices start at £75 for a three-day tour and £139 for a six-day tour.

Haggis Backpackers

11 Blackfriars Street, EH1 (557 9393/fax 558 1177). 1, 6, Bridges buses. **Open** 8am-7pm Mon-Fri; 8am-6pm Sat; 8am-6pm Sun. **Credit** MC, £TC, V. **Map 9 D2**
Interesting, off-beat and laidback tour operator run by travellers for travellers. Just round the corner, and offering similar packages, to Go Blue Banana.
e-mail: info@haggis-backpackers.com

Restaurants

The world's chefs have come banging on Edinburgh's doors – just don't mention the haggis nouvelle.

The days when Scotland could be considered a culinary backwater of haggis, Scotch eggs, too much fat and no vegetables are long past. Edinburgh's restaurants are increasingly diverse in their cuisine: global influences combine with locally sourced produce to create sumptuous and innovative dishes. The Auld Alliance with France finds a particularly delicious expression on this front. Nor are vegetarian options neglected – while there are several completely vegetarian restaurants, most establishments include more than a token option. This chapter has been prepared with the help of *The List* magazine's *Eating and Drinking Guide 1998*, available from newsagents and bookshops price £2.50.

American

Bell's Diner
7 Stephen Street, EH3 (225 8116). 20, 28, 80(A/B) buses. **Open** 6-10.30pm Mon-Fri; noon-10.30pm Sat; noon-4pm, 6-10.30pm Sun. **Average** £8.50. **Credit** MC, £TC, V. **Map 3 D3**
An Edinburgh institution in the one-time hippie heartland of Stockbridge, standing as an ever-reliable benchmark for what real, quality burgers – the house speciality, along with steaks – should taste like. Both beef and chicken varieties come in 4, 6 and 8oz sizes, accompanied by toppings, salads and fries. No less attention is devoted to the veggie versions, rated by many as the capital's best, while portions tend towards the ample side of generous.

Hard Rock Café
20 George Street, EH2 (260 3000). George St buses. **Open** 11.30am-1am daily. **Average** £14. **Credit** AmEx, MC, £$TC, $US, V. **Map 8 B1**
Burgers à gogo at this city-centre Caledonian outpost of the famous rock'n'roll chain, opened in 1998. Choose between five main varieties, then mix'n'match from the array of available side orders. The more adventurous might consider the barbecued ribs, with some unusual sauces on offer, while both smaller appetites and smaller people are well catered for with snacks, sandwiches and salads on the one hand, and a kids' menu on the other. Plus there's the thrill of seeing one of Rod Stewart's old shirts on display.

Mamma's
30 Grassmarket, EH1 (225 6464). 2, 12 buses. **Open** noon-11pm Sun-Thur; noon-midnight Fri, Sat. **Average** £7.50. **Credit** MC, £TC, V. **Map 9 A3**
Billing itself as Edinburgh's home of American-style pizza, this long-established Old Town diner and its newer east-side sister command a loyal, if not diehard, following for the crisp, chewy perfection of its bases and the myriad possibilities offered by the 45 different toppings. With pizza so emphatically centre-stage, the rest of the menu has less to recommend it, but parents will find the child-friendly facilities at

Canonmills a bonus, while the Grassmarket original sits in the midst of that atmospheric street's boisterous pub scene.
Branch: 1 Howard Street, Canonmills, EH3 (558 7177).

Caribbean

Caribbean Connection
3 Grove Street, EH3 (228 1345). 2(A), 12(A) buses. **Open** *winter* 7-10pm Tue-Sat; *summer* 6-10pm Tue-Sat. **Closed** Sun, Mon. **Average** £13.50. **Unlicensed.** **Corkage** free. **Credit** MC, £TC. **Map 5 C7**
An oasis of delights near Haymarket Station, Edinburgh's only Caribbean restaurant is a tiny, wood-panelled cabin decked out in tropical kitsch with steel band music to add to its air of conviviality. The menu offers such curiosities as duppy umbrella – a starter of mushrooms in a sweet, rich sauce; and main courses like Jamaican wet jerk rub – barbecued chicken or pork marinated with herbs and spices. Busy, cheerful and relatively inexpensive.

Chinese

Chinese Home Cooking
34 West Preston Street, EH8 (668 4946). Bridges buses. **Open** noon-2pm, 5.30-11.30pm Mon-Fri; 5.30-11.30pm Sat-Sun. **Average** £7. **No credit cards.** **Map 7 H7**
This friendly little restaurant remains something of a local institution, offering unbeatable value. In addition to favourite dishes such as chicken or duck in bean and chilli sauce, the chef offers daily specials, while fresh seafood, dim sum or vegetarian options can be ordered in advance. The three-course business lunch is a bargain (£4), as is the range of set dinners (two people, two courses £13.80). A favourite student haunt, the restaurant also has a loyal local following.

Loon Fung
2 Warriston Place, EH3 (556 1781). 7A, 8(A), 9(A), 23, 27, 37 buses. **Open** noon-11.30pm Mon-Thur; noon-1am Fri; 2pm-1am Sat; 2pm-midnight Sun. **Average** £12. **Credit** AmEx, JCB, MC, £TC, V. **Map 3 F2**
Situated at Canonmills, a short distance from the New Town and Stockbridge, Loon Fung offers a wide range of meat, fish and vegetarian dishes to suit most pockets. The lengthy opening hours reflect its unfailing popularity. Divided between two tastefully decorated floors, it boasts a busy, yet low-key, atmosphere, while the food ranges from dim sum starters to a bewildering array of speciality main dishes: staff are always happy to advise.

Fish

The Café Royal Oyster Bar
17A West Register Street, EH1 (556 4124). Princes St buses. **Open** noon-10.15pm Mon-Sat; 12.30-10.15pm Sun. **Average** £23. **Credit** AmEx, DC, JCB, MC, £$TC, V. **Map 8 D1**
Oysters and ornate surroundings draw crowds to this

You've got good taste – **Suruchi** *has more to offer than the average curry house. Page 127.*

renowned Edinburgh establishment, where eyes can feast on the splendid Victorian surrounds, while palates are caressed by sumptuously prepared fish and seafood.

Creelers

3 Hunter Square, EH1 (220 4447). Bridges buses. **Open** noon-2.30pm, 5.30-10.30pm Mon-Thur; noon-2.30pm, 5.30-11pm Fri, Sat; 5.30-10.30pm Sun. **Average** *bistro* £15; *restaurant* £25. **Credit** MC, £TC, V. **Map 9 C2**
The city-slicker offshoot of Creelers' long-established restaurant and smokehouse on the Isle of Arran, offering a choice of bistro-style or more formal dining, depending on whether you sit to the fore or rear. The fish-based menu and daily specials are determined by what's fresh and in season, but the seafood platter and bouillabaisse are always popular, while more adventurous creations range from paupiette of turbot filled with salmon mousse to smoked salmon on orange and basil fumet. Imaginative meat and vegetarian dishes also feature on all the menus – bistro, restaurant and table d'hôte lunch – which can often be combined if you ask nicely.
No smoking in restaurant before 2pm or 9.30pm.

Fingal's Cave

24A Stafford Street, EH3 (225 9575). Haymarket buses. **Open** noon-2pm, 6.30-10.30pm Tue-Sat. **Closed** Sun-Mon. **Average** £12.50. **Credit** JCB, MC, £TC, V. **Map 5 C6**
Opened relatively recently in a West End basement, Fingal's Cave provides a haven for lovers of all things fishy. Dishes range across the classic to the contemporary, from grilled lobster (available all year round) to squid ink-dyed black noodles with mussels and scallops in saffron cream. Airy, marine-style blue and white décor picks up the menu's theme, while meat and vegetarian options are always available for pisciphobe companions. A three-course business lunch is available for £5.90 whereas evening meals are à la carte. Home-made ice-cream is a popular house speciality.

Ship on the Shore

24-26 The Shore, Leith, EH6 (555 0409). 1, 6, 10A, 32, 52 buses. **Open** noon-midnight Mon-Thur; noon-1am Fri; 11am-1am Sat; 11am-midnight Sun. **Set lunch** £6.50 three courses. **Average dinner** £20. **Credit** AmEx, MC, £TC, V. **Map 2 Leith**
Decorated to a nautical theme in keeping with its waterfront location, the Ship combines a relaxed bar-cum-restaurant atmosphere with quality fish-led cuisine. Dishes range from the delicate – whole sea bream in dill and lime butter – to the hearty – baked haddock in Orkney cheddar sauce – supplemented by a meat- or fowl-based alternative. A two-course set menu draws a busy lunchtime crowd, while evening diners can choose from both table d'hôte and à la carte selections. The highlighted 'wine of the month' from a diverse list is generally a good-value bet. Breakfasts served at weekends (11am-2pm).

The Shore

3-4 The Shore, Leith, EH6 (553 5080). 1, 6, 10A, 32, 52 buses. **Open** *Bar* 11am-11pm Mon-Sat; 12.30-11pm Sun. *Restaurant* noon-2.30pm, 6.30-10.30pm Mon-Sat; 12.30-3pm, 6.30-10.30pm Sun. **Average** £15. **Credit** AmEx, JCB, MC, £TC, V. **Map 2 Leith**
The Shore's relaxed atmosphere makes it an ideal place for informal dining, whether in the flower-bedecked restaurant or cosy, wood-panelled bar. Fresh fish and seafood are simply presented in dishes such as monkfish tail grilled with leeks and wild mushrooms, while desserts include French-style fruit tarts and sticky toffee pudding. A two-course set lunch is offered for £6.95. A live folk session featuring some of Edinburgh's top players takes place in the bar every Wednesday and Saturday night.
No smoking.

The Waterfront

1C Dock Place, Leith, EH6 (554 7427). 10A, 16, 22A, 32, 52 buses. **Open** noon-9.30pm Mon-Fri; noon-10pm

Sat; 12.30-10pm Sun. **Average** £16. **Credit** AmEx, MC, £TC, V. **Map 2 Leith**
This lively and relaxed bar and bistro, housed in a converted steamship passenger waiting room, features original wooden booths in the bar area, while the beautifully appointed conservatory restaurant has a huge grapevine that shades the view over the dockside. A wide-ranging, consistently tasty fish menu also offers steak, poultry and vegetarian options. During the summer, a pontoon is opened for al fresco dining, along with a marquee serving a tapas menu.
No-smoking conservatory.

French

La Bonne Vie
49-51 Causewayside, EH9 (667 1110). Bridges buses, then 5-min walk. **Open** noon-2pm, 6-11pm Mon-Sat. **Closed** Sun. **Set lunches** £5 two courses, £6 three courses. **Set dinner** £12.95 two courses, £14.95 three courses. **Credit** AmEx, DC, MC, £TC, V. **Map 7 H8**
Offering table d'hôte French cuisine in intimate, stone-walled surroundings, complete with an open fireplace, this local favourite makes full and expert use of Scottish produce. Dishes range from a vinous venison ragout to salmon escalope in lemon and lime butter, while the home-made dessert selection should set the seal on your sighs of satisfaction.

Le Café Saint-Honoré
34 Thistle Street Lane, EH2 (226 2211). Princes St buses, then 5-min walk. **Open** noon-2.15pm, 7-10pm Mon-Fri; 7-10pm Sat. **Closed** Sun. **Average** £22.50. **Credit** AmEx, DC, JCB, MC, £TC, V. **Map 8 B1**
Decorated in traditional French café style, combining elegant mirrorwork with a chequered floor and jazz soundtrack, this grand but welcoming restaurant brings together Scottish ingredients and French traditions, with a Mediterranean twist. It's a consistently rewarding mélange, resulting in dishes like roasted lamb with rosemary and couscous, or steaks garnished with wild mushrooms and garlic, accompanied by an unusually creative vegetable selection. Desserts are an equally strong point, while the décor provides a conducive backdrop for lingering over coffee and cognac. Booking advised for late suppers.
No smoking in main dining area.

Chez Jules
1 Craig's Close, 29 Cockburn Street, EH1 (225 7007). 1, 6, 34, 35 buses. **Open** noon-3pm, 6-11pm Mon-Sat; 6-11pm Sun. **Average** £9. **Credit** MC, £TC, V. **Map 9 C2**
Twin offshoots of the Pierre Victoire chain, offering a Gallic take on the cheap'n'cheerful. Always tending towards the hectic rather than the intimate, the atmosphere can be chaotic – a problem exacerbated, charmingly, by the largely French staff's often limited English. The menu confines itself to just four or five choices for each course, with meat and fish dishes exemplifying the virtues of simple preparation and uncluttered flavours, while the veggie options vary wildly, from sensational to sorely disappointing. The budget-priced set lunch (£5.90 for 3 courses) keeps both places busy during the day.
Branch: 61 Frederick Street, EH2 (225 7983).

La Cuisine d'Odile
The French Institute, 13 Randolph Crescent, EH3 (225 5685). George St buses. **Open** noon-2pm Tue-Sat. **Closed** Sun, Mon. **Average** £6.50 . **Unlicensed**. **Corkage** £1. **No credit cards**. **Map 5 C5**
If you really want to recreate the French art of lunch, this is the place to come, housed downstairs from the cultural embassy of the Institut Français. Closed in the evenings, it offers a daily-changing choice of three starters, entrées and desserts, with the emphasis on local and seasonal ingredi-

ents, plus the eponymous Odile's magic home-cooking touch. Relaxed but proficient service completes a memorably civilised culinary experience: well worth seeking out.

Howie's
75 St Leonard's Street, EH8 (668 2917). Bridges buses, then 5-min walk. **Open** 6-10pm Mon; noon-2pm, 6-10pm Tue-Sun. **Set lunch** £6.95 two courses, £7.95 three courses. **Set dinner** £15.95 three courses. **Credit** AmEx, JCB, MC, £TC, V. **Map 7 H7**
Small and intimate, the three Howie family restaurants – scattered between the South Side, West End and Tollcross areas – offer a warm welcome in casual but extremely civilised surroundings. Atmospheric lighting and simple furnishings complement the Scottish/French menu. Dinner is chosen from a fixed-price, three-course menu, which changes daily, with Howie's priding itself on fresh local produce. Well-judged portions ensure that the requisite wee gap is left for a seductive home-made dessert selection, while the bargain-priced house wine (£4.95 for a bottle) helps wash it all down.
Branches: 208 Bruntsfield Place, EH10 (221 1777); 63 Dalry Road, EH11 (313 3334).

Malmaison
1 Tower Place, EH6 (555 6969). 1, 6, 10A, 32, 52 buses, then 5-min walk. **Open** 7-10am, noon-2.30pm, 6-10.30pm daily. **Average** £15. **Credit** AmEx, DC, MC, V. **Map 2 Leith**
Strikingly housed in a former seaman's mission by the Leith shore, Malmaison offers a welcome alternative to stereotypical hotel fare, illustrated by the fact that most of its diners are non-residents. The atmosphere is one of low-key sophistication, with the brasserie's interior designed by the team behind Glasgow's prestigious **One Devonshire Gardens**. The modestly proportioned menu specialises in expertly prepared French staples like moules marinière and steak frites, alongside more unusual side-dishes such as aubergine frites or braised fennel with ginger, with the emphasis always on bringing out the flavour of quality ingredients.

Pierre Victoire
10 Victoria Street, EH1 (225 1721). George IV Bridge buses. **Open** noon-3pm, 6-11pm daily. **Average** £9. **Credit** MC, £TC, V. **Map 9 B2**
The UK-wide ubiquity of Pierre Levicky's franchise chain made the chef/proprietor one of Edinburgh's best-known success stories. But exponential expansion eventually upset the shrewd balance of decent cooking and ultra-keen pricing that created the winning formula: the chain was in the hands of the receiver at the time of writing. The diversity of flavours in Levicky's recipes mean that there is no such thing as a typical dish but the likes of fanned avocado with crab meat or fillet of red snapper with leek fricassée give an idea.
Branches are too numerous to list here. Consult the *Phone Book* for your nearest.

The Pompadour
Caledonian Hotel, Princes Street, EH1 (459 9988). Princes St buses. **Open** 7-10.15pm Tue-Sat. **Closed** Sun, Mon. **Average** £45. **Credit** AmEx, DC, JCB, MC, £TC, V. **Map 8 A2**
Not for the financially faint-hearted, but an ideal venue for a special occasion or treat, the **Caledonian Hotel's** upstairs restaurant doesn't stint on the luxury trimmings, with its ornate salon-style décor and resident pianist, while the service is impeccably drilled. The menu's central French bias combines with some artful slumming in dishes such as monkfish with confit of tomato and mushy peas and passes the test of a simple classic like asparagus Hollandaise with flying colours, while desserts often centre alluringly on exotic fruits. Not exactly dropping-in-for-a-bite territory – sartorially casual types are probably best giving it a miss – but a real eating experience.

BANN'S

vegetarian cafe

5 Hunter Square
Edinburgh
EH1 1QW
Reservations:
0131 226 1112
http://www.scoot.co.uk/banns/

Take away welcome
Credit cards accepted
LICENSED

Voted "Top budget restaurant in Edinburgh" 1997 and 1998
- By 'The List' readers

"Brilliant combinations of flavours, textures and fresh herbs".
- Scotland on Sunday

"The most exciting salad bar in the city".
- BBC Good Food

"Sophisticated vegetarian food".
- Elle Magazine

"A real find"
- New York Times

Le Sept

7 Old Fishmarket Close, EH1 (225 5428). 1, 6, 34, 35 buses. **Open** noon-2pm, 6-10.30pm Mon-Thur; noon-11.30pm Fri; noon-11pm Sat; noon-10pm Sun. **Average** £13. **Credit** AmEx, DC, JCB, MC, £TC, V. **Map 9 B2**
Tucked away down a close off the middle of the Royal Mile, Le Sept is an Edinburgh favourite, thanks to its pleasing bistro-style décor (with seating outside in summer) and consistently satisfying cooking. Two separate rooms keep smokers and non-smokers amicably apart, while the collection of Robert Doisneau photographs highlights the menu's French foundations. Crêpes are always a popular option, as is the bargain-priced set lunch. Vegetarians are routinely well catered for with dishes such as walnut ravioli with a choice of four sauces.

The Vintner's Rooms

The Vaults, 87 Giles Street, EH6 (554 6767). Great Junction St buses. **Open** noon-2pm, 7pm-midnight Mon-Sat. **Average** £25. **Credit** AmEx, MC, £TC, V. **Map 2 Leith**
One of Edinburgh's most arrestingly-housed restaurants, the Vintner's Rooms occupies a former wine warehouse in Leith. The candlelit dining room takes up the central vaulted space and the adjoining room houses the bar and an open fire and offers a cheaper bill of fare at lunchtime. The main menu reflects Scotland's specialities – oysters, crab, scallops, venison, black pudding and beef. Sauces and garnishes make imaginative use of home-made conserves, rhubarb, heather honey and spices from Asia. The wine list features over 150 varieties, including some excellent value house wines.
No smoking.

Indian

Bombay Bicycle Club

6 Brougham Place, EH3 (229 3839). Bruntsfield buses. **Open** noon-2pm, 5.30pm-midnight daily. **Average** £12. **Credit** AmEx, MC, £TC, V. **Map 6 E7**
High standard Bengali menu that, while catering mainly for the traditionalist, allows the adventurous to break from the norm by way of the chef's specialities. As the name suggests, there is a bicycle theme in evidence here, with prints of bicycles lining the unusual wicker-covered walls.

The Far Pavilions

10-12 Craigleith Road, EH4 (332 3362). 38, 80(B) buses. **Open**. noon-2.30pm, 5.30pm-midnight Mon-Fri; 5.30pm-midnight Sat. **Closed** Sun. **Average** £16. **Credit** AmEx, DC, MC, £TC, V.
Worth the trek from the city centre, the Far Pavilions endeavours to make authentic Indian food accessible without compromise. The one-chilli/two-chilli symbols of hotness indicated in the menu are the real thing: one chilli is serious and two extreme. Concentrating on Goan and Southern Indian recipes, with numerous fish dishes, the Pavs is a tasty reminder of the complexity of Indian cuisine.

Khushi's

16 Drummond Street, EH8 (556 8996). Bridges buses. **Open** noon-3pm, 5-9pm Mon-Thur; noon-3pm, 5-9.30pm Fri-Sat. **Closed** Sun. **Average** £8. **Unlicensed**. **Corkage** free **No credit cards**. **Map 7 G6**
No frills, yet tasty curry. The down-to-earth approach means the surroundings are more akin to a café than a restaurant, but that's part of the beauty of the place. The lamb bhuna and the fish curry are popular, while additions to the menu have increased the choice of starters and veggie dishes.

Mother India

10 Newington Road, EH8 (662 9020). Bridges buses. **Open** 5.30-10.30pm Mon-Thur; noon-2pm, 5.30pm-midnight Fri;

4pm-midnight Sat; 3-10.30pm Sun. **Average** £11. **Credit** AmEx, MC, £TC, V.
A sweeping staircase, fireplaces and three dining areas – spread over two floors and lit by chandeliers – create an intimate but surprisingly relaxed atmosphere in this Georgian townhouse. The sister restaurant to Glasgow's flourishing Mother India, these premises offer a comprehensive selection of authentically prepared dishes. There is a wide choice of starters; main course portions are generous; and the service is attentive without being intrusive. A range of special offers includes a kids' menu (under-12s eat free on Sundays) and a pre-theatre menu (5-7pm Mon-Sat).

Pataka

190 Causewayside, EH9 (668 1167). Bridges buses. **Open** noon-2pm, 5.30-11.30pm daily. **Average** £10. **Credit** AmEx, MC, £TC, V. **Map 7 H8**
The Mackintosh-style exterior of this Southside restaurant provides an unusual contrast to the Bengali-style menu, although the Pataka breathes an air of understated elegance that's matched by the quality of food and service. The menu contains pages of mouthwatering dishes, including vegetarian options, and the food measures up to the puff. The informal atmosphere lends itself to intimate occasions, making Pataka a discreet jewel in Edinburgh's restaurant crown.

Suruchi

14A Nicolson Street, EH8 (556 6583). Bridges buses. **Open** noon-2pm, 5.30-11.30pm daily. **Average** £14. **Credit** MC, V. **Map 7 G6**
The menu at Suruchi (Sanskrit for good taste) is not the familiar list of 50 ways to do a curry. On offer here is a sublime array of intriguing dishes. The recipes originate from throughout India; every three to four weeks Suruchi holds a regional gourmet festival, highlighting a specific regional cuisine and culture. Not much in the way of imaginative desserts, but lassi makes for a refreshing substitute.

Italian

Ciao Roma

64 South Bridge, EH1 (557 3777). Bridges buses. **Open** noon-2pm, 5-11pm Sun-Thur; noon-2pm, 5-11.30pm Fri, Sat. **Average** £13. **Credit** AmEx, DC, JCB, MC, £TC, V. **Map 9 C3**
This 155-seat restaurant on two floors attracts a mixed clientele of students, professionals and families. A popular two-course lunch menu includes a main course with a choice of starter or dessert, plus a complimentary glass of house wine to wash it down, all for £5.50 (Mon-Sat). Ciao Roma offers value for money and fast service. It's also handy for the **Festival Theatre**.

Cosmo

58A North Castle Street, EH2 (226 6743). Princes St buses. **Open** 12.30-2.15pm, 7-10.45pm Mon-Fri; 7-10pm Sat. **Closed** Sun. **Average** £30. **Credit** AmEx, MC, £TC, V. **Map 8 A1**
Soon to celebrate 30 years of offering good food to discerning diners, Cosmo offers first-rate fish dishes and an elegant cocktail bar to a clientele who always return for more. The ambience is pleasantly formal – jacket and tie are advised – and booking is essential.

Raffaelli's

10 Randolph Place, EH3 (225 6060). George St buses. **Open** 12.15-9.30pm Mon-Fri; 6.15-10.30pm Sat. **Closed** Sun. **Average** £22.50. **Credit** AmEx, DC, JCB, MC, £TC, V. **Map 5 C5**
High-class food in sombre surrounds. Dark green walls are hung with Italian architectural prints, music plays softly in the background and the 14 linen-swathed tables are widely spaced. Seafood is a speciality, as is the veal. The whole

unhurried experience (those enjoying lunch can stay all afternoon) can be rounded off with a mound of profiteroles.

La Rusticana
88-90 Hanover Street, EH2 (225 2227). Princes St buses.
Open noon-2pm, 5-11pm daily. **Average** £15. **Credit** AmEx, DC, JCB, MC, £TC, V. **Map 8 C1**
One of the best of the pizza/pasta places in the city centre, Hanover Street's La Rusticana has all the makings of a great night out. The service is exuberantly Italian: a flourish welcomes every dish, along with the obligatory smooth talk. It's just the place for parties of any size, with the restaurant stretching through three rooms. The menu is reasonably priced, with a huge variety of dishes. Booking is advisable at dinner. The Cockburn Street branch tends to attract a younger, livelier crowd.
Branch: 25-27 Cockburn Street , EH1 (225 2832).

Scalini
10 Melville Place, Queensferry Street, EH3 (220 2999). George St buses. **Open** noon-2.30pm, 6-10pm Mon-Sat. **Closed** Sun. **Average** £14. **Credit** AmEx, DC, MC, V. **Map 5 C5**
Scalini is the sister restaurant to the much-admired Silvio's in Leith and, like its dockside counterpart, it boasts an imaginative menu. Traditionalists will coo over old favourites like calf's liver with sage and butter, while the more adventurous will be tempted by dishes such as chestnut tagliatelle. Scalini is perfect for a romantic encounter: quietly intimate and with attentive service that allows you to get on with gazing into each other's eyes. The wine list is well selected and the desserts are gloriously decadent.
No smoking.

Tinelli
139 Easter Road, EH7 (652 1932). London Rd buses, then 5-min walk. **Open** noon-2.30pm, 6.30-11pm Mon-Sat. **Closed** Sun. **Average** £12.50. **Credit** AmEx, DC, MC, V. **Map 4 J3**
A cosy and compact Italian with a reputation big enough to prove that size really does not matter. There is an imaginative menu that ranges from veal to fish to pastas, and a sincere and hearty welcome from the chef/owner and staff who take their art seriously.

Tony's
42 St Stephen Street, EH3 (226 5877). 20, 28, 80(A/B) buses. **Open** noon-2.30pm, 6-11pm Mon-Sat; 6-11pm Sun. **Average** £13.50. **Credit** MC, V. **Map 3 D3**
Enjoy dining in the intimate, atmospheric surroundings of the Tony Roma's Stockbridge original or head for the newer Colinton Road branch for similar cuisine in larger and less distinctive premises. The menu consists of reliable Italian favourites, as well as other Mediterranean-inspired dishes. Stingotto – leg of pork in a rich sauce – may feature, but fish tends to predominate. The usual veal and chicken dishes, as well as two based on duck, round out the menu nicely. The friendly waiters tend to encourage diners to linger over another bottle of wine from the impressive cellar or a splendid espresso
Branch: 19 Colinton Road, EH10 (447 8781).

Vito's
55A Frederick Street, EH2 (225 5052). Princes St buses **Open** noon-2.30pm, 6-11pm Mon-Sat. **Average** £16. **Credit** AmEx, MC, V. **Map 8 B1**
With two compact dining rooms, this busy restaurant, established 25 years ago, is centrally situated and favoured by a mixed clientele. Although below street level, natural light enters the restaurant through bright windows during the day. The ambience is friendly, and the décor Mediterranean. Fish and shellfish, brought fresh from Anstruther daily, are the forte of the house. Served in trencherman quantities, the food is packed with flavour.

Japanese

Daruma-Ya
Commercial Quay (entry via Dock Place), 82 Commercial Street, EH6 (554 7660). 10A, 16, 22A, 32, 52 buses. **Open** noon-2pm, 6.30pm-late Mon-Sat. **Closed** Sun. **Average** £14. **Credit** MC, V. **Map 2 Leith**
Good, affordable Japanese food in the elegantly proportioned surroundings of a former wine warehouse. The friendly, expert waiting staff are happy to talk you through the dishes and explain the structure of Japanese meals, while a selection of set menus provides a ready-designed sampler. A full wine list is supplemented by both sake and Japanese lager.

Tampopo
Japanese Noodle Bar, 25A Thistle Street, EH2 (220 5254). Princes St buses, then 5-min walk. **Open** noon-2.30pm Mon; noon-2.30pm, 6-9pm Tue-Sat; noon-3pm Sun. **Average** £6. **Unlicensed. No credit cards. Map 8 B1**
If you've seen the film *Tampopo*, you'll know what to expect at this busy, friendly and compact noodle bar. The noodles are healthy, filling, made freshly every day and served up in a traditional ramen soup with a variety of toppings, or choose from the range of bento meals – Japanese lunch boxes containing rice, salad, pickles, rolled egg and spicy chicken or pork. With individual dishes modestly priced, and a range of set menus, this is Japanese food at its most affordable. Alcohol cannot be consumed on the premises.

Mexican

The Blue Parrot Cantina
49 St Stephen Street, EH3 (225 2941). 20, 28, 80(A/B) buses. **Open** 5-11pm Mon-Thur; noon-11pm Fri, Sat; 5-10.30pm Sun. **Average** £10. **Credit** MC, £TC, V. **Map 3 D3**
This candlelit basement space has a bohemian air where confident chefs working in the open-plan kitchens prepare generously portioned meals. The bean soup is spicy and pricks the appetite, while the chicken and almond chimichanga is beautifully crisp with a wonderfully juicy filling. The accompanying mounds of rice, guacamole, refried beans and salsa ensure a feeling of repletion. There is also an unusual cocktail called a Piñata: Tequila, lime juice and banana liqueur shaken over ice.

Tex Mex
47 Hanover Street, EH2 (225 1796). Princes St buses. **Open** noon-11pm Mon-Sat; 12.30-11pm Sun. **Average** £16. **Credit** AmEx, DC, MC, £TC, V. **Map 8 C1**
A bustling, spacious basement restaurant, perfectly located for hungry hordes. Most main courses – enchiladas, chimichangas, burritos and tacos – are available in beef, chicken and vegetarian versions. The Tex side of the border is represented by char-grilled steaks, burgers and teriyaki steaks, an idea the menu tells us was brought into California by the Chinese who helped build the railroad. Also a good selection of tempting desserts and a small, though well-appointed, wine list. Booking is essential.

Viva Mexico
41 Cockburn Street, EH1 (226 5145). 1, 6, Bridges buses. **Open** noon-2.30pm, 6.30-10.30pm Mon-Sat; 6.30-10pm Sun. **Average** £11. **Credit** AmEx, DC, JCB, MC, £TC, V. **Map 9 C2**
Traditional and innovative Mexican cuisine, with reliable favourites including beef, chicken or vegetarian burritos, enchiladas and fajitas. The cosily positioned tables, Latin music and lively atmosphere ensure that diners feel part of a veritable fiesta.
Branch: 50 East Fountainbridge, EH3 (228 4005).

Seductive and sophisticated – **The Atrium.**

The Tapas Tree
1 Forth Street, EH1 (556 7118). 7A, 8(A), 9(A), 19, 39 buses. **Open** 11am-11pm daily. **Average** £10. **Credit** AmEx, DC, JCB, MC, £$TC, V. **Map 4 G3**
This Spanish restaurant is a popular choice with bright young things. An intimate yet bustling atmosphere prevails on the ground floor and down in the basement – book ahead to avoid a lengthy wait at the small bar. The menu consists of various tapas: meat (the chorizo sausages are fantastic), fish and vegetarian dishes complement each other well. Eye-catching desserts round off the meal perfectly with uncloying sweetness, and there's a fine selection of liqueurs. A Spanish guitarist plays every Wednesday evening.

Tapas Olé
10 Eyre Place, EH3 (556 2754). 7A, 8(A), 9(A), 19, 23, 27, 37, 39 buses. **Open** 11am-11pm Mon-Sun. **Average** £10. **Credit** MC, £$TC, V. **Map 3 E3**
Set up in late 1997 by a breakaway faction of the popular **Tapas Tree** (*above*). Both flavours and service are robust. The atmosphere is conducive to group eating and it has become popular for hen and stag nights. Booking advised.

Scottish

The Atrium
10 Cambridge Street, EH1 (228 8882). Bruntsfield buses. **Open** noon-2.30pm, 6-10.30pm Mon-Fri; noon-2pm, 6-10.30pm Sat. **Closed** Sun. **Average** £21. **Credit** AmEx, DC, MC, £TC, V. **Map 8 A3**
Firmly established as one of Edinburgh's most stylish restaurants – with its celebrated chef Andrew Radford producing food of a sophistication and originality to match, if not outdo, the clientele – the Atrium has achieved a formidable reputation in its relatively short life and is one of just

two restaurants in Edinburgh to have earned a Michelin red M for its cooking. Despite the wacky décor, it doesn't set out to intimidate, however, rather to seduce then satisfy. Radford rings his own distinctive changes on the Scottish, French, traditional and contemporary spectra, in dishes like game sausages with potato and celeriac mash, or pan-fried sea-bass with rosti.

The Dial
44-46 George IV Bridge, EH1 (225 7179). George IV Bridge buses. **Open** noon-3pm, 6pm-late daily. **Average** £15. **Credit** AmEx, MC, £$TC, V. **Map 9 B3**
Secluded downstairs from the bustle of George IV Bridge, the Dial has the air of a secret and fashionable hangout. The emphasis is on presentation – bright white walls adorned with boldly coloured hangings, floor-set lighting, and snazzy touches like colour-coded cutlery – but the food successfully upstages the décor. The theme is Scottish cuisine with a twist with dishes such as salmon with citrus butter or fillet of Aberdeen Angus served with shallot and Madeira jus. The service is friendly and efficient, neatly matching a stylish, yet informal, dining experience.

Dubh Prais
123B High Street, EH1 (557 5732). 1, 6, 34, 35 buses. **Open** noon-2pm, 6.30-10.30pm Tue-Fri; 6.30-10.30pm Sat. **Closed** Sun, Mon. **Average** £18. **Credit** AmEx, JCB, MC, £TC, V. **Map 9 B2**
While the Old Town is well endowed with informal, quick-eat venues, the more leisured alternative is not that plentiful, rendering the whitewashed basement haven of Dubh Prais a much-prized rarity. Taking its name from the Gaelic word for a blackened cooking pot – an example hangs in the corner – Dubh Prais serves Scottish cuisine prepared with style and skill, sometimes centred on well-known traditional delicacies dressed up afresh, like haggis pan-fried in oatmeal and served with a whisky and leek sauce. Dinner is all à la carte, while a set-price menu is available at lunchtime (£7.50 two courses, £9.50 three courses).

(Fitz)henry: a brasserie
19 Shore Place, EH6 (555 6625). 1, 6, 10A, 32, 52 buses. **Open** 12.30-2.30pm, 6.30-10pm Mon-Thur; 12.30-2.30pm, 6.30-10.30pm Fri, Sat. **Closed** Sun. **Average** £19. **Credit** AmEx, MC, V. **Map 2 Leith**
One of the undisputed stars in Edinburgh's culinary pantheon, tastefully stylish even by Leith's competitive standards, this is the perfect rendezvous for a seductive dinner à deux. Stone-walled, high-ceilinged, sparsely but artfully hung about with velvet and drapes, the converted warehouse setting provides a memorable backdrop for some equally distinguished cooking that has earned it a Michelin red M. Both à la carte and table d'hôte menus reflect the freshest in seasonal produce. Flavours are combined with both originality and assurance, as in langoustine casserole with garlic cream and smoked bacon, or breast of duck on a bed of spinach. The dessert menu is made to make your mouth water and no less inventive, featuring such temptations as baked banana with orange sauce, surrounded by a nutty cocoa sorbet.

Hadrian's
1 Princes Street, EH1 (557 5000). Princes St buses. **Open** noon-2.30pm, 6.30-10pm Mon-Fri; noon-2.30pm, 6.30-10.30pm Sat; 12.30-2.30pm, 6.30-10pm Sun. **Average** £15. **Credit** AmEx, DC, JCB, MC, £$TC, V. **Map 9 C1**
Sculpted in art deco style and illuminated with plenty of subtle lighting, this **Balmoral Hotel** restaurant wears its designer credentials firmly on its sleeve. The menu matches up, with modish but effective touches to the Scottish-based fare – cappuccino of mushroom soup, millefeuille of lemon sole with buttered cabbage and sauce choron, and pot-roasted pork cheek with spiced aromatics and honey.

Haldanes

39A Albany Street, EH3 (556 8407). 7A, 8(A), 9(A), 19, 39 buses. **Open** noon-2pm, 6.30-10pm Mon-Fri; 6.30-11pm Sat, Sun. **Average** £19. **Credit** AmEx, DC, MC, £TC, V. **Map 3 F3**

Haldanes promises 'the country house experience in the city' and diners entering this cosy New Town nook can expect a tranquil meal in traditional surroundings, which do indeed generate a curious sense of remoteness from the capital's bustle. The menu – table d'hôte at lunchtime (£9.75 two courses, £12.50 three courses), à la carte by night – is of a traditional Scots bent, with beef, salmon and venison well represented, complemented by slightly more outré choices such as monkfish and guinea fowl. Dishes are artfully presented – even the bread and butter pudding looks elegant – and the wine list is wide-ranging.
No smoking.

Jackson's

209 High Street, EH1 (225 1793). 1, 6, 34, 35 buses. **Open** noon-2.30pm, 6-10.30pm daily. **Average** £19. **Credit** AmEx, JCB, MC, £TC, V. **Map 9 B2**

Well-heeled local couples and businessmen rub shoulders with visitors in this gourmet's delight situated smack on the tourist trail. The menu makes full use of Scottish produce while the cooking ranges freely between traditional and modern styles. Alongside the reassuring certainties of game terrine, garnished sirloin and beef and venison ragouts, one can find ostrich or fresh tuna, or perhaps a saddle of rabbit wrapped in Parma ham. Excellent service compensates for the rather bland décor, as does the great-value set lunch.

Keepers

13B Dundas Street, EH3 (556 5707). 23, 27, 37, 47 buses. **Open** noon-2pm, 6-10pm Tue-Fri; 6-10pm Sat. **Closed** Sun, Mon. **Average** £17.50. **Credit** AmEx, JCB, MC, £TC, V. **Map 3 E4**

Housed below ground in a 200-year-old vaulted, flagstoned New Town basement, Keepers complements these tradition-soaked premises with a menu that looks both forward and back. Scottish ingredients – meat, game, fish, seafood – exemplify the old-fashioned virtues of freshness and quality, while the cooking unites disparate influences in a thoroughly modern style that's also apparent in an exceptional vegetarian selection.

Kelly's

46 West Richmond Street, EH8 (668 3847). Bridges buses. **Open** noon-2pm, 7-9.30pm Wed-Sat; Mon,Tue by arrangement only; pre- and post-theatre bookings by arrangement. **Set lunch** £9 one course, £12 two courses, £15 three courses. **Set dinner** £20 two courses, £25 three courses. **Credit** MC, £TC, V. **Map 7 G6**

This small dining room housed in a Georgian tenement has a distinctly upmarket atmosphere, but the service is relaxed, the surroundings pleasantly comfortable, and the food will certainly put you at your ease. The fixed-price evening menu looks selective, but is put together with care and attention to detail, together with a modicum of inventiveness.
No smoking.

Martin's

70 Rose Street, North Lane, EH2 (225 3106). Princes St buses. **Open** noon-2pm, 7-10pm Tue-Fri; 7-10pm Sat. **Closed** Sun, Mon; 24 Dec-23 Jan approx; ten days in both May/June and September/October. **Average** £25. **Credit** AmEx, DC, JCB, MC, £TC, V. **Map 8 B1**

Hidden away in a back lane behind Rose Street (between Frederick and Castle Streets), the unassuming exterior of Martin's belies a restaurant dedicated to presenting the very best of Scottish produce, even down to a 30-minute history of the cheeseboard. It has won countless awards since opening in 1983 for its creative use of fish, game and lamb (including three AA rosettes). Proprietor Martin Irons actively encourages healthy eating in his restaurant, keeping fat to a minimum and using organic produce where possible.
No smoking unless a private booking.

Merchants

17 Merchant Street, Candlemaker Row, EH1 (225 4009). George IV Bridge buses. **Open** noon-2pm, 6-10pm Mon-Fri; 6-10pm Sat; 6-8.30pm Sun. **Average** £15. **Credit** AmEx, DC, JCB, MC, V. **Map 9 B3**

Formerly embracing a strong French influence, the cuisine at Merchants has moved more towards Scottish traditions of late. More unusual items might include deep fried mushrooms filled with haggis, while classic quality tells in main courses like fillet of Angus beef cordoned in puff pastry with béarnaise sauce, and collops of salmon served on a bed of crispy leeks with pink peppercorn butter.

Number One, The Restaurant

The Balmoral Hotel, 1 Princes Street, EH1 (557 6727). Princes St buses. **Open** noon-2pm, 7-10pm Mon-Thur; noon-2pm, 7-10.30pm Fri; 7-10.30pm Sat; 7-10pm Sun. **Set lunch** £14.95 two courses, £17.95 three courses. **Set dinner** £32 three courses. **Credit** AmEx, DC, JCB, MC, £STC, V. **Map 8 D2**

Tucked away in the **Balmoral Hotel**, this is one of Edinburgh's most quietly sophisticated restaurants, with tables placed for privacy, while generously curved banquettes invite relaxed conversation. The cooking combines quality ingredients with outstanding modern flair, marrying the likes of smoked Dover sole with roast artichoke and Bresse chicken with veal sweetbread. The wine list runs from good country wines to grande marques, all reasonably priced given the quality. Lunchtime set menus offer a less pocket-walloping treat.

Off the Wall

11 South College Street, EH8 (667 1597). Bridges buses. **Open** noon-2pm, 5.30-7pm (pre-theatre), 7-11pm Mon-Sat. **Closed** Sun. **Average** £16. **Credit** AmEx, MC, £TC, V. **Map 7 G6**

Established in autumn 1997, within a stone's throw of the **Festival Theatre**, this unassuming little restaurant is well worth discovering, its modest décor belying the menu's ambition. Dishes favour a French influence, ranging from the creamily rich to the light and modern. Desserts run a similar gamut, encompassing both palate-fresheners and serious indulgence material, with cheeses supplied by top local fromagier Iain Mellis on hand as an alternative.

Peter's Cellars

11-15 William Street, EH3 (226 3161). Haymarket buses. **Open** noon-2.30pm, 6.30-10.30pm Mon-Fri; 7-10pm Sat. **Closed** Sun. **Set dinner** £13.75 two courses, £15.75 three courses. **Credit** MC, V. **Map 5 C6**

Situated in a West End basement, Peter's Cellars is one of Edinburgh's most enduring bring-your-own-bottle restaurants. Soft lighting and curtained booths offer privacy for intimate evenings, while lunchtimes are livelier, thanks to the local business clientele. In a predominantly Scottish menu, starters like smoked haddock fishcakes or chicken liver pâté with oatcakes give way to venison, duck and salmon-based main courses, garnished with minimal fuss. NHS employees and police officers receive a 10% discount.

Point Restaurant

34 Bread Street, EH3 (221 5555). Bruntsfield buses, then 5-min walk. **Open** noon-2pm, 6-9.30pm Mon-Wed; noon-2pm, 6-10.30pm Thur-Sat. **Set lunch** £6.90 two courses. **Set dinner** £9.90 three courses. **Credit** AmEx, DC, MC, £STC, V. **Map 8 A3**

A bold sense of space makes a real impact in this stylish hotel restaurant, with the prevailing black, white and navy tones offset by big splashes of modern art, while the three-course dinner menu at around a tenner offers outstanding value. Lobster bisque might lead on to an aromatic venison pot au feu, laced with juniper berries and served with seasonal vegetables, while the Point's variants on classic crème brûlée reduce grown men to puddles of gibbering ecstasy.

The Potting Shed

Bruntsfield Hotel, 69 Bruntsfield Place, EH10 (229 1393). Bruntsfield buses. **Open** noon-2pm, 6.30-9.30pm Sun-Fri; noon-2pm, 5.30-9.30pm Sat. **Set lunch** £7.50 two courses, £9.50 three courses Mon-Sat, £9.50 two courses, £12.50 three courses Sun. **Set dinner** £18 three courses. **Credit** AmEx, MC, £TC, V. **Map 6 D8**
A spacious conservatory-style restaurant offering a wide choice from both table d'hôte and à la carte menus. The main courses are fairly traditional but the spirit of adventure shows among the starters and puddings: whet your appetite on bluefin tuna ceviche, or venison and black pudding terrine; get in touch with your inner glutton via mango bavarois with raspberry coulis, or lemon tart with ginger sorbet. *No smoking.*

Quills

Carlton Highland Hotel, North Bridge, EH1 (472 3033). Bridges buses. **Open** noon-2pm, 7-10pm Mon-Fri; 7-10pm Sat. **Closed** Sun. **Average** £18. **Credit** AmEx, DC, MC, £$TC, V. **Map 9 C2**
Amid the Victorian setting of the Carlton Highland Hotel's one-time library, Quills retains a soft-spoken atmosphere – though with only 14 covers, intimacy is pretty much guaranteed, as is attentive service. Duck is a favourite here, while combinations like venison with chocolate sauce reveal a sure hand with the exotic touch. The 'Flavour of Scotland' menu is designed to offer visitors a sampler of Caledonian cuisine.

The Rock

78 Commercial Street, EH6 (555 2225). 10A, 16, 22A, 32, 52 buses. **Open** noon-2.30pm, 6-10.30pm Mon-Sat; 12.30-2.30pm, 6-10.30pm Sun. **Average** £20. **Credit** AmEx, MC, £$TC, V. **Map 2 Leith**
Sounding more like a dodgy pub than an award-winning restaurant, this relative newcomer on Leith's increasingly cut-throat restaurant scene has determinedly muscled to the fore of the pack. The secret of this success lies in mouthwatering Scots-French offerings like roast Barbary duck breast with buttered leeks and a balsamic jus, or crisp fillets of salmon with asparagus spears and vierge sauce, while your dedicated carnivores should make straight for the grill section, which turns out burgers and steaks.

The Round Table

31 Jeffrey Street, EH1 (557 3032). 1, 6 buses. **Open** 10am-10pm Tue-Sat. **Closed** Sun, Mon. **Set dinner** £15.50 four courses. **Credit** AmEx, JCB, £TC, V. **Map 9 D2**
Oversized jars of nuts and seeds, dried flowers hanging from the ceiling and hand-crafted furniture by wood sculptor Tim Stead create a quirky, friendly place to eat. The extensive menu is strong on Scottish influences and fresh seasonal ingredients such as grilled fresh haddock with shrimp and oats, pork sausages and black pudding with mashed potato and onion gravy.

Stac Polly

8-10 Grindlay Street, EH3 (229 5405). Bruntsfield buses. **Open** noon-2pm, 6-10.30pm Mon-Fri; 6-10.30pm Sat; 6-10pm Sun. **Average** £20. **Credit** AmEx, JCB, MC, £TC, V. **Map 8 A3**
Stac Polly has earned a deserved reputation for providing an innovative take on traditional Scottish fare. Its haggis in filo pastry is already legendary, though some may find the plum sauce garnish too innovative. A substantial soup of the day always offers a reliable first-course fallback. Meat, fish and poultry are the staple fodder, with venison, duck, monk-

fish and turbot also served up in some unexpected combinations, followed by a shamelessly sticky range of puds. **Branch:** 29-33 Dublin Street, EH3 (556 2231).

The Stockbridge Restaurant

33A St Stephen Street, EH3 (225 9397). 20, 28, 80(A/B) buses. **Open** 6.30-10.30pm Tue; 12.30-2.30pm, 6.30-10.30pm Wed-Sat. **Closed** Sun, Mon. **Average** £16. **Credit** MC, V. **Map 3 D3**
With its basement premises rendered unexpectedly bright and airy by a white-tiled colour scheme set off with vivid yellows and blues, this establishment has been steadily acquiring a loyal following since it opened in late 1997. Homely Scottish favourites like leek and potato soup rub shoulders happily with French classics like Alsace onion tart, while main courses lead on meat and fish.

Sweet Melinda's

11 Roseneath Street, EH9 (229 7953). 24(A), 40, 41(A) buses. **Open** noon-2pm, 7-10pm Tue-Sat. **Closed** Sun, Mon. **Average** £14. **Credit** MC, £TC, V. **Map 6 F8**
Run by a team who formerly plied their trade at the **Shore** (*see above*), Melinda's lives up to these credentials with a fish and meat-based menu that changes daily according to season and market supplies. Quality ingredients are enlivened by a globe-trotting range of influences, as in a pungent Thai chicken soup. Lunchtimes offer scaled-down dishes along the same lines as the dinner menu, at roughly half the price, and there is always a vegetarian option. Kids are kept amused with a box of toys, though the restaurant's tranquil candlelit ambience precludes any overly boisterous larking.

The Terrace Restaurant

Sheraton Hotel, 1 Festival Square, EH3 (221 6422). Bruntsfield buses. **Open** breakfast 7-11am, *lunch* noon-2.30pm, *dinner* 6-11pm daily. **Average** £15. **Credit** AmEx, DC, JCB, MC, £TC, V. **Map 8 A3**
If you prefer improvisation to formal eating, the Terrace Restaurant is sure to please. The main attraction is the buffet, centrally placed in a theatrical space with a view of the Castle, with a lavish array of salads, soup, cured meats, smoked salmon, relishes and sauces. Chefs will also concoct stir-fries to order, or cook ingredients to your specification, still within the set buffet price. Friday night is seafood night, while a family-friendly brunch is served on Sundays.

36

36 Great King Street, EH3 (556 3636). 23, 27, 37, 47 buses. **Open** noon-2pm, 7-10pm Mon-Fri; 7-10pm Sat; noon-2pm, 7-9.30pm Sun. **Average** £20. **Credit** AmEx, DC, MC, V. **Map 3 E3**
Situated on one of the New Town's grandest thoroughfares, 36 occupies the basement of the plush **Howard Hotel**. Olives and almonds are proffered in the bar on arrival, while the menu reveals an imaginative line-up of international and Scottish dishes. Puddings are nothing short of exquisite: try turning down a gratin of ginger, mango and papaya, doused in icing sugar and accompanied by a delicate arrangement of berries. *No smoking.*

Winter Glen

3A1 Dundas Street, EH3 (477 7060). 23, 27, 37, 47 buses. **Open** noon-2pm, 6.30pm-late Mon-Sat. **Closed** Sun. **Average** £23.95 (Mon-Thur); £25 (Fri, Sat). **Credit** AmEx, MC, £$TC, V. **Map 3 E4**
The elegant and welcoming décor of this stone-walled New Town basement is matched by notably pleasant and proficient service, where Scottish ingredients predominate on a modern-style set menu. With laid-back live jazz, and a special gourmet dinner each month, the place oozes a confidence, comfort and style which has been rewarded by a number of industry awards.

Point Restaurant – *good-value dining and creme brûlées to die for. See page 131.*

The Witchery by the Castle
352 Castlehill, EH1 (225 5613). 1, 6, 34, 35 buses.
Open noon-4pm, 5.30-11.30pm daily. **Average** £25.
Credit AmEx, DC, JCB, MC, £TC, V. **Map 9 A2**
Candlelight and oak panelling, tapestries and flagstones
highlight the Gothic-tinged atmosphere of the Witchery,
whether you eat in the main dining room or the 'Secret
Garden' across the courtyard. Its combination of seriously
good food and unobtrusive service has long ranked this as
one of the capital's top restaurants, popular with students
when the treat's on Mum and Dad. Table d'hôte and à la carte
menus both offer modern-style dishes, such as sauteed king
scallops with spiced cabbage, sweet pepper and chilli sauce,
and the desserts are ruinously tempting. The Witchery's
ancient cellars have won many prestigious awards, but budget-priced luxury can be had by sticking to the pre- and post-
theatre menus.

Swiss

Denzler's
*121 Constitution Street, EH6 (554 3268). 16, 22A, 34
buses.* **Open** noon-2pm, 6.30-10pm Mon-Fri; 6.30-10.30pm
Sat. **Closed** Sun. **Average** £15. **Credit** AmEx, DC, JCB,
MC, £$TC, V. **Map 2 Leith**
Upmarket Swiss style, with cocktails and accoutrements to
suit the more mature dipper into fondues. Cheese with big
holes might be the clichéd view of Swiss eating, but Denzler's
proves that veal and venison are also Alpine favourites.

Thai

Ayutthaya
14B Nicolson Street, EH8 (556 9351). Bridges buses.
Open noon-2.30pm, 5.30-11pm daily. **Average** £12.
Credit AmEx, MC, £TC, V. **Map 7 G6**
Extensive and delicious Thai menu at a venue situated oppo-
site the **Festival Theatre**, and offering a pre-theatre menu.

Siam Erawan
48 Howe Street, EH3 (226 3675). 20, 28, 80(A/B) buses.
Open noon-2.30pm, 6-11pm Mon-Sat; 6-10.30pm Sun.
Average £10. **Credit** MC, £$TC, V. **Map 3 D4**
Packed out with regulars, locals and business folk, booking
is essential at this authentic Thai restaurant, which recently opened a branch in Rose Street. Descending into Siam
Erawan, the whitewashed alcoves, ornate oriental decorations and mint-green walls give a cool feel, while a broad and
authentic range of aromatic dishes are bound to please.
Branch: Erawan Express, 176 Rose Street, EH2 (220
0059).

Sukhothai
23 Brougham Place, EH3 (229 1537). Bruntsfield buses.
Open noon-2.30pm, 5.30-10.30pm daily. **Average** £11.
Credit AmEx, MC, £TC, V. **Map 6 E7**
Sited at the western end of the Meadows, Sukhothai's accent
is firmly on the traditional, with reams of vegetarian dishes,
including steamed dim sum. The vegetarian curries are particularly good and there is a wide range of seafood, chicken
and meat dishes. The house speciality is a fiery minced pork
dish with garlic and tomato.

Turkish

Saray
*72 Commercial Street, EH6 (553 7887). 10A, 16, 22A,
32, 52 buses.* **Open** noon-3pm, 6-10.30pm daily.
Average £17. **Credit** AmEx, DC, JCB, MC, V. **Map 2
Leith**
Located in the newly refurbished area of Leith's Commercial
Quay, Saray offers a comprehensive selection of contemporary Turkish cuisine, all served in a space enhanced by traditional Middle Eastern décor. Approachable staff offer
advice on suitable combinations for sharing. Main courses
range from grills and kebabs to baked fish. Some dishes are
served with rice and salad, but most may require a side order.
Vegetarian options are limited.

Saucy suppers

The abundance of quality fish restaurants in Edinburgh is indicative of its position near the sea on the Firth of Forth. For the true Edinburgh fish experience you must visit a local fish and chip shop. Here fish comes either as a 'supper' (that's fish and chips) or as a single (but don't be surprised if you get a couple of chips with your fish).

What is unique to Edinburgh is that when the fish supper is ready to be wrapped you'll be offered sauce on it, not vinegar. Although this viscous, brown, vinegar-based concoction looks suspiciously as if it could contravene the United Nations chemical weapons limitation treaty, it adds a spicy zing to the supper and should be tried at least once. Edinburgh natives swear by it, but visitors can find the resulting finger-licking experience a bit messy. If you want vinegar, not sauce, just say 'salt and vinegar' when offered 'salt'n'sauce?' – but beware, the offer can sound more like 'serasas?'.

The menu in Scottish fish and chip shops is slightly different to that south of the border. Besides fish, smoked sausage, pie or chicken, on offer are haggis, black pudding and white pudding. All are cooked in batter. Haggis is slightly spicy, black pudding is a blood-based sausage and white pudding is vegetarian.

Another quirk of the Scottish fish and chip shop is that none seem to be able to leave a bag of chips open so that you can eat them walking down the street. No matter how much you ask, it doesn't happen. Even at the best such as these:

Concord Fish Bar
49 Home Street, EH3 (228 1182). Bruntsfield buses. **Open** 11am-2pm, 4.30pm-2.30am Mon-Fri; 11am-2.30am Sat; 4.30pm-2.30am Sun. **No credit cards. Map 6 D7**

Clam Shell Fish and Chip Shop
148 High Street, EH1 (225 4338). 1, 6, 34, 35 buses. **Open** 24 hours daily. **No credit cards. Map 9 C2**

L'Aquila Bianca
17 Raeburn Place, EH4 (332 8433). 20, 28, 80 (A/B) buses. **Open** 11.30am-1-30pm, 4.30pm-12.30am Sun-Thur; 4.30pm-1am Fri-Sat. **No credit cards. Map 2 C3**

L'Alba D'Oro
5 Henderson Row, EH3 (557 2580). 23, 27, 37, 47 buses, then 5-min walk. **Open** 11am-midnight Mon-Fri; 4.15pm-midnight Sat-Sun. **No credit cards. Map 3 D3**

Rapido
79 Broughton Street, EH1 (556 2041). 7A, 8(A), 9(A), 19, 39 buses. **Open** 10.30am-2pm, 4.30pm-1.30am Mon-Thur; 10.30am-2pm; 4.30pm-3.30am Fri-Sat. **No credit cards. Map 3 F3**

Vegetarian

Bann's
5 Hunter Square, EH1 (226 1112). Bridges buses. **Open** 10am-11pm daily. **Average** £11.50. **Credit** AmEx, JCB, MC, £$TC, V. **Map 9 C2**
Situated just off the Royal Mile, Bann's attracts a mixed, mostly young clientele with its relaxed atmosphere and all-vegetarian menu. The global menu is extensive and cosmopolitan, ranging from snacks and cakes to full meals.

Black Bo's
57-61 Blackfriars Street, EH1 (557 6136). 1, 6, Bridges buses. **Open** noon-2pm, 6-10.30pm Mon-Sat; 6-10.30pm Sun. **Average** £12. **Credit** JCB, MC, V. **Map 9 D3**
A hip but subdued restaurant, rustically furnished and candlelit with groovy background music, Bo's is a relaxing venue for a meal with a menu that makes vegetarian food look like the most glamorous cuisine around. Starters include spicy vegetable soup and courgette fritters. For dessert, the ultra-rich home-made chocolate ice-cream is certainly worth dieting for: so intense it's almost bitter! Not cheap, but the innovative menu could please even the most committed meat-eater. *See also chapter* **Bars & Pubs.**

Isabel's
83 Clerk Street, EH8 (662 4014). Bridges buses. **Open** 11.30am-6.30pm Mon-Sat. **Closed** Sun. **Average** £5. **Unlicensed. Corkage** free. **No credit cards. Map 7 G7**
Nestled under the Nature's Gate health food shop, Isabel's offers a modest, low-priced lunch and dinner menu. The sweet stuff is the best bet, with great carrot cake, date slice and cranberry pie. Juices, herbal teas, coffee and hot chocolates are also available. With only one person serving and preparing the meals, things can be slow, so settle back and enjoy the open fire, soft music and reading material. *No smoking.*

Kalpna
2-3 St Patrick Square, EH8 (667 9890). Bridges buses. **Open** noon-2pm Mon-Fri; 5.30-11pm Sat. **Closed** Sun. **Average** £9. **Credit** MC, V. **Map 7 G7**
Healthy, vegetable-based Indian dishes created by owner Mr Barwaj, who makes annual research trips to India in aid of his menus, have earned Kalpna the reputation as one of Edinburgh's best vegetarian restaurants. Thalis are available, as several regional specialities including dosa from Southern India, and a mouthwatering selection of traditional desserts rounds off the experience. Wednesday is gourmet buffet night, and patrons are invited to eat as much as they want for the all-in bargain price of £8.95.

Susie's Wholefood Diner
51-53 West Nicolson Street, EH8 (667 8729). Bridges buses. **Open** 10am-8pm Mon; 10am-9pm Tue-Sat. **Average** £5. **No credit cards. Map 7 G6**
Loud and lively, Susie's is a vegetarian diner offering value for money fodder. Portions are generous, but linger over coffee and cakes and check through the extensive collection of what's-on arts literature available. Although fully licensed, Susie's allows customers to bring their own alcohol if desired. There is often live music in the evenings.

Cafés & Bistros

Tea for two, three or the whole family if you like, at Edinburgh's trendy tearooms and cutting edge cafés.

Blue Moon Café, *in the heart of Broughton, has the best nachos in town. Page 136.*

'You'll have had your tea then', is the mythical greeting of the tight-fisted Morningside matron. The times are less parsimonious now and there are excellent tearooms and cafés dotted around the whole of Edinburgh, whether you want to see the matron in her natural environment or grab a cup of black-as-midnight Jo. If you are on the hoof to the next cultural offering during the Festival, the opening times given here are year round and it is likely that the better establishments will be keeping longer opening hours. Unless otherwise indicated, the average prices given are per person for a two-course, sit-in evening meal without alcohol.

The Arches

66-67 South Bridge, EH1 (556 0200). Bridges buses.
Open 10.30am-11pm Mon-Sat; 10.30am-10.30pm Sun. **Food served** noon-3pm, 5-11pm Mon-Sat; 5-10.30pm Sun. **Average** £10. **Credit** AmEx, DC, JCB, MC, £TC, V. **Map 7 G6**
With its wide-arched windows, in view of the Festival

Theatre, this bistro specialises in venison and seafood with some vegetarian dishes. Good quality cuisine served in a relaxed atmosphere. Set three-course meals are offered for lunch and dinner at £5.75 and £12.95 respectively.

Backstage Bistro

22 Valleyfield Street, EH3 (229 1978). Bruntsfield buses.
Open *July-mid Sept* noon-late daily; *mid-Sept-June* 5pm-late daily. **Average** £12 (dinner). **Credit** MC, V. **Map 6 D7**
This snug little bistro, hidden round the corner from the **King's Theatre**, is owned and run by a former head chef for the Intercontinental chain who has a deft and personal touch with the food. The menu is small but perfectly formed and, as there is no licence, don't forget to bring your own bottle (50p corkage). A pre-theatre menu is available from 5pm to 7pm and a post-theatre menu operates according to the show times at the King's Theatre.

El Bar

15 Blackfriars Street, EH1 (558 9139). Bridges buses.
Open noon-midnight Mon-Fri; 1pm-midnight Sat, Sun. **Average** £6. **No credit cards**. **Map 9 D2**
A Spanish theme is authenticated by the Spanish owner of

this crowded wee tapas bar, just off the Royal Mile, which is popular with local trendies and wandering backpackers alike. The theme extends to the choice of beers, coffee and snacks (served all day). Because of licensing restrictions, alcohol cannot be served without food.

Bewley's
4 South Charlotte Street, EH2 (220 1969). Princes St or George St buses. **Open** 8am-6pm Mon-Sat; 9.30am-6pm Sun. **Average** £4. **Credit** MC, V. **Map 8 A1**
Part of the famous chain of coffeehouses that originated in Dublin in 1840, the large self-service area serves good-value hot food, while the smaller restaurant area offers table-service and an à la carte menu.

Bib & Tucker
2 Deanhaugh Street, EH3 (332 1469). 20, 28, 80(A/B) buses. **Open** 10.30am-5.30pm Mon; 10.30am-9pm Tue-Wed; 10.30am-10pm Thur-Sat. **Closed** Sun. **Average** £9. **Credit** MC, V. **Map 2 C3**
A genteel, basement coffeeshop by day, with the music never played at more than a polite volume. From 6.30pm onwards, it spreads its wings, chalks up a small menu on the blackboard and becomes an unassuming bistro.

Blue Moon Café
36 Broughton Street, EH1 (557 0911). 7A, 8(A), 9(A), 19, 39 buses. **Open** 9am-11.30pm Sun-Thur; 9-12.30am Fri, Sat. **Average** £6. **Credit** MC, V. **Map 3 F3**
Stylish and friendly, this gay-run but straight-friendly café and bistro is home to the best plate of nachos in town. Equally excellent for weekday lunches or a pre-club drink. Inventive, fair-priced vegetarian and child-friendly menu.

The Bookstop Café
4 Teviot Place, EH1 (225 5298). George IV Bridge buses. **Open** 10am-8pm Mon-Sat; noon-8pm Sun. **Average** £4. **Credit** DC, MC, V. **Map 6 F6**
This bookshop-cum-café, opposite Edinburgh University, attracts students and academics during the week and families at the weekend. Books are available to peruse while drinking your coffee – and if you buy a book, the coffee is on the house. Huge selection of very reasonably priced deli sandwiches and salads and light snacks.

Broughton Street Brasserie
2 Broughton Place, EH1 (558 8868). 7A, 8(A), 9(A), 19, 39 buses. **Open** 8am-7pm Mon-Fri; 9am-6pm Sat, Sun. **Average** £10. **Credit** MC, V. **Map 3 F3**
Airy and brightly decorated, with cherubs and a chandelier, this friendly bistro serves a wide range of Scottish, Italian, Spanish, American and Mexican dishes. It's equally good for a Sunday brunch or leisurely coffee.

Byzantium
9 Victoria Street, EH1 (220 2241). George IV Bridge buses. **Open** 10am-5.30pm Mon-Sat. **Closed** Sun. **Average** £5. **No credit cards. Map 9 B2**
Situated above the Byzantium antiques and crafts market (*see chapter* **Shopping & Services**), this large, self-service café offers a good selection of vegetarian and meat curries, mango milk shakes and lassis, alongside more conventional fare. The buffet lunch (11.30am-3.30pm) is particularly good value.

Café Libra
5A Union Street, EH1 (556 9602). Leith Walk buses. **Open** 9am-4.30pm Tue-Fri; 10am-5pm Sat; 10am-3pm Sun. **Closed** Mon. **Average** £4. **No credit cards. Map 4 G3**
This cosy and informal café at the top of Leith Walk serves an excellent selection of all-day breakfasts and a range of light meals. A three-course lunch special, with a choice of dishes, is offered noon-3pm.

Hot java to go at **California Coffee Co**.

Café Procida Espresso Bar
76 Thistle Street, EH2 (226 2230). 19A, 23, 27, 37, 47 buses. **Open** 8am-6pm Mon-Sat. **Closed** Sun. **Average** £4. **No credit cards. Map 8 C1**
This friendly, family-run café/restaurant is popular with a broad mix of shoppers and office workers. It is a particularly relaxing retreat from the bustling Princes and George Streets. Simple Italian dishes, at low prices, with a selection of Italian wines and beers and a takeaway menu.

Café Rouge
43 Frederick Street, EH2 (225 4515). Princes St buses. **Open** 10am-11pm daily. **Average** £8. **Credit** AmEx, MC, V. **Map 8 B1**
Edinburgh's outpost of the successful francophile chain exudes Parisian style. Simple French cuisine, at fairly reasonable prices so long as you don't go for the fussy options, served in a relaxed setting. Top-quality French breakfasts in the morning. 'Le Menu Rapide' is a good value three-course set dinner for £10.

Café WG
16 Brandon Terrace, EH3 (558 7763). 7A, 8(A), 9(A), 19, 39 buses. **Open** 8am-5pm Mon-Sat. **Closed** Sun. **Average** £6. **No credit cards. Map 3 E2**
Situated in Canonmills, this tastefully decorated licensed café attracts a mixed clientele from local business and passing shoppers. Handy for a drink, a coffee or high-quality but reasonably priced bite on the way to the Botanics.
No smoking.

The Caley Bistro
32 Leven Street, EH3 (622 7170). Bruntsfield buses. **Open** noon-2.30pm, 6-10.30pm Tue-Sat; noon-2.30pm Sun. **Closed** Mon. **Average** £12.95. **Credit** MC, V. **Map 6 D7**

A cheery bistro, convenient for the **King's Theatre**, which works equally well for an intimate meal à deux as it does for a group night out. The wine list offers a good choice at sensible prices and there is a choice of à la carte or competitively priced, fixed-price dinner (three courses £15.95).

California Coffee Co
St Patrick's Square, EH8 (228 5001). Bridges buses. **Open** 7.45am-9pm Mon-Fri; 10am-9pm Sat, Sun. **Average** £2. **Credit** MC, V. **Map 7 G7**
These renovated police boxes deliver delicious coffee (only the best Java will do) to those in need of a quick hit on the hoof. More centrally located boxes to be operational soon. Genius!
Branches: Middle Meadow Walk, EH3.; east end of North Meadow Walk, EH8.

Carlyle's
Carlton Highland Hotel, 21 North Bridge, EH1 (472 3113). Bridges buses. **Open** £6. **Credit** AmEx, DC, MC, £TC. V. **Map 9 C2**
A plush, old-style café, complete with chandeliers, ideal for a civilised lunch or afternoon tea. The menu offers continental breakfast, soups, salads, baked potatoes, gourmet sandwiches and hot meals including pasta dishes.

Central Deli
42 Home Street, EH3 (228 8550). Bruntsfield buses. **Open** 8am-6pm Mon-Wed; 8am-9pm Thur-Sat. **Closed** Sun. **Average** £4. **No credit cards. Map 6 D7**
The café lattes and banoffee pie are stupendous, the music's groovy and the staff friendly – this has become more of a café than a takeaway joint, even though it only has seating for ten people.

Chatterbox
1 East Preston Street, EH8 (667 9406). Bridges buses. **Open** 8.30am-6.30pm Mon-Fri; 9am-6pm Sat; 10am-6pm Sun. **Average** £4.65. **No credit cards. Map 7 H8**
A friendly, family-run, traditional Scottish tearoom, with a diverse mix of regulars, professionals, students and swimmers from the nearby Commonwealth Pool. The good, basic menu includes an all-day breakfast and a lunchtime special.

Clarinda's
69 Canongate, EH8 (557 1888). 1, 6 buses. **Open** 9am-4.45pm Mon-Sat; 10am-4.45pm Sun. **Average** £4. **No credit cards. Map 7 G5**
A comfortable, traditional tearoom on the Royal Mile that is renowned for its home-baking, boasting an unrivalled selection of cakes and pies. Full breakfast served 9-10.30am.

Common Grounds
2-3 North Bank Street, EH1 (226 1416). George IV Bridges buses. **Open** 9am-10pm Mon-Fri; 10am-10pm Sat, Sun. **Average** £5. **Credit** AmEx, JCB, MC, £TC, V. **Map 9 B2**
An American-style coffeehouse offering a wide selection of coffees (from the intriguing 'Keith Richards' to the tempting 'Irish Creme'), speciality teas and hot chocolate. The food is good, too, and reasonably priced.

Cornerstone Café
St John's Church, corner of Princes Street and Lothian Road, EH2 (229 0212). Bruntsfield buses. **Open** 9.30am-4pm Mon-Sat. **Closed** Sun. **Average** £4.50. **No credit cards. Map 8 A2**
In the tranquil undercroft of St John's Church, alongside a Christian bookshop and the One World gift shop, this self-service café has a competitively priced vegetarian menu with a good selection of home-baked cakes. Outside tables during the summer and the child-friendly facilities have earned the café and award.
No smoking.

Daniel's Bistro
88 Commercial Street, EH6 (553 5933). 10A, 16, 32, 52, 88(A) buses. **Open** 9am-10pm daily. **Average** £12.50. **Credit** MC, £TC, V. **Map 2 Leith**
One of a row of restaurants opposite the Scottish Office in Leith, Daniel's is worth the detour from anywhere in Edinburgh. The conservatory setting is relaxing and, although busy, the tables aren't too close together. As for the food, it's reasonably priced and exhibits the best tendencies of French provincial cuisine. No-smoking conservatory.

Delifrance
1 Waterloo Place, EH1 (557 4171). Princes St buses. **Open** 8am-6pm Mon-Sat; 10am-5pm Sun. **Average** £7. **No credit cards. Map 4 G4**
Part of the chain of French-style bistro-cafés. Perfect for perusing the papers over coffee and a traditional French breakfast or a selection from the tempting pâtisserie.
Branch: 7-8 Queensferry Street, EH2 (220 0474).

The Elephant House
21 George IV Bridge, EH1 (220 5355). George IV Bridge buses. **Average** £6. **Credit** MC, £TC, V. **Map 9 B3**
A comfortable and airy café that attracts a friendly mix of students, families and professionals with its excellent coffee and good range of light meals and snacks. The non-smoking area at the front helps, while smokers have a view of the Castle from the back room.

Elephant's Sufficiency
170 High Street, EH1 (220 0666). 1, 6, 34, 35 buses. **Open** *winter* 8am-5pm Mon-Sat-Sun; *summer* 8am-10pm Mon-Fri; 9am-10pm Sat-Sun. **Average** £5.25. **No credit cards. Map 9 D2**
A small, bright café, whose name refers to the hearty portions of home-made soups, burgers, sandwiches and other light meals. The atmosphere is buzzing during the Festival, thanks to the High Street location. Tables are provided outside during the summer.

The Engine Shed
19 St Leonard's Lane, EH8 (662 0040). 2(A), 12(A), 21 buses. **Open** 10.30am-3.30pm Mon-Thur; 10.30am-2.30pm Fri; 10.30am-4pm Sat; 11.30am-4pm Sun. **Average** £3.50. **No credit cards. Map 7 H7**
A purely vegetarian café run under the auspices of Garvald Community Enterprises, which provides training and work opportunities for adults with learning difficulties. Simple but pleasant meals and snacks are available to eat; or you can just enjoy a quiet cuppa in this calm environment before traipsing up Arthur's Seat.
No smoking.

La Grande Cafétière
184 Bruntsfield Place, EH10 (228 1188). Bruntsfield buses. **Open** 9am-11pm Mon-Wed; 9am-midnight Thur-Sat; 10am-6pm Sun. **Average** £10. **Credit** MC, £TC, V. **Map 6 D8**
This cosy, family-run establishment is a bustling café, offering a selection of reasonably priced sandwiches and snacks, by day. At 6pm, the café gives way to a bistro-style à la carte evening menu.

Gustos
105 High Street, EH1 (558 3083). 1, 6, 34 35 buses. **Open** *winter* 9am-6pm daily; *summer* 9am-11pm daily. **Average** £6. **Credit** £TC. **Map 9 D2**
This bright, relaxed café, with a good view over the Royal Mile, is a fine pausing point on the tourist trail. Upstairs is the main café area, with a takeaway section downstairs. Light dishes are served all day and the beverages on offer include delicious fruit smoothies and lassis. Tables are provided outside during the summer.

Elephant House – *linger over a jumbo coffee within sight of the Castle. Page 137.*

Helios Fountain

7 Grassmarket, EH1 (229 7884). 2, 12 buses. **Open** 10am-6pm Mon-Sat; noon-4pm Sun. **Average** £4. **Credit** JCB, MC, V. **Map 9 A3**
A relaxed, cosy café located at the back of a shop and offering wholesome vegetarian and vegan food, well priced and tasty, though it's more of a fruit tea than a coffee stop. *No smoking.*

Kaffe Politik

146-148 Marchmont Road, EH9 (446 9873). 24, 40, 41(A) buses. **Open** 10am-10pm daily. **Average** £5. **No credit cards. Map 6 F8**
This stylish café is a popular spot with locals and students. The airy surroundings and wide selection of speciality teas and coffees make it an ideal daytime venue and the all-day full breakfast at weekends is a popular choice for the hungover or just plain hungry.

Kinnells House

36 Victoria Street, EH1 (220 1150) George IV Bridge buses. **Open** 10am-6pm Mon-Sat; 11am-6pm Sun. **Average** £5. **Credit** AmEx, MC, £TC, V. **Map 9 B2**
The 40-plus varieties of coffee beans sold by the pound from the café downstairs give this cosy, art nouveau-style café a distinct, delicious aroma. All the many coffees and tea are available in the café (table service downstairs, counter service upstairs) as well as a selection of home-made food.

Laigh Bake House

117A Hanover Street, EH2 (225 1552). Princes St buses, then 5-min walk. **Open** 8am-4pm Mon-Sat. **Closed** Sun. **Average** £7. **No credit cards. Map 8 C1**
Stone walls, wooden seats, a coal fire, a patio and straight-backed ladies of a certain age make this a genuine Edinburgh nook for the genteel consumption of tea and coffee, with a slightly naughty selection of home-baked cakes and scones.

Lower Aisle Restaurant

St Giles' Cathedral, High Street, EH1 (225 5147). 1, 6, 34, 35 buses. **Open** 9.30am-4.30pm Mon-Fri; 10am-1pm Sun. **Closed** Sat. **Average** £7. **No credit cards. Map 9 C2**
Situated beneath St Giles' Cathedral, this is a peaceful, comfortable self-service restaurant with a small range of wholesome dishes at competitive prices.

Mango & Stone

165A Bruntsfield Place, EH10 (229 2987). Bruntsfield buses. **Open** 8am-8pm daily. **No credit cards. Map 6 D8**
A café-cum-juice-bar with a huge variety of juices, smoothies, yoghurt drinks and speciality coffees and teas, all of which can be blended to your choice. Also a wide range of pastries and sandwiches, all made on the premises. *No smoking.*

Le Menu

248 Dalry Road, EH11 (467 7847). Dalry Road buses. **Open** 10am-9.30pm Mon-Sat. **Closed** Sun. **Average** £4. **No credit cards. Map 5 B7**
Worth a detour from the main drag, this simple, unpretentious bistro operates as a café until 6pm, then offers uncomplicated food at affordable prices.

Metropole

33 Newington Road, EH9 (668 4999). Bridges buses. **Open** 9am-10pm Mon-Sun. **Average** £6. **No credit cards.**
Bright-orange walls and a chic Parisian art deco sense of style have made this hip café a popular hang-out among the young and trendy. A great place to relax with the newspapers, a selection from 20 coffees, 33 teas, hot chocolate or milkshakes and a tempting choice of cakes and scones. Burritos, pizza and sandwiches are available, too. *No smoking.*

Ndebele

57 Home Street, EH3 (221 1141). Bruntsfield buses.
Open 10am-10pm Mon-Sun. **Average** £5. **No credit
cards. Map 6 D7**
Unusual décor, soothing African music, friendly staff and
delicious South African food give this an unique place in the
Edinburgh pantheon of cafés. The food is delicious and it's
also a great nook from which to watch the world pass by.

Number One Brasserie

1 Chambers Street, EH1 (226 7177). Bridges buses.
Open 8am-10pm Mon-Fri; 8am-11pm Sat; 9am-10pm
Sun. **Average** £6.50. **Credit** AmEx, DC, MC, V. **Map 9
C3**
A bright and modern café/bistro with a simple, yet fairly
extensive, menu at very reasonable prices. Well suited for a
relaxed evening meal or a quick daytime snack. Live music
on Thursday nights.

Palm Court Lounge

Balmoral Hotel, 1 Princes Street, EH1 (556 2414).
Princes St buses. **Open** 8am-6pm daily; *breakfast* 8-
10.30am; *afternoon tea* 2.30-6pm; *full afternoon tea*
£10.75. **Credit** AmEx, DC, MC, £$TC, V. **Map 8 D2**
If it's an afternoon tea with style you're wanting, then this
is the place to go. Millionaires lounge on vast armchairs,
obsequious waiters glide among the works of art and the
chandeliers shimmer down on it all. And the afternoon feast
(champagne extra) lives up to the ambience.

Parrots

3 Viewforth, EH10 (229 3252). Bruntsfield buses. **Open**
6-10.30pm Tue-Thur; 5-10.30pm Fri-Sat. **Closed** Sun,
Mon. **Average** £7.50. **No credit cards. Map 6 D8**
An unorthodox bistro, adorned with parrots, in a neo-
Victorian setting. The menu is vast and varied. Quirky
touches add an interesting originality, with inventive
desserts and an extensive choice of non-alcoholic cordials
and cocktails.
No smoking.

Pâtisserie Florentin

*8 St Giles Street, EH1 (225 6267). 1, 6, George IV
Bridge buses.* **Open** 7am-11pm Sun-Thur; 7am-2am Fri,
Sat. **Average** £6. **No credit cards. Map 9 B2**
Bright, sunny décor with an abundance of huge sunflowers
gives this laid-back café a welcoming feel. But it's the cake
and pâtisserie selection that makes the mouth water and
truly satisfies the taste buds.
Branch: 5 North West Circus Place, EH2 (220 0225).

Pigs Bistro

41 West Nicolson Street, EH8 (667 6676). Bridges buses.
Open noon-2pm, 6-10pm Mon-Sat. **Closed** Sun.
Average £12. **Credit** MC, £TC, MC, V. **Map 7 G6**
A fun, unpretentious place where the portions are generous
and the diverse menu apparently unconstrained by any sin-
gle cooking creed. Corkage at £1 for wine and 25p for beer.

The Place to Eat

*John Lewis, Second Floor, St James Centre, EH1 (556
9121). Princes St buses.* **Open** 9.30am-5.15pm Tue, Wed,
Fri; 9.45am-7.15pm Thur; 9.30am-5.45pm Sat. **Closed**
Sun, Mon. **Average** £8. **No credit cards. Map 4 G4**
A nifty hidey-hole from the shopping frenzy, this bright and
airy self-service restaurant and café has splendid views of
Carlton Hill and the Firth of Forth. The selection is wide, rea-
sonably inexpensive and tolerably well prepared
No smoking.

River Café

*36 Deanhaugh Street, EH3 (332 3322). 20, 28, 80(A/B)
buses.* **Open** 9am-6pm Mon-Sat; 11am-6pm Sun.
Average £5.50. **No credit cards. Map 2 C3**

A small, bright basement café in the heart of Stockbridge,
overlooking the Water of Leith, which offers wholesome
equivalents of the traditional greasy spoon café, but without
the oil slick. The Persian owner has also influenced the menu
to include such specialities such as mizra gasemi – baked
aubergine, tomato, egg served with pitta bread.

Seattle Coffee Company

Waterstone's, 128 Princes Street, EH2 (226 3610).
Princes St buses. **Open** 9.30am-8pm Mon-Fri; 9.30am-
7pm Sat; 11am-5pm Sun. **Average** £3. **No credit
cards. Map 8 A2**
Coffee connoisseurs conflict over their choice of Seattle's or
California's Coffee Co for the best cappuccino. But Seattle
boasts a bookshop downstairs, a prime view of the Castle
and an excellent selection of snacks.
Branches: are too numerous to list here. Consult the
Phone Book for your nearest.
No smoking.

Smoke Stack

*53-55 Broughton Street, EH1 (556 6032). 7A, 8(A),
9(A), 19, 39 buses.* **Open** noon-2.30pm, 6-10.30pm Mon-
Fri; noon-10.30pm Sat. **Average** £12. **Credit** AmEx, DC,
MC, V. **Map 3 F3**
The warm, informal atmosphere inside this stylish bistro on
booming Broughton Street contrasts nicely with its discreet
frosted glass fronting and elegantly modernist interior.
Carnivores and vegetarians are all well served by a menu
that is heavily influenced by the American Deep South, both
in flavour and generously sized portions.

The Terrace Café

*Royal Botanic Garden, Inverleith Row, EH3 (552 0616).
7A, 8(A), 9(A), 23, 27, 37 buses.* **Open** 9.30am-6pm
daily. **Average** £7. **Credit** MC, £TC, V. **Map 3 D2**
The splendid setting, beside Inverleith House, gives this
café one of the most stunning views across the city skyline.
In summer, you can enjoy al fresco coffee, a snack or lunch
from a menu that has a 'botanic' feel and Scottish influence.
No smoking.

James Thin Booksellers Café

*57 George Street, EH2 (225 4495). George St
buses.* **Open** 8am-5pm Mon-Sat; 8am-9.30pm Tue;
11.15am-4.30pm Sun. **Average** £5. **No credit cards.
Map 8 B1**
A welcome oasis above the bustle of George Street, this
relaxed café has a real old-fashioned charm and boasts a
tempting selection of home-baking as well as a small selection of hot dishes and snacks.

Valvona & Crolla

19 Elm Row, EH7 (556 6066). Leith Walk buses. **Open**
8am-5pm Mon-Sat. **Closed** Sun. **Average** £8-£12.
Credit AmEx, MC, £TC, V. **Map 4 G3**
A traditional slice of Italian culture in this café, at the far end
of the much-celebrated delicatessen and wine store (*see page
114* **Gourmet's delight**). Bright, bustling and relaxed, the
café begins the day serving a full Italian breakfast (8am-
11am), including house special sausages, before moving on
to a variety of pizzas, chicken, fish and pasta dishes. The
cakes and pastries are a must.
No smoking.

The Vintner's Rooms

*The Vaults, 87 Giles Street, EH1 (554 6767). 1, 6,
George IV Bridge buses.* **Open** noon-2pm, 7-10.30pm
Mon-Sat. **Closed** Sun. **Average** £22. **Credit** AmEx,
MC, £TC, V. **Map 2 Leith**
This elegant bistro is the more informal of the Vintner's
Rooms' two eating spaces. The menus revolve around top-
quality fish, game, beef and lamb, well prepared and imag-
inatively treated.

DAY BY DAY & HOUR BY HOUR

MUSIC CLUBS THEATRE DANCE CINEMA ART

THE LIST

GLASGOW AND EDINBURGH
EVENTS GUIDE

FORTNIGHTLY FROM ALL GOOD NEWSAGENTS £1.90

Arts & Entertainment

Children

Castles and dungeons, water flumes and sea creatures: it's as good as Disneyland, and it's all real. Here's how to make a family visit child's play.

Edinburgh is great from a kid's point of view. Where else does the high street begin with a fantasy castle, slope down past a queen's palace and end up at a volcanic mountain? Not only are many of the interesting sights within walking distance of each other, but it is also a pretty good place to walk around with children in tow. In spite of the hills and traffic, most of the pavements are wide enough to let kids trot along at their own pace without having to grab them out of danger all the time. If short legs get tired a popular alternative is a big black taxi. Fares are reasonable, there are seats for five passengers, all with seatbelts, and pushchairs don't need to be folded. On buses and trains, under-fives go free and five-to-15s pay half price. The open-top guided tour buses, although more expensive, allow you to get on and off all day for the price of a single ticket.

Those with only a day or two in Edinburgh are best off sticking to **Edinburgh Castle** and the Old Town area. Older kids will love the Ghosts and Ghouls tours (*see box* **Murder and mayhem on the Mile** *page 45*). Those staying longer could try the Zoo, Deep Sea World, Inchcolm Island, Dalkeith County Park, Butterfly and Insect World or, in warmer weather, the clean beach at Gullane.

An invaluable guidebook is *Edinburgh for Under Fives*, available from most local bookshops. The *Edinburgh Tourist Board* will send you information on current children's events and staff can give you detailed information about suitable accommodation for families over the phone.

Sites listed in **bold** are described in more detail elsewhere in the guide (*see index*).

Events & entertainment

Many of the annual events listed in the **Edinburgh by Season** chapter include activities for kids. Hogmanay, the Science Festival, the Scottish International Children's Festival, the Royal Highland Show, Meadows Festival, Edinburgh Festival and Fringe, and the Book Festival are all particularly good.

Netherbow Arts Centre often stages plays aimed at children. Most other theatres have some sort of pantomime or children's show at Christmas. There is always an excellent reinterpretation of a classic fairy or folk story aimed at five-to-ten year

olds at the **Royal Lyceum**. The **Theatre Workshop** produces an alternative, often ethnically based, show for the over-fives and the **Traverse Theatre**'s offering usually includes a singalong for small children. For the traditional Scottish panto, complete with dancing girls, dame, best boy and plenty of glitter, the **King's Theatre** comes up trumps.

Two cinemas run Saturday clubs for children. The **ABC Film Centre** on Lothian Road often has a disco followed by a movie at lunchtime. The **Odeon** offers a choice of three films in the morning with drinks and popcorn included in the price. The **Filmhouse** often has programmes that are as suitable for children as they are for grown-ups.

The **City Art Centre** often hosts blockbuster exhibitions that attract children and has a café with high chairs.

Exploring

Central/Princes Street

Edinburgh Castle has loads for kids to do. Take a couple of hours and get there in good time for the One O'clock gun, fired daily (not Sunday) with a satisfyingly big bang and puff of smoke by a stiffly marching soldier. It is still an army HQ so there are plenty of real soldiers about. There's lots of open rocky space for scrambling on, some scary precipices, very exciting dungeony bits, very boring military museums, a teeny church that often has weekend weddings and a spacious cafe with dull but child-friendly food.

The High Street is riddled with alleyways and courtyards that are great for exploring – quite a few lead to open spaces that are good for a run-about or a picnic, particularly Dunbar's Close on the Canongate, which is a secluded seventeenth-century garden.

Worth considering for older kids are the **Camera Obscura**, which has some scary holograms and good telescopes, and the **Brass Rubbing Centre**, a great rainy day standby. The **Museum of Childhood**, the **People's Story** and the **Huntly House Museum** are three free museums in the High Street/Canongate area. The Museum of Childhood can be a little disappointing for wee ones because it is full of marvellous toys they can't get their hands on, but the shop is good. The People's Story is fun with lots of life-size figures and noises, but Huntly House's presentation of local history is a bit dry.

In the western part of Princes Street Gardens (between the Mound and Lothian Road), there's a small, clear plastic-sided bridge over the railway behind the Ross Bandstand. If you wave enough the train drivers will sometimes hoot. There's also a playground and, in summer, an outdoor café.

The **Palace of Holyroodhouse** is best seen by guided tour, a bit dull for little ones, though the grounds are nice. Walk to the end of the Canongate and you'll reach the base of **Arthur's Seat**. To the left is St Mary's Loch, with loads of swans and a large area that's particularly suitable for the flying of kites, gliding of frisbees, kicking around of footballs and general letting off of steam. From here it is quite a long haul to the top. If it is likely to prove too much for weaker legs, get a taxi up to Dunsapie Loch, climb the last bit of hill and then walk down instead.

Calton Hill, with its row of Greek columns on top, is just off the east end of Princes Street. It is a good open space for fresh air and views if you haven't the energy or time for Arthur's Seat. There are a couple of visitor attractions, monuments and lots of grass, but it is not very clean and only just accessible by pushchair from Waterloo Place – if you bump up the first flight of steps.

Southside

The **Royal Museum of Scotland** is perfect for wet days. It has masses of space, gigantic stuffed animals, indoor goldfish ponds, buttons to push, two eating areas and lockers to stash pushchairs and coats.

At the far west end of Chambers Street is the dog statue of Greyfriars Bobby. **Greyfriars Kirkyard** itself will interest older children. South along Forrest Road and Middle Meadow Walk lies the Meadows, a big grassy space with two playgrounds, one at each end, and occasional funfairs. It's a great place to let off steam but watch out for dog mess and speeding students on bikes.

North

The **Royal Botanic Garden** is a godsend for children and their minders: acres of grass, no cars and absolutely no dog mess. There are loads of feedable squirrels and ducks, glasshouses with huge goldfish, a gift shop and a café with high chairs, an outdoor eating area and nappy changing facilities. The Exhibition Hall has some good hands-on educational exhibitions for those who become bored with looking at plants. There's also a playground opposite the West Gate, hidden behind hedges in Inverleith Park.

The Water of Leith walkway is a delightful ribbon of riverside path meandering through the city to the docks. The best bit starts from the bridge on Belford Road, opposite the Hilton International, and goes downstream via the Dean Village to Stockbridge. Exit at India Place. A good itinerary is to visit the **National Gallery of Modern Art** and leave through the path to the rear, then follow the waterside walk downstream past the Hilton and end up in Stockbridge. St Stephen Street has lots of little eateries but **Bells Diner**'s real burgers prove popular all round. Maps and info from Water of Leith Conservation Trust (455 7367; 8.30am-4pm Mon-Fri).

The Shore area in Leith can be interesting for those with older children who are not likely to run off and fall in the water. But be warned, the docks are huge and wandering round them can be very time consuming, although they are home to the **Royal Yacht Britannia**. To the west is Newhaven, with its pretty harbour and the **Newhaven Heritage Museum**, where kids can dress up as fishermen and fishwives.

Shark supper at **Deep Sea World**, *page 144.*

Out of town

A half-hour train trip from Waverley Station brings you to the small East Lothian town of North Berwick, with its harbour, summer boat trips to the Bass Rock, ice-cream shops, rockpools and a shallow sea-water paddling pool on the sandy beach. Gullane, an hour's drive (or bus ride) east of the city, has a good clean beach with toilets.

Eight miles (13km) south-east of the city is Dalkeith Country Park (654 1666; buses to Dalkeith), open between March and October and some winter weekends. It's an astonishing adventure playground for the over-fours with elevated walkways, a good café, woodland paths, intriguing riverside tunnels and flying foxbats.

The seabirds and ancient monastic ruins of Inchcolm Island and Abbey, plus the ferry trip to get there, are sure lures for kids. Take the *Maid of the Forth* boat from South Queensferry (24-hour information line 331 4857).

Outdoor activities
Animal encounters

Though some of the following are a little far away, all are surefire crowd-pleasers.

Bird of Prey Centre
Dobbies Garden World, Lasswade, Midlothian, EH18 (654 1720). LRT 3, SMT 80(A) buses (no Sunday service). **Open** 10.30am-5pm daily. **Admission** £2.20 adults; £1 children; £1.50 concs; group discounts if booked in advance. **No credit cards.**
Half-an-hour's bus ride away from Princes Street, the Bird of Prey Centre is on the same site as Butterfly & Insect World (*see below*), so if aerial violence doesn't get 'em, aerial elegance will. Flying displays are at 1.30pm and 3pm daily. There's a café nearby.

Butterfly & Insect World
Dobbies Garden World, Lasswade, Midlothian, EH18 (663 4932). LRT 3, SMT 80(A) buses (no Sunday service). **Open** 9.30am-5.30pm daily. **Admission** £3.75 adults; £2.65 children; £2.85 concs; £12 family. **Credit** MC, V.
Not just butterflies, too, including scorpions and red-kneed tarantulas.

Deep Sea World
North Queensferry, Fife, KY11 1JR (01383 411 411). North Queensferry rail, then 10-min walk. **Open** 10am-6pm daily. **Admission** £6.15 adults; £3.75 children; £4.25 concs; £16.75 family. **Credit** MC, V.
An award-winning fishy paradise.

Edinburgh Zoo
Corstorphine Road, EH12 (334 9171). Haymarket buses. **Open** *Apr-Sept* 9am-6pm Mon-Sat; 9.30am-6pm Sun. *Oct-Mar* 9am-5pm Mon-Sat; 9.30am-5pm Sun. **Admission** £6.50 adults; £3.50 children; £18-£22.50 family; £4-£4.50 concs. **Credit** MC, £TC, V.
Loads of animals, including all the favourites (pandas, hippos, snakes etc), but the zoo's principal claim to fame is its army of penguins, the most assembled in captivity anywhere. At 2pm, every day between March and October, the penguin parade is one of Edinburgh's most bizarre sights.

Gorgie City Farm
Gorgie Road, EH11 (623 7031). Dalry Rd buses. **Open** 9.30am-4.30pm daily. **Admission** free. **No credit cards.**
A lovely informal spot with all your farmyard favourites plus a good café with high chairs and playground.

Playgrounds

Bruntsfield Links & the Meadows
Off Melville Drive, South Side. **Maps 6 E7** and **7 G7**
Canonmills
Eyre Place. **Map 3 E3**
Inverleith Park
Opposite the Royal Botanic Garden, on the other side of Arboretum Place.
Leith Links
Foot of Leith Walk.
Montgomery Street
Off Leith Walk. **Map 4 J4**
Morningside Park
Balcarres Street.
Pilrig Park
Off Pilrig Street, Leith Walk. **Map 4 G1**
Princes Street Gardens
At the west end, opposite Gap. No swings. **Map 8 2A**
Scotland Yard
Scotland Street, New Town. **Map 3 E3**

Indoor activities

Sports centres and ice-rinks are listed in the **Sport** chapter.

Play centre

Leo's at Forecourt Leisure
14 Ashley Place, Newhaven Road, EH6 (555 4533). 7, 11, 17(B), 25(B) buses. **Open** 9.30am-8pm Mon-Fri; 9.30am-6.30pm Sat, Sun. Café closes daily at 5pm. **Admission** £2.80 2-10s; £2 under-2s. **No credit cards.**
For ten-year-olds and under. It's well organised and staffed and has a slide and ball pool for under-threes and a great climbing, sliding and bouncing area for the over-twos. Children under two must be accompanied, older children can be left while parents use the fitness centre or café. It can get a bit rough if there's a children's party on, so phone first. Good baby-changing facilities and the café has toys.

Swimming

Edinburgh has some great swimming but opening hours are currently limited by a funding crisis so always phone first. The main pools usually sell arm bands and floats.

Leith Waterworld (555 6000) is a state of the-art leisure pool, with flumes, wave machine and a gently sloping 'beach' which is good for babies. There are also family changing rooms, playpens and a bookable crèche. Ainslie Park (551 2400) has a baby pool.

Of the pools listed in the **Sport** chapter, the **Royal Commonwealth Pool** is best for kids as it has flumes (open from 2.30pm). **Glenogle Swim Centre** and **Warrender Baths** have crèches; Genogle's is bookable.

Eating out
Places children will like

Chain inns where a play shed has been tacked on to a pub/diner on the city fringes are hardly inspiring and the food can be awful. But they do provide some kid-free moments. The Cramond Inn (Glebe Road, Cramond Village, EH4; 336 2035), Lauriston Farm Brewers Fayre (Lauriston Farm Road, Silverknowles, EH4; 312 7071) and Hunter's Tryst Restaurant (97 Oxgangs Road, Oxgangs, EH13; 445 3132) are typical. Slightly better food is available at Umberto's (2 Bonnington Road Lane, Leith, EH6; 554 1314), where booth tables form a train, no one minds the kids running around and there's an outdoor playground. **Guiliano's** on the Shore in Leith (554 5272) is another, less gimmicky, Italian; children can create their own pizzas. Fat Sam's (56 Fountainbridge, EH4; 228 3111) has a cartoon barn ambience that youngsters like. For sit-down fish and chips, Harry Ramsden's (Pier Place, Newhaven; 551 5566) is good.

Places parents will like

These restaurants are listed elsewhere (*see index*). They all serve really good food in an adult atmosphere but still welcome children.

Blue Bar & Café
Sophisticated, blond wood and glass, wonderful food, high chairs, half portions and plenty of space. Plus a glass lift down to an indoor courtyard for inter-course amusement.

The Dome
A former bank of grand proportions, with the sort of white-aproned waiters who whip out a high chair and wipe it down for you. And then offer to heat the baby food.

The Outhouse
A trendy bar/restaurant with tables in an open-air courtyard and boules court. No high chairs.

Around the Old Town

Beware – all decent eating places suddenly stop halfway between the Castle and Holyrood Palace. If you haven't fed and watered the weans by the time you get to the High Street/St Mary's Street Junction, retrace your steps. The Canongate is a miserable culinary desert. **See Map 8**

Circles Coffee House
3/4 Lawnmarket, EH1 (225 9505). 1, 6, 34, 35 buses. **Open** 9.30am-6pm daily. **No credit cards.**

Lorenzo's
5 Johnston Terrace, EH1 (226 2426). 1, 6, 34, 35 buses. **Open** noon-2pm, 6-11pm, Mon-Fri; noon-11pm Sat-Sun. **Credit** AmEx, MC, V.
Child-friendly Italian restaurant.

Patisserie Florentin's
(see *chapter* **Cafes & Bistros**)
Delicious pâtissiere and snacks; a bit cramped but worth it.

The Filling Station
(see *chapter* **Pubs & Bars**)

Large American-style diner, MTV, burgers and Mexican. High chairs, nappy-changing area.

Pizza Hut
46 North Bridge, EH1 (226 3038). Bridges buses. **Open** 11.30am-10.30pm Mon-Thur; 11.30am-11pm Fri; 11.30am-midnight Sat; 11.30am-11.30pm Sun. **Credit** AmEx, MC, V.
The standard Pizza Hut package includes a children's menu, crayons and a free toy and helium balloon. High chairs, nappy-changing facilities and understanding staff.

Gusto's
(see *chapter* **Cafes & Bistros**)
Licensed café. Spacious, casual and friendly with a high chair, but small toilets.

Di Placido's
36-38 High Street, EH1 (557 2286). 1, 6, Bridges buses. **Open** 8am-6.30pm Mon-Fri; 8am-6pm Sat; 10am-5pm Sun. **Credit** AmEx, JCB, MC, V.
Italian deli – fab sandwiches to take away and a few tables on the street outside.

Netherbow Arts Centre Cafe
43 High St, EH1 (556 2647). 1, 6 buses. **Open** 9am-5pm Mon-Sat. **No credit cards.**
Nutritious soups and great scones. Very child-friendly, with an outdoor courtyard, toys and books, high chairs and a nappy changing area.

Practicalities for parents
Babysitting/childminding

The top hotels provide their own. Edinburgh Crèche Co-op (*see below*) can provide a baby sitting service in your room, take the child(ren) out for the day and provide mobile crèches for parties and so on. Emergency Mums (447 7744; 8.45am-5pm Mon-Fri) and Guardian (343 3870; 9am-8pm daily) will look after the kids in your home or hotel.

Edinburgh Crèche Co-op
297 Easter Road, EH6 (553 2116). 1, 6, 24(A) buses. **Open** 9am-5pm Mon-Fri. **Charge** £9.76 hourly.

Equipment hire

Baby To Go (01506 824 134; 24 hours daily) will deliver pushchairs, cots, backpacks, car seats and more, as will Baby Equipment Hire (337 7016; 9am-9pm daily).

Shopping

The best toyshop is in **Jenners** department store on Princes Street. For baby supplies Princes Street also has branches of Boots and Mothercare. If the children are with you, nearby Waverley Market is a useful hiding place on a wet day for its glass lifts, statues and pools.

St James Centre has an Early Learning Centre toyshop, and a John Lewis with café and baby changing. Safeway on Pilton Drive, EH5 (315 4970), has a lovely crèche for children between two and ten years old. The **Gyle Shopping Centre** has crèches for children between three months and eight years.

Comedy

Edinburgh is now officially funny all year round. Get your laughing gear here.

For three weeks in August, Edinburgh becomes the undisputed laughter capital of Britain, if not the world, with comedy in all its forms being probably the best-known face of the Festival Fringe.

Until recently, however, the city presented a decidedly dourer aspect throughout the rest of the year; successive attempts by one aspiring promoter or another to establish some kind of ongoing venture foundered repeatedly on the rocks of scant resources, remoteness from the stand-up circuit's London hub and perceived audience apathy.

As of 1995, however, one small club with big ideas and bucketloads of determination – step forward **The Stand**, and take a bow – altered the picture dramatically, staging weekly gigs (now several weekly gigs) in a series of hired pub basements before moving, after three years of rapidly snowballing operation, into its own custom-designed premises in the New Town. With its main-house bills lining up newcomers and rising talents alongside more tried and tested acts, the Stand has encouraged the emergence of a home-grown scene backed by a consistent audience base, latterly forging links with the equally lively north of England circuit. Emboldened by this pioneering example, other regular comedy slots are now beginning to crop up elsewhere in the city.

The talent inevitably comes and goes, but local comics to look out for include Susan Morrison, Frankie Boyle, Vladimir McTavish and Viv & Jill, who have a cabaret club at the Gilded Balloon.

As well as all this indigenous activity, the TV-boosted big guns of the UK-wide comedy scene periodically pass through on tour, usually playing the **Queens Hall** or the **Traverse Theatre**.

The Stand Comedy Club
5 York Place, EH1 (enquiries 558 7373/box office 558 7272). 7A, 8(A), 9(A), 19, 39 buses. **Open** *café-bar* noon-midnight Mon-Fri; noon-1am Sat, Sun; *comedy* times and nights vary. *Red Raw* 8-10pm Mon; *videos/sitcoms* 7pm-midnight Tue; *World of Comedy Quiz Show* 9-11.30pm Wed; *comedy acts* 9-11pm Thur, 9-11.15pm Fri, 9-11.30pm Sat; *Pint Size comedy* (short acts) 8-10pm Sun. **Admission** £1 Mon; free Tue, Wed; £4 Thur; £5 (£3 concs) Fri; £6 (£4 concs) Sat; £2 Sun. **Credit** MC, V. **Map 3 F4**
Housed in a former insurance company document store, the Stand's basement premises comprise two performance spaces. The main cabaret bar is decked out in blues and brick reds, holding audiences of up to 150, while the rather barer studio space can squeeze in around half that number.

Gilded Balloon Theatre/Studio
233 Cowgate, EH1 (226 6550). Bridges buses, then 5 min walk. **Open** *end Sept-mid June* 8-10pm Sat. **Admission** £5 (£4 concs). **No credit cards. Map 9 C3**
One of the major players on the Fringe comedy circuit, the Gilded Balloon stages a varied series of gigs and club nights over the year, featuring a mix of local and imported acts.

Christie's Comedy Cellar
27-31 West Port, EH1 (228 3765). 2(A), 12(A), 28 buses. **Open** *stand-up* 9.30-11.30pm Thur; *Kit-Kat Club Cabaret* 10pm-midnight (free cocktail included) alternate Fri; *spontaneous* 9.30-11.30pm Sun. **Admission** Thur, Fri £4 (£3 concs); Sun £3 (no concs). **No credit cards. Map 8 B3**
Regular weekly servings of in-your-face humour – literally – from up, coming and in-yer-face local acts in an authentically intimate stone-walled cellar bar.

*Take a seat at **The Stand Comedy Club**.*

Film

Trainspotting jacked-up Edinburgh's presence on the silver screen, yet it is Big Sean who is known around the world.

Edinburgh has made it on to the big screen, big time! Well, that's what its denizens would have you believe, and it's all down to that one expression of heroin abuse and nihilism: *Trainspotting*. Forget the fact that it was mostly shot in Glasgow and its characters are repugnant, it was set in Edinburgh and that's what counts.

The city's presence on the silver screen is actually quite strong considering its modest size – even after discounting a certain 007. Sean Connery, probably the most famous Scot in the world, drove his milkfloat up Fountainbridge before finding fame as James Bond. Although Connery comes back to open the odd film at the Film Festival, he is more likely to be found pacing the greens and fairways of Scotland's upmarket golf courses.

Of course, there have been the predictable tourist-oriented short films over the years. And the Disney-tastic excesses of the likes of *Greyfriars Bobby* (1961), which tells the story of the wee Highland Terrier who stayed near the grave of his master, John Gray, in Greyfriars Churchyard for 14 years after he died in 1858.

But there is a small group of movies in which, as David Bruce points out in his book, *Scotland the Movie*, the character of Edinburgh is integral to the feel of the film. *The Battle of the Sexes* (1959) depicts the city as 'cold, hidebound, reactionary and harbouring homicidal tendencies'. Not an altogether fair analysis, but one which Peter Sellers uses to great comedic effect. And also one which is portrayed in *The Prime of Miss Jean Brodie* (1968), adapted from the book by Muriel Spark, which won Maggie Smith the Oscar for Best Actress in 1969.

Part of the problem in portraying Edinburgh is that it is simply too pretty a place. Which is why, when the darker side of life is addressed, the tourist end of town has been spurned for the down-at-heel outer estates. And they have been well reflected. *Conquest of the South Pole* (1989) catches the depression of unemployment in a peculiarly fascinating light when a group of unemployed lads in Leith re-enact Amundsen's Polar journey. Similarly, *Shallow Grave* (1994), the first film from the *Trainspotting* production team, reflected the

Renton gets sick from the number of times Trainspotting *is mentioned in this guide.*

zeitgeist of the early 1990s when yuppie greed seemed capable of anything.

But the problem with shooting movies in Edinburgh is the Scottish film industry has its institutional and practical bases in Glasgow. Edinburgh might have the longest-running film festival in the world (*see chapter* **Edinburgh by Season**), but Glasgow has the government-funded Scottish Film and Locate in Scotland, as well as all the studios.

Practical information

Film programmes change on Fridays. Full listings are carried in *The List* magazine. The *Edinburgh Evening News* and *The Scotsman* carry limited listings. Films are classified as: (U) for universal viewing; (PG) parental guidance advised for young children; (12), (15) and (18) no entry for those aged under 12, 15 and 18 respectively. Most cinemas offer a reduced entry price on weekdays for students, children, OAPs and the unemployed.

Cinemas

Fifty years ago, Edinburgh's cinema-goers had at least 39 different cinemas to choose from. Now there are seven. But these seven have 38 screens between them. And that is not all. The ABC chain is planning to increase the screens at the Lothian Road site to ten. Virgin expects to operate a 13-screen multiplex out at Fountain Park in western Edinburgh and Warner Village will have 12 screens at the Greenside Place entertainment complex between Princes Street and Leith Walk. The problem is that all these screens will probably not increase the choice of films on offer, just the number of different times they can be seen.

ABC Film Centre

120 Lothian Road, EH3 (228 1638/recorded info 229 3030/credit card bookings 228 1638). Bruntsfield buses. **Tickets** £2.80-£3.80 before 6pm; £4.10-£4.80 after 6pm; £2.80-£3.20 concs. **Credit** AmEx, MC, V. **Map 8 A3**
Mainly commercial fare is on show at this city-centre, three-screen cinema. Although the building is getting a bit tatty around the edges the screens more than make up for it in size. Screen One has the best atmosphere in town when packed out on a Friday night for the latest blockbuster. There are two bars — which cannot have changed too many times since the cinema was opened as the Regal in 1938.
Disabled: access; toilets.

ABC Multiplex

Westside Plaza, 120 Wester Hailes Road, Wester Hailes, EH14 (453 1569/recorded info 442 2200/2 4-hour credit card bookings 0541 550 505). Wester Hailes rail. **Tickets** £3-£3.60 before 6pm; £4.20-£5 after 6pm; £3-£3.20 concs. **Credit** AmEx, MC, V.
Modern, eight-screen multiplex out to the west of the city centre. Refreshments are served in an ice-cream bar – no alcohol, but coffee, soft drinks, ice-cream, sweets and sweets should cater for most tastes.
Disabled: access; toilets.

The Cameo

38 Home Street, Tollcross, EH3 (228 4141/recorded info 228 2800/credit card bookings 228 4141). Bruntsfield

buses. **Tickets** £2-£5.20; £2-£3 Mon; £3.50 concs. **Credit** MC, V.
Comfy, cheerful and friendly independent, run from London but showing the imaginative end of the cinematic spectrum. Screen One's airline seats are comfortably spacious, while the good-quality sound can be turned right up for the late night screenings (Thur-Sat) of modern cult movies. Screens Two and Three, on the other hand, are small enough to fit on to an airliner, but the sight lines are good enough. Before 11pm, drinks from the trendy bar may be taken into the film. Top-quality ice-cream – but pricey.
Disabled: access.

The Dominion

18 Newbattle Terrace, Morningside. EH10 (447 4771/recorded info 447 2660/8450/credit card bookings 447 4771). 5, 51, Bruntsfield buses. **Tickets** £3-£4.50 before 6pm; £4.10-£5.50 after 6pm; £3 concs. **Credit** MC, £STC, V.
Cinema-going as she used to be sung! This independent is still run by the Cameron family for whom it was built in 1938. They have a hands-on approach to their cinema and like to make sure their customers are always satisfied. The building is classic art deco, although now divided into four screens. Screen One's Pullman seats are still the comfiest seats in town. Just. The screening policy is in keeping with the douce location in Morningside and oriented towards family entertainment, although commercial realities do not preclude the odd (18)-rated film. Hot snacks available before 6pm in the basement café bar, which stays open until the end of the last film. Drinks may taken into the film.
Disabled: access; toilets.

The Filmhouse

88 Lothian Road, EH3 (228 2688). Bruntsfield buses. **Tickets** £2.90 before 7pm; £3.90 after 7pm; £1.60-£3.60 concs. **Credit** DC, JCB, MC, V. **Map 8 A3**
The British Film Institute's representative cinema in Edinburgh, which means top-quality movies from around the world, the big current arthouse releases and regular screenings for classic movies – although they tend to have short runs. Screen One's sound system is state of the art and powerful. Screen Three's sound system needs to be to drown out the noise of the projector. It is the centre for the Edinburgh International Film Festival and has a relentless round of themed mini-festivals throughout the year including French, Italian, gay and Australian.
Disabled: access; toilets.

The Odeon

7 Clerk Street, EH8 (667 0971/recorded info & credit card bookings 668 2101). Bridges buses. **Tickets** £3.85-£4.60; £2.85-£3.60 concs; £2 Sat am kids' show. **Credit** AmEx, DC, MC, V. **Map 7 G7**
This member of the Odeon chain is centrally located and has five screens. It shows the big commercial movies, with shows for kids on Saturday mornings (no entry without a child) and grown-up late nighters on Fridays and Saturdays. Screen One is huge and all screens are reasonably appointed. Check which seat you're being allocated when you get your ticket or you'll get stuck in the corner.
Disabled: access (cinemas 2 & 3); toilets.

The UCI

Kinnaird Park, Newcraighall Road, EH15 (669 0777/recorded info 669 0711/credit card bookings 0990 888 990). 14(A/B), 32, 52, 88 buses. **Tickets** £3.50 before 3pm; £4.75 after 3pm; £3-£3.50 concs. **Credit** AmEx, MC, V.
Modern multiplex in the Kinnaird Shopping Park about 20 minutes out of town. It lacks the atmosphere of other cinemas, but has good equipment and shows more films for longer runs than its in-town rivals. Good sweet concessions for munchies during the films.
Disabled: access; toilets.

Gay & Lesbian

Out and about in the gay capital of Scotland.

The flower of Scotland's gay scene and a man with a strange habit at **Pride Scotland**.

Whatever your reason for coming to Edinburgh, there's no denying the beauty of the place. Perhaps this is what has made it the centre of gay and lesbian pioneering work in Scotland. Or perhaps it's the city's dour and restrained face, behind which it was possible to hide in the times before the age of consent of 21 was finally adopted into Scots law in 1980 (it is now 18).

Nowadays, the city has a thriving, vibrant and relatively open gay and lesbian community – which has developed a strong commercial element as well as a sound political front. The bars, cafés, clubs and shops in the area, known as the Pink Triangle, surrounding Broughton Street provide a cohesive and successful source of entertainment and information.

Political types have plenty to get on with. The advent of the Scottish Parliament has provided the opportunity to lobby on specifically Scots-related laws. The community's sense of optimism and confidence is obvious from such large-scale productions as the twice-yearly Switchboard Ceilidh held in February and October and the mammoth organising feat behind **Pride Scotland**, held alternatively in Edinburgh and Glasgow in June.

There is plenty of information available without having to look too hard. Posters and flyers advertising all kinds of events can be found at every venue. The best source of news and listings is the free, monthly paper *Gay Scotland*, while *Scotsgay* and *Cruise* are also free and carry listings.

Phone Gay Switchboard on 556 4049 (7.30-10pm daily) or Lesbian Line on 557 0751 (7.30-10pm Mon-Thur) before making your journey, for any major changes.

Broughton Street should be your first port of call at any time of the year. The **Blue Moon** is a good first place to find out what's happening and to link up with the current scene. But although Broughton Street is usually buzzing, don't let it become the only place you visit. There are many more friendly places around town, such as **Black Bo's**, the **Traverse** and the **Festival Theatre**.

Accommodation

All the establishments listed here are either gay- or lesbian-run. A certain level of behaviour is expected (no cruising other guests), but they don't have any restrictions about late entry or who you're travelling with. *See also* the women's section in *chapter* **Directory** for women-only accommodation.

Aries Guest House
5 Upper Gilmore Place, EH3 (229 4669). 10(A), 27, 47 buses. **Rooms** 5. **Rates** B&B £15-£25. **Credit** MC, V. **Map 6 D7**
In the city centre close to all amenities, this small guesthouse is well patronised.

Devon House Guesthouse
2 Pittville Street, EH15 (669 6067). 15(A), 20, 26(A), 66(A), 84 buses. **Rooms** 7 (4 en suite). **Rates** B&B £17-£25. **Credit** DC, JCB, MC, £TC, V.
Well out of town in Edinburgh's seaside district of Portobello. Clean, friendly and within easy reach of Edinburgh city centre by public transport. Ideal if you want both the buzz of a city and the bracing freshness and space of the coast.
Hotel services Continental breakfast. Garden. Multilingual staff. Payphone. Parking (free). Scottish breakfast. Special diets catered for. **Room services** Hairdryer. Tea/coffee-making facilities. TV.

Garlands Guest House

48 Pilrig Street, EH6 (554 4205). Leith Walk buses.
Rooms 6 (all en suite). **Rates** B&B £25-£35. **Credit** MC, £TC, V. **Map 4 H2**
A relatively new place to stay; gay and straight friendly. Clean and comfortable.
Hotel services Continental and Scottish breakfasts. Nio smoking throughout. Parking (free). Payphone. Room services Tea/coffee making facilities. TV.

Mansfield House

57 Dublin Street, EH3 (556 7980). George St buses.
Rooms 5 (2 en suite). **Rates** B&B £30-£40. **Credit** MC, V. **Map 3 F3**
Set in the heart of Edinburgh's Georgian New Town, this substantial guesthouse has five beautifully decorated rooms with continental breakfast served in your room. Tea and coffee are available at any time of the day. Always very clean and always busy, so book in advance.
Hotel services Continental breakfast. Payphone. Room services Refrigerator. Tea/coffee-making facilities. TV.

Rimswell House Hotel

33-35 Mayfield Gardens, EH9 (667 5851). Bridges buses.
Rooms 20 (5 en suite). **Rates** B&B £14.50-£25. **Credit** MC, V.
On a long drag of hotels and guests on the south side of the city, this is not an exclusively gay establishment.
Hotel services Disabled: access with assistance. Lounge. Payphone. Scottish breakfast. Room services Tea/coffee-making facilities. TV.

Letting agency

Clouds Accommodation Agency
16 Forth Street, EH1 (550 3808/fax 550 3807). 7A, 8(A), 9(A), 19, 39 buses. **Open** 9am-6pm Mon-Fri; noon-5pm Sat. **No credit cards. Map 4 G3**
Gay-friendly agency for longer lets and flatshares. Also has flats to let during the Festival.
E-mail cloudsacc@aol.com

Cafés

Blue Moon

See chapter **Cafés & Bistros** *for listings.*
The longest-running gay establishment in Edinburgh. It deserves the good reputation it has gained for a wide menu choice and friendly service. You can easily get into conversation with other customers to find out what's happening. It is licensed and opens until late into the evening as well.

Nexus Café Bar

Lesbian, Gay and Bisexual Centre, 60 Broughton Street, EH1 (478 7069). 7A, 8(A), 9(A), 19, 39 buses. 11am-11pm daily. **Average** £8. **No credit cards. Map 3 F3**
This is the latest revamp of a friendly space that takes you off the street to a bright west-facing room.

Solas

2-4 Abbeymount, EH8 (661 0982). 1, 6 buses. **Open** *Drop-in & Cafe* 11am-4pm Mon-Tue, Thur-Fri; 4-9pm Wed. *Phone* 9am-5pm Mon-Fri. **Closed** Sat, Sun. **No credit cards. Map 4 J7**
The city's HIV/AIDS information and support centre. A wide range of therapies is on offer (counselling and complementary therapies; arts classes; support for children and young people) bookable in advance, plus a good café with a keenly priced menu. See the freebies for details of other gay health agencies.

Clubbing

Traditionally, clubs in Edinburgh have been mixed, that is gay, lesbian and straight. They are not always cruisey, not always druggy, but always safe. The city has a good reputation of bringing together people who want to party – their sexuality is not an issue.

Joy

The legendary 'gay club for happy people' is as busy and lively as ever and now runs once a month on a Saturday at **Wilkie House**. Top guests and a music policy that tends towards the heavier end of house. Info line: *467 2551.*

Luvely

Runs monthly in **Wilkie House**, two weeks after Joy. A fun night out for anyone who is gay, glam or trendy. Lads are strictly not welcome. Big house tunes and glorious fun.

Mingin'

Scots for 'smelly' or 'sweaty', Mingin' runs monthly – on the Saturday between Joy and Luvely – at **Studio 24** and is almost entirely gay. Lighter house music and dressing down. Info line: *467 2551.*

Taste

Attracts an up-for-it and mixed crowd to the **Honeycomb** every Sunday. Hedonism incarnate – if you like your house music to be pumping and uplifting. Dress to sweat, as well as to be seen. Info line: *557 4656.*

Tackno

On the last Sunday of the month at **Club Mercado**, Trendy Wendy attracts an extrovert, mixed crowd to her dressing-up theme nights of trashy disco and '70s kitsch.

Divine Divas

Edinburgh's biggest night for women only, held monthly at the **Venue**. All profits to Lesbian Line. Info: *556 8997.*

Pubs

CC Blooms

See chapter **Nightlife** *for listings.*
The biggest and brashest pub in town, the authentic gay bar. Open early evening, it's busy every night of the week. It has a main bar with lots of seats on the ground floor and a basement with its own dancefloor, good sound system and a variety of DJs and music from disco to house. Keep an eye out for weekly karaoke and strip nights. Exceptionally busy at weekends and Sunday nights.

The Claremont

133/135 East Claremont Street, EH7 (556 5662). 7A, 8(A), 9(A), 19, 39 buses. **Open** 11-1am daily. **Map 3 F2**
A friendly mixed place run by two gay men. It occasionally hosts theme nights and has a restaurant, too.

French Connection

89 Rose Street Lane North, EH2 (225 7651). Princes St buses. **Open** noon-1am daily. **Map 8 B1**
Off the beaten track towards the West End, this tiny bar is the focal point for Edinburgh's TV/TS community.

Newtown

26B Dublin Street, EH3 (538 7775). George St buses. **Open** noon-1am Sun-Thur; noon-2am Fri, Sat. **Map 3 F3**
A well-appointed bar with friendly staff. Almost like a neighbourhood bar, it also opens in the afternoons. Downstairs is **Intense**, A heavy cruise bar famous for its warren of rooms and leather and bear nights.

*For a bloomin' good time, there's nothing like a night on **CC Bloom's** dancefloor.*

Route 66

6 Baxter's Place, Leith Walk, EH1 (524 0061). Leith Walk buses. **Open** 12.30pm-1am Mon-Sat; 3pm-1am Sun. **Map 4 G3**
Just down the road from CC's but attracts a slightly older crowd. It has its own dancefloor, but on ground level. Frequent drink offers and a good range of beers.

Stag and Turret

1-7 Montrose Terrace, EH7 (478 7231). London Rd buses. **Open** 11-1am daily. **Map4 J4**
Out on a limb but still well patronised by locals. Small and friendly, it has a bistro upstairs.

Shops

Fantasies

8B Drummond Street, EH8 (557 8336). Bridges buses. **Open** 10am-9pm Mon-Sat; noon-9pm Sun. **Credit** MC, V. **Map 7 G6**
Downstairs in sexy lingerie outlet Scotland's only licensed sex shop, **Leather and Lace**, Fantasies has lots of things you won't find at your corner store.

Out of the Blue

Basement of the **Blue Moon** (478 7048). **Open** noon-7pm daily. **Credit** MC, V. **Map 3 F3**

PJ's

Part of the **Lesbian, Gay and Bisexual Centre** (*see above*) (558 8174). **Open** 11am-7pm daily. **Credit** MC, V. **Map 3 F3**
Out of the Blue and PJ's carry very much the same sort of stock – and being a stone's throw apart they are in fierce competition with each other. Everything from clothes, gifts, videos and books to toys.

Safety

Whenever we gather together in pursuit of pleasure, the question of safety is not far from our

minds. Outright Scotland, the main political campaigning group, has been working for some years with Lothian and Borders Police. The Gay and Lesbian Liaison Committee ensures that the police will deal fairly and without prejudice with gay and lesbian complaints. There is a Gay and Lesbian Liaison Officer who provides a direct contact for the community and is based at Gayfield Square Police Station at the top of Leith.

Areas within the Pink Triangle, including the area used as a cruising ground between Regent Road and London Road, are policed for the safety of gay men. Cruising areas outside this are not patrolled in this way, although Warriston Cemetery is a cruising ground of long-standing and is relatively safe – but should be avoided at night. Steer well clear of **Calton Hill**. It is notoriously dangerous. Go for the view during the day.

Gayfield Square Police Station

2 Gayfield Square, EH1. (556 9270). Leith Walk buses. **Open** 24 hours daily. **Map 4 G3**

Gay Switchboard

556 4049. **Open** 7.30-10pm daily.

Lesbian Line

557 0751. **Open** 7.30-10pm Mon-Thur.

Sauna

No 18

18 Albert Place, Leith Walk, EH7 (553 3222). Leith Walk buses. **Open** noon-10pm Mon-Sat; 2-10pm Sun. **No credit cards. Map 4 H7**
Edinburgh's only gay sauna and as safe a place as you'll get. The city authorities have a very liberal attitude towards privately run saunas. Attracts all sorts from noon until late. Clean and well run.

Music: Classical & Opera

Imaginative programming and innovative concerts are the hallmarks of Edinburgh's classical music scene.

Lovers of classical music in Edinburgh are pretty well served, even if the really big occasions featuring international symphony orchestras, glitzy soloists and opera to die for tend to happen mainly as part of the Edinburgh International Festival (EIF). There are stunning performances from Scotland's own companies throughout the year. Even though two of the main national companies, the Royal Scottish National Orchestra (RSNO) and Scottish Opera, have their administrative bases in Glasgow they perform regular seasons in the capital. The Edinburgh-based Scottish Chamber Orchestra (SCO), which is enjoying a sensational relationship with principal conductor Joseph Swensen, performs throughout Scotland but gives more concerts in Edinburgh than elsewhere. The BBC Scottish Symphony Orchestra makes occasional forays from the west for one-off events, often featuring music by a specific composer.

The best orchestral venue in the city is the splendid Usher Hall, built in 1913 with £10,000 gifted to the city for the purpose by the beer magnate Sir John Usher. Sadly the hall is out of commission at present, apart from limited use during the EIF, due to internal plasterwork problems with the roof. A failed bid to the Lottery to fund the repairs does not augur well for its future. Outside the Festival, full symphony orchestra performances now take place in the **Edinburgh Festival Theatre** (*see below*), where a specially designed acoustic shell has improved the acoustic for concerts, although it is not an ideal solution for the 90-strong RSNO. A Proms season from the RSNO in the summer brings popular symphonic classics including, as one would expect, nights of Tchaikovsky, Vienna and film music. The RSNO's winter season repertoire on Sunday evenings mixes the familiar with the less familiar, international soloists and conductors adding variety and interest.

The Festival Theatre is, however, excellent for opera. A decent sized pit, one of the largest stages in Europe and an acoustic that's perfect for singers make it popular among Scottish Opera

performers as well as the public. Around eight different operas are mounted by the company annually, mixing past successes with new productions that are generally innovative and often noted for discovering emerging young talent. Puccini has been served particularly well by the company with productions of *Tosca*, *Madam Butterfly* and *La Bohème* in recent years; commissions have included operas by Scottish composers James MacMillan and Judith Weir.

The **Queen's Hall** (*see below*) is a short distance south in a converted Georgian church. The Hall is just right for chamber music but becoming too small for the SCO, whose rehearsing and performing base it is. One of Europe's finest chamber orchestras, the SCO is renowned not only for the quality of its performances but also for its imaginative programming, commissioning policy and education work. Conductor Laureate Sir Charles Mackerras has initiated the orchestra's move into period performance, with natural trumpets and calf-skinned timpani being heard with increasing frequency. It is to be hoped that this side of the orchestra's work will be further developed.

Venues

Edinburgh Festival Theatre

13-29 Nicolson Street, EH8 (box office 529 6000/admin 662 1112). Bridges buses. **Open** *box office/telesales* performance days 11am-8pm Mon-Sat; 4-8pm Sun; non-performance days 11am-6pm Mon-Sat. **Tickets** *opera* £9-£45.50 call for individual event prices. **Credit** AmEx, DC, MC, V. **Map 7 G6**

After years of debating the idea of building a new opera house in Edinburgh, the various powers that be got their act together to bring the old Empire Theatre back to artistic life in June 1994. Scottish Opera, which used to fluctuate between the too-cramped **King's** and the cavernous **Playhouse**, now uses the Festival Theatre for all its Edinburgh performances. Coffees and wines are good enough quality, but interval queuing can be a bore, so remember to order in advance. If not, the Café Lucia at ground level will probably provide the quickest service as staff are more plentiful there. Advance booking is advisable for the best seats – the circle has especially good sightlines.

Glitz, glitter and glamour in Scottish Opera's production of Ariadne auf Naxos.

Les Misérables

THE WORLD'S MOST POPULAR MUSICAL

RETURNS TO EDINBURGH
FOR A LIMITED
SEASON ONLY!

THE EDINBURGH PLAYHOUSE

16 SEPTEMBER - 12 DECEMBER 1998
BOX OFFICE 0131 557 2590 • GROUPS 0131 557 0540

CONTINUES ITS RECORD-BREAKING RUN AT THE PALACE THEATRE LONDON AND NATIONAL TOUR OPENING SOON IN LIVERPOOL AND DUBLIN

Touring companies and the local amateur grand opera society also use the theatre, as do some visiting orchestras and choirs. *(See also chapter* **Music: Rock, Folk & Jazz**.*)*

Queen's Hall

Clerk Street, EH8 (box office 668 2019/admin 668 3456). Bridges buses. **Open** *box office* 10am-5pm Mon-Sat; 6-8pm Sun of performance. **Tickets** £2-£25. **Credit** AmEx, DC, MC, V. **Map 7 H7**

A converted church seating 800 people, which, aside from providing a home for the SCO *(see above)*, also hosts a wide variety of concerts from ensembles and groups of all shapes and sizes. Contemporary and classical chamber music can be heard to great effect here and there are two first-class Steinways in residence. Amateur, youth and school concerts are held regularly and there are short seasons of Wednesday afternoon tea concerts when an extended interval is filled with delicious home-made scones and cakes.

Churches

Many of Edinburgh's churches are suitable for concerts and, indeed, many are used for this purpose during the Fringe. These are the main ones used during the rest of the year.

St Giles' Cathedral

Parliament Square, High Street, EH1 (Visitors' Centre 225 9442). 1, 6, 34, 35 buses. **Open** *spring-autumn* 1.10pm daily. **Organ recitals** 6pm Sun. **Map 9 B2**

Boasts an amazing Rieger organ installed in 1992. On Sundays at 6pm there is an hour of free music and there are regular concerts during spring, summer and autumn (ring the Visitors' Centre for up-to-date information).

Stockbridge Parish Church

Saxe Coburg Street, EH3 (332 0122). 34, 35 buses. **Open** call for dates and times. **Map 3 D3**

The only regularly used concert venue on the north side of the city. Similar in size and architecture to the Queen's Hall, it is used by the Edinburgh Quartet, a number of choirs and for various one-offs. There are no regular concerts, but there is a free mailing list and the church's monthly magazine, *The Bridge*, includes musical events.

St Mary's Episcopal Cathedral

Palmerston Place, EH12 (225 6293). Haymarket buses. **Open** *choral evensong* 5.30pm Mon-Fri; *choral eucharist* 10.30am, *choral evensong* 3.30pm Sun. **Map 5 B6**

At the west end of the city, this is another favourite for organ recitals. Its own choir – the first in Britain to include girl as well as boy trebles – sings at evensong on weekdays during term-time as well as at Sunday services. During the summer, a programme of visiting choirs is offered. Ring the cathedral direct for more information.

St John's Episcopal Church

Princes Street, EH2 (229 7565). Princes St. buses. **Open** *choral eucharist* 9.45am, *choral mass* 11.15am, *choral Evensong* 6pm, *choral eucharist with Taizé music,* 8pm Sun. **Map 6 D5**

Right at the west end of Princes Street, this has a splendid acoustic and is host to a variety of musical happenings.

Greyfriars Tolbooth & Highland Kirk

1 Greyfriars Place, Candlemaker Row, EH1 (225 1900). George IV Bridge buses. **Open** *morning service* 11am, *Gaelic service* 12.30pm Sun. **Map 9 B3**

Choral concerts by professional groups such as Cappella Nova and the Dunedin Consort are often held here. The Kirk produces the quarterly *Greyfriars Programme*, which lists all the events – except for those taking place during the

Festival – and can be picked up from the Tourist Centre or information points in pubs and hotels.

Universities

University of Edinburgh

Contact: concert secretary 650 2423. **Open** 9am-5pm Mon-Fri all year.

An excellent source of free concerts during term-time. High-quality lunchtime chamber music recitals on Tuesdays at the Reid Concert Hall (Bristo Square, EH8, *Oct-May* 1.10-1.55pm) complement Friday lunchtime organ recitals next door at the McEwan Hall (Bristo Square, EH8, *Oct-May* 1.10-1.55pm), where a more unusual repertoire is programmed. Reid Hall also houses the unique **Edinburgh University Collection of Historic Musical Instruments**. The working exhibits of the **Russell Collection of Early Keyboard Instruments**, just down the road at the eighteenth-century St Cecilia's Hall in the Cowgate, are used for public performance once a year.

*The **Edinburgh Festival Theatre** page 152.*

Music: Rock, Folk & Jazz

Innovation and style lead the way on the live music front – proving that size is not everything.

Leaving to one side the colossal impact of the Bay City Rollers in the 1970s, in rock and pop music terms, the capital has always been upstaged by its old rival Glasgow. In terms of long-term commercial success, Edinburgh's recent past is a catalogue of also-rans like Win and Goodbye Mr Mackenzie, whose backup vocalist Shirley Manson nonetheless found fame fronting Garbage, and whose guitarist, 'Big' John Duncan, reached the lofty heights of playing second guitar with Nirvana on their final tour. There are the odd, proud exceptions. The Proclaimers have achieved international recognition with a sound that owes as much to Memphis as it does to the vocal and lyrical tradition of their homeland. Stardom also beckons for pop-reggae singer Finley Quaye whom won the Best Solo Male Brit Award for his debut album.

Edinburgh's relatively small population means that, despite its importance as a capital city, there hasn't been a record industry infrastructure strong enough to compete with the bigger cities. Local record labels are small, hand-to-mouth businesses with very limited clout, and the music business (such as it is) could do with a focal point to rally around. In mid-1997, however, the mood shifted. People were going out more, both to dance in clubs and to support their local bands at rock venues. The record label Equipe Ecosse opened for business; the first major label subsidiary with its head office in Scotland. The unfeasibly sparkling Magicdrive signed a major deal. At the In the City festival (an annual feeding-frenzy for the A&R departments of major record companies), the popularly acclaimed bands were from Edinburgh or other parts of the east coast. The time seems to be right for Annie Christian (Equipe Ecosse's first signing), Idlewild, Cruyff and the Cherry Fire Ashes.

But even though Edinburgh acts have scored low on the commercial potential scale, the innovative spirit that infused such early-1980s bands as Josef K and the Fire Engines still sparks the city. There is a history of maverick combos whose music is frequently as interesting as, if not more than, their counterparts' on the west. Bands from Edinburgh might find it hard to scale the corporate ladder, but that doesn't mean you can't pop into one of the smaller venues and hear some fine, spirited, often inspired bands. And, interestingly, they rarely have anything but their city of origin in common. There isn't, and never has been, an 'Edinburgh sound'.

The dance scene is in good health, with re-mix artists like Huggy (Burger Queen) and George T (Tribal Funktion) making their names on the national and international house music circuits, while the likes of Aqua Bassino and Wreckage do the same for big beat. Old stalwarts Finitribe are constantly mutating to keep ahead of the game.

There's no shortage of guitar bands either. The latest crop include Huckleberry, Chickweed and Solaris as well as the In the City favourites mentioned above. And their number is constantly being augmented. Regular Edinburgh audiences know that if any band fails to last the course there'll be another one along in a minute.

Medium-sized touring bands are spoilt for choice when it comes to playing in Edinburgh. In fact the only real cloud is the fact that the Playhouse Theatre, once a booming rock venue, is block-booked with stage musicals: the biggest-selling bands now miss Edinburgh out of their itineraries altogether, forcing fans to travel 40 miles to the SECC or Barrowland in Glasgow to see them.

Goodbye also-rans, hello Garbage.

FOLK AND ROOTS

But if Edinburgh's rock scene is a bit low key, the folk scene is flourishing like never before. Scotland has witnessed a remarkable flowering of folk and roots-based music in recent years, with Edinburgh firmly at its epicentre. The political potency of traditional music may have diminished since the banning of the bagpipes – on pain of death – as an instrument of war following the 1745 Jacobite Rebellion. Yet the popular debate over cultural identity, at a time of renewed momentum for Scottish self-government, has undoubtedly been the key catalyst in folk music renaissance. Add the widespread interest in acoustic and 'ethnic' music, fostered by the world-beat vogue, and you get a new generation of sounds that embodies Scotland's revitalised self-confidence.

This is inventive stuff, too. Bands like Shooglenifty, Martyn Bennett, the Tartan Amoebas and the Peatbog Faeries blend traditional forms with all manner of rock, dance, jazz and global influences to create music that leaves hoary old finger-in-the-ear folk stereotypes floundering in the dust.

As the undisputed hub of all this cosmopolitan crossover, Edinburgh has become a folk music mecca for those in the know. Edinburgh-born musicians are outnumbered by emigré Highlanders and Hebrideans, folk from Fife and the north-east, and a good sprinkling of Orcadians and Shetlanders for good measure. All of whom add their own traditions to the melting pot. As does the vibrant local jazz and club circuit and the wealth of international cross-currents jointly supplied by the Festival, tourism and an extensive academic community. All told, a recipe for some exhilarating musical adventures.

Cutting-edge fusions aside, Edinburgh's folk scene has many other faces: Pipers in full Highland dress busk on Princes Street; 'traditional' Scottish evenings play nightly during the summer in the big chain hotels; a cappella singers and instrumental duos perform in pub cellars; and the famously raucous late-night ceilidhs held at the Fringe Club during the Festival are routinely packed out with sweatily mad-for-it revellers. The city's musicians cater for the genre's full spectrum of tastes.

Paradoxically the music can take some seeking out. Decent gigs are often thin on the ground. Edinburgh may be abundantly supplied with performers, but the kind of small and mid-scale venues generally best suited to their skills seem to be stuck in the rock and house music circuit. The **Bongo Club**, **La Belle Angele** and **Café Graffiti** are honorable exceptions with an eclectic and frequently interwoven mix of live local acts and club nights, often with an experimental twist.

The city's two folk clubs offer a solid and reasonably diverse diet of traditional and contemporary

All around my hat

For some of the best and surest-fire fun you can have with your clothes on, there is nothing to beat a good ceilidh, as anyone who's survived a Strip the Willow will tell you. This venerable variety of Caledonian intercourse – some popular dance figures are reckoned to date back to pre-Christian days – has enjoyed a remarkable new lease of life in recent years. Gone are the days when the word automatically denoted the kind of embarrassing tartan-bedecked kitsch familiar from the TV Hogmanay specials. A new generation of dancers and bands are lining up to take the floor and the stage – the monthly ceilidhs held at Edinburgh's Assembly Rooms, for instance, regularly sell out well in advance and most of the people on the dancefloor are well under 30. On many weekends there are three or four such events taking place throughout the city.

To the uninitiated the ceilidh can appear a decidedly daunting prospect. But, the seething melee of birling bodies is nothing like as complicated (or perilous) to negotiate as it looks. The beauty of the ceilidh set-up lies in its power to demolish customary – especially in Britain – barriers of reserve and inhibition. A partner is generally the first requirement, but asking or being asked to dance by strangers carries none of the usual potential pick-up connotations, despite the degree of physical contact involved. Many ceilidh bands feature a caller, who shouts out the various moves and steps from the stage before the dance, proper, begins. In the absence of such instruction simply watch and copy those couples who evidently know what they're doing – and don't take offense to the odd friendly shove in the right direction. Listening to the music – basic as it might sound – is the other key point to remember, as the tunes and rhythms themselves will often guide you through the moves.

Hair of the dog – Martyn Bennett takes a peek with Cuillin Music. Page 157.

sounds during most of the year. Among the bigger venues, the **Festival Theatre**, the **Queen's Hall** and the **Assembly Rooms** all stage occasional gigs by Celtic and world-music acts. The last-mentioned is also home to a highly popular monthly series of ceilidhs, held throughout the spring and autumn.

Authentic informal pub sessions tend, by definition, to be spontaneous and are therefore moveable feasts. Some pubs can generally be relied on for a tune, however. The Royal Oak on Infirmary Street (557 2976); Sandy Bell's on Forrest Road (225 2751); Ensign Ewart on the Lawnmarket (225 7440); the Shore Bar on the Shore, Leith (225 2751); and the Hebrides on Market Street (220 4213) are all good bets for a session.

JAZZ

Edinburgh has nurtured a respectable roster of important jazz musicians over the years, including the iconoclastic clarinetist Sandy Brown and the Royal High Gang, of the late 1950s, and saxophonist Tommy Smith, now the most important jazz musician Scotland has ever produced. If they have sometimes seemed to thrive in spite of, rather than thanks to, the city's jazz scene (or simply had to go elsewhere), that is not unique to Edinburgh. Provision for jazz has often been better than in many bigger cities.

The current scene ranges from Dixieland in pubs to international jazz at the **Queen's Hall**, although Assembly Direct's programmes there have become disturbingly erratic. The latest development is an active local late-night club scene, centred on Kulu's Jazz Joint (where jazz-hip hop fusion is a speciality, but acoustic jazz gets an occasional look in – actually hearing it in this noisy basement can be another matter), and the Midnight Blue and Lizzard Lounge club nights at the popular but threatened Café Graffiti. The motivating forces here are an overlapping combination of bands such as Basic Collective, El Cometas and Blackanized, who operate within a loose collective of acts known as the East Coast Project. Wherever they end up will be one of the most vital venues in the city.

For straight-ahead and contemporary jazz, the best option is the Edinburgh Jazz Project's series at the **Tron Tavern and Ceilidh House**, featuring good local and touring artists. There are also a number of well-established free residencies in pubs and restaurants, covering various styles of jazz. The first week of August ushers in the Edinburgh International Jazz Festival. Its reputation as a trad jazz stronghold was partly broken down with the inclusion of the likes of Sun Ra and Pat Metheny, and the festival is now co-produced with Assembly Direct, Scotland's major jazz promoter, who used to run its own Round Midnight festival. The first joint effort in 1997 was a predictable hybrid of the two, but more interesting developments may emerge.

The Leith Jazz Festival is a much more modest event in musical terms, but provides a lively, usually convivial weekend in early June, when the pubs and restaurants around the Shore move into raucous swing mode. The events are free, and there is a genuine buzz around the port, especially if the rain stays away.

Venues

Assembly Rooms

54 George Street, EH2 (box office 220 4349/admin 220 4348). George St buses. **Open** *box office 10am-8pm Mon-Sat; 11am-6pm Sun; admin 10am-5pm Mon-Fri.* **Tickets** £2-£25. **Credit** AmEx, DC, MC, V. **Map 8 B1**
Beyond the Festival, this former Georgian society rendezvous retains its faintly Jane Austen-esque aura. The main room's ceiling is too high, so the acoustics can go awry, along with the atmosphere. But the large ballroom across the landing, with chandeliers and a civilised atmosphere, makes even the scuzziest of crowds feel special. Hosts a popular monthly ceilidh season from October to May, and the occasional rock, folk, jazz and world-music gigs by Scottish and international artists.

La Belle Angele

11 Hasties Close, Cowgate, EH1 (225 7536). Bridges buses, then 5-min walk. **Open** *9pm-1am during gigs.* **Tickets** £3-£6. **No credit cards. Map 9 C3**
The concrete walls and floor of the long L-shaped main room can be a bit of a downer, but the effect is mitigated with arty flourishes. Cool enough to be used by record companies for Scottish showcases, La Belle hosted the debut Edinburgh performances of Oasis, Radiohead and Jeff Buckley.

The Bongo Club

14 New Street, EH8 (556 5204). 1, 6 buses, then 5-min walk. **Open** *10pm-3am Wed, Fri, Sat, monthly Sun.* **Tickets** £2-£6. **No credit cards. Map 7 G5**
Not fancy by any means, this small venue is run as a charity by a hugely eclectic and fiercely independent collective who will put on any kind of music from left-field classical to dance to the hinterlands of post-rock. It really comes to life during the Festival, but there are gigs on here most weeks.

Café Graffiti

Mansfield Place Church, East London Street, EH7 (557 8003). 7A, 8(A), 9(A), 19, 39 buses. **Open** *9.30pm-2am Fri, Sat.* **Admission** £4-£6. **No credit cards. Map 3 F3**
An artful and bohemian-tinged blend of live music (folk, Latin, jazz, world and most bases in between) and clubs, plus a smattering of theatre and dance, housed in an architecturally splendid deconsecrated church – sadly scheduled for eviction/closure in spring 1999, due to planned restoration work.

Canon's Gait

232 Canongate, EH8 (556 4481). 1, 6 buses. **Open** *noon-11pm Mon-Wed; noon-1am Thur-Sun.* **Admission** £2-£4. **No credit cards. Map 7 H5**
Currently one of the best pubs to catch local bands starting out, whether in an indie, soft or hard rock vein, but the most unlikely surroundings to do so.

Cas Rock

104 West Port, EH3 (229 4341). 2, 12, 28 buses. **Open** *9pm-1am Sat, Sun.* **Tickets** £3. **No credit cards. Map 6 E6**
For all the love/hate relationship that its patrons have with it, the Cas Rock is practically an institution, a small space specialising in the noisiest, most obscure bands ever to crawl out from under a rock – along with some of the most exciting local talent.

The Cavendish
West Tollcross, EH3 (228 3252). Bruntsfield buses.
Open 10pm-3am Fri, Sat. **Tickets** £5-£6. **No credit
cards. Map 6 D7**
Once a roller disco, with springy floor, the current management have restricted it to '60s and '70s nostalgia acts and
tribute bands. Enviable space for seating. Respectably
dressed over-25s only.

The Jaffacake
*28 King's Stables Road, EH1 (229 7986). Bruntsfield
buses, then 10-min walk.* **Open** 9pm-1am during gigs.
Tickets £3-£8. **No credit cards. Map 8 B3**
Squatting under a bridge on the way to the Grassmarket,
this building has had a chequered history, but as The
Jaffacake it may now be finally getting into its stride. Clean,
modern, spacious interior, with an abundance of seating.

Kulu's Jazz Joint
*Henry's Cellar Bar, 8 Morrison Street, EH3 (221 1288).
Bruntsfield buses.* **Open** noon-3am daily. **Tickets** £2-£5.
No credit cards. Map 8 A3
Lively basement club where Kulu presides over the emerg-
ing jazz-hip hop fusion scene. Live bands are different each
night of the week, but are usually booked on a residency
basis for at least a month. DJs carry on until the wee hours.

The Liquid Room
*9C Victoria Street, EH1 (225 2564). George IV Bridge
buses.* **Open** 10pm-1am during gigs.**Tickets** vary. **No
credit cards. Map 9 B2**
A name change and refit have made this a serious contender
for live bands. The upstairs bar and gallery give a great view
of the stage. Now used regularly by the better local bands
and medium-sized out-of-towners.

Playhouse Theatre
See chapter **Theatre.**
An excellent 3,000-seater venue – when not block-booked
with big-budget, crowd-pulling musicals.

The Subway
*69 Cowgate, EH1 (225 6766). Bridges buses, then 5-min
walk.* **Open** 8pm-3am daily. **Tickets** *Mon-Fri* £1,
students free; *Sat, Sun* £2; students free. **No credit
cards. Map 9 C3**
A subterranean hall of debatable acoustic qualities, situated in the sleaziest quarter of the Cowgate. Mostly filled by
young bands still at the stage when they are happy to play
anywhere: there's always the chance of stumbling across
fresh local talent.

The Tap O'Lauriston
*Lauriston Place, EH3 (229 4041). 23, 27, 28, 37, 45, 47
buses.* **Open** noon-midnight Mon-Wed; noon-1am Thur-
Sun. **Admission** varies. **No credit cards. Map 6 E7**
Once a year, when punks flood into Edinburgh from Europe
and even further afield, they converge on the Tap. From the
outside it is an unpromising, windowless concrete block.
Inside, the DJs and bands are on the noisy side of raucous.

Tron Tavern and Ceilidh House
See chapter **Bars & Pubs.**
Specifically set up by its beneficent proprietor to be a folk-
and jazz music hub and musicians' haven. On the folk side
it attracts many a high-calibre local player to its regular session nights, together with plenty of punters in the know. Also
hosts the best modern jazz promotion in the city, run by the
Edinburgh Jazz Project, on Thursdays at 8.30pm (with occasional variations).

The Venue
15 Calton Road, EH8 (557 3073). Leith Walk buses.
Open 10.30pm-3am daily. **Tickets** £3-£10. **No credit
cards. Map 7 G5**
The main floor is a classic dark and dingy rock dive that has
expanded over the years but retains the atmosphere that
small-to-medium-sized touring rock bands thrive on. When
big names are playing, the dancefloor can get very packed
and sweaty. Local, triple-band packages are a staple of its
programme, and sometimes sell surprisingly well.

Teen idols and original tartan terrorists – the Bay City Rollers. Page 156.

Nightlife

From house to disco, dressing up to dressing down, Edinburgh offers a plate full of fun to the late-night party animal.

Even the most inveterate seekers after nightlife would be forgiven for pausing before partaking of their nocturnal pleasures in Edinburgh – if all they had to go on was the Tourist Board's cosy, tartan image of the city. Those with a smattering of literary or cinematic knowledge would, however, have an inkling that, behind the elegant façade and grey, moral rectitude, there lies something a little more interesting. Once the sun has set, the wildlife comes out to play.

The wildlife is at its most obvious in the West End, Lothian Road, the Grassmarket and the Cowgate, which all throng with revellers on Friday and Saturday nights. Bare-legged girls with high heels, higher hem lines and WonderBra busts queue nonchalantly for clubs and teeter out of pubs. The lads, chinos, check shirts and too much aftershave, stagger and pose manfully in their wake.

Edinburgh does have style, too, although not in in the same self-consciously designer-led conspicuousness of Glasgow. It's more discreet and based on taste and individuality – not the ability to spot a label before it becomes hip. It is obvious in the bars around Broughton Street, at **EH1** on the High Street and in **Iguana,** opposite Bristo Square, all places where the soundtrack of club music prepares drinkers for a night on the dancefloor.

The club scene itself is thriving. Small enough to have kept out the supermarket attitudes of the super-club, Edinburgh is large enough to have a wealth of home-grown talent. Tribal Funktion, Pure, Joy, Taste, Tackno, Going Places, Manga and Disco Inferno have all made their individual marks on the cluberati over the years without becoming stale. New clubs are constantly springing up. What Edinburgh does lack is the motivating and unifying force that a strong independent record label, such as Glasgow's Soma, can have on a city. Instead, there are a good number of DJs, all talented in their chosen areas of dance music, who are dedicated to creating a name for themselves in the city and in Scotland, rather than around the world. This is as true for the cutting-edge dance clubs as it is for the retro-cool.

Thanks to Scotland's half way decent licensing hours, at the same time that London is struggling home with a lager carry-out and a greasy kebab, Edinburgh is just getting into the swing of things and wondering which club to go to. Most pubs and bars are open until midnight, many are open until 1am and a few carry on serving right up until 3am. The down side is that, except under special circumstances, the city's guardians of its moral fibre have decreed that 3am is the absolute limit. In clubs, this is annoying, to say the least.

In general terms, Friday night clubs tend to be about going out, getting sweaty and dancing the tensions of the week away. Saturday nights see a far more sartorially elegant approach. Sunday clubs cater for those full-on party animals who can afford to ignore Monday morning. Weekday clubbing tends more towards the alcohol-fuelled boogie than the hard-core club fanatic.

Because of the ephemeral nature of the club scene, no written guide will ever be up to date, including *The List*'s club information, which is not as reliable as the rest of its listings. Club runners do spend a lot on advertising, however. Posters tied on lamp-posts and railings around the city centre give a good idea of the bigger events. Flyers piled in bars like the **City Café** and in record shops help point out the rest. **Underground Solushun** is always a good place to hang out – the staff are both knowledgeable and friendly.

But nightlife takes many forms and after dark pleasures are far from a modern phenomenon. Although Robert Louis Stevenson is reputed to have based his *Strange Case of Dr Jekyll and Mr Hyde* on the grisly history of Deacon Brody, it is more likely that the primary inspiration came from his own experiences. Late at night, he would steal away from the drawing rooms of the New Town to purchase his pleasures up Lothian Road, in the Old Town and down in Leith. This was Edinburgh's knicker-free posterior guarded by the warming fur coat. 'I love night in the city', he wrote, 'the lighted streets and the swinging gait of harlots. I love cool pale morning, in the empty by-streets . . .'

Nowadays, the purchasing of fleshly pleasures has been banished to the city's saunas, which are licensed under the city health and safety regulations, much to the outrage of the moral minority. While this certainly makes life safer and less unhealthy for workers in the sex industry, it does not reduce exploitation and has an unquantifiable effect on demand.

The uncharitable would also argue that it allows the great and good of Edinburgh to indulge themselves with ease and in private. The viewing of flesh continues, but not in private, at a couple of seedy dives in the West Bow and a lap-top bar in Tollcross.

Which is neither the wholesome image the Tourist Board would like to present nor a typical representation of Edinburgh at play. Whatever your mood and whatever your predilection, this is a city where the night time is the right time for dancing.

Dress me up before I go go

It all started as a joke. A club called Misery – a drinking den riposte to the late 1980s rave scene – had just closed because it was becoming too popular to be cool. The promoters decided to put on the most naff event possible and Going Places (at the **Assembly Rooms**) was born. A place to wear horrible clothes from the 1940s and 1950s, while grooving away to an easy listening soundtrack of Frank and Shirley. Cigars, cocktails and bri-nylon were in; Marlboro Lights, ecstacy and rave tops were out. But by being so wrong, they actually got it right: the club became so popular it had to move to a bigger home. After flirting with the ABC on Lothian Road, they finally ended up at the Assembly Rooms.

Meanwhile a DJ called Trendy Wendy had moved into town and started her own night, Tackno (at **Mercado**), where she played the kind of music that Pam's People used to hand jive to; songs which have actions to go with the words. Where Wendy made her mark, though, was to give every night a theme. Sporty Tackno, Sexy Tackno and the Tackno to put all others in the shade, Abba Tackno, allowed the clubbers to really put some effort into their dressing up. And the more effort they made, the more fun they had.

Other clubs have joined in. Vegas goes for a glamorous edge at the **Shooting Gallery**. The long-running Disco Inferno (fortnightly, Saturdays at the **Venue**) puts on specials, also at the Assembly Rooms, where the stage is big enough for the original disco stars to come out and play. And best of all, Edinburgh's second-hand clothes emporia, charity shops or car boot sales are the perfect places to find something silly to wear. So there's no excuse for not dressing up.

Nightlife

Club venues

Club nights come and go. Those mentioned here have a reasonable chance of lasting. Prices vary wildly, with most venues charging very little, or not at all, midweek. The higher prices are for non-members on Fridays and Saturdays. Expect to pay even more during the Festival, when clubs tend to extend their opening nights.

The Assembly Rooms
George Street, EH2 (220 4348). George St buses. **Open** varies. **Admission** varies. **Map 8 B1**
Occasional one-off clubs like Going Places and Disco Inferno. (*See box:* **Dress me up before I go go**).

The Attic
Dyer's Close, Cowgate, EH1 (225 8382). Bridges buses, then 5-min walk. **Open** 11pm-3am daily. **Admission** £2-£4. **Map 9 B3**
A smallish space that doubles as a live venue for the indie rock scene in the early evening. The clubs tend to be student oriented in a retro-pop vein with a bit of dance thrown in midweek.

La Belle Angele
11 Hasties Close, Cowgate, EH1 (225 7536). Bridges buses, then 5-min walk. **Open** 8pm-3am Thur-Sat. **Admission** £3-£6. **Map 9 C3**
This former gallery, tucked away in a little square at the end of a close and surrounded by centuries-old buildings, was once home to the renowned Yip Yap. Now the only remaining strong dance night is the drum 'n' bass Manga (monthly, Fri). Otherwise it's mostly on the big beat, new indie tip with a strong contingent of under-21s eyeing each other up.

The Bongo Club
14 New Street, EH8 (558 7604). 1, 6 buses. **Open** 10pm-3am Wed, Fri, Sat, monthly Sun. **Admission** £3-£5. **Map 7 G5**
A multimedia arts space above the old bus station that can hit a truly underground vibe with dub reggae from the mighty Messenger Sound System (fortnightly, Sat). Otherwise, it's pretty bohemian and highly eclectic. An adjoining café is open 11am-6pm Tue-Sat.

Café Graffiti
Mansfield Place Church, East London Street, EH7 (557 8003). 7A, 8(A), 9(A), 19, 39 buses. **Open** 9.30pm-2am Fri, Sat. **Admission** £4-£6. **Map 3 F3**
Under threat from the conversion of the church into offices, this old crypt is a cracking, Weimar Republic-style space. Live jazz and a soul/world music influenced vibe have made it heaving with an older crowd on Saturdays.

The Cavendish
3 West Tollcross, EH3 (228 3252). Bruntsfield buses. **Open** 9.30pm-4am Wed; 10pm-3am Thur-Sat. **Admission** £2.50-£3.50. **Map 6 D7**
Once a roller disco, with springy floor, the current management have restricted it to 1960s and 1970s nostalgia acts and tribute bands. Enviable space for seating, for those who'd rather drink and talk. Respectably dressed over-25s only.

CC Blooms
23 Greenside Place, Leith Walk, EH1 (556 9331). Leith Walk buses. **Open** 6pm-3am Mon-Thur; 11am-3am Fri, Sat. **Admission** free. **Map 4 G3**
The downstairs dancefloor of this busy gay bar gets mobbed over the weekend. Everything from karaoke to disco, house and striptease delights the scene.

The Citrus
40-42 Grindlay Street, EH3 (622 7086). Bruntsfield buses. **Open** 11pm-3am Thur-Sat; 10pm-3am Sun. **Admission** £2-£4. **Map 8 A3**
Small, indie and retro-oriented club that does well from its student clientele.

Henry's Cellar Bar
8 Morrison Street, EH3 (221 1288). Bruntsfield buses. **Open** 10pm-3am daily. **Admission** £3-£5. **Map 8 A3**
Experimental beats and breaks with live bands and eclectically minded DJs give this small venue opposite the **ABC Film Centre** a cutting-edge, bohemian vibe.

The Honeycomb
36 Blair Street, EH1 (220 4381). High St or North Bridge buses. **Open** 11pm-3am Thur-Sun. **Admission** free-£10. **Map 9 C3**
This well-appointed venue has one of the city's best sound systems and two good dancefloors with lots of seating area. The only club to go the distance is Sunday night's hedonistic, pumped-up Taste. Otherwise the strong and usually classy nights vary from house anthems to soulful garage.

The Jaffacake
28 King's Stables Road, EH1 (229 7986). Bruntsfield buses, then 10-min walk. **Open** 10pm-3am Thur-Sat. **Admission** £2-£4. **Map 8 B3**
Very busy, keeping the students off the streets and dancing very drunkenly on cheap drinks promos to the usual indie pop mix. Saturday's Love Shack packs 'em in.

JP's
3 Semple Street, Tollcross, EH3 (229 7733). Bruntsfield buses. **Open** 9.30pm-3am Fri-Sun. **Admission** £2-£5. **Map 6 D7**
Catering for the well-dressed, older crowd (over-21s only) and early evening office workers.

The Liquid Room
9C Victoria Street, EH1 (225 2564). George IV Bridge buses. **Open** 10.30pm-3am Wed-Sun. **Admission** £2-£5. **Map 9 B2**
Although the mix gets quite housed-up on Saturday, this is really aimed at the alcohol-using set.

Mercado
36-39 Market Street, EH1 (226 4224). Princes St buses, then 5-min walk. **Open** 10pm-3am Wed, 5pm-3am Fri, 11pm-4am Sat, Sun. **Admission** free-£10. **Map 9 C1**
The excellent dance-floor, good seating and quick-witted bar staff make up for the lights and sound system. Saturdays fortnightly is the dressed-up, party house of Colours of Love. Tackno sees dressing up of a different sort on the last Sunday of the month (*See box:* **Dress me up before I go go**).

Po Na Na
43B Frederick Street, EH2 (226 2224). Princes St buses, then 5-min walk. **Open** 8pm-3am Thur-Sat. **Admission** £2 after 11pm Thur; £3 after 11pm Fri, Sat. **Map 8 B1**
An after-work drinking hole for local office workers in the early evening, this warren of alcoves below the Café Rouge picks up the clubby crowd mid-evening when the DJ gets to work and starts to charge at 11pm, when the dancefloor can get very packed.

Revolution
31 Lothian Road, EH1 (229 7670). Bruntsfield buses. **Open** 11pm-3am Wed-Sun. **Admission** £3-£5. **Map 8 A2**
Formerly Century 2000, a venue boasting white stilettos, testosterone and fights in the girls' loos, this venue is due to reopen on 17 September after a £2.5-million facelift.

Three dancefloors (including one with a hydraulic lift floor) are promised; a VIP bar and the added attraction of Boy George (in his DJ incarnation) playing a regular monthly date.

The Rocking Horse

4 India Buildings, Victoria Street, EH1 (225 3326). George IV Bridge buses. **Open** 11pm-3am Thur-Sun. **Admission** £3. **Map 9 B2**
Three floors of seriously non-house music to dance to. Everything from air-guitar, to punk, to metal and a bit of bagginess on the bottom floor. Massively popular.

The Shooting Gallery

32A Broughton Street, EH1 (478 7434). 7A, 8(A), 9(A), 19, 39 buses. **Open** 11pm-3am certain Fri, Sat (ring for dates). **Admission** £5-£8. **Map 3 F3**
A rather claustrophobic, two-floored space in an old masonic lodge. Hosts a varied assortment of independently promoted nights from hip hop to dressing-up disco and house. Mostly very good, with Vegas, once a month on Saturdays, being wildly popular.

Studio 24

24 Calton Road, EH8 (558 3758). Leith Walk buses, then 5-min walk. **Open** 11pm-3am monthly Sat. **Admission** £5. **Map 7 H5**
A concrete-floored barn downstairs, but more intimate and with a better dancefloor up. Has been through many incarnations, currently the sole remaining venue for happy hardcore and bouncy, tartan techno (once a staple of the city's youth) in the capital.

The Vaults

15-17 Niddry Street, EH1 (558 9052).Bridges buses. **Open** 11pm-3pm Wed; 10.30pm-3am Thur, Sat; 9.30pm-3am Fri. **Admission** £3-£10. **Map 9 D2**
A warren of dancefloors and bars in the vaults under the arches holding up South Bridge. Fridays is unpretentiously hot and sweaty, whatever the club, although they usually play hard house or techno. Saturdays is the more commercial Red on Red where a dressed-up dress code applies and the DJs are big-named superstars spinning house anthems.

The Venue

17-21 Calton Road, EH8 (557 3073). Leith Walk buses, then 5-min walk. **Open** 10.30pm-3am daily. **Admission** £6. **Map 7 G5**
Three floors which can be run independently from each other. The **Cooler** is a surprisingly warm chill-out zone; the ground floor the dark embodiment of a truly underground venue; and the top floor has bright lights and well-sprung dancefloor. Fridays is Pure, still playing a fresh mix of house and techno after all these years and welcoming some quality guests. Saturdays alternate between the underground house of Tribal Funktion (superb) and the drunken antics of Disco Inferno, the original retro-disco drinking den.

Wilkie House

207 Cowgate, EH1 (225 2935). Bridges buses, then 5-min walk. **Open** 10.30pm-3am Wed-Sat. **Admission** £3-£10. **Map 9 C3**
A good, airy space with bar and balcony overlooking the well-sprung dancefloor. Chill-out room upstairs to the back. Fridays have jostled into the hard house/techno market. Saturdays alternate between four classy, housed-up monthly nights. Joy, the happy club for gay people, with a pumping nu-NRG soundtrack leads the way. Used as a theatre venue during the Festival.

EHI – *where clubbers meet to plan the night ahead. See chapter* **Bars & Pubs.**

Sport & Fitness

Football, rugby and golf absorb Edinburgh's sports fans.

Whether Edinburgh can be classed as a 'sporting' city is a moot point. Its citizens are so preoccupied with football, rugby and golf that when success in these fields is proving elusive, particularly at a national level in football and rugby, then pessimism clouds their perception of all sports.

If the fans could only look more closely, they would see that Edinburgh's sporting successes tend to be concentrated in the 'minor' sports such as cycling. So the reality is that, compared to many other cities, the fans are ambivalent and unambitious. Nor is much of the city's wealth invested in sport.

That said, when Heart of Midlothian Football Club brought joy to their success-starved fans in 1998 by winning the Scottish Cup, some 100,000 people lined the streets the following day to welcome back the cup and the team.

Scottish Sports Council

Caledonia House, South Gyle, EH12 (317 7200). **Open** 9am-5pm Mon-Fri.
Doubles up as the headquarters for a number of sports, such as basketball and hockey. Produces a quarterly calendar of sports events throughout Scotland, called *Touchline.*

American football

Gridiron has been played at an amateur level in Scotland for years, but the arrival of the Scottish Claymores – fully professional and with a strong NFL presence – put the sport on the map. A sprinkling of Scottish players has helped establish a vibrant relationship with the public. The Claymores play in the NFL European league between April and June. Home games are played at both Murrayfield Stadium and Hampden Park in Glasgow.

Scottish Claymores shop

137 George Street, EH2 (478 7200/ticket hotline 0500 353 535). George St buses. **Open** 9am-5pm Mon-Fri; 10am-5pm Sat. **Tickets** £12 adults; £6 concs; £4 children. **Credit** AmEx, MC, V. **Map 8 B1**
Sells team merchandising and tickets for the games.

Basketball

An Edinburgh franchise has been accepted into the Budweiser League and will compete in the 1998/99 season – games will be played on Sunday afternoons at the **Meadowbank Sports Centre** (*see below*). Outdoor and indoor courts can be booked at the MSC.

Cricket

Cricket may not be the sport most readily associated with Scotland, but it is beginning to acquire a higher profile. The national side has given the game a boost by qualifying for the 1999 World Cup in England. And the playing standard at club level should be improved by the decision to replace regional leagues with a nationwide structure.

Scottish Cricket Union *(317 7247).*

Cycling

The City of Edinburgh team is Britain's crack track outfit, based at the velodrome at the Meadowbank Sports Centre (*see below*). In the 1997 Great Britain senior championships they picked up six gold medals. Highlights of the local track calendar include the East of Scotland Grand Prix (end of June) and the Festival meeting (mid-August). Both incorporate British League events. The velodrome is also home to the Scottish Cyclists' Union (625 0187), which can advise on all the cycling sports, from mountain biking to the track disciplines. *See also chapter* **Directory.**

Football

The Scottish football season runs from August to May with three main domestic competitions: the League, the Cup and the League Cup. The two professional football clubs in Edinburgh, Heart of Midlothian and Hibernian, have both been perennial underachievers. The Glasgow clubs, Celtic and Rangers (collectively known as the Old Firm), soak up the lion's share of the trophies. Hearts had an excellent 1997/98 season, winning the Cup and placing third in the League, but Hibernian were relegated.

There isn't nearly the same money swilling around the Edinburgh pair as there is around the Old Firm and, equally, not the same poisonous rivalry based on 'what foot you kick with' (parlance for religious affiliation). To those for whom it matters (and, thankfully, it is becoming fewer), Celtic and Hibernian are the Roman Catholic clubs, while Rangers and Hearts are the Protestant ones. But the bigotry is subsiding and all-seater stadia have encouraged more families to attend matches. Most games are pay-at-the-turnstile, but it is

Philosophy football – fans mobbed Hume's statue when **Heart of Midlothian** *won the cup.*

advisable to phone and confirm first. Old Firm games and local derbies are likely to be all-ticket.

There is a flourishing amateur and semi-professional scene throughout the city; the women's game is growing steadily; and the best place for a kickabout on the grass is the Meadows on a Sunday afternoon.

Heart of Midlothian FC

Tynecastle Park, Gorgie Road, EH11 (200 7200/tickets 200 7201). Dalry Rd buses. **Open** 9am-5pm Mon-Fri; 10am-3pm matchdays. **Tickets** £14; £7 concs. **Credit** MC, V.
Situated to the west side of the city. Average crowd: 15,000.

Hibernian FC

Easter Road Stadium, Albion Place, EH7 (661 2159). 1, 6, 24(A) buses. **Open** 9am-5pm Mon-Fri; 10am-3pm matchdays. **Tickets** £11-£13; £6 concs. **Credit** MC, V. **Map 4 J2**
Situated to the east side of the city. Average crowd: 13,000.

Golf

Scotland is a great place for golf and Edinburgh has numerous courses both within and outside the city boundary. St Andrews, the home of the game's governing body, the Royal and Ancient, is an hour-and-a-half's drive away. Along the coast in East Lothian are some of the finest links courses in the world, including Muirfield, a venue for the British Open. Nearer the city, Musselburgh Links hosted some of the first Open championships and Mary, Queen of Scots is said to have 'hit a golf ball' there as early as 1567. To the west, Dalmahoy was, in

1992, the scene of a famous Solheim Cup triumph for the women of Europe over the USA.

Golf is very much a people's game in Scotland. While there are a few snooty clubs, the majority welcome visitors with open arms. Don't turn up to a course and expect to play straightaway. Demand often outstrips supply – so book in advance.

The Edinburgh Tourist Board offers a discount pass (seven-day pass £5; call 557 1700) for the single-minded golfer hoping to cram in as many rounds of golf at as many courses as possible. There are also a number of practice ranges.

Braids

Braid Hills Approach Road, EH10 (447 6666). 11, 15(A) buses. **Open** 7am-8.45pm daily. **Green fee** £8.50. **Club hire** £7; £10 deposit. **Credit** £TC.
These municipal courses are two of the best in the city with some excellent holes and superb views of Edinburgh.

Lothianburn

Biggar Road, EH10 (445 2288). 4 bus. **Open** 8am-7.30pm. **Green fee** midweek £15; weekend £21. **Club hire** £10. **Credit** AmEx, MC, V.
A hillside course, again affording great views of the city. One of the cheaper private courses to play.

Mortonhall

Braid Road, EH10 (447 5185). 11, 15(A) buses. **Open** dawn-dusk daily. **Green fee** £30 per round; £40 per day. **Club hire** by prior arrangement. **Credit** MC, V.

Murrayfield

43 Murrayfield Road, EH12 (337 3479). Haymarket buses. **Open** 8am-7pm Mon-Fri. **Green fee** £25 per round, £30 per day. **Club hire** £12-£14. **No credit cards**.
The sixth hole is the best for views of the city. Closed to visitors at weekends.

Gullane

West Links Road, Gullane, EH31 (01620 842 255). SMT bus 124. **Green fees** £14-£54 round. **Club hire** £20 per round. **Credit** AmEx, MC, V.
Three courses and, no matter what time of year, the greens are always in excellent condition. The third course is the shortest, but the fairways are narrower. A beer at the nearby Old Clubhouse makes a pleasant end to the day.

Musselburgh Links

Balcarres Road, Musselburgh, EH21 (665 5438). 15(A), 43, 44 buses. **Open** 8am-8pm daily. **Green fee** £7. **No club hire. No credit cards.**
Nine holes in the middle of the racecourse.

Muirfield

The Honourable Company of Edinburgh Golfers, Muirfield, Gullane, EH31 (01620 842 123). **Open** to visitors: Tue & Thur only. **Green fee** £65 per round; £85 per day. **Minimum handicap required** 18 (men), 24(women).
Book six months in advance to play this prestigious course.

St Andrews

West Sands Road, St Andrews, Fife, KY16 (01334 466666 – 24-hour reservation facility for the Jubilee, Eden & Strathtyrum courses). **Green fee** £16-£72.
Six courses – Old, New, Jubilee, Eden, Strathtyrum and Balgove (nine holes). First come, first served at the New Course, fitting in with tee times booked in advance. Same for Balgove. Ballot available for tee times on Old Course – phone by 2pm the day before (or Saturday if for Monday). Otherwise, reserve at least a month ahead. Handicap certificate required for Old Course. A round on the Old Course in high season (after April 1) costs £72. On Strathtyrum, a round costs £16.

Braid Hills driving range

Liberton Drive, EH16 (658 1111). 31(A), 62, 64(A), 65(A/B), 81(A/B), 87(A), 88(A) buses. **Open** 10am-9pm Mon-Fri; 10am-6pm Sat-Sun. **Cost** £2.50 per 50 balls. **Credit** MC, V.

Port Royal golf range

Eastfield road, Ingliston, EH28 (333 4377). 16, 18, 19, 31, 37, 38 buses. **Open** 10am-9pm Fri-Mon; 10am-10pm Tue-Thur. **Cost** *range* £2 per basket; *pitch & putt* £4; £2 concs. **No credit cards.**

Gyms & fitness centres

Body Talk Health & Fitness Centre

7/9 Ponton Street, EH3 (228 2426). 1, 6, 28, 34, 35 buses. **Open** 7am-10pm Mon-Fri; 9am-6pm Sat-Sun. **Admission** £3.50; *membership* £25 per month. **Credit** MC, V. **Map 6 D7**
The centre has a gym (members only at night, but there are classes open to the public), a beauty room and sun beds. **Branch:** 54A Fountainbridge, EH3 (228 2426).

Pleasance Sports Centre

46 Pleasance, EH8 (650 2585). 60 bus. **Open** 8.30am-9.50pm Mon-Fri; 8.50am-5.50pm Sat; 9.50am-5.50pm Sun. **Admission** *during student holidays* £4; *membership* £122 per year. **Credit** MC, V. **Map 7 G6**
A sports centre attached to Edinburgh University with a gymnasium, squash and badminton courts and fitness suite. During term-time you must be a member, but during vacations the guest fee of £4 gives access to the fitness suite.

Meadowbank Sports Centre

139 London Road, EH7 (661 5351). London Rd buses. **Open** 9.30am-10.30pm Mon; 9am-10.30pm Tue-Sun. **No credit cards.**

Opened for the Commonwealth Games in 1970, the MSC has facilities for badminton, squash, basketball, football and a cycling velodrome. There are classes for children, adults and the over-50s in everything from archery to various martial arts. Call for more information on rates and classes. Telephone bookings for members only.

Horse racing

The sport of kings takes place at five racecourses in Scotland. One, Musselburgh, is six miles (ten kilometres) east of Edinburgh city centre. Further afield, the rural courses of Perth, to the north, and Kelso, to the south, make a pleasant day out. Ayr, on the west coast, stages the bigger races in Scotland, such as the Scottish Grand National.

Musselburgh

Linkfield Road, EH21 (665 2859). 15(A), 43, 44 buses.. **Admission** *grandstand* £6; *club stand* £12; £3 concs; free accompanied children under-16 ; half-price disabled, free carers. **No credit cards.**
Scotland's oldest racecourse hosts 22 meetings per year, some in the evening, which are well attended. The Pinkie Bar was opened in 1997 by the legendary jockey Lester Piggott. Popular events include the Saints and Sinners charity meet at the end of February and Gold Cup day in June.

Ayr

(01292 264 179).
Scotland's biggest course hosts 25 meetings per year. A slightly more expensive Club Badge provides entry to the pleasant Western House at the bottom of the course. The biggest events of the year are the Scottish Grand National (Apr) and the Ladbroke Ayr Gold Cup (Sept).

Kelso

(01668 281 611).
Wonderful traditions in rural splendour. Visit the Tin Hut bar, no more than a chicken shed where the locals gather. About 12 meetings per year. The biggest events of the year are the Scottish Borders National (Jan) and the Hennessy Cognac Special Series Final (Mar).

Perth

(01738 551 597).
Frequently voted the 'best small racecourse in the north', Perth hosts about ten meetings per year. Enjoy the garden party atmosphere and maybe catch a pre-meet game of polo. The biggest event of the year is the Perth Festival in April.

Hamilton

(01698 283 806).
Scotland's most urban course hosts about 18 meetings per year, many in the evening, and is known as the 'Royal Ascot of the north'. Advice: dress to thrill.

Ice-skating

Murrayfield Ice Rink

Riversdale Crescent, EH12 (337 6933). Haymarket buses. **Open** 2.30-4.30pm, 5-7pm, 7-9pm Mon-Fri; also 7.30-10.30pm Fri; 10am-noon, 7.30-10.30pm Sat; 10-11.30am Sun. **Admission** £2.50-£3.20; *disco skating* £4.70. **No credit cards.**
The rink is home to Murrayfield Royals ice hockey team. The times given can vary and some sessions are for beginners, so call before going. The admission fee includes the hire of skates. An unlicensed café is open on Wednesdays, Fridays and at the weekend. Friday and Saturday nights are disco sessions and attract a young crowd.

Rugby union

Union is the preferred code of rugby in Scotland. The national team plays at Murrayfield Stadium (346 5000): the venue for Scotland's two home games during the Five Nations championship each year. Tickets are very hard to come by for these games and must be booked well in advance.

Edinburgh, as a centre of rugby, differs from other parts of the country because its club scene is so closely linked to a group of prestigious, fee-paying schools. The days when only former pupils could play for the likes of Edinburgh Academicals, Heriot's, Stewart's Melville and Watsonians are long gone. But the school-based rivalries remain.

Edinburgh also has a growing summer-based touch rugby scene, administered by *Scottish Rugby* magazine (554 0540).

Rock climbing

The National Rock Climbing Centre of Scotland is under construction and, when completed (late 1999), will boast 2,500 metres of indoor surfaces and 5,000m of outdoor. **Meadowbank Sports Centre** (*see above*) has a small wall, otherwise try:

Alien Rock
8A Pier Place, EH6 (552 7211). 7, 11, 16, 17(A), 22, 25(B) buses. **Open** *summer* noon-10pm Mon-Fri; 10am-7pm Sat-Sun; *winter* noon-11am Mon-Fri; 10am-9pm Sat-Sun. **Admission** *peak* £5 adults; £2 children; *off-peak* (before 4pm weekdays, before 5pm weekends) £3 adults; £2 children. **No credit cards. Map 2 Leith**
A 10m-high wall located in a former church. All equipment is available for hire, including footwear. For experienced climbers a session costs £3-£5 (excluding boot and harness hire). A two-hour introductory course for novices costs £18, including equipment hire. There is a café, shop and a bouldering room with a 4m-high wall.

Snooker

The Angle Club
Jordan Lane, EH10 (447 8814). 5, 11, 15, 16, 17, 23, 57, 51 buses. **Open** 11am-midnight daily. **Cost** *snooker* £3.60-£3.84 per hour; *pool* £3.96-£4.20. **No credit cards.**
Ten snooker tables, five pool tables and a bar/café.

Marco's snooker halls
55 Grove Street, EH3 (228 2141). 1, 6, 34, 35, then 5-min walk. **Open** 8am-11pm daily. **Cost** *snooker* £3.90 per hour; *pool* £4.50. **Credit** MC, V. **Map 5 C7**
Marco's has 15 snooker and 18 pool tables and a bar/café. **Branch**: 146 Slateford Road, EH14 (443 2211).

Skiing

Midlothian Ski Centre
Hill End, EH10 (445 4433). 4 bus. **Open** 9.30am-9pm Mon-Fri; 9.30am-7pm Sat-Sun. **Cost** *main slope* £6 adults first hour, £2.50 per additional hour; £4, £1.60 children. **Credit** MC, JCB, £TC, V.
Situated to the south of Edinburgh, the centre has Europe's longest artificial ski slope at 400m. Prices include hire of

boots, skis and poles and use of the chairlift. For novices, the nursery slopes cost adults £3.70 for the first hour.

Swimming

Edinburgh boasts a range of excellent swimming pools. Many are a legacy from the city's far-sighted Victorian forebears, including Warrender Baths in Marchmont and Glenogle Swim Centre in Stockbridge. Newer pools are generally found in the housing estates on the fringes of the city, such as Ainslie Park.

All the pools run classes and special sessions so it is advisable to call first.

Royal Commonwealth Pool
Dalkeith Road, EH16 (667 7211). 2, 12, 14(A/B), 21, 30, 33 buses. **Open** 9am-10pm (last entry 9pm) Mon-Tue, Thur-Fri; 10am-10pm Wed; 10am-4pm Sat-Sun. **Admission** *pool* £1.80 before 2.30pm; £2.35 after 2.30pm; *fitness suite* £4.25 (including swim); *sauna* £6.15. **No credit cards. Map 7 J8**
Built for the 1970 Commonwealth Games and housing Olympic-size swimming and diving pools, fitness and sauna suites. Flumes in operation after 2.30pm.

Glenogle Swim Centre
Glenogle Road, EH3 (343 6376). 20, 28, 80 buses, then 10-min walk. **Open** 8am-7.40pm Mon-Fri; 8am-3.40pm Sat; 9am-3.40pm Sun. **Admission** *pool* £1.40 adults; 85p children; *gym* £2.75; *sauna* £3.25. **No credit cards. Map 3 D2**
This Victorian building houses a 25yd (23m) pool, sauna, gym and crèche. Various sessions and restrictions operate throughout the week, so call first.

Portobello Swim Centre
57 The Promenade, EH15 (669 6888). 2, 12, 15, 20, 26, 46, 52 buses. **Open** *pool* 7am-10pm Mon-Fri; 9am-4pm Sat-Sun. Closed 8-9am Tue, Thur; 2-3pm Mon. *Turkish baths* women 3-9pm Mon; 9am-9pm Wed, Fri; men 9am-9pm Tue, Thur; 9am-4pm Sat; mixed 9am-4pm Sun. **Admission** *pool* £1.40 adults; 85p children; *Turkish baths* £5. **No credit cards.**

Warrender Baths
Thirlestane Road, EH9 (447 0052). 5, 24, 40, 41 51 buses. **Open** 8am-10pm Mon-Fri; 9am-4.30pm Sat. **Admission** *pool* £1.40 adults; 85p children; *sauna* £3.25; *gym* £2.75; crèche. **No credit cards.**

Anslie Park Leisure Centre
92 Pilton Drive, EH5 (551 2400). 1, 6, 27 buses, then 5-min walk. **Open** 10am-10pm Mon-Fri; 9am-6pm Sat-Sun; *women only* 6-10pm Mon. **Admission** *pool* £1.80 adults; £1 children; *gym* £4.25; *sauna/steam room* £4.40; creche. **No credit cards.**

Tennis

Craiglockhart Tennis & Sports Centre
177 Colinton Road, EH14 (sport 443 0101/tennis 444 1969).10(A), 27, 45, 47 buses. **Open** 9am-10pm Mon-Sun. **Cost** *fitness suite* £4.25; *squash* £6.75 per hour; *badminton* £7.30 per hour; *step & aerobic classes* £3; *tennis* outdoor £6 per hour; indoor £14 per hour. **No credit cards.**
The sports centre has a fitness room, badminton and squash courts, a crèche and runs step and aerobics classes. The tennis centre has six indoor and eight outdoor courts.

Theatre

All the world's a stage – or most of Edinburgh, at any rate.

Judging by the prevailing response of the English-based press, you'd be forgiven for thinking that while Edinburgh erupts in an annual, three week-long glut of theatrical over-indulgence every August, for the rest of the year its denizens make do with decidedly meagre dramatic rations. But, while it can't pretend to compete numerically or resources-wise with London's thespian artillery, Edinburgh's home-based theatre scene offers a wide-ranging bill of quality attractions to suit most pockets and persuasions. Admittedly, the musicals are of the London West End touring variety, but from cutting-edge contemporary drama to honest, workmanlike revivals and fringe, student and community-based work, Edinburgh's own companies and theatres are able to stage some quality productions throughout the year.

Of the city's two main producing houses, the world-famous **Traverse Theatre** specialises in new writing. Its little'n'large twin spaces are programmed with a selection of touring drama, dance and comedy beside its own productions. Even if you don't like what you see, it be a waste of time. Artistic director Philip Howard continues the tradition of nurturing home-grown Scottish and Edinburgh-based writing talent, a policy that has brought its own rewards with the likes of Stephen Greenhorn's Passing Places going on to a national tour and the launch of David Greig's and David Harrower's careers. As you'd expect, the Traverse tends to attract the younger, more adventurous end of the theatre-going population, their post-show numbers swollen by the arts and media types who frequent its hip but laid-back café-bar.

Much Ado About Nothing *at the* **Royal Lyceum** *(page 170).*

Fulfiling the capital's mainstream-rep brief, the **Royal Lyceum** stages between six and eight productions over its spring and autumn subscription seasons, plus a Christmas show, a short season of touring shows in May/June and a summer season in June/July. The theatre manages to juggle populist appeal with the natural inclination of artistic director Kenny Ireland towards adventure by integrating a mix of classics and adaptations with new works and new writing. Production values are never less than solid, though the productions themselves can tend towards the workmanlike.

For many years the weakest part of Edinburgh's claim to staging the world's greatest arts festival was its lack of a truly grand-scale, fully appointed space for international productions. This somewhat glaring gap was more than handsomely filled in 1994 when the 1,900-seat **Edinburgh Festival Theatre** was opened. The Council-backed refurbishment of this former Victorian variety house included the restoration of the interior to its original, opulent glory, the introduction of state of the art technical specifications (including the biggest stage in Britain) and the addition of an emphatically modern, three-storey-high, glass frontage, housing the box office, café and bars.

Bricks and mortar aside, it's fair to say that the Festival Theatre has experienced something of a bumpy ride over its first few years of operation, struggling to meet financial targets despite the determinedly all-encompassing span of its programming. The choice of productions on offer ranges from grand opera to the *Solid Silver 60s Show*; from ballet and contemporary dance of an international standard to Ken Dodd or old-style Scottish music hall, along with big-name touring theatre (be it popular musicals or Royal Shakespeare Company classics), orchestral concerts and occasional pop and folk gigs.

The **Festival Theatre**'s advent initially appeared to spell trouble for the smaller **King's Theatre**: the two were competing in similar market sectors, but a co-management deal thrashed out by the local authority (which backs both venues) brought them under the unitary control of the Festival City Theatres Trust in 1998. Budget problems mean that the King's will be dark for some of the year, but it will continue to host the majority of touring drama, while the Festival Theatre will be Edinburgh's lyric theatre, taking opera, music and ballet – along with drama productions big enough to fit its stage.

As for the **Playhouse**, the commercially run theatre has been making vast sums for its owners as Edinburgh's receiving house for the large-scale touring musicals, if not doing anything to enhance its artistic credibility.

Occupying a radically different – but widely respected – position on the theatrical spectrum, **Theatre Workshop** specialises in high-quality community-based work – both education- and performance-based – and books a lively mix of touring drama and dance. A recently formed in-house company combines the talents of able-bodied and disabled actors under the direction of artistic director Robert Rae. Among the city's fringe venues, the Edinburgh University Theatre Company stages three shows as term at their **Bedlam Theatre**. The **Netherbow** and **St Bride's** Centres both periodically stage new and experimental work.

In addition to venue-based work, Edinburgh is also home to several of Scotland's top touring companies, including the much-feted, multi-award-winning Communicado, the adventurously hard-hitting Boilerhouse and the women-led Stellar Quines.

TICKETS

Tickets for many major venues are bookable through the **Ticketline** network (220 4349 10am-8pm Mon-Sat; 11am-6pm Sun); otherwise contact individual box offices as listed below.

Bedlam Theatre
2A Forrest Road, EH1 (225 9893). **Open** *9.30am-midnight during productions.* **Tickets** *£3.50-£6.50.* **No credit cards. Map 6 F6**

Edinburgh Festival Theatre
See chapter **Music: Classical and Opera** *page 152.*

Edinburgh Playhouse
18-22 Greenside Place, EH1 (557 2590/credit card bookings 557 8444). Leith Walk buses. **Open** *box office* 10am-6pm Mon-Sat; *phone* 9am-9pm Mon-Sat; 10am-9pm Sun. **Tickets** £7.50-£29.50. **Credit** AmEx, DC, V. **Map 4 G3**

King's Theatre
2 Leven Street, EH3 (220 4349). Bruntsfield buses. **Open** *box office* 10am-5pm Mon; 10am-8pm Tue-Sat. **Tickets** £12-£16. **Credit** AmEx, DC, MC, V. **Map 6 D7**

Netherbow Arts Centre
43 High Street, EH1 (556 9579). 1, 6, Bridges buses. **Open** *box office* 9.30am-8pm during performances. **Credit** MC, V. **Map 9 D2**

Royal Lyceum
Grindlay Street, EH3 (248 4848). Bruntsfield buses. **Open** *box office* 10am-7pm Mon-Sat. **Tickets** £1-£16. **Credit** AmEx, MC, V. **Map 8 A3**

St Bride's Centre
10 Orwell Terrace, EH11 (346 1405). Dalry Road buses. **Open** *box office* 9am-5pm Mon-Fri. **Tickets** 50p-£10. **Credit** MC, V. **Map 5 B7**

Theatre Workshop
34 Hamilton Place, EH3 (226 5425). 20, 28, 80 buses. **Open** *box office* 9.30am-5.30pm Mon-Sat. **Tickets** £3-£6.50. **Credit** MC, V. **Map 3 D3**

Traverse Theatre
10 Cambridge Street, EH1 (box office 228 1404). Bruntsfield buses. **Open** 10am-6pm Mon, 10am-11pm Tue-Sun. **Tickets** £4-£8. **Credit** JCB, MC, V. **Map 8 A3**

Glasgow

Glasgow Today

Britain's coolest city – and we're not talking temperature.

Glasgow was voted the coolest city in Britain in a recent nationwide survey by *The Big Issue*. Literally so, because it topped the worst weather category, but also metaphorically as the best base for students and twenty-somethings in the late 1990s. Over the past decade the renaissance of style – as a sophisticated notion of selfimage – has been a major factor in explaining this burgeoning allure. As the millennium approaches, the regeneration of Glasgow as a designer city, as much as any architectural or cultural regeneration, has helped to sideline the pervading but dated postwar image of 'no mean city' – when drunkenness and violence seemed to be the two main qualities attributed to Glaswegians by outsiders. Although some negative traits will possibly never change – the city's poor heart disease record, its sectarian divisions or the deprivation in the outlying housing estates – there has never been a better time to enjoy Glasgow's largely unsung tourist potential.

Scotland's largest city, with a population of 623,000, lies a mere 50 miles (80km) west of Edinburgh along the M8 – an hour's journey by car, 50 minutes by train. For many, that modest distance is enough to place Scotland's two main cities poles apart. Rather than celebrate their differences and co-exist peacefully, Glasgow and Edinburgh traditionally 'enjoy' the splenetic relationship of warring neighbours. Denizens of Edinburgh refer to 'Weegie soap-dodgers'; Glaswegians trumpet their city's friendly reputation – in contrast to Edinburgh's aloof coldness. And so the sweeping generalisations persist.

TONGUE-POKING AND RIVALRY

Ironically, the 'my city is better than your city' tongue-poking has erupted anew since 1997's devolution referendum – a development that should have brought Scots closer together. Although the capital was always the obvious choice to host the new Scottish Parliament, the decision process provoked the inevitable sparring. And the bickering continued loud and long into the debate over where the Parliament's temporary home should be until the its permanent building is ready. In spring 1998, Glasgow received a double blow: first political pride was hurt when it was announced that the temporary home would also be in Edinburgh; then artistic pride was bruised when plans for a National Gallery of Scottish Art in Glasgow were shelved.

While these recent developments give an example of civic rivalry, they have little bearing on Glasgow's attractiveness as a city to live in or visit. Its position as 1999's City of Architecture is a more useful pointer. Pausing cheekily to note that Edinburgh, whose classic city centre will already be familiar to many a shortbread-tin owner, was one of the shortlisted cities that lost out on the accolade, the title is a timely symbol of Glasgow's dynamism as it powers towards the millennium.

Although it boasts as rich a history as its East Coast neighbour, Glasgow is not as ensnared by its own heritage as the tourist-pleasing Edinburgh. Nevertheless, Glaswegians are proud of their social, political and industrial history (just check out the **People's Palace Museum** on Glasgow Green), and convictions run deep for many of Glasgow's staunch Labour-voting population. The city's size and personality are its main advantages. It is large and dynamic enough to always be offering new experiences for its residents. Yet it is intimate enough for no one to feel lost or alienated. Visitors to Glasgow are warmly invited to participate in its culture and there is little doubt that, with a larger population to amuse, there is more going on in Glasgow. The City Council's 'Glasgow's Alive' catchphrase may be naff, but it is certainly true.

The 'Glasgow patter', slang banter kept alive by nostalgic raconteurs like Jimmy Logan and Dorothy Paul, is a feature that baffles and delights non-natives. But ultimately it promotes the idea that Glasgow is an approachable city, full of punters happy to tell you their life story. While the TV comedy series *Rab C Nesbitt*, with its heavy-drinking, vest-wearing eponymous anti-hero and parade of Glaswegian caricatures, is closer to the truth than some might care to admit, it also shows that Glasgow can laugh at its own stereotypes.

REBIRTH OF COOL

However, it is the city's rebirth of cool that has had the most striking influence on its image in recent years. Glasgow's history as a style conscious town stems from the days when the Tobacco Lords would prioritise the purchase of the 'right' clothing over feeding their families. In recent times, it had a successful tenancy as European City of Culture in 1990, when big-name artists visited the city, new cultural venues sprang up and bars and clubs opened late into the night. This promoted the idea that Glasgow was a place to party rather than

Who needs a sensible name if you're a rising star of the rock'n'pop vanguard? **Mogwai**...

lock up your daughters after dark, and kick started a decade that saw Glasgow blossom from a city living down its unsavoury elements to become the hippest urban centre outside London.

The most obvious expression of this hipness is the influx of designer clothing outlets that have recognised that Glasgow is simply *the* place to be. With a city centre choice of Katharine Hamnett, Versace, Armani, Hugo Boss and home-grown style emporium **Cruise** for all your Paul Smith and Patrick Cox needs, it's no surprise that moneyed Glaswegians wear their labels with pride. Nor are they in danger of eclipsing the dynamic street style culture, fuelled by local clubby designers and superlative retro-clothing shops.

If Glaswegians are conscious of wanting to look good, they want places to look good in. Another 1990s development is the proliferation of 'style' bars and clubs. The trend, which has now reached saturation point, began with **Bar 10**, designed by the team behind Manchester's Haçienda club, and the **Tunnel**, a club whose look was inspired by the audacious architecture of Barcelona. Restaurants and hotels like **Malmaison** and the **Brunswick** have followed, with many in the supercool Merchant City.

RISING STARS

While there will always be a poseur element to clubbing, the hippest dance meccas are those, like the **Arches** and the **Sub Club**, that concentrate on the music. Here, the epicentre of the action is the dancefloor, not the bar area.

and **Urusei Yatsura**.

'Trendiness' in music is harder to pin down. The best bands are so cool they shun fashion and get on with making idiosyncratic records and blitzing the nation's venues. Bands like Mogwai, Belle and Sebastian and Urusei Yatsura are among Britain's rock and pop vanguard; venues like the **13th Note**, **Nice'n'Sleazy** and **King Tut's** carry on supporting the new wave of rising stars.

Glasgow may never acquire the world-class tourist credentials of Edinburgh. It is not the capital and it doesn't boast the world's largest arts festival, although its specialist festivals and plethora of social hangouts give it a year-round buzz. If it is flourishing as a place which non-natives want to make their home, they are simply picking up on what Glaswegians have known for some time: that in terms of the latest hip urban destination, Glasgow is the new Glasgow.

History

'The Clyde made Glasgow and Glasgow made the Clyde.'

Early history

For the earliest settlers, the River Clyde provided a plentiful supply of food. In more recent times, as trade boomed and Glasgow became the second city of the Empire after London, its waters became crowded with cargo ships carrying riches to and from every corner of the globe. Today, Glasgow has a population of 623,000 and is Scotland's largest city and the fourth largest in Britain.

It was a ford across the Clyde, as one of the lowest and easiest places to cross the river, that became the centre for early development. Used from prehistoric times right up to the Roman invasion, today it is the site of Albert Bridge and Glasgow Green. Early activity centred on hunting and fishing as small nomadic tribes foraged for food across the Clyde basin. By 4,000BC, both the river and the shelter provided by the surrounding hills began to attract more permanent settlers. A neolithic axe was found in Sauchiehall Street in 1848, while several boats from this time have also been discovered and can be seen in the city's **Hunterian Museum**. The scattered Roman settlements along the Clyde became more concentrated as the legions consolidated their position with a line of forts between the Forth and the Clyde, about 100 miles (160km) north of Hadrian's Wall. These fortifications, known as the Antonine Wall, kept the local Damnonii tribe at bay and remains can be found in Glasgow's northern suburbs. One fort was positioned roughly where the Royal Infirmary now stands. A stone slab erected by legionnaires to record the length of the wall is in the **Kelvingrove Art Gallery and Museum**. The area was peaceful and trade flourished until AD163, when the Roman Empire began to wane and the armies retreated south.

Little is known of the area's development in the ensuing centuries, but the facts that do exist explain the eventual prominence of Glasgow over the neighbouring tribal villages. In the late sixth or early seventh century, a monastery was founded one mile to the north of the Clyde on the site of an old cemetery beside the Molendinar Burn, which runs into the Clyde. It became the religious focus for the area – today Glasgow Cathedral is on the same site.

The monastery also helps to explain the origins of the name Glasgow. A holy man, called St Kentigern or St Mungo, was given land known as

'glas cau' or 'the green hollow' by the King of Strathclyde to found a retreat. Another theory has it that the land was called 'glas cu', or 'dear green', which would explain modern Glaswegians' fondness for calling their city 'the dear green place'. St Mungo's followers settled in the green hollow and the saint's tomb can be visited in the Cathedral.

THE MIRACULOUS ST MUNGO

An expert in minor miracles, St Mungo revived a dead robin, found a queen's ring lost in the Clyde after catching a salmon, and caused a frozen bush to catch fire. He brought a bell back from Rome after a pilgrimage. These images appear in Glasgow's coat of arms, designed in Victorian times, while the fish can be seen adorning ornate lamp-posts. It was also he who, in an early sermon, said 'Let Glasgow Flourish', a phrase now used as the city's motto.

A second settlement, primarily of salmon fishermen, developed alongside the religious community on the northern bank of the river near today's Saltmarket. In time, these two equally buoyant settlements grew together to form the hub of a rapidly expanding town.

Trade also grew throughout the period, encouraged in the late 1170s when William the Lion granted the bishop a Charter and the town became a burgh. With the Charter came grants of lands and the increasing export of hides, wool, herring and salmon. By 1172, the town had grown sufficiently to be referred to in a papal bull as a city.

Glasgow slumbered through the Middle Ages and Scotland's Wars of Independence in the thirteenth century. William Wallace is said to have performed some of his heroics against English invaders nearby, but there is little evidence he did so. There are few archeological remains from medieval Glasgow, although the city's oldest building, the fifteenth-century **Provand's Lordship** where Mary, Queen of Scots stayed, still stands and is now a museum.

A crucial element in the city's success was the founding of Glasgow University (1451) by Pope Nicholas V. The college buildings were erected near the Cathedral in Rottenrow or 'the road of kings'. Nothing remains of the original university on this site. It was replaced first by a college in the High Street and then moved in Victorian times to its present grand position in the West End. However, its influence as the second university in

Shipping on the Clyde carried passengers 'doon the water' and goods all over the world.

Scotland after St Andrews ensured that scholars flocked to Glasgow. Today, the old site is dominated by Strathclyde University, founded in 1796 as the Anderson Institute.

Trading place

In the 1500s, few people outside Britain had heard of the bustling market town of Glasgow, whose 5,000 residents clustered around a handful of streets from Rottenrow to the Trongate.

In the early 1600s, the town was dominated by craftsmen. By 1746, when Bonnie Prince Charlie visited Glasgow during his retreat from England, the city's name was becoming increasingly well known and the population had swollen to 20,000 and, 30 years later, to 40,000.

The reason for this growth? Trade. Coal, cloth and Clyde red herrings were shipped to Ireland and France in return for meal, oats, butter, salt, pepper and prunes.

In 1707, the Act of Union joined England and Scotland together. Although fervently opposed by Glaswegians, it unlocked the door to the fantastic wealth of the British colonies. Glasgow was the closest British port to the West Indies and the Americas and city merchants seized the opportunity. In 1775, the Clyde was widened and deepened up to the Broomielaw Quay to allow ships access to the heart of the city.

THE TOBACCO LORDS

Sugar, rum and tobacco from the colonies were sold at great profits throughout Britain and Europe and, before long, half of all tobacco imported to Britain came up the Clyde. Glasgow tobacco merchants became so rich they were known as the Tobacco Lords and wore special three-cornered hats, white wigs and scarlet cloaks as a badge of their importance. They were responsible for building the first pavement in the city, in front of the Tolbooth at the foot of the High Street. Known as the 'planestanes', the merchants met there to talk business or parade in their finery.

One of the greatest Tobacco Lords, Stephen Mitchell, left his fortune to found the public **Mitchell Library**, opened in Ingram Street in 1877. A few years later, it moved to Miller Street before taking up its current position in grand buildings in North Street in 1911. It is now Europe's largest reference library.

As Glasgow flourished, it grew; wealthy merchants moved west, first to the Merchant City and then beyond. Glasgow began to acquire an infrastructure of banks, insurance companies, warehouses and docks that would provide the backbone of future expansion.

The Industrial Revolution

One of Glasgow's greatest achievements has been to constantly reinvent itself to sustain development. This became vital after 1775 when American colonies revolted against British rule and declared their independence. With the tobacco traders facing bankruptcy, the focus of trade shifted to the factories that, since the early 1700s, had been making cloth, refining sugar and brewing ale. These were joined by printing, pottery, carpet manufacture, dye and chemical works. Charles Mackintosh invented a chemical process that produced the first waterproof material – giving his name to the raincoat. The Industrial Revolution found its first home in Glasgow.

Throughout the first half of the nineteenth century, cotton was king in Glasgow until supplies failed during the American Civil War (1861-5). As trade suffered, Glaswegians turned the nearby coal and iron ore deposits into a new source of wealth, providing the raw material for the rapid expansion of engineering. Heavy industry developed quickly and shipbuilding and locomotive manufacture dominated for the next century. Glasgow-built railway engines ran on lines across the world as far away as India and China. Shipbuilding spread along the Clyde from the heart of the city in Govan to the mouth of the Clyde Estuary at Greenock and Port Glasgow. Between 1780 and 1880, the population increased to over 500,000 and, at its height, half the workers of the city were involved in shipbuilding or factories. Some of the world's greatest liners, including the *QE2* and the recently decommissioned **Royal Yacht *Britannia***, were launched into the Clyde.

This increasing population was bolstered by a huge influx of poor immigrants escaping the poverty of the Highlands or the misery of the Irish potato famines – creating a social mix that encompassed both Catholics and Protestants, rich, poor and very poor. In 1831, one in six of the population was estimated to be Irish. One offshoot of this was the establishment of Celtic Football Club (1888) by Catholics to raise money for the poor. Celtic's great rivalry with Glasgow Rangers has become one of the most passionate in European football, although it has also been a focus for sectarian rivalries. Beneficiaries of the Industrial Revolution followed the example of the Tobacco Lords and moved out of the rapidly expanding city centre to large mansions in western suburbs, such as Partick, Dowanhill and Hyndland, which were upwind of the city's industrial smog.

TEA TIMES

Living in great style and with plenty of money, Glasgow's richer citizens enjoyed an expansive social life comprising tea and supper parties, theatre trips, concerts and lectures. One of the more genteel ways to socialise was by visiting one of the many tearooms that opened at this time. The most famous of these was owned by the formidable Miss Cranston, who opened the world's first such establishment in 1875 and who employed the services of architect Charles Rennie Mackintosh to design her tearooms. So strict was her demand for cleanliness that she was reputed to inspect the underwear of her waitresses every morning before opening time. Her legacy lives on in the **Willow Tea Rooms**, which contains some original Mackintosh features.

As the city expanded, the city centre also took on a new form. The narrow streets of the Merchant City were unsuited to the needs of business, so wider streets were built to the west of George Square on a grid system that mirrored those of Chicago. During the Victorian era city buildings took on an elaborate splendour. Hospitals, schools, churches and ornate public buildings of all descriptions were raised to proclaim their power and wealth. The increased leisure time of its citizens was reflected in the proliferation of over 70 parks and gardens throughout the 'dear green place'. The elaborate **City Chambers** in George Square, opened in 1888 by Queen Victoria, epitomise the era's confident splendour. By the late nineteenth century, Glasgow's population was over one million. In the 1880s, trains and trams ran throughout the city and, in 1896, one of the earliest underground systems in Britain (now known affectionately as the Clockwork Orange) was built. The pride and confidence of the city was symbolised in the 1888 International Exhibition held in Kelvingrove Park.

TENEMENT LIVING

However, away from the splendour of the city centre and the western suburbs, there was a darker side. The poor moved into the new four-storey tenements that were built from the 1830s. Today, the European-influenced red and blond sandstone buildings dominate the city and are much admired for their style, particularly in the affluent areas where no expense was spared to add flourishes of grandeur including stained-glass windows and ornate, tiled stairwells. These latter buildings were occupied by clerks and artisans, but the multitude of smaller tenement flats housed the poorest.

By the late 1800s, these homes were more noted for their abject squalor and overcrowding. It was not unusual for entire families to live in one or two rooms with little sanitation. The tenements in areas such as the Gorbals became slums and had to be managed by a system of ticketing. Flats were inspected, measured and a metal ticket placed beside the door prescribing the number of people over the age of eight who were allowed to sleep in them. Night inspectors checked these tenements weren't overcrowded, and if they were, landlords and tenants could be fined. The system was hated by Glaswegians.

The worst tenements became breeding grounds for crime and diseases such as smallpox. In 1866, the City Improvement Trust was given the power to demolish the worst slums and build new tenements with wash-houses and better sewage. **Tenement House**, with its original fittings, can be visited today in Buccleuch Street.

End of an era

Despite widespread poverty, Glasgow entered the twentieth century on the crest of a wave. Some 60,000 men worked on the Clyde, and no one could conceive of the tragic fall to come with the Great Depression of the 1930s. However, the darkest cloud over Glasgow was the impending decline of the shipbuilding industry, which saw thousands plunged into unemployment.

The end of World War I triggered the city's demise. Shipyards geared up to operate at maximum capacity faced a post-war slump. This created tensions among the workforce and the stirrings of industrial action by the radical socialist group, the Red Clydesiders, who organised their first strike in 1915. More followed as unemployment rose to 80,000 in 1922 and the Depression bit.

World War II brought an industrial upturn, with the increased need for battleships and armaments, and the war boom continued to bolster industry into the 1950s. However, the 1960s and 1970s saw shipyards along the length of the Clyde closing in droves. The underlying reason was Glasgow's early industrialisation. From the 1870s, Britain faced competition from America, Germany and, after 1945, Japan. The city's dependence on exporting ships and engineering products made these industries vulnerable to slumps in the world economy and new technology quickly outstripped earlier working practices. Today, only two shipbuilders remain and these are dogged by closure rumours. The one area where Glasgow remains a world leader in the maritime industry is in ship management.

A lasting memorial to this bygone era is the Finnieston crane, which has become one of the city's best-known landmarks. Over 164 feet (50m) high, it was used to lift steam locomotives onto ships bound for India, Russia and Africa.

THE SOCIAL WHIRL

Despite the recession, the social life of the city has enjoyed a boom throughout the twentieth century. Once the preserve of the rich, the dance hall quickly became the social focus for the working classes. The first purpose-built dance hall was the Assembly Rooms (1796), funded by the Tobacco Lords. By the 1920s, Glasgow had 11 ballrooms and over 70 small dance halls. The biggest and most popular was the **Barrowland**, opened on Christmas Eve, 1934. Its huge, neon sign was taken down during World War II after German planes used it to navigate by. Today, the venue stills thrives as a concert hall for rock bands.

The flip-side of Glasgow's thriving social life is its image as 'no mean city' dogged by drink-fuelled violence and gang warfare. The razor gangs of the 1960s remain an enduring image of Glasgow to this day and violence is still present on the streets. However, the image is stronger than the reality, and Glasgow is no more violent than many other major cities – less so than most.

As unemployment grew and conditions in the inner-city slums worsened, Glasgow followed the lead of other post-industrial cities with a radical rethink of housing policy. In the 1950s and 1960s, some 85,000 old tenements in the east of the city were demolished. Tenants were moved into council estates and high-rise tower blocks, or decamped into new settlements on the outskirts of the city such as Drumchapel and Easterhouse. The optimism that these moves would improve conditions for the poor was not realised. People felt isolated in the new settlements, which had few shops or facilities. Today these areas are rife with poverty, unemployment, vandalism and crime. The talk is once again of moving people back into the empty areas left by receding industry. In the last decade, Glasgow has enjoyed a renaissance based not on the traditional heavy industries, but on the architectural legacy of its heyday, a flourishing arts scene and the aggressive marketing of the city as a key European tourist attraction. Ambitious programmes to restore, rather than demolish, the city's fine tenements were introduced. The buildings, parks and cultural scene have captured the imagination of fellow Europeans, who first came to the city in 1988 for the International Garden Festival and returned in droves in 1990 when Glasgow, to the amazement of its residents, became the European City of Culture.

The city has become more cosmopolitan and, despite the wet climate, has taken on the mantle of a vibrant, multicultural European city with trend-setting galleries, bars, clubs and restaurants. Ambitious projects such as the extension to the **Scottish Exhibition and Conference Centre**, nicknamed 'the Armadillo', have further heightened Glasgow's positive image.

With new motorways providing faster links between the city and the rest of Britain, Glasgow continues to thrive. Some have criticised the latest resurgence of Glasgow as short-lived, while others believe the arrival of a Scottish Parliament in Edinburgh will lead to decline. However, Glasgow is set to hold the mantle of the UK City of Architecture and Design in 1999 and, with an eye on its past successes, it is well placed to enter the next millennium with new-found confidence.

Architecture

Mackintosh dominates, but a Victorian aesthetic is being revealed as Glasgow prepares to revel in its other architectural highpoints.

Glasgow has suffered from a reputation over the last 50 years as the ugly and brutish industrial neighbour of genteel Edinburgh. Certainly, the M8 approach to the city, flanked by HM Prison Barlinnie and Blochairn gas works, is unlikely to make the hairs on the back of your neck stand up with aesthetic appreciation, but don't be discouraged. The city has for too long believed in its own bad publicity, precipitated in large part by post-war town-planning decisions (or lack of them) to destroy whole areas of the city, much of it tenement housing. High-rise flats and major roads replaced the tenement communities, the most famous example being the Gorbals area of Hutchenstown, where not only do the streets have no name, but there are no real streets at all.

Yet the last ten years have seen something of a recovery of the civic pride for which the city is so famed, and attempts to right some of these wrongs have been, and continue to be, vitally addressed.

BOLD, UNFUSSY AND SCARY BY NIGHT

Daniel Defoe described Glasgow in 1724 as 'the cleanliest, beautifullest, and best-built city in Britain, London excepted'. Unfortunately, little remains of Glasgow's early architectural flourish, due in no small part to the progressive, yet marauding, nature of the Victorian urban renewal programme. All that remains of the mediaeval city to the east is Glasgow Cathedral, begun in the early thirteenth century and subject to much alteration over time, with the Victorians lopping off two towers on the west front for aesthetic reasons. It's no blockbuster as cathedrals go, but it's bold, unfussy and quite scary at night when viewed from its dramatic rise in the south-east.

Directly across from the Cathedral, the oldest house in Glasgow, **Provand's Lordship** (1471), stands as a sadly solitary example of a late-mediaeval townhouse. Similarly, very little exists of early-seventeenth-century Glasgow following the Reformation. The Tolbooth Steeple (1626) at the busy High Street junction is about it.

The eighteenth-century Merchant City continued the development in the east, and grew out of Glasgow's prominence as a busy trading port. Of the early mercantile town, the outstanding existing monuments are Hutcheson's Hall (1802) on Ingram Street, a mixed bag of classical and Renaissance styles by David Hamilton, a signifi-

cant Glasgow architect. Hamilton was also responsible for the portico addition to the Cunninghame Mansion (1778), strikingly situated at the end of Ingram Street in Royal Exchange Square, and now the **Gallery of Modern Art**.

St George's Church (1807) is as important symbolically as it is in its eccentric design. The church stands on Buchanan and George Streets and marks the end of the growth of the old town to the east and the beginning of the city's westward expansion following a grid plan patterned on Chicago's map, thus shaping the city into its present character. The domestic terrace buildings of this period, west of Charing Cross, are among the city's most superb features and well worth a leisurely stroll. Highlights are Park Circus (1857-63) and Park Terrace (1855), and further west, flanking Great Western Road, Great Western Terrace (1867), the definitive Glasgow terrace designed by one of the city's most important architects, Alexander 'Greek' Thomson.

IT'S ALL GREEK

Thomson contributed arguably more than any other single architect to the defining personality of Glasgow, which is essentially a Victorian city. A sizeable part of his work remains, and a tour of Thomson's architectural legacy is an excellent way to explore. Buildings to look out for include his magnificent, classical-fronted warehouse and office developments in the city centre such as the Egyptian Halls (1871) on Union Street and the Grosvenor Building (1861) on Gordon Street; domestic terraces such as Great Western Terrace and Moray Place; villas, the most striking of which is Holmwood (1858) in Cathcart (currently being restoredi and due to open to coincide with 1999's major Thomson exhibition), combining the classical and picturesque, and arguably anticipating Frank Lloyd Wright's Prairie Houses (1901-10) with their low-pitched roof and overhanging eaves; and his two remaining churches – Caledonia Road Church (1856) on Caledonia Street, which is currently only a shell, and St Vincent Street Church (1859), one of the most recognisable landmarks in the city with its amazing mix of classical, Egyptian and Indian-style motifs, and which has recently joined the Taj Mahal as one of the 100 most-endangered sites on the World Monuments Watch List.

Maximum Mackintosh

The legacy of Charles Rennie Mackintosh looms large over the city of Glasgow. City-centre bins, benches and just about every other street accessory designed for or after 1990 is an ersatz variation on a Mackintosh stylistic theme, affectionately known as 'Mockintosh'. The Mackintosh phenomenon reached fever pitch in 1996 when Glasgow's favourite son was the subject of a major exhibition, which toured the Metropolitan Museum, New York, Art Institute of Chicago and Los Angeles County Museum to dramatic success. As a result of this collective pride (or clever marketing opportunity), Mackintosh-style typeface declares everything on the menu at Henry Healy's to Pure Dead Brilliant (thatμ's local for nice) on T-shirts stretched across many a Glaswegian beer gut.

Mackintosh mania aside, the recent phenomenal success of the exhibition in the US reinforces his rightful international reputation as one of the most original and dynamic architects and designers of the twentieth century and one of the pioneers of the Modern movement.

His greatest public buildings can be seen in and around Glasgow and his masterpiece, the **Hill House**, involves an essential trip to Helensburgh, just outside Glasgow.

Mackintosh's pièce de résistance is the **Glasgow School of Art** (*pictured*), a twentieth-century icon of modern design. The must-views are the façades of the north and west wings, and particularly the library beyond. If there is only one thing you are able to do on your visit, then a tour of this building is it. It's glorious in its spatial innovations and, along with Hill House, this is as near as one gets to a pure example of continuous harmony. Other Mackintosh buildings to see include:

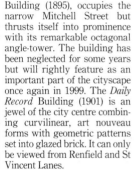

• **Martyrs' Public School** Just north of the Cathedral, this 1896 edifice is an early example of Mackintosh's architectural designs, and now houses the conservation department for Glasgow Museums.

• **Queen's Cross Church (1899)** The headquarters of the Charles Rennie Mackintosh Society nods more in the direction of free-Gothic-style building with splashes of art nouveau form.

• *Glasgow Herald* and *Daily Record* **Buildings** A stone's throw from each other in the city centre. The earlier of the two, the *Herald* Building (1895), occupies the narrow Mitchell Street but thrusts itself into prominence with its remarkable octagonal angle-tower. The building has been neglected for some years but will rightly feature as an important part of the cityscape once again in 1999. The *Daily Record* Building (1901) is an jewel of the city centre combining curvilinear, art nouveau forms with geometric patterns set into glazed brick. It can only be viewed from Renfield and St Vincent Lanes.

• **Scotland Street School (1904)** Best viewed at night to achieve the full illuminated impact of its glass Scots-baronial-type turrets.

• **The Willow Tea Rooms (1904)** In Sauchiehall Street, these retain their simple and understated façade, and many of the original features in the Salon de Luxe remain.

• **The Ladies' Luncheon Room** Reconstructed from the Mackintosh-designed Ingram Street Tea Rooms (1900), it formed the centrepiece for the exhibition that toured the US. The remaining six rooms and connecting halls, which were shamefully dismantled in the early 1970s, have been partially salvaged and are being reconstructed by Glasgow Museums.

Nineteenth-century Glasgow was at the centre of a great commercial and industrial boom. Iron became increasingly important, particularly architecturally in the iron-framed warehouses of the city centre. Gardner's Warehouse (1856) on Jamaica Street is the best example, mainly by virtue of its beautifully simple, classically proportioned bays. It's easy to miss as it's so understated; the Ca'd'Oro

building (1872) on Union Street is not, being a flamboyant interpretation of the Venetian Doge's Palace in iron and glass. The Doge's Palace makes another appearance in the guise of one of the most striking and quirky buildings of the period, Templeton's Carpet Factory (1889) on Glasgow Green. Designed by William Leiper, the building is one of the greatest examples of decorative brickwork in existence, and a rare find in an essentially stone city. The superb intricate design reflects the carpets that were manufactured there.

BIG PINK WEDDING CAKE

Thankfully, the Gothic revival was not generally embraced by discerning Glaswegians, although there is one notable exception, namely Gilbert Scott's University of Glasgow main building (1866-86), which incensed Thomson into delivering a public lecture attacking the building as a betrayal of Scotland's, and indeed Glasgow's, architectural tradition. Across the River Kelvin is the **Kelvingrove Art Gallery and Museum** (1901), a red sandstone, wedding cake of a building, which every taxi driver will duly inform you is built back to front – an urban myth.

Glasgow's art deco legacy has not fared particularly well. One cracking exception is the former **Beresford Hotel** (Sauchiehall Street), now student accommodation for the University of Strathclyde. Resembling the evil Emperor Ming's headquarters in *Flash Gordon*, it was known at the time as 'Glasgow's first skyscraper hotel'.

Recent buildings worth more than a glance are the **Burrell Collection** (Barry Gasson, 1983), where the interior courtyard on a sunny day illustrates that natural light is the essential material of meaningful architecture; also, Glasgow's own Sydney Opera House on the banks of the Clyde, the Sir Norman Foster-designed **Scottish Conference Centre,** or 'Armadillo'. It has its detractors, but it's a vibrant addition to a previously run-down area.

1999 – UK City of Architecture

Glasgow, in the 1990s, has had more stabs at re-inventing itself than Madonna. In 1990, Glasgow was the European City of Culture; this was also the golden age of Mr Happy, the Council's corporate logo, proclaiming that 'Glasgow's Miles Better'. The City of Culture gave way to the city of just about anything that springs to mind, and Mr Happy was given the elbow, ignominiously replaced by a faceless campaign declaring Glasgow as 'the Friendly City'. In 1999, the Friendly City will have the distinction of being the UK City of Architecture and Design.

The aim of Glasgow 1999 is to celebrate international architecture and design, and to highlight new ideas and developments. An ambitious programme of exhibitions focusing on some of the great movers and shakers of twentieth-century modernism – Frank Lloyd Wright, Mies van der Rohe, and Alvar Aalto – is promised, as well as the long-awaited exhibition on the work of Thomson. The Thomson show will christen, in May 1999, the Lighthouse, Scotland's Centre for Architecture Design and the City, one of the pivotal projects associated with the 1999 programme.

The Lighthouse project involves the conversion of the Mackintosh-designed *Glasgow Herald* Building by local architects Page and Park, with interiors by Barcelona-based designer Javier Mariscal, best known for his Cobi mascot for the 1992 Olympics. The redevelopment is designed to become a focus for discourse on architecture and design issues. This rejuvenation of often-dilapidated existing buildings into contemporary and functional spaces has been one of the more forward-thinking initiatives of 1990s Glasgow. A number of successful precedents can currently be seen, the most outstanding example being the remodelling of the 1930s former Luma Lamp Factory (which can be seen on the south side of Glasgow from the M8) into state-of-the-art housing with an office suite in the tower.

Homes for the Future is the most ambitious project being undertaken for the 1999 programme. It plans to redevelop the derelict land between St Andrew's Square and Glasgow Green in the city's East End, and develop 200 homes. The initiative is described as 'an exploration of innovative responses to changes in urban living', by examining ecological concerns, changes in the family structure and living patterns. Private and public developers will work with local, national and international architects to build what is hoped will be a model for housing in Scotland for the next century. The first phase of the project of up to 50 homes is to be completed in time for 1999 and part of the proposal is to allow the public the chance to see the construction processes in progress.

Glasgow as the UK City of Architecture and Design does make a lot of sense. It is a bountiful city, in architectural and design terms, and is sufficiently confident in itself to pull the celebration off. Thankfully, the accompanying promotion is not replete with asinine publicity informing us, as it did in 1990, that 'There's a lot Glasgowing on' in, yes, Mackintosh-style typeface. The city is older and wiser and not so anxious to prove itself. Glasgow 1999 even has its own customised typeface.

Sightseeing

***From the Clyde to the Kelvin, the Acropolis to Pollok Park and
Barras to the University, art and architecture reflect a vibrant heart.***

City centre

Glasgow's city centre is laid out in an easy grid pattern, although it would be a courageous motorist who braved the baffling one-way system before becoming familiar with the area. But the centre is so fascinating that there's no substitute for negotiating it on foot. The streets are thronged with shoppers, students and *The Big Issue* sellers. Skateboarders practise on all available inclines.

Arrival at Queen Street Railway Station plunges the visitor right into the thick of Glasgow. The station stands on the north side of George Square with its grassy lawns and 80-foot (25-metre) central column topped by a statue of Sir Walter Scott. Statues of the likes of Robbie Burns and Queen Victoria are dotted about. The magnificent City Chambers (0141 221 9600), built in Italian Renaissance style and capped by a 213-foot (66-metre) tower, dominate the east side of the square. The Chambers were opened by Queen Victoria in 1888 when Glasgow was rich enough to be known as the 'second city' of her vast Empire. The bas-relief sculp-

tures covering the façade represent the British nations and colonies. The interior is equally grand, with a vista of gleaming Italian marble and Peterhead granite inside the entrance and sumptuous rooms, arched ceilings and friezes.

MERCHANT CITY

Spreading away from the south-east of George Square is the Merchant City, formerly the centre for Glasgow's sugar and tobacco traders, who brought the city its prosperity. After suffering from neglect during the early twentieth century, the area became trendy in the yuppie years of the 1980s and since then has enjoyed a boom of chic and trendy gentrification. Its buildings have been cleaned up, whole blocks have been knocked down and revamped with only the façades remaining and the designer clothing shops and trendy brasseries have moved in.

Seen from a pavement café table on a sunny day, Royal Exchange Square shows Glasgow at its most continental. At the centre is the **Gallery of Modern Art** (*see below*) – GOMA. Since its 1996

The **City Chambers**, *in George Square, were built in 1888 and opened by Queen Victoria.*

CANDLERIGGS

The **City Hall**, Glasgow's main concert venue until the building of the Royal Concert Hall in 1990, is on Candleriggs. Looking past it, up Ingram Street, you can see the Ramshorn Church, which is supposed to have acquired its name from St Mungo's miracle of turning a ram's head into stone, and is now a theatre.

The Old Fruitmarket at the top of Albion Street has, since 1969, found a new use as a covered arena for events such as the Glasgow Jazz Festival. Also on Albion Street is Café Gandolfi, which has an attractive interior with wooden furnishings by Tim Steadman and stained-glass windows by John K Clark, whose work can also be seen in Queen's Park Synagogue on the South Side.

To the south lies Trongate, marked by the 126-foot (39-metre) Tolbooth Steeple (1626) at the intersection of five roads in the heart of old Glasgow. It is where tolls were collected for entering the city, and was the jail mentioned in Sir Walter Scott's *Rob Roy*. The Mercat Cross is here, too, a 1929 copy of the original that stood until 1659 and marked the first Glasgow market in the twelfth century. Turning eastwards into Trongate, which forms the beginning of Argyle Street, the brown clock steeple belongs to the **Tron Theatre**. The steeple is all that remains of the original church, which was burned down in 1793 by members of the local branch of the Hellfire Club. Argyle Street has the edge over Sauchiehall Street for the title of Glasgow's best mainstream shopping drag, as it boasts the **St Enoch Centre** (1989). This is Europe's largest glass-covered shopping area and the roof, held up by a forest of white girders, uses a system of blinds to prevent sunlight from baking the shoppers inside. Opposite lies the Argyle Arcade, a narrow but airy Victorian-style thoroughfare, lined with jewellers' shops, which links through to Buchanan Street.

ART & ANTIQUES

For less mainstream goods, the streets just behind the Tron, such as Parnie Street, are full of shops selling old books, records and science fiction paraphernalia. This and the adjoining King Street are a centre for art galleries, with the Transmission Gallery, Art Exposure, Framemaker Gallery, Sharmanka Gallery of Kinetic Sculptures, Glasgow Print Studio and Streetlevel Photowork all crammed into the small area. With a number of studios above the galleries themselves, this is one of the more bohemian, fascinating parts of the city centre. Further down is King's Court Antiques and Collectibles Market, a row of indoor stalls in the shadow of a railway bridge. Paddy's Market lies just over the road, a traditional market whose romance is tarnished by the daily detritus left behind. Along the gentle curve of the railway line towards the Clyde is Bridge Gate, one of the old-

Gallery of Modern Art. *See page 184.*

opening, the gallery has attracted a record amount of controversy and disapproval from art critics for its populist selection policy and design. Glaswegians know what they like, however, and it has also attracted a record number of visitors. Eastwards, along Ingram Street and into the heart of the Merchant City, the mood of upwardly mobile Glasgow is captured in the **Italian Centre**, a yuppie heaven decorated with statues of Mercury and housing numerous designer-label shops.

The area between Ingram and Argyle Streets was once a busy market district and many of the old premises have found modern uses. On Virginia Street is **Virginia Galleries**, a high-ceilinged hall with three floors of stalls selling antiques, second-hand books, cheap videos and clothing. The grand classical façade and green dome of Trades House, designed in 1794 by Robert Adam and the second-oldest building in the city, dominates Glassford Street (No.85, 0141 552 2418; open 10am-5pm Mon-Fri). It still serves its original function as the headquarters of the Glasgow trade guilds. The coats of arms of the individual guilds (tailors, weavers, hammer men and the like) are emblazoned on walls, chairs, stained-glass windows, the cupola of the dome itself and on a ten-yard (nine-metre) long bench by the entrance, which was carved by Belgian refugees during World War I.

est parts of the city. It's a typically Glaswegian set of contrasts, with an upmarket hairdresser practically next door to a scrapyard. The cream and green building, the Briggait – towered over by the 160-foot (50-metre) Merchant's Steeple – is, sadly, closed, but is crying out for a new lease of life. Its wrought iron interior can be glimpsed through the gates. Closer to the the Clyde is the Clutha Vaults, a drinkers' institution, and, like the 250-year-old **Scotia Bar** on Stockwell Street, a mecca for folk music and traditional Scottish culture.

NAUTICAL INFLUENCES

Down by the riverside, the Clyde Walkway is a pleasant stroll underneath the numerous city centre bridges. The regeneration of Glasgow brought with it some splendid buildings on the banks of the Clyde, a few with a discernible nautical influence, such as the flats on the corner of Clyde Street and Stockwell Street with their black curved balconies and mast-like posts and the shiny metal and glass construction of 1 Atlantic Quay, a little further west. The Gothic St Andrew's Cathedral (1816) nestles modestly on Clyde Street. Broomielaw is where passenger steamers used to depart 'doon the watter' for the Glasgow Trades Holidays, but now the main things to see are Custom House (1840) and the pedestrian suspension bridge.

Away from the Clyde, the renovation of Central Station, once famous only for having the largest signal box in the world to cope with its traffic, has a concourse that's almost chic by railway station standards. The streets in the immediate vicinity of the station have some notable buildings. The Ca' d'oro, on the corner of Gordon Street and Union Street, is a fabulous Venetian-looking construction – rows of arches supported by Doric pilasters, with big windows at street level. Practically next door is the Egyptian Building by Alexander 'Greek' Thomson (1817-75). Although ornate, with fascinating decorative detail, in comparison with nearby buildings it looks grubby and unloved. One block along, on Mitchell Street, is an early Charles Rennie Mackintosh building (1895) that once housed the *Glasgow Herald*. The former *Daily Record* building is on Renfield Lane. If all this architectural appreciation becomes thirsty work, the **Horseshoe Bar** on Drury Street is reputed to have the longest continuous bar in Europe.

SHOPPING IN STYLE

The pedestrianised Buchanan Street, two streets east, provides more upmarket shopping than Argyle Street and Sauchiehall Street. It contains **Princes Square**, a stylish shopping mall that shows what can be achieved with wood, metal, glass, the shells of existing buildings – and, of course, a little inspiration from Mackintosh. At the north of Buchanan Street stands the **Royal**

Tolbooth Steeple – the heart of old Glasgow.

Concert Hall, one of Glasgow's most impressive modern buildings. Just before that, on the right, is the Buchanan Galleries, a sprawling behemoth of a shopping centre that only goes to make the rundown George Hotel opposite look even seedier: the 'London' hotel scenes of *Trainspotting* were filmed in here.

Sauchiehall Street is legendary – the mere mention of it can bring a tear to the eye of an expatriate Glaswegian. It has also become a byword for crowded. The wide, bustling, semi-pedestrianised thoroughfare gives the impression that if you stand there for long enough all human life will stream past. Needless to say, it's to be avoided when the pubs and clubs spill out. The **Willow Tea Rooms**, above Henderson's jewellery shop, is an exact reproduction (right down to the cutlery) of a tearoom designed by Mackintosh, and a gorgeous place to stop for coffee and cake. Nearby are the **McLellan Galleries** (*see below*) and the **Centre for Contemporary Arts** (*see below*), which both host a range of touring and temporary shows from new artists and international celebrities. The eight-storey Baird Hall of Residence on the corner of Garnet Street is an eye-catching splash of art deco, its verve rivalled only slightly by the truck protruding from the wall above the **Garage**, a medium-sized rock venue close by.

The blocks south of Sauchiehall Street mainly comprise office space, with the occasional discreet gallery. There are a few exceptions. The **King's Theatre** is a red sandstone building on Bath Street, with the ever-expanding Griffin pub diagonally opposite. The black, Roman-looking building on the corner of Bath and Pitt Streets is the former Elgin Place Congregational Church, now Follies, a nightclub that has hung around far longer than is respectable. **King Tut's Wah Wah Hut**, one of the city's best live music venues, is on St Vincent Street.

GARNETHILL

On the north side of Sauchiehall Street, a sharp incline leads up to Garnethill, a mainly residential area that's the centre of Glasgow's Chinese community and also contains Garnethill Synagogue, the oldest Jewish place of worship in the city. **Glasgow School of Art** (*see below*), one of the boldest and most splendid of Mackintosh's designs, balances on this perilously steep hill. Over its brow is **Tenement House** (*see below*), the preserved home of Agnes Toward, who lived there from 1911 to 1965 without changing the interior. Those with traditional tastes can bone up on military history at the nearby **Regimental Museum of the Royal Highland Fusiliers** (*see below*).

A little further down, the M8 motorway cuts a huge swathe through the centre of the city, leaving Stow College looking lonely and isolated at its edge. But in the shadow of the grey flyovers gleam the vivid colours that mark the entrance to the Chinatown Glasgow Shopping Mall. The area from here westwards is Cowcaddens and is known throughout Scotland as the home of Scottish Television. It is also the home to several places of entertainment. The **Glasgow Film Theatre** is on Rose Street; the attractive brick-and-glass edifice on Renfrew Street is the **Royal Scottish Academy of Music & Drama**; opposite that, on Hope Street, lies the **Theatre Royal**. Finally, the **Pavilion Theatre** is on the corner of Renfrew Street and Renfield Street.

Little of old Glasgow is left standing north-east of George Square, an area that has become the college district. Glasgow College of Building and Printing, Central College of Commerce, Glasgow College of Food Technology and the University of Strathclyde are all found along Cathedral Street, which runs along the back of Queen Street Station. The University of Strathclyde's campus is centred around Rottenrow, where, in 1451, Bishop William Turnbull founded its rival, the University of Glasgow.

Centre for Contemporary Arts

350 Sauchiehall Street, G2 (0141 332 7521). Cowcaddens tube. **Open** *gallery* 11am-6pm Mon-Sat;

noon-5pm Sun; *centre* 9am-11pm Mon-Wed; 9am-midnight Thur-Sat; noon-6pm Sun. **Admission** free. **Credit** MC, V. **Map 1 C2**
Glasgow's focus for contemporary visual, performance (payment required) and multimedia art. Closed for a year from March 1999 for a £10million refurbishment that will triple its exhibition space.

Gallery of Modern Art

Queen Street, G1 (0141 229 1996). Buchanan St tube. **Open** 10am-5pm Mon-Sat; 11am-5pm Sun. **Admission** free. **Credit** AmEx, DC, MC, £TC, V. **Map 1 D3**
Opened in 1996 and separated into four themed spaces – earth, air, fire and water – the gallery has attracted a barrage of disapproval from critics and artists for its populist stance and design. It's an eclectic place, where the rotund ladies of Beryl Cook's paintings co-exist with serious meditations on breast cancer by Jo Spence. Scottish artists are well represented by Peter Howson, Ken Currie and John Bellany, while the rooftop café has been decorated in the distinctive style of Adrian Wizniewski.

Glasgow School of Art

167 Renfrew Street, G3 (0141 353 4500). Queen St rail or Cowcaddens tube. **Open** *tours* 11am, 2pm Mon-Fri; 10.30am Sat; *shop* 10am-5pm Mon-Fri; 10am-noon Sat. **Tours** £3.50 adult; £2 concs. **Credit** AmEx, MC, £TC, V. **Map 1 D2**
One of the boldest and most splendid of Mackintosh's designs. Initially more appreciated in Europe than at home, it's a building of contrasts between the utilitarian and the fanciful, the approachable and the stern, the linear and the asymmetrical. The intimidating air of the severe west wall, with its grille-covered windows, and the stark east wall, is relieved by the wrought iron embellishments and generous studio windows on the north side. Inside, excellent use has been made of timber, especially in the library. The interior is open to the public via guided tours only, but it's worth seeing not only for the timber inside but for the collection of Mackintosh paintings, architectural plans and furniture. The School is closed for exams in the last three weeks of June each year.

McLellan Galleries

270 Sauchiehall Street, G2 (0141 331 1854). Buchanan St tube. **Open** 10am-5pm Mon-Sat; 11am-5pm Sun. **Admission** free. **Credit** AmEx, MC, £TC, V. **Map 1 C2**
Named after the art-loving coach-maker Archibald McLennan, who bequeathed his collection, very strong on sixteenth- and seventeenth-century Italian masterworks, along with the building they were kept in, to the city. The collection became the basis of Glasgow's main art gallery, which was based here before moving to Kelvingrove. These remain some of Glasgow's most important art spaces, hosting a whole range of shows from young artists to international celebrities, along with some more unusual pop-culture oriented exhibitions, in a succession of grand, high rooms. Admission charged for some exhibitions.

Regimental Museum of the Royal Highland Fusiliers

518 Sauchiehall Street, G2 (0141 332 0961). Charing Cross tube. **Open** 9am-4.30pm Mon-Thur; 9am-4pm Fri. **Admission** free. **Map 1 C2**
The story of the three regiments – the Royal Scots Fusiliers, the Highland Light Infantry and the 74th Highlanders – which merged into one and won more battle honours than any other British regiment, is told in a series of interlinked and recently refurbished galleries. The building was designed by the architects Honeyman, Keppie and Mackintosh and many features both in the façade and the interior reflect the latter's style.

Tenement House

145 Buccleuch Street, G3 (0141 333 0183). Cowcaddens tube. **Open** *1 Mar-31 Oct* 2-5pm daily. **Admission** £3.15 adults; £2.10 concs; £8.40 family (2 adults & 6 children); free NT members. **No credit cards.**
Map 1 C1
The preserved home of Agnes Toward, who lived here from 1911 to 1965 without changing the interior. The flat provides a fascinating snapshot of Glasgow tenement living.

Old Town & East End

East of the shopping thoroughfares and chic bars and restaurants of the Merchant City beats the city's historic heart, fanning eastwards from the intersection of Trongate, Gallowgate, High Street and Saltmarket – namely **Glasgow Cross**.

This area was the old centre of the city before the nineteenth-century surge westwards and, although it lacks the social vibrancy of Merchant City, it has rich pickings for anyone with an interest in Glaswegian history. Glasgow was effectively founded at the point where the Molendinar Burn flowed into the Clyde, now the site of the High Court, but further up the High Street at the point where it becomes the High Street stands the quintessential symbol of old Glasgow, the 126-foot (39-metre) Tolbooth Steeple. Here royal proclamations were read and condemned prisoners hung, Bonnie Prince Charlie marched his troops in 1745, and farmers and, later, merchants met to talk shop.

DEAR GREEN PLACE

Saltmarket, so named because it was where salt was sold to cure salmon, stretches south from the steeple to the river and was the site of Glasgow's first post office and bank in the eighteenth century. Now the sight of its blackened tenements is only alleviated by a glimpse of St Andrew's by the Green, Scotland's oldest Episcopal Church, which is now home to a housing association. The High Court and city mortuary are located on the right on the approach to the river, with the McLennan Arch on the left. Originally the main entrance to the Ingram Street Assembly Rooms, the arch was relocated when the rooms were pulled down and now marks the entrance to the city's most famous public space, Glasgow Green. This stretch of parkland may look unspectacular, but as Europe's oldest public park, it supports over 800 years of memories and experiences. Originally known as Jail Square, it was renamed Jocelyn Square after the bishop who founded the Glasgow Fair. It doubled as both fair site and hanging place. Some of the executed were buried where the city mortuary now stands, including the last victim of the gallows, Dr Edward Pritchard, a Sauchiehall Street doctor convicted in 1865 of poisoning his wife and mother-in-law.

Glasgow Green has also been a drying green for the local wash-houses. You can still see the 'iron men', 33 posts forming a drying green. According to the terms of a fourteenth-century charter, the

Templeton's Carpet Factory – built in 1889 and modelled on the Doge's Palace in Venice.

The People's Palace – *tales of the city.*

Green can only be used as a place of leisure: the annual Bonfire Night fireworks display, Glasgow Fair Festival and rock concerts have honoured this. The **People's Palace** (*see below*) and **Winter Gardens** are the main permanent attractions on the Green. The 144-foot (44-metre) Nelson Monument has the distinction of being the first major British monument to honour Admiral Lord Nelson's naval victories. It dates from 1806 (15 years before Nelson's Column in London) and was erected by public subscriptions of £2,000. Elsewhere on the green, the terracotta Doulton Fountain is the only remnant of the 1888 Great Exhibition in Kelvingrove Park.

BARRAS BARGAINS
Across the road from the People's Palace is Glasgow's most over-the-top architectural spectacle, Templeton's Carpet Factory. The ornate, colourful brickwork and mosaic tiling goes beyond pastiche – Templeton's has to be seen, if not necessarily appreciated. To the north-west of the Green lie the twin thoroughfares of Gallowgate and London Road. A stroll here after dark can be a hair-raising experience, but these two streets form the boundary for Glasgow's famous weekend market, the Barras, which is a whole Sunday morning bargain-hunting expedi-

tion in itself. The site was acquired for vending purposes in 1920, but has its roots in the Victorian era when goods were sold from barrows. The cut-price shops and spit-and-sawdust pubs in the area add to the community flavour. The famous **Barrowland** adjoins the market. It's used as a venue for rock concerts, but became notorious as a ballroom in the 1960s by association with the serial killer Bible John, who quoted scripture before strangling the female victims he would pick up at the ballroom's Thursday night session – traditionally, the night when married folk would head to the hall for an extra-marital pick-up. The murderer was never caught and the case lingers in the popular imagination. It was recently reopened to examine inconclusive DNA evidence.

On a lighter note, there are several artists' studios in the area, belying the hard-man reputation of the East End. There is little for the sightseer further east. The East End was formerly the industrial heart of the city. One of its main attractions now is the shopping and cinema complex Parkhead Forge, built on the site of the original forge, the area's biggest employer last century. For about half the city's population, the football ground Parkhead is synonymous with the agony and ecstasy of supporting Glasgow Celtic Football Club, whose stadium dominates the area. The only other landmark in the vicinity is the Umbrella at Bridgeton Cross, a cast iron pavilion donated late last century by the owners of the Sun Foundry.

MEDIAEVAL ATTRACTIONS
The area to the north of Glasgow Cross is a contradictory mix of derelict buildings and expensive new flats. The High Street snakes quaintly from the Tolbooth Steeple, past the intersection with Duke Street – Britain's longest street – which is now just waste ground but was the site of Glasgow Castle and the thirteenth-century Battle o' the Bell o' the Brae, in which William Wallace defeated the English. Castle Street contains a cluster of mediaeval attractions: the **Cathedral, Necropolis, Provand's Lordship** and the **St Mungo Museum** (*see below*).

Frowning over the entire area is the formidable Royal Infirmary, originally established in 1792 on the site of the Bishop's Castle. In 1865, the combination of Joseph Lister and carbolic acid was enough to ensure the Infirmary's place in medical history books as the location of the world's first antiseptic surgery. The current, impressively brooding structure was designed by Robert and James Adam and completed in 1915. Alexandra Parade runs behind it and it is there, in residential Dennistoun, that you will find the former Will's cigarette factory, where many of *Trainspotting's* interior scenes were filmed, bringing Glasgow's oldest quarter bang up to date.

Glasgow Cathedral

Castle Street, G4 (0141 552 6891). Buchanan St buses.
Open *summer* 9.30am-6pm Mon-Sat; 2-5pm Sun; *winter* 9.30am-4pm Mon-Sat; 2-4pm Sun. **Admission** free.
Map 1 F2
Glasgow's patron saint St Mungo founded Glasgow Cathedral in 543 on burial ground consecrated by St Ninian, and his tomb can be found in the crypt. Parts of the current building date from the twelfth century, making it one of Scotland's oldest mediaeval churches. The pristine Cathedral Square out front was formerly Bishop's Castle, Glasgow's first public hanging place, and the macabre atmosphere pervades the Old Churchyard. However, the serious gravedigger will check out the neighbouring Necropolis cemetery.

The Necropolis

Glasgow Necropolis Cemetery, G4 (0141 552 3145).
High St tube. **Open** 24 hours daily. **Admission** free.
Map 1 F2
Scotland's first non-denominational 'hygienic' graveyard, was inspired by the famed Père Lachaise cemetery in Paris to give the industrialists and merchants of the nineteenth century a dignified resting place. John Knox's statue dominates the skyline, over 200 feet (62 metres) above the Clyde. Leading from Cathedral Square, Glasgow's own Bridge of Sighs – so called because of all the funeral processions that passed over it – spans what was formerly the Molendinar Glen, now the rather more functional Wishart Street. Frustrated poets may find succour in the cemetery's romantic design; patients in the neighbouring Royal Infirmary less so.

The People's Palace/Winter Gardens

Glasgow Green, G4 (0141 554 0223). Bridgeton rail.
Open 10am-5pm Mon-Sat; 11am-5pm Sun. **Admission** free. **Map 1 F4**
The red sandstone People's Palace, built in 1898, originally served as a municipal and cultural centre for the city's working class and now houses one of Glasgow's most cherished exhibitions, covering all aspects of Glaswegian life, particularly its social and industrial history. A recent £1million facelift to coincide with its centenary has given the exhibits a more interactive bent. The adjoining Winter Gardens was severely damaged by fire in 1998.

Provand's Lordship

3 Castle Street, G4 (0141 552 8819). High St tube. **Open** call for details. **Map 1 F2**
Glasgow's oldest and only surviving mediaeval house was built in 1471 under the auspices of Bishop Andrew Muirhead. Mary, Queen of Scots is believed to have slept here; nowadays its rooms house period displays from the sixteenth century to 1914. The adjoining St Nicholas garden was added in 1995. Provand's Lordship was closed in April 1998 due to structural damage and is not expected to reopen until spring 1999.

St Mungo Museum of Religious Life and Art

2 Castle Street, G4 (0141 553 2557). High St tube. **Open** 10am-5pm Mon-Sat; 11am-5pm Sun. **Admission** free.
Map 1 F2
The St Mungo Museum completes the culture trail round Cathedral Square. The main reason to visit is to see Dali's awesome *Christ of St John of the Cross*, relocated from its erstwhile home in the Kelvingrove Art Gallery. Despite Glasgow's undesirable sectarian predilections, this is a multifaith museum with its own Zen garden for some instant karma. The Religious Art gallery contains some beautiful examples of stained glass and, although its bias is mainly Christian, there are pieces representing oriental, Egyptian, tribal African and native North American beliefs. The Religious Life Gallery is a darkened room with a compact display relating each of the six major world religions.

South Side

Glasgow's South Side is made up of several small and friendly communities. The cosmopolitan areas of today were originally disparate parishes and villages south of the city boundaries on land belonging to wealthy Renfrewshire families. Starting with the burghs nearest the river – Govan and the Gorbals – they were gradually accumulated by the city as twentieth-century suburbia took shape.

Now the South Side encompasses areas such as the multi-ethnic Govanhill with its colourful sari shops, the deprived housing estates of Castlemilk and Pollok, where community culture thrives regardless, and the upper-middle-class Newton Mearns and Giffnock. The majority of the South Side is residential and dotted with the largest parks in a city that boasts more parks per head of population than anywhere else in Europe. The tenement lifestyle of yore has changed and the sandstone edifices that dominate much of the South Side are home to everyone from students to Glasgow's various ethnic communities – Asian, Chinese, Italian. The West End may be the city's bohemian hub, but the South Side has a dynamic, cosmopolitan outlook, too. It also boasts two of Glasgow's best arts venues: the **Tramway**, a theatre and gallery space in a former tram shed in

Mackintosh House. See page 193.

Full steam ahead at the **Museum of Transport** *Page 193.*

Pollokshields, and the **Citizens' Theatre**, founded in 1943 by James Bridie and occupying the city's oldest theatre building, situated on Gorbals Main Street. A cultural experience of a different kind can be had down the road at the Plaza, a ballroom-turned-nightclub venue at Eglinton Toll.

GORBALS STORY

The Gorbals has a colourful history. A leper colony before becoming one of Glasgow's first suburbs in the nineteenth century, its name has been translated variously as 'beautiful town' and 'rough plot of ground'. Its desirability as a residential area has fluctuated, too. Its greenbelt surroundings made it initially fashionable, but the arrival of industry and immigrants led to slum overcrowding. Only recently, with the construction of the 'New Gorbals Village', are the disastrous post-war housing initiatives being rectified.

Gorbals riverside landmarks include the imposing modern Sheriff Court, the Glasgow College of Nautical Studies with its masts and planetarium dome, and Carlton Place, an elegant terrace of Georgian townhouses, including the Prince and Princess of Wales Hospice and Laurieston House, a double mansion recently restored by Strathclyde Building Preservation Trust. The skyline is dominated by the minaret and golden dome of Glasgow's Central Mosque, one of Europe's largest, opened in 1984 on the site of an old distillery. Further west along the river is one of Glasgow's most ornate buildings, the former Scottish Co-operation Wholesale Society headquarters, built in 1879 by architects Bruce and Hay. Drivers crossing Kingston Bridge get the best view of its French Renaissance façade.

Mackintosh's **Scotland Street School Museum** (*see below*) is not far from here, as are other Glaswegian landmarks, such as Harry Ramsden's fish and chip restaurant and the **Grand Ole Opry** at Paisley Road Toll, modelled half-heartedly on the Memphis original. It stands at the head of Paisley Road West, a former toll road, known in the past as 'the great road'. The district of Govan nestles next to the river and shares many similarities to the Gorbals – mediaeval roots, a population explosion last century, a rough reputation and current redevelopment. In the sixteenth century, Bishop Leslie declared Govan to be a place 'where ale is wondrous guid' and its most famous inhabitant, TV's string-vest-wearing philosopher Rab C Nesbitt, would probably agree. The area's best-known landmark is arguably the Pearce Institute, built at the turn of the century for the people of Govan by shipyard chairman Sir William Pearce. The former Harland & Wolff shipyard is closed but not forgotten: it has hosted two memorable large-scale 1990s theatrical happenings, *The Ship* and *The Big Picnic*.

PARK LIFE

The South Side's parks include Bellahouston, where the Pope said mass in 1982 and where you will find Mackintosh's **House for an Art Lover** (*see below*); Rouken Glen near the Ayr Road with its own bijou Gatehouse Gallery, butterfly farm and garden centre; Cathkin Braes, with its city-wide vista, situated 600 feet (185 metres) above sea level and Pollok Park, Glasgow's largest at 361 acres (146 hectares), which was the estate of the Maxwell family until gifted to the city in the 1960s. The eighteenth-century mansion Pollok House was open to the public until autumn 1997, and its future is under discussion, with the National Trust among the interested parties. One of the South Side's main attractions, the **Burrell Collection** (*see below*), is also situated in the park. The history of Queen's Park, named after Mary, Queen of Scots, and its environs centre on the Battle of Langside (1568), when Mary saw her forces defeated by the Regent Moray from the lookout of Cathcart Castle, which was demolished in 1980. The commemorative Langside Monument was built in 1887 on the site where her generals surrendered, and the village (now district) of Crossmyloof is reputed to be named after the sign of the cross Mary made in the palm ('loof') of her hand.

Mary also casts a historical shadow over Crookston Castle in Pollok, west of Pollok Park. It is Glasgow's last surviving castle and oldest building after the Cathedral, built in the early fifteenth century by Sir John Stewart of Darnley on the site of an earlier wooden castle dating from the twelfth century. This rather modest stone fortification was at the centre of a siege in the late fifteenth century when the first Stewart earls rose in rebellion against James IV. Mary is said to have plighted her troth to Henry, Lord Darnley, under a yew tree there. The South Side is home to some of the best examples of Alexander 'Greek' Thomson's architecture. The Caledonia Road Church in the Gorbals was inspired by the Acropolis but its future has remained uncertain since a fire in 1965 destroyed the painted interior, leaving only the portico and tower intact. The double villa in Mansionhouse Road, Langside, was built in 1856, shortly before Holmwood in Netherlee, which is regarded as Thomson's finest villa. It is being restored by the National Trust and is only open on selected occasions, such as September's Doors Open Day, when you can see inside other local attractions such as Greenbank House, an eighteenth-century Tobacco Lord's mansion that's now the headquarters of the National Trust for Scotland. The Thomson-designed terraces of Regent Park in the district of Strathbungo, to the west of Queen's Park, have been designated a conservation area since the 1970s. Both Thomson and Mackintosh lived there.

Another (unrelated) conservation area is the village of Carmunnock, situated south of Castlemilk housing estate and just within the city boundaries. The parish was established by St Cadoc in the sixth century. Today its charm is its preserved eighteenth-century houses clustered round the parish church.

No round-up of the attractions south of the city would be complete without mention of its stadia: **Ibrox**, home of Glasgow Rangers; Shawfield, last bastion of greyhound racing; and national football stadium Hampden Park, home of Scotland's oldest team, Queen's Park. Hampden is undergoing extensive refurbishment, including the building of a new south stand due to be completed in autumn 1999, which will also house a national football museum.

The Burrell Collection

Pollok Park, 2060 Pollokshaws Road, G43 (0141 649 7151). Pollokshaws East rail, then 10-min walk. **Open** 10am-5pm Mon-Sat; 11am-5pm Sun. **Admission** free.
Sir William Burrell gifted his prodigious collection of art and artefacts to the City of Glasgow in 1944, but it took so long to find a suitable site to house his treasures that he did not live to see their public display in the purpose-built gallery in the grounds of Pollok Park. The Queen opened the Burrell Collection in 1983 and it remains one of the jewels in Glasgow's cultural crown. Among its treasures are Egyptian, Greek and Roman earthenware and sculpture, china from various Chinese dynasties, many sixteenth- and seventeenth-century artefacts, huge European tapestries and English furniture, armour and paintings by Boudin, Degas, Bellini and Sisley – a collection only bettered by the Kelvingrove Art Gallery. The enormous Warwick Vase, a large, restored Roman marble urn dating from the second century and found in Hadrian's Villa at Tivoli, has come to symbolise the collection, not all of which can be displayed at any one time, although provision is also made for temporary and visiting exhibitions.

House for an Art Lover

Bellahouston Park, 10 Dumbreck Road, G4 (0141 353 4791). Ibrox tube. **Open** 10am-5pm Sat, Sun; call for week times. **Admission** £3.50; £2.50 concs.
For almost 90 years, Mackintosh's House for an Art Lover remained a design submitted in 1901 to a competition set by a German magazine, until local Mackintosh enthusiast Graham Roxburgh – responsible for the restoration of nearby Craigie Hall and its early Mackintosh interiors – and architect Professor Andy Macmillan realised the plans on the former site of Ibrox Hill House in Bellahouston Park. The plans established Mackintosh's reputation in Europe, but of the interior, only the main hall, dining room, music room (where the piano is played for ambience) and Oval Room have been reproduced. Since their completion in 1996, the work of researching further refinements continues, only partially justifying the rather steep entry fee.

Scotland Street School Museum

225 Scotland Street, G5 (0141 429 1202). Shields Rd tube. **Open** 10am-5pm Mon-Sat; 2-5pm Sun. **Admission** free. **Map 1 B4**
A more substantial Mackintosh experience than the HFAAL, both architecturally and in terms of content, offering a hands-on history of Glaswegian schooling in the first half of the century. In addition to an exhibition covering aspects of school life, from the 'janny' (janitor) to playground games, there are replica classrooms and a spacious cookery room. Visitors can take in the stunning stairwell windows with their view of the Glaswegian skyline.

West End

Dominated by the university and its large student population, the West End is also the most bourgeois and artistic area of the city. But if the West End is smug, it at least has something to be smug about in the sheer pleasure of its stunning architecture and the cultural vibe and the lively streets. The West End Festival (late June) features a colourful carnival parade down Byres Road, complete with startling costumes, steel bands and dancers.

The huge dome and imposing façade of the **Mitchell Library** (*see below*), with its statue of Minerva overlooking the motorway, unofficially divides the West End from the city centre. To the north and west, across Sauchiehall Street, lies the Park Conservation Area, a fine piece of town planning consisting of three-storey yellow sandstone terraces that extend up Woodlands Hill to Park Circus. It contains some of the most elegant houses in Glasgow, built for the Victorian elite, most of which have been converted to offices, student halls and youth hostels. At Park Circus Place, the Park Church, of which only the striking white tower remains (it was controversially replaced by a bank in 1968), was built in 1858 by JT Rochead.

Mitchell Library – *need a reference? P193.*

GREAT WESTERN

Further to the north lies the long Great Western Road, started in 1836 after relentless pressure from the Glaswegian middle classes, who wanted a route out of the overcrowded, industry-polluted city centre. Now it contributes to that pollution. West along the road are Lansdowne Parish Church, a splendid Gothic revival building, and St Mary's Episcopal Cathedral, which had its beautiful blue stained glass added a few years ago. North from St George's Cross on St George's Road is the stunning St George's-in-the-Fields, which was converted into flats in the late 1980s. It resembles a Greek temple and has a grand Victorian front carving of the loaves and fishes parable by WB Rhind. Across Garscube Road is the Glasgow branch of the Forth & Clyde Canal Path, which dates back to 1790. The canal is not the most salubrious area, but on a sunny day this stretch makes for an unusual walk with views of waste grounds, factories and the odd swan. Further on, it gives good views of the city and it is possible to walk along the towpath to the Lochburn Road junction, turn left on to the Westbound canal and drop down to the Kelvin Walkway at the impressive Kelvin Aqueduct. From there, the walkway follows the River Kelvin downstream towards the Botanic Gardens. Upstream, it eventually leads to the West Highland Way: Scotland's first long distance footpath, which ends 92 miles (147 kilometres) away in Fort William.

A shorter route is to turn off at Fir Park, the home of Partick Thistle, the city's 'third' football team, and return via Firhill Street to Garscube Road. Here, the Queen's Cross Church (1898) is the headquarters of the Charles Rennie Mackintosh Society – and members are happy to show you round. This was Mackintosh's only church; dwindling congregations in the late 1970s led the Church of Scotland to lease it out to the Society to use as a monument to his work. It looks fairly conventional on the outside, but inside its airy lines create an unusual atmosphere and upstairs on the balcony the full effect is magnificent. The Society runs a small tearoom, a bookshop and an exhibition of Mackintosh's work.

THE HEART OF THE WEST END

The Botanic Gardens – the place to be seen during Glasgow's short summer – are dominated by the huge dome of Kibble Palace (summer 10am-4.45pm, winter 10am-4.15pm Mon-Sat; noon-4.15pm Sun). It was originally a conservatory built for Victorian eccentric John Kibble, who is said to have brought it from his estate on the shores of Loch Long, up the River Clyde on a huge raft drawn by a steamboat. Its greenhouses contain many rare species, palm trees and tropical plants and are a great place to sit when it rains. Outside, there's another large greenhouse housing orchids and cacti, a herb garden and well-maintained flower beds. Down from the Gardens is the top of Byres Road, the real heart of the West End, both for shopping and for students. The most interesting stores are in the little lanes leading off the main street (Ashton, Dowanside and Cresswell) and

*Motor on down to the **Museum of Transport** to see polished cars, trams and bikes.*

there are loads of cafés, which range from the cheap and cheerful to the swanky. The Dowanhill/Hyndland area, off the main thoroughfare, contains several impressive buildings, such as Thomson's Great Western Terrace, many with the West End's characteristic stained glass.

The University of Glasgow is up the hill to the east of Byres Road. Its beautiful Gothic towers are by noted architect Sir George Gilbert Scott, who also designed the Bute Halls, a gorgeous and intimidating setting where generations have suffered through their exams. To the west of the main buildings is the grand University Chapel and the Lion and Unicorn Stair, part of the original college of 1690. It looks on to Professor's Square, once home of Lord Kelvin, a major patron of the university, which now houses college offices. The elegant quadrangles in the main section are pleasant to stroll around, particularly in autumn when the falling leaves give them a suitably melancholy feel. The university's lesser buildings are mostly horrid 1960s concrete things. Next to the tall main library tower is the bizarre-looking Mackintosh House and **Hunterian Art Gallery** (*see below*).

To the east of the University is Kelvingrove Park, an 85-acre sprawl of paths dotted with patriotic statues. The park was first laid out as a pleasure grounds in the 1850s. On a hot day it instantly becomes packed. Although people do cut through the park at night, it's not really advisable. Small bridges span the muddy Kelvin, and lead to a rollerskating area and the Scottish Gothic Fountain (1872) by John Mossman, which commemorates Lord Provost Stewart and the water supply he instigated from Loch Katrine. The south end of the Park is dominated by the wedding cake fantasy architecture of the **Kelvingrove Art Gallery & Museum** (*see below*), over Argyle Street from which is the huge Kelvin Hall sports complex, next door to the quirky **Museum of Transport** (*see below*).

The River Clyde is about fifteen minutes walk south from here and the **Scottish Exhibition and Conference Centre** (SECC) is in sight of the huge hammerhead crane known as the Finnieston Crane. The SECC is known by locals as the 'big red shed' and is a venue for big concerts, trade shows and international gatherings. The recently added extension has already earned the nickname of The Armadillo.

Hunterian Art Gallery & Museum

University of Glasgow, Hillhead Street, G12 (0141 330 5430). Hillhead tube. **Open** 9.30am-5pm Mon-Sat. **Admission** free.

The art gallery contains an important collection of works by James McNeill Whistler as well as a collection of his equipment and furnishings. There's also a good collection of nineteenth- and twentieth-century Scottish art, some French impressionists and Scotland's largest print collection. The gallery leads on to the Mackintosh House (entry charge), a recreation of the architect's home in Southpark

The 'Armadillo' extension to the SECC.

Avenue from 1906-1914, which was demolished in the 1960s. Built in 1807, the Hunterian is Scotland's oldest public museum. Like the Gallery, it was donated to the university by former student William Hunter. Its archaeological treasures include Roman coins, and its zoological collection has loads of fossils and several dinosaurs – as befits the Scottish Centre for Dinosaur Research.

Kelvingrove Art Gallery & Museum

Kelvinhall, G3 (0141 287 2700). Partick rail or Kelvinhall tube. **Open** 10am-5pm Mon-Sat; 11am-5pm Sun. **Admission** free.

Every Glaswegian will gleefully tell you how this turreted red sandstone splendour was mistakenly built back to front by dozy workmen, which so horrified the architect that he leapt to his death from a top-floor window – but this tragic story is complete mince: the route of the road was changed at the last minute. The museum was built to hold the 1901 International Exhibition, mostly from public subscription at a time of municipal confidence, though there was an outcry when the design competition was won by an English firm. The ground floor houses a rather dull collection of armour, natural history specimens and stuffed animals of varying interest – the feuding stags by the side stairs are rather a sight as is the *Star Wars* stormtrooper. Upstairs is divided into smaller rooms, some housing the permanent collection, which is particularly strong on seventeenth-century Dutch art, Victorian history paintings, the Impressionists and, of course, pre-modern Scottish art including the Glasgow Boys' school. The museum also has a tearoom and on some Sunday afternoons holds fantastic free organ concerts.

Mitchell Library

North Street, G3 (0141 287 2999). Charing Cross tube. **Open** 9am-8pm Mon-Thur; 9am-5pm Fri, Sat. **Map 1 B2**

With over one million books and documents, this is the largest reference library in Europe. The Glasgow and Burns Collections are invaluable for researchers. In spring, it's full of students cramming for exams.

Museum of Transport

Kelvinhall, G3 (0141 357 3929). Partick rail or Kelvinhall tube. **Open** 10am-5pm Mon, Wed-Sat; 11am-5pm Sun. **Admission** free.

Britain's best transport museum, full of colourful, beautifully maintained trams, buses, bikes and luxury motors. There's a reconstruction of a 'typical' street from the 1930s, complete with coffee shop, newspaper vendors, cinema and carefully hidden little jokes (look out for the bakery buns). The Clyde Room celebrates, as well as mourns, Glasgow's shipbuilding industry, with fascinating models of ships such as the *QE2*.

Accommodation

Audacious conversions vie with ultra-modern concrete edifices for Glasgow's new tourists.

Glasgow has experienced a resurgence in hotel accommodation since the industrial grime was carefully removed from its fine Victorian and Georgian buildings in the 1980s and the mantle of 1990 European City of Culture brought a wave of tourists. New arrivals such as the **Malmaison**, **Glasgow Hilton** and the audacious **Brunswick Merchant City Hotel** have spurred on hoteliers across the city, sparking refurbishments and a constant battle for talented head chefs. Visitors on a budget benefit from the greatly enhanced B&B choice, where off-peak season deals are plentiful.

The **Greater Glasgow and Clyde Valley Tourist Board** (*see chapter* **Directory**) will book accommodation in the city, answer general enquiries and supply details of special rates in its brochure.

Top dollar

Copthorne Hotel

40 George Square, G2 (0141 332 6711/fax 0141 332 4264). Buchanan St tube or Queen St rail. **Rooms** 140 (all en suite). **Rates** *single* £116; *double* £126; *suite* £145 (peak season; weekend rates by request). **Credit** AmEx, DC, JCB, MC, V, £$TC. **Map 1 E2**
Completed in the 1950s, this 'B'-listed building occupies pole position on the north side of George Square. The inside has been revamped recently – the low-lit, indigo, curved walls and divides in the restaurant smack of copycat Conran. La Mirage bar, popular with Glaswegians for its cocktail happy hour, is the social hub of the building and contrasts sharply with the classy reception area – where a TrafficMaster screen monitors the main routes in central Scotland. The rooms remain old fashioned and hi-tech amenities minimal – just one of the eight meeting rooms has an ISDN link and only the gym has fully embraced the benefits of technology. Queen Street Railway Station is next door, but double glazing keeps the noise of the trains down to a low rumble.
Hotel services *Babysitting. Bar (2). Business services. Conference facilities (100 people). Concierge. Currency exchange. Fax. Garden. Gym. Laundry. No-smoking rooms. Restaurant. Safe.* **Room services** *Cable TV. Hairdryer. Ironing facilities. Modem line. Radio. Room service (24 hours). Tea/coffee. Trouser press.*

Glasgow Hilton

1 William Street, G3 (0141 204 5555/fax 0141 204 5004). 8, 6, 16 buses, then 10-min walk orCentral rail, then 5-min taxi ride. **Rooms** 319 (all en suite). **Rates** (midweek/weekend) *queen double* £171/£105; *king double* £180/£115; *executive* £205/£145. **Credit** AmEx, DC, JCB, MC, V, £$TC. **Map 1 C2**
Opened in 1992, the Hilton's 20 storeys house a mini shopping mall, a gym and leisure suite and a floor geared to business needs. No expense has been spared on the décor in a range of themed dining areas, including Mama Minsky's Brasserie, styled on the tearooms of Belle Epoque New York. Bygone trad-

Malmaison – classic and modern.

ing links between Glasgow and East Asia are reflected in the colonial ambience of Raffles, modelled on Singapore's famous drinking spot. Rates reflect the jet-set quality – this is an international-standard Hilton and rock stars Oasis count among past guests. Proximity to the city's motorway system is countered by double glazing and all 319 rooms have adjustable air conditioning, marbled bathrooms and two phones.
Hotel services *Air-conditioning. Babysitting. Bar (2). Beauty salon. Business services. Conference facilities (1,000 people). Concierge. Currency exchange. Disabled: access; toilets. Fax. Gym. Laundry. Multilingual staff. No-smoking rooms. Free parking. Restaurants (2). Safe. Swimming pool.* **Room services** *Hairdryer. Minibar. Modem line. Radio. Room service (24 hours). Rooms adapted for disabled (4). Tea/coffee. Trouser press.*

Malmaison

278 West George Street, G2 (0141 572 1000/fax 0141 572 1002). Buchanan St tube. **Rooms** 76 (all en suite). **Rates** *single/double* £95; *suites* £120-£420. **Credit** AmEx, DC, MC, V, £$TC. **Map 1 C2**
A converted church with a stylish extension, and a high quotient of celebrity guests – the band Cornershop, Keanu Reeves, Janet Jackson and Ewan McGregor have all checked

in. The décor is classic and modern: a wrought iron interpretation of Napoleonic soldiering forms the banister of the central staircase, while discreet monochrome photographs of Gothic features in the city's architecture adorn the bedroom walls. Original features from St Jude's Church are retained within, notably the tiled floor and 'strawberry Gothic' ceiling of the brasserie, formerly the crypt. *Tatler* magazine voted it the best hotel in the world for under £100.
Hotel services *Air-conditioning. Babysitting. Bar. Business services. Conference facilities (20 people). Currency exchange. Disabled: access; toilets. Fax. Gym. Laundry. Multilingual staff. No-smoking rooms. Restaurant (2). Safe. Swimming pool.* **Room services** *CD player. Hairdryer. Ironing facilities. Minibar. Modem line. Radio. Room service (24 hours). Rooms adapted for disabled (5). Tea/coffee. Trouser press.*

One Devonshire Gardens
1 Devonshire Gardens, G12 (0141 339 2001/fax 0141 337 1663). 11, 20, 51, 66 buses. **Rooms** 27 (all en suite). **Rates** *single* from £140; *double* from £165; *suite* from £190 (weekend rates on request). **Credit** AmEx, DC, MC, V, £$TC.
In the exquisite drawing rooms of Glasgow's most exclusive hotel the plush sofa chairs invite you to take it easy while the coal fire crackles and wine chills in a distressed iron ice bucket. The emphasis is on 'quality time', right down to the fresh tulips placed daily in the rooms, many of which have four-poster beds. Scottish produce with a French edge is the starting point for the four-course, set-menu dinner, which changes daily and costs £40. Amid all the ostentation – the stained-glass windows, walk-in wardrobes and black-marble bathrooms – only the in-house sommelier is truly intimidating, but once collared he can offer expert advice on the vast range stocked in the wine cellar.
Hotel services *Babysitting. Bar (2). Conference facilities (50 people). Concierge. Currency exchange. Disabled: access with assistance; toilet. Fax. Garden. Laundry. Multilingual staff. Parking (free). Restaurant. Safe.* **Room services** *CD player. Hairdryer. Minibar. Radio. Room service (24 hours). Rooms adapted for disabled (1).*

Moderate

Brunswick Merchant City Hotel
106-108 Brunswick Street, G1 (0141 552 0001/fax 0141 552 1551). 66A/B/C buses. **Rooms** 23 (all en suite). **Rates** (incl continental buffet breakfast) *single* £55; *double* £55; *twin* £75; *penthouse* (sleeps 5) £395. **Credit** AmEx, DC, MC, V, £$TC. **Map 1 E3**
New architecture in the Merchant City district doesn't come more state-of-the-art than this landmark hotel, completed by Elder & Canon in 1995. Ru Paul, Boy George and Billy Connolly have all stayed in the penthouse suites, which are fully adaptable for private parties, while the restaurant and basement bar are crammed year round with 'stylish' professionals. The stamp of interior design agency Graven Images is visible everywhere from the leather-padded wall in the café to the cute Italian lamps in the rooms. The standard single/double and twin rooms with en suite shower are relatively cheap due to their ultra-compact layout, but all contain double beds. Italian, Cajun, Mexican and Japanese dishes take precedence on the eclectic menu.
Hotel services *Air-conditioning. Bar. Business facilities. Conference facilities (30 people). Disabled: access; toilets. Fax. Multilingual staff. Restaurant. Safe.* **Room services** *Modem line. Room service (24 hours). Rooms adapted for disabled (2).*
e-mail: brunhotel@aol.com
http: www.scotland2000.com/brunswick

Cathedral House Hotel
28-32 Cathedral Square, G4 (0141 552 3519/fax 0141 552 2444). High Street rail, then 2(A), 37 buses. **Rooms** 8 (all en suite). **Rates** (incl breakfast) *single* £49/£59

(twin beds); *double* £69. **Credit** AmEx, DC, JCB, MC, V, £TC. **Map 1 F2**
This hotel began its life in 1877 as a half way house for a local prison, before being transformed into the regional diocese headquarters of the Catholic Church. It opened as a hotel in 1990. It's rumoured to have a ghost, but sceptics put it down to the combined impact of too many whiskies and the natural nocturnal creaking of the wooden spiral staircase. All eight rooms are done out in minimalist Scottish chic. The split-level café bar downstairs is a popular lunching spot for office workers, while the first-floor restaurant is one of Glasgow's best-kept secrets, with chef John Quinn serving up a sumptuous menu of Mediterranean, Chinese and Japanese cuisine.
Hotel services *Air-conditioning. Bar (2). Disabled: access; toilets. Fax. Laundry. No-smoking rooms. Parking (free). Restaurant. Safe. Special diets catered for.* **Room services** *Hairdryer. Radio. Tea/coffee. Trouser press.*

Charing Cross Tower Hotel
10 Elmbank Gardens, G2 (0141 221 1000/fax 0141 248 1000). Charing Cross rail. **Rooms** 282 (all en suite). **Rates** *single* £34.50-£44.50; *double/twin* £50-£59.50. **Credit** AmEx, DC, JCB, MC, V, £$TC. **Map 1 B2**
The 12-storey Charing Cross Tower was converted from office block to hotel in 1996 and provides efficient, streamlined facilities. Considering their price, the rooms are spacious, with fashionable furnishings and great views of the city from the upper floors. Sports fans congregate in Bill's Bar for matches shown on its large screen and the premises function as home to the Scottish Claymores team during the American Football season. The large dining area offers an unremarkable menu of traditional and continental dishes, but licensed vending machines and a free delivery service from Sannino's pizza parlour are available for en suite dining after a hard day's sightseeing. Otherwise, there are bars and restaurants of every variety in nearby Sauchiehall Street.
Hotel services *Air-conditioning. Bar. Conference facilities (50 people). Currency exchange. Disabled: access; toilets. Fax. Laundry. No-smoking rooms. Parking (free). Restaurant. Safe.* **Room services** *Hairdryer. Ironing facilities. Minibar. Tea/coffee. Satellite TV.*
e-mail: cxt@cims.co.uk

Glasgow City Travelodge
5-11 Hill Street, G3 (0141 333 1515/fax 0141 333 1221). Cowcaddens tube, then 10-min walk. **Rooms** 93 (all en suite). **Rates** *single/double* £55.95; family rates on request (under-12s free). **Credit** AmEx, DC, MC, V, £TC. **Map 1 C1**
Opened in May 1998, this Travelodge is situated near to the Glasgow School of Art but aimed at business travellers and overseas package tourists. Beige-on-green décor throughout cements the corporate atmosphere and the three conference rooms are kitted out with hi-tech presentation gear. It offers appetising, value-for-money cuisine with Scottish breakfasts prepared by the chef and light, continental meals served in the Lounge Bar until 6pm. The bistro's table d'hôte and à la carte menu incorporates a decent vegetarian selection and changes monthly. Roast chicken filled with haggis and served with a whisky and Arran-grain mustard sauce typifies the Scottish main course dishes on offer.
Hotel services *Babysitting. Bar. Business services. Conference facilities (35 people). Disabled: access. Fax. No-smoking rooms. Restaurant. Safe.* **Room services** *Ironing facilities. Hairdryer. Rooms adapted for disabled (2). Tea/coffee. Trouser press.*

Holiday Inn
161 West Nile Street, G1 (0141 332 0110/fax 0141 332 7447/reservations 0141 352 8305). 45(A) buses. **Rooms** 113 (all en suite). **Rates** *single* £82-£95; *double* £82-£95; *suites* from £140. **Credit** AmEx, DC, JCB, MC, V, £$TC. **Map 1 D2**
Modelled on La Tour D'Argent in Paris, this 113-room hotel

Town House Hotel – *it'll be all white on the night.*

replaced the ugly, tower-block Holiday Inn in 1996 and makes a fair impression architecturally. La Bonne Auberge, its air-conditioned cocktail bar, is decked out with a wrought iron surround by local sculptor Andy Scott. The view from the French windows of the adjacent L'Orangerie is less pleasing – a road junction and grey buildings. Complimentary sherry, fruit juice and cheeses await you in the three penthouse suites – named Degas, Monet and Matisse. The décor falls short of inspirational, but they do contain a personal safe, minibar and Jacuzzi. Elsewhere, the rooms are spacious and functional with limited room service delivering full or continental breakfast and a fitness suite to work off the excesses of French cuisine.
Hotel services *Babysitting. Bar. Business services. Conference facilities (120 people). Currency exchange. Disabled: access; toilets. Fax. Gym. Laundry. Multilingual staff. No-smoking rooms. Restaurant. Safe.* **Room services** *Hairdryer. Guestlink. Minibar (executive rooms & suites only). Modem line. Radio. Room service (24 hours). Rooms adapted for disabled (6).*

Quality Central Hotel

99 Gordon Street, G1 (0141 221 9680/fax 0141 226 3948/central reservations 0800 44 44 44). Central rail.
Rooms 222 (all en suite). **Rates** *single* £66.50; *double* £80.25; *suite* £107 (special offers on request). **Credit** AmEx, DC, MC, V, £$TC. **Map 1 D3**
A product of Glasgow's halcyon era as the second city of the Empire, this hotel rises proudly above Central Station and is popular with overseas visitors. Since opening in 1888 it has hosted some major events – John Logie Baird, the Scotsman who invented television, transmitted his first TV broadcast signal from one of the upper rooms. Laurel & Hardy and JFK were guests and an early celebrity stunt saw Roy Rodgers's horse, Trigger, paraded up the stairs. Today, the ambience falls between grandiose (the largest function suites are resplendent with marble balustrades and a domed ceiling) and jet set (pool, beauty salon and a Klaus Kobe jewellery stand). The Ailsa Lounge and Entresol Carvery offer unpretentious drinking and dining. The 222 bedrooms are decorated in warm hues.
Hotel services *Babysitting. Bar. Beauty salon. Business*

services. Conference facilities (500). Currency exchange. Disabled: access; toilets. Fax. Gym. Laundry. Multilingual staff. No-smoking rooms. Restaurant. Safe/safety deposit boxes. Swimming pool. **Room services** *Hairdryer. Minibar (premier rooms only). Radio. Room service (24 hours). Rooms adapted for disabled (7).*
e-mail: admin@gb627.u-net.com

Budget

The Albion Hotel

407 North Woodside road, G20 (0141 339 8620/fax 0141 334 8159). Kelvinbridge tube. **Rooms** 16 (all en suite). **Rates** (incl breakfast) *single* £42; *double* £52; *family* £62-£82. **Credit** AmEx, DC, MC, V, £TC.
A licensed bar serving light evening meals and a spacious reading room stocked with books and magazines give the Albion Hotel an edge over the average B&B. The curfew-free premises has coded entry to the main door and rooms for added security. Spotless formica dressing tables and bedside units give the décor an inadvertently kitsch feel. Bay windows in many of the rooms afford fine views of the River Kelvin out front and a wooded entry to the rear.
Hotel services *Café bar. Disabled: access; toilets. Fax. Patio. No-smoking rooms. Parking (free). Safe.* **Room services** *Hairdryer. Ironing. Radio. Tea/coffee. Trouser press.*

Hillview Hotel

18 Hillhead Street, G12 (0141 334 5585). Hillhead tube. **Rooms** 11. **Rates** (incl breakfast) *single* £23; *double* £38; *triple* £55; *quadruple* £60; *family rooms* £45-£60. **Credit** JCB, MC, V, £$TC.
A young, family-run hotel at the residential end of the central thoroughfare of Glasgow University. Three, pristine bathrooms service the 11 bedrooms. The rooms are incredibly large and amply furnished with comfy chairs, dressing tables and porcelain basins. Understated paintwork flatters the preserved cornices and ceiling roses. A rear extension houses the dining area, where guests can watch their breakfast being cooked in the

open-plan kitchen. Pine fittings, overhead skylights and a stone garden rising from the back window give the place an unaffected, homespun feel. Pet- and children-friendly. No curfew. **Hotel services** *Babysitting. Business services. Concierge. Disabled: access. Garden. Parking (free).* **Room services** *Hairdryer. Ironing facilities. Tea/coffee.*

Kelvingrove Hotel

944 Sauchiehall Street, G3 (0141 339 5011/fax 0141 339 6566). 42, 57(A) buses. **Rooms** 21 (19 en suite). **Rates** (incl breakfast) *single* £34.50; *double* £53. **Credit** AmEx, DC, JCB, MC, V, £TC. **Map 1 B2**
Price is a selling point of this hotel, but it doesn't compensate for having to deal with a short-tempered manager and the chemical stench of cheap air-freshener. Satellite TV in the rooms is the only distraction from the clashing décor. Hairdryers, two-seater sofas in the rooms and a decent breakfast room are paltry plus points. But this second-rate business soldiers on – largely due to advance overseas bookings and a prime location at the western end of Sauchiehall St. **Hotel services** *Business services. Concierge. Garden. Laundry. Multilingual staff. No-smoking rooms. Parking (free). Safe.* **Room services** *Hairdryer. Minibar. Modem line. Room service (24 hours).*

Lomond Hotel

6 Buckingham Terrace, Great Western Road, G12 (0141 339 2339/fax 0141 339 5215). Kelvinbridge tube, then 5-min walk. **Rooms** 17 (7 en suite). **Rates** *single* £25-£36; *double* £42-£52; *family* £54-£60. **Credit** AmEx, DC, MC, V, £TC.
A quiet, family-run hotel occupying two, formerly separate houses on this 'A'-listed Victorian terrace. No curfew operates. Scottish breakfasts are cooked to order, but a room-only rate is available. Understated furnishings allow the rooms' original features to stand out. **Hotel services** *Continental breakfast. Disabled: access with assistance. Fax.* **Room services** *(no telephones) Tea/coffee. TV. Washbasin.*
http: www.s-h-systems.co.uk/hotels/lomond.html

The Old School House

194 Renfrew Street, G3 (0141 332 7600/fax 0141 332 8684). 20, 21, 23, 61, 66 buses. **Rooms** 17 (16 en suite). **Rates** (incl breakfast) *single* from £30; *double* £48; *family* £65-£75. **Credit** MC, V, £TC. **Map 1 C2**
Built to house a Tobacco Lord in the last century, this newly opened B&B's interior is now unobtrusively modern, with ornate woodwork and the occasional cherub-laden cornice hinting at bygone elegance. One limitation is en suite facilities are shower or bath, not both. But breakfast is fantastic. **Hotel services** *Fax. Multilingual staff.* **Room services** *Hairdryer. Rooms adapted for disabled (3). Tea/coffee.*

Regent Guest House

44 Regent Park Square, G41 (0141 422 1199/fax 0141 423 7531). Queens Park/Pollokshields West rail, then 5-min walk. **Rooms** 7. **Rates** (incl breakfast) *single* £20; *double* £40. **Credit** AmEx, MC, V, £TC.
A three-floor house in a leafy, residential area. Location is its main asset –the grand Queens Park, a prime example of stately, Victorian-era public works, is across the road, and Pollok Park, which houses the Burrell Collection and Haggs Castle, is a five-minute bus ride away. Unexceptional, if neatly furnished, this family-run guest-house represents good value for money. **Hotel services** *Disabled: access with assistance. Completely no smoking.* **Room services** *(no telephones) Hairdryer. Tea/coffee. TV. Washbasin.*

Town House Hotel

21 Royal Crescent, G3 (0141 332 9009/fax 0141 353 9604). 42, 57(A) buses. **Rooms** 19 (17 en suite). **Rates** (incl breakfast) *single* £23-£35; *double* £48; *triple* £60; *family* £70. **Credit** DC, JCB, MC, V, £TC. **Map 1 A2**

This conversion of two adjoining houses in an elegant Edwardian crescent opened in November 1997 and offers excellent value for money in palatial surroundings. Rooms have pine floorboards and smart, modern furnishings. The basement dining room has a self-service cereals and juice counter alongside the cooked breakfast menu. **Hotel services** *Disabled: access. Fax. Laundry. Multilingual staff. No-smoking rooms. Parking (free).* **Room services** *Hairdryer. Room service (24 hours). Rooms adapted for disabled (4).*

Hostels

Berkeley Globetrotters Independent Hostel

63 Berkeley Street, Charing Cross, G3 (0141 221 7880). Charing Cross rail, then 10-min walk. **Beds** 60. **Rates** *1 night* from £9.50; *week* from £56. **Credit** £TC. **Map 1 B2**
This centrally located hostel has filled a vacuum in the self-catering market in the two years since it opened. No curfew operates and the three communal living rooms have TV, VCRs and satellite channels. Sleeping arrangements come in two basic varieties: bunk beds in the six dormitory rooms (four of which are unisex) or a bunk bed and a single bed in the two lockable private rooms. Free toast and fruit juice are laid on in the morning; no charge is made for tea and coffee. No frills, but plenty of friendly advice and company to survive on.

Glasgow Youth Hostel

7-8 Park Terrace, G3 (0141 332 3004/fax 0141 332 5007). 11, 23, 44, 59, 74 buses, then 5-min walk. **Beds** 160 (all en suite). **Rates** *1 night* £9.95 (under 18), £11.50 (over 18). Non-SYHA members pay an extra £1.50. **No credit cards. Map 1 A1**
A Georgian townhouse and formerly a hotel, which accounts for the en-suite-as-standard facilities in this popular hostel. A swipe-card system controls the doors. Most rooms have five-eight beds. The standard YHA rate of £11.50 (£12.50 July/Aug) includes a continental breakfast. Meals for groups can be booked in advance. Payphones, vending machines and lockers big enough to fit two or three suitcases take care of the essentials, while a TV room, common room and games room provide some R&R space. There's even a conference room. A 2am curfew operates – probably worth it, given the spotless sheen of the place.
e-mail: glasgow@syha.org.uk
http: www.syha.org.uk

Private apartments

West End Apartments

401 North Woodside Road, G20 (0141 779 4427/fax 0141 779 4800). Kelvinbridge tube. **Open** 9am-5pm Mon-Fri. **Rooms** 4 apartments. **Rates** £210-£280 per week (nightly rate on request). **Credit** MC, V, £TC.
Four apartments housed in an elegant, sandstone building in Kelvinbridge. Each flat has a payphone, TV, coin-meter electric heating and kitchen. A shared laundry room serves the building. Children are welcome.

Seasonal lets

University of Strathclyde *50 Richmond Street, G1 (0141 553 4148/fax 0141 548 4149). 6, 8, 41 buses.* **Open** 9am-5pm Mon-Fri. **Map 1 E2**
e-mail: rescat@com.strath.ac.uk
University of Glasgow *81 Great George Street, G12 (0141 330 5385/fax 0141 334 5465). Hillhead tube, then 5-min walk.* **Open** 9am-5pm Mon-Fri.
e-mail: conf@gla.ac.uk
Both universities let a wide range of affordable accommodation to let, mainly during student holidays (June-Sept).

Pedestrians
←

Possibilities
↓

 London's Living Guide.

http://www.timeout.co.uk

Restaurants & Cafés

Internationalism is the name of the game in Glasgow's modern restaurant culture.

The Rogano – *fabulous for fish. Page 203.*

Once Glasgow had only its reputation for curry houses on the culinary front. The curries are still fantastic, but the modern cuisine extends a lot further than the Indian subcontinent, as you can see in this selection, compiled with the help of *The List's Eating and Drinking Guide 1998*.

Balbir's

51 West Regent Street, G2 (0141 331 1980). Buchanan St tube, then 5-min walk. **Open** noon-12.30am Fri, Sat; 2-11.30pm Sun. **Average** £12. **Credit** AmEx, DC, MC, £TC, V. **Map 1 D2**
Housed in an impressive art deco building, this restaurant is the love-child of Balbir, one of Glasgow's best-known restaurateurs. A tradition of employing quality ingredients and culinary innovation, accommodating Scottish tastes while upholding traditional Asian methods, has set Balbir's up with a reputation for providing top-notch food at very reasonable prices. There is plenty of variety in the menu, with a fair amount of vegetarian choice. Balbir has played host to many famous people, including Ravi Shankar and Gary Rhodes.

The Battlefield Rest

55 Battlefield Road, G42 (0141 636 6955). Mount Florida rail, then 5-min walk. **Open** 10am-10pm Mon-Sat. **Closed** Sun. **Average** £10. **Credit** AmEx, MC, £TC, V.
This green-and-white tiled restaurant used to be a tram-workers' bothy. Now it successfully blends Scots and Italian cultures and cuisine. The large, thin-based pizzas, such as the Piemontese (with spinach, sun-dried tomatoes, roasted peppers and mozzarella), are arguably the best in Glasgow. The wine list is well chosen and reasonably priced. Since everything is freshly cooked, it is a place for a relaxed meal rather than a quick bite. It is popular, so booking is essential.

Brunswick Café-Bar

106-108 Brunswick Street, Merchant City, G1 (0141 552 0001). Argyle St or High St rail, then 5-min walk. **Open** 7am-10pm daily. **Average** £15. **Credit** AmEx, MC, £TC, V. **Map 1 E3**
The Brunswick manages to combine state-of-the-art design with comfort, even homeless – a rare feat indeed. The chef is vegetarian and it shows: there is no cursory nod to vegetarians here. A great deal of care has gone into this menu, which includes a selection of dishes from around the globe such as dim sums, sushi, grilled jackfish with coconut sauce or roast vegetables on polenta, followed by sirloin stroganoff with home-made buckwheat pasta and pumpkin ravioli with a cream sauce. The sweets are no less interesting, either.

Café Cossachok

10 King Street, G1 (0141 553 0733). Argyle St rail or St Enoch tube, then 5-min walk. **Open** 10.30am-midnight Mon-Sat; 11.30am-midnight Sun. **Average** £10. **Credit** JCB, MC, £TC, V. **Map 1 E3**
This delightful and original café/restaurant seeks to promote Russian culture and traditions, both culinary and musical. Patrons will often enjoy live folk tunes as they sample the authentic cuisine or indulge in a perfectly chilled, flavoured vodka. The emphasis in Cossachok is on simple, wholesome dishes, such as borscht, a hearty rustic soup made with cabbage, tomato, beetroot and garlic. The friendly, welcoming service is mirrored in the warm décor – a glorious mix of primary colours and beautifully carved wood.

Café Gandolfi

64 Albion Street, G1 (0141 552 6813). Argyle St or High St rail, then 5-min walk. **Open** 9am-11.30pm Mon-Sat; noon-11.30pm Sun. **Average** £14. **Credit** MC, £TC, V. **Map 1 E3**
Café Gandolfi is a well-established port of call in the Merchant City with a large and devoted following of diners who can enjoy the bohemian atmosphere and Tim Stead-designed polished wood décor as they choose from a wide variety of dishes with a Scottish flavour. Current favourites include the cullen skink starter and the smoked venison with gratin dauphinois. It's a relaxed, laid-back kind of place, where they are equally as happy to see you nip in for a coffee as a full meal.

Café Sergei

67 Bridge Street, G5 (0141 429 1547). Bridge St tube. **Open** noon-2.30pm, 5-11pm Mon-Sat; 6-11pm Sun. **Set lunch** £4.80 two courses (desserts £1.70 extra). **Set dinner** £7 two courses (up to 7pm), £13.50 three courses. **Credit** MC, £TC, V. **Map 1 C4**
Café Sergei is a popular and lively restaurant, housed in a former bank on the south side of the river, serving Greek and Mediterranean cuisine to a varied clientele. As well as a wide range of kebabs and rice dishes, there are a number of house specialities, including kleftiko (lamb on the bone) and kota

*Take a break from the art in the calm and civility of **Burrell Café & Restaurant**. Page 204.*

arabike (pan-fried chicken). On Fridays, it's dance night: for £17 per head, patrons are treated to a three-course meal plus coffee, dance demonstrations (Greek and ceilidh dancing) and audience participation.

City Merchant

97-99 Candleriggs, G1 (0141 553 1577). Argyle St or High St rail, then 5-min walk. **Open** noon-11pm Mon-Sat; 5-11pm Sun. **Average** £18. **Credit** AmEx, DC, JCB, MC, £TC, V. **Map 1 E3**

With its beautiful wood interiors, fresh Scottish ingredients and welcoming atmosphere, City Merchant is a very reliable restaurant. Fish and shellfish are the house specialities, with Loch Etive providing delicious mussels and oysters; but don't ignore the game dishes, particularly an awesome breast of duck. Highly recommended – booking essential.

Cottier's

93-95 Hyndland Street, G11 (0141 357 5825). Kelvinhall St tube. **Open** 5-10.30pm Sun-Thur; 5pm-12.30am Fri, Sat. **Average** £15. **Credit** AmEX, DC, £TC, V.

The lively Mexican menu at Cottier's sits oddly with its sub-dued décor: many elements of the church originally housed in the building have been retained, but the contrast is pleas-ant rather than jarring. Specialities on the menu include Caribbean chicken pepper pot with cornmeal dumplings, or rum-soaked fillet of pork with pineapple salsa. The choice is not huge for vegetarians, but the vegetable fajitas are worth the trip in themselves. Portions are generous and families are a regular part of the clientele.

Fratelli Sarti

121 Bath Street, G2 (0141 204 0440). Bath St buses. **Open** 8am-10.30pm Mon-Sat; noon-10.30pm Sun. **Average** £11. **Credit** AmEx, DC, MC, £TC, V. **Map 1 C2**

Priding itself on its '100% authentic Italian' motto, these fam-ily-run restaurants are exactly that. Café Sarti, hidden away at the quieter end of Bath Street, offers a welcome oasis to

the weary city-centre diner. Informal, bustling, yet still retaining a sense of intimacy, this charming eaterie strad-dles the restaurant/bistro/deli dividing lines. Whether it's a quick pre-theatre bite or a luxuriously long meal, Sarti caters for both adequately. Often busy, especially at weekends, so advance booking is advisable.

Branch: 133 Wellington Street, G2 *(enquiries* 0141 248 2228/*bookings* 0141 204 0440).

Ho Wong

82 York Street, G2 (0141 221 3550). Anderston rail. **Open** noon-2pm, 6pm-midnight Mon-Sat; 6pm-midnight Sun. **Average** £20. **Credit** AmEx, DC, MC, £TC, V. **Map 1 B3**

This upmarket restaurant with opulent décor is renowned for excellent Cantonese cuisine. A house speciality is crispy aromatic duck with pancakes. A set four-course dinner is available at all times, priced £25 per person.

Kama Sutra

331 Sauchiehall Street, G2 (0141 332 0055). Sauchiehall St buses. **Open** noon-midnight Mon-Thur; noon-1am Fri, Sat; 5pm-midnight Sun. **Average** £13. **Credit** AmEx, DC, JCB, MC, £TC, V. **Map 1 D2**

Part of the renowned Ashoka empire, the Kama Sutra is a self-consciously stylish eaterie, but not oppressively so. Above all, it offers the stylish twenty- to thirty-something set a welcome respite from the standard flock-wallpaper and sitar-soundtrack experience. All the favourite regional Indian dishes are on offer, as well as more unusual North-eastern Frontier dishes, such as Tibetan hot pot and Sing Sing chas-ni. Especially popular is the buffet deal on Monday nights, at which diners can gorge themselves for only £9.95.

Killermont Polo Club

2022 Maryhill Road, G20 (0141 946 5412). 18(A), 21(C), 61 buses. **Open** noon-2pm, 5-11pm Mon-Sat; 5-11pm Sun. **Average** £13.50. **Credit** AmEx, DC, MC, £TC, V.

Sophisticated but friendly, the award-winning Polo Club is

trying to improve the undeserved reputation that Indian food is somehow samey and uninteresting. The setting is a large townhouse with roaring fire and huge bay windows that has the feel of an upmarket hotel. The evening buffet (£9.95 Mon-Thur) is legendary for both quality and quantity, but it's the restaurant's à la carte menu that truly shines. Tandoori salmon is recommended as is the tender lamb in a cashew and pistachio sauce.

Mojo

158A Bath Street, G2 (0141 331 2257). Bath St buses. **Open** noon-midnight Mon-Sat; 6pm-midnight Sun. **Average** £14.50. **Credit** AmEx, MC, V. **Map 1 D2**
Mojo boasts an absolute gem of a restaurant, overseen by head chef John Quigley, who has travelled the globe catering for the music biz aristocracy. It is one of only five restaurants in Scotland to be recommended by *Gourmet* magazine, and with good reason. The menu is compact but eclectic, offering modern British cooking with an oriental influence. Special mention goes to the roast turbot with spiced pak choi, prawn toasts and Hollandaise sauce. Considerable emphasis is placed upon presentation, but the dishes are not minimalist: these are hefty, generous portions.

Nairns

13 Woodside Crescent, G3 (0141 353 0707). Charing Cross rail, then 10-min walk. **Open** noon-2pm, 6-10pm Tue-Sat. **Closed** Mon. **Set lunch** £13.50 two courses, £17 three courses. **Set dinner** £23.50 three courses. **Credit** AmEx MC, £TC, V. **Map 1 B1**
Nick Nairn casts a long shadow in the world of Scottish cuisine and this restaurant, housed within an elegant nineteenth-century townhouse hotel, can only add to that reputation. The food is contemporary Scottish, taking on board influences from North Africa, the Mediterranean and Asia. Portions are in proportion, the sauces are light and well balanced, and the ingredients are as fresh as the Scottish countryside can provide. This is relaxed dining and, for the quality on offer, the prices are pretty hard to beat.

One Devonshire Gardens

1 Devonshire Gardens, G12 (0141 339 2001). 11, 20, 51, 66 buses. **Open** noon-2pm, 7.15-9.45pm Sun-Fri; 7.15-9.45pm Sat. **Average** £40 (four courses). **Credit** AmEx, DC, MC, £$TC, V.
Dining at One Devonshire Gardens is a truly special, luxurious occasion; from the pre-dinner drinks in the fabulous sitting room to eating in the opulent Morris-esque dining room. The food is excellent, entirely worthy of its Michelin one star (the only one in Glasgow) and fairly priced. The menu changes daily, focusing on traditional Scottish primaries prepared with a contemporary French influence. In all, meals are superbly judged and exquisitely presented. The wine list is interesting and has been expertly chosen, although the mark-up is rather steep.
No smoking.

La Parmigiana

447 Great Western Road, G12 (0141 334 0686). Kelvinbridge tube. **Open** noon-2.30pm, 6-11pm Mon-Sat. **Closed** Sun. **Average** £20. **Credit** AmEx, DC, MC, £TC, V.
One of Glasgow's standout restaurants, La Parmigiana is an elegant and well-respected, upmarket Italian, which specialises in fresh fish such as sea bass, lemon sole, Dover sole, and veal and game dishes when available. The management also prides itself on the extensive range of Italian wines. Served on crisp white tablecloths in a dining room decorated with tiles and rich dark wood, dinner at La Parmigiana offers very fine Italian cuisine in handsome surroundings.

The Rogano

11 Exchange Place, Buchanan Street, G1 (0141 248 4055). Buchanan St tube or Queen St rail. **Open** *restaurant* noon-2.30pm, 6.30-10.30pm daily; *café* noon-11pm Sun-Thur; noon-midnight Fri-Sat. **Average** £30. **Credit** AmEX, DC, MC, £TC, V. **Map 1 D3**
Boasting a full restaurant, café and bar, the Rogano is a fabulous example of art deco style and a must-visit. The restaurant's menu is handsome and traditional. Fish is the thing: from great fish soup, to glittering platters of fruits de mer, lobster thermidor and oysters, all at serious prices. You'll usually find lamb, beef and game on the menu, and vegetarian options are available. Service is impeccable. Downstairs is Café Rogano, a rather different and much more affordable kettle of fish. It too has elegant décor, although much more recent than the main restaurant. The menu is also a little more modern, with trendy Pacific Rim ingredients making occasional appearances.
No smoking before 2pm or 10pm.

Sal-e Pepe

18 Gibson Street, G12 (0141 341 0999). Kelvinbridge tube. **Open** 9.30am-11pm Mon-Sat; 11am-11pm Sun. **Average** £10. **Credit** AmEx, MC, V.
Sal-e Pepe makes a departure from the tried-and-tested spaghetti-and-meatballs formula, with an enjoyable Tuscan atmosphere. The thin-crust pizza with spicy sausage served here is one of the best around, closely followed, in terms of popularity, by the moist meatloaf and creamy mash. There is also a good line in seafood and game dishes, and the duck is particularly recommended. The dessert menu is a treat.

Thai Fountain

2 Woodside Crescent, G3 (0141 332 2599). Charing Cross rail, then 10-min walk. **Open** 11am-2.30pm, 5-11pm Mon-Fri; 11am-midnight Sat. **Closed** Sun. **Average** £16. **Credit** AmEx, JCB, MC, V. **Map 1 B1**
Popular with business people during the day and a mixed clientele in the evenings, this welcoming restaurant suggests booking ahead. Recommended dishes include fried king prawn with chilli paste, tam yam kung soup and the sweet and hot Thai curries. All main courses are half price when ordered before 7pm on weekdays or 6.30pm on Saturdays.

The 13th Note

50-60 King Street, G1 (0141 553 1638). Argyle St or High St rail, then 5-min walk. **Open** noon-11.45pm Mon-Sat; 12.30-11.45pm Sun. **Average** £5.50. **Credit** MC, V. **Map 1 E3**
The vegan café at the 13th Note is frequented by students and those of the 'gently alternative' crowd in the relaxed atmosphere of the cinema-like building. The café has the laidback look of an American diner and the menu offers a fairly varied selection of dairy-free snacks and main dishes. Vegan Society members receive a 10% discount.

Two Fat Ladies

88 Dumbarton Road, G12 (0141 339 1944). Kelvinhall tube, then 5-min walk. **Open** noon-2pm Fri-Sat; 6-10pm Tue-Sat. **Closed** Sun-Mon. **Set lunch** £9.95 two courses, £13.95 three courses Fri-Sat. **Set dinner** *pre-theatre* £9.95 two courses Fri-Sat; £24.50 three courses. **Credit** MC, V.
Named after the bingo-caller's nickname for 88 (and not after the motorbike-borne television cooks) Two Fat Ladies offers an adventurous and expertly prepared menu that has earned it a deservedly high reputation across Scotland. An informal setting with only nine tables, reservations are virtually essential. The emphasis of chef/proprietor Calum Mathieson's cuisine is firmly on fish and seafood. Typical starters include mussels and Loch Fyne oysters; main courses are likely to include monkfish, scallops and halibut.

The Ubiquitous Chip

12 Ashton Lane, G12 (0141 334 5007). Hillhead tube. **Open** noon-2.30pm, 5.30-11pm Mon-Sat; 12.30-2.30pm, 6.30-11pm Sun. **Set lunch** £18.60 two

Film

Guide

'Without doubt, the "bible" for film buffs.'
British Film and TV Academy News

Updated annually to include over 11,500 films from around the world and fully cross-referenced with extensive indexes covering films by genre, subject, director and star, this A-to-Z directory is the ultimate guide for movie lovers.

The *Time Out* Film Guide is available at a bookshop near you.

courses, £23.60 three courses. **Set dinner** £26.60 two courses, £31.60 three courses. **Credit** AmEx, DC, MC, £TC, V.

The Ubiquitous Chip is a Glasgow institution. The building is a converted mews stable: a number of tables are in the cobbled courtyard, with its lush greenery and fish pond. The constantly evolving menu makes use of seasonal Scottish produce. Typical offerings include cullen skink, clapshot, howtowdie, wood pigeon, venison, haggis and, on the cheeseboard, Lanark blue and Cairnsmore. All meals are table d'hote and include coffee and an appetiser. The wine list is justly famous and there are some 150 malt whiskies.

Mackintosh and muffins – **Willow Tea Rooms**.

Cafés

Art Gallery & Museum

1 Argyle Street, G12 (0141 287 2700).
Kelvinhall tube, then 10-min walk. **Open** 10am-4.30pm Mon-Sat; 11am-4.30pm Sun. **Average** £4. **No credit cards.**
Popular destination for families and bus-loads of school kids. There is self-service with a range of snacks and kids' lunch boxes; drinks are all 'soft'.
No smoking.

The Burrell Café & Restaurant

Pollok Country Park, G43 (0141 632 3910).
Crossmyloof rail, then 34(A) bus. **Open** *café* 10am-4.30pm Mon-Sat; 11am-4.30pm Sun; *restaurant* noon-4pm daily. **Restaurant average** £8. **Credit** AmEx, MC, £TC, V.
Baked fillet of Scottish salmon and grilled mozzarella and tomato on ciabatta bread are a taster of the delicacies served up in the restaurant, while the café is self-service with a lively menu – ideal for a quick, restorative snack.
No smoking.

Café Alba

61 Otago Street, G12 (0141 337 2282). Kelvinbridge tube. **Open** 10am-5pm Mon-Sat. **Average** £4.50. **Unlicensed. Corkage** free. **No credit cards.** **Map 1 A1**
Café Alba's regular home-baking (with a great vegeburger meal for £2.75) attracts a busy lunchtime crowd. Students can also take advantage of a 10% discount.

Café Cosmo

GFT, 12 Rose Street, G3 (0141 332 6535). Sauchiehall St buses. **Open** noon-7pm Mon-Sat; *bar only* 2-9pm Sun. **Average** £5. **No credit cards. Map 1 C2**
A meeting place for arthouse film-goers and students – **Glasgow School of Art** is situated just around the corner. The gooey Mississippi mud pie is superb .

CCA Café Bar

350 Sauchiehall Street, G2 (0141 332 7864). Sauchiehall St buses. **Open** 9am-11pm Mon-Wed; 9am-midnight Thur-Sat; noon-6pm Sun. **Average** £7.50. **Credit** AmEX, DC, MC, £TC, V. **Map 1 C2**
The buzzing but laid-back nerve-centre of the **Centre for Contemporary Arts**, the café is also a popular hang-out for Glasgow's arts crowd. The café has an eclectic, but much improved, menu.

Gallery of Modern Art

Royal Exchange Square, G1 (0141 221 7484). Buchanan St tube or Queen St rail. **Open** 10am-4.30pm Sun-Wed; 10am-4.30pm, 6.30-10pm Thur-Sat. **Set dinner** £16.95 two courses, £19.50 three courses. **Credit** AmEx, MC, £TC, V. **Map 1 D3**
This two-tier café has terrific views of the city's skyline. Recommended on the lunch menu is the salmon salad.
No smoking.

Grosvenor Café

31/33 Ashton Lane, G12 (0141 339 1848).
Hillhead tube. **Open** 9am-7pm Mon; 9am-11pm Tue-Sat; 10.30am-5.30pm Sun. **Average** £7. **No credit cards.**
The Grosvenor's cheery atmosphere and low prices have made it a West End institution, appealing to everyone from students and artists to pensioners.

University Café

87 Byres Road, G11 (0141 339 5217). Hillhead or Kelvinhall tube. **Open** 9am-10pm Mon, Wed-Fri; 9am-10.30pm Sat; 10am-10pm Sun. **Closed** Tue. **Average** £3. **No credit cards.**
Famous for its fab 1950s-style décor and hearty food. The ice-cream has won innumerable awards, and the knickerbocker glory is particularly spectacular.

Willow Tea Rooms

217 Sauchiehall Street, G2 (0141 332 0521). Sauchiehall St buses. **Open** 9.30am-4.30pm Mon-Sat; noon-4.15pm Sun. **Average** £4.50. **No credit cards. Map 1 D2**
Remarkable for its Charles Rennie Mackintosh-designed premises only. Expect the old standards: toasties, baked potatoes, filled croissants and baguettes, as well as Scottish fare such as smoked salmon and haggis, neeps and tatties.
Branch: 97 Buchanan Street, G1 (0141 204 5242).

Internet cafés

Internet Café

569 Sauchiehall Street, G3 (0141 564 1052). Sauchiehall St buses. **Open** 9am-11pm Mon-Fri; 10am-11pm Sat, Sun. **Credit** AmEx, MC, V. **Map 1 C2**
Web design and Internet business services go on behind the scenes in these anodyne premises near Charing Cross. There are a variety of training courses, surfing costs £2.50 (£2 concs) per half hour and e-mail accounts start at £1. The café sells a range of snacks and soft drinks.
e-mail: tim@linkcafe.co.uk
http: www.linkcafe.co.uk

Java Café

152 Park Road, G12 (0141 337 6814).
Kelvinbridge tube. **Open** 9am-10pm daily. **Average** £5. **Unlicensed. Corkage** *wine* £2.50; *beer* free. **No credit cards.**
Serving a first-rate selection of fresh coffee and vegetarian/wholefood dishes, the upstairs café has six terminals and hosts occasional poetry and comedy nights. Surfing from £1.75 (£1.50 concs) per half hour, e-mail accounts for a flat fee of £5 and a Surf Addicts club: £95 will buy you Net access between 11pm-8.30am, plus breakfast in the morning.
e-mail: java@javacafe.co.uk

Bars & Pubs

If ye fancy a wee swally, here's a few we've drunk in earlier.

Although the image of the drunken Glaswegian has gone far enough, no one would deny that the city's population enjoys a drink or three and a convivial environment in which to do so. There are bars to suit every taste, whether for a lively pre-club 'swally', a quiet chat in comfort or the opportunity to be seen with the designer set in the flourishing 'style' bars scene. This is a selection of the best bars in the two main drinking areas of the city – the centre and the West End.

The Attic

44-46 Ashton Lane, G12 (0141 334 6688). Hillhead tube. **Open** 8am-11pm Mon-Thur, Sun; 8am-midnight Fri-Sat.
The latest addition to the Ashton Lane pub crawl occupies the attic space of the **Cul De Sac** (*see below*). Open rafters are a feature, boxes of junk and dampness are not, in this dimly lit snug with an island bar. Quaff a designer beer with trendy West Enders, sample a refreshing draught from the fruit and vegetable juice bar or, if you're an early bird, nibble some cinnamon toast from the breakfast menu.

Babbity Bowster

16-18 Blackfriars Street, G1 (0141 552 7774). High St rail, then 5-min walk. **Open** 11am-midnight daily. **Map 1 E3**
It's a hotel, it's a restaurant, but it's also a comfortable pub with a traditional feel, more than capable of holding its own against the style bar onslaught in the Merchant City. The stark, white walls are adorned sparingly with paintings and drawings of Glaswegian scenes. Don't look for the jukebox; any music in Babbity's comes from the folk musicians and groupies who hang out here to sup real ale in one of Glasgow's few beer gardens.

Bar Booshka

41 Old Dumbarton Road, G3 (0141 357 1830). Kelvinhall tube, then 5-min walk. **Open** noon-11pm Sun-Thur; noon-midnight Fri-Sat.
Glasgow's only vodka bar – where a large number of customers insist on consuming pints of lager, rather than the vast range of vodka brands and over 50 flavoured vodkas: chilli, curry or garlic flavours for the more aniti-social drinker; parma violets or sherbet lemon for the fragrant. Plot the next violent riots (if you can hear yourself over the pumping dance music) in one of the booths in this den of a West End bar decorated with Soviet paraphernalia.

Bargo

80 Albion Street, G1 (0141 553 4771). High St or Argyle St rail, then 5-min walk. **Open** 11am-midnight Mon-Sat; 10am-midnight Sun.
In the hip Merchant City, Bargo and its regulars are the hippest. Clubby sorts, business high-flyers and voluble bohemians sup pricey designer beers to the strains of the latest club sounds. Despite the size of this airy, post-modern bar, which scooped the 1997 Pub Design Award for its City of Lost Children-inspired industrial/maritime interior, it fills up quickly at weekends with expectant clubbers getting into dancing mood. A cosmopolitan food menu is served until 7pm (8pm Thur-Sat).

Bar 10

10 Mitchell Lane, G1 (0141 221 8353). St Enoch tube, then 5-min walk. **Open** 10am-12.30am daily. **Map 1 D3**
A city centre hive of activity tucked down a New York-esque lane off Buchanan Street. A particular mecca for clubbers and a haunt of the gay community. Led the way in Glasgow's style-bar stakes, with a compact interior and quirky features designed by Ben Kelly, the man behind Manchester's Haçienda nightclub. It's wall-to-wall beautiful people at the weekend, but many prefer to visit midweek for a quieter drink or a leisurely lunch.

Bar 91

91 Candleriggs, G1 (0141 552 5211). George Square buses or Argyle St rail, then 5-min walk. **Open** 11am-midnight Mon-Sat; 12.30pm-midnight Sun. **Map 1 E3**
A staple of any Merchant City pub crawl. Ideal for twenty- and thirtysomethings who enjoy stylish surroundings but baulk at the idea of trendier-than-thou, style-bar culture. Intimate but uncluttered candlelit bar with beautiful design features such as high-backed chairs and pipes behind the bar that look like Kate Bush's cloudbusting machine.

Blackfriars

36 Bell Street, G1 (0141 552 5924). High St or Argyle St rail, then 5 min walk. **Open** 11.30am-midnight daily. **Map 1 E3**
A cosy, traditional pub in the Merchant City which is popular with the students from nearby Strathclyde University and fans of real ale. Offers a busy programme of free live music, mainly jazz, in the bar. The basement venue hosts one of Glasgow's longest-running comedy nights on Sundays.

Bon Accord

153 North Street, G3 (0141 248 4427). Charing Cross rail. **Open** 11am-11.45pm Mon-Sat; 12.30pm-11pm Sun. **Map 1 B2**
A real ale pub that is deceptively large once you fight your way through from the bar. Convenient for the Mitchell Library and a sampling of the extensive range of cask ales in a chatter-friendly environment after a study session.

Brel

39-43 Ashton Lane, G12 (0141 342 4966). Hillhead tube. **Open** 10am-11pm Sun-Thur; 10am-midnight Fri-Sat.
In honour of the Belgian crooner Jacques Brel, this bijou, rustic bar exudes a continental feel, reflected in the food menu and the al fresco drinking that breaks out in Ashton Lane whenever there's a hint of sunshine. Handy for the **Grosvenor Cinema** (*see chapter* **Arts & Entertainment**). Various DJs and musicians play here regularly.

Budda

142 St Vincent Street, G2 (0141 221 5660). St Vincent St buses. **Open** noon-midnight Mon-Sat; 6pm-midnight Sun. **Map 1 D2**
A style bar with a Mediterranean/North African/Middle Eastern hybrid décor. More importantly, there is an abundance of comfy armchairs and a soundtrack of sweet soul and funk music with which to replicate that home drinking environment. At weekends you'll be sharing that home with a rabble of other imbibers and paying over the odds for your round, but midweek it's an oasis of calm and comfort.

Cottier's

93-95 Hyndland Street, G11 (0141 357 5825). Kelvinhall tube. **Open** 11am-11pm Mon-Thur; 11am-midnight Fri-Sat; noon-11pm Sun.

A spacious, converted church in the heart of the West End that is hugely popular, probably because it's the only watering hole in the heart of a residential area and there's a theatre and restaurant in the same building. Gets very busy with bohemian locals at weekends, but there's usually a niche to be found for you and your glass of Soave.

Cul De Sac

44-46 Ashton Lane, G12 (0141 334 8899). Hillhead tube. **Open** noon-11pm Mon-Thur; noon-midnight Fri-Sat; 12.30-11pm Sun.

An Ashton Lane institution with a ground-floor bistro attracting a cosmopolitan range of people. The buzzing, first-floor bar is mainly frequented by students hanging loose after lectures, so bottled beers, DJs and the latest dance tracks are the order of the day. The more stylish Cul De Sac Southside (1079 Pollokshaws Road; 0141 649 4717) in Shawlands attracts an older crowd wanting an alternative to the spit-and-sawdust local hostelries.

Curlers

256 Byres Road, G12 (0141 338 6511). Hillhead tube. **Open** 10.30am-11pm Sun-Thur; 11am-11.45pm Fri-Sat.

Old school pub right in the thick of the West End. The Byres Road location attracts students, shoppers and locals all wanting a refreshing pint. The ground-floor bar has attempted to move with the times and adopt some style-bar trappings, while the upstairs bar is a wholesome, straightforward beer-drinking environment. Local bands play Tuesdays.

Delmonica's

68 Virginia Street, G1 (0141 552 4803). Buchanan St tube, then 5-min walk. **Open** noon-midnight daily. **Map 1 E3**

Falling midway between a traditional pub and a style bar, this spacious bar is renowned as a gay hangout with a straight-friendly policy. Opinions differ as to the extent of the predatory atmosphere, but the emphasis is mainly on a fun drinking experience, with extensive happy hours, DJs and karaoke to facilitate this.

Flares

73 Bath Street, G2 (0141 331 5160). Bath St buses. **Open** 11am-midnight Mon-Sat; 5pm-midnight Sun. **Map 1 D2**

This 1970s theme bar overloads on the multicoloured décor: purple and orange predominate. Bar staff wear Afro wigs and flares (naturally), serve colourful cocktails and attend to the perpetual soundtrack of disco hits, broken only by the occasional live band – playing 1970s covers. Although it would like to think it has *Shaft*'s retro cool, Flares has more of a holiday camp atmosphere. Don't go looking for a quiet drink in the corner – you'll only be coerced into joining the disco dancing competition. Naff but lively.

The Griffin

226 Bath Street, G2 (0141 331 5171). Bath St buses. **Map 1 C2**

Few pubs in Glasgow have a genuinely varied clientele, but this is one of them. All ages together from students to blue-rinsed old ladies fresh from a musical at the **King's Theatre** (*see chapter* **Arts & Entertainment**) across the road. Choose between the main Griffin bar, a traditional affair with booths, fruit machines and a video screen for the footie, the cosy Griffinette for a seat and a chat (if you're lucky – weekends can be very busy), or the Griffiny lounge, which, like **Curlers** (*see above*), has succumbed to style-bar design to disgruntled mutterings from the regulars who like their Griffin to stay the same.

The Halt Bar

160 Woodlands Road, G3 (0141 564 1527). Kelvinbridge tube. **Open** 11am-11pm Mon-Thur; 11am-midnight Fri-Sat; 12.30-11pm Sun.

Another well-loved traditional bar with three spaces to choose from – the bright, bustling main bar, the narrow snug with its poster-covered walls and the laid-back lounge where rock, pop and blues bands play on a regular basis. Its West End location, on the pub-strewn Woodlands Road, makes it the haunt of a cross-section of pleasure-seekers – mainly students and ex-students, twenty- and thirtysomething locals and musicians who congregate for political and cultural chat. Or just to get pissed.

Havana

50 Hope Street, G2 (0141 248 4466). Hope St buses. **Open** noon-1am daily. **Map 1 C3**

A sumptuous new drinking experience for pale Glaswegians, situated right next to Central Station. Havana wrings every last exotic drop out of its Cuban theme – rich décor, animal print furniture, Latino background music, tropical cocktails, Hispanic food menu and the house speciality – hand-rolled Cuban cigars. Even the telephone hold music is Latin and listenable! Unlike many theme bars, it's tastefully done.

Heraghty's

708 Pollokshaws Road, G41 (0141 423 0380). Pollokshields East rail. **Open** 11am-11pm Mon-Thur; 11am-midnight Fri-Sat; 12.30-11pm Sun.

This spit-and-sawdust Irish bar on the Southside is in danger of becoming famous for one thing – being the pub that Jack McLean drinks in. The gruff *Scotsman* columnist is a loyal advocate of Heraghty's fabled pint of Guinness, but then so are all its regulars. This old man's pub is the place to head to watch a Celtic match on the box or listen to some genuine Irish blarney, rather than the manufactured flavour of the city-centre's Irish theme bars.

The Horseshoe

17 Drury Street, G2 (0141 229 5711). Buchanan St or St Enoch tube, then 5-min walk. **Open** 11am-midnight Mon-Sat; 12.30pm-midnight Sun. **Map 1 D3**

In a city of drinking institutions, this is the one to end them all. Tucked down a lane near Central Station, the Horseshoe boasts the longest continuous bar in the UK (horseshoe-shaped, of course) – the *Guinness Book of Records* attests to the fact. More important is the friendly atmosphere of its traditional surroundings. The ground-floor bar is large, but the huge bar means it's not spacious on a weekend night. The lounge bar upstairs sells the quickest and cheapest three-course lunch in town and hosts very serious karaoke evenings where drunken exhibitionists are not encouraged.

Jinty McGinty's

23 Ashton Lane, G12 (0141 339 0747). Hillhead tube. **Open** 11am-11pm Mon-Thur; 11am-midnight Fri-Sat; 12.30-11pm Sun.

The place where all the Irish bar fans flock to drink their pints of Guinness al fresco. In the style-conscious Ashton Lane pub crawl, Jinty's is a great leveller, but it remains a mystery why hardy souls insist on quaffing their drinks outside even on cooler evenings. It's perfectly cosy inside with its dark wood and Emerald Isle feel.

The Living Room

5-9 Byres Road, G11 (0141 339 8511). Hillhead tube. **Open** 11am-11pm Mon-Thur; 11am-midnight Fri-Sat; noon-11pm Sun.

Designed by trendy Glaswegian company Graven Images, this was one of the leaders in the style stakes of recent years. Close to Partick Cross in the West End, it is now one of the more established, hip watering holes in the city. Divided into two rooms, it combines mock-baronial décor with beautiful, wrought iron fireplaces to create a trippy take on the hunting lodge theme. Crowded at nights, its limited space is more conducive to a relaxed lunch.

McChuills

40 High Street, G1 (0141 552 2135). High St rail. **Open** noon-midnight daily. **Map 1 E3**
This atmospheric Merchant City pub is a great champion of live music of all styles and the vibe changes according to who's playing. Vintage record sleeves adorn the walls and there's a cavern feel due to the low roof and arched portals and abundant seating around candlelit, thick wooden tables for the youngish clientele of mainly students, young professionals and locals. For those West Enders not prepared to make the journey across town, there's a sister pub, McChuills Way Out West (14 Kelvinhaugh Street, G3; 0141 221 5569).

Nice'n'Sleazy

421 Sauchiehall Street, G2 (0141 333 9637). Charing Cross rail. **Open** 11.30am-11.45pm daily. **Map 1 C2**
Named after a Stranglers song, Sleazys is perfect for those looking for the young and funky who want to bypass the pretensions of the style-bar set. The walls are painted in a variety of psychedelic, 1960s patterns and the furniture has an American diner look, with groovy jukebox to match. An inexpensive place to drink, made cheaper by the generous happy hours, so it's unsurprisingly busy, even during the traditional midweek lull. Boasts a largely student clientele with a coterie of twenty-something regulars trying to stave off the onset of maturity by checking out the local band scene, much of which either drinks in the bar or plays in the scarlet dive venue downstairs.

Oblomov

372-374 Great Western Road, G12 (0141 339 9177). Kelvinbridge or St George's Cross tube. **Open** 11am-11pm Mon-Thur; 11am-midnight Fri-Sat; noon-11pm Sun. **Map 1 B1**
A classy addition to the West End that attracts a cosmopolitan crowd to its compact bar and adjoining restaurant. The food and drink theme is Eastern European, so it's blinis and vodka for those who want to get into the spirit of things. The layout means the place gets crowded very easily. You may have to shout to make your remarks about the latest Wim Wenders film heard, but civility reigns overall.

The October Café

Third Floor, Princes Square, Buchanan Street, G1 (0141 221 0303). St Enoch tube. **Open** 11am-midnight Mon-Sat; 12.30-6pm Sun. **Map 1 D3**
The setting, up in the gods in Princes Square, makes this popular with shoppers looking for lunch and a small libation. By day its glass ceiling gives it an airy, almost colonial feel, but by night it fills up with young dressed-up clubbers eager to lubricate the palate for their night out.

The Polo Lounge

84 Wilson Street, G1 (0141 553 1221). Buchanan St tube, then 5-min walk. **Open** noon-1am Mon-Thur; noon-3am Fri-Sun. **Map 1 E3**
Just round the corner from Delmonica's (*see above*), this is a more recent, welcome addition to Glasgow's limited gay bar scene. Unsurprisingly, it has quickly established itself with a slightly older crowd than its more raucous neighbour. There's a club downstairs, but the large bar area on the ground floor is equally popular. As the name suggests, it has a luxurious baronial lodge feel. Less of a hunting ground atmosphere than Delmonica's.

Rab Ha's

83 Hutchinson Street, G1 (0141 572 0400). Buchanan St tube or Argyle St rail, then 5 min walk. **Open** 11am-midnight daily. **Map 1 E3**
Named after Robert Hall, a fabled Glaswegian character with a prodigious appetite, this cosy bar and its acclaimed

Scottish restaurant are dedicated to satiating your culinary and alcoholic needs, particularly those of malt whisky lovers. Its Merchant City situation means you get the best of both worlds – comfy tradition and hip, youthful punters. There's usually good, new music emanating from the CD player at the bar but it won't impose on the lively chatter.

The Saracen Head

209 Gallowgate, G1 (0141 552 1660). 61(A/B/C), 62(A/B/C/D) buses. **Open** 11am-11pm Mon-Thur; 8am-midnight Fri-Sat; 12.30-11pm Sun. **Map 1 F3**
A glorious spit-and-sawdust bar that has nevertheless begun submitting to the karaoke onslaught. Usefully situated for pre- and post-**Barrowland** (*see chapter* **Arts & Entertainment**) drinks, so a large proportion of the clientele changes according to who is playing across the road. On the other hand, some of the more 'mature' East End regulars never change.

The Scotia

112 Stockwell Street, G4 (0141 552 8681). Argyle St rail or St Enoch tube, then 5 min walk. **Open** 11am-midnight Mon-Sat; 12.30pm-midnight Sun. **Map 1 D3**
This traditional bar, situated close to the river, claims to be Glasgow's oldest public house. It is the busiest and most famous of the three bars that make up the 'Stockwell Village' – the others are the Clutha Vaults further down the road and the **Victoria Bar** (*see below*) – an associative term for the musical and literary life to which the pubs play host. Numerous folk sessions, residencies, and live bands on Saturday afternoons and Wednesday evenings. The likes of Booker Prize-winning author James Kelman have been spotted propping up the perpetually busy bar, so it obviously carries out its self-imposed artistic remit.

Solid Rock Café

19 Hope Street, G2 (0141 221 1105). Hope St buses. **Open** 11am-midnight Mon-Sat; 12.30pm-midnight Sun. **Map 1 C3**
This might look quite ordinary, but it performs a special function as the long-term primary hangout for rockers and bikers in the city centre – in fact, there's usually a few gleaming motorbikes parked outside. A diet of heavy rock plays inside but you won't be checked for the quality of your leathers on the way in – all are welcome, regardless of the length of your hair.

The Tap Bar and Coffee Huis

1055 Sauchiehall Street, G4 (0141 339 8866). Sauchiehall St buses. **Open** noon-11pm Mon-Thur; noon-midnight Fri-Sat. **Map 1 A2**
A popular haunt at the west end of Sauchiehall Street that overlooks Kelvingrove Park. Although still dedicated to hearty real ale consumption, the Tap has undergone a facelift to create a warm-hued mellow vibe in which West End punters of all persuasions can kick back and enjoy regular DJ sets and live jazz on a Saturday night. The end result is a sort of all-in cultural experience popular with, for example, the staff of the nearby **Kelvingrove Art Gallery** (*see chapter* **Sightseeing**).

Tennent's

191 Byres Road, G12 (0141 341 1024). Hillhead tube. **Open** 11am-11pm Mon-Thur; 11am-midnight Fri-Sat; 12.30-11pm Sun.
A no-nonsense pub which provides those most basic functions necessary in a pub: a warm place in which to drink beer and watch the footie on the telly. Despite the fact that both these goals can be achieved by staying at home, a wide variety of locals and tutorial-dodging students – and their tutors – populate this traditional bar, which is part of the Tennent's chain. If you asked anyone around the world to envisage a typical British pub, Tennent's would, most probably, be what they came up with.

*If you've got it, flaunt it. Stylish **Bargo** in the Merchant City certainly does. Page 206.*

The Ubiquitous Chip
12 Ashton Lane, G12 (0141 334 5007). Hillhead tube.
Open 11am-11pm Mon-Thur; 11am-midnight Fri-Sat;
12.30-11pm Sun.
The intimate, traditional bar area of this West End institution is as popular and renowned as the expensive restaurant it is situated above. Attracts an older crowd than the other Ashton Lane bars, including a mix of cosmopolitan locals, BBC employees, university staff and many other arty and creative types who congregate to see who can talk the loudest about their latest project while consuming as much wine, beer and malt whisky as possible. Achieves that rare feat of being civilised and boisterous at the same time.

Uisge Beatha
232 Woodlands Road, G3 (0141 332 0473). Kelvinbridge tube. **Open** 11am-11pm Sun-Thur; 11am-midnight Fri-Sat. **Map 1 A1**
A tasteful Scottish bar that looks like three parts of a Highland hunting lodge – pantry with solid wooden tables, welcoming hallway and intimate smoking room where you can swill a dram or two. The Uisge Beatha, meaning 'water of life' (whisky), manages to incorporate tartan, stuffed stags' heads and log fires into the décor without being naff. Its varied clientele is testament to its enduring popularity.

Variety Bar
401 Sauchiehall Street, G2 (0141 332 4449). Charing Cross rail. **Open** 11am-midnight daily. **Map 1 C2**
Predating the style-bar onslaught with some idiosyncratic deco style of its own, Variety Bar is a firm favourite with groovy twentysomethings on the Sauchiehall Street pub crawl. Relax on the semicircular couches, prop yourself on the upright tables at the back of the room or congregate round the crowded bar – wherever you can wedge yourself in on the busier nights. A pumping soundtrack of varied dance sounds makes it an atmospheric prelude to a night's clubbing. During the day there's a curious metamorphosis: flat-capped old men, refusing to believe their traditional haunt has changed, still patronise the pub.

The Victoria Bar
159 Bridgegate, G1 (0141 552 6040). Argyle St rail, then 5-min walk. **Open** 11am-midnight daily. **Map 1 E4**
Along with the **Scotia** (*see above*), the intimate Victoria Bar helps to liven up the riverside area, which otherwise offers slim pickings for revellers. Again, music is a feature with spontaneous acoustic jams breaking out from time to time. It is one of Glasgow's most quintessential drinking experiences. No fancy design trappings, just a straightforward wood-panelled old man's bar and lounge. But as it is populated by actors, staff and punters from the Citizens Theatre just across the river and decorated with posters of past and upcoming artistic events, it has a creative vibe.

Whistler's Mother
116 Byres Road, G12 (0141 576 0528). Hillhead tube.
Open 10am-11pm Sun-Thur; 10am-midnight Fri-Sat.
Younger West Enders and students looking for an alternative to the union bar tend to head here for a pre-club drink in lively, unpretentious surroundings. The bar gets packed out at weekends when its large windows reveal a hubbub of people. The adjoining lounge area tends to be mellower. During the day, it is ideally situated for a shopper's lunch or coffee break.

Yo Yo
31 Queen Street, G1 (0141 248 8484). Buchanan St tube or Queen St rail. **Open** 5pm-12.30am Mon-Thur; noon-12.30am Fri-Sat; 5pm-12.30am Sun. **Map 1 D3**
A new concept in themed drinking – the sports style bar. Thankfully, athletic credentials do not need to be established for admittance to this long, narrow bar with a reasaonably sized lounge area at the back, although you'd be forgiven for thinking that designer dressing was compulsory. As it is situated next to and owned by the nightclub **Archaos**, it attracts roughly the same clientele, who rub sunbed-tanned shoulders and drink imported bottled lagers on the busy weekend nights. During the week, the vibe is a lot more laid back – the low lighting and the comfy lounge area make it a doubly attractive option.

Shopping & Services

With designer stores aplenty in the label-infested Italian Centre and Princes Square, Glasgow is pure dead shopping central.

Arts & entertainment

Books

Caledonia Books
483 Great Western Road, G2 (0141 334 9663). Kelvinbridge tube. **Open** 10am-6pm Mon-Sat. **No credit cards.**
The best in second-hand books: beat poetry, Irish fiction, film, crime novels, art – every visit turns up an irresistible gem.

John Smith & Son
57 St Vincent Street, G2 (0141 221 7472/fax 248 4412). Buchanan St tube. **Open** 8.30am-6pm Mon-Wed, Fri; 8.30am-7pm Thur; 8.30am-5.30pm Sat; 1-5pm Sun. **Credit** AmEx, MC, £$TC, V. **Map 1 D2**
Founded in 1751, Scotland's sole national bookseller covers every base, including university set texts, and also gives committed support to new Scottish material and cult fiction. **Branches** are too numerous to list here. Check the telephone directory for your nearest.
e-mail: 57@johnsmith.co.uk
http: www.johnsmith.co.uk

Voltaire & Rousseau
18 Otago Lane, G12 (0141 339 1811). Kelvinbridge tube. **Open** 10am-6pm Mon-Sat. **No credit cards. Map 1 A1**
Full of decrepit charm and antiquarian curiosities.

Waterstone's
153-157 Sauchiehall Street, G2 (0141 332 9105/fax 331 0478). Buchanan St tube. **Open** 8am-10pm Mon-Fri; 8am-8pm Sat; 10.30am-7pm Sun. **Credit** AmEx, DC, MC, £TC, V. **Map 1 C2**
The national chain's new flagship store offers five floors with Internet café, reading areas, back-rubs and a coffee shop.
e-mail: sauchiehall@waterstones.co.uk

Music

Fopp
358 Byres Road, G12 (0141 357 0774). Hillhead tube. **Open** 9.30am-7pm Mon-Sat; 11am-6pm Sun. **Credit** AmEx, MC, £TC, V.
Retro rock, guitar-based contemporary, jazz and leftfield dance. Some vinyl, but better for obscure CDs.

HMV
Debenham's Building, Argyle Street, G1 (0141 204 4787). St Enoch tube. **Open** 9am-6pm Mon-Wed, Fri; 9am-7pm Thur; 8.30am-6.30pm Sat; 11am-5.30pm Sun. **Credit** AmEx, DC, MC, £TC, V. **Map 1 D3**
A huge selection of mainstream CDs, games and videos, as well as an impressive selection of 12in vinyl.

Missing
9-11 Wellington Street, G2 (0141 400 1776). Buchanan St tube or Central Station rail, then 10-min walk. **Open** 8am-7pm Mon; 9am-7pm Tue-Sat; 11am-6pm Sun. **Credit** AmEx, MC, £TC, V. **Map 1 C3**
Indie vinyl and CD heaven with a branch in the West End as well as the city centre. Second-hand and new releases. **Branch:** 685 Great Western Road, G11 (0141 400 2270).

Tower Records
217 Argyle Street, G2 (0141 204 2500). Central Station rail or St Enoch tube. **Open** 9am-midnight Mon-Sat; 11am-midnight Sun. **Credit** AmEx, DC, JCB, MC, £TC, V. **Map 1 D3**
Glasgow's biggest music store with CDs, videos, books, merchandise and computer games. There's a small range of vinyl and this is also one of the few places to do laser discs and world music. More expensive than the others.

23rd Precinct
23 Bath Street, G2 (0141 332 4806). Bath St buses. **Open** 9.30am-6pm Mon-Sat; noon-5pm Sun. **Credit** AmEx, DC, MC, £TC, V. **Map 1 D2**
Knowledgeable dance specialists. Most of the staff DJ around town, so a good place for information on the local club scene.

Sport & outdoor

Boardwise
1146 Argyle Street, G3 (0141 334 5559). Kelvinhall tube, then 5-min walk. **Open** 10am-6pm Mon-Fri; 9am-5pm Sat. **Credit** AmEx, MC, V. **Map 1 A2**
Sales, hire and accessories for surf and snowboarding. Provides a daily weather report for snow and surf conditions.

Highrange Sports
200 Great Western Road, G4 (0141 332 5533). Kelvinbridge or St George's Cross tube. **Open** 9.30am-5.30pm Mon-Wed, Fri, Sat; 9.30am-7pm Thur. **Credit** MC, V. **Map 1 B1**
Very good for skiing, mountaineering and camping gear.

Tiso
129 Buchanan Street, G1 (0141 248 4877). Buchanan St tube. **Open** 9.30am-5.30pm Mon, Tue, Fri, Sat; 10am-5.30pm Wed; 9.30am-7pm Thur; noon-5pm Sun. **Credit** AmEx, JBC, MC, £TC, V. **Map 1 D2**
Centrally located and the city's largest in its field.

Millets
71 Union Street, G1 (0141 221 1678). Central Station rail or St Enoch tube. **Open** 9am-5.30pm Mon-Fri; noon-5pm Sun. **Credit** AmEx, MC, £TC, V. **Map 1 D3**
Branch of the chain store carrying outdoor supplies and its own-brand, Peter Storm range.

Dedicated followers of fashion should head for Buchanan Street.

Department stores

Debenhams
97 Argyle Street, G2 (0141 221 0088). St Enoch tube.
Open 9am-6pm Mon-Wed; 9am-8pm Thur; 9am-7pm Fri, Sat; 11am-5.30pm Sun. **Credit** AmEx, DC, MC, V, £TC. **Map 1 D3**
Household goods, clothes and restaurant franchises over three floors in the city centre.

House of Fraser
21-45 Buchanan Street, G1 (0141 221 3880). St Enoch tube. **Open** 9.30am-6pm Mon-Sat; 9.30am-8pm Thur; noon-5.30pm Sun. **Credit** AmEx, DC, MC, V. **Map 1 D3**
Classic department store.

Fashion

Aspecto
20 Gordon Street, G1 (0141 248 2532). Buchanan St tube. **Open** 9am-6pm Mon-Sat; noon-5pm Sun. **Credit** AmEx, JCB, MC, £TC, V. **Map 1 D3**
Scotland's only outlets for the Manchester-based store with two shops principally for men. The first is for expensive brands like Duffer and more formal shoes; the second branch (*below*) sells an outdoor-wear selection of shoes and some clothing.
Branch: 34 Gordon Street, G1 (0141 248 6900).

Bankrupt
63-67 Queen Street, G1 (0141 226 6822). Buchanan St tube or Queen St rail. **Open** 9.30am-5.30pm Mon-Wed, Fri; 9.30am-7pm Thur; noon-5pm Sun. **Credit** MC, £TC, V. **Map 1 D3**
Cut-price jeans shop down from Queen Street Station with many brands you have never heard of as well as better-known makes.

Clan
45 Hyndland Street, G11 (0141 339 6523). Kelvinhall tube. **Open** 10am-5.30pm Mon-Sat. **Credit** MC, V.
Small, friendly, West End shop carrying its own brands as well as the better skateboard and snowboard labels.

Concrete Skates
20 Wilson Street, G1 (0141 552 0222). Buchanan St tube. **Open** 10.30am-6pm Mon-Fri; 10am-6pm Sat; noon-5pm Sun. **Credit** MC, V. **Map 1 E3**
The best store in town for the more underground labels and for clothes that people actually use to skateboard in, rather than simply pose.

Cruise
180 Ingram Street, G1 (0141 552 9989). Buchanan St tube. **Open** 10am-6pm Mon-Wed, Fri; 10am-7pm Thur; 9am-6pm Sat; 1-5pm Sun. **Credit** AmEx, DC, JCB, MC, £TC, V. **Map 1 E3**
The best range of men's and women's designer gear in the city from the largest independent retailer in Europe.
Branches are too numerous to list here. Check the telephone directory for your nearest.

Diesel
116-120 Buchanan Street, G2 (0141 221 5255). Buchanan St or St Enoch tube. **Open** 10am-6pm Mon-Wed, Fri; 10am-7pm Thur; 9.30am-6pm Sat; 11.30am-5.30pm Sun. **Credit** AmEx, MC, £TC, V. **Map 1 D3**
Italian designer label with a young, modern retro feel in the city centre on two floors for men and women.

Dr Jives
111-113 Candleriggs, G1 (0141 552 5451). Argyle St rail. **Open** 10am-6pm Mon-Sat. **Credit** AmEx, DC, MC, £TC, V. **Map 1 E£**
This trendy Merchant City shop stocks exclusive brands for men and women and is Glasgow's only Stussy outlet.

MODERN PAINTERS

Major British and American writers contribute to the U.K.'s most controversial art magazine:

- JULIAN BARNES

- WILLIAM BOYD

- A.S.BYATT

- PATRICK HERON

- HILTON KRAMER

- JED PEARL

- CHARLIE FINCH

- MATTHEW COLLINGS

- DAVID SYLVESTER

Britain's best-selling quarterly journal to the fine arts.

High & Mighty
18-20 West Nile Street, G1 (0141 221 0749). Buchanan St tube. **Open** 10am-5.30pm Mon; 9am-5.30pm Tue-Sat. **Credit** AmEx, DC, MC, £TC, V. **Map 1 D2**
Catering for the king-size man with sportswear, suits and shoes from sizes 12 to 15.

The Gap
167-201 Argyle Street, G2 (0141 221 0629). St Enoch tube. **Open** 9am-6pm Mon-Wed, Fri, Sat; 9am-7pm Thur; noon-5pm Sun. **Credit** AmEx, MC, £TC, V. **Map 1 D3**
The Gap's flagship store in Scotland for casual preppy wear for men, women and children.

Jigsaw
61 Buchanan Street, G2 (0141 248 9004). Buchanan St or St Enoch tube. **Open** 10am-6pm Mon-Wed, Fri, Sat; 10am-8pm Thur; noon-5pm Sun. **Credit** AmEx, MC, £TC, V. **Map 1 D3**
Cool style, reasonable quality, casual and business wear in the modern-with-a-hint-of-retro look.

Karen Millen
46 Buchanan Street, G1 (0141 226 5113). Buchanan St tube. **Open** 10am-6pm Mon-Wed, Fri, Sat; 10am-7pm Thur; noon-5pm Sun. **Credit** AmEx, DC, JCB, MC, £TC, V. **Map 1 D3**
Quite expensive, but the smart business wear is worth it for any young female professional looking for something beyond the basic high-street look.

Long Tall Sally
43 West Nile Street, G1 (0141 221 8474). Buchanan St tube. **Open** 9.30am-5.30pm Mon-Wed, Fri, Sat; 9.30am-7pm Thur; noon-5pm Sun. **Credit** AmEx, DC, MC, V. **Map 1 D2**
Casual and formal wear for women over 5ft 8in.

TK Maxx
The Basement, Sauchiehall Street Centre, G2 (0141 331 0411). Sauchiehall St buses. **Open** 9am-5.30pm Mon-Wed, Fri; 9am-7pm Thur; 9am-6pm Sat; noon-5pm Sun. **Credit** AmEx MC, £TC, V. **Map 1 C2**
A designer discount superstore selling a variety of labels for men, women and kids.

Dress hire

Geoffrey (Tailor)
309 Sauchiehall Street, G2 (0141 331 2388). Sauchiehall St buses. **Open** 9am-5.30pm Mon-Wed, Fri, Sat; 9am-7pm Thur; 11am-4pm Sun. **Credit** AmEx, DC , MC, £TC, V. **Map 1 D2**
Helpful outlet for traditional Scottish regalia.

Moss Bros
25 Renfield Street, G2 (0141 248 7571). Union St buses. **Open** 9am-6pm Mon-Wed, Fri-Sat; 9am-7pm Thur; 10am-5pm Sun. **Credit** AmEx, DC, MC, £TC, V. **Map 1 D3**
Old favourite suit hire shop with courteous service.

Slater Menswear
165 Howard Street, G1 (0141 552 7171). St Enoch tube. **Open** 8.30am-5.30pm Mon-Wed, Fri, Sat; 8.30am-7.30pm Thur. **Credit** AmEx MC, £TC, V. **Map 1 D3**
Hidden behind the **St Enoch Centre** (*see below*), Slater offers the biggest selection of suits in Scotland.

Smiths
14-16 Renfield Street, G2 (0141 221 0603). Buchanan St tube. **Open** 9.30am-6pm Mon-Wed, Fri, Sat; 9.30am-7pm Thur. **Credit** AmEx, DC, JCB, MC, £TC, V. **Map 1 D2**
A more designer and fashion-orientated range of suits and smart menswear than the mighty Slater.

Second-hand

Flip of Hollywood
70-72 Queen Street, G1 (0141 221 2041). Buchanan St tube or Queen St rail. **Open** 9.30am-5.30pm Mon-Wed; 9.30am-6pm Thur-Sat; noon-5pm Sun. **Credit** JCB, MC, £TC, V. **Map 1 D3**
Massive store in the city centre with vast second-hand, retro Americana selection, as well as groovy new gear.

Nicol's Originals
8 Chancellor Street, G11 (0141 337 6994). Kelvinhall tube. **Open** 10am-6pm Mon-Wed; 10am-7pm Thur-Sat. **Credit** AmEx, DC, MC, £TC, V.
Men's and women's second-hand and vintage clothes.

Starry Starry Night Vintage Clothes
19 Downside Lane, G12 (0141 337 1837). Hillhead or Kelvinbridge tube. **Open** 10am-5.30pm Mon-Sat. **No credit cards.**
Antique and vintage clothing for men and women.

Shoes

Schuh
118-120 Argyle Street, G2 (0141 248 7331). St Enoch tube. **Open** 9am-6pm Mon-Wed, Fri, Sat; 9am-8pm Thur; noon-5.30pm Sun. **Credit** AmEx, MC, £TC, V. **Map 1 D3**
Scottish chain with fashion shoes for men and women – excellent for outlandish styles such as tartan Doctor Martens. **Branch:** 43-45 Union Street, G1 (0141 221 1093).

Pied à Terre
Unit 10, Princes Square, G1 (0141 221 0463). St Enoch tube. **Open** 10am-6pm Mon; 10am-7pm Tue-Sat; noon-5pm Sun. **Credit** AmEx, DC, JCB, MC, £TC, V. **Map 1 D3**
Smart and fashionable women's shoes and accessories in a large store to the west of the city centre. **Branch:** House of Fraser, 21-45 Buchanan Street, G1 (0141 221 3880).

Food & drink

Drink

Oddbins
26 Hope Street, G2 (0141 248 3082). Hope St buses. **Open** 9am-7pm Mon-Sat. **Credit** AmEx, JCB, MC, £TC, V. **Map 1 D3**
Well stocked with a better whisky selection than others. **Branches** are too numerous to list here. Check the telephone directory for your nearest.

The Whisky Shop
Unit 12, Princes Square, G1 (0141 226 8446). St Enoch tube. **Open** 10am-6pm Mon; 10am-7pm Tue-Sat; 12.30-5pm Sun. **Credit** AmEx, JCB, MC, £TC, V. **Map 1 D3**
With over 500 malt whiskies in-store and an assortment of decanters and flasks, this is the first stop for 'uisge beatha' connoisseurs. Popular tipples Lagavulin and Talisker retail for around £25, but customers can pick up a 40-year-old Bowmore for £4,000.

The Wine & Whisky Shop
116 Saltmarket, G1 (0141 552 3892). High St rail or St Enoch tube. **Open** 10am-9.30pm Mon-Thur; 10am-10pm Fri, Sat; 12.30-7pm Sun. **No credit cards.** **Map 1 E3**
A compact store in the city centre's East End, with a good variety of miniature whiskies and bottled curios and a fine selection of wine.

The Ubiquitous Chip Wine Shop
12 Ashton Lane, G12 (0141 334 5007). Hillhead tube.
Open noon-10pm Mon-Fri; 11am-10pm Sat. **Credit**
AmEx, DC, MC, £TC, V.
Offers the best wine selection in the West End along with
140 malt whiskies and a big brandy range.

Gourmet groceries

IJ Mellis Cheesemonger
492 Great Western Road, G12 (0141 339 8998).
Kelvinbridge tube. **Open** 9.30am-6pm Mon-Wed; 9.30am-
6.30pm Thur-Fri; 9.30am-5.30pm Sat. **Credit** AmEx, MC,
£TC, V.
Advance orders can be telephoned in to this renowned West
End establishment where Scottish speciality cheeses com-
pete bullishly with the continental big bruisers.
Branches are too numerous to list here. Check the
telephone directory for your nearest.

Henry Healy
243 Argyle Street, G2 (0141 248 9816). Argyle St rail or
St Enoch tube. **Open** 8am-5pm Mon-Sat. **No credit**
cards. Map 1 D3
Selling Scotch pies dripping with fat, cheap cuts of chick-
en and ham, square sausage, all to be washed down with a
can of Irn Bru, this low-cost chain gives the high-choles-
terol diet that still prevails in west Scotland a branded presence on the high street.
Branches are too numerous to list here. Check the
telephone directory for your nearest.

Pâtisseries & bakeries

The Auld Alliance
493 Great Western Road, G12 (0141 576 0220).
Kelvinbridge tube. **Open** 8.30am-6pm Mon-Fri; 8.30am-
5.30pm Sat; 11.30am-5pm Sun. **No credit cards.**
Popular for its selection of sweet biscuit flans and host of
organic breads.

Gregg's
Unit 2B, St Enoch Centre, G1 (0141 248 5162). St
Enoch tube. **Open** 8am-5pm Mon-Sat. **No credit cards.**
Map 1 D3
Customers recommend the cheese and onion pasties, while
staff will offer advice on pronouncing 'scones' correctly.
Branches too numerous to list. Check the telephone
directory for your nearest.

Pâtisserie Françoise
Italian Centre, 45 Cochrane Street, G1 (0141 552 7330).
Buchanan St tube or Queen St rail. **Open** 9am-7pm Mon-
Sat. **Credit** AmEx, MC £TC, V. **Map 1 E3**
As in Paris, pricey cakes and petite buns.
Branch: 138 Byres Road, G2 (0141 334 1882).

Gifts & antiques

Henderson the Jeweller
217 Sauchiehall Street, G2 (0141 331 2569). Sauchiehall
St buses. **Open** 9am-5.30pm Mon-Sat; noon-5pm Sun.
Credit AmEx, DC, MC, £TC, V. **Map 1 D2**
Renowned for its extensive range of silver jewellery and gifts
fashioned in the style of Charles Rennie Mackintosh, who
also designed the building that houses the recreated **Willow**
Tea Rooms upstairs.

Lansdowne Antiques
10 Park Road, G4 (0141 339 7211). Kelvinbridge tube.
Open 10.30am-5.30pm Mon-Fri; 11am-5pm Sat, Sun.
Credit MC, £$TC, V.

Pamper yourself at **Rita Rusk International.**

Vintage wood furnishings, lamps and ornaments. Collectors
will accept the hefty price tags for objects so well preserved.

Papyrus
296-298 Sauchiehall Street, G2 (0141 353 2182).
Sauchiehall St buses. **Open** 9am-5.30pm Mon-Sat. **Credit**
AmEx, MC, £TC, V. **Map 1 C2**
A plentiful, eclectic gift and card range with Mackintosh
motifs and jewellery.
Branch: 374 Byres Road, G12 (0141 334 6514).

Robin Hood Gift House
11 St Vincent Place, G1 (0141 221 7408). Buchanan St
tube. **Open** 9am-5.30pm Mon-Sat. **Credit** AmEx, JBC,
MC, £TC, V. **Map 1 D2**
Near to George Square, it does a brisk trade in clan histories,
shortbread, whisky and books on Robert Burns.

Scotch on the Rocks
Unit 61, St Enoch's Centre, G1 (0141 248 1502). St
Enoch tube. **Open** 9am-6pm Mon-Wed, Fri, Sat; 9am-8pm
Thur; 11am-5.30pm Sun. **Credit** AmEx, MC, V. **Map 1**
D3
From tartan cufflinks and china Nessies to Celtic jewellery
and Caithness glass, all the goods here are hand-crafted in
Scotland.

Health & beauty

City Beach
29 Royal Exchange Square, G1 (0141 248 8282).
Buchanan St tube or Queen St rail. **Open** 9am-10pm
Mon-Fri; 9am-9pm Sat; 10am-7pm Sun. **Credit** DC, JCB,
MC, £TC, V. **Map 1 D3**
Beauty's a science at this central salon where CACI facial
regeneration and body wrap treatments can be supplement-
ed with non-needle electrolysis, massages and sunbeds.

Crabtree & Evelyn
Unit 16, Princes Square, G1 (0141 204 0797). St Enoch
tube. **Open** 10am-6pm Mon; 10am-7pm Tue-Sat; noon-
5pm Sun. **Credit** AmEx MC, £TC, V. **Map 1 D3**
Affordable but classy, the full C & E toiletries range stocked
here is a magnet for bodycare fanatics.

Holland & Barrett
94 Sauchiehall Street, G2 (0141 331 1188). Buchanan St
tube. **Open** 9am-5.30pm Mon-Sat. **Credit** AmEx, MC,
£TC, V. **Map 1 D2**
Groceries and dietary produce for the health-conscious.

Rita Rusk International
49 West Nile Street, G1 (0141 221 1472). Buchanan St
tube, then 5-min walk. **Open** 9am-6pm Tue-Wed, Fri;

9am-8pm Thur; 9am-5pm Sat. **Credit** AmEx, MC, £TC, V. **Map 1 D2**
For pampering with a rarefied frisson, the award-laden Ms Rusk's spacious city-centre salon on West Nile Street fits the bill.

Hairdressers & barbers

City Barbers
99 West Nile Street, G1 (0141 332 7114). Buchanan St tube, then 5-min walk. **Open** 8am-5.30pm Mon-Fri; 8am-5pm Sat. **No credit cards. Map 1 D3**
No-nonsense gents' cuts.

DLC
10A Mitchell Lane, G1 (0141 204 2020). Buchanan St tube, then 5-min walk. **Open** 9am-5pm Tue, Sat; 9am-8pm Wed; 9am-9pm Thur; 9am-6pm Fri; noon-6pm Sun. **Credit** MC, V. **Map 1 D3**
Local, city-centre company with a youthful, international outlook without too many pretensions.

Daniel Field
61 Cresswell Street, G12 (0141 339 0526). Hillhead tube. **Open** 9am-6pm Mon-Wed, Fri; 9am-7pm Thur; 9am-5pm Sat (student discount Tue,Wed). **Credit** AmEx, JCB, MC, V.
Hair and beauty parlour with an inexpensive, in-house range of treatments.

Hairlynks
433 Great Western Road, G4 (0141 339 9748). Kelvinbridge tube. **Open** 10am-5.30pm Tue-Sat. **No credit cards.**
West End emporium with more than a decade of experience. The emphasis is on Afro hair.

Italian Centre – *for the labels that matter.*

Toni & Guy
96 St Vincent Street, G2 (0141 248 9243). Buchanan St tube or Queen St rail. **Open** 8.30am-6pm Mon-Wed, Sat; 8.30am-8pm Thur, Fri. **Credit** JCB, MC, V. **Map 1 D2**
Recent, super-chic addition to the city.

Shopping centres

Italian Centre
7 John Street, G1 (0141 552 6368). Buchanan St tube or Queen St rail. **Open** 8am-6pm Mon-Sat. **Credit** varies. **Map 1 E3**
At the northern end of Merchant City, this compact hub of boutiques and cafés exerts a magnetic power upon the Versace-, Sisley- and Armani-clad denizens of Glasgow.

Princes Square
48 Buchanan Street, G1 (0141 221 0324). St Enoch tube. **Open** 9am-1am Mon-Sat; 11.30am-5.30pm Sun. **Credit** varies. **Map 1 D3**
A replica of Foucault's Pendulum is the centrepiece of this city-centre mecca of 'must visit' shops and restaurants ranged over six floors. The range of upmarket outlets is over-whelming, so be careful with that credit card.

St Enoch Centre
55 St Enoch's Square, G1 (0141 204 3900). St Enoch tube. **Open** 9am-6pm Mon-Wed, Fri, Sat; 9am-8pm Thur; 11am-5.30pm Sun. **Credit** varies. **Map 1 D3**
High-street chains and speciality outlets with car park.

Sauchiehall Centre
177 Sauchiehall Street, G2 (0141 332 0726). Sauchiehall St buses. **Open** 9am-5.30pm Mon-Wed, Fri; 9am-7pm Thur; 9am-6pm Sat; noon-5pm Sun. **Credit** varies. **Map 1 C2**
Central, with affordable high-street chains and car park.

Virginia Galleries
33 Virginia Street, G1 (0141 552 9994). Buchanan St tube or Argyle St rail. **Open** 10.30am-6pm Mon-Sat. **Credit** varies. **Map 1 E3**
Worth visiting for vintage clothing and the vibrant street fashions of enterprising local designers.

Services
Chemists

Boots the Chemist
55 St Enoch Centre, G1 (0141 248 7387). St Enoch tube. **Open** 9am-6pm Mon-Wed, Fri, Sat; 9am-8pm Thur; 11am-5.30pm Sun. **Credit** AmEx, DC, JCB, MC, £TC, V. **Map 1 D3**
Branches are too numerous to list here. Check the telephone directory for your nearest.

Computers
Clydeforth
Unit 25 Anderston Centre, Blythswood Court, G2 (0141 248 7523). Charing Cross rail, then 5-min walk. **Open** 9am-5pm Mon-Fri. **Credit** MC, V. **Map 1 C2**
Best in the city for PC repairs.

Scotsys Apple Centre
74 Victoria Crescent Road, G12 (shop 0141 339 9627/technical support 01698 846 003). Hillhead tube. **Open** *shop* 9am-5pm Mon-Fri; *technical support line* 8.30am-5.30pm Mon-Fri. **Credit** AmEx, JCB, MC, V.
Mac specialists.

Princes Square – *a wrought iron temple of consumer pleasures. See page 215.*

Laundrettes & drycleaners

Dowanhill Laundrette and Drycleaners
17 Dowanhill Street, G11 (0141 339 8385). Kelvinhall tube. **Open** 8.30am-6pm Mon-Fri; 9am-3.30pm Sat, Sun. **No credit cards**.

Speedclean
85 Candleriggs, G1 (0141 552 2888). Buchanan St tube or Argyle St rail. **Open** 8am-5.30pm Mon-Fri; 9am-5.30pm Sat. **Credit** AmEx, MC, V. **Map 1 E3**
Merchant City's best dry cleaners. Alterations/repair service.

Opticians

The Eye Clinic
28-36 Renfield Street, G2 (0141 221 9090). Buchanan St tube. **Open** 8.45am-7pm Mon-Thur; 8.45am-5.45pm Fri, Sat. **Credit** MC, V. **Map 1 D2**

Lizars
101 Buchanan Street, G1 (0141 221 8062). Buchanan St tube. **Open** 9am-5.30pm Mon-Wed, Fri, Sat; 9am-7pm Thur. **Credit** MC, V. **Map 1 D3**

Vision Express
Unit 59, St Enoch Centre, G1 (0141 204 3978). St Enoch tube. **Open** 9am-6pm Mon-Wed, Fri-Sat; 9am-8pm Thur; noon-5pm Sun. **Credit** MC, V. **Map 1 D3**

Photographic

Quigg's
7-11 Parnie Street, G1 (0141 552 6823). Argyle St rail, then 5-min walk. **Open** 9.15am-5.30pm Mon-Fri. **Credit** AmEx, MC, V. **Map 1 E3**
Serious camera shop with excellent repair service.

Tom Dickson
87 Renfield Street, G1 (0141 332 0556). Union St buses. **Open** 9am-5.30pm Mon-Sat. **Credit** AmEx, MC, V. **Map 1 D2**
Top-notch local shop catering for the serious snapper.

Stationery

Nash's
94 Miller Street, G1 (0141 221 4724). Buchanan St or St Enoch tube. **Open** 8.30am-5.30pm Mon-Sat. **Credit** AmEx, JCB, MC, V. **Map 1 D3**
City-centre store offering an array of services including stationery, gifts, a wide range of office and student supplies and a fully functional post office.

Travel

Campus Travel
Glasgow University, The Hub, Hillhead Street, G12 (0141 357 0608). Hillhead tube. **Open** 9.30am-5pm Mon, Tue, Thur, Fri; 10am-5pm Wed. **Credit** AmEx, JCB, MC, £TC, V.
Independent travel specialists catering predominantly for students and young people.
Branch: Strathclyde University, 122 George Street, G1 (0141 553 1818/fax 0141 553 1919).

STA Travel
184 Byers Road, G12 (0141 338 6000/fax 338 6022). Hillhead tube. **Open** 9.30am-5.30pm Mon, Tue, Thur, Fri; 10am-5.30pm Wed; 11am-5pm Sat. **Credit** AmEx, MC, £TC, V.
Dealing in rail, road and air tickets largely outside the UK, STA also issues ISIC and Young Scot cards.
Branch: Strathclyde Student Union Building, 90 John Street, G1 (0141 552 8808/fax 552 2639).

Arts & Entertainment

Although Glasgow's cultural offerings are eclipsed in the national consciousness by Edinburgh's annual arts beano, the city still has plenty to offer.

For listings information, call the venues direct or peruse *The List* (published fortnightly), *The Glasgow Evening Times* or the weekend supplements of the Scottish broadsheets. The **Ticket Centre** (*below*) sells tickets for many different venues and events and some of the following listings simply have its phone number to contact.

Film

Glasgow is the home of the Scottish film industry, and the BBC and STV have their headquarters in the city, but cinematic representations of Glasgow are fairly thin on the ground. Early Bill Forsyth films such as *That Sinking Feeling* and *Comfort and Joy* presented a humorous, even whimsical look at the city. The Gillies Mackinnon-directed *Small Faces* pulled few punches in its portrayal of the razor gangs of the 1960s and David Hayman's *The Near Room* went for a noir-ish approach to the city's avenues and alleyways. Ken Loach's *Carla's Song* departed from the more typical 'no mean city' representation of Glasgow, and, although set in Edinburgh, Irvine Welsh's *Trainspotting* was partly filmed in Glasgow. The city is also home to Robert Carlyle, one of Britain's most successful screen actors of recent years.

Glasgow Film Theatre 'shares' some of the premières and special events of the Edinburgh Film Festival, and hosts annual festivals of French (November), Italian (April), Spanish, Latin American and gay cinema.

Commercially, the multiplex cinemas in outlying areas are sweeping all before them at the expense of city-centre complexes, but the arthouse scene continues to thrive on the demand for something beyond the diet of big-budget blockbusters.

ABC

380 Clarkston Road, Muirend, G44 (0141 633 2123/info 637 2641). Muirend rail. **Tickets** £3 (£2 before 5pm Mon-Fri); £2.20 concs. **No credit cards.**
This three-screen cinema is the sole surviving suburban picture house in the city and, although Southsiders might enjoy its convenience, old-fashioned charm and cheap tickets, its

programme doesn't offer anything you can't get with better sound and comfier seats in a multiplex.

ABC Film Centre

326 Sauchiehall Street, G2 (0141 332 9513/credit card bookings 332 1592). Sauchiehall St buses. **Tickets** £4 (£3.20 before 5pm); £3 concs; £2.70 children. **Credit** AmEx, MC, V. **Map 1 D2**
Big, five-screen sibling to the ABC (*see above*). Despite its central location, its future is threatened by the bigger, louder ethos of the larger cinemas.

Glasgow Film Theatre

12 Rose Street, G3 (0141 332 8128). Sauchiehall St buses. **Tickets** £3.25-£4.25; £2-£3 concs. **Credit** MC, V, **Map 1 C2**
The place to see independent, arthouse and foreign releases. A listed building, this cinema, formerly known as the Cosmo, has been refurbished to enhance its art deco look.

The Grosvenor

Ashton Lane, Hillhead, G12 (credit card bookings 0141 339 4298). Hillhead tube. **Tickets** £4; (£3.50 Mon); £3 concs; £2 children. **Credit** MC, V.
There are two similarly sized screens (the Ashton and the Kelvin) at this popular West End haunt that meets the mainstream and the arthouse midway in its programming. It has, arguably, the comfiest cinema seats in the city.

Odeon City Centre

56 Renfield Street, G2 (0141 332 3413/credit card bookings 333 9551). Buchanan St tube, then 10-min walk. **Tickets** £4; £3 concs; £2.75 children/OAPs; £11 family ticket. **Credit** AmEx, MC, V. **Map 1 D2**
This six screen, city-centre cinema is always packed on weekend nights, so arrive early for new openings. The choice is mostly mainstream, but an unexpected independent often appears on selected release. The premiere for *Trainspotting* provided the cinema with a dash of glitz.

Odeon At The Quay

Paisley Road West, G5 (0141 418 0111/credit card bookings 418 0345). Cessnock tube. **Tickets** £4.50 (£3.50 before 5pm); £3 concs; £2.75 child/OAP; family ticket £11. **Credit** AmEx, MC, V.
Although it lacks the personal touch, this 12-screen multiplex, just south of the river, is comfortable and has excellent sound. The extensive selection means you can turn up on spec and usually find something worth viewing.

Showcase Cinema

Langmuir Road, Bargeddie (01236 434 434/credit card bookings 01236 438 880). Bargeddie rail. **Tickets** £4.25; £3 before 6pm Mon-Fri and first show Sat, Sun); £3 concs. **Credit** AmEx, MC, V.

Griffin Avenue
Phoenix Business Park, Paisley (0141 887 0011/info 887 0020). 17A, 29 buses. **Tickets** *£4.25; £3 10.30am-6pm Mon-Fri; £3 concs.* **Credit** DC, MC, V.
Two multiplexes boasting 28 screens between them. If you don't mind making the journey, the Showcase cinemas are occasionally the only places to see short-run films.

UCI Clyde Regional Centre
23 Britannia Way, Clydebank, G81 (0141 951 1949/info 951 2022/credit card bookings 0990 888 990). Clydebank tube. **Tickets** *£4.65 (£3.25 before 5pm); £3.25 students (Mon-Thur); £3 children/OAPs.* **Credit** AmEx, MC, V.

UCI Olympia Mall
Rothesay Street, East Kilbride, G74 (013552 49622/info 013552 49699/credit card bookings 0990 888 990). East Kilbride rail. **Tickets** *£4.65 (£3.25 before 5pm); £3.60 concs.* **Credit** AmEx, JCB, MC, V.
Ten and nine screens respectively in these UCI multiplexes that stick to mainstream releases, kids' matinées and the usual late-night fare.

Virgin Cinema
The Forge, 1221 Gallowgate, Parkhead (0141 556 4282/credit card bookings 0541 555 136). 3A, 46, 61, 62, 89 buses. **Tickets** *£4.10 (£3.20 Mon-Thur); £2.80 concs.* **Credit** AmEx, MC, V.
Seven-screen multiplex in the East End of the city. Only really accessible if you're based out there or have a car.

Gay & Lesbian

The scene has two main clubs – the long established **Bennet's** and the **Polo Lounge & Club** – as well as weekly or monthly club nights at otherwise straight venues, such as Love Boutique on the first Saturday of the month at the **Arches**.

Less specifically gay-oriented than the capital, Glasgow's café-bar scene includes Caffé Latte (58 Virginia Street; 0141 553 2553; open 11am-midnight Mon-Sat; noon-midnight Sun) and QC's Café in the **Glasgow Gay & Lesbian Centre**. Both are brightly decorated and reasonably priced, if a little over-generous with the background music.

Of the scene bars, Austin's (183A Hope Street; 0141 332 2707; open 4pm-midnight Mon-Fri; 2pm-midnight Sat-Sun) is a basement bar with nightly entertainment, principally karaoke; **Delmonica's** mainly attracts a younger crowd; and Sadie Frost's (8-10 West George Street; 0141 332 8005; open noon-midnight Mon-Sat; 2pm-midnight Sun) is also popular.

The city's larger art galleries and museums can get quite cruisey, especially on a sunny Sunday afternoon, as are the major parks – but personal safety remains an issue.

Gay Scotland, a free monthly tabloid, has the most extensive listings section, while *Cruise* and *Scotsgay* (both free) also carry listings.

Glasgow has its own biennial lesbian and gay arts festival, Glasgay! (30 Oct-8 Nov 1998; 29 Oct-7 Nov 1999; 31 Oct-9 Nov 2000 – 1999/2000 provi-

sional dates only) and **Pride Scotland** alternates yearly between Edinburgh and Glasgow.

Bennet's
80-90 Glassford Street, G1 (0141 552 5761). St Enoch tube. **Open** *11.30pm-3am Tue-Sun.* **Admission** *£2.50-£6; £1.50-£5 concs.* **No credit cards.** **Map 1 E3**

Gay & Lesbian Switchboard
(0141 332 8372). **Open** *7-10pm daily.*

Glasgow Gay & Lesbian Centre
11 Dixon Street, G1 (0141 221 7203). St Enoch tube. **Open** *10am-11pm Mon-Sat; 11am-6pm Sun.* **Map 1 D3**
Home to QC's café-bar and a contact for Glasgay!

Polo Lounge & Club
84 Wilson Street, G1 (0141 553 1221). Argyle St rail or St Enoch tube. **Open** *bar noon-1am Mon-Thur; noon-3am Fri-Sun; club 10pm-3am Fri-Sun.* **Admission** *club before 11pm free; after 11pm £5.* **Credit** MC, V. **Map 1 E3**

Music

The British press occasionally touts Glasgow as the hip city for music. In fact, Glasgow has a permanent love affair with music. The transatlantic pull is strong – Scotland gave America its traditional folk music and, years later, the US returned the favour and Glasgow grasped country music to its bosom. Its influence can be heard in bands from Del Amitri to Teenage Fanclub.

The American east and west coasts (in the shape of Velvet Underground and the Beach Boys) still make their influence felt on the likes of Belle and Sebastian and Adventures in Stereo, as do the lo-fi sounds of Sonic Youth and Pavement on the city's trendiest guitar slingers, Urusei Yatsura and Mogwai.

Glasgow is always crawling with bands and musicians, be they an indie group playing their first gig in one of the city's excellent smaller venues or a band with the international stature of Texas or Wet Wet Wet.

The last few years have been healthy ones for the grassroots music scene: many bands have adopted a DIY approach and independent labels such as Chemikal Underground, Creeping Bent, Flotsam & Jetsam and Vesuvius have sprung up in force.

Barrowland and the SECC provide suitably sized venues for major rock acts' only dates in Scotland. *The List* magazine carries gig listings and for tickets try **Tower Records**, the Virgin Megastore on Argyle Street or:

Ticket Centre
Candleriggs, G1 (0141 287 5511/7777). Buchanan St tube, then 5-min walk. **Open** *office 9.30am-6.30pm Mon-Sat; 10am-5pm Sun; phone 9am-9pm Mon-Sat; 10am-5pm Sun.* **Credit** AmEx, MC, V. **Map 1 E3**

Roll out the **Barrowland** – *the place to see the stars.*

Venues

Barrowland

244 Gallowgate, G4 (0141 552 4601). 61(A/B/C), 62 (A/B/C/D) buses. **Open** 7-11pm. **Admission** varies; tickets must be purchased in advance. **Map 1 F3**

This former East End ballroom is now a spacious concert venue that retains its glitterball without the associated glamour. The place to see bigger name bands – David Bowie, Mötorhead and the Chemical Brothers have all played here. The dive environment is not for the faint-hearted, but the electric atmosphere is what counts.

The Cathouse

15 Union Street, G1 (0141 248 6606). Central rail/St Enoch tube. **Open** 11pm-3am Wed-Thur; 10.30pm-3am Fri-Sun. **Admission** £2-£4; £1.50-£2.50 concs. **No credit cards. Map 1 D3**

This 350-capacity club vies with **King Tut's** (*see below*) to showcase the best bands, although it lacks the *je ne sais quoi* that makes for a no-holds-barred night out. Originally a venue for rock and metal bands, including early Oasis and Pearl Jam gigs, it has branched out to embrace the likes of Man Or Astroman? and the Dandy Warhols.

The Garage

490 Sauchiehall Street, G2 (0141 332 1120). Sauchiehall St buses. **Open** 10.30pm-3am daily. **Admission** £3-£5; £2-£4 concs. **Credit** AmEx, MC, V. **Map 1 C2**

This popular student-orientated club is the place to see bands before they make the leap to Barrowland – anyone from Finley Quaye, the Stereophonics, Fun Lovin' Criminals to Prince, who performed a secret aftershow gig here a few years ago. The surroundings are far from stunning, but that doesn't impinge on the celebratory air of a packed gig.

Grand Ole Opry

2/4 Govan Road, Paisley Road Toll, G4 (0141 429 5396). 4, 9A, 23(A), 39(A) buses. **Open** 6.30pm-12.30am Fri-Sun. **Admission** £2.50. **No credit cards. Map 1 A4**

A Glaswegian institution nestling south of the river. Country fans of all ages don their gingham and denim and gather each weekend in this tacky hall, decorated in Confederate memorabilia, to imbibe cheap liquor, line-dance to the live band, witness the fake shoot-out and, in a surreal twist, play bingo. Arrive early for ringside seats and wear rhinestones.

King Tut's Wah Wah Hut

272A St Vincent Street, G2 (0141 221 5279). St Vincent St buses. **Open** noon-1am Mon-Sat; 6pm-1am Sun (if a

band is playing). **Admission** varies. **Credit** MC, V. **Map 1 C2**

Tut's secured its place in rock history as the venue where Oasis was spotted and signed. It's an established live venue catering for all musical tastes: Blur and Radiohead played early shows here and, given the T in the Park organisers own it, this personable, 350-capacity venue carries a lot of clout on the touring circuit.

Nice'n'Sleazy

421 Sauchiehall Street, G2 (0141 333 9637/333 0900). Sauchiehall St buses. **Open** 11.30-3.45am Thur-Sat. **Admission** £3. **No credit cards. Map 1 C2**

This psychedelically decorated pub is the hangout of choice for Glasgow's alternative music population. Take in the lively chatter and sounds of the city's best jukebox in the bar, or head downstairs to the scarlet-hued venue for leftfield sounds from punk to dance delivered by mainly Scottish acts, and all for a minimal door charge.

Scottish Exhibition & Conference Centre/Clyde Auditorium

Finnieston Quay, G3 (0141 248 3000). Exhibition Centre rail. **Open** 9am-5.30pm Fri. **Admission** varies. **Credit** AmEx, MC, V.

This soulless, aircraft hangar of an arena is the main venue for the biggest touring groups that come to Scotland. The Spice Girls, Oasis and Manic Street Preachers have all battled against its volatile acoustics. The newer 3,000-seater 'Armadillo' auditorium provides the same service for more 'mature' performers such as Shirley Bassey, Tom Jones and Yes.

The 13th Note

50-60 King Street, G1 (0141 553 1638) & 260 Clyde Street, G1 (0141 221 0414). St Enoch tube. **Open** *café-bar* noon-midnight daily, *club* 9pm-3am daily. **Admission** free-£5. **No credit cards. Map 1 E3**

A grassroots institution which has recently spread its wings to become a cosy art deco café-bar (on King Street) and a laid-back club (Clyde Street). Both host cheap nights of live music and most of Glasgow's hip new bands such as Mogwai and the Delgados started life (and still hang out) here. The Clydeside club has a vibrant atmosphere at weekends and, if you arrive early enough, entry is free.

Pubs & bars

In addition to the larger venues, the pubs and bars of Glasgow are enthusiastic supporters of free live

music. Try your luck at any of the following for rock, pop, blues, country and jazz:
The Baby Grand (3-7 Elmbank Gardens; 0141 248 4942; open 7.30pm-midnight Mon-Thur; 7.30pm-2am Fri; 10am-2am Sat; noon-midnight Sun); **Blackfriars**; **Brel**; **Curlers**; **Halt Bar**; **McChuills**; MacSorleys (42 Jamaica Street; 0141 572 0199; open 11.30am-midnight Mon-Sat; 12.30pm-midnight Sun); State Bar (148 Holland Street; 0141 332 2159; open 11am-midnight daily); **The Tap Bar**. *See also chapter* **Glasgow Bars & Pubs**

Folk

Glasgow's pre-eminence in the folk and traditional music field during the last major revival of the 1960s has been ceded to Edinburgh in recent years. Virtually all the leading younger bands base themselves in the capital. But the Celtic Connections Festival is the one area in which the west coast folk scene predominates.

Other festival events in Glasgow also frequently have a folk music element, including the city's Hogmanay celebrations, which are on a smaller scale than Edinburgh's extravaganza, but still quite a party.

There is also a lively session scene based around the bars on Stockwell Street: the Clutha Vaults (0141 552 7520; open 11am-midnight Mon-Sat; 12.30pm-midnight Sun); **Scotia Bar** and **Victoria Bar**. *See also chapter* **Glasgow Bars & Pubs**.

Celtic Connections Festival

Contact Glasgow Royal Concert Hall, 2 Sauchiehall Street, G2 (details 0141 332 6633/credit card bookings subject to service charge 0141 287 5511). Sauchiehall St buses. **Date** 13-31 Jan 1999; 13-30 Jan 2000.
This two-and-a-half week festival is held in mid-January every year. It easily ranks as one of the world's biggest and most prestigious roots festivals and has played host to top international acts such as David Byrne, James Taylor, the Chieftains, Steve Earle and the Hothouse Flowers. Spread over a number of city-centre venues, it also enjoys a truly mighty reputation for the post-concert craic that rages nightly at the Festival Club, housed in the venerable Central Hotel. Programme details and a list of performers for the Festival are available from October.
http: www.scotnet.co.uk/grch

Venues

The Ferry

Clyde Place, G1 (0141 553 0606). Central rail/St Enoch tube, then 10-min walk. **Open** 9pm-2am Fri Ceilidh. Occasional bands (check *The List*). **Admission** *ceilidh* £5/; £3 concs; otherwise varies. **Map 1 C3**
This former Clyde paddle steamer, now permanently moored on the river's south bank, provides a highly distinctive setting for occasional folk gigs and weekly ceilidhs; its windows offer a river vista of summer sunsets.

The Riverside Club

Fox Street, G1 (0141 248 3144). St Enoch tube. **Open** 7.30pm-midnight (ring for dates). **Admission** £5. **No credit cards. Map 1 D3**
The weekend ceilidh dances consistently attract a lively crowd. Arrive early for a seat and wait for the halls to transform from chilly to sweaty.

New Dawn Folk Club

Queen's Club, Queen Street, G1 (0141 221 6389). Buchanan St tube or Queen St rail. **Open** 8-11pm Thur. **Admission** varies. **No credit cards. Map 1 D3**
Weekly small-scale concerts by Scottish and touring artists.

Classical & Opera

Glasgow is home to Scottish Opera, Scottish Ballet, the BBC Scottish Symphony Orchestra and the Royal Scottish National Orchestra.

City Hall

Candleriggs, G1 (0141 287 5511). Buchanan St tube or Queen St rail, then 5-min walk. **Open** 9am-9pm Mon-Sat; 10am-5pm Sun. **Tickets** £6-£14 (for SCO concerts). **Credit** AmEx, MC, V. **Map 1 E3**
This municipal hall has been superseded by the **Glasgow Royal Concert Hall** (*see below*), in terms of comfort as much as programme, as the city's main classical venue. However, the Scottish Chamber Orchestra mounts a vibrant programme.

Glasgow Royal Concert Hall

2 Sauchiehall Street, G2 (0141 353 4131). Buchanan St tube or Queen St rail. **Open** box office 10am-6pm daily. **Tickets** *summer proms* £2.50-£19; *winter proms* £8-£21. **Credit** MC, £TC, V. **Map 1 D2**
The place to hear the big names and the international orchestras. Home to the Royal Scottish National Orchestra, which makes full use of the excellent acoustics. Regally situated at the top of Buchanan Street, it also hosts the annual **Celtic Connections Festival** (*see above*), some terribly civilised rock concerts and the occasional hormone-drenched teenybop gig in its 2,400 capacity auditorium and the smaller Strathclyde Suite.

Royal Scottish Academy of Music & Drama

100 Renfrew Street, G2 (0141 332 5057). Cowcaddens tube. **Open** 9am-8.30pm Mon-Fri; 9am-4.30pm Sat; noon-4.30pm Sun (longer at weekends according to concerts). **Admission** varies. **Credit** MC, V. **Map 1 D2**
The RSAMD has two halls for recitals, masterclasses and guest soloists. Hip composer James MacMillan teaches here.

Theatre Royal

282 Hope Street, G2 (0141 332 9000). Cowcaddens tube. **Open** box office 10am-6pm Mon-Sat. **Admission** varies. **Credit** AmEx, MC, V. **Map 1 D2**
This sumptuous venue is the home of Scottish Opera, with about eight productions in any one season, and where Scottish Ballet premières productions. Respected touring theatre and ballet companies frequently visit, too. Rattle your jewellery in the expensive seats or head to the back of the balcony for a mere £3.50. No dress code.

Nightlife

While Glasgow is famed for its fertility in rock and pop, dance music is no less vibrant, born of a healthy club scene and some resourceful independent record labels such as Limbo and Soma (which was the first to release Daft Punk's 'Da Funk'). Promising studio acts like DJ Q and club overlords Slam produce their own music as much as play other artists. If the music makers are doing well, it's because the club scene they come from is so strong. From mammoth superclubs to smoky underground venues, there's more than enough choice for anyone wanting to strike a pose when the sun goes down. Compared to Edinburgh, Glasgow has a larger scene, with more mainstream clubs and a greater emphasis on dressing-up.

The majority of clubs open around 11pm, but don't get going until after the pubs have closed. Many city centre and West End bars host pre-club events with live DJs. The dress codes on the door are quite open minded, with smart casual being the general inclination. Since 1993, there has been a curfew and all clubs are required to close their doors at 1am. This is the law, so don't push it. All the clubs are open until 3am and some keep going until 5am, but with no alcohol sold after 3am.

Cleopatra's (508 Great Western Road; 0141 334 0560), Victoria's (98 Sauchiehall Street; 0141 332 1444), Penelope's (18 Jamaica Street; 0141 400 1423) and Follies (Pitt Street; 0141 332 7322) are all probably best avoided unless you have a satsuma tan or look good in slingbacks.

Archaos
25 Queen Street, G1 (0141 204 3189). Buchanan St tube or Queen St rail. **Open** 10pm-3.30am Wed; 10pm-3am Thur-Fri; 11pm-3am Sat-Sun. **Closed** Mon-Tue. **Admission** £4-£8; £2.50-£6 concs. **Map 1 D3**
Archaos attracts a young, sartorially elegant crowd to its three-storey club for a weekly diet of mainstream house. It has a hip hop room at the weekend and Sunday's Shirley's Temple night is a haven of glammy, hard house.

The Arches
Midland Street, G1 (0141 221 4001). Central Station tube or St Enoch tube. **Open** 11pm-3am Fri-Sat; 11pm-3am first and last Thur in the month. **Admission** £6-£15. **Map 1 D3**
One of the largest clubs in Glasgow, situated in renovated railway arches beneath Central Station. A rotating selection of local club promoterss host the Saturday night clubs, which are of a principally hard house/techno persuasion. Everyone gets an extensive search that can take some time, so expect to queue. No dress code. *See also* **Theatre** (*below*).

The Sub Club
22 Jamaica Street, G1 (0141 240 4600). St Enoch tube. **Open** 11pm-3am Wed-Fri, Sun; 10.30pm-5am Sat. **Admission** £3-£8; £3-£5 concs. **Map 1 D3**
This ten-year-old club is one of the best in the country for deep house on a Saturday night. Thursday nights are gaining a reputation for top hip hop and drum 'n' bass, while Fridays and Sundays are for harder house and techno.

Trash
197 Pitt Street, G2 (0141 572 3372). Sauchiehall St buses. **Open** 11pm-3am Wed-Sun; 10.30pm-3am Tue. **Admission** £2-£7; £3-£5 concs. **Map 1 C2**
Largish club that aims itself at the middle ground of night owls who don't want anything too heavy, fancy dressing up a bit and aren't that keen on going all the way into town. House and R&B music over three rooms.

The Tunnel
84 Mitchell Street, G1 (0141 204 1000). St Enoch tube. **Open** 10.30pm-3.30am Thur; 11pm-3.30am Fri; 10.30pm-4am Sat. **Admission** £4-£11; £2.50-£5 concs. **Map 1 D3**

As near to a super-club as you get in Glasgow, hosting nights by Cream on the last Saturday of the month and regularly welcoming the biggest names on the dance circuit. A dressy crowd inhabits this stunning venue, which has a fairly strict door policy.

Velvet Rooms
520 Sauchiehall Street, G2 (0141 332 0755). Sauchiehall St buses. **Open** 11pm-3am Tue, Thur, Sun; 10.30pm-3am Wed; 10pm-3am Sat. Closed Mon. **Admission** £3-£6; £2-£3 concs. **Map 1 C2**
Busy club playing house in the main room and laid-back grooves in the front room to a dressy, older crowd.

Sport

Think Glasgow and, inevitably, the Old Firm football giants, Celtic and Rangers, come to mind. The two clubs have dominated the Scottish Premier Division – Rangers winning the title nine consecutive times before Celtic brought a halt to the run in 1998. The sectarian rivalry between the two is legendary – Rangers represent the Protestants, Celtic the Catholics. The crowd violence associated with this rivalry has calmed in recent years, but the Old Firm derbies are always fiercely contested. The Scottish season runs from August to May and matches are normally played on a Saturday afternoon at 3pm. Rangers play at Ibrox (0141 427 8800), which has a 50,000 capacity. Celtic play at Celtic Park (0141 551 8653), which has a capacity of 60,000. Old Firm games are difficult to acquire tickets for, but for other games call the numbers listed. Glasgow is also home to Partick Thistle, who play at Firhill Park (0141 945 4811). The Scottish national team play at Hampden Park, which is being upgraded and will reopen, complete with a football museum, in spring 1999.

Leisure centres

Tollcross Park Leisure Centre
Tollcross Park, Wellshot Road, G31 (0141 763 2345). 20A, 90 buses. **Open** *pool* 7am-9pm Mon-Wed ; 10am-10pm (6-10pm women only) Thur; 7am-9pm Fri; 9am-5pm Sat; 9am-4pm Sun; *gym* 7am-10pm Mon-Wed, Fri-Sun; 10am-10pm Thur. **Admission** *pool* £1.60 adults; 80p children; 50p concs; *gym* £3.70 adults; £2.30 children; £1.45 concs. **No credit cards**.

Kelvinhall International Sports Arena
1445 Argyle Street, G3 (0141 357 2525). Kelvinhall tube, then 5-min walk. **Open** 9am-9.15pm Mon, Wed, Fri; 7.30am-9.15pm Tue, Thur; 9am-6pm Sat; 9am-10pm Sun. **Credit** MC, V. **Map 1 A2**
Badminton courts, five-a-side football, a gym, aerobic classes and a 200m running track, all indoors and only ten minutes away from the city centre.

Scotstoun Leisure Centre
Danes Drive, G12 (0141 959 4000). Scotstounhill rail, then 5-min walk. **Open** 7.30am-10pm Mon, Wed, Fri; 9am-6pm Tue, Sat, Sun; 10am-10pm Thur; *ladies night* 6-10pm Tue. **No credit cards**.
This West End leisure centre contains a 25m swimming pool, gym, sauna, Jacuzzi, steam room, badminton courts, indoor

and outdoor tennis courts, athletics track, indoor football, children's soft play area and a café-bar.

Theatre

Glasgow has a clutch of critically acclaimed venues and a loyal theatre-going audience. The 1990 Year of Culture sparked a wave of enthusiasm for theatre in the city and the following year Mayfest – a month-long festival – was inaugurated. But it proved to be too much, too soon and the festival folded in 1997.

Although many venues are struggling to stay open all year round, due to tight budget cutbacks, they are still producing a full range of work from the experimental to the classical. More importantly, there's a cultural strength in the city, with its tradition of good writing and acting, that bodes well for a future renaissance. Larger touring shows by big names such as the Royal Shakespeare Company often visit the **Theatre Royal** (*see above*). Tickets for most venues can be bought at the **Ticket Centre** (*see above*).

The Arches

30 Midland Street, G1 (0141 221 4001). Central Station rail or St Enoch tube. **Open** *box office* noon-8pm Mon-Sat. **Closed** Sun. **Tickets** £6.50; £3.50 concs. **Credit** JCB, MC, V. **Map 1 D3**
The Arches enjoys a young, hip image thanks to it sharing its home with music and club venues. Besides the smallish touring productions, the resident company produce unusual contemporary shows and modern classics. The huge, cavernous space adds atmosphere to the theatre's occasional promenade productions. *See also* **Nightlife** (*above*).

Centre for Contemporary Arts

350 Sauchiehall Street, G2 (0141 332 0522). Sauchiehall St buses. **Open** *box office* 10am-6pm Mon-Sat; noon-5pm Sun. **Tickets** £1-£6. **Credit** MC, V. **Map 1 C2**
The arts complex houses a small theatre for mostly experimental productions with an emphasis on the sort of dance and performance art that, if not handled well, veers more towards the pretentious than the innovative.

Citizens' Theatre

119 Gorbals Street, G5 (0141 429 0022). 5(A), 12(A), 31, 66(A/B/C), 74 buses. **Open** *box office* 10am-5pm Mon-Fri; *performance season* 10am-9pm Mon-Sat. **Tickets** £2-£8. **Credit** MC, V. **Map 1 D4**
The 'Citz' is the best theatre in Scotland and is renowned for its risk-taking and lively productions. It has a tradition of being a theatre for the people: it is housed among high-rise flats in a deprived area which used to be Gorbals slum and the ticket prices are a bargain. The 600-seater main stage specialises in barn-storming versions of British and foreign work. Sexy reinterpretations of Restoration plays and other forgotten classics are always popular with the loyal, local audience. The tiny Circle and Stalls studios – seating 120 and 60 respectively – cram the audience right up against the actors for sometimes brilliant, sometimes awful, new or obscure plays.

Cottier's Theatre

93 Hyndland Street, G12 (0141 357 3868). Kelvinhall tube, then 5-min walk. **Open** *box office* 4.15-8pm Tue-Sun. **Closed** Mon. **Tickets** prices vary. **Credit** AmEx, MC, V.

An unusual venue, this beautiful converted church shows a varied mixture of cabaret, comedy and small-scale touring shows. It can be cold and draughty unless you're sitting right next to a heater.

King's Theatre

294 Bath Street, G2 (0141 287 5511). Bath St buses. **Open** 9am-9pm Mon-Sat; 10am-5pm Sun. **Tickets** vary. **Credit** AmEx, MC, V. **Map 1 D2**
Glasgow's home of the musical. Thanks to local amateur shows and popular touring productions, this is the place to see chorus girls become stars and cats burst into song. The impressive façade of the theatre is late nineteenth century.

Pavilion

121 Renfield Street, G1 (0141 332 1846). Cowcaddens tube, then 5 min walk. **Open** *box office* 10am-8pm Mon-Sat. **Closed** Sun. **Tickets** prices vary. **Credit** AmEx, MC, V. **Map 1 D2**
Cheery, end-of-the-pier type shows predominate at this large, traditional venue, with Scottish favourites Dorothy Paul, the ineffable country crooner Sydney Devine and hypnotist acts all regular visitors. They also produce shows and revues, usually on nostalgic themes, that don't trouble any artistic boundaries.

Tramway

25 Albert Drive, G41 (0141 422 2023/box office 423 3298). Pollokshields East rail. **Open** *box office* 3 hours before performances. **Tickets** £6-£10; £4-£8 concs. **Credit** MC, V.
Tramway was famously rescued from demolition in 1988 by impresario Peter Brook who saw the former transport museum as an 'industrial cathedral' ideal for staging his mammoth, multicultural production of Indian epic *The Mahabharata*. A huge, empty space with no fixed stage and spindly seating banks, in which visiting productions by the likes of Robert Lepage, Jonathan Miller, Brith Gof and the Wooster Group have helped it gain an international reputation as a cutting-edge venue.

Tron

63 Trongate, G1 (0141 552 4267). Argyle St rail or St Enoch tube. **Open** *box office* 10am-8pm Mon-Sat; 1-8pm Sun. **Tickets** £9; £4 concs. **Credit** MC, V. **Map 1 E3**
The tiny stage is regularly visited by small-scale productions with a couple of strong in-house shows every year. The intimacy has been a definite benefit in memorable versions of *Macbeth* with Iain Glen and Angels in America. Recent renovations have further improved the excellent café-bar and there are occasional comedy and music events, too.

Scotland's finest – **Citizens' Theatre.**

Trips Out of Town

Trips Out of Town

From the rolling hills of the Borders to the wild, open mountains of the Highlands, Scotland's lochs, beaches and glens are beautiful.

Having got to Edinburgh, it would be a shame to leave without seeing something of the rest of Scotland. There are many fine places within easy striking distance of the capital in Lothian, Fife and the Borders, which, if they aren't quite the Highlands and Islands, at least give a good indication of how the land lies. And, if you've got a bit more time, it is possible to get right out into the wilds with comparative ease.

Planning a trip

The best place to start is at the Scotland Desk of the **Edinburgh and Lothian Tourist Board**. However, while the staff are friendly and helpful, they are only able to provide information, not give an opinion, which can be irritating if you want to find out if a particular area is worth visiting. But if you already have a good idea of where you want to go, the office is a good first contact to work out how to get there.

A good map, besides being an invaluable source of information while you are in Scotland, is also an interesting souvenir of the trip. Ordnance Survey (OS) has the whole of Great Britain mapped in intimate detail. The two series that are likely to prove of greatest use are the Landranger (scale 1: 50,000, one and a quarter inches to the mile/two centimetres to the kilometre) and the Pathfinder (scale 1:25,000, two and a half inches to the mile/four centimetres to the kilometre).

Edinburgh and Lothian Tourist Board
3 Princes Street, EH2 (473 3800). Princes St buses. **Open** Nov-Mar, Apr, Oct 9am-6pm Mon-Sat, 10am-6pm Sun; May, June, Sept closes one hour later; July, Aug closes two hours later. **Map 8 D2**

The Stationery Office Bookshop
71 Lothian Road, EH3 (228 4181). Bruntsfield buses. **Open** 9am-5pm Mon-Fri; 10am-5pm Sat. **Credit** MC, £TC, V. **Map 8 A3**
Stock OS maps covering the whole of Scotland and a good selection of the more esoteric guides to the country's monuments, including some published by Historic Scotland, as well as business and computing books. The official outlet for government publications.

Getting there

The only real problem is transport. Some rural areas are lucky if they're served by two buses. A week. Although these do tend to be in the most remote places. If you are going to use the public bus service you will need to time your trip carefully to make sure you are able to get back to Edinburgh. You will probably also have to do a bit of walking at the far end to get where you are going. The rail system is almost as sporadic, although you will be able to get further, faster, but at greater expense and you will still need to do some walking. Hiring your own transport is often the best option, although it does not leave the driver with much chance of looking at the view. For details of **Waverley Railway Station** and **St Andrew Square Bus Station** *see page 251* **Getting Around Edinburgh**. Details of bicycle, car and motorbike hire are given on page 254.

If you are going further afield, several companies organise tours. Many of these are rather sedate and involve a lot of sitting on a coach while the country rolls past and a tour guide runs through their paces. There are several companies that will tailor a tour to suit your needs if you are in a large group. Others cater for independent travellers, either alone or in small groups (*see chapter* **Shopping & Services**, travel section).

Surviving

Scotland's mountains are incredibly beautiful and provide pleasure for thousands of people. They can also be very dangerous if they are not treated with respect. Always observe the basic rules – accidents will happen but their effects can be minimised. Always tell someone where you are going and what time you plan to get back. Take a map and a compass. Wear suitable footwear and take waterproofs. Carry a water bottle (which you can refill from a burn or small stream if necessary) and emergency rations. Take a torch. The real problem is that the weather changes very quickly, so if it looks like turning bad, get off the mountain quickly. Reputable sports and outdoor equipment shops (*see chapter* **Shopping & Services**) will be able to give advice on mountain conditions.

Leering down the years – the Apprentice Pillar in **Rosslyn Chapel**. *Page 226.*

East Lothian

Lothian Region stretches from Cockburnspath on the North Sea coast in the east to Blackness on the Forth in the west, and covers an area about 15 miles (24 kilometres) deep, south of the Firth of Forth. The main east coast road into Lothian from England is the A1. It is a dreary route that gives little indication of the area's natural and historical surprises so it is best to keep to the coast or smaller inland roads wherever possible. Lothian's rich farmland and proximity to the capital has produced some particularly fine country houses and castles. Summer sets East Lothian ablaze with flaming yellow whin (gorse) while the moors and reservoirs of the Pentland and Lammermuir Hills are reminiscent of parts of the Highlands. East Lothian is served by Eastern Scottish buses from St Andrew Square Bus Station. A local branch line runs from Haymarket, through Waverley to Musselburgh, Prestonpans, Longniddry, Drem and North Berwick. Some East Coast mainline services call at Dunbar. Cycling is a viable mode of travel, with some signposted routes and designated trails (mostly along disused railway lines) leaving Edinburgh.

The Pentland Hills

Wildlife and rural solitude are surprisingly easy to find in Lothian, as the hazard warning sign on the A702 – !Badgers for 3 Miles! – testifies. The Pentlands are the closest hills to Edinburgh and the scar of the Hillend dry ski slope at the **Midlothian Ski Centre** is visible from the city. There's a golf course and country park here, too, and it is within easy striking range from the city centre by public transport (LRT bus No. 4). But to get away from the madding crowd go along the A702 to the sign for Castle Law Hill Fort. This is a prehistoric Iron Age fort, accessible through a small gate into an underground passage. Nearby is a path to Glencorse Reservoir, a picturesque spot surrounded by Scots pines and hidden from Edinburgh by heathery hills. There is, however, a rather menacing area set aside for army target

practice. But in spring, if the red flags aren't flying, lambs use the whole range as a playground. It is possible to walk for some distance in the Pentlands, which are littered with reservoirs, but best to take a map.

Rosslyn Chapel

For architecture that is heavily flavoured with mystery and speculation Rosslyn Chapel (0131 440 2159), only six miles (ten kilometres) south of Edinburgh, is a must. Founded in 1446 by Sir William St Clair, a prince of Orkney, the chapel is a fantastic blend of pagan, Celtic, Christian and Masonic symbolism. It has more 'green men' than any other building in Britain – over 100 have been counted. There is a bizarre twisted pillar for which its maker is said to have been killed, representations of the seven sins and virtues, whole orchestras of carved musicians and what may be the death mask of Robert the Bruce.

Questions abound. Why are there carvings of new world plants, such as Indian corn, carved over 100 years before Columbus 'discovered' America? Was the chapel built as a copy of Solomon's Temple in Jerusalem and thus have little to do with the New Testament? What lies beneath its floors – the Scrolls of the original Temple, the Ark of the Covenant, the true Stone of Destiny, 20 barons or Knights Templar or even the head of John the Baptist? And where is the secret entrance to the crypt? Diverse theories attract an equally diverse range of visitors. Despite its uniqueness, a grave mistake was made in the 1950s when the interior was lime-washed to 'protect' the carvings. About £2 million is being spent to undo this error, which has caused the stones to become saturated with water. Hence the scaffolding and canopy, but while work is in progress, visitors can climb up for a bird's-eye view of the exterior. The chapel has a visitor centre, shop and tearoom. It is also worth walking down to the ruins of Rosslyn Castle and the beautiful woodlands of Roslin Glen. This area was a favourite with Romantic writers and painters including Sir Walter Scott and JMW Turner.

With all this mystery, it is not particularly surprising to discover that near here is the Roslin Institute, where Dolly, the first cloned sheep, was created.

Dalkeith

This pretty town is steeped in history and is only a few minutes south-east of Edinburgh. Dalkeith Country Park (0131 654 1666) has a fine nineteenth-century orangery and a walk that takes you through tunnels and arches by the river. Dalkeith House is owned by the University of Wisconsin. St Mary's Episcopal Church contains Scotland's only water-powered Hamilton organ,

but is rarely open. Edinburgh **Butterfly and Insect World** (0131 663 4932) just outside Dalkeith is a must for all lovers of exotic creepie crawlies and fluttery things. This is the biggest collection of butterflies in Scotland. There are between 25 and 35 species in the tropical greenhouse at any one time alongside hummingbirds, finches, fish, terrapins and iguanas. Baby butterflies are on display in the Caterpillar Room while the Bugs and Beasties Area houses the traditionally less attractive members of the insect world. Handling sessions allow visitors to cuddle Chilean tarantulas – Carmen and Rosie will show even the most committed arachnophobes that spiders can be cute. Next door is the **Bird of Prey Centre** (0131 654 1720). The centre has a gift shop and is attached to the huge Dobies Garden Centre, where there is a restaurant.

Castles near to Dalkeith include Crichton Castle Pathhead (01875 320 017), a well-preserved ruin of which the most spectacular part was erected by the Earl of Bothwell between 1581 and 1591. The faceted stonework is in an Italian style. A few miles east along the A6093, in Pentcaitland, is the Glenkinchie Whisky Distillery. It is the most southerly distillery in Scotland and was founded in the 1830s. Tours run throughout the year and a large visitor centre deals not only with the history of Glenkinchie, one of United Distillers' six classic malts, but with the whole story of whisky. Nearby, to the north, is Winton House (01875 341 309), a fine example of Scottish Renaissance architecture with unique stone carving and a collection of antique furniture. Viewing is by appointment only.

King Coal

Cistercian monks at Newbattle Abbey started to mine coal in the thirteenth century and have provided the earliest written record of mining in the country. Although unemployment in the area is high, because mining and other heavy industry used to play such an important and large part in the economy of the area, now that it has gone, the real surprise is that it is not higher.

The award-winning Scottish Mining Museum (0131 663 7519) at Newtongrange is one of the best industrial heritage museums in the UK. The Lady Victoria Colliery closed in 1981 after 90 years, having produced more coal than any other colliery in Britain – 40 million tons. Visitors don hard hats and ex-miners guide them through the works explaining everything from the rather depressing role of canaries to the mechanics of the giant colliery winding machine – Scotland's largest steam engine. £5 million of Lottery money means that more of the nineteenth-century buildings will be restored and a new visitor centre opens in July 1999. Unfortunately this also means that the role of the guides will be reduced by 'magic helmets'. 'Talking tableaux' and an award-winning hands-on activity zone make this museum a favourite with children. The shop specialises in all things to do with mining, including Welsh coal sculptures, and the tearoom has home-baking and soup.

Pot Arses

Less funding makes Prestongrange Colliery at Prestongrange Industrial Museum (0131 653 2904), on the B1348 coast road between Musselburgh and Prestonpans, much less accessible. But it is free and the guides are well informed. Between 1829 and 1947 miners burrowed two miles under the sea from the pithead. Of the many local industries which developed using the coal – Prestonpans Soap Works, Belfield's Pottery, Fowler's Brewery, the Salt Works and Prestongrange Brickworks – only Cockenzie Power Station survives. The miners' bath-house, built shortly before the pit's closure in 1962, the massive beam engine and parts of the brick works, including the kilns, are all still on site. The beam engine ran from 1874 to 1954 and was used to pump water out of mines 800 feet (250 metres) below the surface. There is a minimal snack shop and a visitor centre Look for the petrified tree trunk by the door. Known as 'pot arses' by miners, these three million-year-old stone stumps often lodged in the roofs of mines had a tendency to fall.

Inveresk Gardens (01721 722 502) at Inveresk village seem a world away from the pits. The terraced garden surrounds seventeenth-entury Inveresk Lodge (not open to the public), the oldest house in the picturesque village, populated by peers and rich foreigners. The public are allowed a nosey into some of the other village gardens on certain days under Scotland's Garden Scheme.

Haddington

A particularly well-preserved and elegant market town, 13 miles (20 kilometres) east of Edinburgh on the A1, Haddington's sites include the impressive fourteenth-century St Mary's Collegiate Church (01620 825111), but it is as the birthplace of John Knox, architect of the Scottish Reformation, that it has gone down in history. The Jane Welsh Carlyle Museum (01620 823 738) is a Regency-style house and gardens that was the childhood home of Jane Welsh, wife of Thomas Carlyle. Born in 1801, a doctor's daughter, she was an intellectual in her own right, but is only now being recognised as such with a number of American female academics holding her up as an early feminist.

A mile south of Haddington is the romantically named Lennoxlove House (01620 823 720), originally called Lethington Tower. The name was changed to 'Lennox love to Blantyre' in 1702 for a woman who never lived there. Frances Duchess of Lennox was admired throughout her life as a wondrous beauty, despite her disfigurement from smallpox. Even Charles II fancied her but, although she accepted his gifts, she never consented to be his mistress.

The house was bought in 1946 by the Duke of Hamilton, so most of the furnishings come via his family. The fifth Duke was not short of mistresses. There are several portraits of them (reputedly) in his bedroom, each wearing the same blue dress. The elaborate Goan bed belonged to Napoleon's sister, who was a mistress of the tenth Duke. Mary, Queen of Scots did not sleep in this bed, but Princess Anne did. The house does contain the almost obligatory Mary relics including a ring, a casket that stored the forged letters implicating her in the murder of her husband Lord Darnley and what is said to be her deathmask. The castle dates from the fourteenth century with the latest additions being made early this century by Sir Robert Lorimer, quite the most fashionable architect of the period. Outside, beautiful white Cadzow cattle, one of only two breeding herds in Scotland, graze beyond the ha-ha. Clarissa Dickson Wright (of the *Two Fat Ladies* TV cookery show fame) recently opened a café (Tue-Sat), which is proving so popular it's advisable to book.

For top nosh in Haddington, the Poldrate Restaurant (01620 826 882), set in a beautifully renovated mill, is worth every penny. Imaginative cooking and quality ingredients (sea bass, scallops and fish cakes to die for) are offset by a choice of elegant interiors, river views or courtyard dining. For cheaper fare and plenty of history there's the Tyneside Tavern (01620 822 221) next door, but beware the owner's non-PC taste in calendars.

The Lammermuir Hills

Further south of Haddington, past Lennoxlove, is the exquisite model village of Gifford built by the Marquis of Tweeddale in the seventeenth century for his estate workers. John Witherspoon, the first Moderator of the Presbyterian Church of America and the only clergyman to sign the American Declaration of Independence, was born in the manse of the church. Of the two obvious places to eat in the town, the one with the sign of the levitating yogic goblin, Goblin Ha' (01620 810 244), gets its name from a legend of Yester Castle, much fuelled by Sir Walter Scott in *Marmion*. The ruins of the castle are no longer accessible (nor is the tallest beech tree in Britain) since the estate is now in the hands of a very privacy-conscious Italian composer.

The Lammermuir Hills are easily accessible from nearby Longyester from where there is a track up to the picturesque Hopes Reservoir, snuggling under Lammer Law. This provides a much more satisfying route on to the Lammermuirs than simply driving up to the top along the road to Duns. While these hills are sneered at by those who consider nothing less than a Munro to be worth climbing, they are close to the city and can make an exhilarating day out.

East Linton, five miles (eight kilometres) east of Haddington, is another lovely Lothian village although the Phantassie Doocot is not as exciting as it sounds, unless you are a pigeon perhaps, but it is very pretty. Nearby, Hailes Castle, dating from the thirteenth century, is a beautiful spot. Behind the castle is Traprain Law with its Iron Age fort, once the home of the Votadini or Gododdin Tribe. There's not much to see at the top except the view.

North of the A1

The area north of the A1 between Cockenzie and Dunbar is rolling countryside, bounded by golden beaches to the north-west and high cliffs to the north-east. This is the agriculturally rich, so-called breadbasket of Lothian.

On the hills north of Haddington looking out on to all this agricultural splendour is the Hopetoun Monument, a prominent tower built in 1824 to the memory of the fourth Earl of Hopetoun. There is a path to the summit of the hill, but take a torch if you intend climbing to the top of the tower. Of rather more historical interest is the village of Athelstaneford, west of the tower on the B1343. If there's a nice blue sky, with plenty of little fluffy clouds, imagine the clouds uniting to form a giant cross. It is said that this is what King Angus, leader of a Pictish/Scots army, saw in 832 just prior to a battle with a much larger Saxon force under Athelstan. Since the cross was diagonal, he took this as a sign from St Andrew and vowed that the martyr could be patron saint of Scotland if he would let the smaller army win. They did and St Andrew became the patron of bonnie Scotland and his cross (or Saltire) the Scottish flag – the oldest in Europe and the Commonwealth. In the churchyard there is a 1965 memorial to the flag's birthhand, behind the church, a sixteenth-century dovecote, which was converted into a Flag Heritage Centre in 1996 by the Scottish Flag Trust. If it's open, inside there is a four-minute audio-visual dramatisation of the traditional origin of the flag. Athelstaneford itself was built much later, in the eighteenth century, by Sir David Kinloch as a model village for his estate workers. It is said to have been a particularly happy village where even the drunks were not aggressive.

Walkin' on the beaches

Beaches, golf courses, country houses, castles and villages make the coastal roads by the Firth of Forth vastly preferable to the A1. One way to explore this area is along the beach, almost unbroken between Longniddry and North Berwick. Overlooking Gosford Bay, a mile west of Aberlady, is Gosford House (01875 870 201) standing like a mirage from the Arabian Nights among sea-bent bushes and shrubs. Sadly, it is only fleetingly open, during June and July, but glimpsed from the road, it's hard to resist. With so many flamboyant additions, it is hard to think of this as an Adam house. William Burn and, in the 1890s, William Young, the architect of Glasgow's City Chambers, both made their marks. The three storey Italian marble hall is certainly familiar. The house has been nearly demolished, part-demolished, burnt out, used as a hotel and by the army and was not lived in by the Wemyss family, who had it built, until 1890 – almost 100 years after it was started. The present Lord and Lady Wemyss live in part of the house.

Naturalists and naturists

The Aberlady wildlife sanctuary is reached by crossing the footbridge from the car park just east along the coast from Aberlady. The sandy mudflats are a good spot to see wading birds and are a favourite with naturalists. The sandy dunes, on the other hand, behind the beach and before Gullane Point, are an unofficial naturist playground. If you're passing don't be too perturbed by the site of gooseflesh, but if you wish to join in, discretion is advised. The beach at Gullane, about a mile past the Point, is more family-oriented and has a large car park behind.

Gullane has often hosted the Scottish Open golf tournament and the various courses at **Gullane** and the very exclusive **Muirfield** are a mecca for golfers. The Heritage of Golf Museum (01875 870277) contains a mixture of golfing memorabilia and can be visited by prior arrangement. East of Gullane, Dirleton is a pretty English-looking village presided over by Dirleton Castle (01620 850 330). Dating from the thirteenth century, with later additions, it is empty inside, but the gardens, first recorded in the sixteenth century, have some fascinating features including an early-twentieth-century Arts and Crafts garden and a restored Victorian garden. A small road goes to Yellowcraig, which is a good viewpoint for Fidra Island and its lighthouse.

Salem of Scotland

North Berwick is still accessible by train from Edinburgh, the station is about 15 minutes walk from the town centre. The town is the Salem of Scotland. In the sixteenth century nearly 100 people, including the Earl of Bothwell, were arrested for taking part in the now infamous Witches' Sabbat in the old kirk on 31 October 1590. It all began with an insomniac girl and grew into claims of a plot to kill King James VI and I. It was said that the devil himself was made incarnate and that over 200 witches (women and men) had sailed to North Berwick in sieves. Despite these special skills, many of them were strangled and burned or burned alive on Edinburgh's Castle Hill where King James himself presided over their doom. The

The Bass Rock – *a basalt bastion of guano and gannets.*

remains of the church where it was all supposed to have taken place are by the harbour, an interesting area where the long-closed outdoor swimming pool attests to the times when North Berwick was where Edinburgh went on holiday.

North Berwick Museum (01620 895457) examines the town's long history as a holiday resort and has one room devoted to golf and another to the omnipresent Bass Rock. There are a number of small islands off North Berwick, but Bass Rock, a Gibraltar-like natural bastion three and a half miles (six kilometres) offshore, is by far the most spectacular. This lump of basalt is evidence, like Arthur's Seat, North Berwick Law and Traprain Law, of the region's volcanic beginnings. It has been a prison, a fortress and monastic retreat and is summer home to so many gannets that their Latin name, *sula bassana*, is taken from the rock. The gannets (known locally as solan geese) were once hunted for food, but are now in the care of the RSPB. Regular boat trips around the rock leave from North Berwick harbour, but landings must be arranged in advance (01620 893 863). You can see gannets all season, but May and June are the best time for guillemots, razorbills and puffins. It takes about an hour to get to the top of North Berwick Law where there is a strange collection of structures ranging from a whalebone arch to bits of a Napoleonic watchtower. North Berwick is well appointed in terms of refreshments with the omnipresent tearoom being particularly well represented, but the Quadrant is a quirky new bar and coffeehouse.

Cliff hanger

Three miles (five kilometres) east of North Berwick is Tantallon Castle (01620 892 727), a formidable fortification almost hanging off the cliffs. The combination of salt air and vertigo can make the ancient battles that the castle experienced ring in your ears without the aid of modern, interactive, computer-aided devices. With its earthwork defences and a massive fourteenth-century curtain wall, its bulky architecture is the man-made equivalent to the Bass Rock. Five miles (eight kilometres) south of the castle, there is a turning left off the A198 to Tyninghame Links and a beautiful but sedate walk out to St Baldred's Cradle, where there is a stone bench that is ideally suited for watching the gannets fly past the end of the point.

Tyninghame is on the north-west edge of the John Muir Country Park, which stretches across Tyne Mouth and Bellhaven Bay to the cliffs round the north of Dunbar to end at Dunbar harbour. With its salt marshes, lagoons and a long sandy beach, it is home to a wide variety of birds. John Muir, after whom the park is named, was born in Dunbar. There is a small museum dedicated to him in the town, at John Muir House (01368 862 585) where he was born and lived until he was three. There is not much to see, but it's free and the interpretive boards and video are interesting. Dunbar is reputed to be the sunniest place in Scotland. Which didn't stop John Muir and his family from leaving for America where this explorer, naturalist and writer is best

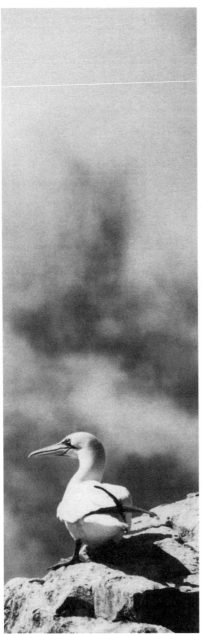
'*Who said* sula bassana?' *Page 229.*

known today as the founding father of the National Parks system. Ironically Scotland has no national parks, although England does.

Drunk monks

On the way into Dunbar is the small village of Bellhaven, home to the Bellhaven Brewery (01368 862 734), founded in 1719 by local monks. An independent concern, it produces a fine pint of 80/-. While distilleries have their 'angel's share', Bellhaven boasts the ghosts of drunk monks. Tours of the brewery can be arranged during the week, but phone well in advance. The pub in Bellhaven is the best place to sample the ale. Dunbar has a very unusual harbour built between rocks and castle ruins that is most attractive. The nearby Volunteer Arms is decorated with old postcards of Dunbar and specialises in seafood.

The beaches past Dunbar are very pleasant, but they are dominated by the grey bulk of the Torness Nuclear Power Station (0800 250 255). The station was the scene of modern-day battles in the late 1970s when anti-nuclear protesters took nonviolent direct action. Although the protesters ultimately failed, some still claim to have photographs of cracks in the gas cooled reactor's basement to anyone who cares to listen.

Flights of fancy

Back towards Edinburgh from Dunbar are two unusual museums: Scotland's National Museum of Flight (01620 880 308), at East Fortune Airfield, and the Myreton Motor Museum (01875 870 288), two miles from Aberlady. Neither are what you would call typical museums.

The Museum of Flight, housed in old aircraft hangars at the disused airfield, is part of the National Museums of Scotland. It has some fascinating exhibits ranging from flights of fancy to aircraft art. During WW I, the airfield was a base for British airships including the Scottish-built R34, which made the first two-way flight across the Atlantic, from East Fortune, in 1919. The airship required the skins of 600,000 animals to make its 19 gas bags and harboured the first ever airborne stowaways, a disappointed airman who had worked on the ship in Scotland and a kitten called Whopsie, smuggled aboard as a mascot. The museum's oldest exhibit is a glider built in 1896 by Glasgow-born Percy Pilcher. Sadly it was also his last, as he died when it broke up during flight in 1899. Sheila Scott OBE was more successful: beµtween 1965 and 1972 she broke 104 light aircraft records and flew round the world three times. Ironically, a car crash ended her aeronautics. Her stylish 1960s suits, a bizarre array of lucky charms and the fuselage of her single-engine Piper Commanche, Myth Too, are on display. There is a shop, an imaginative interactive area for kids, a café and a range of special events during summer. Open days enable visitors to see parts of the collection normally in storage.

Myreton Motor Museum, about five miles (eight kilometres) along the B1377, past Drem, is a wonderful, 30-year-old hotch-potch of vehicles and everything to do with vehicular transportation. Many exhibits have been lovingly restored by the owner. Each car is labelled with its own personal history and a photo of its anorexic condition before reaching Myreton. Cars range from an 1899 electric car from Philadelphia, more carriage than car, to the 1923 Alvis with a boat-like rear and top speed of 100mph (160kph) and a 1935, two-seater Singer that 'goes like the proverbial cat'. Motorbikes include the foldable Welbike used for parachute drops in WWII and capable of 90 miles on 6.5 pints (40 kilometres per litre) while there are also plenty of bicycles for those who prefer leg power to petrol power. Throughout the museum old road signs, petrol pumps (anyone for a gallon of Pratt's petrol?) and adverts (all the French cycle promotions require a naked woman for some unexplained reason) complete the picture. Jumbled into some farm buildings, this museum has an atmosphere and character that no amount of high-tech designing could reproduce.

West Lothian & Central

Although Cramond is technically part of Edinburgh, this pretty village with its Roman remains and small island that is cut off at high tide, makes a good starting point to explore the Firth of Forth shoreline to the west of the city. Cramond is served by LRT buses 40, 41 and 41A. There has been a village here since the Romans arrived in AD 142. The Cramond Inn (0131 336 2035) is a good hostelry and it caters for children. The four-mile (six-and-a-half-kilometre) walk back from the village towards Newhaven along the sea front is rather dreary but is easy cycling. Across the small marina at the mouth of the River Almond (there is a rowing boat ferry which operates during the summer) is Dalmeny House (0131 331 1888), a Gothic revival mansion designed by William Wilkins in 1814 and home of the Earl of Rosebery whose family have owned the estate since 1662.

The original thirteenth-century Barnbougle Castle built by the Mowbray family is not open to the public, but Dalmeny is definitely worth a visit for its extravagant Gothic interiors, historical treasures and intriguing stories. There is a portrait of Nell Gwyn, the Covent Garden orange seller who became the mistress of Charles II, and also a picture of the third Earl of Rosebery who, to disguise his baldness, had three wigs of differing lengths so that when he went to Edinburgh 'for a haircut' he could wear the long one and return in the short. His father had run off with a laundry maid. Sadly the house is only open during July and August, but the coastal path runs through the grounds.

Further along the coastal path, South Queensferry is also accessible by train from Edinburgh and is an excellent place to view the twin engineering feats of the Forth Rail and Forth Road Bridges. There is a footpath along the road bridge that gives a spectacular view of the rail bridge. But quite the best place to view the 50,000 tons of rust-red steel that went into the bridge is from right under the base of the most northerly span, on the north side of the Forth at North Queensferry. South Queensferry is also a very pretty town with an interesting museum and a unique annual custom that occurs on a Friday in early August. The Burry Man is clad top to toe in a prickly costume made of burrs and parades around the streets for nine hours. The Hawes Inn was immortalised by Robert Louis Stevenson in *Kidnapped*.

Crimson dreams

West of South Queensferry is the grandiose Hopetoun House (0131 331 2451), designed by William Bruce in 1699 for Charles Hope, the first Earl of Hopetoun and enlarged by William Adam in 1721. The elegant symmetry of the building belies nothing of the overstated opulence within. Inside, there are ceilings covered in naked cherubs that look like they might drop something on you, so convincing is the trompe l'oeil painting. Even the service stairs are spectacular. And as for the Bruce Bedchamber – it would give you hellish nightmares if you could get to sleep in all that red. The red drawing room is arranged in the eighteenth century style, known as 'parade' where the specially designed furniture is arranged with the backs against the wall. The rococo plaster ceiling is one of the finest in Scotland. A more intimate rococo masterpiece is the Dutch clock in the Garden Parlour. Just before the hour the windmill springs to life and the orchestra plays a tune. A rooftop viewing platform helps to give an idea of the vast dimensions of this palatial building. The grounds, which can be visited separately, were laid out by the architects in 1720. They comprise 100 acres (40 hectares) of formal woodlands, mainly exotic trees. There are three wee follies, views of the Forth and a herd of red deer. The Stables Restaurant does tasty lunches and afternoon teas in the stables courtyard and there is a tasteful gift shop.

South of the Forth, but still staying with the water, the Edinburgh Canal Centre (0131 333 1320/1251) at Ratho, near the airport, offers a variety of cruises on the Union Canal. Built by, among others, the infamous bodysnatchers Burke and Hare, the Union Canal was opened in 1822 and it would not be entirely surprising to see bodies floating in parts of the canal today – although an injection of millennium money means the canal, which was closed to through traffic in 1965, is enjoying a renaissance. The centre's two restaurant boats are modern, but the *Ratho Princess* started life in 1923, cruising on the Norfolk Broads. All three travel three and a half miles (five and a half kilometres) west along the canal to the Almond Aqueduct, the third largest in Britain. The centre also has the largest collection of vintage fire engines in Scotland, which 'perform' on the first Sunday in May, when they come together and squirt water into the canal. This unique behaviour is called the Pumpathon. Another bizarre event is the Annual Scottish Open Canal Jump Competition (third Sunday in June) when lunatics attempt to vault across the canal using a variety of means. Not many have, however, made it.

Lost unicorns

Linlithgow, also on the Union Canal, is on the edge of Lothian and really belongs to the industrial central belt, but it is easily accessible by train from Edinburgh and the spectacular lochside palace makes the visit worthwhile. It was in Linlithgow Palace (in the King's apartments) that both James V and his daughter Mary, Queen of Scots were born, in 1512 and 1542, so there is no doubt that she slept here. If more ceilings had survived, it is likely that there would be whole herds of unicorns prancing around the place. As it is, only three bosses survive depicting James's symbol. The soft stone of which the building is made means that the unicorn (though not the mermaid) has disappeared entirely from the fountain in the courtyard. Luckily Queen Victoria had a replica made for Holyrood. On special occasions the fountain was made to flow with red wine.

Outside the palace is St Michael's Church, which dates back to the thirteenth century and has strong associations with the royals. Mary, Queen of Scots was probably baptised here, while her grandfather, James IV, is said to have seen a vision warning him not to go to war with England. Ignoring

this, he shortly afterwards died at Flodden with 10,000 of his army, while his wife, Margaret Tudor, waited in vain in Queen Margaret's Bower at the top of the palace's north-west turnpike stair.

The spire on St Michael's is a surprisingly effective 1960s addition. The same cannot be said of the hideous houses by the loch. A heritage trail combined with a booklet and an audio guide direct visitors to more picturesque old Linlithgow. Ask at the Linlithgow Tourist Office (01506 844 600), which also has some displays. For a fuller history of the town visit the Linlithgow Story situated in a handsome Georgian house in the town centre.There is also a fascinating canal museum and a choice of boat trips. Linlithgow has a wealth of tea-shops, including one at the canal museum. Unusually for this part of Scotland, Linlithgow stages a Common Riding (*see box* Riding roun teh bounds of history) in June.

Just up the road, on the Forth, is Bo'ness, where the Bo'ness and Kinneil Railway runs steam trains along the shoreline on a seven-mile (11 kilometre) round trip to Birkhill Claymines during the summer. East of Bo'ness is Blackness Castle (1506 834 807) spectacularly situated on a promontory in the Forth, which was built in the 1440s, strengthened in the sixteenth century and restored in the 1920s. With its infamous pit dungeon, it was used as a prison for nobles and more recently was the setting for Zefferelli's *Hamlet*. Inland from here is the House of the Binns (1324 613 777). not a museum of waste-paper baskets but the historic home of the Dalyells including General Tam Dalyell who raised the Scots Greys here in 1681 and was known by some as a 'friend of the de'il'. The current Tam Dalyell, an MP, is notorious for asking the paradoxical 'East Lothian Question' about Scottish devolution in the House of Parliament. Most of the house dates from the seventeenth century but the furniture is largely eighteenth and nineteenthth century. The tower on the hill in the grounds has fine views over the Forth.

Six miles west of Falkirk is the unremarkable village of Bonnybridge. Remains of the Antonine Wall, the Romans' most northerly defence intended to keep out the wild Highlanders from the rest of the Empire, are visible here, but only with some imagination. Which is what is needed to see Bonnybridge's other attraction – Unidentified Flying Objects: the town appeals to aliens, allegedly. Since 1992, when Councillor Billy Buchanan took up the concerns of a local businessman who had come across a UFO on the road home from Falkirk, the village (pop. 9,000), depressed by the closure of heavy industry and with only two pubs

Disney's got nothing on **Thirlestane Castle.** *Page 236.*

and one hotel, has become internationally known as a centre of extra-terrestrial activity, a 'window area', as some UFO experts believe. According to Councillor Buchanan about 6,000 people have seen unexplained lights of all colours and shapes including a 'Toblerone'-shaped object reported by Andy Swan, a cable layer for Scottish Power, in 1994. Some of these events have even been captured on film. American Fox TV made a documentary and the Japanese produced a programme that was watched by 50 million people, but Buchanan believes the British government is not taking the events seriously enough. In true *X-Files* style he thinks they know something, but they're not telling. He has asked the Ministry of Defence – which received only two reports of 'unexplained' aerial objects in 1997 – written to John Major and more recently faxed Tony Blair. Buchanan's recently released song, *The Lights of Bonnybridge*, which ends in 'But I stand up for the people, I stand up for the youth, and I only hope in my lifetime, they will know the truth' has not, as he expected, shot straight to number one, but he has sung it outside Number Ten. If the proposed visitor centre, the Bonnybridge Encounter Centre, is built it will certainly help alleviate the area's high unemployment. The word on the street is that the locals are more scary than any alien and many villagers have become irritated by the constant jokes. However there's a lady down the chip shop swears she saw a flying saucer above her house two years ago.

The Borders

Tourist info – 01750 20555

Gentle, pastoral landscapes and time-warped towns make the Borders a fascinating, unique and often–overlooked corner of Scotland. Here the antagonistic history of the Scots and English comes alive. Moving south towards the border with England, Scottish flags start to appear and the River Tweed, which has powered the area's famous woollen mills, twists lazily by like a watery no-man's land. This is the area that Sir Walter Scot made his own, in which he built his home and was, indeed, a pillar of the community.

Peebles

Peebles for pleasure is the motto of this sleepy little town nestling in the Borders hills and it is more than alliteration. Universal happiness was on the mind of Peebles-born John Veitch, Victorian professor of logic, rhetoric and metaphysics when he warned, 'Never to blend your pleasure...with suffering of the nearest thing that feels.' No one seems to be suffering in Peebles's woollen shops and rooms, but they are hardly stimulating. The town does hold some surprises, however.

Peebles for plastering

The Secret Room of the Tweeddale Museum and Art Gallery, in the Chambers Institute on the High Street, is a unique opportunity to study parts of the Parthenon Frieze (just don't call them the Elgin Marbles) you never knew existed. They may be plaster copies, but are nonetheless impressive. Also displayed is a copy of the Alexander Frieze, executed in 1812 by Danish sculptor Bertel Thorvaldsen for the Palazzo Quirinale in Rome. The allegorical subject celebrates the arrival of Napoleon and is based on sections of the Parthenon frieze. It's possible to try plastering yourself at the Cornice, Scottish Museum of Ornamental Plasterwork (01721 720 212). The museum not only recreates a plasterer's casting workshop at the turn of the century, but continues as a business and has been in the Grandison family for over 100 years.

There are a number of drinking holes in Peebles where you can carry on getting plastered in the good old British sense. The Bridge Inn has character, some interesting old photos of Peebles and a useful Chinese restaurant above. For contrast try the elegant Tontine Hotel in the middle of the High Street, which was built by French prisoners of war between 1806 and 1808. The Peebles Hydro Hotel (01721 720 602) is a throwback to the Victorian belief in water as a cure for all. It commands great views of the town and for its facilities – swimming pool, whirlpool, tennis courts, health and beauty salon – is reasonably priced.

Just outside Peebles on the River Tweed is picturesque Neidpath Castle (01721 720 333), built in the fourteenth century and the ancestral home of the Lords of Tweeddale. It has inspired poetry by William Wordsworth and Sir Walter Scott. The latter's 'The Maid of Neidpath' tells a tragic tale of male insensitivity and female frailty. Beyond Neidpath on the B712 is Dawyck Botanic Garden (01721 760 254), an arboretum which is an outstation of the **Royal Botanic Garden** in Edinburgh. Trees date back to the seventeenth century and the outstanding conifer collection includes two Douglas Fir Trees grown from original seed collected by David Douglas in the American Northwest. Rhododendrons and azaleas bloom from March to July. There is a small tearoom, gift shop and plant nursery.

Further west in Broughton is the John Buchan Centre, a fairly home-made assemblage of artefacts and displays set up in a church and dedicated to the life of author John Buchan. Although remembered as the author of *The Thirty-Nine Steps*, he was also Governor-General of Canada.

The back road to Innerleithen from Peebles goes past Kailzie Garden (01721 720 007), 17 acres (seven hectares) of trees, shrubs and walled garden. Springtime at Kailzie, which means 'wooded place', brings a succession of flowery carpets, beginning with snowdrops, then daffodils and finishing with bluebells in May. Although the estate dates back to the twelfth century and contains some larch trees planted in 1725, the current garden was laid out in the 1970s by the owner. There are impressive plants and vegetables for sale and a licensed restaurant (01721 722 807) in the old coachhouse.

Health in the water

In 1822 a Dr Fyfe launched the sleepy village of Innerleithen on a career as a Victorian spa town by claiming that its well waters had health-giving properties. The water was said to be beneficial for everything from scurvy to sterility and was even reported to have restored the sight to two blind girls. In 1842 Sir Walter Scott used Innerleithen as a setting for his novel *St Ronan's Well* thus making the resort popular among the literati. The village adopted St Ronan – traditionally depicted as attacking Satan with his crook (Cleiking the De'il) –as its patron saint. This rather bizarre story has led to the Cleikum Ceremonies, which are held with the St Ronan's Border Games in July. The water can be tasted at the St Ronan's Wells Interpretative Centre (01721 720 123). Another unusual attraction is Robert Smail's Printing Works (01896 830 206), a turn-of-the-century printing shop where visitors can try setting type by hand.

Just outside Innerleithen is 1,000-year-old Traquair House (01896 830 323), the oldest inhabited house in Scotland. It was used as a hunting lodge by Scottish royalty, served as a refuge for Catholic priests and a stronghold of Jacobite sentiment. Mary, Queen of Scots not only stayed here in 1566 (where hasn't she slept in Scotland?) but may have embroidered the bedspread. In 1745 the fifth Earl wished his guest, Prince Charles Edward Stuart, a safe journey and rashly promised that he would not reopen his gates until the Stuarts were restored to the throne. Visitors and family still use the 'temporary' drive because the gates, topped by their toothy stone bears, have remained closed.

Not only is the house a fascinating insight into Scottish history, but it includes some bizarre artefacts such as a tongue scraper, a list of the fourth Countess's 17 children in her own hand and a rosary that belonged to Mary, Queen of Scots. Traquair is also famous for its seventeenth-century embroidery that 'reads' like a medieval Herbal or Bestiary. The grounds include a rather impressive maze, a croquet lawn, a brewery and a number of unusual craft workshops set up in the old stables. Particularly fine home-made food is available at the teashop. Ale has been brewed at Traquair for centuries. Drink it on site or, if the house isn't open, try it at the Traquair Arms Hotel, Innerleithen.

Galashiels & Melrose

Galashiels is not the most attractive Borders town, but it has a buzz about it that makes it a bit more 'real' than its more twee neighbours. With a population of nearly 14,000, it is the second largest settlement in the Borders and more centrally located than Hawick. Galashiels continues to be a manufacturing centre of tweed (the word comes from a misreading of tweel, the Scottish word for twill, not from the name of the river) although electronics production is now a bigger part of the economy. The Scottish College of Textiles and the Borders College, the latter split between Galashiels and Hawick, gives the town an unusual injection of youth and fashion.

Loch Carron/Peter Anderson (01896 752 091) is one of only four textile manufacturers to have survived from the 30 that were based in the town during Galashiels's golden years. There is a small museum devoted to tweed and tartan and regular tours provide a good overview of the process except for spinning, which is done elsewhere.

Fantasy gothic

Essential viewing on any trip to the Borders is Abbotsford (01896 752 043), Sir Walter Scott's romantic, fantasy Gothic house, built between 1818 and 1822. Situated on the banks of the Tweed, it was built partly to show off his collection of historic relics, and was financed by the Waverley Novels. However turgid these tales may seem today, the ornate interior of Abbotsford will not fail to impress. Objects of interest include Rob Roy's gun, Montrose's sword, Prince Charlie's quaich and over 9,000 rare volumes. American author Washington Irving (*Rip Van Winkle*), based his Hudson River house, Sunnyside, on Abbotsford.

A pig playing the bagpipes is the most unusual medieval carving on Melrose Abbey. Reputed to be the resting place of Robert the Bruce's heart and burial site of Michael Scott, the wizard, the Abbey is probably the most interesting of the four Borders Abbeys. Founded in 1136 by monks from the Cistercian Abbey of Rievaulx in Yorkshire, it was dedicated to the Blessed Virgin Mary a decade later. Historic Scotland has created an audio tour which makes the place a bit more human and points out parts easily overlooked. Teddy Melrose, Scotland's Teddy Bear Museum (01896 822 464), contains all you need to know about British teddy bears from the early 1900 Bruins to today's top designer teddies – for sale in the shop. The museum includes a huge collection of teddies from all over the world and an astonishing array of teddy trivia. Collectors' teddy fairs are held in May and August.

Rolling hills

The Eildon Hills, legendary burial ground of King Arthur, are not high, but in the rolling Borders country create a distinctive landmark.

The lion leaps tonight – plasterwork at **Thirlestane Castle**. *Page 236.*

Dryburgh Abbey – *raised by monks and razed by the English.*

They were immortalised by Sir Walter who often admired them from a viewpoint near Bemersyde – Scott's View – and are said to have been split in three by the wizard Michael Scott. The view is almost as good from the Wallace Statue, a gargantuan effigy of William Wallace. The visitors' book contains an array of nationalist rants and eulogies to Mel Gibson. At the foot of the hills, the Roman army made its Southern Scotland HQ during the first and second centuries AD. The Trimontium Exhibition (01896 822 651) in Melrose contains artefacts and models and runs guided walks.

The serene ruins of Dryburgh Abbey by the River Tweed hardly hint at the ferocious raids of the English that finally devastated the building in the 1540s. The Abbey was founded in 1150 by the White Canons of the Premonstratensian Order, founded in France by St Norbert in 1121. It was their first home on Scottish soil and was followed by five others. Dryburgh is probably most celebrated today as the burial site of Sir Walter Scott.

Thirlestane Castle (01578 722 430) near Lauder is on the A68, a good return route to Edinburgh from Dryburgh. This is a spectacular building originally constructed as a defensive fort in the thirteenth century, rebuilt in the sixteenth and dramatically extended in the nineteenth. Of the one Duke and several Earls of Lauderdale, only the Duke's ghost haunts the castle, which continues to be the home of the Maitland family. As the man in charge of the King's works at Holyrood Palace, the Duke deployed some of

Europe's finest craftsmen to decorate his ceilings, making them among the best examples of Restoration plasterwork in existence. Look out for the flamboyant lion leaping out of a flower in Bonnie Prince Charlie's room. Part of the family crest, lions abound at Thirlestane, mainly in the kind of pose young girls are told not to sit in. Stories are also numerous – ask for the one about Midside Maggie who freed the Duke from the Tower of London. Children can dress up and play in the nurseries and there's a slightly dated Border country life exhibition.

Selkirk & Hawick

Selkirk is a pretty town just south of Galashiels on the A7. Halliwell's House Museum (01750 20096) contains a re-creation of an old ironmonger's shop and there are displays about the history of this royal burgh. Victorian Selkirk is represented at Robert Clapperton's Daylight Photographic Studio (01750 20523), one of the oldest photo studios in the country. It has an extensive archive and the present proprietors, the fourth generation, demonstrate old techniques. A whole other side of Scott's life can be experienced at Sir Walter Scott's Courtroom (01750 20096). Not content with tartanising Scotland and being a blockbuster novelist, the writer was Sherriff of Selkirkshire from 1799 to 1832, but not in the Wild West sense – sherriffs are Scottish judges. Selkirk is also famous for its bannock, a deliciously rich currant loaf that is best tasted toasted. There are several bannock bakeries in town, but Camerons on the High Street bakes the best. For a dose of traditional Borders bigotry try the Fleece pub. The Rolling Stones were refused service here because their hair was too long, and if women ask for a pint they'll be served two halves as it's more ladylike.

Houses and wizards

East out of Selkirk along the A708 is Bowhill House and Country Park (01750 22204), the Borders home of the Duke and Duchess of Buccleuch. It has a variety of experiences to offer including a tiny theatre. Unfortunately, the house, with its internationally renowned paintings and furniture and intriguing royal and literary relics, is only open during July. The theatre has spring and autumn seasons, however, and the extensive grounds, open throughout the summer, offer woodland and lakeside nature trails, as well as views of the stately home. For contrast, a bit further south is Aikwood Tower (01750 52253), a fine sixteenth-century towerhouse restored as the family home for MP Sir David Steel. It is also the legendary home of Michael Scott, a thirteenth-century scholar, scientist and alchemist who translated Aristotle from Arabic (the original Greek text had been lost) into Latin and is referred to in Dante's *Inferno* as being in the seventh circle of hell with his face reversed. He was known as a wizard and it is said that, having been turned into a hare by

Reiven' in the years

If your name is Elliot, Kerr, Armstrong, Nixon, Johnson, Scott, Burns or Carlyle (to name but a few), you are descended from a bunch of professional cattle-thieves, racketeers and all-round pillagers known as the Border Reivers. These feuding families raided each other from both sides of the border in a kind of no-man's land that had its own law for many centuries. When a family was raided and goods stolen, locals joined forces on horseback and, picking up a piece of smouldering peat, set out on the 'hot trod' whereby those who were robbed 'may lawfully follow their goods either with a sleuth hound the trod (track) thereof, or else by such means as they can best devise'. The reivers have also bequeathed us the word 'blackmail'. To get on their 'hot trods' call Jedburgh's tourist office on 01835 863 435 (website: sbtb@scot-borders.co.uk).

a neighbouring witch, he set her feet moving so that she and her husband's workforce were turned mad from dancing until the spell had been lifted. Aikwood Tower and its wizard were an inspiration to poet and writer James Hogg, the Ettrick Shepherd, who was a contemporary of Sir Walter Scott's. There is an exhibition here about Hogg's life, most remarkable due to his lack of a formal education. His best-known book, *Confessions of a Justified Sinner*, was way ahead of its time in terms of structure and equally as anti-establishment as *Trainspotting* in its own way. A black cat called Michael Scott joins the guided tours of the tower.

High hill views

Some of the most beautiful scenery in the Borders is around St Mary's Loch, which is further east out of Selkirk along the A708. This area was a favourite haunt of Hogg. The Tibbie Shiels Inn at the head of the loch serves a good pint, and you can imagine the poets sitting around swapping verses in doggerel. The Grey Mare's Tail is a lovely waterfall in the hills above.

Hawick (pronounced hoyk) has an air of being time-warped in the 1950s. With a population of nearly 16,000 this is no Brigadoon, but it is certainly the most traditional of the Borders towns, some say archaic. It is the home of Pringle of Scotland, manufacturers of sports and leisurewear of the golfing variety. Hawick is also famous for its rugby. Testosterone and oval balls reach a peak in mid-April when the Rugby Sevens are played. While all the other Borders Ridings of the Marches (*see box* **Common Ridings**) have admitted women to the ceremonies, Hawick only allowed its female citizens to participate in 1997 after some serious legal battles. However, they are still only able to take part in some of the less important processions. To the idle tourist such sexism might seem quaint, but it is hardly likely to attract people to settle in the town. Hawick Museum and the Scott Gallery (01450 373 457) give a taste of Hawick history. One of the most interesting exhibits is the re-creation of a study of Sir Walter Elliot, a Victorian gentleman who collected flora, fauna and artefacts from all over the world. For more local history visit Drumlanrig's Tower (01450 377 615), a museum that doubles as a tourist office.

Kelso & Jedburgh

Kelso is the site of Scott's publishers, Ballantynes, whose bankruptcy in 1826 left the writer £130,000 in debt (£3 million in today's terms). On the quirky side, there is a horseshoe embedded in Roxburgh Street (outside Safeways), said to mark the spot where Bonnie Prince Charlie's horse cast a shoe in 1745 – perhaps a portent of the better-known loss at Culloden.

As Kelso Abbey is the closest to the English border, there is not much left of it, although it makes a most evocative Romanesque ruin. Like Jedburgh, it was founded by David I, in 1128, for a community of French monks from Tiron, near Chartres. The octagonal parish church built in 1773 is also worth a visit. The town also has a racecourse. For pubs in Kelso try the Queen's Head where you'll see that cricket is not just an English sport.

Visions of *Brideshead Revisited* and other Evelyn Waugh novels spring unbidden to mind at Floors Castle (01573 223 333), situated on the banks of the Tweed. It is Scotland's largest inhabited castle and the home of the Duke and Duchess of Roxburgh, but you're unlikely to see any family members when the castle is open. The house was started by William Adam in 1721, but owes its flamboyance to William Playfair who remodelled and extended it from 1837 to 1842. The floors of Floors are packed with priceless antiques – seventeenth-century Gobelin tapestries, paintings by Henri Matisse and Odilon Redon, eighteenth-century Chinoiserie and over 400 stuffed birds, including the now extinct American passenger pigeon. After staggering round that little lot, there's a restaurant to recover in before exploring the extensive grounds with their walled gardens, garden centre and historic holly tree marking the death site of King James II in 1460. Floors is enclosed by a high stone wall built by French prisoners of war after the Battle of Waterloo. Another reminder of that battle is the wonderfully phallic Waterloo Monument on a hill near Jedburgh. It was built by the sixth and seventh Marquises of Lothian and can be reached through Harestanes Country Park (01835 830 306), which has other pleasant walks and an exceptional visitor centre.

Robert Adam and Charles Rennie Mackintosh are probably Scotland's most influential and famous architects. If you could only ever see one Adam house in in Scotland it would either have to be Culzean Castle in Ayrshire or Mellerstain House (01573 410 225) near Kelso. Started in 1725 by William Adam and finished years later by his son, Robert, some say the interior of the library represents Adam at the zenith of his career. Certainly this is one of Adam's most intact interiors, containing most of the original period furniture and paintings by such masters as Gainsborough, Van Dyck and Scotland's own Romantic, Alexander Naysmyth. There is also a unique collection of dolls. Unusually, the surrounding landscape was designed by Adam – note the alignment of the lake and the folly on the hill, which was built as an 'eyecatcher.' The Italian-style terrace gardens were added in 1911. The grounds also hold a Hansel-and-Gretel style thatched cottage and a pet cemetery.

Riding round the

There are 11 towns in the Borders that stage a Common Riding festival every summer. Each has its own peculiarities, but all feature town notaries doing obscure ceremonial things, hordes of riders charging around the streets and lots of folk getting drunk. The practice of riding the town's marches or boundaries to preserve burgh rights reflects the turbulent history of the area. Most of the celebrations started this century, the Coldstream Civic Week as late as 1952. The highlight of the week (first week in August) is the ride to Flodden Memorial to commemorate the dead of 1513 when the Scots, having gained a toehold in Northumberland, were defeated by the English army. Lauder (last week in July) was one of the original Common Ridings, reference being made to it in 1686 and features the only boundary stone still in existence. Selkirk Common Riding (mid-June) dates back 400 years. The casting of the colours commemorates the sole survivor of 80 Selkirk men from Flodden. He returned with a captured English flag, but having raised it aloft, quickly cast it down again. At Duns (mid-June), riders follow a 'reiver' to the top of Duns Law on Monday and on Friday a game of 'handba' ' is played between married men and bachelors of the town. Jedburgh's celebrations last a whole two weeks (end-of-June to mid-July) and involve homage to a tree, while Kelso Civic Week (early-July) has a raft race and a meeting of whipmen (not as exciting as it sounds). Hawick (early-June) is the one where women can't take part in the main rides, while in Galashiels the event is known as the Braw Lads Gathering (second-last week in June) although there is a braw lass too. In 1337 some Gala lads killed English raiders in a field of wild plums, and 'soor plooms' became the Burgh emblem. Peebles's Beltane Week (mid-June) incorporates a fair, Melrose Festival Week (mid- June) culminates in the Abbey and for some reason West Linton has a Whipman Play (early-June). Linlithgow, in West Lothian also has a Common Riding. To take part in some of these events, horses can be hired from local riding stables. It's expensive, but charging about the town, up hills and through rivers with a herd of up-for-it Borders riders mounted on ponies and horses of all shapes, sizes and behaviour standards is an unforgettable experience.

bounds of historic Borders

Jedburgh is one of the most colourful Borders towns. Founded, like many, on the tweed industry, today its principal product is coathangers. Jedburgh Abbey is the best preserved and most dramatically situated of the Borders Abbeys. It was started soon after 1138 for some Augustinian monks. By founding it here David I was demonstrating that his rule extended up to the English Border and that the Scots, too, could build on a grand scale. The Abbey suffered from devastating English attacks during the sixteenth century, but after the Reformation (1560) it continued to be used as the parish church, which ensured its maintenance. Two beard/moustache combs made of walrus ivory and depicting vicious mythical beasts are on show in the visitor centre and indicate the care medieval gentlemen lavished on their facial hair. Mary, Queen of Scots House (01835 863 331), a sixteenth-century bastel house, has exhibits that provide everything that anyone ever wanted to know about M,Q of S (except how many beds she slept in). The original Jedburgh Castle was destroyed by the Scots in 1409 to keep it out of the hands of the English, but the newer Jedburgh Castle Jail and Museum (01835 863 254) presents a fascinating insight into Victorian crime and punishment. Convicts destined for Australia spent up to six weeks in these cells prior to transportation and these were the days when you could get life imprisonment for stealing a horse. For pubs try the Jedburgh Arms. Ask why there are rats crawling round the fountain that commemorates Queen Victoria. The locals will give you some entertaining answers including theories on the difference between a rock and a stone.

Duns & Eyemouth

Duns has the dubious honour of being the birthplace, in 1266, of John Duns Scotus, a medieval scholar who taught philosophy at the University of Paris. When his teachings were discredited, his name became associated with stupidity and it is thanks to him we have the word 'dunce'. The town, surprisingly, still honours him in the shape of a statue and plaque. But locals are far more proud of champion racing driver Jim Clark (1937-68), who lived at nearby Chirnside. The Jim Clark Room (01361 883 960) in Duns contains a unique collection of racing memorabilia. James Hutton (1726-97), now known as the father of geology, was another Duns man who was far from dim. He described the Borders as 'the most important geological site in the world' and challenged the theory of Creation. There is self-catering accommodation in Duns Castle (01361 882 015), whose grounds are managed as a nature reserve by the Scottish Wildlife Trust. Two miles east of Duns, Manderston House and Gardens (01361 883

450) epitomises fine, if over-the-top, Edwardian living: its splendours include the only silver staircase in the world and a marble dairy.

Paxton House (01289 386 291), five miles (eight kilometres) from Berwick-on-Tweed and a stone's throw from England, is the result of a failed love affair. After university in Leipzig, Patrick Home became the darling of Fredrick the Great's court in Berlin and even captured the heart of the tsar's daughter, Charlotte de Brandt. However despite the austere neo-Palladian house that Home built for his sweetheart in 1758 the marriage never took place. Today it contains Scotland's finest collection of Chippendale furniture and some elegant Adam interiors. Paxton also has the largest private country house picture gallery in Scotland, which was added by George Home in 1812 to house his uncle's collection. Today the space is leased by the National Galleries of Scotland, which displays a changing array of its lesser known works that are often far more intriguing than the famous ones.

Those with a penchant for mannequins in uniform will want to visit the Coldstream Museum (01890 882 630) to explore the history of the Coldstream Guards. The regiment was named after its stay in the town in 1659. If the museum isn't open, the pub closest to England, the Besom, has a fine collection of memorabilia. Just outside Coldstream, the museum and craft centre at Hirsel Country Park (01890 882 834), offers fascinating facts about pigeons and neeps, Scottish jaspers and agates and old farming methods.

Eyemouth, one time stronghold of tobacco and booze smuggling, is not the most picturesque fishing village on Scotland's east coast, but it's worth stopping at the museum (01890 750 678) to look at the Eyemouth Tapestry, which commemorates the 1881 fishing disaster when 189 local fishermen were drowned during a storm. The next fishing village north along the coast is St Abbs, which has the full quota of picture postcard tweeness on a balmy summer afternoon. But when the waves start rolling in, mean and grey, off the North Sea, the thought of having to negotiate the harbour entrance in a small fishing boat is daunting. North of the port, the cliffs rise up to St Abbs Head, which still features on the shipping forecast. There is a well-trodden pathway near the cliff edge and an inland track. The whole of the headland is a nature reserve and during spring it is home to whole cities of guillemots, razorbills and puffins. Also in the cliffs is evidence that over 400 million years ago Scotland and England were parts of different land masses, Scotland being joined to what is now North America. This is hard to see without the trained eye of a geologist, but just north of here, at Sicar Point, is the place where James Hutton finally formulated his 'Theory of the Earth' in 1788.

Fife & Dundee

Tourist information – 01334 472 021

Just over the Forth road and rail bridges from Lothian is the Kingdom of Fife, so called because it is the only one of the seven original Scottish kingdoms to retain its border's, mostly because it is bounded so precisely to the south, east and north by the Firth of Forth, the North Sea and the Firth of Tay. Fife is well served by buses and trains and there is a walk linking the towns along the coast. The coastal road is promoted as a Tourist Route but, unless you are into coal-mining heritage and industrialisation, the stretch as far as Kirkaldy and Buckhaven is not the most attractive of roads. However there are some little gems tucked between the high-rises and factories and, once the East Neuk of Fife is reached at Lower Largo, the villages become ridiculously picturesque.

North Queensferry is the best place to look back at the railbridge that inspired Iain Banks' nightmare vision of *The Bridge*. The port is also home to **Deepsea World** (01383 411 880), an impressive aquarium with sharks and a 367 foot (112 metre) underwater tunnel with moving walkway. From the harbour a ferry runs to Inchcolm Island, the 'Iona of the East'. Inchcolme Abbey was founded in 1123 and its ruins incorporate a thirteenth-century octagonal chapterhouse, but it is really the setting that is most impressive.

Continuing round the coast, fourteenth century Aberdour Castle (01383 860 519) is complete with seventeenth-century doocot (Scots for dovecot – pigeons were essential winter food when it was built) and terraced gardens. Nearby St Bridget's Kirk is a minor oasis with fine views over the Forth. The oyster shells in the mortar were not only a useful building material but were said to ward off evil. Further on Burntisland has a reproduction Edwardian fairground display in its library.

There has been a fair at Kirkcaldy every year since 1305, and the Links Fair in April is still an excellent funfair. Kirkcaldy is the largest town on this section of coast and was once the world's biggest producer of linoleum, which is still a significant industry. A remarkable number of important people were born here: Adam Smith, moral philosopher and political economist has given his name to the local theatre, Sir Sandford Fleming, inventor of Standard Time, and William Adam and his son Robert, eighteenth century architects extraordinaire are also Kirkcaldy-born. Less well known are the Reverend Shirra, who successfully prayed for wind to take the American navy away during the War of Independence, and Michael Scott, the wizard who made such a mark on the Borders. The Kirkcaldy Museum and Art Gallery (01592 412 860) has displays on all these people as well as an amazing collection of work by Scottish artists amassed over the last 50 years.

The East Neuk

Lower Largo is the first hamlet of the East Neuk, or 'nook' of Fife, undoubtedly the bonniest part of the Kingdom. Although the area has been adversely affected by the reduction in fishing quotas, the small ports and harbours are still the sorts of places where you can buy fish on the quayside. Alexander Selkirk, the prototype for Daniel Defoe's Robinson Crusoe, was born in Lower Largo, where a statue

Incredible hulk – the frigate **Unicorn** *in Dundee harbour. Page 244.*

of him clad in goatskins marks his birthplace. The Crusoe Hotel (01333 320 759) has taken up the theme and has a helpful display. Earlsferry and Elie are also pretty, and from here on, names like 'niblick' and 'links' herald golf territory. St Monan's has a beautiful church where the real Venus Peter grew up, although Ian Sellar's 1989 film *Venus Peter* was made and set on Orkney. The East Neuk's other big cinematic connection is that the sandy beaches were used in *Chariots of Fire*. More recently, Alan Rickman's *The Winter Guest* used the even more picturesque harbour of Pittenweem as its location.

Although the East Neuk Fishing Fleet is currently based at Pittenweem, Anstruther is a bigger, livelier place and home of the Scottish Fisheries Museum (01333 310 628). Eat at the Cellar for really good seafood or queue at the renowned Anstruther Fish Bar to which fish and chip fans flock from around the world. Boat trips (01333 310 103) run from here to the Isle of May, the site of St Adrian's martyrdom and Scotland's oldest lighthouse, built in 1636. The island is now a nature reserve and in summer there are thousands of puffins and grey seals. Crail is the most easterly and probably the cutest of East Neuk's villages. From here, the best way of continuing to St Andrews is along the coastal path, a distance of about 12 miles (19 kilometres).

The East Neuk has some interesting inland places too. Five miles from Crail is the Secret Bunker (1333 310 301) an underground, cold-war nuclear command centre, built in 1953 and cunningly disguised as a farmhouse. Kellie Castle (1333 720 326), near Pittenweem, dates from the twelfth century and in the nineteenth century was bought by the Lorimer family, who have lovingly restored and enhanced it.

St Andrews

Founded on God, Golf and Graduation, St Andrews has attracted pilgrims of one sort or another for many centuries. While God has taken a back seat, badly dressed people continue to hit balls with sticks and terminally traditional students wear red gowns and throw flour at each other. Best start with God. What was to be the largest and wealthiest cathedral in Scotland was begun in 1160 by Bishop Arnold and dismantled from 1559 onwards following a particularly rousing sermon by John Knox. Climbing to the top of St Rule's Tower provides impressive views of the medieval town walls. St Rule (or Regulus) was the semi-mythical bonebearer who is said to have brought bits of St Andrew from Greece. More likely, the relics came via Hexham from St Wilfrid, who picked them up in Rome. Bones or no bones, there is a magnificent Pictish sarcophagus in the cathedral museum which could have held them. The Kingdom of Fife Tourist Board have devised a way to combine God and golf with their St Andrews Golf Pilgrim Guide,

available from the tourist office: you can go dead golfer spotting in the cemetery.

St Andrews Castle, dating from the twelfth century, was built as the bishops' palace. It was, however, hardly a place of peace and goodwill, more the first flowering of sectarianism. Protestants who protested at the wealth and hypocrisy of the Catholic church (Archbishop Hamilton paraded around with his mistress and illegitimate children) were burned for their beliefs. In retaliation Cardinal David Beaton was murdered and the castle besieged in 1546. The two sides tried to dig their way to victory. The resulting mine and countermine are open for exploration. With its dank and justifiably dreaded bottle-dungeon and clifftop latrine, a hole cut in stone that empties straight into the sea, the castle oozes with medieval malevolence.

There were other ball and stick games prior to golf, but it was the Scots who thought of hitting the balls into holes in the ground. The British Golf Museum (01334 478 880) surprisingly interesting even to non-golfers.

As for the Graduates, the University of St Andrews, founded in 1410-11, is the oldest in Scotland and has a legacy of atmospheric old buildings. Interpretive boards and leaflets from the tourist office help to explore them. Most interesting are St Salvator's Chapel (1450), St Leonards (1512) and St Mary's (1537), where Mary, Queen of Scots' thorn tree is still growing. The St Andrews Museum (01334 412 690) covers the university's history as well as other aspects of the town. The St Andrews Sealife Centre is built around a 1906 outdoor swimming pool and features the Kingdom (of course) of the Seahorse. The nearby West Sands are a much nicer walk than the East Sands but don't stand in a jellyfish when the tide is out.

Leuchars is not only the nearest you can get to St Andrews by train, but has an unusual twelfth century Norman church, St Athernase, and nearby Tentsmuir forest and beach, which is a wonderful area for seal-watching. South of Leuchars is the pretty market town of Cupar, just south of which is the National Trust for Scotland's property of Hill of Tarvit (01334 653 127). Built in 1906 for Dundee jute baron Frederick Bower Sharp as a treasure chest for his valuable art collection, the house contains some fantastic furniture, tapestries and paintings. Just outside the well-kept grounds is the centuries-old keep, Scotstarvit Tower, where eminent cartographer Sir John Scott did his mapping. The key is kept at Hill of Tarvit house.

Crail harbour *in the East Neuk of Fife.*

Dundee

Tourist office – 01382 434664)

Dundonians call it the City of Apathy, the tourist board calls it City of Discovery. The key to enjoying Dundee (pop. 150,300), situated on the north bank of the Tay, is keeping an open mind. The city was founded on three Js – Jute, Journalism and Jam. Today it is the largest manufacturer of cash dispensing machines in the world. Only journalism continues to flourish, the jute industry having been whittled down to a mere two companies and the jam (actually marmalade discovered by the thrifty Janet Keiller in the 1790s) having shifted production to Manchester. In 1309 Robert the Bruce was made king here. The city has been destroyed twice, first during the Civil War and again following the Restoration. As a major centre for shipbuilding, whaling and jute manufacture, Dundee docks built one of history's most famous boats – the Royal Research Ship *Discovery* (01382 201 245)– used by Captain Scott on his first expedition to the Antarctic (1901 to 1904) when the ship spent two years in the ice before bringing the expedition home. She was the first ship to be constructed specifically for scientific research and is now moored at Discovery Quay, where her story and that of her crew is told in a spectacular and entertaining way before you board the ship herself. The frigate *Unicorn* is also moored, quiteunostentatiously, in the harbour. She was built as a warship in 1824 and was in service until 1968.

Daughters of Dundee

'Over-dressed, loud, bold-eyed girls' was the way Reverend Walker described Dundee mill girls in the late 1800s. Unusually for a Victorian city, in 1861 female death rates were higher than male, while in 1854 the lasses out-ladded the lads by totalling 730 disorderly behaviour convictions, compared to a puny 650 from the men. Women wore the trousers when it came to jute production, creating a unique, near-matrilineal society where men became 'kettle bilers' and looked after the 'wains'.

With such an independent lifestyle, it is no surprise that Dundee was the first Scottish city where suffragettes were imprisoned and went on hunger-strike, nor that it was in the mills that Mary Slessor

Munros and midges

Midges may be minuscule, but they are wee terrors, the scourge of the Highlands, probably Scotland's most deadly weapon and a constant bane for tourism. Of the 152 species of biting midge in Britain, one third feed on mammals' blood and 37 of these live in Scotland.. If you are planning a trip to the Highlands and Islands, it is best to know your enemy.

The Highland Midge, *ulicoides impunctis*, attacks Highlanders, the Garden Midge, *culicoides obsoletus* plagues lowlanders. Only the female bites, the males preferring flowers to blood. Midges are born in boggy ground and the population peaks in late May/early June and late July/early August with estimates of up to 10 million midge larvae per acre (24 million per hectare). They are most active in the two hours before sunset, preferring humidity and stillness. The good news is that, although the bites are itchy and a swarm of biting midges can drive you mad, the bites themselves rarely swell and midges do not transmit diseases to humans. The bad news is that, since the 1940s, government-funded research programmes have been unable to come up with an effective chemical control or repellent.

Unless your clothes are more protective than a beekeeper's, these hints will help. Citronella or herb oils such as thyme or bog myrtle are deterrents. Midges prefer dark to light coloured cloth-ing and detest smoke. Either get the barbecue going or take up smoking. And if all else fails bear in mind that along with the Scottish weather and a few toothless government bodies, they are the chief guardians of some of the country's wildest and most scenic places. If it wasn't for the midge it's likely you wouldn't be there anyway.

One good reason to brave the midge is the lure of the Munro. These are hills over 3,000 feet (914 meters) in Scotland. There are 284 of them and they were first listed by Sir Hugh Munro, an original member of the Scottish Mountaineering Club, in 1891. Before then there were assumed to be around 30. However, controversy has surrounded the definition of a separate hill as opposed to a top and the Munro Tables have been revised several times. Climbing all of them (Munro bagging) has become a sport, some would say an obsession, among hillwalkers. The first person to climb the full complement was thme Reverend AE Robertson, who, on completing his final summit in 1901, described the experience as 'a desultory campaign of ten years'. Nonetheless Munro's list continues to inspire anoraks from all over the country with a kind of 'because-it's-there' attitude.

Frankly, many of these hills would have been ignored by walkers altogether had it not been for Sir Hugh. Munros vary vastly, from the dull hills of Drumochter, better for ski-mountaineering made her living before setting out to West Africa as a missionary. Her death in Nigeria in 1915 caught the attention of the world, but produced only a short obituary in the *Dundee Advertiser*. Margaret Fenwick MBE (1920-1992) started as an apprentice weaver at 14 and was quick to get a pay rise on the grounds that she was being discriminated against due to her youth. By 1971 she was the first woman general secretary of a British trade union. Arbroath-born, Margaret Fairlie (1891-1963) was Scotland's first woman professor. Educated at St Andrews University, she went on to specialise in gynaecology and obstetrics and by 1940 she not only had a successful practice in Dundee but was Professor of Gynaecology and Midwifery at University College. Probably Dundee's best known heroine today, is world champion runner Liz McColgan, but Liz was not the only Dundonian to achieve fame at the 1996 London Marathon. While Liz was first over the line, Jenny Wood Allen, at the age of 84, was the oldest person to take part. That was her 24th marathon, completed in 7.5 hours, and she holds a number of world records for her age group.

Scots and read all over

Journalism is still big in Dundee. DC Thomson & Co. is the only Scottish-controlled company among Scotland's principal newspaper publishers. In the 1870s, William Thomson bought in to the Dundee newspaper industry. By 1886 he controlled it and made his son, DC Thomson, a partner. The family company now produces more than 260 million newspapers and magazines a year and is Britain's largest comic paper empire. Children all over Britain grew up with comic characters Dennis the Menace (born, 1951 in *The Beano* as a kind of 1950s Bart Simpson) and Desperate Dan of *The Dandy* (born 1937). *The Dundee Courier and Advertiser* is one of the most successful provincial newspapers in Britain, with daily sales around 115,000. The *Sunday Post* is in the *Guiness Book of Records* as the 'Most Read Newspaper', with an estimated readership of six out of ten of the entire population of Scotland, aged 15 and over. This is not due to its insissive journalism, but rather to the popularity of the family cartoons *Oor Wullie* and *The Broons,* whose couthy comments and asinine antics are adored the world over.

than walking, to the spectacular jagged ridges of the Cuillins on Skye, which include the notorious 'inaccessible pinnacle' for which a rope is needed. The most southerly Munro is Ben Lomond, on Loch Lomond. Close to Glasgow, it can be busy in summer, but with a near sea-level start, it's a long day. Isolated Ben Hope is the most northerly Munro and a shorter walk. If size is not important Corbett-bagging can be equally rewarding. Corbetts are hills between 2,500 and 3,000 feet, which can offer shorter, but equally spectacular walks with fewer people. Considering that many of the Gaelic names translate as body parts – mamore means big breast and a toul is a penis – it is not particularly surprising that some couples are rising to the challenge of munro-shagging. Not, it must be said, a winter sport.

Scotland's hills are some of the world's oldest. Once they looked like the Himalayas. But, even if they're not as big now, the unpredictable weather can still make them dangerous. Whatever you choose to bag, respect the mountain. If you can't use a map or, more importantly, a compass, don't go if the cloud base is below 2,000 feet (600 meters). There won't be a view anyway. In winter take ice-axes, thermals, plenty of food, a survival bag and even crampons depending on the route. Always wear proper boots, take food and take a waterproof even if it's hot and sunny at the base of the hill. There are books on Munros and Corbetts, but these are no substitute for a map. Burn water is generally OK to drink. Above all, don't become obsessive. If, for instance, you want

to do six Munros in Knoidart, take a tent or stay in a bothy and do them in two days instead of one. Finally, always let someone know where you're going. Scotland's 26 mountain rescue teams cope with an average of 330 call-outs per year.

Directory

Facts and figures on Edinburgh, Glasgow and the Scottish experience: a research resource for planning and profiting from your stay.

Essential Information

This chapter contains information on visiting Scotland in general, plus essential contacts for visitors to Edinburgh. For Glasgow-specific information, *see page 264* **Glasgow Resources**.

Emergencies

In the event of a serious accident, fire or incident, call **999** and specify whether you require **ambulance, fire service** or **police**.

Consuls

For a list of foreign consular offices in Edinburgh consult the phone book or *Yellow Pages* and look under Consuls and/or Embassies.

American Consulate General

3 Regent Terrace, EH7 (556 8315/fax 557 6023). **Telephone enquiries** 8.30am-noon, 1-5pm, Mon-Fri. **Personal callers** (emergencies only) 1-4pm Mon-Fri or by appointment. **Map 4 H4**
Offers a limited service such as assistance with repatriation, return of bodies, hospitalisation and arrest, as well as giving out general information, advice and official forms. Does not issue visas or replacement passports. For replacement passports telephone 0171 499 9000; for visa enquiries telephone 0891 200 290 (calls charged at 50p per minute at all times). *e-mail: ch1congenedinburgh. demon.co.uk.*

Australian Consulate

555 4500.
A new Edinburgh office is due to be established by the end of 1998.

Meanwhile, calls to the number above will be automatically diverted to the Australian High Commission in London.

French Consulate General

11 Randolph Crescent, EH3 (general enquiries only 225 7954/fax 225 8975/visa enquiries 220 6324/visa enquiry line 0891 600 215 24 hours daily; calls cost 50p per minute/passports 225 3377/legal 220 0141). Haymarket buses.
Open visas 9.30am-12.30pm, passports/ID cards 9.30am-1pm, by appointment 2-5pm, Mon-Fri. **Map 5 L5**

Consulate General of the Federal Republic of Germany

16 Eglinton Crescent, EH12 (337 2323/fax 346 1578). Haymarket buses, then 10-min walk. **Open** 9am-noon, by appointment 1-5pm, Mon-Fri. **Map 5 B6**

Italian Consulate General

32 Melville Street, EH3 (226 3631/220 3695/fax 226 6260). Haymarket buses, then 5-min walk. **Telephone enquiries** 9.30am-5.30pm Mon-Fri. **Personal callers** 9.30am-12.30pm Mon-Fri.
An emergency service for Italian nationals only is offered 9.30am-12.30pm Sat. **Map 5 L5**

Spanish Consulate

63 North Castle Street, EH2 (220 1843/fax 226 4568). Princes St buses. **Telephone enquiries** 9am-4pm Mon-Fri. **Personal callers** 9am-12.30pm, 1-3pm, Mon-Fri. **Map 8 B1**

Customs

When entering the UK, non-EU citizens and anyone buying duty-free goods have the following import limits:

● 200 cigarettes or 100 cigarillos or 250 grams (8.82 ounces) of tobacco
● 2 litres still table wine plus either 1 litre spirits or strong liqueurs (over 22% alcohol by volume) or 2 litres fortified wine (under 22% abv), sparkling wine or other liqueurs
● 60cc/ml perfume
● 250cc/ml toilet water
● Other goods to the value of: £75 for EU citizens purchasing from another EU country or £145 for travellers arriving from outside the EU

The import of meat, poultry, fruit, plants, flowers and protected animals is restricted or forbidden; there are no restrictions on the import or export of currency.

Since the Single European Market agreement came into force at the beginning of 1993, people over the age of 17 arriving from an EU country have been able to import limit-less goods for their own personal use, if bought tax-paid (ie not duty-free).

However, the law sets out guidance levels for what is 'for personal use' (and it's not as much as you might expect or hope), so if you exceed them you must be able to satisfy officials that the goods are not for resale. Just remember, they've heard it all before.

HM Customs & Excise

Edinburgh Airport (344 3196). **Open** 6am-11pm daily.

Disabled travellers

The older parts of Edinburgh can be hard for wheelchair users to get around: listed buildings are not allowed to widen their entrances or add ramps, and parts of the Old Town have very narrow pavements. However, equal opportunity legislation requires new buildings to be fully accessible – step forward the **Festival Theatre** and the new **Museum of Scotland**. The newer taxis can all take wheelchairs and the bus fleet is gradually being upgraded to low-floor models, though currently the only reliable low-floorroute reliably plied by these is the No.66. For more information, contact one of the following organisations.

Disability Scotland
Princes House, 5 Shandwick Place, EH2 4RG (telephone enquiries 229 8632 9am-1pm Mon-Fri/fax 229 5168). Princes St buses. **Open** 9am-5pm Mon-Fri. **Map 5 C5**
Scotland's primary disabled agency can advise travellers on access and other facilities throughout the country. It can also refer you to specialist agencies.

Lothian Coalition of Disabled People
Norton Park, 5 Albion Road, EH7 (475 2360/fax 475 2392). **Telephone enquiries** 9am-5pm Mon-Fri.
The Coalition publishes the free *Access Guide* to Edinburgh, which does exactly what it says. Call to ask for a copy.

Insurance

You should arrange insurance to cover personal belongings before travelling, as it is difficult to organise once you have arrived. Non UK-citizens should ensure that medical insurance is covered in their travel insurance. If your country has a reciprocal medical treatment arrangement you will have limited cover, but you should make sure you have the necessary documentation before you arrive. If you cannot

access the information in your own country, contact the Primary Care Department in Edinburgh (536 9000).

Money

Britain's currency is pounds sterling (£). One pound equals 100 pence (p). 1p and 2p coins are copper; 5p, 10p, 20p and 50p coins are silver; the £1 coin is yellowy-gold; the £2 coin is silver with a yellowy-gold surround. There are three Scottish clearing banks, all of which issue their own paper notes: the Bank of Scotland, the Royal Bank of Scotland and the Clydesdale Bank. The colour of paper notes varies slightly between the three, but an approximation is as follows: green £1 (Scotland only; England and Wales have done away with the £1 note); blue £5; brown £10, purple/pink £20, red or green £50 and, unique to Scotland, a bold red £100. You can exchange foreign currency at banks or bureaux de change.

It's a good idea to try to use up all your Scottish currency before leaving the country: the further south you go, the more wary people will be of accepting it.

Banks

Banks have variable opening hours, depending on the day of the week. Minimum opening hours are 9am-4pm, but some are open until 5.30pm. Cashpoint machines, usually situated outside a bank or building society (most building societies operate as banks), give access to cash 24 hours a day.

Banks generally offer the best exchange rates, although they can vary considerably from place to place and it pays to shop around. Commission is sometimes charged for cashing travellers' cheques in foreign currencies, but not for sterling travellers' cheques, provided

you cash them at a bank affiliated to the issuing bank (get a list when you buy your cheques). Commission is charged if you change cash into another currency. You always need identification, such as a passport, when cashing travellers' cheques.

There are branches of the three Scottish clearing banks and cash machines throughout the city. There are, however, few branches of the English clearing banks. These are situated at:

Barclays Bank
1 St Andrew Square, EH2 (557 2733). Princes St buses. **Open** 9.30am-5pm Mon-Wed, Fri; 10am-5pm Thur. **Map 8 D1**

Lloyds Bank
113-115 George Street, EH2 (226 4021). George St buses. **Open** 9am-5pm Mon-Tue, Thur-Fri; 9.30am-5pm Wed. **Map 8 B1**

Midland Bank
76 Hanover Street, EH2 (456 3200). Princes St buses. **Open** 9.30am-4.30pm Mon-Fri. **Map 8 C1**

National Westminster Bank
80 George Street, EH2 (226 6181). George St buses. **Open** 9am-5.30pm Mon, Tue, Thur, Fri; 9.30am-5.30pm Wed. **Map 8 C1**

Bureaux de change

You will be charged for cashing travellers' cheques or buying and selling foreign currency at a bureau de change. Commission rates, which should be clearly displayed, vary.

Banks, travel companies and the major rail stations have bureaux de change, and there are many in tourist areas. Most are open standard business hours (9am-5.30pm Mon-Fri), but one which is open longer is FEXCO Ltd, situated inside the **Edinburgh and Scotland Information Centre** (*see below* **Tourist information**).

Lost/stolen credit cards

Report lost or stolen credit cards immediately to both the police and the 24-hour services

Directory

listed below. Inform your bank by phone and in writing.

American Express *(personal card 01273 696 933/corporate card 01273 689 955).*

Diners Club/Diners Club International *(general enquiries & emergencies 01252 513 500/0800 460 800).*

Eurocard *(00 49 697 933 1910). This German number will accept reversed charges in an emergency.*

JCB *(0171 499 3000).*

MasterCard *(0800 964 767).*

Visa *(0800 895 082).*

Money transfers

The information centre above the **Waverley Shopping Centre** can advise on Western Union money transfer. Alternatively contact your own bank to find out which British banks it is affiliated with; you can then nominate an Edinburgh branch to have the money sent to.

Western Union
0800 833 833.

Police & security

The police are a good source of information about the locality and are used to helping visitors find their way around. If you have been robbed, assaulted or involved in an infringement of the law, look under 'Police' in the phone directory for the nearest police station, or call directory enquiries (free from public payphones) on 192.

Dial 999 only in an emergency.

If you have a complaint to make about the police, be sure to take the offending officer's ID number, which should be prominently displayed on his or her epaulette.

You can then register a complaint at any police station, visit a solicitor or Citizens' Advice Bureau or contact The Complaints Department, Police Headquarters, Lothian and Borders Police, Fettes Avenue, Edinburgh, EH4 1RB (311 3377).

Violent crime is relatively rare in Edinburgh, but, as in any major city, it is unwise to take any risks. Thieves and pickpockets specifically target unwary tourists. Use common sense and follow these basic rules:
● Keep your wallet and purse out of sight. Don't wear a wrist wallet (they are easily snatched). Keep your handbag securely closed.
● Don't leave a handbag, briefcase, bag or coat unattended, especially in pubs, cinemas, department stores or fast food shops, on public transport, at railway stations and airports, or in crowds.
● Don't leave your bag or coat beside, under or on the back of your chair.
● Don't wear expensive jewellery or watches that can be easily snatched.
● Don't put your purse down on the table in a restaurant or on a shop counter while you scrutinise the bill.
● Don't carry a wallet in your back pocket.
● Don't flash your money or credit cards around.
● Avoid parks after dark. Late at night, try to travel in groups of three or more.

Postal services

Compared to some other countries, the UK has a reliable postal service. If you have a query on any aspect of Royal Mail services contact Customer Services on 0345 740 740/fax 550 8360 (Edinburgh) or 0345 740 740/fax 0141 242 4120 (Glasgow). Lines open 8am-8pm Mon-Fri; 8.30am-12.30pm Sat. For business enquiries contact the Royal Mail Business Centre for Scotland on 0345 950 950/fax 0141 242 4652. Lines open 8am-6pm Mon-Thur; 8am-5.30pm Fri. You can ask for a Royal Mail Fact File and any post office leaflets to be sent to you.

Post office opening hours are usually 9am-5.30pm Mon-Fri; 9am-12.30pm Sat, with the exception of St James Post Office (8-10 Kings Mall, St James Centre, EH1; 556 0478; Princes St buses), which is open 9am-5.30pm Mon; 8.30am-5.30pm Tue-Fri; 8.30am-6pm Sat. Listed below are the main central offices. Consult the phone book for other offices within Edinburgh:

Hope Street Post Office *7 Hope Street, EH2 4EN (226 6823). Princes St buses.* **Map 8 A1**

Frederick Street Post Office *40 Frederick Street, EH2 (226 6937). Princes St buses.* **Map 8 B1**

Poste restante

If you intend to travel around Britain, friends from home can write to you care of a post office, where mail will be kept at the enquiry desk for up to one month. The envelope should be marked 'Poste Restante' in the top left-hand corner, with your name displayed above the address of the post office where you want to collect your mail. Take ID when you collect your mail. The Hope Street office offers this service.

Stamp prices

You can buy stamps at post offices and at any newsagents that display the appropriate red sign. Stamps can be bought individually (post offices only) or, in the case of first class (for next-day delivery within mainland Britain) or second class (two- to three-day delivery time in mainland Britain), in books of four or ten. At the time of writing (June 1998), prices were 20p for second-class letters (inland only) and 26p for first-class inland letters and letters up to 20g in weight to EU countries. Postcards cost 26p to send within the EU and 31p to countries outside Europe. Rates for other letters and parcels vary according to weight and destination.

Express delivery services

All companies can arrange pick-up.

DHL
Unit 15/4-15/5 South Gyle Crescent, South Gyle Industrial Estate, EH12 (0345 100 300). South Gyle rail. **Open** 24 hours daily. **Credit** AmEx, DC, MC, V.
Worldwide express delivery service. Next-day deliveries can be made within the EU (not guaranteed), and the USA if booked before 2pm.

Federal Express
c/o Securicor, 23 South Gyle Crescent, South Gyle Industrial Estate, EH12 (0800 123 800). South Gyle rail. **Open** 24 hours daily. **Credit** AmEx, MC, V.
FedEx can deliver next day by 8am to certain destinations across the USA (mainly New York and other major cities). More than 210 countries are served.

UPS
30 South Gyle Crescent, South Gyle Industrial Estate, EH12 (0345 877 877/fax 316 2920).
South Gyle rail. **Open** 8am-8pm Mon-Fri; 9am-2pm Sat. **Credit** AmEx, MC, V.
UPS offers express delivery to more than 200 countries; cheaper, slower services are also available. Deliveries to some destinations can be guaranteed to arrive by 8.30am or 10.30am the next day.

Public holidays

On public holidays (known as bank holidays) many shops remain open, but public transport services are less frequent. The exception is Christmas Day, when almost everything closes down.

Public Holiday Mon 21 Sept 1998; Mon 20 Sept 1999.
Christmas Day Fri 25 Dec 1998; Sat 25 Dec 1999.
Boxing Day Sat 26 Dec 1998; Sun 26 Dec 1999.
Bank Holiday Mon 28 Dec 1998; Mon 27 Dec 1999.
New Year's Day Fri 1 Jan 1999; Sat 1 Jan 2000.
Bank Holiday Mon 4 Jan 1999; Mon 3 Jan 2000.
Good Friday Fri 2 Apr 1999; Fri 21 Apr 2000.
Easter Monday Mon 5 Apr 1999; Mon 24 Apr 2000.
May Day Holiday Mon 3 May 1999; Mon 2 May 2000.

Victoria Day (Spring Bank Holiday) Mon 31 May 1999; Mon 30 May 2000.

Public toilets

The Mound
Princes Street, EH2. **Open** 10am-10pm Mon-Sun. Disabled access 24 hours using National Key Scheme. **Map 8 C2**

Waverley Shopping Centre
Waverley Bridge, EH1. **Open** 10am-10pm daily. **Map 8 D2**

Telephones

The code for Edinburgh is 0131. If you're calling from outside the UK, dial the international code, followed by 44 (code for Britain), then the ten-digit number starting with 131 (omitting the first 0). The code for the Glasgow area is 0141.

International dialling codes
Australia 00 61; **Belgium** 00 32; **Canada** 00 1; **France** 00 33; **Germany** 00 49; **Ireland** 00 353; **Italy** 00 39; **Japan** 00 81; **Netherlands** 00 31; **New Zealand** 00 64; **Spain** 00 34; **USA** 00 1.

Operator services

Operator
Call **100** for the operator in the following circumstances: when you have difficulty in dialling; for an early-morning alarm call (not cheap); to make a credit card call; for information about the cost of a call; and for international person-to-person calls. Dial **155** if you need to reverse the charges (call collect) or if you can't dial direct. Be warned, this service is very expensive.

Directory enquiries
Dial **192** for any number in Britain, or **153** for international numbers. Phoning directory enquiries from a private phone is expensive, and only two enquiries are allowed per call. If you phone from a public call box, directory enquiries calls are free.

International telemessages/telegrams
Call **0800 190 190** to phone in your message and it will be delivered by post the next day (£8.99 for up to 50 words, an additional £1 for a greetings card). There is no longer a domestic telegram service, but you can still send telegrams abroad. Call the same number.

Public phones

Public payphones take coins, credit cards or prepaid phonecards (and sometimes all three). The minimum cost is 10p, but some payphones (such as counter-top ones found in many pubs) require a minimum of 20p.

British Telecom phonecards
From post offices & many newsagents. **Cost** 10p per unit; cards in denominations of £2, £5, £10 and £20.
Call boxes with the green Phonecard symbol take prepaid cards. A notice in the box tells you where to find the nearest stockist. A digital display shows how many units you have remaining on your card.

Telephone directories

There is one alphabetical phone directory for Edinburgh; it lists business and commercial numbers as well as private phone numbers and is available at post offices and libraries. Hotels will also have them and they are issued free to all residents with telephones, as is the *Yellow Pages* directory, which lists businesses and services.

Time & the seasons

Every year in spring (28 March 1999, 26 March 2000) Scotland, in common with the rest of the UK, puts its clocks forward by one hour to give British Summer Time (BST). In autumn (25 Oct 1998, 31 Oct 1999, 29 Oct 2000) the clocks go back by one hour to rejoin Greenwich Mean Time (GMT).

The British climate is unpredictable. For daily, updated forecasts for the British Isles and international holiday destinations ring Weather Check on 0891 333 111 (50p per minute at all times).

Thanks to its coastal situation, Edinburgh has a temperate climate, and escapes

Directory

Scots, as she is spoke

The Scottish tongue is a whole language to itself and its regional variations are legendary. The Edinburgh vernacular is constantly being transformed by incomers from all over Scotland.

Barry – good, excellent, attractive. A general term of acclaim.
Bampot – a nutter.
Ben – the back room of the house.
Chum – to accompany.
Couthy – plain or homely (of a person); agreeable, snug, comfortable (of a place).
Dod – a small amount, a dab. Often used in conjunction with 'wee'.
Douce – kind, gentle, soothing (pejoratively – sedate).
Dreich – wet, dull, tedious, dreary– of the weather or a person. The 'ch' is pronounced as in the German composer Bach.
Eejit – a fool (pejorative).
Gallus – cheeky, self-confident or daring. In Glasgow: stylish or impressive.
Get – to go with (as in the phrase 'shall I get you down the road?').
Haar – sea mist, especially from the North Sea.
Hen – a female (informal).
Ken – know, understand – also interpolated (seemingly at random) into speech.
Laldy – as in the folk music phrase 'to give it laldy' – to play vigorously.
Loch – a lake. There are only two lakes in Scotland.
Lugs – ears.
Messages – shopping, groceries.
Nash – to leave precipitously (as in 'I better nash, the pub's about to close').
Oxter – armpit.
Pished – drunk.
Radge – barmy, mad, a bit too extrovert for comfort.
Scran – food.
See – take, for example (as in 'see that wee jimmy, he's well radge'.
See you! – 'Hey!', 'Oi you!' or 'I say, old chap!'
Slater – woodlouse.
Stay – place of habitation (as in 'where do you stay?').
Stushie – a fight, an altercation.
Teuchter – someone from the Highlands (pejorative).
Wee – small, a small quantity.
Weejie – a Glaswegian (highly derogatory).
Youze – the plural of 'you'.

the low winter temperatures of the Highlands. It's cold, but it rarely snows or freezes for very long. Equally, summers are fairly dry and seldom uncomfortably hot, though they're often cloudy. The weather can change abruptly, so it's a good idea to bring a rainproof and extra layer even in summer. In January the average minimum temperature is 2°C and the maximum 6°C; in July the figures are 10° and 18°C. Glasgow is noticeably warmer year-round but notoriously wet.

Tipping

In Britain it is accepted that you tip in taxis, minicabs, restaurants (some waiting staff are forced to rely heavily on gratuities), hairdressers, hotels and some bars (not pubs) – 10 to 15 per cent is normal. Be careful to check whether service has been added automatically to your bill – some restaurants include service and then also leave the space for gratuity on your credit card slip.

Tourist information

The Edinburgh and Lothians Tourist Board operates the information centres listed below. You can also access information on 24-hour electronic information units found at the Edinburgh and Scotland Information Centre and in Rutland Place at the west end of Princes Street. Alternatively, visit the Tourist Board website: *http://www.edinburgh.org* For more websites, *see page 257* **Internet**.

Edinburgh and Scotland Information Centre

above Waverley Shopping Centre, 3 Princes Street EH 1 (473 3800). Princes St buses. **Open** *Oct-Apr* 9am-6pm Mon-Sat; 10am-6pm Sun; *May, June, Sept* 9am-7pm Mon-Sat; 10am-7pm Sun; *July-Aug* 9am-8pm Mon-Sat; 10am-8pm Sun.
Map 8 D2

Edinburgh Airport Tourist Information Desk

Edinburgh Airport, EH12 (333 2167). **Open** *Apr-Oct* 8.30am-9.30pm Mon-Sat; 9.30am-9.30pm Sun; *Nov-Mar* 9am-6pm Mon-Fri; 9am-5pm Sat; 9.30am-5pm Sun.

Visas

Citizens of EU countries do not require a visa to visit the UK; citizens of other countries, including the USA, Canada and New Zealand, require only a valid passport for a visit of up to six months.

To apply for a visa, and to check your visa status **before you travel**, contact the British Embassy, High Commission or Consulate in your own country.

A visa allows you entry for a maximum of six months. For information about work permits *see below* **Working in Edinburgh**.

Home Office

Immigration & Nationality Department, Lunar House, 40 Wellesley Road, Croydon, CR9 2BY (0181 686 0688).
Telephone enquiries 9am-4.45pm Mon-Wed; 10am-4.45pm Thur; 9am-4.30pm Fri.
The immigration department of the Home Office deals with all queries about immigration matters, visas and work permits for citizens from the Commonwealth and a few other countries. Croydon, in case you're wondering, is south of London.

Getting Around Edinburgh

Edinburgh is best explored on foot to fully appreciate the beauty, elegance, charm and contrasts of the city centre and its environs. To the south of Princes Street, the Old Town is characterised by narrow wynds and tortuous stairways. The more spacious and orderly New Town, north of Princes Street, is set out according to a grid plan and offers some spectacular views across the Firth of Forth towards Fife.

Walking around Edinburgh is safe and can provide a rewarding experience, but do exercise the usual caution at night (*see chapter* **Edinburgh Resources: women**). Individuals with a nervous disposition should avoid the areas of the city with abundant and rowdy nightlife such as Lothian Road and the Cowgate.

A useful way to orient yourself and to get an overview of the major tourist sights is on one of the guided bus tours (*see below*) or themed walking tours (*see chapter* **Royal Mile**). Since the introduction of the Greenways scheme (*see below*), getting around the centre of Edinburgh by bus has become faster and more reliable; an extensive network of bus routes ensures that most of the city is easily accessible.

Driving around Edinburgh (*see below*) can be more hassle than it's worth, especially as city-centre parking can prove problematic; taxis are numerous, if rather pricey; and cycling is a fast and efficient way of getting around, both in the city centre and further afield (*see box page 254*).

Arrival/departure
By air

Edinburgh Airport
333 1000.

Situated 10 miles to the west of the city centre, Edinburgh Airport is about 20 minutes' drive from Princes Street. The airport services flights from the Continent and English airports. Flights leave Edinburgh for the north and Highlands and Islands of Scotland.

The quickest way to travel from the airport is by Edinburgh Airport Taxis (344 3344/3153). The service covers every flight in and out of the airport (approx 5am-11pm); journey time is 15-20 minutes, although this rises to 30 minutes during rush hours (7.30-9am and 4.30-6pm). The fare is about £12, depending on time of day and number of passengers. All taxis have one seat adapted for disabled passengers.

Two fast, frequent (about every 15 minutes) and reliable bus services travel between the airport and Waverley Bridge. Both operate seven days a week, with a journey time of about 30 minutes. All timetables and prices are subject to change, so phone to check current information.

Airline 100
555 6363.
These blue and white buses stop at Gogarburn, Maybury, Corstorphine, Edinburgh Zoo, Murrayfield and the West End. Buses leave the airport 6.30am-10.30pm Mon-Fri; 7.30am-10.30pm Sat, Sun; the service from Waverley Bridge runs 6am-10pm Mon-Fri; 6.45am-10pm Sat, Sun. Buses are double-deckers with ample luggage space. Collapsible wheelchairs can be carried but, due to union regulations, staff are unable to physically assist disabled customers (for safety reasons). **Tickets** £3.20 adult/£2 child (5-16) one way; £5 adult/£3.40 child day return; free under-5s; Airline Day Saver £4 adult/£2.65 child – allows one journey to or from the airport and unlimited travel for a day over most of the Lothian Regional Transport (LRT) bus network (*see below*).

Airbus Express
Operated by Guide Friday (556 2244).
Green and cream buses. Stop at

Ingliston, Gogarburn, Maybury, Drum Brae, Corstorphine, Edinburgh Zoo, Murrayfield, Roseburn, Haymarket and the West End. Buses leave the airport 8.37am-8.35pm Mon-Fri; 8.37am-7.35pm Sat; 8.37am-8.35pm Sun; services to the airport from Waverley Bridge run 7.45am-8pm Mon-Fri, Sun; 7.45am-7pm Sat. **Tickets** £3.50 single, £5.50 return; £1.50 5-12s single, free under-5s. Keep your Airbus tickets to receive a discount off the full price of a Guide Friday tour (*see below*). Buses have generous luggage space; staff will assist disabled passengers.

By coach

St Andrew Square Bus Station
Clyde Street, EH1. **Map 8 D1**
Coaches arriving in Edinburgh from England and Wales are run by Britain's most extensive coach network, National Express (0990 80 80 80). Coaches serving the whole of Scotland are run by Scottish Citylink (0990 50 50 50). Located in the city centre, the bus station is not a place to linger long, but is not far from Edinburgh's extensive bus network, taxis or Waverley Station.

By train

Waverley Station
Waverley Bridge EH1 (train information 0345 48 49 50). **Map 8 D2**
Edinburgh's central railway station serves the East Coast main line to London, as well as connections to the West Coast main line via Glasgow. Scotrail services leave Waverley for stations throughout Scotland. Local services go to East and West Lothian.

Haymarket Station
Haymarket, EH12 (train information 0345 48 49 50). Haymarket buses. **Map 5 B6**
On the main line to Glasgow. Most trains north from Waverley stop here, as well as local services to West Lothian.

Public transport

Travelling by bus, cycle or taxi around Edinburgh has become faster and more efficient since the introduction of the first phase of Edinburgh City Council's Greenways scheme in August 1997. With two

Directory

Bus basics

Throughout this guide, we have listed Edinburgh's buses as follows: 8(A/B) indicates that the number 8 bus, plus numbers 8A and 8B, will take you where you want to go; 8A indicates that only the 8A goes that way. Where several buses follow the same route for much of their journey, we have grouped them together as listed below. All buses listed are operated by Lothian Regional Transport.

Princes St buses: 2, 3, 4, 11, 12, 15, 16, 17, 21, 25, 26, 30, 33, 36, 37, 38, 43, 44, 63, 69, 85, 86.

Bridges buses: 3, 7, 8, 9, 14, 21, 30, 31, 33, 36, 62, 64, 69, 80, 87, 88.

George IV Bridge buses: 23, 27, 28, 37, 40, 41, 42, 45, 46, 47.

George St buses: 13, 19, 34, 35, 39, 40, 41, 43, 47, 55, 82.

Leith Walk buses: 2, 7, 10, 11, 12, 14, 16, 17, 22, 25, 87, 88.

Haymarket buses: 2, 3, 4, 12, 18, 21, 22, 25, 26, 30, 31, 33, 36, 37, 38, 43, 44, 61, 63, 66, 69, 85, 86.

Great Junction St buses: 1, 6, 7, 10, 14, 17, 22, 25, 87, 88.

Bruntsfield buses: 11, 15, 16, 17, 23, 37, 45.

London Road buses: 4, 5, 15, 26, 43, 44, 45, 51, 63, 66, 75, 85, 86.

Dalry Road buses: 2, 3, 4, 12, 21, 22, 25, 28, 30, 33, 43, 44, 61, 65, 66.

Greenways routes to the east and west of the city centre, the scheme encourages the use of public transport by improving the reliability of bus services and cutting journey times by 10 per cent. In the long term it aims to create a fully integrated public transport system that will reduce city-centre congestion, pollution and road accidents.

Greenways lanes are painted green with red road markings showing when and where stopping is permitted; buses, licensed taxis and cycles all have unrestricted access to green lanes at all times. Private vehicles have restricted access during rush hours and at peak times. The City Council hopes that by investing in 'green' buses, encouraging the use of public transport and discouraging the use of private vehicles, Edinburgh's poor air quality will improve.

Cyclists say that the green lanes are faster and safer but during rush hours buses and taxis have a tendency to crowd cyclists when they overtake on the left.

Disabled travellers

For travellers with mobility difficulties, Edinburgh City Council publishes the booklet *Transport in Edinburgh: A Guide for Disabled People*. This gives information on transport accessibility and services and assistance available to disabled people; it also includes a list of useful contact addresses and phone numbers. The booklet can be picked up free of charge from Lothian Regional Transport Travelshops (*see below*) or

requested from Traveline on 0800 23 23 23 (local calls) or 225 3858 (national calls). In addition, the Lothian Coalition of Disabled People, 8 Lochend Road, EH6 (555 2151) may be able to give information and advice.

Lothian Regional Transport is gradually replacing all its buses with low-floor versions, but currently the only route with a reliable low-floor service is the No.66 along Princes Street.

Buses

Edinburgh has extensive bus networks that give ready access to most of the city by day and night. The ubiquitous maroon and white buses are run by Lothian Regional Transport (LRT), which has a 24-hour, seven-day telephone enquiry service, Traveline, on 0800 23 23 23 (local calls) or 225 3858 (national calls).

LRT Travelshops provide free maps and details of all local public transport services in Lothian, and they can be found at:

LRT Travelshops
27 Hanover Street EH2 (554 4494). Princes St buses. **Open** 8.30am-6pm Mon-Sat. **Map 8 C1**
Waverley Bridge. Princes St buses. **Open** *May-Oct* 8am-7.15pm Mon-Sat; 9am-4.30pm Sun; *Nov-April* 9am-4.30pm Tue-Sat. **Map 8 D2**

Edinburgh's other main bus company is FirstBus, which incorporates SMT, Eastern Scottish, Lowland Omnibuses and Midland Scottish. For information call 663 9233.

Fares & travelcards

Bus fares are based on a stage system; fare stages are listed on individual service timetables. Bus drivers won't give change, so ensure you have the correct fare before boarding. There is no on-the-spot fine for travelling without a valid ticket or pass but action may be taken later.

Adult fares

Single tickets start from 50p (1-2 stages), and for this you will be able to travel around most of the city centre. Travelling 3-8 stages costs 65p; 9-13 stages 85p; 14-21 stages £1.10; 22-27 stages £1.30; 28 or more stages £1.50. A Day Saver Ticket, purchased from the bus driver of the first bus you board, costs £2.20 and allows unlimited travel around the LRT network for a day.

Child fares

Children under five travel free (up to a maximum of two children per adult passenger). Children's fares are charged for ages 5 to 15 inclusive. Photo ID cards, if desired, can be purchased for the cost of £1 from the LRT Travelshop at 27 Hanover Street upon production of a birth certificate. Child fares are 50p for 1-13 stages and 70p for 14 or more. Child Day Saver tickets are £1.50.

Travel passes

If you plan to take several bus journeys during your stay, the most economical way to travel is to buy a Ridacard. These give unlimited travel on ordinary LRT services but are not valid on night buses, services to special events, Airline 100 buses or tours. For adults, a one-week Ridacard costs £10, 2 weeks £20, 4 weeks £29; Junior Ridacards (ages 5-15 inclusive) are one-week £6, 2 weeks £12, 4 weeks £17. Purchase Ridacards at LRT Travelshops.

Touristcard

A Touristcard is more flexible for the visitor to Edinburgh than the Ridacard. In addition to unlimited travel on all LRT city bus services, including the **Edinburgh Classic Tour**, the Touristcard offers reductions on LRT coach tours and discounts on city restaurants and tourist attractions. The prices of Touristcards are: for 2 days £11 (£5.50 5-15s), 3 days £13 (£7 child), 4 days £15 (£8.50), 5 days £17 (£10), 6 days £19 (£11.50), 7 days £21 (£13). Prices, offers and concessions are likely to change so contact a Travelshop for information.

Tokens

LRT Travelshops sell travel tokens in denominations of 10p, 25p, 30p and 50p. If buying a Day Saver, Ridacard or Touristcard is not financially worthwhile, tokens can avoid the need to search for change.

Night buses

Night buses run seven days a week from about midnight-4am Mon-Thur, Sun nights and midnight-3am Fri, Sat. There is a flat fare of £1.50, which allows one transfer to be made to another night service at Waverley Bridge, on production of a valid ticket. A free map and timetable can be picked up at LRT Travelshops.

Sightseeing tours

Guide Friday (556 2244) and Edinburgh Classic Tour (run by LRT; 554 4494) both run sightseeing bus tours of the centre of Edinburgh, which leave from Waverley Bridge. They are a good way of seeing the middle of Edinburgh quickly and efficiently if you are short of time.

Scotrail

Most rail services in Scotland are run by Scotrail. Details of services and fares are available from **National Rail Enquiry Scheme** (0345 48 49 50, 24 hours daily). The information desk in Waverley Station (*see above*) has timetables and details of discount travel, season tickets and international travel.

Driving

In conjunction with the Greenways Scheme, a system of one-way streets and pedestrian-only areas is being introduced into central Edinburgh. This can make driving in the city centre frustrating.

Driving in Edinburgh can be a time-consuming, difficult business. Like other large cities, Edinburgh has many one-way streets; thus a good road map will be essential. The main thoroughfare through the city centre, Princes Street, has limited access for private vehicles and is best avoided if possible; a knock-on effect of the prohibition of private vehicles from Princes Street is that the surrounding roads are becoming increasingly busy, and slow-moving traffic is the norm, especially during the rush hours. In addition to overcrowded roads and traffic jams you will find stringent parking restrictions, and the whole driving process could well leave you feeling harassed and frustrated.

If you park illegally, you will probably get a £20 parking ticket; if your car is causing an obstruction, it will probably be towed away and impounded. The good news is that in Scotland the clamping of vehicles has been ruled illegal; don't let that lull you into a false sense of security, however, as traffic wardens patrol the city centre.

Vehicle removal

If your car has been impounded, expect to pay a stiff fine: a fee of £105 is levied for removal, plus a £12 storage fee for every day the vehicle remains uncollected. And of course you'll have to pay £20 for the parking ticket.

24-hour car parks

Greenside Car Park
Greenside Row, EH1 (558 3518). **Rates** £1.10 for 2 hours; £1.80 overnight (6pm-9am).**Map 4 G4**

National Car Parks
Castle Terrace, EH1 (229 2870). **Rates** 70p for 1 hour; £1.40 for 2 hours; £1.90 for 3 hours; £2.50 for 4 hours; £4.60 for 4-6 hours; £6.40 for 6-9 hours; £8 for up to 24 hours; £1 overnight (5pm-9am).**Map 6 D6**

St James Centre
EH1 (556 5066). **Rates** £1 for 2 hours; £1.70 for 3 hours; £2.70 for 4 hours; £4.20 for 5 hours; £8.25 for 5-7 hours; £13 for 7-9 hours; £16 for 9-24 hours. **Map 4 G4**

1 Festival Square
EH3 (229 9131). **Rates** £1.50 for 2 hours; £2.50 for 4 hours; £6 for 6 hours; £12 for 24 hours. **Map 8 A3**

Waverley Car Park
New Street, EH8 (557 8526). **Rates** £1 for 2 hours; £2.50 for 4-12 hours; £5 for 4-12 hours; £10 for 24 hours; £2 overnight (8pm-8am); £18 weekly permit. **Open** unlimited access 6am-10pm; between 10pm-6am access by pre-arrangement only. **Map 7 G5**

On your bike

Do not be put off by the hills: Edinburgh is a great place to cycle around thanks to some successful lobbying by the local cycle campaign, Spokes (232 Dalry Road, EH11, 313 2114, www.btinternet.com/~spokes/). The city council has invested wisely in both off-road cycle paths and road-edge cycle lanes. Although it is not compulsory for motorists to observe the latter, the lanes ease the flow of cyclists during rush hours and make some of the more tricky roads safer. Cyclists can travel freely along all the bus lanes – including Princes Street.

Admittedly, some of the hills are a bit strenuous – but it is quite acceptable to walk up them – and the strong winds in winter can make exposed spots like North Bridge rather treacherous. Be sensible when tethering a bike in the street: the Grassmarket, Rose Street and other pub-infested areas are prone to bouts of drunken vandalism and, as everywhere, theft is a problem. Otherwise, the only real worries are for those cyclists not on mountain bikes are the cobbled streets around the New Town, which can give buttocks a bit of a buffeting. From Frederick Street down towards Stockbridge is particularly numbing.

The joy of cycling in Edinburgh is that you can fly from one side of town to the other in minutes – even when the streets are blocked during the Festival. A bike also makes trips outside the city centre remarkably accessible. Spokes' Cycle Map shows all the cycle routes and cycle paths. There are good paths out to Crammond from Roseburn, out towards East Lothian, starting at the Innocent Cycle Path in Holyrood Park, and a bike is the perfect way to explore the Water of Leith walkway.

Edinburgh Bicycle Co-operative

8 Alvanley Terrace, Whitehouse Loan, EH9 (228 1368). **Open** *summer* 10am-7pm Mon-Fri; 10am-6pm, Sat-Sun; *winter* 10am-6pm Fri-Wed; 10am-7pm Thur.
Extensive equipment and own-brand bikes for sale. Repair service.

Edinburgh Cycle Hire & Bike Café

29 Blackfriars Street (off Royal Mile, opposite Holiday Inn Crowne Plaza) (556 5560 phone/fax). **Open** *Nov-Apr* 9am-6pm Mon-Sun; *May-Oct* 9am-9pm Mon-Sun. **Hire** From £10 first day; weekly rates and discounts available. **Deposit** £100 per bike. **Credit** AmEx, DC, MC, V (for deposit); cash/cheque preferred for rental.
Mountain bikes, road bikes, city tourers and tandems are all available – with helmets and locks included as standard – plus panniers, trailers, and lightweight tents. All women's models are fitted with anatomically-designed gel saddles, which can also be mounted on men's bikes. In addition to renting you the pedal-power, staff can also sell you maps, suggest routes and offer a range of day excursions and longer tour-packages to suit all pockets. A drop-in cafe offers loan of repair kits, informed advice and a space to hang out with other cyclists.

Central Cycle Hire

11 Lochrin Place (228 6333). **Open** *Nov-Apr* 10am-5.30pm Mon-Sat; *May-Oct* 9am-7pm Mon-Sat. **Hire** £10 first day; £20 second day; £50 seven days. **Deposit** £100 per bike. **Credit** V, MC.
A wide range of cycles, helmets, child seats, trailers, car racks; maps and guides for sale.

Sandy Gilchrist Cycles

1 Cadzow Place, Abbeyhill (652 1760). **Open** 9am-5.30pm Mon-Wed, Fri-Sat; 9am-7pm Thur.
Hires out mountain bikes, plus a range of accessories.

Breakdown services

If you are a member of a motoring organisation in your home country, check to see if it has a reciprocal agreement with a British organisation.

AA (Automobile Association)

Fanum House, 18/22 Melville Street, EH1 (enquiries 0990 444 444/breakdown 0800 887 766/insurance 0800 444 777/new membership 0800 919 595). **Open** 24 hours daily.
Credit MC, V.
You can call the AA if you break down and become a member on the spot for £90. The first year's

roadside service membership starts at £40. **Map 5 C5**

Environmental Transport Association

Freepost KT 4021, Weybridge, Surrey, KT13 8RS (0193 282 8882). **Open** *office* 8am-6pm Mon-Fri; 9am-4pm Sat. *Breakdown service* 24 hours daily. **Credit** AmEx, DC, MC, V.
The green alternative, if you don't want part of your membership fees used for lobbying the government into building more roads, as happens with the AA and RAC. Basic membership is £20 per year for individuals and £25 for families.

RAC

Great Park Road, Bristol, BS12 4QN (enquiries 0345 331 133/breakdown 0800 828 282/motor insurance 0800 678 000/new membership 0800 550 550). **Open** *office* 9am-5pm Mon-Fri; *breakdown service* 24 hours daily. **Credit** AmEx, DC, MC, V.
Membership costs from £39 to £130, plus £75 for European cover.

Taxis

Black cabs

Edinburgh's licensed taxis are black cabs. When a taxi's yellow For Hire sign is switched on, it can be hailed in the street. Many taxi companies have credit card facilities, but check when you book or get in.

Taxis can be found in the *Yellow Pages*; a selection of the larger companies, all of which have facilities for the disabled traveller and offer a 24-hour service, are:
Capital Castle Taxis *228 2555*
Central Radio Taxis *229 2468*
City Cabs *228 1211*
Edinburgh Taxis *228 8989*
Radio Cabs *225 9000*

Minicabs

Minicabs (saloon cars) are generally cheaper than black cabs, but the drivers are unlicensed and may be uninsured; mini cabs are not permitted to use the Greenways routes. The following private-hire companies have facilities for disabled passengers. It's a good idea to call round to get the best price.
Bluebird Private Hire *467 7770*
Dunedin Private Hire *229 6661*
Leith Private Hire *555 6556*
Persevere Private Hire *552 2322/555 3377*

Complaints or compliments about a taxicab or private hire company journey can be made to The Cab Inspector, The Cab Office, 33 Murrayburn Road, Wester Hailes, Edinburgh, EH14 2TF (529 5800). Make a note of the date and time of the journey and the licence number of the vehicle.

Transport hire

Cars

To hire a car you must have at least one year's driving experience and be in possession of a current full driving licence with no serious endorsements. Overseas visitors, particularly those whose national driving licence is not readily readable by English speakers, are recommended to acquire an International Driving Licence before travel.

Prices for car hire vary, and may be subject to change, so ring round to find the deal that suits you best. A few of

the more reputable companies are given below. Check exactly what insurance is included in the price.

National Car Rental

(central reservations 0990 365 365, 24 hours daily). Branches at Edinburgh Airport (333 1922), Edinburgh City (337 8686). **Credit** AmEx, DC, MC, V.
A wide range of manual and automatic vehicles, one-way rates and a delivery and collection service. Cheapest rental, all inclusive, is £37.28 per day; £83.43 weekend; £218.96 seven days. To hire, you must be between 21-75.

Hertz

(central reservations 0990 996 699, 24 hours daily). Branches at Edinburgh Airport (333 1019), Edinburgh City (556 8311/8312) and Waverley Station (557 5272). **Credit** AmEx, DC, MC, V.
Services available include a wide range of manual and automatic vehicles, corporate accounts, one-way rates, collection and delivery. Cheapest rental, all inclusive, is £33.52 per day; £94.36 weekend; £214.11 seven days. You must be 25 or over to hire here.

Arnold Clark

553 Gorgie Road EH11 (444 1852). **Open** 8am-8pm Mon-Fri; 8am-5pm Sat; 11am-5pm Sun. **Credit** AmEx, DC, MC, V.
A full range of vehicles is available for hire. One-way rates upon request; corporate accounts; free courtesy coach to and from Edinburgh Airport. Cheapest rental rates are £16 per day; £39 weekend; £112 seven days. You must be between 23 and 75 to hire here; a deposit of £100 is required. See the phone book for other branches.

Cycles

See box page 254.

Motorbikes

Alvins

9B Springfield Street (off Leith Walk), EH6 (555 1039/fax 553 3093). **Open** 9am-5.30pm Mon-Fri; 9am-7pm Thur; 9am-5pm Sat. **Deposit** £50 booking deposit (non-refundable); £350 on credit card before collection. **Credit** MC, V. **Map 4 H1**
You will need a full driving licence, and you must be aged 25 or over to hire from here. Hire rates are inclusive of VAT, insurance and breakdown recovery service. Waterproofs and luggage may be hired, but you will need to purchase

or bring your own helmet. Other services offered here are bike sales, parts and accessories and a workshop. Sample hire rates are: GS 500 Suzuki £55 per day (aged 30 and over), £65 per day (25-29 years); for a RG 900 Suzuki £80 per day (30 years and over), £90 per day (25-29 years). Harley-Davidson rates on request.

Left luggage

Edinburgh Airport
333 1000.
There is a left luggage facility located outside the main terminal building, opposite parking zone E. Open 6am-10pm daily.

Waverley Train Station
550 2711.
24-hour left luggage facility adjacent to Platform 11.

St Andrews Bus Station
Left luggage lockers are located beside Platform A1; 24-hour access.

Lost property

Always inform the nearest police station if you lose anything (to validate insurance claims). A lost passport should also be reported to your embassy.

Airport

Edinburgh Airport
333 1000. **Open** 6am-10pm daily.
The lost property office is located outside the main terminal building, opposite parking zone E. For items lost on the plane, contact the airline or handling agents.

Bus

Lothian Region Transport
Lost Property Office, 1-4 Shrub Place, Leith Walk EH6 (554 4492). **Open** 10am-1.30pm Mon-Fri. **Map 4 H2**

Railway stations

If items have been lost in railway stations or trains in Scotland, contact:
Scotrail *(0141 332 9811).* **Open** 24 hours daily.

Taxis

Edinburgh Police Headquarters
Fettes Avenue, EH4 (311 3141). **Open** 9am-5pm Mon-Fri.
All property that has been lost in a registered, licensed black cab gets sent here.

Directory

Media

Most of Scotland's newspapers – and much of its TV output – operate on a quasi-national basis, pitched somewhere between the regional media and London's self-styled 'national' press.

The attitudes and arguments on display both reflect and illuminate the current state of that nebulous beast known as Scottish identity. From the time-honoured east/west rivalry – perpetuated in the battle between *The Scotsman*, published in Edinburgh, and the Glasgow-based *Herald* for the title of Scotland's national broadsheet daily – to the thorny question of the tabloid *Daily Record*'s Rangers affiliations; from Radio Scotland's Sony award-winning output to the famously surreal couthiness of the *Sunday Post* letters page, the cultural divergences that impelled the long campaign for devolution continue to pervade the Scottish media.

Print

Newspapers

The Scotsman

Edinburgh-based broadsheet. Somewhat more establishment in tone than its Glasgow rival, but recent new ownership has shifted its editorial line towards the mid-market. *www.scotsman.com*

The Herald

Glasgow-based broadsheet. Has the edge in terms of news coverage (though many would argue the opposite, and the balance shifts back and forth in any case) and certainly enjoying the upper hand in terms of sales. Any Glasgow bias in its arts and features coverage complements *The Scotsman*'s east-coast orientation. *www.theherald.co.uk*

Daily Record

Glasgow-based tabloid. Scotland's best selling daily is now published by the Mirror Group. Lots of froth but some good campaigning journalism. *www.record-mail.co.uk*

Evening News

Edinburgh's evening daily tabloid. The latest headlines from around the world are combined with a strong local Edinburgh flavour. On Saturday the *Pink* carries all the sports results.

Evening Times

Glasgow's daily evening tabloid.

Scotland on Sunday

The Scotsman's sister publication, enjoying the status of 'Scotland's only quality Sunday newspaper'. Has come under fire for frothing up/dumbing down its style under the new regime. Good analysis of Scottish issues.

Sunday Mail

Sunday sister to the *Daily Record*, with which it shares strong sports coverage and a campaigning instinct.

Sunday Post

This Dundee-published Sunday treat that was once a by-word for couthy tittle tattle and reactionary opinion has become increasingly – and blandly – like the other Sunday tabloids of late. At least it's still the home of the Oor Wullie comic strip.

Sunday Times

London-based pioneer of the 'supermarket' approach to Sunday newspapers. Its ever-expanding multi-section format includes a reasonable Scottish supplement, *Ecosse*, comprising features, reviews and listings.

Magazines

Chapman

Established for more than a quarter of a century and currently appearing four times annually, *Chapman* is a highly regarded platform for new writing (fiction and poetry) as well as offering reviews and general debate on contemporary Scottish culture.

Cencrastus

Subtitled 'Scottish and International Literature, Arts and Affairs', this thrice-yearly publication has been moving in a more satirical direction of late, doubtless sharpening its teeth for the advent of the Scottish Parliament.

Edinburgh Review

By far the oldest of Edinburgh's literary magazines, founded in 1802, the *Review* now appears twice a year and features fiction, poetry, criticism and literary/cultural argument.

Gay Scotland

Having switched from its former colour-magazine format, this Edinburgh-based publication now appears as a monthly tabloid, distributed free, covering events related to the lesbian and gay community, as well as comprehensive entertainment listings.

Listings

The List

Fortnightly listings magazine for Edinburgh and Glasgow (published Thursdays). Most visitors to either city will find that a copy of this local arts and listings magazine will provide many a valuable shortcut when planning their time. It gives details of everything from mainstream cinema releases to readings by local writers, concerts of all sizes and genres to soccer or speedway fixtures. On the whole it's both reliable and comprehensive, though it's always worth phoning ahead to double-check before setting off to an event. Switches to weekly issues for the Festival when its time-banded sections and extensive preview coverage offer a useful – though by no means infallible – guide through the bewildering plethora of attractions on offer.

Television

On the broadcasting front, both the BBC and ITV in Scotland opt in and out of the UK-wide output, BBC Scotland and the independent Scottish Television (STV) each also contributing regularly to their respective networks.

BBC Scotland's TV drama has been on something of a winning streak of late, with both one-off and serial dramas – *Rab C Nesbitt* being only the best-known – while also venturing successfully into the film business with the critically acclaimed *Small Faces* and *Mrs Brown*. On the factual side, its arts documentary strand, Ex-S, has also picked up a good many plaudits.

STV, meanwhile, produces a diverse range of home-grown special-interest programmes such as *Get It On* (fashion), *Don't Look Down* (arts) and *Scottish Passport* (holidays), in addition to mainstream popular drama. Both stations also broadcast much of their own, Scottish-centred sports coverage – especially in the football season.

Radio

At the time of writing, bids were being submitted to run a new radio frequency covering central Scotland, with a range of music- and talk-based proposals vying for the contract.

BBC Radio Scotland

(92.4-94.7 FM, 810 MW)

Enjoying particularly widespread popularity and respect for its mix of talk- and music-based programming, Radio Scotland's news coverage offers an illuminating alternative to the reports from London, while its arts, documentary, sports and short-story strands are all worth listening to. The nightly rotation of music shows ranges from the *Brand New Opry*'s country selection, to folk and traditional-based sounds in *Celtic Connections* and *Travelling Folk*.

Radio Forth

(97.3 FM and 1548 MW)

Music-oriented Edinburgh-based commercial station. Wins awards for both its frequencies. FM and MW cater for the younger and maturer ends of the mainstream/chart audience respectively. Does feature local and Scottish acts and is a must for travel news.

Scot FM

(101.1 FM)

Country-wide, fairly downmarket approach to talk radio. Its early attempts to introduce Scotland to the shock-jock formula enjoyed mixed results, to say the least.

Alternative

The fringe media scene in Edinburgh has been expanding steadily, if gradually, in recent years, boosted both by Scotland's lively cultural/political mood and the impact of the IT revolution. Probably the best-known publication in this context is *Rebel Inc*, famously the first to publish the work of one Irvine Welsh back in the early 1990s, and now generally recognised as a landmark force in new Scottish writing.

These days the magazine itself operates online (*www.canongate.co.uk*), as well as lending its name to an imprint of Edinburgh independent publishers Canongate, championing the same ilk of authors in book form. The 'little magazine' sector features three main Edinburgh-based titles – *Chapman*, *Cencrastus* and *New Edinburgh Review*, each mixing its own combination of fiction, poetry, reviews, interviews, features and essays. 'Zines and fanzines come and go periodically – though they can be hard to find – catering for

tastes from Riot Grrls to football supporters.

Edinburgh's proudest alternative media creation is the infamous *Shaver's Weekly*.

Internet

Scotland

www.holiday.scotland. net/

Official site of the Scottish Tourist Board, with information on accommodation, restaurants, arts events, nightlife and more in your choice of format, from data-only to fully plugged in.

Lots of accommodation of all kinds, with a disabled option, but the search could be better constructed and there's no booking facility. Some very useful links, though.

www.scotland.net

Scotland Online: a magazine of Scottish essentials (news, features, tartan guide, a searchable golf database) and a travel site produced in conjunction with the STB with data on accommodation, events and so on in all the major cities.

www.scotsman.com/ index.html

News, sport and arts from Edinburgh-based newspaper *The Scotsman*. Good for tuning into local opinion and issues (especially the archive), but doesn't include any city guides or what's on elements.

www.theherald.co.uk/

Daily news and sport from the electronic version of the *Glasgow Herald*. It's bright, fast and simple but again doesn't go beyond the usual paper content.

www.record- mail.co.uk/rm/

In-yer-face tabloid take on news and sport from the *Daily Record* and *Sunday Mail*. Inclues Discover Scotland, the papers' professionally engineered visitor site, with split screen, good searches (accommodation etc) and maps for each entry (we liked the 'locate nearest pub' option). Also contains useful what's on and gig and pub guides.

www.scotweb.co.uk.

This is primarily an on-line sales forum for Scottish goods and services, but there's lots else of interest, too: consult the Tartan (yellow) Pages or the white (e-mail) pages, read *Piping World* or *Scottish Life* and browse Whisky Web or the Scotweb history site.

www.historic- scotland.gov.uk

Home pages for the government body in charge of Scotland's historic monuments. Strong databases on listed buildings, tourist attractions, literature and calander events. Updated every three months.

http://scotch.com/

The ultimate whisky lover's guide: beautifully illustrated musings on all aspects and varieties of the noble drink.

www.timeout.co.uk

Click on the Edinburgh & Glasgow button for *The List* and *Time Out*'s directional pick of local arts and entertainment. Updated every two weeks.

Edinburgh

www.edinburgh.org

The home base of the Edinburgh Tourist Board was long on looks but short on solid info when we visited: an improved accommodation database is planned. Some useful links.

www.eae.co.uk

Edinburgh's main publicity distribution company, responsible for most of the posters and leaflets you'll see around, also runs this 'virtual leaflet rack', proffering details of forthcoming arts and entertainment fixtures. Coverage is patchy: when we visited there were four (useful) folk listings but improbably 'no events' under cinema.

www.go-edinburgh.co.uk

Full details of Edinburgh's major annual festivals. Thorough background and good information (including a page for would-be performers), and a text-only option. Come here for the fringe programme on-line.

www.electrum.co.uk/ pubs/

Take a virtual jaunt through Edinburgh's watering holes in the company of a wasted youth, a history geek or an architecture appreciator. Slow and scanty, but fun and pretty frank with useful maps.

Glasgow

www.glasgow.gov.uk/cgi- glasgow/citylive/cgi/eve nts.pl/

City Live – a what's on guide for Glasgow divided into sections for theatre, music, clubs, visual arts, family and festivals. Search by date or topic: either way listings are brief but useful. Links are provided to booking agencies.

Directory

Edinburgh Resources

Directory

Business

Information

Edinburgh Chamber of Commerce and Enterprise
152 Morrison Street, EH3 8EB (477 7000/fax 477 7002). **Open** 9am-5pm Mon-Fri.
One of the fastest-growing Chambers in the United Kingdom, with international trade near the top of its agenda.
e-mail: info@ecce.org
http: www.ecce.org

The Scottish Office
St Andrews House, Regent Road, EH1 3DG/Victoria Quay, EH6 6QQ (556 8400). **Open** 8.30am-5.30pm Mon-Fri.
A good starting point from which to reach the relevant department, such as Enterprise & Tourism or Economic & Industrial Affairs.
e-mail: ceu@isd01.scotoff.gov.uk
http: www.scotland.gov.uk

Lothian and Edinburgh Enterprise
Apex House, 99 Haymarket Terrace, EH12 5HD (313 4000/fax 313 6120). **Open** 9am-5pm Mon-Fri.
A Government-funded economic development, training and environmental improvement agency with responsibility for the Lothians (which includes Edinburgh).
e-mail: lothined@scotent.co.uk
http: www.leel.co.uk

Conferences

Edinburgh Convention Bureau
4 Rothesay Terrace, EH3 7RY (473 3666/fax 473 3636). **Open** 9am-5pm.
Part of the business and tourism division of the Edinburgh & Lothians Tourist Board, the ECB offers impartial advice on finding a conference venue and help with the organisation.
e-mail: convention@edinburgh.org
http: www.edinburgh.org/conference

Edinburgh International Conference Centre
The Exchange, 150 Morrison Street, EH3 8EE (300 3000).
Telephone enquiries 8am-6pm Mon-Fri.
In the modern surroundings of the city's new financial centre, the Exchange can accommodate up to 1,200 delegates and offers in-house catering as well as business services.

Equipment hire

Sound & Vision AV
11B South Gyle Crescent, EH12 9EB (334 3324/fax 316 4975). **Open** 8.30am-5.30pm Mon-Fri; 24-hour technical cover daily.
Will hire out anything required for a presentation, including PCs, and can produce graphics. Also has the unique (in the UK) service of a van full of equipment ready to go in case of emergencies.
http: www.sound-and-vision.co.uk

PC World
1-17 Glasgow Road, EH12 8NL (334 5953/fax 334 6102). **Open** 9am-8pm Mon-Fri; 9am-6pm Sat; 10.30am-5pm Sun.
PC World doesn't hire out equipment, but has a dedicated business centre within the store, PC World Business Direct, with a stock of 12,000 lines.

Import & export

Companies House
Argyle House, 37 Castle Terrace, EH1 2EB (535 5800/fax 535 5820). **Open** 9am-5pm Mon-Fri.
Companies House incorporates new limited companies, and to export goods you must be registered here. Also information on Scottish companies and foreign companies registered in Scotland.

Customs & Excise
Scotland Head Office, 44 York Place, EH1 3JW (469 2000/fax 469 7349). **Open** 8.30am-5pm Mon-Fri.
Customs & Excise also deals with VAT enquiries, with a public counter open from 9.30am-4pm Mon-Fri and a freephone line (0345 442 266) open during their regular office hours.

Office space

Regus
Conference House, The Exchange, 152 Morrison Street, EH3 8EB (200 6000/fax 200 6200). **Open** 8.30am-6pm Mon-Fri.
Conference House contains one-person to 67-person office suites, starting at £1,000 per month. A fully furnished office can be provided, with phones, PCs, secretarial support and catering. Conference space can also be hired by the day or hour.

Rutland Square House
12 Rutland Square, EH1 2BB (228 2281/fax 228 3637). **Open** 8.30am-5.30pm
Twelve fully furnished offices, from

£400 per month. All are hired on a three-month minimum basis.

Edinburgh Office Business Centre & Conference Venue
16-26 Forth Street, EH1 3LH (550 3700/fax 550 3701). **Open** 8.30am-5.30pm Mon-Fri; 8.30am-5pm Fri.
Over 60 office spaces, ranging from 85 to 775sq ft. Rates start at £150 month.

Secretarial

Alva Business Centre
82 Great King Street, EH3 6QU (557 2222/fax 557 2861). **Open** 9am-5pm, Mon-Fri.
Doesn't actually hire out staff, but provides secretarial and word-processing services, as well as photocopying, document binding, fax broadcasting, translation and interpreting (with prior notice). E-mail can be forwarded here too.
e-mail: alvaedin@aol.com

Office Angels
95 George Street, EH2 3ES (226 6112/fax 220 6850). **Open** 8.30am-6pm, Mon-Fri.
Supplies everything from mailroom staff to the chairman's PA, except qualified accountants and IT specialists – and only to offices, not businesses run from home.

Reed Employment
13 Frederick Street, EH2 2EB (226 3687/fax 220 1322). **Open** 8am-6pm Mon-Fri.
Reed supplies office, secretarial, call centre and catering staff.
http: www.reed.co.uk
Accountancy branch: 25 Frederick Street, EH2 (226 3686/fax 225 5817)

Translation

Berlitz
24-26 Frederick Street, EH2 2JR (226 7198/fax 225 2918). **Open** 9am-5pm Mon-Fri.
Berlitz will translate out of or into all languages under the sun. Rates vary according to language.

Integrated Language Services
School of Languages, Heriot Watt University, Riccarton, EH14 4AS (451 3159/fax 451 3160). **Open** 9am-5pm Mon-Fri.
All European languages and most others can be translated. ILS also supply interpreters and all necessary interpreting equipment for conferences. Rates on request.

Health

National Health Service (NHS) treatment is free if you fall into one of the following categories:
● European Union (EU) nationals, plus those of Iceland, Norway and Liechtenstein.
● European Economic Area (EEA) nationals living in an EEA state.
● Nationals/residents of countries with which the UK has a reciprocal agreement.
● Anyone who at time of receiving treatment has been in the UK for the previous 12 months.
● Anyone who has come the UK to take up permanent residence.
● Students on full-time recognised courses of study from anywhere in the world.
● Refugees and others who have sought refuge in the UK.
● Anyone formally detained be the Immigration Authorities.

There are no NHS charges for the following:
● Treatment in accident and emergency departments.
● Emergency ambulance transport.
● Diagnosis and treatment of certain communicable diseases, including STDs.
● Family planning services.
● Compulsory psychiatric treatment.

If you do not fit into any of the above categories, but wish to find out if you may still qualify for free treatment, contact:

Primary Care Department, *Lothian Health, Stevenson House, 555 Gorgie Road, EH11 (536 9000).*

Accident & emergency

The 24-hour casualty department serving Edinburgh is located at:

Royal Infirmary of Edinburgh, *Lauriston Place, EH3 (536 4000). 23, 27, 28, 37, 45, 47 buses.*

Chemists

See chapter **Shopping**. Many drugs cannot be bought over the counter. A pharmacist will dispense medicines on receipt of a prescription from a doctor. An NHS prescription costs £5.80 per item at present. A late-opening dispensing chemist is Boots The Chemist, 48 Shandwick Place, EH2 (225 6757), open 8am-9pm Mon-Sat; 10am-5pm Sun.

Contraception/abortion

Abortions are free to British citizens on the National Health Service (NHS). This also applies to EU residents and foreign nationals living, working or studying in Britain. Two doctors must agree that an abortion is justified within the terms of the Abortion Act 1967, as amended, whether it is on the NHS or not. If you decide to go private, contact one of the organisations below.

Lothian Brook Advisory Centre

2 Lower Gilmore Place, EH3 (229 3596). **Open** *office 9am-5pm Mon-Fri; clinic noon-2.30pm Mon, Tue, Thur, Sat; 4-6pm Mon, Tue, Thur; noon-3.30pm Fri.*
Advice on contraception, sexual problems and abortion with referral to an NHS hospital or private clinic.

Family Planning & Well Woman Services

18 Dean Terrace, EH4 (343 6243/332 7941). Clinics operate strictly by appointment only (except for emergency treatment); *switchboard* 8.30am-7.30pm Mon-Thur; 9.30am-4pm Fri; *young people's clinic* (under 25s) 9.30am-1pm Sat. Clinics give contraception advice, abortion referral, post-termination counselling, pre-menstrual syndrome advice and support, menopause information, psycho-sexual counselling, vasectomy operations and female sterilisation advice

Dental services

Dental care is free only to UK citizens in certain categories. All other patients, NHS or private, must pay; certain categories of people from some countries may be eligible for reduced dental costs. For advice, and to find an NHS dentist, contact the **Primary Care Department** (*see above*). Emergency dental treatment can be obtained at:

Edinburgh Dental Institute

Level 7, Lauriston Building, Lauriston Place, EH3 (536 4913). 23, 27, 28, 37, 45, 47 buses. **Open** 9am-3pm Mon-Fri.
Free walk-in emergency clinic.

Western General Hospital

Crewe Road South, EH4 (537 1338). 19, 20, 28, 38, 39, 55, buses. **Open** 7pm-10pm Mon-Fri; 10am-12noon.
Free walk-in emergency clinic.

Doctors

If you are a British citizen or working in the city, you can to to any GP. People who are ordinarily resident in the UK, such as overseas students, can also register with an NHS doctor. For names of GPs in your area, contact the **Primary Care Department** (*see above* **Health**).

If you are not eligible to see an NHS doctor, you will be charged cost price for medicines prescribed by a private doctor.

Opticians

For dispensing opticians, *see chapter* **Shopping & Services**.

Princess Alexandra Eye Pavilion

Chalmers Street, EH3 (536 3753). For emergency eye complaints, the Eye Pavilion operates a free walk-in service.

STDs/HIV/AIDS

The Genito-Urinary Medicine (GUM) clinic (listed below) is affiliated to the Royal Infirmary of Edinburgh. It provides free, confidential advice and treatment of STDs and non-sex related problems, such as thrush (yeast infections) and cystitis (urinary tract infections). It also offers information and counselling on HIV and STDs, and can conduct a confidential blood test to determine HIV status. Government and Health Education pamphlets – *AIDS: The Facts, Safer Sex and the Condom* and *AIDS: The Test* – are available from the GUM clinic and by post from: Health Education Board for Scotland, Woodburn House, Canaan Lane, EH10. *See also below* **Helplines & information**.

SOLAS
2-4 Abbeymount, EH8 (661 0982). **Open** 11am-4pm Mon, Tue, Thur, Fri; 5-9pm Wed.
Scottish HIV/AIDS Information Centre.

Genito-Urinary Medicine
Lauriston Building, Lauriston Place, EH3 (males 536 2103/ females 536 2104). **Open** 8.30am-4.30pm Mon-Wed, Fri; 8.30am-6.30pm Thur.
Walk-in clinic, free and confidential. Offers counselling for people who are HIV positive.

Helplines & information

AIDS Helpline
0800 567 123. **Open** 24 hours daily.
A free and confidential information service. Staff speak several languages.

Alcoholics Anonymous
225 2727. **Open** 24 hours daily.
Confidential, around-the-clock help and advice.

Childline
0800 1111. **Open** 24 hours daily.
Free and confidential national helpline for children and young people in trouble or danger.

Citizens' Advice Scotland
26 George Street, EH2 (667 0156). **Open** 9am-5pm Mon-Fri.
Citizens' Advice Bureaux are run by local councils, offering free advice on legal, financial and personal matters. The above office does not offer advice itself but staff will direct callers to their nearest CAB. Alternatively, check the *Yellow Pages* or the phone book for the nearest one.

Crew 2000
32 Cockburn Street, EH1 (220 3404).
Harm-reduction drug information.

Edinburgh Bisexual Group
58A Broughton Street, EH1 (557 3620).

Edinburgh Rape Crisis Centre
556 9437.
Free, confidential rape counselling.

Edinburgh & Lothian Women's Aid
229 1419.
Refuge referral for women experiencing domestic violence. An after-hours answerphone gives numbers for immediate help.

Gamblers Anonymous
0171 384 3040. **Open** 24 hours daily.
Advice is offered by members of the fellowship. Referrals to meetings.

Health Information Service
0800 665 544. **Open** 10am-5pm Mon-Fri.
A free telephone information service which gives details about local NHS services, waiting times, common diseases, conditions and treatments.

Narcotics Anonymous
661 9770.

The Rights Office
Southside Community Centre, Nicholson Street, EH8 (667 6339). **Open** 10am-12.30pm Mon, Wed.
Free, confidential advice and advocacy.

Samaritans
0345 909 090. **Open** 24-hour emergency line.
The Samaritans will listen to anyone with an emotional problem. You may have to ring several times before you get through.

Simpson House
52 Queen Street, EH2 (225 1054/225 6028).
Drugs counselling, family counselling and related services.

Lothian Gay & Lesbian Switchboard
556 4049.

Victim Support
14 Frederick Street, EH2 (225 7779/8233/fax 225 8456).
Victims of crime are put in touch with a volunteer who provides emotional and practical support, including information on legal procedures and advice on compensation. Interpreters can be arranged.

Women Unlimited
4a Downfield Place, EH11 (337 5543). **Open** *drop-in service* 9am-5pm Mon-Fri; 24-hour telephone answer service.
Support, advice and counselling for women on all issues.

Legal Aid & immigration advice

If a legal problem arises, contact your embassy, consulate or high commission, go to a **Citizens' Advice Bureau** or the **Rights Office** (*for both see above*) or contact one of the organisations listed below. Ask about Legal Aid eligibility. For leaflets explaining how the system works, write to the **Scottish Legal Aid Board** (*see below*).

Scottish Legal Aid Board
44 Drumsheugh Gardens, EH3 (226 7061). **Open** office 9am-5pm Mon-Fri; switchboard 8.30am-5pm Mon-Fri.
Publishes information leaflets on Criminal and Civil Legal Aid; can advise on how to make a complaint against the Scottish Legal Advice Board.

Libraries

Central Library
George IV Bridge (225 5584/fax 225 8783). George IV Bridge buses. **Open** 10am-8pm Mon-Thur; 10am-6pm Fri, 9am-1pm Sat.
The library stocks a selection of American and European publications including *Le Monde, Repubblica, El Pais* and *Frankfurter Allgemeine Zeitung*, as well a large refernece section. Proof of identity is required to join the lending library. Edinburgh Room and the Scottish Room are dedicated to local and Scottish material.

University of Edinburgh Main Library
George Square (650 3384/fax 650 3380). **Open** *term-time* 9am-10pm Mon, Tue, Thur; 10.15am-10pm Wed; 9am-5pm Fri-Sat; noon-5pm Sun; *vacations* 9am-5pm Mon, Tue, Thur, Fri; 9am-9pm Wed.
With a valid matriculation card or ISIC, international students not studying at the University may use the library for reference purposes only. Alternatively full membership is available at £26 for 3 months, £46 for 6 months or £65 for 12 months.

Religion

Baptist
Charlotte Baptist Chapel
West Rose Street, EH2 (225 4812). **Open** *office* 9am-5pm. **Services** 10am (*prayer meeting*), 11am, 5.45pm

(*prayer meeting*), 6.30pm, Sun; 8pm (*prayer meeting*) Tue.

Buddhist
There is no central meeting place for Edinburgh's diverse Buddhist groups, which tend to share space with other faiths or organisations. Phone 332 7987 for information.

Catholic
St Mary's Cathedral
Top of Broughton Street, EH1 (556 1798). **Open** 7am-6pm Mon-Fri, Sun; 7am-7pm Sat. **Services** 7.30am, 10am (*Eucharist*), 12.45pm, 6pm (*feast days or holidays of Obligation*), Mon-Fri; 7.30am, 10am (*Eucharist*), 12.45pm, 6pm, Sat; 7.30am, 9.30am, 11.30am, 7.30pm, Sun. **Confessions heard** 10.30-11.30am, 1.15-2pm, 5-5.45pm, Sat.

Church of Scotland
St Giles Cathedral
Royal Mile, EH1 (225 4363). **Open** *Easter-Sept* 9am-5pm; *Sept-Easter* 9am-7pm. **Services** 8am, noon, Mon-Fri; noon, 6pm (*Holy Communion*), Sat; 8am (*Holy Communion*), 10am (*Holy Communion*), 11.30am, 8pm, Sun.

Episcopalian
The Cathedral Church of St Mary
Palmerston Place, EH12 (225 6293). **Open** 7.15am-6pm Mon-Sat; 7.30am-6pm Sun (*closes 9pm in summer*). **Services** 7.30am (*Eucharist*), 1.05pm, 5.30pm (*choral evensong*), Mon, Tue, Wed, Fri; 7.30am (*Eucharist*), 11.30am (*Eucharist*), 1.05pm, 5.30pm (*choral evensong*), Thur; 7.30am Sat; 8am (*Eucharist*), 10.30am (*choral Eucharist*), 3.30pm (*choral evensong*), Sun.

Hindu
Edinburgh Hindu Mandir and Sanskritik Kendra (Temple and Community Centre)
St Andrew Place (former St Andrew's Church), Leith, EH6 (667 6064/663 4689). **Open/services** 4-6pm every second Sunday; noon-2pm every fourth Sunday.

Islamic
Mosque and Islamic Centre
50 Potterow, EH8 (667 1777/fax 668 4245). **Open** dawn-dusk. **Services** phone for details.

Jewish
Synagogue Chambers
4 Salisbury Road, EH16 (667 3144). **Open/services** phone for details.

Methodist
Nicolson Square Methodist Church
Nicolson Square, EH8 (662 0417). **Open** *basement chapel & café*

8.30am-3.30pm Mon-Fri; *church* open for view at lunchtime over summer. **Services** 11am, 6.30pm, Sun.

Quaker
Quaker Meeting House
7 Victoria Terrace, EH1 (225 4825). **Open** 9am-10pm. **Services** 11am, Sun; 12.30pm Wed.

Sikh
The Sikh Temple
1 Mill Lane, EH6 (553 7207). **Open** phone in advance. **Services** noon-3pm Sun.

Students

Renowned worldwide and with an unbeatable reputation for medicine and scientific research, a degree from Edinburgh University certainly does carry hefty academic kudos. Founded in 1583, and with 15,608 full-time students, the University boasts an impressive roll-call of former pupils, including Sir Walter Scott, Robert Louis Stevenson and Charles Darwin.

There are eight faculties with departments scattered across town, while the Old College boasts some stunning architecture. With this impressive baggage, Edinburgh University also has an – arguably justifiable – reputation for a disproportionate number of yahs (snobs of predominantly Southern English origin). On the flip side, Edinburgh is also home to a number of newer colleges and former polytechnics.

Universities/colleges
Edinburgh College of Art
Lauriston Place (221 6000/fax 221 6028).
One of the most prestigious art colleges in the UK: competition for places here is stiff. Studies on offer include a wide range from film to textiles and sculpture.

Heriot-Watt University
Riccarton Campus, Currie (449 5111/fax 451 3190).
A vocational university specialising in business, finance, languages, science and engineering subjects.

Moray House College of Education
Holyrood Campus, Holyrood Road (556 8455/fax 557 3458).
Predominantly a teacher training college, which also offers courses in leisure and physical education.

Napier University
Craiglockhart Campus, 219 Colinton Road (444 2266/fax 455 4666).
Founded in 1964 and named after mathematical whizz-kid John Napier, this former polytechnic with a reputation for a more eclectic (and down-to-earth) student body than Edinburgh University was granted university status in 1992. Offering predominantly vocational courses, its employment record for graduates is second to none.

Queen Margaret College
Corstorphine Campus, Clerwood Terrace (317 3000/fax 317 3256).
An assortment of predominantly degree courses – everything from nursing, nutrition and tourism to management, business and drama.

University of Edinburgh
Old College, South Bridge (650 1000/fax 650 2147). *International office: 57 George Square (650 4300/fax 668 4565)*. **Open** 9am-1pm, 2-5pm, Mon-Fri.
One of the UK's oldest and most reputable universities offers a staggering range of academic degree courses. There's also a good selection of part-time special interest courses in the day and evening.

Language courses
A full list of the vast number of schools offering English language courses can be found in the *Yellow Pages*. This is a small selection of some of the best and most well known.

Berlitz
24/26 Frederick Street (226 7198/fax 225 2918).
Group programmes start at £395 for 30 hours' tuition, while semi-private tuition with a maximum of three students per group starts at £455 for 17 hours tuition. Not cheap, but the Berlitz method gets results.

Edinburgh Language Centre
10B Oxford Terrace (343 6596 phone/fax).
A range of language courses tailored to your exact requirements include beginner weekends at £32, intensive TEFL weekend courses at £129 and four-week summer courses with two sessions per week at £52. Year-round

Directory

courses cost from £67 for 10 weeks to £91 for 14 weeks. Student discounts are available on all these.

Institute for Applied Language Studies

21 Hill Place (650 6200/fax 667 5927).
Part of Edinburgh University, this well-established language school offers 20 hours per week general or business English classes for £167. It also runs TEFL and more specialist academic courses.

Moray House English Language Centre

Moray House Institute of Education, Heriot-Watt University, Holyrood Road (558 6332/fax 557 5138).
A branch of Herriot-Watt University, the language centre offers a two-week, 30-hour general English course from £261, a two-week, 30-hour summer vacation course at £331 (or £441 including activity programme) and a summer festival course (available 16-29 Aug).

Regent Edinburgh

29 Chester Street (225 9888/fax 225 2133).
Running courses throughout the UK and with a reputation for getting results, Regent offers individual tuition at £35 for 50 minutes.

Stevenson College

Sighthill Campus, Bankhead Avenue (535 4600/fax 535 4666).
English language courses offered from £125 for seven weeks part-time group. Full-time study prices from £725 for seve weeks.

Student travel

Campus Travel

5 Nicolson Square (668 3303/fax 667 3855). **Open** 9am-5.30pm Mon, Tue, Thur, Fri; 10am-5.30pm Wed; 10am-5pm Sat.

Edinburgh Travel Centre

92 South Clerk Street (667 9488/fax 662 1035); 3 Bristow Square (668 2221/fax 667 8618). **Open** 9am-5.30pm Mon-Fri; 10am-1pm Sat.

Books

James Thin

53-59 South Bridge (556 6743); 57 George Street (225 4495); King's Buildings, West Mains Road (667 0432).
The main academic booksellers in town, Thins stocks most of the texts prescribed by the city's colleges and universities, covering everything from childcare to astro-physics. Also a nice range of fiction.

Women

Security

Despite the night-time nuisance-factor engendered by the still-popular stereotype of the red-blooded Scottish male, with its attendant macho drinking culture, Edinburgh – central-ish Edinburgh, at least – is a pretty safe and civilised place for women. The worst hassle you're likely to encounter is of the passing verbal variety, from groups of lagered-up lads.

With its compact centre and a lively late-night entertainment scene, there's generally a reasonable safety-in-numbers feel on the streets throughout Edinburgh's main drag and its immediate hinterland, even into the wee small hours.

The main areas best avoided by women on their own at night are Lothian Road (a preponderance of decidedly laddish pubs and a history of violence at chucking-out time), the dockside and backstreet areas of Leith (one of Edinburgh's main red-light districts) and the Meadows. The latter is a south-lying park whose brightly lit paths prove deceptively long and tree-screened once you actually set off down them; it has been the scene of several assaults in the past.

The Royal Mile, too, perhaps more unexpectedly, has seen its share of such incidents, mainly thanks to the cover provided by the innumerable narrow alleys, or 'wynds', leading off it: highly picturesque by day, spookily dark and shadowy at night.

Further afield, if you go to one of the city's big peripheral housing schemes, take local advice, and get your directions firmly sorted – the geographical layout of these areas is frequently bewildering, to say the least, and the levels of social deprivation to be found in some of them present a starkly different face of Edinburgh to the economic and architectural wealth of the centre.

Eating out

Eating, drinking and accommodation wise, Edinburgh these days caters for enough visitors of every variety to be pretty easy-going and flexible about different travellers' circumstances. For a relaxed solo meal, though, cafés can often be a better (and cheaper) bet than restaurants, with several good city-centre ones opening late into the evening.

Try Bann's (5 Hunter Square, 226 1112; 10am-11pm daily) or **Susie's Wholefood Diner** (51 West Nicolson Street, 667 8729; 10am-8pm Mon; 10am-9pm, Tue-Sat) for a tasty array of vegetarian snacks and meals, cakes and pastries, or the **Blue Moon Café** (36A Broughton Street, 557 0911; 9am-11.30pm Mon-Thur, Sun; 9am-12.30am Fri-Sat), a gay-run but straight-friendly establishment serving everything from toasties to Mexican dishes, plus a children's menu and a good veggie range.

Accommodation

Edinburgh is sorely lacking in women-only or specifically designated women-friendly establishments. What you will find, fortunately, is a sufficient quantity and diversity of places to lay your hat so that finding something secure and suitable should pose no real problem.

The bigger chain hotels, of which Edinburgh boasts several, tend to be well geared up to the needs of lone female guests, while many of the abundant B&Bs and guest-houses offer single rooms along with the kind of welcome that has made Scottish hospitality famous. Some B&Bs do take a decidedly starchier or stingier approach: do sound out your prospective landlady (it's generally a she) with some care.

One hostel that offers accommodation to women and married couples only is the Kinnaird Christian Hostel, which accepts women whatever their circumstances. Two other recommended women-run guesthouses are the Amaryllis and the Armadillo.

Kinnaird Christian Hostel
13-14 Coates Crescent, West End, EH3 (225 3608).

Amaryllis Guest House
21 Upper Gilmore Place, EH3 (229 3293).

Armadillo Guest House
12 Gilmore Place, EH3 (229 6457).

Getting around

Edinburgh's bus services add up to a pretty comprehensive (and safe) network covering the city and its environs (*see chapter* **Getting Around**). Many of Edinburgh's (black) taxi firms have now signed up to a policy of giving priority to lone women, whether they're phoning up or flagging down. Bear in mind, though, that taxis routinely become gold-dust scarce between midnight and 3am at weekends, when the post-pub and club traffic is at its peak; book in advance or be prepared to wait – or walk.

Activities

For those curious about women's often overlooked place in Edinburgh's long and colourful history, the Central Library on George IV Bridge (*see above* **Libraries**) has a good booklet describing a 'Herstory Walk of the Royal Mile', starting at the Castle with St Margaret's Chapel, the oldest building in use in Edinburgh, and ending at Holyrood Palace, home to Mary Queen of Scots.

It takes in nearly 40 different sites en route, linked to women as diverse as the fishwives of Newhaven,

independent traders who routinely carried creels weighing up to 140 pounds (64kg) from the sea-port to Fishmarket Close, and legendary feminist writer Rebecca West, whose first published article on women's suffrage – written when she was just 13 – was published in *The Scotsman* in 1904 and whose childhood home lies on the Lawnmarket.

Health & advice

For more women's crisis support services *see above* **Helplines & information**; for more contraception and sexual health agencies *see above* **Health**.

Edinburgh and Lothian Women's Aid
97-101 Morrison Street (229 1419). **Open** 10am-3pm Mon, Wed, Fri; 1.30-3.30pm Tue; telephone enquiries only 10am-3pm Thur.
Help, advice and information for woman suffering physical, mental or sexual abuse from their partners. Precariously limited funding means that hours and services may be subject to change.

Lothian Brook Advisory Centre
2 Lower Gilmore Place, EH3 (229 3596). **Open** *office* 9am-5pm Mon-Fri; *clinic* noon-2.30pm Mon, Tue, Thur, Sat; 4-6pm Mon, Tue, Thur; noon-3.30pm Fri.
Contraception, sexual advice and counselling for young people up to the age of 25, including pregnancy advice and emergency contraception. For visitors based outside most Scottish regions, a £15 consultation fee is payable, plus any prescription costs.

Family Planning & Well Women Services
18 Dean Terrace, EH4 (343 6243/332 7941). Clinics operate strictly by appointment only (except for emergency treatment); *switchboard* 8.30am-7.30pm Mon-Thur; 9.30am-4pm Fri; *young people's clinic* (under 25s) 9.30am-1pm Sat.
Confidential advice, contraceptive provision and pregnancy tests. As an NHS-run clinic, covered under the European Union E111 scheme, it provides most services free, though some charges may apply to overseas visitors.

Finding a summer job in Edinburgh, or temporary employment if you are on a working holiday, can prove a long, drawn-out process. If you can speak English and at least one other language well, and are an EU citizen or have a work permit, you should be able to find something in catering, bar/restaurant or shop work.

Graduates with an English or a foreign language degree could try teaching. If your English is not too good, you could try distributing free leaflets. Ideas can be found in *Summer Jobs in Britain*, published by Vacation Work, 9 Park End Street, Oxford (£7.99 plus £1.50 p&p). The Central Bureau for Educational Visits & Exchanges (*see below*) has other publications.

To find work, look in *The Scotsman*, local and national papers and newsagents' windows, or write, phone or visit employers. Employers advertise vacancies on Jobcentre noticeboards; there is often temporary and unskilled work available; look in the *Yellow Pages* under Employment Agencies.

For office work, sign on with temp agencies. If you have shorthand, typing or wordprocessing skills, such agencies may be able to find you well-paid assignments.

Work for foreign visitors

With few exceptions, citizens of non-European Economic Area (EEA) countries need a work permit before they are legally able to work in the UK. One of the advantages of working here is the opportunity to meet people, but for any employment it is essential that you speak reasonable English. For office work you need a high standard of English and relevant skills.

Directory

Work permits

EEA citizens, residents of Gibraltar and certain categories of other overseas nationals do not require a work permit. However, others who wish to come to the UK to work must obtain a permit before setting out.

Prospective employers who have a vacancy that they are unable to fill with a resident or EEA national must apply for a permit to the Department for Education & Employment (*see below*). Permits are only issued for jobs that require a high level of skill and experience. The employer must be able to demonstrate to the DfEE that there is no resident/EEA labour available.

There is a Training & Work Experience Scheme that enables non-EEA nationals to come to the UK for training towards a professional or specialist qualification, or to undertake a short period of managerial level work experience. Again, this should be applied for before coming to the UK. Listed below are other possibilities.

Au pairs

The option of au pairing is only open to citizens of certain countries (*see below*) who are aged between 17 and 27. Try contacting an agency in your own country or look in the *Yellow Pages* under Employment Agencies. Such work usually provides free accommodation, but wages tend to be low. The following countries are included in the Au Pair Scheme: Andorra, Bosnia-Herzegovina, Croatia, Cyprus, Czech Republic, Faroe Islands, Greenland, Hungary, Macedonia, Malta, Monaco, San Marino, Slovak Republic, Slovenia, Switzerland and Turkey.

Sandwich-course students

Students at a recognised UK university or college can undertake work placements which are essential to obtain their qualifications. Approval for such placements must be obtained by the college from the DfEE's **Overseas Labour Service** (*see below*).

Students

Visiting students from the US, Canada, Australia or Jamaica can often get a blue BUNAC card enabling them to work in the UK for up to six months. BUNAC cards are not difficult to obtain, but you must get it before entering the country. Contact the Work in Britain Department of the Council on International Educational Exchange or call BUNAC (*see below*), a non-prof-it-making organisation that arranges work exchange programmes for students from these countries. BUNAC students should obtain and application form OSS1 (BUNAC) from BUNAC before starting work in the UK. This should be submitted to the nearest Jobcentre to obtain permission to work.

Non-EEA nationals in the UK as students who wish to take casual part-time or vacation employment unconnected to their course of study must obtain the permission of their local Employment Service Jobcentre. The Jobcentre will provide an applica-tion form (OSS1) for completion by the student, their college and the prospective employer.

Voluntary work

Voluntary work in youth hostels provides board, lodging and some pocket money. For advice on voluntary work with charities contact the **Home Office** (*see below*).

Working holidaymakers

Citizens of Commonwealth countries, aged 17-27, may apply to come to the UK as a working holidaymaker. This allows them to take part-time work without a DfEE permit. They must contact their nearest British Diplomatic Post to obtain the necessary entry clearance before travelling to the UK.

Useful addresses

Aliens Registration Office
10 Lamb's Conduit Street, London, WC1 (0171 230 1208). Holborn tube. **Open** 9am-4.45pm Mon-Fri. It costs £30 to be registered, if you have a work permit.

BUNAC
7-9 Blackfriars Street, EH1 (558 9313/558 9314).
See above **Students**.

Central Bureau for Educational Visits & Exchanges
3/4 Bruntsfield Crescent, EH10 (447 8024/fax 452 8569). **Open** 9.15am-5pm Mon-Fri.
Deals with the organisation of visits outside the UK, but you can obtain copies of its useful publications.

Council on International Educational Exchange Work in Britain Department
205 East 42nd Street, New York, NY 10017, USA (001 212 661 1414).

Department for Education & Employment Overseas Labour Services
Level 5, Moorfoot, Sheffield, S1 4PQ (0114 259 4074). **Telephone enquiries** 9am-5pm Mon-Fri. Not open for personal visits, but you can call the above enquiry line. Employers seeking work permit application forms should phone 0990 210 224.

Home Office
Immigration & Nationality Directorate, Lunar House, 40 Wellesley Road, Croydon CR9 9BY (0181 686 0688). **Open** 8.30am-4pm Mon-Fri.
Will give advice on whether a work permit is required.

Glasgow Resources

Most countries have their Scotland consulate in Edinburgh; *see page 246* **Essential Information**. This is unlikely to change, once the Edinburgh Parliament opens.

Banks/bureaux de change

Some English and Irish banks are thin on the ground in Scotland, but most of the majors do have at least one Glasgow branch.

Barclays Bank
90 St Vincent Street, G2 (0141 221 9585). Buchanan Street tube/Queen Street rail, then 5-min walk.

Lloyds Bank
12 Bothwell Street, G2 (0141 248 4661). Central Station/St Enoch tube, then 5-min walk.

Midland Bank
120 West Regent Street, G2 (0141 531 1700). Buchanan St tube, then 5-min walk.

National Westminster Bank
14 Blythswood Square, G2 (0141 221 6981). 6(A), 8(A), 9(A), 16(A) buses.

Thomas Cook Travel
Unit 19, Central Station, G1 (0141 204 4496/fax 248 6524). Central Station rail/St Enoch tube.
Bureau de change and travel centre.

Post offices

There are post offices all through the city, the majority operating within usual shop hours. To get information about your nearest one, call their helpline on 0345 22 33 44 (9am-6pm Mon-Fri; 8.30am-4pm Sat).

A late-opening post office near the city centre, which offers all the usual postal facilities as well as a bureau de change, is:

Anniesland
900 Crow Road, G13 (0141 954 8661). Anniesland rail. **Open** 8am-10pm Mon-Sat; 9am-8pm Sun. **No credit cards.**

Security

Glasgow's city centre is pretty safe, even at night. The streets are well lit and CCTV and a high police visibility ensure few breaches of the peace. Be more careful around the parks, where the lighting is poorer, and in the East End. The usual big-city precautions apply, but for more general advice on security, *see page 246* **Essential Information.**

Telephones

The area code for Glasgow and environs is 0141.

Tourist information

The Greater Glasgow and Clyde Valley Tourist Board
11 George Square, G2 (reservations 0141 221 0049/general enquiries

Bus basics

In this guide, we have listed Glasgow's buses as follows. All routes are operated by Greater Glasgow Bus Company.
Bath St buses: 11, 16, 18, 23, 42, 44, 57, 59, 66, 74.
Hope St buses: 4, 18, 21, 23, 38, 39, 41, 44, 45, 48, 53, 54, 55, 57, 59, 61.
St Vincent St buses: 6, 8, 14, 16, 20, 31, 66.
Sauchiehall St buses: 11, 18, 20, 21, 23, 42, 44, 48, 51, 53, 54, 55, 57, 59, 61, 66.

0141 204 4400/fax 0141 221 3524). Buchanan Street tube, then 5 min walk. **Open** *Oct-Apr* 9am-6pm Mon-Sat; *May* 9am-6pm Mon-Sun; *June* 9am-7pm Mon-Sun; *July-Aug* 9am-8pm daily; *Sept* 9am-7pm daily. **Credit** JCB, MC, V. **Booking fee** £2, plus 10% deposit. **Map 1 E2**
The tourist board will take credit-card bookings for accommodation throughout the city. It also answers general enquiries about sightseeing and events and supplies details of special rates in its brochure.
e-mail: tourismglasgow@ GGCVTB.org.uk

Getting around
Arrival/departure
Plane
Glasgow is served by Glasgow Airport (0141 887 1111), eight miles (14km) south-west of the city, at Junction 28 of the M8.

Coach
Buchanan Street Bus Station (0141 332 7133), on Killermont Street, is where long-distance coach services arrive and depart. It's central and well served by both public transport and taxis.

Train
Glasgow has two main-line train stations, Queen Street, which serves Edinburgh and the north of Scotland, and Central, serving the West Coast and south to England. The stations are centrally located and walking distance apart. For rail enquiries call the national number: 0345 484 950.

Public transport

As with most worthwhile cities, the best way of seeing Glasgow is definitely on foot: it's compact enough for this to be

easily possible as well as pleasant. But if this doesn't appeal, there is a good bus service and two local train systems, the Low Level, serving the suburbs, and a single line underground (tube), affectionately known as the 'Clockwork Orange', which loops between the centre and the West End.

For information on all three, call or visit the conveniently located St Enoch Travel Centre (St Enoch Square, G1; 0141 226 4826. Open 9am-5pm Mon-Sat).

For information on Glasgow buses and their routes, *see box page 103.*

Taxis

Like Edinburgh, Glasgow is served by a fleet of capacious black taxi cabs – and they're cheap.

Car rental

Should you wish to drive in Glasgow, or head out of town.

Arnold Clark
459 Crow Road, G11 (0141 434 0480). 6(A), 16(A) buses. **Open** 8am-6pm Mon-Fri; 8am-5pm Sat; 11am-5pm Sun. **Credit** AmEx, DC, MC, V.
Has the best deals starting from £16 per day, £80 per week for Micras

Europcar incorporating BCR
Terminal Building, Glasgow Airport, Inchinnan Road, Paisley, PA3 2RP (0141 887 0414/fax 889 3815). **Open** 7am-10.30pm daily. **Credit** AmEx, DC, MC, £TC, V.

You must be aged 23 or over to hire from here, with a minimum of one year's driving experience. Rentals (subject to change; ring to confirm) start from £49 per day, £210 weekly, for a Vauxhall Corsa with unlimited mileage and full AA breakdown recovery service included.

Mitchell's Self Drive
47 McAlpine Street, G2 (0141 221 8461). 62(B/C/D), 64(A/B) buses. **Open** 8am-6pm Mon-Thur; 8am-7.30pm Fri; 8am-5.30pm Sat; 8am-12.30pm Sun. **Credit** AmEx, DC, JCB, MC, V. **Map 1 C3**

Health

The following two infirmaries have accident and emergency departments (both obviously open 24 hours every day of the year).

The family planning and dental clinics offer free advice and treatment.

Glasgow Royal Infirmary NHS Trust
84 Castle Street, G4 (0141 211 4000). High Street rail, then 2(A), 37 buses. **Map 1 F2**

Western Infirmary NHS Trust
Dumbarton Road, G11 90141 211 2000). Kelvinhall tube.

Family Planning Clinic
2 Claremont Terrace, G3 (0141 211 8130). Bath St buses, then 10 min walk. **Open** *switchboard* 8.30am-5pm Mon-Fri; *clinics* 9am-7.30 pm Mon-Thur; 9am-3.30pm Fri, Sat.* **Map 1 A1**

Glasgow Dental NHS Trust
378 Sauchiehall Street (0141 211 9600). Sauchiehall St buses. **Open** *emergency clinic* 9am-3pm Mon-Fri. **Map 1 C2**

Libraries

Glasgow is extremely well served by local libraries. Consult the telephone directory for your nearest, or make tracks for one of the two major places listed below.

The Mitchell Library
North Street, G3 (0141 287 2938). Charing Cross rail, then 5 min walk. **Open** 9am-8pm Mon-Thur; 9am-5pm Fri, Sat. **Map 1 B2**

The front part of this impressive building facing Charing Cross was completed in 1911 and, together with the rear extension, houses five reference-only departments: science and technology, arts, social sciences, business information and the History and Glasgow room. Newspapers, periodicals, UK press archives and the British Humanities Index on CD-Rom can also be accessed here.

Stirling's Library
62 Miller Street, G1 (0141 221 1876). Buchanan Street or St Enoch tube/Queen Street rail. **Open** 11am-7pm Mon-Tue, Thur; 9am-5pm Wed, Fri, Sat. **Map 1 D3**
With mainstays of fiction, history, sport and children's books, membership for those who live, work or study in Glasgow (or another local authority) can be obtained by producing ID showing your address and signature.

Universities & colleges

Glasgow has a large student population, which helps to explain the thriving arts, nightlife and (naturally enough) bars scenes.

Glasgow Caledonian University
City Campus, Cowcaddens Road (331 3000/fax 331 3005).
Founded at the turn of the century and granted university status in1993, Glasgow Caledonian is keen to encourage overseas students to enrol. The three faculties are business, health and science and technology.

Glasgow School of Art
167 Renfrew Street (353 4500/fax 353 4746).
Offering a variety of BA honours and post-graduate courses in art and design and architecture, the School of Art was established in 1845 under the name of School of Design for Industry. There are currently 1,400 full-time students. Former pupils of note include Charles Rennie Mackintosh, actor and film director Peter Capaldi, actor Robbie Coltrane, and writers Liz Lochead and Carol Smillie.

University of Glasgow
University Avenue (339 8855/fax 330 4808).
Scotland's oldest university after St Andrews, Glasgow University was founded in 1451 by papal bull and, with its impressive Gothic

architecture, it's one of the city's best-known landmarks. It also has a good reputation world-wide for research.

University of Paisley
High Street, Paisley (848 3000/fax 848 3333).
Having celebrated its centenary last year, this former college, which was granted university status in 1992 as part of a UK-wide policy, boasts a good track record in graduate recruitment.
The eight faculties offer courses ranging from media, business and tourism to science and technology, nursing and teacher training.

University of Strathclyde
John Anderson Campus, George Street (552 4400/fax 552 0775).
Regarded unfairly as slightly scuzzy by the Glasgow Uni elite – many of the students here come from the surrounding area and thus continue to live at home. The degree courses take in the whole spectrum of academic as well as a plethora of vocational subjects. Famous former pupils include writer James Kellman and African explorer David Livingstone.

Travel agents

For **Thomas Cook Travel,** *see page 265 above.*

Campus Travel
Glasgow University
The Hub, Hillhead Street (357 0608). **Open** 9.30am-5pm Mon, Tue, Thur, Fri; 10am-5pm Wed.
Strathclyde University
122 George Street (553 1818/fax 553 1919). **Open** 9.30am-5pm Mon, Tue, Thur, Fri; 10am-5pm Wed; 10am-5pm Sat.
Independent travel specialists catering predominantly for students and young people and offering cheap flights abroad. Campus ssues ISIC and Young Scot cards – available to the under 26s and hugely useful for discount travel and other perks.

STA Travel
84 Byers Road (338 6000/fax 338 6022). **Open** 9.30am-5.30pm Mon, Tue, Thur, Fri; 10am-5.30pm Wed; 11am-5pm Sat.
Student Association Building, 90 John Street (552 8808/fax 552 2639). **Open** 10am-5.30pm Mon, Tue, Thur, Fri; 10.30am-5.30pm Wed.
Dealing in rail, road and air tickets largely outside the UK, STA, with a mainly student market, also issues ISIC and Young Scot cards. It does also, however, offer non-students an excellent service.

Directory

Further Reading

Whole tomes have been filled with quotations from transfixed visitors about the 'Windy City', 'Auld Reekie' and the 'Athens of The North'. But for a taste of the real Edinburgh, the one which you won't really get to know until you've stayed here a while, start with the many modern, popular fiction books set here.

The classics

Hogg, James: *Confessions of a Justified Sinner*
Old (first published in 1824) but kicking description of Edinburgh in the early seventeenth and eighteenth centuries in an almost post-modern double narrative. It's an ironic jibe against religious bigotry that also happens to have a peculiarly haunting description of Arthur's Seat in the haar. The *Canongate Classics* edition contains a useful introduction.
Scott, Walter: *The Heart of Midlothian*
Contains, amongst other things, an account of the Porteous lynching of 1736.
Spark, Muriel: *The Prime of Miss Jean Brodie*
Practically the official Edinburgh Novel. Edinburgh-born Spark has created an enduring icon in Jean Brodie, who makes a stand against the city's moral intransigence.

Modern fiction

Banks, Iain: *Complicity*
Fife-based Banks has a reputation for acutely visceral observation, and the bodies littering the text of this, the closest he has come to a thriller, does nothing to alter that idea. The body count might be exaggerated, but the characterisation (of both city and protagonists) is so good that several *Scotsman* journalists were accused of being the basis for his reporter on a fictional Edinburgh-based broadsheet (the *Caledonian*).
Boyd, William: *New Confessions*
Fine portrait of turn-of-the-century Edinburgh, as seen by a young boy growing up in an austere household.
Butlin, Ron: *Night Visits*
Set in 'an Edinburgh at its grandest, coldest and hardest… as if nothing less than such a stony grip and iron inflexibility were needed to prevent unimaginable pain,' as the *TLS* so eloquently put it.
Jardine, Quentin: *Skinner* novels
Another local genre writer of detective fiction, notorious for his high body count. Jardine's Skinner is a bit too perfect for comfort, but reflects the morally aloof side of the Edinburgh psyche. *Skinner's Festival* is the best.
Meek, James: *MacFarlane Boils The Sea*
Meek's poetic yet merciless description of Edinburgh in winter gets into every corner of the city and will be recognisable to every trendy (and not so trendy) young thing who lived or worked there in the late 1980s.
Rankin, Iain: *Inspector Rhebus* novels
Quality, genre, detective fiction for which Rankin has won the Gold Dagger award. His hard-bitten cop inhabits an Edinburgh that is the reality for most of its residents. All of the series carry their weight, but the earliest reveal Edinburgh at its most gritty. *Black and Blue* and *Mortal Causes* are a good place to start.
Warner, Alan: *The Sopranos*

An elliptical look at Edinburgh, from the point of view of a group of choirgirls down from Oban for a singing competition – but intent on drinking their way out of the final. Wry, cheeky and brilliantly observed.
Welsh, Irvine: *Trainspotting*
The first, and best, of Welsh's novels about the culture of drugs, clubs and unemployed youth that Edinburgh's more genteel residents do their beset to ignore. His later work is more self-indulgent than cutting-edge but his observation of language is spot on.
Kevin Williamson, Ed: *Children of Albion Rovers*
Short stories that grip grimly the Edinburgh underbelly – from where there are surprisingly revealing views. Williamson's Rebel Inc imprint is famous for giving vent to the young, radge generation's splenetic prose.

History & politics

Daitches, David: *Edinburgh*
Highly readable, academically sound, history.
Gray, Alasdair: *Why Scots Should Rule Scotland*
A well-constructed argument to just that point.
Prebble, John: *The King's Jaunt* Everything you could want to know (and more) about George IV's agenda-setting visit of 1822.
Smout, TC: *A History of the Scottish People 1560-1830*
The definitive social history of Scotland.

Culture

Bold, Alan: *Scotland – A Literary Guide*
And about as complete a guide as you will need.
Daiches, David: *The New Companion to Scottish Culture*
A useful encyclopedia.
Dale, Michael: *Sore Throats and Overdrafts*
The Fringe, as told by its administrator from 1978-'85.
Dudley Edwards & Richardson (Eds): *Edinburgh*
One of the better literary anthologies on Edinburgh
Lamond and Tucek: *The Malt Whisky File*
All the distilleries and nearly every commercially available malt reviewed, with useful tasting notes giving marks for sweetness, peatiness and availability.
Mackie Albert: *Speak Scotch or Whistle*
'A braw wee book, ken, wie yu fair smatterin' o wureds yous can yuze'.
Hardy, Forsyth: *Slightly Mad and Full of Danger*
The history of the Film Festival by one of its founders.

Glasgow

Burgess, Moira: *Imagine a City – Glasgow in Fiction*
An informed and entertaining examination of the books and the writing that reflect the city.
Gray, Alasdair: *Lanark*
A surreal description of Glasgow in the 1940s and '50s and a fascinating examination of the Scottish Psyche.
Scott, Walter: *Rob Roy*
Contains several observations on the Merchant City in the early eighteenth century.
Torrington, Jeff: *Swing Hammer, Swing*
Set in the slums of the Gorbals as they were demolished in the 1960s.

Directory

Index

Advertisers' Index

Maps

Street Index

Edinburgh

Trips Out of Town

0   75 miles

© Copyright Time Out Group 1998

North Ronaldsay
Westray
Rousay   Sanday
Stronsay
Stromness

Cape
Wrath   Hoy
Pentland
Firth
Durness   John
Skerray   Thurso   o' Groats   South Ronaldsay
Portskerra
Port of Ness   Balchrick   Tongue
Western   Altnaharra   Mybster   Wick
Isles   Kinbrace
Culkein   Unapool   Kinbrace   Lybster
Stornoway   Loch
Isle of   Lochinver   Shin   Lairg
Lewis
Ullapool   Brora
Dornoch
Taransay   Firth
Harris   Gairlo   Kincardine   Dornoch   Moray   Lossiemouth
Braemore   Invergordon   Firth   Elgin   Buckie   Macduff   Fraserburgh
North   Junction   Cromarty   Forres   Keith   Mintla
Uist   Rona   Achnasheen   Nairn   Peterhead
Inverness   Grantown-   Craigelliachie   Huntly
Benbecula   on-Spey   Inverurie   Eilon
Skye   Raasay   Drumnadrochit   Loch   Dyce
Scalpay   Ness   SCOTLAND   Grampian   Aberdeen
South   Inner   Kyle   Aviemore
Uist   Hebrides   Canna   Rum   Invermoriston   Cairngorm Mtns. Dee   Banchory
Ardvasar   Invergarry   Kingussie   Braemar   Stonehaven
Barra   Muck   Mallaig   Loch   Newtonmore
Eigg   Lochy   Dalwhinnie   Lautencekirk
Loch   Johnshaven
Coll   Shiel   Fort   Grampian   Mountains   Brechin
Tobermory   Glencoe   William   Pitlochry   Forfar   Montrose
Tiree   Ulva   Aberfeldy   TAYSIDE   Arbroath
Mull   Oban   Loch   Loch   Blairgowrie   Carnoustie
Iona   Avich   Tay   Dundee   Firth of
Colonsay   Jura   Callander   Perth   Tay   NORTH
ATLANTIC   Dunblane   Cupar   St Andrews
OCEAN   Central   Stirling   Alloa   Glenrothes   Fife   SEA
Islay   Denny   Cowdenbeath
Helensburgh   Stenhousemuir   Firth of Forth   North Berwick
Sound   Dunoon   Dumbarton   Glasgow   Falkirk   Edinburgh   Dunbar
of   Rothesay   Greenock   Paisley   Livingston   Haddington   Eyemouth
Jura   Bute   See   Motherwell   Lothian   See   Berwick-upon
Arran   Larger   Hamilton   Larger   -Tweed
Brodick   Map   Strathclyde   Peebles   Map   Melrose
Troon   Kilmarnock   Biggar   Galashiels   Coldstream
Prestwick   Muirkirk   Borders   Kelso
Campbeltown   Ayr   Cumnock
Turnberry   New Cumnock   Southern   Uplands   Cheviot Hills
Giants   Rathlin I.   Maybole
Causeway   Sanquhar   Kielder   Morpeth
Thornhill   Dumfries and   Northumberland
Londonderry   NORTHERN   Ballantrae   New   Galloway   Lockerbie   Newcastle
(Derry)   IRELAND   Galloway   Dumfries   Gretna   -upon-Tyne
Kirkcolm   Newton   Annan   Carlisle   Tyne &
Larne   Stranraer   Stewart   Dalbeattie   Alston   Wear
Antrim   Glenluce   Kirkcudbright   Solway Firth   Durham   Durham
Lough   Whithorn   Cumbria
Neagh   Bangor   Drummore   Luce   Wigtown   Keswick   Penrith
BELFAST   Bay   Bay   Darlington
Workington   Northallerton
Armagh   Windermere   Hawes
Monaghan   Ramsey   Kendal   North Yorkshire
Isle of Man
Dundalk   Douglas   Morecambe   ENGLAND
Castletown

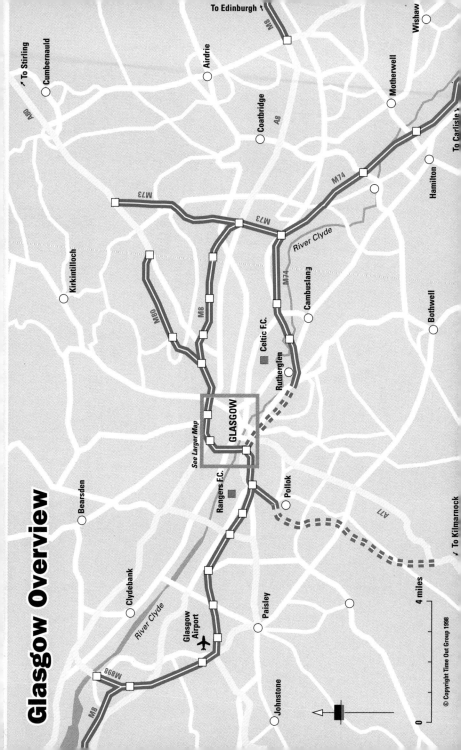

Glasgow Overview

To Edinburgh

To Stirling

Cumbernauld

A80

Airdrie

Wishaw

Motherwell

Coatbridge

A8

To Carlisle

M73

M73

M74

Hamilton

Kirkintilloch

River Clyde

M80

M8

M74

Cambuslang

Bothwell

Celtic F.C.

Rutherglen

GLASGOW

See Larger Map

Bearsden

Pollok

A77

Rangers F.C.

To Kilmarnock

Clydebank

River Clyde

Glasgow Airport

Paisley

4 miles

M898

M8

Johnstone

© Copyright Time Out Group 1998

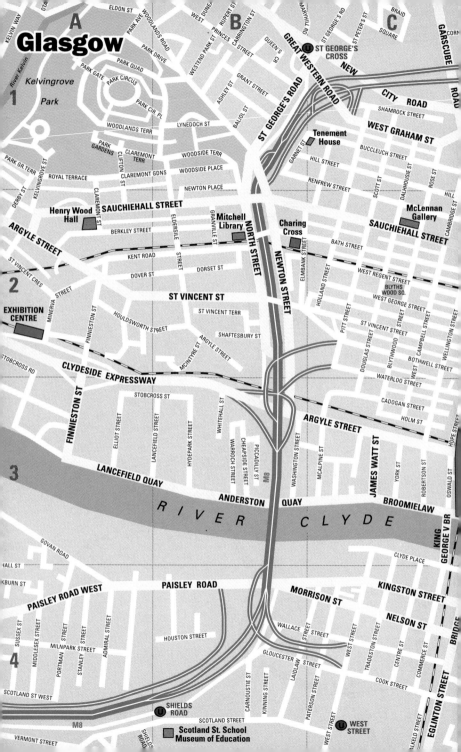

Glasgow

A

KELVIN WAY
OTA...
ELDON ST
Park Ave
WOODLANDS ROAD
PARK DRIVE
PARK QUAD
Park Gate
PARK CIRCUS
PARK CIR PL
PARK CIR PL
Park Gardens
WOODLANDS TERR
LYNEDOCH ST
CLAREMONT TERR
CLAREMONT GDNS
WOODSIDE TERR
WOODSIDE PLACE
NEWTON PLACE

River Kelvin

Kelvingrove Park

1

Park Gr Terr
Royal Terrace
Derby St
Kelvingrove St
Clifton St
Claremont St

Henry Wood Hall

SAUCHIEHALL STREET

BERKLEY STREET
ELDERSLIE
GRANVILLE ST
Mitchell Library
Charing Cross

ARGYLE STREET

ST VINCENT CRES
KENT ROAD
DOVER ST
DORSET ST

NORTH STREET
NEWTON STREET
ELMBANK STREET
HOLLAND STREET

BATH STREET

2

MINERVA STREET

EXHIBITION CENTRE

FINNIESTON ST
HOULDSWORTH STREET
ST VINCENT TERR
SHAFTESBURY ST

ST VINCENT ST

ARGYLE STREET
McINTYRE ST

STOBCROSS RD

CLYDESIDE EXPRESSWAY

B

WEST DUNE...
RUPERT ST
WEST PRINCES
CARRINGTON STREET
QUEEN'S CR
WESTEND PARK ST
PRINCES ST
ASHLEY ST
GRANT STREET
BALJOL ST

ST GEORGE'S ROAD

GREAT WESTERN ROAD

NEW

GARNET ST
HILL STREET
RENFREW STREET

Tenement House

C

BRAID SQUARE
ST GEORGE'S RD
ST PETER'S ST
ST GEORGE'S CROSS
GARSCUBE ROAD

CITY ROAD

SHAMROCK STREET

WEST GRAHAM ST

BUCCLEUCH STREET

SCOTT ST
DALHOUSIE ST
CAMBRIDGE ST
ROSE ST
HILL

McLennan Gallery

SAUCHIEHALL STREET

WEST REGENT STREET
BLYTHS WOOD SQ.
WEST GEORGE STREET
PITT STREET
ST VINCENT STREET
DOUGLAS STREET
BLYTHWOOD
CAMPBELL STREET
WELLINGTON STREET
BOTHWELL STREET
WATERLOO STREET
WEST

CADOGAN STREET
HOLM ST

ARGYLE STREET

3

FINNIESTON ST
STOBCROSS ST
ELLIOT STREET
LANCEFIELD STREET
HYDEPARK STREET
WHITEHALL STREET
WARROCH STREET
CHEAPSIDE STREET
PICCADILLY ST
M8
WASHINGTON STREET
McALPINE ST

LANCEFIELD QUAY

ANDERSTON QUAY

BROOMIELAW

JAMES WATT ST
YORK ST
ROBERTSON ST
OSWALD ST
HOPE STREET

R I V E R   C L Y D E

KING GEORGE V BR
BRIDGE

GOVAN ROAD
...HALL ST
...KBURN ST

CLYDE PLACE

PAISLEY ROAD

MORRISON ST

KINGSTON STREET

PAISLEY ROAD WEST

SUSSEX ST
MIDDLESEX STREET
PORTER STREET
MILNPARK STREET
PORTMAN
STANLEY ST
ADMIRAL STREET
HOUSTON STREET

WALLACE STREET
STREET
WEST STREET
TRADESTON ST
CENTRE ST
COMMERCE ST

NELSON ST

4

GLOUCESTER STREET
LAIDLAW STREET
CARNOUSTIE ST
KINNING STREET
PATERSON STREET
WEST STREET

COOK STREET

EGLINTON STREET
...ALKELD STREET

SCOTLAND ST WEST

SHIELDS ROAD

SCOTLAND STREET
SHIELDS ROAD

Scotland St. School Museum of Education

WEST STREET

VERMONT STREET
M8

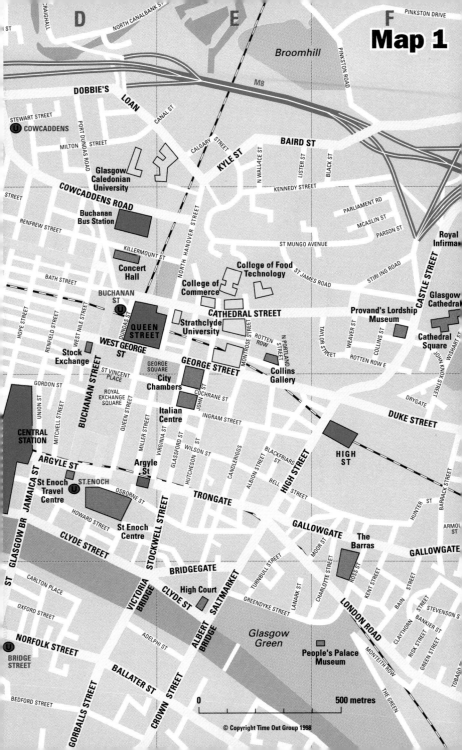

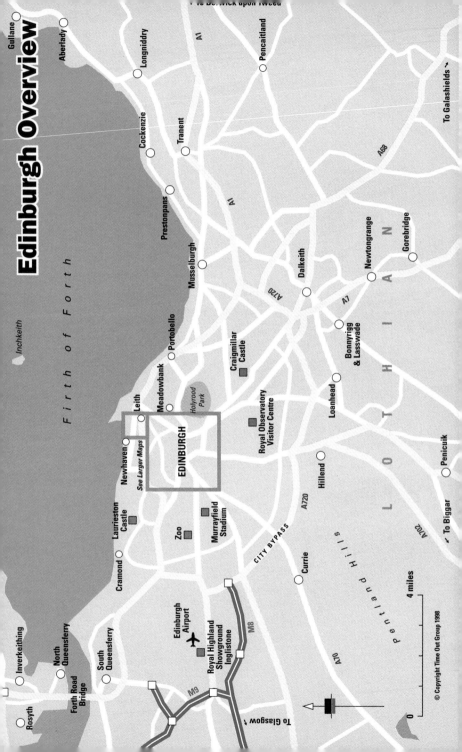

Edinburgh Overview

Gullane
Aberlady
Longniddry
Pencaitland
To Galashields →
Cockenzie
Tranent
A1
A68
Prestonpans
A1
Newtongrange
Gorebridge
Musselburgh
Dalkeith
A720
A7
L O T H I A N
Portobello
Craigmillar Castle
Bonnyrigg & Lasswade
Meadowbank
Loanhead
Firth of Forth
Inchkeith
Leith
Holyrood Park
Royal Observatory Visitor Centre
Newhaven
See Larger Maps
EDINBURGH
Hilland
Penicuik
Laurieston Castle
A720
CITY BYPASS
Cramond
Zoo
Murrayfield Stadium
Currie
To Biggar
A702
Inverkeithing
North Queensferry
South Queensferry
Edinburgh Airport
Royal Highland Showground Inglistone
M8
Pentland Hills
A70
Rosyth
Forth Road Bridge
M9
To Glasgow ↑

4 miles

© Copyright Time Out Group 1998

0

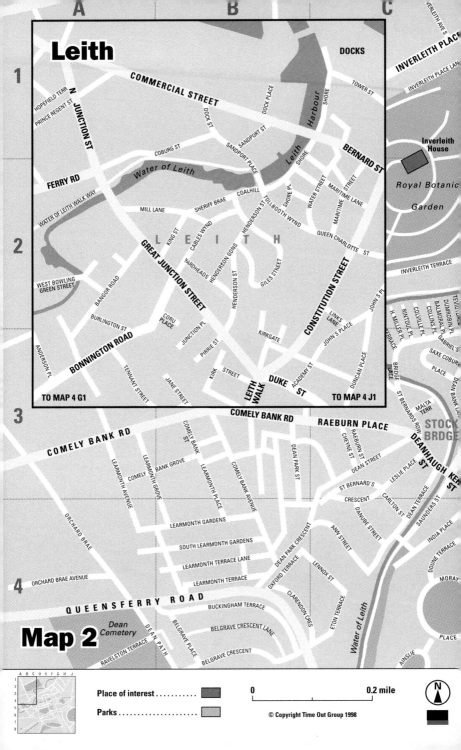

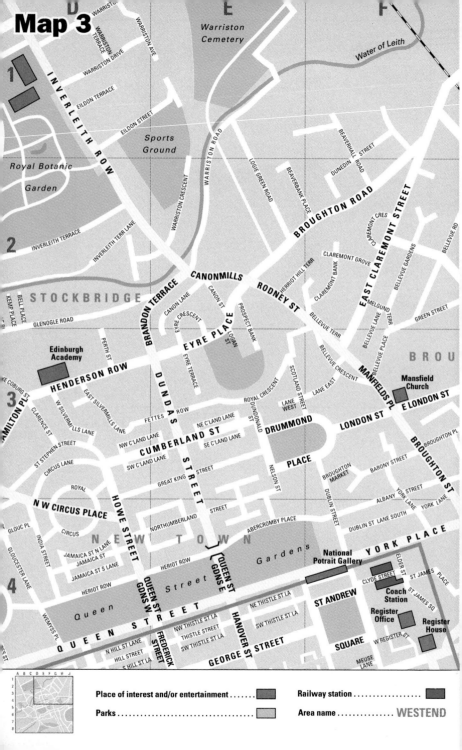

Map 3

Warriston Cemetery

Water of Leith

WARRISTON TERRACE

WARRISTON AVE

WARRISTON DRIVE

EILDON TERRACE

WARRISTON ROAD

WARRISTON CRESCENT

EILDON STREET

Sports Ground

INVERLEITH ROW

BEAVERHALL ROAD

DUNEDIN ROAD

LOGIE GREEN ROAD

BEAVERBANK PLACE

BROUGHTON ROAD

EAST CLAREMONT STREET

CLAREMONT CRES

BELLEVUE RD

Royal Botanic Garden

INVERLEITH TERRACE

INVERLEITH TERR LANE

CLAREMONT GROVE

CLAREMONT BANK

BELLEVUE GARDENS

2

CANONMILLS

HERIOT HILL TERR

RODNEY ST

BELLEVUE TERR

MELGUND TERR

GREEN STREET

BELL PLACE

KEMP PLACE

GLENOGLE ROAD

STOCKBRIDGE

BRANDON TERRACE

CANON LANE

CANON ST

CANON CRESCENT

EYRE PLACE

EYRE CRESCENT

LOGAN ST

PROSPECT BANK

BELLEVUE LANE

BELLEVUE PLACE

MANSFIELD PL

BROU

Mansfield Church

E LONDON ST

Edinburgh Academy

PERTH ST

HENDERSON ROW

DUNDAS STREET

EYRE TERRACE

BELLEVUE CRESCENT

KE COBURG ST

W SILVERMILLS LANE

EAST SILVERMILLS LANE

FETTES ROW

ROYAL CRESCENT

SCOTLAND STREET

LANE EAST

3

HAMILTON PL

CLARENCE ST

NE C'LAND LANE

NW C'LAND LANE

CUMBERLAND ST

DUNDONALD STREET

LANE WEST

DRUMMOND

LONDON ST

BROUGHTON PL

ST STEPHEN STREET

SE C'LAND LANE

SW C'LAND LANE

PLACE

NELSON ST

BROUGHTON ST

CIRCUS LANE

GREAT KING STREET

BROUGHTON MARKET

BARONY STREET

ROYAL

STREET

YORK STREET

N W CIRCUS PLACE

HOWE STREET

NORTHUMBERLAND

ABERCROMBY PLACE

DUBLIN STREET

ALBANY STREET

YORK LANE

GLOUC PL

CIRCUS

DUBLIN ST LANE SOUTH

YORK PLACE

INDIA STREET

NEW TOWN

Gardens

National Portrait Gallery

ELDER ST

ST JAMES PLACE

GLOUCESTER LANE

JAMAICA ST N LANE

JAMAICA ST

HERIOT ROW

QUEEN ST GDNS E

CLYDE STREET

Coach Station

ST JAMES SQ

4

JAMAICA ST S LANE

HERIOT ROW

Street

QUEEN ST GDNS W

NE THISTLE ST LA

ST ANDREW

Register Office

ST JAMES PLACE

WEMYSS PL

Queen

QUEEN STREET

FREDERICK STREET

NW THISTLE ST STREET

THISTLE STREET

SW THISTLE ST LA

SQUARE

W REGISTER ST

Register House

N HILL ST LANE

HILL STREET

S HILL ST LA

HANOVER ST

GEORGE ST

MEUSE LANE

A B C D E F G H J

Place of interest and/or entertainment ....

Parks ....

Railway station ....

Area name .... **WESTEND**

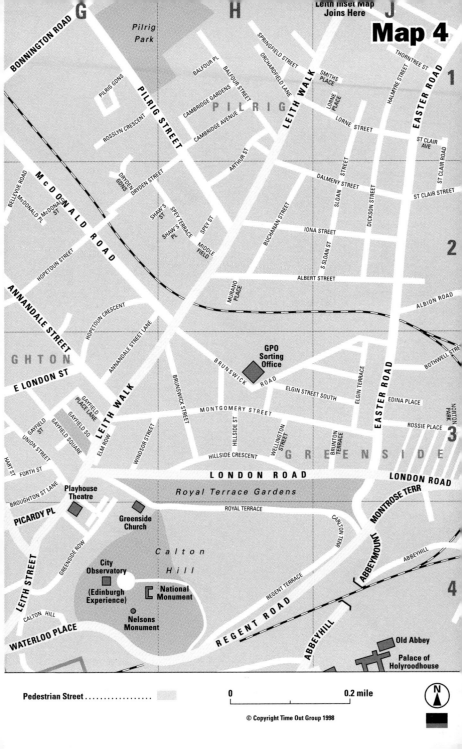

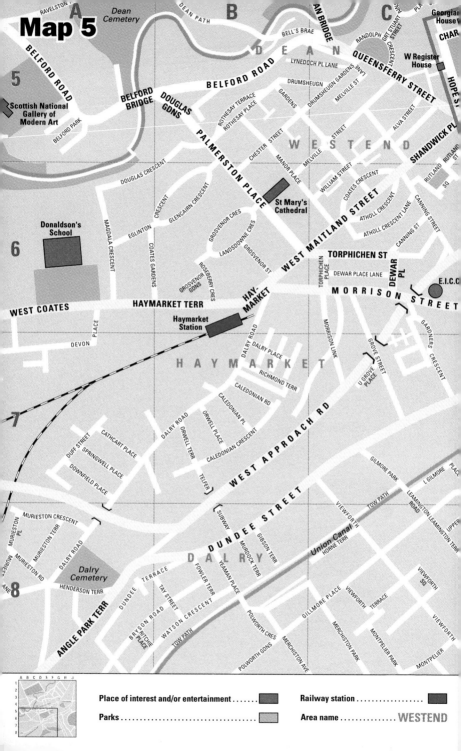

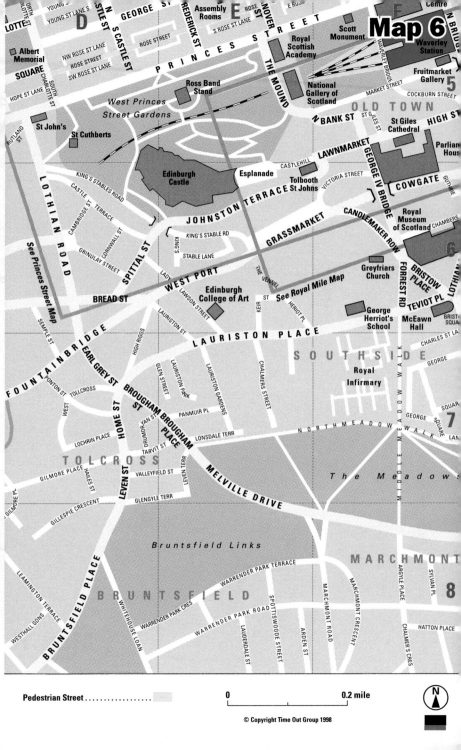

Map 6

YOUNG S
CHARLOTTE
D E
GEORGE ST
FREDERICK ST
HANOVER ST
E ROSE ST
Centre
N BRIDGE

YOUNG ST LANE S
S CASTLE ST
ROSE STREET
Assembly Rooms
S ROSE ST LANE
ROSE ST
F

Albert Memorial SQUARE
NW ROSE ST LANE
ROSE STREET
SW ROSE ST LANE
PRINCES STREET
Royal Scottish Academy
Scott Monument
WAVERLEY BRIDGE
Waverley Station
5

HOPE ST LANE
SOUTH CHARLOTTE ST
West Princes Street Gardens
THE MOUND
National Gallery of Scotland
MARKET STREET
COCKBURN STREET
Fruitmarket Gallery

RUTLAND ST
St John's
St Cuthberts
Ross Band Stand
N BANK ST
ST G ILES ST
OLD TOWN
St Giles Cathedral
HIGH ST

LOTHIAN ROAD
CASTLE TERRACE
KING'S STABLES ROAD
Edinburgh Castle
Esplanade
CASTLEHILL
LAWNMARKET
GEORGE IV BRIDGE
Tolbooth St Johns
VICTORIA STREET
COWGATE
Parliam Hous

See Princes Street Map
CAMBRIDGE ST
CORNWALL ST
GRINDLAY STREET
SPITTAL ST
KING'S STABLE RD
KING'S
STABLE LANE
JOHNSTON TERRACE
GRASSMARKET
CANDLEMAKER ROW
Royal Museum of Scotland
CHAMBERS
6

BREAD ST
WEST PORT
LAWSON STREET
LADY
Edinburgh College of Art
THE VENNEL
KEIR ST
See Royal Mile Map
HERIOT PL
Greyfriars Church
FORREST RD
BRISTO PLACE
LOTHIAN

SEMPLE ST
LAURISTON ST
HIGH RIGGS
Edinburgh College of Art
LAURISTON PLACE
George Herriot's School
McEwan Hall
TEVIOT PL
BRIST SQUA

FOUNTAINBRIDGE
EARL GREY ST
HOME ST
BROUGHAM ST
GLEN STREET
LAURISTON PARK
LAURISTON GARDENS
CHALMERS STREET
SOUTHSIDE
Royal Infirmary
MEADOW WALK
CHARLES ST LA
GEORGE

PONTON ST
WEST
TOLLCROSS
BROUGHAM PLACE
DRUMDRYAN ST
VAN ST
PANMUIR PL
GEORGE
SQUARE
LAN
7

LOCHRIN PLACE
TARVIT ST
LONSDALE TERR
NORTHMEADOW WALK
SQUAR

GILMORE PLACE
TOLCROSS
LEVEN ST
HALES ST
VALLEYFIELD ST
LEVEN TERR
MELVILLE DRIVE
The Meadows

GILLESPIE CRESCENT
GLENGYLE TERR

LEAMINGTON TERRACE
BRUNTSFIELD PLACE
WHITEHOUSE LOAN
Bruntsfield Links
WARRENDER PARK TERRACE
MARCHMONT
8

WESTHALL GDNS
BRUNTSFIELD
WARRENDER PARK CRES
WARRENDER PARK ROAD
SPOTTISWOODE STREET
LAUDERDALE ST
ARDEN ST
MARCHMONT ROAD
MARCHMONT CRESCENT
ARGYLE PLACE
SYLVAN PL
HATTON PLACE
CHALMER'S CRES

Pedestrian Street . . . .

0   0.2 mile

© Copyright Time Out Group 1998

5

G

CALTON ROAD

OLD TOLLBOOTH WYND

EAST MARKET STREET

JEFFREY STREET

CRANSTON ST

NEW STREET

C A N O N G A T E

The People's Story

H

Huntly House

BULL'S CLOSE

HORSE WYND

J

Palace of Holyroodhouse

BLAIR ST

NIDDRY STREET

BLACKFRIARS ST

SOUTH BRIDGE

ST MARY'S ST

C A N O N G A T E

ST JOHN STREET

HOLYROOD ROAD

DUMBIEDYKES ROAD

QUEEN'S DRIVE

RADICAL ROAD

INFIRMARY STREET

CHAMBERS ST

S COLLEGE ST

Edinburgh University Old College

DRUMMOND ST

ROXBURGH PLACE

ROXBURGH ST

W ADAM ST

E ADAM ST

RICHMOND PLACE

THE PLEASANCE

Holyrood

Park

6

POTTER ROW

Festival Theatre

NICOLSON SQUARE

NICOLSON STREET

HILL PLACE

W RICHMOND ST

RICHMOND ST

RICHMOND LA

BRISTO SQUARE

W NICOLSON ST

GEORGE SQUARE

W CROSS CAUSEWAY

E CROSS CAUSEWAY

ST BEAUMONT PL

ST LEONARD'S HILL

ST LEONARD'S LANE

ST LEONARD'S STREET

ST LEONARD'S BANK

RADICAL ROAD

QUEEN'S DRIVE

7

BUCCLEUCH PLACE

MEADOW LANE

BUCCLEUCH STREET

CLERK STREET

ST PATRICK SQ

GIFFORD PARK

RANKEILLOR ST

MONTAGUE ST

BERNARD TERRACE

PARKSIDE ST

HENRY ST

MELVILLE DRIVE

SUMMERHALL

S C I E N N E S

MELVILLE TERRACE

LIVINGSTON PL

GLADSTONE TERRACE

SCIENNES

SOUTH CLERK ST

LUTTON PLACE

OXFORD ST

W PRESTON ST

BLACKWOOD CR

NEWINGTON RD

EAST PRESTON ST

PARKSIDE TERRACE

HOLYROOD PARK ROAD

8

SCIENNES ROAD

HATTON PLACE

LAUDER ROAD

TANTALLON PL

ST CATHERINE'S PL

CAUSEWAY SIDE

SALISBURY PL

GRANGE ROAD

SALISBURY ROAD

Map 7

A B C D E F G H J

1 2 3 4 5 6 7 8

Place of interest . . . .

Parks . . . .

0

0.2 mile

© Copyright Time Out Group 1998

N

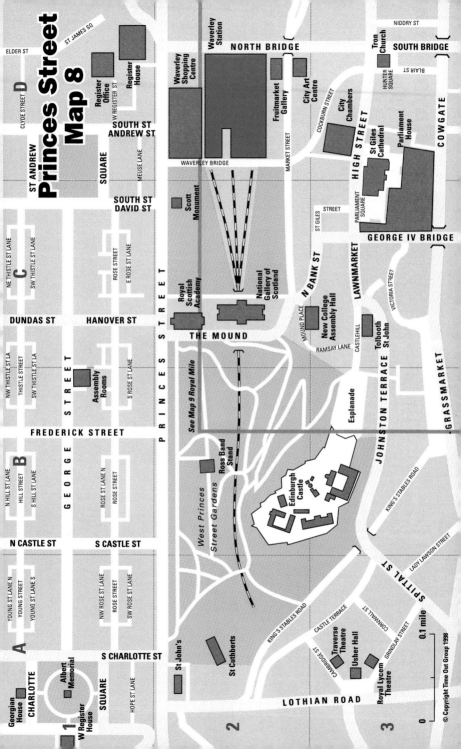

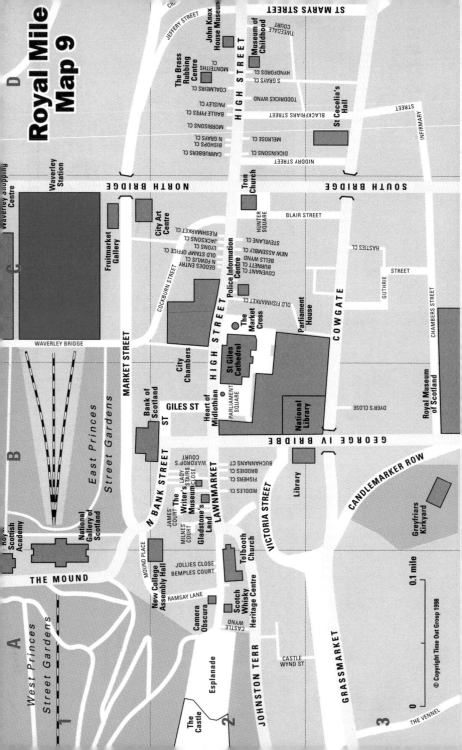

Royal Mile
Map 9

D **C** **B** **A**

1 **2** **3**

ST MARYS STREET

John Knox House Museum

TWEEDALE COURT

Museum of Childhood

The Brass Rubbing Centre

MONTEITH CL

COALMEIRS CL

TWEEDALE CT

HYNDFORDS CL

S GRAYS CL

PAISLEY CL

BAILIE FYFES CL

MORRISONS CL

N GRAYS CL

BISHOPS CL

CARRUBBERS CL

H I G H   S T R E E T

St Cecelia's Hall

BLACKFRIARS STREET

MELROSE CL

DICKINSONS CL

NIDDRY STREET

INFIRMARY STREET

JEFFERY STREET

TODDRICKS WYND

Waverley Shopping Centre

Waverley Station

NORTH BRIDGE

Tron Church

SOUTH BRIDGE

City Art Centre

FISHMARKET CL

BLAIR STREET

HUNTER SQUARE

HASTIES CL

Fruitmarket Gallery

GEDDES ENTRY

N FOWLIS CL

OLD STAMP OFFICE CL

LYONS CL

JACKSONS CL

STEVELAW CL

NEW ASSEMBLY CL

BELLS WYND

BURNETT CL

COVENANT CL

STREET

GUTHRIE STREET

CHAMBERS STREET

COCKBURN STREET

Police Information Centre

OLD FISHMARKET CL

COWGATE

WAVERLEY BRIDGE

MARKET STREET

The Market Cross

Parliament House

DYER'S CLOSE

Royal Museum of Scotland

East Princes
Street Gardens

City Chambers

H I G H   S T R E E T

St Giles Cathedral

Bank of Scotland

GILES ST

Heart of Midlothian

PARLIAMENT SQUARE

National Library

GEORGE IV BRIDGE

National Gallery of Scotland

N BANK STREET

WARDROP'S COURT

LADY STAIRS CLOSE

The Writer's Museum

BUCHANANS CT

FISHERS CL

BRODIES CL

RIDDLES CL

Library

CANDLEMARKER ROW

Royal Scottish Academy

JAMES' COURT

MILNES COURT

Gladstone's Land

LAWNMARKET

Tolbooth Church

VICTORIA STREET

Greyfriars Kirkyard

MOUND PLACE

JOLLIES CLOSE

BEMPLES COURT

RAMSAY LANE

Camera Obscura

Scotch Whisky Heritage Centre

CASTLE WYND

THE MOUND

New College Assembly Hall

West Princes Street Gardens

JOHNSTON TERR

Esplanade

The Castle

CASTLE WYND ST

GRASSMARKET

0   0.1 mile

THE VENNEL

© Copyright Time Out Group 1998